Sam cooper

1327 S.e. 78th ave.

paul g.   paul g.

☮ Sam Cooper ☮

234-3585

1327 se. 48th Avenue

Portland, Oregon
97215

Introduction to Business

Raymond E. Glos, Ph.D., C.P.A.   *School of Business Administration*
Chairman, Department of Business   *Miami University, Oxford, Ohio*

Harold A. Baker, Ph.D.   *School of Business*
Formerly Professor of Marketing   *John Carroll University, Cleveland, Ohio*

Consulting Editor: **Arthur J. Noetzel,** *Dean*
School of Business, John Carroll University

 Published by

SOUTH-WESTERN PUBLISHING COMPANY

Cincinnati   Chicago   Burlingame, Calif.   Dallas   New Rochelle, N. Y.

G70

SIXTH EDITION

Introduction to Business

A TEXTBOOK FOR THE FIRST COURSE IN BUSINESS ON THE COLLEGIATE LEVEL

Preface

The rapidity and extent of changes in the business world in recent years require that a text designed to impart an understanding of this important area of human activity be revised rather frequently. The introduction of computers on a large scale, the increasing use of automation, new types and locations of retailers, a greater awareness of the social responsibilities of industry, and the growing influence of government, to name a few factors, have contributed to what might be termed a revolution in established business procedures. Collegiate preparation for business has kept pace with these new trends as reflected by substantial revisions of content and emphasis in many of the traditional courses as well as in the introduction of new ones. A first course in business, to be of maximum value, must recognize the extensive changes that are taking place in both the academic and business worlds.

In this, the Sixth Edition of *Introduction to Business,* the authors have attempted to reflect the current trends in collegiate education for business as well as to update all relevant materials from earlier editions. To accomplish these objectives, a new chapter, Data Processing, has been incorporated in Part VII, Quantitative Controls for Decision Making. The chapter on Business and Environmental Factors, which was new in the Fifth Edition, has been expanded in line with the increasing recognition of the interaction of these two elements. The chapter on Management and Organization presents some of the newer concepts in this area; more emphasis has been placed on business ethics; and the chapter on the International Aspects of Business has been revised to reflect the growing importance of our business with and in other countries. Consistent with the limitations inherent in a first course in business, greater attention has been given to management uses of business information and how it arrives at decisions. Short cases for each chapter, as well as a new comprehensive case, are provided.

Despite these changes, the authors believe that an introduction to business text must contain a substantial amount of descriptive and basic information. To this end we have tried to explain what business is all about and, in so doing, have attempted to convey to the student some of the dynamic and fascinating aspects of our capitalistic system. Frequent references are made to specific situations, and examples drawn from the business world have been widely used.

The basic objectives of an introduction to business course, which have been stressed in previous editions, are, we believe, still valid and worthy of being repeated. These may be itemized as follows:

1. The student should obtain an understanding of the whole area of activity known as business. For those who continue in a business curriculum, this complete view will provide him with a framework into which he can fit the segments as he subsequently studies in greater detail such subjects as accounting, marketing, finance, and management.
2. The student will acquire a vocabulary of business terms. This acquisition will prove invaluable in later courses as well as in reading newspapers and magazines or listening to the radio or television on topics related to business.
3. The student will learn what capitalism is and how it functions, which seems to be misunderstood by large segments of our population. As a result, he should be a better citizen of this country.
4. Both by direction and indirection, the student will have his attention focused on the many and varied careers available in the business world. His ability to make an intelligent vocational choice will be enhanced.
5. The student will acquire some understanding and gain some experience in the methods and procedures used by businessmen to arrive at decisions.

In striving to produce a text that will be of maximum assistance to the student in attaining these objectives, the authors have attempted to present a balanced description and analysis of the various functions. We do not believe that our treatment of any subject can be termed superficial but, at the same time, considering the survey nature of this text, it does not attempt to delve too deeply into any one segment of the total business picture. The pathway between too little and too much is a narrow one, but the authors hope that those who use this text will agree that we have consistently remained on course.

To the many users of previous editions who have submitted suggestions and constructive criticisms, the authors are deeply grateful. We also wish to thank the numerous business firms and organizations who have permitted us to reproduce charts, graphs, pictures, and other materials from their publications. Our special thanks go to Dean Arthur J. Noetzel, our Consulting Editor, who has not only made numerous suggestions for the improvement of the text but has also contributed a substantial amount of manuscript copy.

R. E. G.

H. A. B.

Contents

I / BUSINESS: ITS NATURE, ENVIRONMENT, AND OPPORTUNITIES

CHAPTER

1 The Nature of Business   3

2 Business and Environmental Factors   27

3 Opportunities in Business   47

II / OWNERSHIP, MANAGEMENT, AND ORGANIZATION

4 Sole Proprietorships and Partnerships   67

5 Corporations   89

6 Management and Organization   109

III / MARKETING

7 Marketing—Its Nature and Scope   133

8 Wholesaling and Retailing   155

9 Prices and Pricing   181

10 Advertising Problems   203

11 International Aspects of Business   227

IV / OPERATIONAL FACTORS

CHAPTER

12   Location and Layout   **251**

13   Purchasing and Inventory Control   **277**

14   Production Problems   **297**

V / PERSONNEL

15   Employee Selection and Training   **321**

16   Employee Compensation   **343**

17   Labor Problems and Legislation   **363**

VI / FINANCE

18   Long-Term Financing   **389**

19   Short-Term Financing   **411**

20   Security Exchanges and Financial News   **433**

21   Risks and Insurance   **453**

22   Financial Problems and Policies   **475**

VII / QUANTITATIVE CONTROLS FOR DECISION MAKING

23   Accounting and Financial Statements   **497**

24   Business Statistics   **519**

25   Data Processing   **539**

26   Budgeting and Forecasting   **557**

VIII / LEGAL AND REGULATORY ENVIRONMENT OF BUSINESS

CHAPTER

27   Business Ethics and Law   **579**

28   Regulation of Competitive Business   **599**

29   Regulated Industries   **617**

30   Taxation and Business   **637**

COMPREHENSIVE CASES

Case 1   Bozart Metal Company   **657**

Case 2   Farr Soap Company   **663**

Appendix—Careers in Business   **671**

Index   **675**

Foreword

WHERE'S THE CHALLENGE
IN AN AIR-CONDITIONED OFFICE?

Even surrounded by creature comforts in modern office buildings, you'll find there's a special kind of excitement and satisfaction in business. Here's the way Robert O. Anderson, Board Chairman of Atlantic Richfield Company, tells it:

A few years ago someone asked me why I had chosen to involve myself in the "dull world" of commerce and industry. I replied that, in my opinion, any activity that did not give me a personal sense of achievement would be dull indeed. But the world of business, as I've experienced it, affords countless opportunities for achievement, creative expression, effective social interaction, the use of imagination and intelligence, and the challenge of effectively using financial—and human—resources.

In business, one can serve his community as well—and meet challenges more sophisticated than those in most social service projects. Instead of mixing mortar for a community center, one may develop the materials that go into it—or market the fuel that heats it—or compute the corporate taxes that will maintain it.

Moreover, the world of business is competitive. It's certainly no place for a man unwilling to take risks, or to face up to a rigorous accounting of his stewardship. For accepting the risks, however, the personal rewards, psychological as well as economic, can be substantial.

Dull world? Never for me. "Exciting," "challenging," "demanding," "rewarding" are words that I find appropriate. Business involves all man's talents; I can see no dullness in it.*

* Reproduced with permission from *Time,* December 16, 1966.

Robert O. Anderson, who made petroleum refining his first career, is now also Board Chairman of the Aspen Institute for Humanistic Studies and the Kennedy Center for the Performing Arts. He is a trustee of the University of Chicago and regent of New Mexico State University.

x

Part I

BUSINESS: ITS NATURE, ENVIRONMENT, AND OPPORTUNITIES

CHAPTER

1 The Nature of Business

2 Business and Environmental Factors

3 Opportunities in Business

PROLOGUE TO PART I

BUSINESS: ITS NATURE, ENVIRONMENT, AND OPPORTUNITIES

The aims of the three chapters in this introductory part are to assist students in understanding the principles upon which the economy of this country is based, to develop an appreciation of the relationships between business and its environment, and to present briefly the opportunities for employment that await the collegiate student of business.

Chapter 1, The Nature of Business, presents a brief overview of capitalism, the economic system that prevails in this country. The important characteristics of current business practices are also presented.

Chapter 2, Business and Environmental Factors, emphasizes the fact that business does not operate in a vacuum, but rather as a part of a singularly complex environment, in which governmental influence and change are among the most potent factors. The interrelationships between business and the different components of its environment are stressed.

Chapter 3, Opportunities in Business, brings to the attention of students the wide range of occupational choices that are to be found in business. Implicit in this presentation is the hope that it may encourage students to think about their future careers as they may bear on the different fields of business activity that are presented in the remaining chapters of this book.

Chapter 1

THE NATURE OF BUSINESS

The people of a nation require a great number of goods and services in order to survive and in order to sustain and improve their standard of living. In a primitive society, men with crude tools provide but little more than the barest essentials of living. In more civilized areas with higher standards of living, however, people strive to produce and to distribute the goods and services that are requisite for their well-being, comfort, safety, and happiness and which are of benefit to society as a whole. These individual and joint efforts are referred to as *business*.

The purpose of this book is to consider in a systematic manner the methods by which businesses in the United States are organized and managed so as to earn a profit by satisfying the wants of the people. This study will begin with an examination of capitalism, which is the term customarily applied to the economic system under which American business operates. This system is in contrast to alternative economic systems, such as socialism or communism.

communism - can't own property
no freedom choice
no private enterprise

■ What Is Capitalism?

Capitalism is an economic system in which individuals, with comparative freedom from external restraint, produce goods and services for public consumption under conditions of competition and with private profit or gain as the principal motivating force. These goods and services move from producers to consumers by means of an exchange (or sales) procedure in which the common medium of payment is usually money or some acceptable substitute for it, such as credit.

At the outset, it should be understood that capitalism is an economic, not a political, system. Capitalism flourishes best, however, in a country with a democratic form of government. The importance of understanding

3

our kind of capitalism cannot be overemphasized in view of the attacks that have been leveled against this institution, both at home and abroad, within recent years. Not only have the proponents of communism, consisting of the spokesmen of Russia, Red China, and countries behind the "Iron Curtain," decried capitalism as an economic system and a way of life, but in this country voices other than those of American communists have been raised to call into question many of the fundamental tenets of our economic order. To evaluate these criticisms properly, our economic system must be thoroughly understood.

Capitalism, in its purest form, is what emerges in a situation where the outstanding circumstance is freedom. This type of capitalism is often called *laissez faire*, a French term that signifies noninterference by government in the conduct of business by individual businessmen and firms. American business, in the earlier years of its existence, probably typified laissez faire capitalism to a considerable extent. In recent years, however, the increase in restraints by government upon business has been such that our economy is frequently referred to as a "modified capitalism." In fact, since the early 1930's, the trend toward the abridgement of freedom in many phases of business has been a notable aspect of the twentieth century. There is reason for believing that the future will witness a continuance of this trend, particularly with regard to the federal government. Vigorous enforcement of the antitrust laws, the Civil Rights Act of 1964, minimum-wage laws, and the growing power of governmental agencies, such as the Federal Trade Commission, are in line with this trend.

In order to facilitate an examination of the characteristics of capitalism, the fundamental factors in the system will be considered in three groups— the basic freedoms of capitalism, the role of individuals in capitalism, and other aspects of capitalism.

■ The Basic Freedoms of Capitalism

The following factors comprise the basic freedoms of capitalism:

1. Private property
2. Private enterprise
3. Freedom of choice

1 / Private property. Capitalism can operate only where the institution of *private property* prevails. This means that individuals and business firms have the right to purchase, own, and sell property of all kinds, including land, buildings, machinery, and equipment. It also implies that business-men have the right to ownership of the goods which they produce and to any profits which may come about through the sale of these goods.

   2 / Private enterprise. The second important freedom of capitalism is *private enterprise,* which means that most business ventures in this country are owned by individuals who have invested their own funds in businesses of their own choosing, from the operation of which they hope to realize gains (or profits) for themselves. This is true regardless of the size of the companies. Large enterprises such as General Motors Corporation, Standard Oil Company of New Jersey, and National Cash Register Company, as well as such small businesses as a hardware store or a barber-shop, are all private enterprises. In no sense are they public or government projects, such as the Federal Post Office, police and fire departments, county homes, and the Tennessee Valley Authority.

   Even though a corporation must go through certain routine formalities to secure a charter to conduct its business, it is still a private enterprise. The state, in granting a charter, does not enter into partnership with the corporation, does not supply any of the capital, nor does it agree to share in any of the losses that may be suffered. Nor may the state ordinarily require that the concern applying for a charter show that there is any need for its being brought into existence, or refuse a charter if such proof is not forthcoming.

   Thus this characteristic of capitalism, private enterprise, pertains to ownership and indicates that business is owned by private individuals rather than by public bodies, such as federal, state, or local governments. Private sources of capital are used to secure the needed funds to start and operate a business. The dealings between businesses are private transactions and, if not illegal in nature, they are customarily not of public concern. The efforts put into the management of business are those of private individuals whose judgments and decisions determine the paths that the business follows.

   3 / Freedom of choice. An outstanding characteristic of capitalism, especially in a country with a democratic form of government, and one which differentiates it from all other economic systems, is the extent to which everyone affected by it has, to a considerable degree, freedom of choice in his economic actions. The businessman is free to choose the field of business in which he will engage and to manipulate the factors of land, labor, capital, and management as he sees fit in order to achieve the highest measure of profit. He may also choose his customers with almost complete freedom.[1] Workers are at liberty to choose the jobs that they wish, in the trades or callings that they prefer, and in the companies that offer them the best returns for their efforts. Consumers are singularly free in their choices of the goods and services that they wish to buy because there is no compulsion for them either to purchase or to refrain from so doing. This freedom of choice is found at all economic levels; the chief limiting factor, as a general rule, is that of the financial resources of the individuals themselves.

A variant on the concept of freedom of choice is that of *freedom of contract*. This means that individuals or firms are free to enter into contracts that call for the performance of services or the delivery of goods, provided that there is no violation of law involved, in accordance with the dictates of their own best judgments. Likewise, they may decline to enter such contracts on the same basis.

■ The Role of Individuals in Capitalism

Four groups of individuals play essential roles in capitalism:

1. Entrepreneurs
2. Management
3. Workers
4. Consumers

1 / **Entrepreneurs.** The term applied to the individual, or group, who engages in business under the capitalistic system is entrepreneur. This is a French word for which no completely accurate or satisfactory counterpart exists in the English language. The word "enterpriser," a fairly literal translation, is not at all in common usage.

An *entrepreneur* may be regarded as the one who, having the necessary capital or being able to secure it, enters business in some form in which he believes that there is an opportunity for profit to himself. Subject to certain outside influences, such as competition, laws, government action, and chance, he manages the business as he wishes.

The entrepreneurial functions may be performed by a single individual in the form of a sole proprietorship, or by several individuals, either as a partnership, corporation, or some other form of business ownership.

The entrepreneur brings his business into being and operates it because he believes that he can secure a profit by so doing and he is willing, at least tacitly, to accept the risk of loss. He knows that the more efficiently

---

[1] The Civil Rights Act of 1964, as well as several state laws, prohibits places of public accommodation from refusing to serve their customers on the basis of race, religion, color, or national origin. This prohibition includes hotels, motels, restaurants, cafeterias, and theaters.

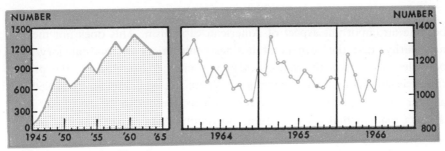

Source: *Graphic Trends.*

Commercial Failures
Annually 1945-1965; Monthly 1964-1966

Profit is the entrepreneur's goal, but he must be aware of the possibility of failure.

he can operate his business, the larger will be his profits and the better his chances of surviving competitively. Therefore, he keeps a close watch on his costs of doing business and is ever alert to new and cheaper ways of operating. Lower costs frequently result in lower prices and enhanced quality of the goods and services available to consumers. The entrepreneur thus is seen as the prime initiator of all economic activity in a capitalistic system.

Among the critics of our economic system are those who would substitute some measure of governmental ownership and operation of certain types of business enterprise for private entrepreneurship. This is particularly true in the field of public utilities, notably the generation and distribution of electric power. It should be pointed out, however, that the government is neither equipped nor intended to assume the risks of enterprise, nor are the incentives to more efficient operation present when the government runs a business.

2 / **Management.** The individuals charged with the responsibility of operating business enterprises and of endeavoring to do so profitably are commonly referred to as *management*. In the earlier days of business in this country, the owners were also the management, a circumstance that is still to be found in small-scale firms. In most of the larger companies, however, particularly those with great numbers of shareholders (or owners), the managements have come to consist of individuals who may not own any stock in the companies that they operate. Management, in these instances, comprises groups of salaried persons, whose incentives for the efficient direction of the enterprises with which they are connected come from the expectation of higher salaries and possibly job security, rather than from profits.

The separation of management and ownership in large businesses has become an important aspect of American capitalism. This does not mean, necessarily, that the owners of business enterprises in this category are powerless to control the actions of management, particularly if the profit return is not up to their expectations. There are ways, to be discussed in a later chapter, whereby situations such as these can be rectified. But the fact remains that the day-to-day operation of many businesses is in the hands of salaried managers and that the control function of ownership has been largely delegated to management.

The importance of management in the setting of American capitalism can scarcely be overemphasized. The decisions made by management, acting either as owners or as top-ranking employees, are vital to the successful functioning of our economic system. This has become increasingly apparent in recent years as many business firms have grown markedly in sales, number of employees, variety of products, physical plants, and financial requirements. Indeed, some students of American business believe that the further growth of many of these companies will be limited by their ability to discover or develop managerial personnel capable of successfully directing these enterprises.

3 / **Workers.** Capitalism is dependent upon a large group of individual workers who must perform the actual physical and mental labor that is necessary to bring into being all of the many and varied types of goods and services that the system produces. Included among the worker group are those that are skilled, semiskilled, and unskilled. One definition of workers might be that they are those who have no authority over other workers, for as soon as an individual achieves control over other workers, he ceases to be a worker and becomes a part of management.

4 / **Consumers.** The role of the consumer in a capitalistic economy is a dual one. In the first place, every individual is a consumer. Each one of us must consume a minimum amount of food and drink in order to sustain life. Upward from this lowest point of consumption are various gradations of consumptive levels. Any modern economic system, such as capitalism, exists for the primary purpose of providing the goods and services required by the consumers who are a part of it. Consumer demand for the products of the system, however, determines the success or the failure of the individual firms that comprise the economic organization of the country, and, to a considerable degree, the level of business activity in the nation. *Consumer demand* may be defined as the desire for goods and services coupled with the requisite purchasing power.

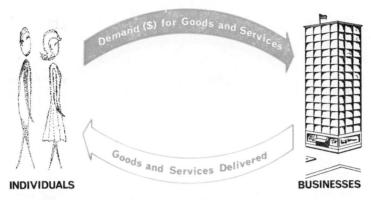

INDIVIDUALS   **BUSINESSES**

Individuals as Consumers

In order that a person may consume goods in our economic system, he must possess purchasing power so that he may buy those things which he needs and wants. In most instances this purchasing power comes into being when its possessor is paid for doing (producing, in the broad sense of the term) something, whether the payment is in the form of wages, rent, profits, or other types of income. The consumer thus emerges in a second role, that of a producer. For various reasons, some historic and some psychological, consumers have generally thought of themselves as producers first, and consumers second. In their attempts (either singly or in groups, such as labor unions) to better their economic status, consumers have customarily sought greater rewards in their roles as producers, such as higher wages, rather than by endeavoring to achieve the same objectives through the improvement of their positions as consumers, by way of more prudent purchasing. Attempts that have been made by various individuals and groups to interest consumers in becoming more efficient purchasers have met with little success.

INDIVIDUALS   **BUSINESSES**

Individuals as Producers

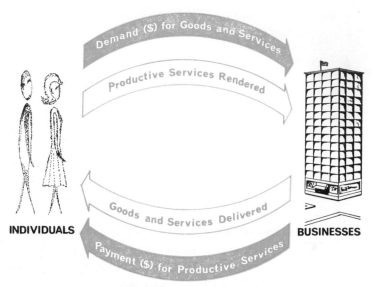

The Circular Flow of Economic Activity

■ Other Aspects of Capitalism

A number of additional items are essential to an understanding of the operation of capitalism:

1. Capital
2. Production
3. Distribution of goods

4. Price
5. Competition
6. Risk

7. Profit

1 / **Capital.** Capital can best be understood in terms of its two forms— capital goods and capital funds. *Capital goods* consist of such things as tools, equipment, buildings, fixtures, patents, and land, as well as raw materials in the process of manufacture, and merchandise for sale. *Capital funds* refers to money that is available from individual savers or from groups through savings institutions for investment in business enterprises. The capital needed by a business may be obtained through the investment of the entrepreneur, by borrowing from others, and by using the funds resulting from business profits and retained in the business.

The owners of capital, known as capitalists, contribute their resources to a business either as owners or creditors. If they assume the risks of entrepreneurship, they are interested in profits; if as creditors, in interest on their investment. In either event, capital funds or goods will not be forthcoming unless the capitalists see an opportunity for a satisfactory

Expenditures by Business for New Plant and Equipment
(Billions of Dollars)

YEAR	AMOUNT
1960	35.71
1961	34.36
1962	37.24
1963	39.05
1964	44.86
1965	51.86
1966	*60.84

* Estimated

Source: U. S. Department of Commerce—Securities and Exchange Commission.

return on their investment or loan. If such a return does not appear to be in prospect, the investment or loan will not be made and the business project in question will not be initiated or continued. It is probable that the term "capitalism" owes its origin and meaning to its dependence upon the decisions and actions of the owners of capital.

2 / **Production.** _Production,_ as used in its broadest economic sense, means the furnishing by the entrepreneur of some economically valuable goods or services that are to be sold to others. Economists commonly speak of production as the creation of utilities. Production, in this sense, includes not only the manufacture of such products as automobiles, food, radios, and so on, but also their transportation and their distribution at wholesale and retail.

In its narrower and more common business usage, production refers to the physical manufacture of goods, whether this be a simple extractive process, such as fishing, farming, lumbering, or mining, or the highly complex types necessary to produce rubber tires, washing machines, and electrical appliances. It is in this latter sense that production will be used in this text.

3 / **Distribution of goods.** _Distribution_ may be regarded as the ways by which the output of production is made available to its users, the consumers. From the standpoint of the capitalistic system, the entrepreneur in distribution is one who seeks profit by providing the facilities whereby

products may reach their destination. He, like the entrepreneur in production, will use the factors of land, labor, capital, and management in those combinations that appear to him best from the standpoint of profits.

The production entrepreneur usually must undertake some of the duties of the distribution entrepreneur in order to dispose of his product; whereas the latter only occasionally enters the field of production. Chain stores and others who have undertaken the manufacture of some of their own branded goods both produce and distribute. This latter development, noticeable in the last few years, is the result of the seeking of greater profits by distribution entrepreneurs.

4 / Price. Under capitalism, the movement of goods from the producer to the consumer takes place on an exchange basis; or, to use the customary phrase, a sale takes place. The buyer gives something of value to the seller in exchange for the goods that the seller has available for sale. In our economy this "something of value" is money, our medium of exchange; and the amount of money for which a good or service is exchanged is the price.

The *price* at which a commodity is bought and sold is partly determined by demand and supply. As the price of a commodity increases, the supply of that commodity tends to increase and its demand to decrease. Contrariwise, as the price of that commodity decreases, the demand tends to increase and the supply to decrease. According to one school of economic thought, the price at which a commodity is bought and sold is the one for which the quantities supplied for sale and demanded for purchase are equal.

Presumably over a period of time the prices that sellers receive will be high enough to cover their costs of doing business and yield them their desired profits. If prices are too low, the sellers will supposedly withdraw from their present business and enter more profitable fields. On the other hand, it is presumed that the prices that the buyers will pay over a period of time must at least equal the satisfaction or usefulness that they will receive from the purchase of the goods. If prices are too high, buyers will withhold their purchases or transfer them to other, lower-priced goods.

While the above-mentioned supply-and-demand situation unquestionably has a certain amount of validity, it would be an oversimplification to presume that it was the only explanation of this phenomenon of capitalism. The factors that enter into the determination of prices are exceedingly complex, involving a large number of elements, psychological as well as economic. A more extensive discussion of this phase of capitalism will be presented in Chapter 9.

5 / **Competition.** Under capitalism, the entrepreneurs in each line of business compete with each other in the sale of their products or services.[2] Thus *competition* is basic to the capitalistic system. The institution of free, private enterprise implies freedom on the part of any entrepreneur to enter any field of business and to compete with those already established therein for the favor of the buyers in the market.

Early economists propounded the concept of *pure competition*. Four criteria were assumed under this concept: (1) a large number of sellers are in the market, all selling an identical product; (2) all buyers and sellers are completely informed about all markets and prices; (3) there is free movement in and out of the market by buyers and sellers; and (4) no individual buyer or seller is able to influence the price, which is determined by supply and demand, or the total of the actions of all of the buyers and sellers. Under these assumptions competition was solely on the basis of price. Over time it became evident that, except for a few farm products, such as wheat, corn, and soybeans, pure competition simply did not exist. Eventually supplanting it was the theory of imperfect competition, which can be divided into oligopoly and monopolistic competition.

Oligopoly assumes a market situation in which comparatively few firms produce identical or similar products, and where individual firms have the ability to influence price. *Monopolistic competition* assumes that there are many makers of goods with identical end usage who brand their products to differentiate them from those of their competitors. This practice is known as *product differentiation.* In this manner the producers of these branded goods hope to convince consumers that their products are different from, and presumably better than, those of their competitors in some important aspect so that they may escape having their goods compared with those of other manufacturers of similar wares. Through this practice producers endeavor to create a "brand loyalty" among consumers, so that they may avoid the rigors of strictly price competition. The large number of different brands to be found among consumer goods lends credence to this theory.

OTHER CONCEPTS OF COMPETITION. Born of the depression of the 1930's, there came into being what is known as *handicap competition,* the purpose of which was to lessen the impact of price competition on identical goods between large and small retailers—those who sell directly

---

[2] There are certain exceptions to this rule, as in the case of such public utilities as electric power, gas, water, telephone, and transportation companies, which enjoy a more or less monopolistic situation, subject to regulation by some governmental agency.

to consumers. Laws were passed in many states [3] that, in effect, prevented the large retailers from offering these goods at lower prices than the small ones. Thus the small retailers were given assistance in their competition with the large operators. Many of these laws are still in effect.

A phenomenon that first appeared in the middle 1940's has given rise to a still further classification of competition. The growth of supermarkets, discount houses, suburban shopping centers, self-service, and a host of new products (or older ones redesigned) has been given the name of _innovistic competition._ This type of competition subordinates, to some extent, the role of price and stresses instead customer convenience and novelty, both in goods and the places where they may be purchased. It is a dynamic type of competition that threatens the status quo of many of the historic competitive practices in the area of consumer goods. Many observers believe that innovistic competition will be the rule for the foreseeable future.

IMPORTANCE OF PRICE. There is, however, a strong conviction that price will continue to retain its preeminence as a base for competition, despite the inroads of innovation, service, convenience, prestige, and reputation. An entrepreneur endeavors to gain a competitive advantage by lowering his prices. This action causes his competitors to try to meet the new lowered prices and, in some instances, to go below them. The extent to which this price-cutting activity will go is determined largely by two factors, the demand and the operating costs of the entrepreneurs concerned. If the demand is great enough to take all of the products of the producers in a given field, the competitive price will tend to be that at which all producers are making at least a satisfactory profit. If the demand is not great enough for this purpose and if it can be increased by lowering the price, then the operating costs of the entrepreneurs enter the picture. Obviously the producers with the lowest costs can go farther in the direction of lowering prices than can their less efficient competitors. It should be equally apparent that, when the price goes below the production and distribution costs of any producer, he cannot long remain in business unless he can reduce his costs and thereby become more efficient in his operations.

This situation provides the clue to the presumably beneficent social character of competition. Through its operation, people are supposed to secure their goods and services at the lowest possible prices based on the highest attainable efficiency of the producers. Those entrepreneurs who

---

[3] A further discussion of these laws will be found in Chapter 9.

are unable to achieve this standard of efficiency are assumed to retire from business; thus the public is rid of the high cost of inefficient producers. There is also, according to this presumption, a never-ending effort on the part of all producers to lower their costs, both to increase their profits and to give them a possible competitive advantage thereby.

This is obviously a simplification of this part of our economic system, as there are many factors operating to offset and supplement this more or less purifying competitive movement. But it is still basically true in a large segment of our economic life, and the student's attention is directed to it at this point in order that he may understand something of the stronger trends that characterize capitalistic economics.

In spite of the lip service that is paid to competition by businessmen, the fact of the matter is that many of them do not like it so far as their being exposed to it is concerned. They want the sellers from whom they buy to compete in order that the prices which they have to pay may be as low as possible; and they likewise desire competition among their buyers in order that they may sell at the highest possible prices. But they do not care for a competitive situation into which they themselves must fit.

6 / Risk. *Risk* is always present in private enterprise. Of greatest importance is the risk of complete failure—of bankruptcy—in which case the entrepreneur stands to lose all of his investment. In the case of the sole proprietorship or partnership he may possibly also lose his personal property and savings. This risk is apt to be greater when a new business is being launched than after it is well established. A similar danger exists, however, when an old concern fails to keep abreast of the times and loses out to newer, more wide-awake competitors.

At all times a firm must be aware of the risks that are inherent in competition—chances for loss through shifts in the price level, changes in style and fashion, and the appearance of substitutes on the market that sometimes render present models obsolete. The switch from steam to diesel power in railroad locomotives is a good example of the risk involved in the use of substitutes for materials formerly used. The market for coal has been substantially reduced by this changeover. When the development of atomic power reaches the stage where it can be adapted generally to industrial operations, it is likely that all other forms of energy will be adversely affected.

The appearance of innovistic competition in the past couple of decades has markedly enhanced the risk aspects of entrepreneurship in all economic areas. Especially is this true in the field of small business where the effect of mergers of large firms, the increase in number and types of goods, and the speed with which these phenomena have come into being, have added to the risk burdens of small entrepreneurs. Two other factors are noteworthy as contributors to risk. These are automation, which involves the substitution of mechanical for human effort with a frequently resulting reduction in cost; and electronic data processing through the use of computers, which permits of the assembling and use of large amounts of vital information by management.[4] For those firms unable or unwilling to utilize either or both of these factors, the risk of falling behind competitively may be serious.

Other sources of potential loss are to be found in changes in the desirability of business locations, in distribution methods, and in public demand. All of these risks must be accepted by entrepreneurs as integral parts of capitalism. On their ability to meet the situations surrounding these hazards will depend their success or failure in their respective enterprises.

Certain other risks can be met to a considerable degree through insurance. These include losses from such items as fire, theft, flood, wind, death of important executives, and accidents for which the business must assume responsibility. Any risk that can be shifted to others by insurance or other devices, however, is not of the type regarded as implicit to entrepreneurship.

7 / Profit. For all practical purposes, business *profit* may be considered to be the excess of the income of an enterprise over the costs of its operation. Profits or the anticipation of profits constitute the inducement to capitalists to invest in private enterprise in an ownership capacity. It is not necessary at this point to enter into an analysis of what may be properly considered as the costs of operating a business. The significance of profits in the present discussion lies in their role as determinants of action by the owners of capital.

The question may well be raised as to the amount of profits, in any given instance, that is required to induce capitalists to invest in the enterprise in question. No absolute quantitative answer can be given, and there are wide variations among different lines of business. The question, however, is not unanswerable if attention is directed to the term that signifies the opposite of profits, namely, losses.

Losses arise when the income of a business is insufficient to cover its costs; they are an ever-present possibility of risk in any private enterprise under capitalism. The entrepreneur accepts the risk of loss when he enters

---

[4] Automation is treated in Chapter 14 and electronic data processing in Chapter 25.

business in the quest for profits. Some writers in the field of economics have claimed that profits are justified as inducements to the entrepreneur to assume the risks of loss in any private enterprise. Whether or not there is any justification, moral or social, for profits is not of any moment in this discussion, but it is here that the clue may be found to the answer to the question presented above. Speaking broadly, it may be said that in order to induce entrepreneurs to enter any given business, they must be convinced that the prospective profits are potentially greater than the possible losses. The expectation of profits and the fear of losses provide incentives for effective management, risk-taking, and innovation.

The advertisement on page 18 by a well-known advertising agency is an attempt to explain the role of profit.

■ The Economist's Concept of Capitalism

For many years economists, who study the operation of economic systems, have propounded various theories designed to explain the operation of capitalism. These theories have ranged all the way from explanations of the functioning of capitalism as an organic whole (macro-economics) to a consideration of the decisions to be made by individual firms with regard to prices and profits (microeconomics). Not infrequently some of these theories have been at variance with others put forth at earlier times. This has been particularly true of those theories which have undertaken to explain the reasons for the varying levels of business activity, the more or less cyclical periods of prosperity and recession that have occurred throughout the history of our economy.

It is not within the province of this text to undertake a minute scrutiny of these theories but rather to set forth briefly the basic elements of the two that economists have most recently had under discussion. The older, or *classical theory of capitalism,* makes the following assumptions: (1) normally there is full employment of labor and, if this condition does not exist, it is only a temporary deviation; (2) all income from the production of goods and services will be spent immediately to buy the current goods and services required, or invested in capital goods such as materials, machinery, and buildings, and consumer goods that are destined to be put into inventories of sellers; and (3) the production of goods creates an equivalent amount of demand, and therefore aggregate supply and demand will always be equal. A conclusion which the classical theory propounds, then, is that the forces of supply and demand, together with investment, are adequate to keep the economy operating at its highest level and in a state of equilibrium.

Is profit a dirty word?

It's not a dirty word to a little boy or girl who puts a dollar in a bank and expects to get more than that out.

It's not a dirty word to a newsboy who charges more for his papers than they cost him.

It's not a dirty word to a widow who puts her and her husband's life savings in blue-chip stocks.

It's not a dirty word to people who compile dictionaries—who define profit with words like "good . . . beneficial . . . reward."

Profit is what makes our society go around. By making research and development possible, it makes new products possible . . . and improved products . . . and lower-cost products. It secures jobs and creates new ones. It's essential. It's good.

Then why do so many businessmen seem ashamed of the word? Why, in annual reports and financial statements and publicity releases, do they hide the word and the idea of profit? Why do they call profit "earnings" . . . or "net"? Why don't they call it *profit*?

A banker doesn't apologize for paying 4% interest. Why does a businessman feel the need to apologize when he pays a 4% dividend?

We're proud of profit. It's what we're paid to create. It's a good thing to create. It's good, if new products are good . . . if improved products are good . . . if jobs are good . . . if our society is good.

Let's tell people about profit. They'll understand. It helps them, too.

Marsteller Inc.

The more recent theory, called the *income-expenditure analysis*,[5] differs from the classical theory in several respects. It holds that the economy can be in equilibrium without full employment. This theory states that the level of business activity, and also of employment, at any one point in time, is based on the volume of demand for goods and services by both consumers and businessmen, and the volume of investment by business- men in economic goods of all kinds. Inasmuch as the level of consumption is presumed to be fairly steady for any level of income, the rate of business activity and the level of employment depends upon the amount of invest- ment. Consumers, however, may not spend all of their incomes for goods and services but save some for various reasons. This will tend not only to reduce consumption but, unless the savings are invested in economic goods, will also tend to lower the investment rate. Therefore, it is held that if the rate of consumption, and particularly the rate of investment, is not great enough to ensure relatively full employment, government spend- ing must provide the additional expenditures necessary to raise the level of employment.

The federal government has for many years embraced the concept of the income-expenditure theory with respect to its responsibility for achieving and maintaining full employment in the country. As a means of attaining this objective, a long series of annual deficits have been incurred, which may or may not have produced the desired result. One of the results of this course of action has been a steady increase in the national debt and interest on that debt. There are sharp differences of opinion among economists and businessmen regarding the desirability of the continuance of this situation and of its eventual effect on the economy of the country.

The foregoing brief explanation of the classical and income-expenditure theories should help to explain some of the fiscal policies of the federal government and the recommendations in this area that have been made by economists who embrace the income-expenditure analysis.

◾ Characteristics of Present-Day Business

Business in this country has developed several special characteristics that illustrate its dynamic nature. They are:

1. Specialization
2. Mass production
3. Large-scale industry
4. Growing importance of research

---

[5] This theory is also known as the national income theory or the Neo-Keynesian theory.

1 / **Specialization**. The trend toward specialization in industry has been noteworthy at all levels. Workers have tended to specialize and the jack-of-all-trades, so common years ago, has been largely replaced by the specialist, the worker who is trained to excel at one, relatively small, task. Thus the all-round machinist, who could operate all types of machine tools, has given way to the individual who is equipped to run only a lathe or a drill press. The machines are adjusted and made ready for operation, not by the general machinist, but by a set-up man, a specialist in grinding and setting the cutting tools by which the work is shaped into the finished product. The advent and growth of automation and of computers has required the commensurate development of highly trained and skilled specialists who are capable of performing the intricate tasks involved in preparing, operating, adjusting and, where necessary, repairing these complicated devices.

Companies have also developed along specialized lines. There are many firms that produce items which have no separate utility in themselves, but which must be combined with other goods to form some sort of a whole that is useful to man. For example, an automobile is made up of a great many parts which, apart from the car, have little usefulness. Spark plugs, tubeless tires, upholstery fabric, cotter pins, and piston rings are a few parts that are the products of specialized industries. While it is true that the great motor car manufacturers, such as Ford and General Motors, have tended to produce more of the items that go into their cars, a large number of parts are still made by firms that produce nothing else. This tendency is an outstanding characteristic of business in this country.

2 / **Mass production**. This phenomenon of our industry is responsible, to no small degree, for the availability, at low cost and in large numbers, of such goods as airplanes, telephones, radios and television sets, and many other commodities that help to give us the highest standard of living known to man.

Mass production does not merely mean the producing of a large number of any given item. It involves a manufacturing technique that not only results in the creation of a great quantity of goods but also brings about a reduction in unit costs, which, in turn, permits lower prices and greater sales. This technique consists mainly of a standardization and interchange-ability of parts; the use of the assembly line, whereby the item to be produced moves slowly along a belt or chain and undergoes a series of additions of component parts until it emerges at the end completely assembled; and the subdivision of the labor element into a series of simple, repetitive operations. This process probably originated in the automobile industry but has spread to many other fields. The production technique known as automation, which is described in Chapter 14, is particularly applicable to mass-production industries.

3 / Large-scale business. Most businesses start on a relatively small scale, and many never experience more than a moderate growth. Some, however, have grown to great size. Among the large-scale businesses in manufacturing are the General Electric Company, Texaco, Inc., and Bethlehem Steel Corporation. In the merchandising field are Sears, Roebuck & Co., Macy's, and Safeway Stores. Large public utilities include the American Telephone and Telegraph Company and the Consolidated Edison Company of New York. Financial institutions in this size grouping are the Bank of America, Chase Manhattan Bank, and the Continental Illinois National Bank and Trust Company. Their capital, sales, properties, and number of employees are all on a vast scale. Some are mass production companies; while others, the nonmanufacturing group, are not. Their size, which is one of their outstanding characteristics, is a development of the last fifty years or more.

4 / Growing importance of research. A characteristic of present-day business that has increasingly manifested itself in recent years is that of research. *Research* may be defined as the systematic investigation of the facts surrounding any given situation with the hope that more effective methods may be found. Research in business is carried on in production methods, materials, personnel, marketing, products, packaging, and advertising. The ever-growing pressure of competition is the major force behind this increased emphasis on research. In order for producers to remain competitive, as well as to survive, it becomes imperative for them continuously to engage in research, both to discover better and cheaper methods of manufacture and distribution and to search for new products and improvements in their present product lines.

The term *research and development*, often shortened to R and D, has become quite common as descriptive not only of the research aspect of this activity but also of the application of the results of the research to cost-saving methods, to the adding of new products, or to the enhancing of the sales value of old ones. Large sums of money are committed annually to R and D projects and, to an ever-increasing extent, the judgments and decisions of top management are being influenced by the findings of research in business. One aspect of this field, *operations research*, which is the application of certain statistical and mathematical procedures to the solution of business problems, has been gaining in usage.

■ **Size of Business Firms**

American business is carried on by firms that range in size from the small enterprise in which a single person conducts his business, such as a shoe repair or an upholstering shop; through medium-sized firms, such as grocery wholesalers or paper box manufacturers; to such industrial and commercial giants as the General Motors Corporation and the Great Atlantic and Pacific Tea Company, whose sales volumes amount to billions of dollars annually and who employ many thousands of workers. In the chapters that follow attention will be given to companies of all sizes.

Over 98 percent of all enterprises in the United States can be classified as small businesses according to Congressional definition. A retail store

The Twenty Largest Industrial Corporations
Ranked by Sales, 1965

RANK	COMPANY	SALES	ASSETS	EM-PLOYEES	PROFIT AS % OF SALES
		(THOUSANDS OF DOLLARS)			
1	General Motors	20,733,982	12,586,170	734,594	10.3
2	Ford Motor	11,536,789	7,596,834	364,487	6.1
3	Standard Oil (N. J.)	11,471,529	13,073,437	148,000	9.0
4	General Electric	6,213,595	4,300,440	300,000	5.7
5	Chrysler	5,299,935	2,934,488	166,773	4.4
6	Mobil Oil	4,907,504	5,212,380	80,600	6.5
7	U. S. Steel	4,399,590	5,451,740	208,838	6.3
8	Texaco	3,779,406	5,342,903	56,960	16.8
9	I. B. M.	3,572,825	3,744,918	172,445	13.3
10	Gulf Oil	3,384,742	5,210,833	55,200	12.6
11	Western Electric	3,362,149	2,303,354	168,846	5.0
12	E. I. du Pont de Nemours	3,020,758	2,847,762	109,336	13.5
13	Swift	2,750,957	634,193	52,800	.6
14	Bethlehem Steel	2,579,384	2,609,869	130,000	5.8
15	Shell Oil	2,562,209	2,671,464	34,548	9.1
16	Standard Oil (Ind.)	2,471,988	3,514,102	41,158	8.9
17	Standard Oil of California	2,442,453	4,165,825	44,434	16.0
18	Westinghouse Electric	2,389,909	1,711,516	115,141	4.5
19	International Harvester	2,336,719	1,814,491	111,980	4.3
20	Goodyear Tire & Rubber	2,226,256	1,637,812	103,664	4.9

Reprinted from the July 15, 1966, *Fortune Directory* by special permission: © 1966, Time, Inc.

or a dealer in services whose annual sales do not exceed $1 million is classified as a small business. A wholesaler whose annual sales do not exceed $5 million is a small businessman. A manufacturing company that does not have more than 250 employees is ordinarily classified as a small business; and under some circumstances, it retains that classification even though it employs up to 1,000 workers. Small businesses, therefore, are very important in our economy.

The table on page 22 presents certain pertinent data for the 20 largest industrial corporations in the United States for 1965. Of particular note are the wide variations between different firms in assets, employees, and specifically in profit as a percent of sales.

■ Classification of Business

Two basic classes of business firms are industrial and commercial. *Industrial businesses* include all businesses that are engaged in producing things—by extraction from the earth, by fabrication in the factory, or by construction on a building site. In the classification of *commercial businesses* are to be found firms engaged in marketing, such as wholesalers and retailers; in finance, such as banks and investment concerns; and in the service field, which includes communication, transportation, gas, electric power, water supply, hotels, and theaters. The following table presents selected data concerning manufacturing, service industries, retail trade, and wholesale trade for a recent year.

Number of Units, Dollar Volume of Sales, and Number of Employees for Selected Types of Business

TYPE OF BUSINESS	NUMBER OF UNITS	SALES (BILLIONS OF DOLLARS)	NUMBER OF EMPLOYEES
Manufacturing	313,000	399,120	16,859,000
Service Industries	1,061,673	44,586	7,949,000
Retail Trade	2,032,000	244,201	8,410,000
Wholesale Trade	308,177	358,385	3,088,000

Source: 1963 *Census of Business.*

At the close of 1962 more than 4.7 million business firms were in operation in this country. This was an increase of 22,000 over the number doing business at the end of the preceding year. In 1962 approximately 43 out of every 100 businesses were engaged in retail trade, as contrasted to 19 in service industries, 9 in construction, and 7 each in manufacturing and in wholesale trade. The greatest increase in number of firms since

1946 has occurred in the retail industry. There has also been a steady increase in the number of wholesale firms. The number of manufacturing firms has shown a decline since 1957.

■ Other Economic Systems

Socialism and communism are the principal noncapitalistic economic systems in the world today. Both socialism and communism in their pure forms provide for government ownership of business enterprises, as opposed to the private enterprise of capitalism. This means that the direction of economic activity is in the hands of the government and that workers are government employees. In such an economy there would, of course, be no profits as this term is understood under capitalism. Competition would not exist, nor would the element of entrepreneurial risk.

Perhaps one of the most outstanding points of difference is that of incentives. In our capitalistic economy, a number of built-in incentives play a significant role in inducing workers at all levels to exert their best efforts at their jobs and in persuading those who have saved funds to invest in business enterprise. These inducements are both monetary and social. They include not only profits for entrepreneurs, wage incentives and opportunities for promotion for employees, but also the prestige that attaches to success in almost all lines of economic endeavor. Under socialism and communism, workers are supposed to do their best for the state without personal incentives. If extra effort is required, it is presumed to be forthcoming because the government has ordered it and not because of any personal gain that may be achieved by the workers.

BUSINESS TERMS

The following business terms have been introduced in this chapter. Check the list to make certain that you can define or explain and give an example of each term. The numbers in parentheses following the terms are page references.

(a) business (3); capitalism (3), laissez faire (4)
(b) private property (4), private enterprise (5), freedom of contract (6)
(c) entrepreneur (6), management (7)
(d) consumer demand (8)
(e) capital goods (10), capital funds (10)
(f) production (11), distribution (11)
(g) price (12)
(h) competition (13), pure competition (13)
(i) oligopoly (13), monopolistic competition (13)

(j) product differentiation (13), handicap competition (13), innovistic competition (14)
(k) risk (15), profit (16)
(l) classical theory of capitalism (17), income-expenditure analysis (19)
(m) mass production (20)
(n) research (21), research and development (21), operations research (21)
(o) industrial businesses (23), commercial businesses (23)

QUESTIONS FOR DISCUSSION AND ANALYSIS

1. Do you believe that there will ever be a reversal of the trend away from laissez faire in this country? Why?
2. Name several areas of economic activity where private enterprise is not usually found. What reasons can you give for these situations?
3. The footnote on page 13 points out that public utilities are normally not subjected to competition. Do you think that this is a desirable condition? Why?
4. Should the federal government put a limit on the amount of profits that business firms can earn? Why?
5. If the role of profits in business is not understood by the public, how would you suggest that this situation be rectified?
6. Which is more important, the wages paid to labor or the profits and interest to capital? Explain.
7. If research and development is vital to the survival of the large firms that can afford it, what will happen to those smaller firms that cannot? Explain.
8. In view of the growing size of the leading companies in practically all areas of business, would you expect small businesses to disappear over the years? Explain.
9. Do you think that the concepts of handicap and innovistic competition will ever become as important as price competition? Why?
10. Some years ago a prominent corporation president stated publicly that "what's good for business is good for the country." Do you agree with this statement? Why?

PROBLEMS AND SHORT CASES

1. A prominent industrialist, who was the chief executive of a firm that is the largest manufacturer of its kind in the world, distinguished himself and his company by an employee compensation system that resulted in the workers receiving, on the average, approximately twice the annual wages paid in the field of production. The philosophy of this man has been summed up in the following statements made by him from time to time:

"There is no limit to the production capacity of a human being."
"The worker who is assured the fruits of his labor will find a thousand and one ways to increase production."
"Man is inherently lazy. He must have the proper incentive to produce more than just enough to live."
"The worker should be worthy of his hire, but his hire should be proportionate to his ability to produce."
"The goal of an organization must be this—to make a better product to be sold at a lower and lower price. Profit cannot be the goal. Profit must be the by-product."

After analyzing these statements, be prepared to answer and discuss the following questions:

(a) Could the philosophy of this man and his company be adopted by all businesses? Why?

(b) Do these statements imply a negation of the historic role of profit in capitalism? Why?

(c) Do you believe that these statements are contrary to the basic tenets of capitalism? Explain.

2. In the past few years the size of some companies, such as the General Motors Corporation and the Great Atlantic and Pacific Tea Company, has been viewed with disfavor by some politicians, labor leaders, and spokesmen for small business. Their complaint has been that the great growth of these and other concerns creates the danger of monopolies, of driving small firms out of business, and of raising prices to unreasonable heights in the country. Defend or criticize the presence of large companies in this country, in accord with your own point of view. Give reasons for the stand that you take.

3. Refer to page 22 and compute (a) the ratio of sales to employees and (b) the ratio of assets to employees for (1) General Motors, Ford, and Chrysler and for (2) Standard Oil (N.J.), Mobil Oil, Texaco, and Gulf Oil. What do you infer from your figures?

SUGGESTED READINGS

Bach, G. L. *Economics: An Introduction to Analysis and Policy,* Fourth Edition. Englewood Cliffs, New Jersey: Prentice-Hall, Inc., 1963.

Hailstones, T. J., and J. H. Dodd. *Economics: An Analysis of Principles and Policies,* Fifth Edition. Cincinnati: South-Western Publishing Company, 1965.

McConnell, C. R. *Economics: Principles, Problems, and Policies,* Third Edition. New York: McGraw-Hill Book Company, 1966.

Samuelson, P. A. *Economics: An Introductory Analysis,* Sixth Edition. New York: McGraw-Hill Book Company, 1964.

Magazines: *Business Week, Dun's Review,* and *Fortune.* Current information on business topics that will be considered in this course may be obtained from a number of magazines. These will be identified in the Suggested Readings for the various chapters.

Chapter 2

BUSINESS AND ENVIRONMENTAL FACTORS

A meaningful inquiry into the purposes, methods, institutions, results, and philosophy of American business would be inadequate without first giving consideration to its relationship to the environment in which it functions. This relationship is a mutual one in which the forces of business and its environment interact continuously upon each other and determine to a considerable extent the attitude of the public and of government toward business as an institution. This, in turn, affects the decisions and actions of businessmen as they attempt to perform their economic function, which is that of satisfying the needs and wants of the people of this country and thereby earning a profit for themselves.

This mutual relationship is not a static entity but is subject to constant modification, reflective of the variations that arise in the public thinking and of the changes in business techniques and policies that the pressures of competition and progress create. It is therefore important for students of business to be aware of the dynamic character of the environment of business and to recognize that changes may come about with startling rapidity.

■ Historical Setting

An understanding of the factors that make up the environment in which business functions will be aided by a brief consideration of two historical aspects of the situation.

> 1. The land and the people
> 2. The industrial revolution

1 / The land and the people. The United States comprises a very large territory, with a widely varied climate and vast natural resources of timber, metal ores, waterways, water power sources, and fertile farmland.

At the time that the first white settlers began arriving, these resources were almost completely undeveloped. This was virgin land, admirably adapted to support an agricultural and industrial population.

With few exceptions, the people who migrated to this country in the early days of its history were strong, courageous, adventurous, and self-reliant. In many instances they came here to be free from oppression—political, economic, or religious. Deeply ingrained in many of them was an intense suspicion of and dislike for a strong central government, coupled with a belief in the dignity of hard work. While they naturally brought with them from England and Europe many of the customs and habits of thought of their native lands, they were confronted with new problems, in strange surroundings, that demanded of them new and different approaches to the solution of questions of survival and of making a satisfactory living. The attitude taken by the ruling groups in England and elsewhere that the settlements in America were to have the status of colonies, contributing needed materials to the mother countries and at the same time remaining always dependent upon and subservient to them, aroused a deep sense of resentment among the colonists and served as a stimulus to them to become more completely self-sustaining and politically independent of the countries from which they and their parents had come.

Thus was the attitude of self-reliance and independence developed here. It manifested itself in the belief that a man's success in life was, in a large measure, due to his own energy, courage, and resourcefulness. It spawned the concept of "going into business for one's self" that was a dominant characteristic of our economic thinking for many years, and which survives even to the present.

An important by-product of this type of thinking was the general attitude that private business enterprise was important. Success in business was regarded highly, and successful businessmen were honored and respected as leaders in their communities. Even though the doctrine of *caveat emptor,* let the buyer beware, was generally accepted by the people, they accorded honor and prestige to the leading entrepreneurs of the times.

2 / The industrial revolution. The middle of the 18th century has been commonly, if possibly somewhat inaccurately, accepted as the time of the onset of what is called the *industrial revolution.* Stated briefly, this revolution consisted of the application of mechanical power to productive processes hitherto derived from human or animal sources; the extensive development of machinery to which the new power sources could be applied; and the establishment of the *factory system,* under which production workers were assembled in a central location as opposed to the precedent *domestic system*, under which the workers performed their productive tasks in their own homes. The effect of the industrial revolution was to bring about a far-reaching change in business organization. Whereas formerly production was carried on in small, family groups, with minimal capital requirements, now the advent of mechanical power, complicated machinery, and extensive factory buildings called for large amounts of capital and, to an increasing extent, for more competent managerial personnel.

The industrial revolution developed principally in England but moved, within a relatively short time, to America where it had a profound impact on the industrial development of the country. Prior to this time, business had been conducted on a local basis to a large extent, with most firms of relatively small size. Furthermore, the philosophy of laissez faire was predominant here, as it was abroad. The industrial revolution brought about a gradual increase in the size and scope of manufacturing establishments that was accelerated by the demands for war matériel generated by the Civil War. After the war, with the progressive opening up of the western parts of the country to a growing population, with a consequent broadening of markets and of business activity, large companies began to appear and the dominance of the corporation began to emerge. Along with this trend there came a gradual weakening of the laissez faire idea, brought about by the competitive practices of some of the large concerns, which were believed to be inimical to the best interests of the country. This development was the source of many of the business environmental factors of the present time.

Business and Society

Business does not operate in a social vacuum. Basic to an understanding of business is a recognition of its integral relationships with that entity which is commonly referred to as society. The purpose of the remainder of this chapter is to inquire into the nature of these relationships.

1. Public opinion
2. Business and government
3. Labor and government
4. Business cycles
5. Big and little business
6. Foreign competition
7. The role of economists
8. Statism or the welfare state

1 / Public opinion. In a democracy the influence of public opinion makes itself felt in many ways, among which are letters to the editors of newspapers and periodicals; editorials that reflect the impact of these letters on the editors and publishers of a free press; the writings of observers and commentators on public affairs; demands upon government made by interested groups for action to protect them from some actual or imagined dangers; the election or defeat of candidates for political office on the basis of the positions that they have taken regarding current issues of public interest; and, occasionally, through more or less spontaneous uprising of members of the public in support of or against certain issues that affect them.

All of these methods have been employed at one time or another as a means of bringing the power of public opinion to bear on the actions and policies of the business community. In many, if not most instances, public opinion has been instrumental in bringing about changes in business practices of which the public disapproved.

There is a strong reason to believe that there exists a rather broad misconception of the role of profits in our economy, coupled with a suspicion that while profits are possibly necessary, they are too high for the public good in some instances. The belief persists that many business firms, particularly the larger ones, could reduce their prices substantially without endangering their continued existence. The statements of dollar profit volume before taxes, which are issued periodically by many large companies, publicize amounts that are frequently beyond the comprehension of many people and serve to confirm the suspicion that profits are too large.

It is quite probable that large segments of the general public, particularly those who do not own or manage business enterprises, are quite ignorant of the economics of business operation, know little about accounting and finance, and hence are unable to understand the relationships between capital investment and the need for an adequate return to investors. Many educators and businessmen are aware of this situation and have been trying to do something about correcting it, but with little apparent success. Doubtless the disparity between the income of the average citizen and those of business executives, which are published from time to time, tends to accentuate this attitude.

(a) THE CONSUMER AS FINAL ARBITER. Another important aspect of public opinion is the summation of the actions of individual consumers in accepting or rejecting products and services that business offers to them. Without legislation or regulatory bodies, consumers show their approval or disapproval of goods and services by the simple process of buying or not buying them. This is one of the most potent methods of making certain that the products and the services provided by business are those which are needed and desired by the public. Although the determination by producers of the acceptability of their products prior to their being offered for sale presents a most difficult problem, the decision of the public will come, quickly and definitely, once the products are available for purchase. While there is no complete agreement on the exact percentages involved, it has been frequently said that 8 out of every 10 new products that appear on the market fail to win public approval and are relegated to the scrap heap. This aspect of the business environment is one of which all makers and sellers of goods and services are constantly aware.

(b) THE CORPORATE IMAGE. A factor in the environment of both large and small business, but particularly in the case of the former, is what has come to be known as the *corporate image concept.* This refers to the impression of a corporation that is held by the public, which may be either good or bad. A firm may be regarded as beneficent, ruthless, public spirited, progressive, conservative, reliable, or any one of a number of favorable or unfavorable characterizations. No small part of the activities of public relations firms consists of endeavoring to create and preserve favorable corporate images for their clients. For small businesses, the image that the public has of them is important, but somewhat less so than with big business, possibly because of the personal contacts that small businessmen have with their customers.

2 / Business and government. When the people of this country believe that something should be done which they are unable to do for themselves, they usually turn to some branch of government to secure the desired action. At the federal level, nearly all types of business that engage in interstate commerce have been affected by government action to some extent, frequently through some form of regulation. In many instances, the pattern has been for the Congress to pass certain laws designed to regulate some field of business or phase of business activity, and then to establish federal agencies to administer these laws. For example, the Interstate Commerce Commission was established in 1887 to regulate the railroads under the Interstate Commerce Act. The Federal Trade Commission was set up in 1915 to administer the Federal Trade Commission Act and the Clayton Act. In the same manner, the Federal Communications Commission, the Federal Power Commission, the Food and Drug Administration, and many others were created by Congress to handle problems in their respective fields.

An interesting aspect of this form of governmental action is that the decisions reached by these agencies, in dealing with matters which properly come within their authority, have the force of law and are, in fact, commonly referred to as *administrative law*. Thus, it becomes clear that a part of the environment of business consists of edicts of administrative agencies issued under the authority of laws passed by the Congress. These rulings may be just as important as the original law and may require an equal degree of compliance. Since many of these administrative agencies will be discussed in some detail in certain chapters that follow, no attempt will be made here to list all of them or the areas over which they have jurisdiction.

Another contact that government has with business is the administration of the Sherman Antitrust Act of 1890 by the Department of Justice. Also, the area of taxation at all governmental levels is a significant factor in this phase of the business environment. The monetary and fiscal policies of the federal government, bearing on such matters as interest rates, foreign aid, and the federal budget, affect business in many different ways. The trend toward governmental ownership and operation of power generating and transmission facilities is one of concern to private business in this area, as well as to the users of electric power.

The powers of the federal government to levy and adjust the duties on goods from other countries has a profound effect upon the impact of foreign competition on domestic manufacturers. The farm price-support program, whereby the prices of certain agricultural products have been supported at levels above those which would be obtained in a free market, affects those whose business requires them to deal with these commodities.

Since the days of the so-called New Deal of the early 1930's, there has been a growing belief in government circles that the maintenance of a prosperous economy and of high-level employment is the concern and, to a considerable extent, the responsibility of the federal government. Successive administrations and Congresses have followed this concept with increasing intensity. The underlying philosophy of government action in this area has been that of endeavoring to provide a favorable governmental and economic climate, rather than to undertake the actual manipulation of the business system itself. The income tax and excise tax reductions of the past few years are indicative of this approach.

The civil rights legislation is not without its relevancy to business. Procedures for the avoidance of discrimination in the hiring and promoting of employees must be established. Also the prospect of increased incomes for the minority groups indicates greater sales in many categories of consumer goods.

3 / **Labor and government.** With the passage of the National Labor Relations Act of 1935, organized labor, which had hitherto played a somewhat minor role in the business environment, grew in size and importance. Employers were required to bargain with the unions that represented their employees, and such vast industrial areas as the steel and automobile fields were thoroughly unionized. Union membership rose rapidly from a low of around 3 million members in 1934 to approximately 18 million in 1964. The New Deal of the 1930's and the so-called Fair Deal of the immediate post-World War II period encouraged the growth of organized labor's economic and political power, with the result that the traditional freedom of action and decision in the area of labor relations, which businessmen had long enjoyed, was greatly curtailed, and the owners and managers of business firms discovered in the new-found strength of labor a formidable opponent in bargaining and in politics.

The exemption of labor from the antitrust laws, under the Clayton Act of 1914, has given the unions an advantage in their dealings with business that many businessmen regard as unfair but about which they have been able to do nothing to date. Some of the more liberal labor leaders have suggested that the profits of certain companies are too large and have called into question the methods by which their costs are allocated and their prices computed. A small group of labor leaders have even suggested that labor should have a voice in the management of business enterprises. The growth in the influence of labor is a significant item in the environment of business.

4 / **Business cycles.** The history of business activity in this country has been one of alternate prosperity and depression. This movement has been termed the *business cycle*. During periods of prosperity, the volume of production, employment, profits, and prices rise. In times of depression, they decrease. For many years the belief prevailed in business and governmental circles that these cyclical movements were inevitable and there was little that anyone could do about them. When the downward movement of the business cycle was slight and of short duration, the term *recession* was applied. After each depression (or recession) the recovery usually reached a higher level than in the past.

The depression of the 1930's, which was one of great severity and which followed the post-World War I era of prosperity, brought a change in the thinking of governmental officials and many businessmen. Instead of merely waiting for the downward trend of the cycle to run its course, attempts were made through a number of legislative enactments to induce a recovery. Whether or not these had any effect on the depression is uncertain, as the approach of World War II brought with it a substantial measure of recovery and the entrance of this country into the conflict late in 1941 raised the level of production to a new high and dispelled all thoughts of depression for several years.

In the postwar years several recessions of relatively brief duration occurred, each followed by a recovery period. One notable aspect of these times, however, was that unemployment, which had historically increased during depressions and decreased during prosperity, failed to improve during the recovery periods of these years but, in the opinion of many officials in the government, remained abnormally high. This situation led to a widespread discussion of the emerging effect of business cycles on employment and of the part that government might be able to play in decreasing unemployment.

The Employment Act of 1946, a federal law, sometimes referred to as the *full employment act,* placed upon the federal government the responsibility for taking such measures as seem advisable to maintain the economic health of the nation. A federal Council of Economic Advisers was established to "develop and recommend to the President national economic policies to foster and promote free competitive enterprise, to avoid economic fluctuations or to diminish the effects thereof, and to maintain maximum employment, production, and purchasing power." It prepares an Annual Economic Review for the President, who transmits an Economic Report to the Congress. Thus the current discussion regarding unemployment is not over the role of government, as such, but over the solution to the problem of unemployment in an era of prosperity. The question seems to be whether this is due to *structural unemployment*, which refers to the difficulties involved in matching available people and jobs, or to an inadequate growth of aggregate demand in the country.

5 / Big and little business. The presence of very large firms with huge resources, well-trained managerial and operative personnel, and extensive research facilities has brought about an intensification of competition that has been apparent at all levels of business. Small firms in many lines of business must follow the lead of the large firms in order to compete successfully, a factor in the environmental picture that has been emphasized by the relatively high rate of failures among small companies.

For big business, the problem of competing with alert small firms is always present, but the pressure involved is much less than it is for small companies. However, there is an aspect of this situation that many large firms, particularly in retailing, have had to meet and learn to live with. This concerns certain types of legislation, passed at the behest of small businesses, that have been designed to equalize the competitive advantages that the large firms would otherwise enjoy. Examples include laws to prevent price cutting by retailers, to prevent price discrimination by sellers, and to establish price floors for certain commodities; and chain-store tax laws. Whether or not these laws are in the best interest of the public is an open question. The legislative bodies involved apparently thought so at the time that they were enacted. Thus the environment of big business is affected by the presence of a large number of small firms.

There are numerous instances where a project, either government sponsored or under private auspices, utilizes the facilities of both large and small companies. For example, in the fabricating of Telstar, our first communications satellite, 1,249 companies participated either as subcontractors or suppliers, under the leadership of the Bell Telephone System, which underwrote the project.

For big business, competition is rugged; for small business, it has become a life-or-death matter. In an attempt to help the small business-man meet the rigors of competition, the Small Business Administration was established by Congress in 1953. Many of the laws mentioned earlier were adopted to relieve the pressure of competition on small businesses. In some instances, a few large firms have sought relief from the severity of competition through collusion with their competitors, mainly in the area of prices. This is illegal and has resulted in fines for the companies and, in one case, imprisonment of the officials involved. The extent of this practice is unknown, but it is evidence of the strenuous nature of competition in this country.

There is an area, however, in which small businessmen have been able to achieve a remarkable measure of success. This is called *franchising*, a procedure by which companies with well-known names grant franchises or licenses to small businessmen with some capital to invest, which permits the latter group not only to be in business for themselves but also to benefit from the reputations, guidance, and know-how of the franchising companies. Among the types of business where franchising is to be found are restaurants, gas stations, soft-drink bottlers, car rentals, and coin-operated laundries and dry cleaning establishments. Some of the well-known franchisers are Howard Johnson's, Avis, Hertz, and Dairy Queen. The International Franchise Association has been organized to establish and maintain a strict code of ethics for the industry.

6 / Foreign competition. A sizable volume of foreign trade, both in exports and imports, has long been regarded as a favorable item in the nation's business complex. Certain products of foreign lands have always found a market in this country, some encountering competition from domestic producers and others catering to a demand not being adequately supplied here. An example of the latter is the Volkswagen, which has had a phenomenal sale, in a size class that our car manufacturers had previously generally ignored. English bone china dinnerware, French perfumes, and Swedish glassware fall into the same category. When producers in this country have been affected by foreign competition, in some instances tariff walls have been erected to equalize the competition between our manufacturers and those in other countries with lower costs.

The Marshall Plan of 1948 was designed to help the war-ravaged countries of Europe to reestablish their economies. Under its operation, these nations were given modern tools and instruction in how to use them. The consequence of this action over the years has been to create strong competitors in Europe, who are capable of delivering goods in this country, even allowing for tariffs, at prices equal to, and in many cases below, those of our own manufacturers. The range of goods involved has been broadened with the result that a considerable number of American producers have been forced to add foreign competition to an already tough domestic competitive situation. With the possible extension, both in numbers and power, of the European Common Market, this competition could become even more rigorous, although attempts are being made by the Administration in Washington to reach agreements with the Common Market countries that will counterbalance this to some extent through a growth in our exports.

7 / The role of economists. Until the depression of the 1930's, economists were generally thought of as cloistered savants, whose theories and attitudes appeared to have little visible influence on business practices and governmental policies. There had been a number of depressions in the history of the country from which the economy had always emerged; and, while certain economists had occasionally suggested that these recoveries were needlessly delayed, it appears that neither businessmen nor governmental officials paid much attention to their proposed remedies for business slumps. The depression of the 1930's was different, apparently, and by 1933 not only had many businessmen despaired of a quick recovery, but also they turned to the federal government in the hope of some sort of a solution to the continuing low level of business activity.

At about this time, an English economist, John Maynard Keynes, proposed that the federal government should embark on a program of spending, the purpose of which was to stimulate the recovery of the economy. Some of the details of Lord Keynes' theory have been described in Chapter 1. The federal government followed Keynes' suggstions to some extent, and there was a visible improvement in the level of business activity. Whether this was due in any considerable measure to the Keynesian theory has been a matter of dispute among economists, businessmen, and government officials. The onset of World War II in 1939 and the involvement of this country after Pearl Harbor in December, 1941, provided a stimulus to business that overshadowed any prior government spending for recovery. But during the late 1930's, and to a large extent thereafter, economists became active in government and their theories and viewpoints came to exert an increasing measure of influence on federal economic and fiscal policy.

Since the end of World War II, the theories of Lord Keynes have achieved even greater attention. The persistently high level of business activity, with a few minor deviations, is largely credited to the fact that the federal government, guided to a considerable extent by economists, has adopted policies that have permitted business and consumers to take those steps deemed most likely to keep the economy in high gear. It appears that there is a substantial measure of agreement among economists that the Keynesian doctrines point the way toward continued prosperity in the country; and many businessmen have come to accept, if not embrace, the role of economists and their theories in the mosaic of business environment.

The effect on the economy of such events as the war in Viet Nam, with its abnormal drain on men, money, and materials, and the success of such steps as the government may take to prevent an inflation will indicate whether the economists have the means of achieving such a goal within the doctrines of Keynesian economics. It appears that these theories can operate successfully to brake a downward economic trend, but only the future will reveal if it is economically and politically possible to reverse the upward trend and still maintain an acceptably robust level of business activity.

8 / Statism or the welfare state. Under the philosophy of laissez faire, the assumption was implicit that the well-being of individuals was achieved through their own efforts and accomplishments and that the status of each person was more or less a reflection of his energy and ability. Over the years from the start of the industrial revolution until the depression of the 1930's, there had been a gradual shift in public opinion away from this reliance on the individual toward the belief that there are some circumstances where action by government would bring about more certain relief from troublesome situations. The 1930's, with the crushing weight of high unemployment and failure of many businesses, appear to have accelerated this trend, and to have brought about a fairly widespread belief that it was the function of government to assume responsibility for the welfare of its citizens and to take such steps as seemed necessary to implement this obligation. The terms *welfare state* and, more recently, *statism* came into being as descriptive of this new role of government. Such items as aid to the unemployed, social security, racial desegration, aid to education, public housing, slum clearance, urban renewal, and many other projects came into being under the philosophy of this new belief.

Writers and commentators claim that they discern a breaking away from the pioneering spirit of earlier days, particularly on the part of younger men, and that security rather than achievement has become their goal. On the other hand, the proponents of still further extension of governmental welfare action maintain that conditions are different than they were years ago, and that only action by the government can prevent widespread distress and economic dislocation within the country. Actually no one expects, and probably few really hope for, a return to the pre-1930 hands-off governmental policies; but the argument between the proponents and the opponents of the welfare idea, together with the actions already taken in its behalf, constitute a formidable segment of the current environment in which business functions.

A factor that may be an indication of a growing tolerance, if not complete approval, of this development is found in the increasing number of prominent business executives who have accepted important posts in the federal government, many of cabinet rank.

■ Change as an Environmental Ingredient

The element of change is inescapable, and it is most unwise for any businessman to ignore it. The pervasive nature of change affecting so many aspects of the business scene has suggested the observation that the only permanent element in the environment of business is change. Of particular importance are the changes related to the following factors:

1. Automation
2. Science
3. Electronic data processing
4. Simulation and models
5. The shift in emphasis from production to distribution
6. Defense contracts and space technology
7. Population growth and suburbanization
8. The shift from an industrial to a service economy

1 / Automation. Since the beginning of the industrial revolution, there has been a continuous search by entrepreneurs, ~~businessmen~~ both individual and corporate, for ways in which to cut costs and thereby to achieve either competitive price advantages or larger profits. This has brought about the progressive substitution of machines for human labor, permitting a greater measure of production with the same labor force, or maintaining the same productive output with fewer workers. The past twenty or more years has witnessed a notable acceleration of these efforts, and the term *automation* has come to be applied to it. This phenomenon has made itself felt in the environment of business in a number of ways. Competition among companies that have been able to automate and those that have not has become more severe. The accelerated obsolescence of machinery has presented many firms with serious financial problems since they have been compelled to replace their present machinery with the newer tools of automation. The personnel aspects of the automation problem have been singularly difficult. The introduction of automated machinery has frequently brought about the abolition of the jobs of many skilled and semiskilled workers for whom the problem of finding new jobs has been quite difficult. In unionized industries the resistance of the labor leaders to the dismissal of their members has placed additional burdens on the managements of the companies involved whose competitive survival hinged on their ability to achieve the cost savings that automation offered. At the same time there appeared, in many instances, a shortage of the highly skilled workers whose abilities were required to set up, adjust, and repair the new machines.

2 / Science. In the past two decades, there has been a remarkable advance in the area of science, particularly in the productive techniques of business. Stimulated both by the uncertainties of the international situation, such as the so-called cold war, and the growing competition from those nations that were more or less devastated by World War II, research in the physical and technological sciences has been extended under both governmental and private auspices.

Items of consequence involve the discovery and growth of atomic fission as a source of power; the development of artificial substances called plastics; new techniques in manufacture, such as the use of oxygen in the production of steel; and the promise of greater advances in metallurgy and allied fields resulting from the space program.

The environmental aspects of this advance in science are that manufacturers are and will be in ever greater danger of some scientific breakthrough that may place upon them the burden of scrapping some of their current productive equipment in order to remain competitive, or of falling behind if they are financially unable to keep abreast of competition. New products will doubtless arise, which will render obsolete some well-established ones. Progress in the fields of electronics and miniaturization will offer attractive opportunities for alert manufacturers. From the standpoint of personnel, technically trained manpower is in ever-increasing demand; and at the executive and managerial levels, the problems to be met will require administrative abilities of a high order.

Many economists believe that _innovation_, in the form of new processes, products, machinery, or techniques, is essential to the continued growth of our national economy. It brings about an increase in production, employment, and income, all of which serve to spur the economy to greater heights of activity. While some decline in volume of business may follow eventually, it is believed that this decline will be of less intensity than the expansion and that further innovation will result in an ever-higher rate of production.

A further development in this area is the result of inquiry into the contributions that the _behavioral sciences_ might be able to make to business. Leaders in the fields of economics, sociology, psychology, and cultural anthropology have joined with forward-looking executives in exploring the areas of business in which the principles of their professions might be helpful.

3 / Electronic data processing. With the development of electronic data processing equipment, called computers, great stress is being placed on the assembling and analysis of the quantitative aspects of business operations. While close attention has long been paid to this area of business information, the tremendous increase in the amount of quantitative data that can be assimilated by these machines, plus the speed with which they operate, has provided management with noteworthy assistance in decision making.

Computers have come into constructive usage in an ever-increasing number of business areas. Users of computers have found the following advantages in their installation: saving of clerical labor costs, saving of time in preparing reports, greater accuracy, and the development of new information. Computers had, at first, been utilized to perform routine recording operations, such as billing, preparing payrolls, cost compilations, and maintaining inventory data. More advanced applications are the costing and scheduling of complex technical projects; the revealing of the fastest and most economical routes for incoming and outgoing goods; the analysis of the effectiveness with which salesmen are covering their territories; the scheduling of machines in a factory so as to achieve the optimum production; a recording and analysis of sales; the most advantageous location for branch plants and sales offices, considering the sources of raw materials, transportation costs, and customer locations; and the practically instant retrieval of reports previously stored in the so-called "memory" of the computer. The attempt has even been made, but without too great a measure of success, to use computers to discover the best advertising media for certain products.

4 / Simulation and models. A comparatively new development, and one that has been made possible by the introduction of computers, is the use of _simulation_ or _business games_ and the development of _models_ or mathematical equations designed to represent desired business situations. These devices have been used in management training courses in which the participants are given certain data concerning the company and are asked to make decisions regarding future actions. These decisions are then referred to the computer, which has been previously programmed as to the consequences of these various moves, and the trainees can then determine whether their choices are wise or not.

5 / The shift in emphasis from production to distribution. The advances in productive techniques, partly the result of the advance in science, has made it possible to produce more goods than can be sold profitably. While it is recognized that substantial segments of our people have substandard incomes and that the rate of unemployment is doubtless too high, there is probably sufficient idle productive capacity to take care of the needs and wants of these unfortunates were their incomes to rise to an acceptable level. This situation points up one of the emerging aspects of the business environment—the shift in emphasis from production to distribution. Ways must be found, within the attainable limits of average incomes, to dispose profitably of the goods that our productive capacity is capable of producing.

6 / Defense contracts and space technology. One of the key items in the changing environment of business is the presence of an increasing volume of contracts for research, development, and manufacture of defense hardware, awarded by the federal government. During the different wars in which this country has participated, the weapons required for their prosecution have been furnished, in the main, by private business. At the conclusion of these conflicts, until the end of World War II, it was customary for the companies concerned to return to the manufacture of their former lines of peacetime products. Since 1945, however, with the onset of the cold war, the development of nuclear energy for weaponry and propulsion, and the growth of interest in the exploration of space, an ever-increasing number of federal defense and space research, development, and production contracts have been awarded to qualified business concerns. In many instances, very large companies are devoting all or most of their productive facilities to the handling of these contracts, which amount to many billions of dollars annually.

7 / Population growth and suburbanization. The years immediately following World War II witnessed a marked upturn in the birthrate in this country, which reached its peak in 1957. Since that time there has been a steady decline with demographers wondering if the present trend will continue or whether it will reverse itself again as it has done from time to time in the past. Regardless of the direction of the birthrate in the future, the growth in population has resulted in a sizable increase in the demand for goods and services of all kinds, as well as the ever-growing necessity of creating jobs for those who reach working age. Now, with the birthrate falling, the shift in the types of goods and services required will reflect the decreasing demand for the classifications of goods needed by children, and this will move in a sort of ebbing tide as the years pass and the young people grow up.

The so-called "population explosion" of the post-World War II years is apparently slowing down, but the overall effect of the population increase will mean that there will be about 250 million people in this country by 1980, according to the estimates of the Census Bureau of the United States. And with the continued growth in personal income, indicated in the chart on page 43, it appears that business will benefit through the combination of these two factors.

There has also been a marked migration of families from the cities to the suburbs. This trend has affected the construction industry, both in the building of homes and in the requisite facilities, such as shopping centers, service stations, medical buildings, schools, and hospitals. Those industries which manufacture the articles that go into the furnishing and equipping of these structures have shared in the increase of business in their areas. Many firms have moved their offices from the cities to the suburbs in order to be nearer to where their employees live and, in cases of expansion, to provide greater parking facilities for them and for the firms' customers. There has been a noteworthy growth of industrial parks in the suburban areas, apart from the residential sections, that has markedly affected many of the operational phases of industries.

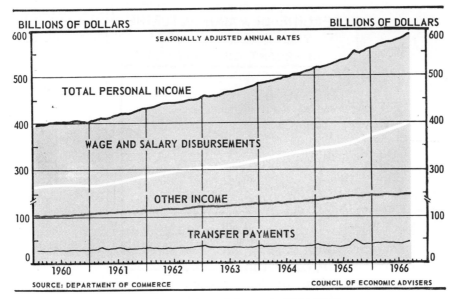

BILLIONS OF DOLLARS

BILLIONS OF DOLLARS

SEASONALLY ADJUSTED ANNUAL RATES

TOTAL PERSONAL INCOME

WAGE AND SALARY DISBURSEMENTS

OTHER INCOME

TRANSFER PAYMENTS

SOURCE: DEPARTMENT OF COMMERCE   COUNCIL OF ECONOMIC ADVISERS

Growth in Personal Income, 1960-1966

The top line of this chart indicates the continued growth in personal income. The next line indicates the principal source of personal income—wage and salary disbursements. Other income includes business, professional, and rental income; dividends and personal interest; and farm proprietors' income.

8 / The shift from an industrial to a service economy. Historically the economy of the United States has been regarded as devoted principally to the production of goods rather than of services. This concept has been based on the impact of the industrial revolution on the manufacture of and demand for goods of all kinds. It has also been affected by the historic preponderance of employment in industry as contrasted to the workers in the services. Dating from around 1953, and brought about by the growth of automation and other technological developments, it has been possible to turn out more and more goods with fewer workers, with the result that more people are employed in the service fields than in the production of goods. And this condition is expected to become accentuated as progress in the technology of manufacture continues.

The *service industries* include business, professional, and repair services; and government. The consequences of this situation are not entirely clear, but among them appear to be an increase in the number of women employed and a possible weakening of the influence of labor unions, which are somewhat less important in the service industries than in manufacturing.

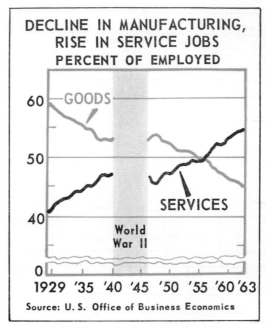

DECLINE IN MANUFACTURING, RISE IN SERVICE JOBS
PERCENT OF EMPLOYED

Source: U. S. Office of Business Economics

■ The Social Responsibilities of Business

The impact of business on society is such that certain social responsibilities devolve upon it. There is, however, no general agreement among those interested as to the specific nature and extent of these responsibilities. Questions such as the following have been raised and their eventual answers will go far toward delineating the extent of the social obligations of business:

Should business take care of its superannuated employees?

Does business have any responsibility toward those of its employees whose jobs disappear because of technological advances?

Should business be concerned with the problems of education and the financial difficulties of educational institutions?

Should a small firm be required to pay its employees a legally established minimum wage even though to do so may endanger its solvency?

In the matter of plant relocation, quite common in recent years, is the decision to move exclusively that of management, or does a firm have an obligation to its workers who might be disemployed because of the proposed move, or to the community whose economy might be adversely affected by the loss of the enterprise?

Are there any business decisions in which representatives of labor or the local communities are entitled to a voice?

BUSINESS TERMS

(a) caveat emptor (28) buyer beware
(b) industrial revolution (28); factory system (28), domestic system (29)
(c) corporate image concept (31)
(d) administrative law (32)
(e) business cycle (33), recession (33)
(f) full employment act (34), structural unemployment (34)
(g) franchising (35)
(h) welfare state (38), statism (38)
(i) automation (39)
(j) innovation (40); behavioral sciences (40)
(k) simulation (41), business games (41), models (41)
(l) service industries (43)

✱ ✓ all

QUESTIONS FOR DISCUSSION AND ANALYSIS

1. Do you think that the doctrine of caveat emptor is a characteristic of present-day business? Why?
2. If the early settlers of this country had come from communist countries, do you think that our economy would have developed as it has? Explain.
3. What opinions do the members of your class in school have with regard to the size of business profits in this country?
4. Should business be required to find jobs for workers who are displaced by automation? Explain.
5. Do you think that the federal government should assume responsibility for maintaining a high level of business activity? Why?
6. Why is there disagreement among economists with regard to the proper relationships between government and business? Explain.
7. Can a business afford to operate with a disregard for public opinion? Explain.
8. Is the concept of a welfare state consistent with the basic principles of capitalism? Explain.
9. Do you believe that this country is moving toward complete regulation of business by government? Explain.
10. Should prominent businessmen be encouraged to enter government service? Why?

PROBLEMS AND SHORT CASES

1. A prominent labor leader in this country has repeatedly expressed the opinion that labor should have a voice in the management of business, particularly big business. His rationale for this point of view is that the workers, through their efforts both mental and physical, have

made an investment in business that is at least as valuable to its success as is the money invested by the shareholders. He feels, therefore, that they deserve the right to participate with management and shareholders in the major decisions that are made by the latter groups. This notion, of course, is completely at variance with the accepted procedure along this line in actual business practice, where the ultimate control rests with the shareholders or owners, who delegate this authority to management. The only investment which business recognizes from the standpoint of control is that of ownership, and quite obviously the exerting of efforts by employees, however valuable to the success of business, does not qualify as ownership. When the labor leader points out that, without the intelligent and more or less dedicated efforts of the workers, a business might fail, management replies that the workers are doing only what is expected of them and in accord with the decisions of management. You are asked to discuss the viewpoints of both the labor leader and business from the standpoint of one to whom this dispute has been presented for an opinion.

2. The struggle for the survival of small business in view of the increasing severity of competition from big business has brought about congressional action that is designed to aid small business in order to preserve competition. The Small Business Act of 1953 established the Small Business Administration with 14 regional offices throughout the United States. The aid to small business is achieved through preferential treatment in the bidding for government procurement; by loans; by providing counseling service on a wide variety of managerial problems; by assistance by small business investment companies; and through preferential treatment as subcontractors for government business.

You are asked to prepare a short paper justifying or condemning the Small Business program, giving reasons. Consult the *Readers' Guide to Periodical Literature* and the *Business Periodical Index* in your school library to secure source material for your paper.

⌐SUGGESTED READINGS

Anderson, R. A. *Government and Business,* Third Edition. Cincinnati: South-Western Publishing Company, 1966.

Lebergott, S. *Manpower in Economic Growth.* New York: McGraw-Hill Book Company, Inc., 1964.

Walton, S. D. *American Business and Its Environment.* New York: The Macmillan Company, 1966.

Withers, W. *Business in Society.* New York: Appleton-Century-Crofts, Inc., 1966.

Magazines: *Newsweek, Time, U.S. News and World Report.* Each of these weekly news magazines includes articles on business and economics or a section devoted to these subjects.

Chapter 3

OPPORTUNITIES IN BUSINESS

The continuing growth of population in this country and the accompanying increase in the level of business activity present an ever-widening span of career opportunities for ambitious and qualified young people. It should be recognized that competition, which is such a prominent part of the business picture, extends also into the preemployment area and profoundly affects those who are looking forward to careers in business at the termination of their formal education. This phase of competition is a two-way operation—business firms compete for the best qualified students, and the students compete among themselves to secure the jobs that appear to offer them the best career opportunities.

The wide variety of opportunities in the various fields of endeavor and the almost complete freedom of entrance into many of them place before students the problem of deciding upon a life work—a problem that truly reflects the complexity of our economic system. In many areas of business, preparation in the form of course specialization, over and above the liberal arts, can serve as a distinct advantage to graduates of junior colleges and universities both from the standpoint of their initial jobs and from that of their subsequent progress in the companies where they are employed.

Most of the students who read this textbook probably will enter some functional field of business, but many of them have not decided whether they wish to go into production, marketing, personnel, finance, or accounting in some form upon their graduation. In order that their aptitudes and preferences may be used to the best advantage, choices which they make should be based, as far as possible, on a knowledge of the different fields of business, of the character of the jobs immediately available, and of the future opportunities that can be reasonably anticipated. The purpose of this chapter is to offer aid to all students in choosing a *vocation*—the occupation in which they will earn a living—with emphasis on careers in business. For those students who use this text as a means of learning something about business, but whose vocational aims are those of teaching, government service, law, engineering, science, or architecture, this chapter may be helpful in providing information concerning the types of positions that exist in the different sectors of our economy.

■ Specialization in Business

One of the first facts about modern-day business that a student who is selecting his future vocation needs to realize is that we are in an era of specialization. *Business specialization* means that practically all firms perform limited functions, such as selling groceries, producing steel, or transporting goods. Even within these rather narrow business activities, individuals who are employed by these firms are assigned to one type of work. Business wants broadly trained men and women, but it assumes that these individuals will start their careers in a specific activity, such as selling, purchasing, or office work.

This situation poses a serious problem for the individual who is interested in business generally but who has no idea of the type of work for which to prepare. Firms hesitate to hire a person when there is an apparent indecision as to whether their job interests the applicant. The situation is aggravated by the fact that a first job assignment is frequently limited to a small segment of the total activity of the company. That assignment can serve as a stepping-stone for the person who sees in it the beginnings of a desirable career. Furthermore, although the college-trained person is frequently considered a trainee for an executive position, he or she is expected to prove worthy of promotion.

The preferable solution to the problems created by specialization in business is to adapt college training to meet job requirements at all levels of employment. Nonprofessional subjects and professional courses in all phases of business can provide a background that will enable the individual to view a first job in its proper perspective. This background will prove most useful when managerial duties are attained. In addition, specialized work in his or her field will prove especially valuable in making good on the initial job and in shortening the time for earning promotions.

■ A Typical Experience

The career of Ken Williams is perhaps typical of many college students. When Ken was admitted to the college of his choice, he had no

PERCENT DISTRIBUTION BY YEARS OF SCHOOL COMPLETED
FOR PERSONS 25 YEARS & OVER

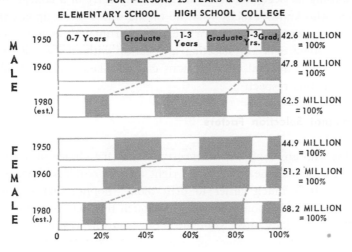

ELEMENTARY SCHOOL   HIGH SCHOOL COLLEGE

MALE
1950   0-7 Years   Graduate   1-3 Years   Graduate   1-3 Yrs.   Grad.   42.6 MILLION = 100%
1960   47.8 MILLION = 100%
1980 (est.)   62.5 MILLION = 100%

FEMALE
1950   44.9 MILLION = 100%
1960   51.2 MILLION = 100%
1980 (est.)   68.2 MILLION = 100%

0   20%   40%   60%   80%   100%

SOURCE: BUREAU OF THE CENSUS

The Conference Board *Road Maps of Industry.*

decided preference as to the type of work in which he would engage in the future. His father was an architect, but Ken had no interest in that field. He had, however, worked as a carryout boy in a supermarket near his home on Saturdays and during his vacation periods while he was in high school, and this experience had given him some interest in retailing. For this reason, among others, when the time came for him to elect a major at college, he chose marketing, which included courses in retailing.

After completing his course, Ken was chosen by a large chain variety store organization as a member of their executive training group. This involved starting as a stockman in one of their stores. Within less than a year he was advanced to the position of assistant manager of a small store in the chain and from there to a similar job in a much larger store. As the company was increasing the number of stores in the chain, Ken was made the manager of one of the new outlets about four years after his initial employment with them. At this point his knowledge of marketing generally, as well as such fields as accounting, statistics, personnel, finance, and government regulations, became as important to his success as was his training in retailing. His subsequent progress was to the managership of a large store, then to the position of field supervisor over a group of the company's stores, and eventually he was appointed to an executive position in the merchandising division of the home office.

This brief account of Ken Williams' business career indicates the advantage of choosing an occupational field reasonably early in a college course. The student who knows exactly what he or she wants to do upon entering college is the exception rather than the rule. Fortunately in most schools there can be some delay in selecting a vocation without loss of time or credit. During this interval, definite steps can be taken that will lead to a wise choice in this respect.

■ Occupational Selection Factors

Students who are confused or uncertain as to the choice of a vocation should realize that the search for the right answer requires time, energy, and thought. It is much easier to drift along, hoping that the proper vocation will suddenly loom into view. Although this may happen, a decision that will materially affect your life, both from the viewpoint of financial rewards and the enjoyment of living, should not be left to chance. Some suggestions for a positive approach to this problem of choosing a vocation or occupation are included in the discussion of the following:

1. Personal evaluation
2. Work experience
3. College courses
4. Vocational literature
5. Industry contacts
6. Biographies, business histories, and magazine articles
7. Placement bureaus

1 / Personal evaluation. Some of the following appraisals of your qualifications for a vocation can be measured objectively; other evaluations require a subjective treatment.

(a) MENTAL ABILITY. *Intelligence tests* are available that can measure accurately your mental capacities in relationship to other college students. If you have not already taken such tests, they are available at most schools or in private counseling agencies in larger cities. Scores, and their meanings, should be obtained from persons competent to interpret them properly.

There are different types of mental ability, too. If you find mathematics enjoyable and easy, perhaps you should find employment in market research. If English is your forte, you might be a good copywriter for an advertising agency.

(b) APTITUDES AND INTERESTS. The extent of the ability of a person to learn how to perform certain jobs can be measured by *aptitude tests*. These tests measure such items as finger and manual dexterity, numerical aptitude, and eye-hand coordination. A very bright young lady who thought she wanted to be a secretary found that her eye-hand coordination was so poor that she could not learn to type rapidly without making mistakes.

Two tests that measure these aptitudes are the Differential Aptitude Tests of the Psychological Corporation and the General Aptitude Test Battery of the United States Employment Service. The latter test is available to job applicants who register with the State Employment Service.

Interest tests are also available that measure the extent of your concern with different vocations. The best-known interest tests are the Kuder Preference Record and the Strong Vocational Interest Blank. These tests are usually available wherever general intelligence tests are given.

In vocational guidance centers, which are to be found in most cities, in state employment service offices, and at most colleges and universities, there are individuals with graduate degrees in psychology or guidance counseling who are trained to diagnose mental ability, aptitudes, and potential for achievement in a job. They are equipped to administer tests designed to measure intelligence, reasoning power, reading comprehension, and interests. They are also informed regarding the areas of opportunities and the job requirements of applicants for these positions. You may wish to compare results obtained from two sources. Fees incurred for professional service of this type may well pay dividends in later life.

(c) PERSONALITY. *Personality traits* are important in the selection of a vocation. The ability to make friends easily and to get along well with other people and a good character are a few personality elements that are necessary for success in all types of work. Other traits, such as initiative, judgment, emotional stability, and physical size and fitness, are frequently more important in one type of work than in another. Although tests and self-rating scales are available, it is doubtful if personality traits can be measured with as much accuracy as can intelligence, aptitudes, and interests.

(d) AVOCATIONS. It is not at all unusual for students to gain a useful clue to their future choice of vocations through an introspective analysis of their avocations or hobbies. Many individuals have certain likes and dislikes that are frequently manifested in the activities in which they engage. Students who enjoy art, writing, mathematics, working with tools, or constructing things may well find that these interests offer useful suggestions in the choice of their college majors and eventual vocational selections.

2 / Work experience. Some work experience either during the school year or in vacations is desirable. To the extent possible, consistent with financial necessity, a variety of jobs is most satisfactory. Working in a factory, an office, and a retail store, for example, will give you a first-hand contact with various jobs. This procedure should help you to make some positive choices as well as to eliminate others.

3 / College courses. As you progress through this course and others in business subjects, you will learn a great deal more about the various areas of business activity and the functions performed in each. In most instances, these activities can be translated into job opportunities. There may be some particular kind of work that, prior to your contact with it during your course of instruction, was unknown to you. It may prove to be the right answer to your problem of a vocation. A young man studied motion and time study in a course in industrial management. Although this type of work had never occurred to him as a career opportunity, he became so interested in this technique that it became his vocational choice.

4 / Vocational literature. A wealth of vocational literature is available in your college library as well in the public libraries of your home communities. At the end of this chapter some general references about the selection of a vocation are given, and in an appendix at the back of this book many pamphlets and books that cover specific vocations are itemized.

A useful reference in investigating specific jobs is the *Dictionary of Occupational Titles* (1965) prepared by the United States Employment Service. It lists almost 22,000 occupations with more than 35,000 occupational titles and classifies them under the following nine headings: (1) professional, technical, and managerial occupations; (2) clerical and sales occupations; (3) service occupations; (4) farming, fishery, forestry, and related occupations; (5) processing occupations; (6) machine trades occupations; (7) bench work occupations; (8) structural work occupations; and (9) miscellaneous occupations.

Three samples from this dictionary give some idea of the type of information provided about the jobs listed.

EMPLOYMENT INTERVIEWER. Interviews applicants to determine their suitability for employment with company: Records information and impressions gained from applicants and evaluates information to determine suitability for employment. Administers tests and interprets results. Prepares rating on applicants and makes recommendations for future consideration of those not immediately employed. Supplies such information to applicants as company and union policies, duties, responsibilities, working conditions, hours and pay, and promotional opportunities. Prepares and maintains records of those interviewed, accepted or rejected, and those declining appointment. Discusses hiring activity with supervisors to determine adequacy of selection techniques or recruitment program. Observes jobs to obtain first-hand information of job requirements and needs.

MARKET-RESEARCH ANALYST. Researches market conditions in local, regional, or national area to determine potential sales of a product or service: Examines and analyzes statistical data on past sales and wholesale or retail trade trends to forecast future sales trends. Gathers data on competitors and analyzes their prices, sales, and methods of operation. Collects data on buying habits and preferences of prospective customers. May specialize in advertising analysis and be designated Advertising Analyst.

PROGRAMMER, BUSINESS. Converts symbolic statement of business problems to detailed logical flow charts for coding into computer language and solution by means of automatic data-processing equipment: Analyzes all or part of workflow chart or diagram representing business problem by applying knowledge of computer capabilities, subject matter, algebra, and symbolic logic to develop sequence of program steps. Confers with supervisor and representatives of departments affected by program to resolve questions of program intent, output requirements, input data acquisition, extent of automatic programming and coding use and modification, and inclusion of internal checks and controls. Writes detailed logical flow chart in symbolic form to represent work order of data to be processed by computer system, and to describe input, output, and arithmetic and logical operations involved. May convert detailed logical flow chart to language processable by computer. Devises sample input data to provide test of program adequacy. Prepares block diagrams to specify equipment configuration. Observes or runs tests of coded program on computer, using actual or sample input data. Corrects program errors by such methods as altering program steps and sequence. Prepares written instructions (run book) to guide operating personnel during production runs. Analyzes, reviews, and rewrites programs to increase operating efficiency or adapt to new requirements. Compiles documentation of program development and subsequent revisions. May specialize in writing programs for one make and type of computer.

5 / **Industry contacts.** Whenever the opportunity presents itself, preferably through class trips planned by the instructor, visit a factory, or a store, or a bank, and see business in action. Try to imagine yourself in some of the jobs you see others filling. Also talk with employees at all levels of management about their jobs. Try to find out what they believe is important for success in their particular line of endeavor. Friends of your family and acquaintances may give you some worthwhile ideas.

6 / **Biographies, business histories, and magazine articles.** A great many books have been written about businessmen and outstanding business firms. Many of these not only make fascinating reading but also provide a description of an industry or an individual who achieved success. Articles such as those that appear in *Fortune, Business Week, Time,* and other magazines also provide information about companies and jobs.

7 / Placement bureaus. Many colleges and universities maintain placement bureaus whose primary purpose is to provide the facilities through which prospective graduates and the recruiting officers from business may meet and discuss job availabilities. These bureaus frequently post on bulletin boards notices of employment opportunities offered by firms whose personnel officers visit the campus or request help in filling vacancies. Knowledge of the types of openings that will become available to you when you approach graduation will be helpful in stimulating your thinking along vocational lines. Also, many of the firms who recruit college graduates have compiled brochures describing their opportunities and positions, and these are usually available in the placement bureau office.

■ Areas of Employment Opportunities

All businesses have some common activities, such as selling products or services and record keeping, but their major functions vary considerably. Retailers do not manufacture goods; transportation companies do not accept deposits from their customers. Various classifications of these diverse areas of business activity can be made. The classification used below follows, in general, the several parts of this text:

1. Going into business for yourself
2. Marketing
3. Manufacturing
4. Personnel
5. Finance
6. Accounting and statistics
7. Office management
8. Transportation and public utilities
9. Government service

1 / Going into business for yourself. Some of the vocational opportunities suggested by Part II, Ownership, Organization, and Management, center around going into business for yourself. If you believe that you want to make your career in your own organization, several factors should be given consideration. Some of these are strictly personal, and others are related to the type of business activity chosen. Personal factors include willingness to work hard, perseverance in the face of discouragements, and the ability to make friends of customers and employees. Factors related to the business include the amount of capital needed, the experience necessary for a reasonable expectation of success, and the mental and physical qualities demanded by the type of business selected.

Most young men and women who go into business for themselves find that the better opportunities are in their local communities and in a business that sells goods or services to the public. The operation of a motel, a tearoom, a television and radio repair shop, and a ladies' accessories shop are a few examples of such enterprises. Occasionally new manufacturing operations are established to produce a good, but such enterprises are less common than the retailing of goods and services. The growth of franchising has provided a new field of self-employment for persons who have the requisite capital and abilities.

Many individuals who hope to go into business for themselves realize that they must have certain resources, both personal and financial, but they fail to consider that they should have some experience in the proposed line of endeavor or one related to it. Unless such experience has been acquired by the time the person completes college training, it may well be the wisest course of action to work for someone else who is established in the same or a related business. Going into business for yourself offers opportunities for great rewards, but the risks are much higher than when working for someone else. Before deciding to operate your own business, be sure that you have the necessary personal qualities, have access to adequate capital funds, and possess the requisite experience for the type of business selected.

In 1964 managers, officials, and proprietors numbered about 7.5 million, an increase of more than one-quarter since 1947. . . . Opportunities for proprietors declined considerably during the postwar period. In the years ahead, this declining trend is expected to level off. . . . The trend toward formation of larger businesses is expected to continue and restrict the growth in the total number of firms. The replacement of small grocery and general stores and hand laundries (often run as family businesses) by supermarkets and large chains may reduce the opportunities for proprietors in the next decade. Offsetting these trends somewhat will be the expansion of business opportunities for proprietors in small franchised owner-operated businesses in such fields as quick-service grocery stores, self-service laundries and drycleaning shops, hamburger and frozen custard drive-ins, dance studios, and slenderizing salons.

On the other hand, the need for managers and other salaried officials—such as buyers, department store heads, and purchasing agents—is likely to go on increasing fairly rapidly in business organizations and government. As a result of these diverse trends, the manager-proprietor group as a whole may increase by slightly more than one-fourth between 1964 and 1975—about the same rate of increase as for all occupations. This rate of increase is somewhat faster than that which took place during the past decade and a half.[1]

[1] *Monthly Labor Review*, April, 1965, p. 380.

2 / Marketing. The field of marketing offers numerous as well as widely varied vocational opportunities for both men and women. Salesmen are needed by manufacturers, wholesalers, retailers, and all others who produce and sell goods and services. With the exception of a very few goods that require technical training as a background for their sale, college-trained personnel with a business background are sought by many types of firms. Men predominate in the selling of industrial goods, but both sexes are well represented at the retail level.

Because of the large number of salesmen employed, advancement possibilities are excellent. In the industrial field, openings such as sales supervisor, district sales manager, divisional sales manager, and sales manager are available to those who have achieved outstanding sales records and possess supervisory abilities. Department stores usually promote salesmen first to the rank of assistant buyer and then to buyer for a particular department of a store. Recognizing the need for a larger number of competent and trainable personnel than is to be found in their employee ranks, many department stores are instituting executive training programs to fill their future requirements at the managerial level. In this they are following the lead of Macy's and a few other stores that established such programs many years ago.

Advertising is another area of marketing that offers a number of possibilities. Openings are available in the advertising departments of large firms and also in advertising agencies. Duties may involve copy writing and layout, or they may deal with such problems as buying or selling space. Advancement in the advertising department of a firm can be to an assistant advertising manager and to advertising manager. In agencies, the first step might be to an account executive or to the managership of one of the departments or branches of the business.

There is an increasing demand for competent personnel in marketing research. College graduates with a background in marketing and statistics are sought after both by marketing research firms and by the marketing research departments of many companies. The initial positions might be as interviewers or in questionnaire construction, with possible eventual promotion to supervisor or editor. A knowledge of statistics can lead to positions in the area of sample construction and validation.

With the expansion of international trade that has taken place during the last two decades, particularly the growth of firms with branch offices and factories in other countries, there have appeared opportunities for those who can qualify for positions in international marketing management. The duties involved in these positions will be described in Chapter 11. It is coming to be recognized by the firms involved that careful selection and training of these individuals will be required, and that considerable pioneering in both of these areas will be necessary. Aside from this, export and import houses located in coast cities have openings that may lead to overseas assignments after some experience has been acquired.

3 / Manufacturing. Industries engaged in manufacturing employ approximately one fourth of all workers in the United States. Within these organizations, both large and small, there are numerous opportunities for college-trained students of business. Some graduates begin as machine operators and advance to such supervisory positions as foreman, production supervisor, and plant manager. Others work in motion and time study, inspection, and planning departments. Production control, inventory control, shipping, warehousing, and plant maintenance offer career possibilities.

Purchasing for a factory offers an excellent opportunity for students of business. The opening wedge may be a clerical position in the purchasing department or work in some other phase of factory operations. Promotions to assistant purchasing agent, purchasing agent, and even to a rank such as vice-president in charge of purchasing are advancement possibilities.

4 / Personnel. Although the openings in the field of personnel and labor relations are limited, this area has been one of great interest to business students in recent years. Most of the larger factories maintain personnel departments; and employment possibilities in this field are greater in industry than they are in mercantile, financial, and other nonmanufacturing enterprises. Personnel departments usually prefer to select new people from other departments of the firm. Once a connection has been made, advancement possibilities include heading a division, such as training, recruitment, welfare, employment, or safety. From one of these posts an outstanding individual should be able to secure a position as personnel manager, and many firms now have a vice-president in charge of labor relations.

Women are more likely to find opportunities in this field in department stores, offices, and government service. A student who decides to choose personnel as a vocation should recognize the fact that entry into the field usually follows some years of experience with the company in the area of its major activity.

5 / Finance. The field of finance offers a wealth and variety of vocational opportunities for both men and women with collegiate training in business. The majority of such openings involve indoor work. They require an individual who has some liking for and ability to handle figures, but at the same time many positions involve meeting the public. Integrity, accuracy, and reliability are some of the personal traits especially necessary for success.

Both manufacturing and retailing firms employ men and women for positions in their credit and collection departments, and similar jobs can be secured in finance companies and credit-investigating agencies. Most openings are clerical in nature at the outset, but they lead to such positions as credit manager, collection manager, or manager of a branch office.

Commercial banking offers many opportunities to both sexes. Advancement possibilities include cashier, branch manager, and loan officer. All of these positions involve meeting the public, and a good personality is essential for success. Positions are also available in governmental banking agencies, including that of a bank examiner.

One of the largest fields of endeavor for college-trained people is insurance. Life, property, and casualty insurance companies are continually looking for salesmen, and other types of work are also available in the home and branch offices of these financial institutions. Those who sell frequently prefer to retain this status because earnings are based on commissions received and, if a good clientele has been developed, such individuals do not care to give up a lucrative business. Others move on to positions as supervisors and agency managers. Nonselling jobs include adjusters, agency supervisors, actuaries, and all types of office management.

The broad area of finance also includes many other types of openings. Investment banks and brokerage firms employ college men to sell stocks and bonds, to handle accounts, and to perform tasks involving the analysis of securities. If an industrial concern operates employee insurance programs and handles its own security transfers and registration, job opportunities exist in these areas as well as the financial department of the firm.

The field of real estate properly falls in the financial category, and both selling and property management are involved. Several types of financial institutions, such as savings and loan associations, sales finance companies, and trust companies, have openings for those who possess the necessary experience.

6 / Accounting and statistics. Accounting is a large field with three major subdivisions—public, private, and governmental. Public accounting is a profession, and the usual goal is to qualify as a Certified Public Accountant. This designation is given by all states to those who pass an examination and have gained the required experience. The method of acquiring experience is to secure employment as a junior accountant with a public accounting firm with the expectation that, over the years, progress will lead to a partnership in the firm, or the individual may open his own office.

In addition to C.P.A.'s there are a number of accountants who perform services of a somewhat comparable nature except that their clients are usually smaller organizations and they may do more detailed work for them.

Private accounting embraces the accounting activities of all types of firms. A major subdivision of this classification is industrial accounting, including cost accounting for manufacturing firms. Many companies also employ internal auditors whose duties are somewhat similar to those performed by public accountants. Although many starting positions are clerical, such as handling receivables or payrolls, opportunities for advancement are excellent. Many corporation treasurers and controllers have risen to their positions from routine jobs.

Governmental accounting positions are open in numerous branches of state and federal activities. Positions in the Federal Bureau of Investigation and in the Internal Revenue Service are available to graduates of collegiate schools of business who have majored in accounting. Other agencies, such as the armed services, Atomic Energy Commission, and Department of Agriculture, employ accountants, who then attain a civil-service status.

Persons qualified as statisticians are needed by industry, research organizations, and the government. Many large firms maintain their own statistical department and recruit college graduates into this field. All types of research organizations have trained statisticians on their staffs. Numerous civil-service appointments as statisticians are available to qualified men and women. A number of beginning jobs require the services of tabulating equipment operators, investigators and interviewers, and statistical clerks. Advancement to more responsible positions may lead to such managerial posts as chief statistician or director of research.

The fairly widespread adoption of computers for data processing has provided a growing field for people who have a good background of accounting courses. Many schools of business offer courses in the programming and operation of computers.

7 / Office management. This area has attracted considerable interest and attention with the recent introduction of data processing equipment, computers, instant duplication of records, mechanical sorting and handling of paperwork, and the growing emphasis on work simplification in offices and the development of standards by which the effectiveness of the work of office personnel can be measured. While historically men have been predominant in office management, an increasing number of women have entered this field. A person with an orderly turn of mind, an aptitude for systematic procedures, and a liking for office work may find office management a most rewarding line of endeavor. The growth of computerization has created a host of new opportunities in this field also. Included in this group are director of data processing, management operations analyst, computer programmer, business-systems coordinator, program manager, and many others. Many of these positions require mathematical aptitude and ability. It would appear that this area is one that will experience steady growth as new applications for computerization are found and the hardware becomes more sophisticated.

8 / **Transportation and public utilities.** The railroad industry has recently begun a recruiting and training program that should offer attractive opportunities to college men. Many problems in the management area in the railroad business remain to be solved, not the least of which is the deeply entrenched seniority system. But these difficulties should be worked out in time, and this industry should take its place among those offering interesting careers to college-trained people.

Other forms of transportation, particularly air and highway, have positions of interest to college-trained people. Highway bus and truck companies maintain numerous offices in which both clerical and supervisory positions are available. The airlines hire college men and women as reservation clerks, ticket sellers, dispatchers, and the like. Advancement to manager of a department or division is a reasonable expectation. Many young women are interested in becoming airline hostesses. Those who make a career in this field can move up to supervisory levels after they have had some years of experience.

Public utilities have a wide variety of openings for college men and women with a business training. The telephone companies make use of college people as adjusters, complaint specialists, new business salesmen, and branch managers. Gas and electric companies maintain large offices with all types of related problems and opportunities for positions in office-type work. Although seniority does not play the same role that it does with the railroads, business opportunities are not spectacular but, on the other hand, progress can be steady and reasonably sure.

9 / **Government service.** With the increased emphasis on governmental activities in recent years, new bureaus, administrations, departments, and

Trends in Government Employment Annual Averages, 1929 – 64 [12]

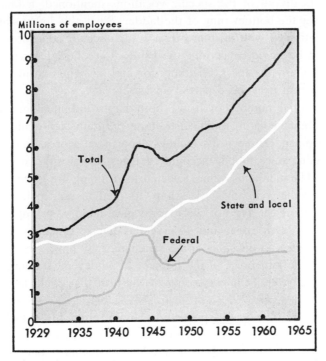

1 Beginning with 1959, data include Alaska and Hawaii, and are therefore not strictly comparable with previous years.
2 1964 figures are preliminary.

Monthly Labor Review, March, 1965.

Note: Federal data relate to civilian employment only.

commissions have come into being and old ones have increased in size. Many types of employment opportunities exist in these organizations at both state and national levels. Jobs usually carry a state or federal civil-service classification. Increases in salary and grade can be earned by those whose performance on the job merits recognition.

College men and women who expect to make their careers with the federal government should take the special examinations that are given periodically. Individuals who score the required grade are employed as management trainees in a manner somewhat comparable to the training programs available in many industries. Starting salaries approximate those offered by business and, whereas promotion will probably be slower than that in private firms, job security is very high. ← Govt

■ Training Programs

In practically all of the specific vocations mentioned, a first job will be on or near the bottom rung of the ladder. Since this lowly status might have been attained with no more than a high school education, a logical question can be raised concerning the value of a collegiate preparation for business. In many instances, eligibility for and participation in an industry training program provides a partial answer.

A substantial number of firms, both large and medium-sized, have found it advantageous to establish training programs for qualified college men and women. These firms include department stores, manufacturers, insurance companies, public accounting firms, chain store organizations, and banks. The men and women selected for training are given a thorough knowledge of the company's operations, its methods and policies, and the various duties of the type of work for which they were employed. This opportunity to learn about and observe the diverse functions of the various departments and divisions of the company may have a bearing on the ultimate specific job choice of the trainee. In any event, training programs provide for an overall understanding of the firm that could not otherwise be acquired.

The purpose of industry-sponsored training programs is to hasten the development of executive talent. Those persons admitted to these programs are selected with this potential in mind. For the most part, graduation from a junior college or university is expected, and many firms expect their trainees to have a basic knowledge of business and of the particular field that they are entering. Even if this requirement is not so stated, competition among the trainees is keen, and a person with an adequate and suitable college background has a better chance to complete the training period with a distinguished record than one whose education has been terminated earlier.

■ Vocational-Aim Values

Your main purpose in attending college is to prepare for living in our society and for your lifework. Training for good citizenship is important, and your enjoyment of life can be enhanced by nonprofessional courses. Also, courses in business that seem unrelated to a vocational aim may turn out to be the most important subjects in the years ahead. At the management level a knowledge of all fields of business and of the world in which we live is essential to success. The growing trend toward diversification in industry gives added emphasis to this requirement. Nonetheless, a vocational aim can give a meaning to all types of courses that is in sharp contrast to studying subjects merely because they are required.

The selection of a career will also assist you in planning your college program. The choice of a major or an area of concentration in your academic career has an important bearing on the courses required and on appropriate electives. One of the purposes of a course in introduction to business is to assist students in selecting a major within the field of business.

BUSINESS TERMS

none

(a) vocation (47)
(b) business specialization (48)
(c) intelligence tests (50), aptitude tests (50), interest tests (51)
(d) personality traits (51)

QUESTIONS FOR DISCUSSION AND ANALYSIS

1. Several surveys have recently revealed that a rather large number of college graduates hold jobs with three or more companies before finding the one with whom they will spend most of their business careers. Why should this be?
2. In what way does business specialization make the choice of a vocation more difficult?
3. What should a student do who finds, at the end of his college career, that he has no particular preference as to his future vocation?
4. Do you think that franchising offers a fruitful field for students who want to go into business for themselves? Why?
5. Are personality traits more important for success in business than in other fields, such as engineering, science, or one of the professions? Discuss.
6. What should a college graduate do if he discovers that there are no immediate employment opportunities in the vocational area in which he has taken his major?
7. Should the varying financial opportunities of different vocational areas be predominant in influencing a student's choice? Why?
8. Should a student take advantage of the opportunities for interviews with representatives of different fields, even though he has decided on a vocational choice? Why?
9. Should a vocational-guidance counselor make specific job recommendations to students? Why?
10. Should all students take aptitude and interest tests before deciding on their vocations? Explain.

PROBLEMS AND SHORT CASES

1. A considerable number of students, upon graduating from high school, are undecided as to what their future life's work is to be. Two alternative courses of action are open to them: (1) enroll in a college in the hope that through the content of their courses, or contact with the school's vocational guidance center, a desirable vocational area will be revealed to them; (2) postpone college entrance for a year or more and secure jobs in various fields in the hope of discovering some vocation that is appealing, and then go to college with the objective of selecting the major that will best fit them for their chosen vocations. Discuss these alternative possibilities, pointing out the strong and weak points of each.

2. Until shortly before World War I (1914-1918) a common ambition of young men was to go into business for themselves, either immediately after completing their formal education or as soon as they could accumulate sufficient capital and experience to be able to afford setting out on their own. Since then, however, there has been a trend away from this objective and toward that of becoming employees of large firms in the hope of advancing to positions of authority and eminence as rapidly as possible. Write a short report giving the reasons for this change, indicating whether or not you believe that it is a desirable circumstance and what might be done to persuade more young men to look forward to owning and operating their own firms.

3. For college students who, upon completing their first two years, are uncertain as to the vocational area in which they wish to specialize, the suggestion has been made that they drop out of school for a few years and try out jobs in a number of different fields. Then, when they have found the type of work that they like, they should return to college and spend their last two years there in taking courses that will help them in their chosen work area. Evaluate this suggestion in a short paper, setting forth the arguments both for and against it, and then stating your own conclusions as to its merit.

SUGGESTED READINGS

Careers Incorporated. *Careers for the College Man, The Annual Guide to Business Opportunities.* Published Annually.

Forrester, G. *Occupational Literature.* New York: H. W. Wilson Company, 1964.

King, A. G. *Career Opportunities for Women in Business.* New York: E. P. Dutton & Co., Inc., 1963.

United States Department of Labor. *Dictionary of Occupational Titles,* Volumes I and II. Washington: United States Government Printing Office, 1965.

United States Department of Labor. *Occupational Outlook Handbook.* Washington: United States Government Printing Office, 1966.

Part II

OWNERSHIP, MANAGEMENT, AND ORGANIZATION

CHAPTER

4   **Sole Proprietorships and Partnerships**

5   **Corporations**

6   **Management and Organization**

OWNERSHIP, MANAGEMENT, AND ORGANIZATION

Private enterprise is an important freedom of a capitalistic society. This means that the vast majority of business organizations in this country are owned by individuals who risk their own funds in enterprises of all types. One person may be the sole owner of a business unit or he may share the ownership with one, two, or even thousands of individuals who wish to participate in the rewards available from successful business operations. As a corollary to ownership, these firms are managed and organized by individuals who may be either the owners of the enterprise or their employees.

An understanding of the forms that are used for business ownership in this country is basic to an understanding of how business functions. Chapter 4 discusses unincorporated types, which are predominately either sole proprietorships or partnerships. Chapter 5 describes the corporation and some other incorporated forms of business ownership. Although corporations do not dominate the business scene in terms of numbers, they are the most important form of business ownership as measured by total business receipts, net profits, employment, and impact on our economy.

Chapter 6 emphasises the role that management and organization play in the successful conduct of business firms regardless of the forms of ownership that they adopt. Decision making is discussed in the light of the most recent thinking in this area. In addition to an explanation of the basic factors involved, the gradual emergence of organization and management theory is brought to the students' attention.

Chapter 4

"Get Back"—
Beatles

SOLE PROPRIETORSHIPS AND PARTNERSHIPS

Private enterprise is one of the basic freedoms of capitalism. This means that the millions of business firms in this country which operate to make a profit are owned by one or more individuals. While it is true that the federal, state, and local governments do own and operate some businesses, such as the post office or a municipal parking lot, the overwhelming number of business units are in private hands. By contrast, under communism or socialism government ownership of factories and stores, for example, is the rule rather than the exception.

The forms that business ownership may take are predominately three in number. These include two unincorporated types, the sole proprietorship and the partnership, and the corporation. This chapter will explain the first two as well as discuss briefly a few special types of partnerships and other unincorporated forms of ownership. Chapter 5 will be devoted primarily to the corporation although other types of ownership involving securing a federal or a state charter will also be described.

An understanding of the forms of business ownership is fundamental to an understanding of business. When a business enterprise is being formed, the prospective owner or owners must decide which ownership form is best suited to their purposes. A great many factors may enter into this decision, and the ultimate success or failure of the business may hinge on the form of business ownership selected. Many sole proprietorships, for example, have floundered or even failed for want of adequate capital, a situation that might have been avoided by organizing as a partnership or a corporation. On the other hand, many partnerships have come to grief possibly due to the incompatibility of the owners, and stockholders of a corporation have been known to outvote the very individuals who were instrumental in organizing the business.

67

SOLE PROPRIETORSHIPS

A *sole proprietorship* is a business owned by one person and operated for his profit. The term "sole proprietorship" is interchangeable with "individual proprietorship," "sole ownership," "individual enterprise," and "single proprietorship."

■ Characteristics of a Sole Proprietorship

Although a few large proprietorships do exist, typically the sole proprietorship is the ownership form for the small-town restaurant, the neighborhood grocery store, the local TV and radio repair shop, and the bakery. The owner, aided by a few employees, conducts a small business that usually caters to the consuming public. Although the owner may employ someone to manage his business, more commonly he is the active manager of his firm.

The capital necessary for operating the business is normally provided by the sole proprietor from his own wealth, frequently augmented by borrowing. Responsibility for all decisions is his, and he usually makes them personally rather than by delegating them to employees. The business may well be his sole source of livelihood and, if it is, his ability to operate it at a profit is vitally important to him and his family.

Some sole proprietorships can be identified by the name used for the firm, such as Bob's Garden Center, Robert Gordon, Proprietor; but in most instances the public does not know the form of business ownership used by the small businesses they patronize. Sole proprietorships can take names such as The University Men's Shop or even Maplegrove Wallpaper Company. In the latter case, since there is an implication that the firm is a corporation, registration of the name may be required by the state.

In the United States over five and a half million individuals engage in business on their own account either on a part-time or full-time basis. To this total could be added three and a half million persons, primarily farmers, who are also working for themselves. The table on page 69 shows the number of sole proprietorships by industrial divisions and also the annual volume of business and profit in each category. An analysis of these figures shows that the total receipts for the average sole proprietorship are slightly less than $26,000 and that the average net profit is approximately $3,500.

A comparison of these figures with similar data provided for partnerships and corporations will reveal another important characteristic of the sole proprietorship form of business ownership. Although constituting

Sole Proprietorship Income Tax Returns

Number, Business Receipts, and Net Profits by Industrial Divisions

INDUSTRIAL DIVISIONS	NUMBER OF RETURNS	BUSINESS RECEIPTS	NET PROFIT (LOSS)
		(THOUSANDS OF DOLLARS)	
ALL INDUSTRIAL DIVISIONS..	5,738,470	$148,220,341	$20,198,836
Mining	34,987	987,483	(63,855)
Construction	687,187	15,539,360	2,108,195
Manufacturing	180,805	6,710,267	654,001
Transportation, Communication, and Sanitary Services.	283,955	4,241,309	642,210
Wholesale and Retail Trade .	1,888,602	88,977,310	5,836,878
Finance, Insurance, and Real Estate	472,674	5,172,284	1,638,461
Services	2,132,751	26,079,027	9,289,343
Business Not Allocable	57,509	513,301	93,603

Source: United States Treasury Department, Internal Revenue Service, *Statistics of Income—1962-1963*. Agriculture, Forestry, and Fisheries omitted.

almost 75 percent of all forms of ownership, the volume of business done by sole proprietorships is less than 14 percent of the total of all three types.

" *Pinball Wizard* "- the Who

■ **Advantages of the Sole Proprietorship**

Why is the sole proprietorship the most common form of business ownership? Aside from the innate urge many people have to go into business for themselves, some with the hope of high profits and others merely because they enjoy being the "boss," sole proprietorships have several advantages as the following list indicates.

1. Ownership of all profits
2. Ease and low cost of organization
3. Freedom and promptness of action
4. Tax savings
5. Personal incentive and satisfaction
6. High credit standing
7. Secrecy
8. Ease of dissolution

1 / Ownership of all profits. No other form of organization permits one person to own 100 percent of the profits earned by the business. In a partnership or a corporation the amount shared with others may be limited if one person has a substantial ownership percentage, but some portion of the profits will be distributed to other individuals. A man going into business may debate whether to borrow funds needed beyond his own wealth or to find a partner with sufficient cash to provide the necessary amount. If he adopts the first course of action, all of the profits will be his. If he enters into a partnership agreement, however, some of the profits will be divided as long as the business continues in that form.

2 / Ease and low cost of organization. Anyone can usually go into business without "red tape" or special legal procedures. For example, a farm hand who finishes painting a barn in the evening decides that he likes painting better than other farm chores, and the next morning he quits the farm to become a house painter. He can work by himself or, if his services are much in demand, he may hire others to work for him. In the latter case he may dignify his occupation by calling himself a painting contractor.

Restrictions on becoming a businessman are not numerous or serious. Of course, the type of business chosen must be legal. In some instances a license is required by the state, city, or county. For example, in most states barbers must be licensed, and no one may practice medicine without state authority. Some cities issue licenses to operate pool halls, restaurants, or retail stores. In most states banks may not be organized by a single proprietor.

A sole proprietorship is also easy to organize because there is little or no cost involved. By contrast, partnerships usually incur legal fees in drawing up a partnership agreement, and a corporation must pay a fee to the state from which it receives its charter.

3 / Freedom and promptness of action. A sole proprietor has the maximum of freedom in his actions. He is the "boss"; his decisions are final. He may expand his business at will; he may add new products or discontinue old ones at his discretion; he may sell or close his business as he wishes; and he may change from one kind of business to another as he pleases. Furthermore, these decisions can be made promptly because he need not consult others nor secure approval from any other individual or group. For the individual who does not work well with or for others, the sole proprietorship is the ideal form of business ownership.

A sole proprietor is also free from government control to a greater extent than is any other form of business ownership. He is usually allowed to do business in states other than the one in which he resides without special permission; he can work as many hours a day or week as he chooses; and he may pay himself a large or a small salary. This freedom, however, is not complete. He must abide by state and federal labor laws as they apply to his employees; he must file reports if they are requested by authorized government agencies; and he cannot ship certain merchandise into states that prohibit such shipments. Such government restrictions affect some sole proprietorships more than others, but for the vast majority they have little effect on the owner's freedom of action.

4 / Tax savings. As contrasted with corporations, special taxes are not levied against an individual in his role as a sole proprietor. He must pay regular individual and business taxes, such as those on his income, his property, and his payroll, but these are not levied as special taxes against the form of business ownership. Furthermore, if his profits are so high that he would be subject to federal income taxes larger than those that would be levied against a corporation, he can elect to be taxed as a corporation.

5 / Personal incentive and satisfaction. A man in business for himself has everything to lose if his efforts are not successful; this makes him willing to devote a maximum amount of time, thought, and energy to the successful prosecution of the activity for which his firm was organized. If his business is successful, the owner has a sense of accomplishment that cannot be matched when the glory must be shared with others.

6 / High credit standing. Anyone who extends credit to a business owned by one person may look beyond the value of the firm to the nonbusiness wealth of the owner. In contrast, an extension of credit to a corporation must be based entirely on the ability of the business to repay the debt. Assuming that a sole proprietorship and a corporation are identical in size and in the nature of the wealth owned, the credit standing of the sole proprietor usually will be better than that of the corporation unless the individual involved owns no assets beyond those invested in his business.

7 / Secrecy. In some businesses the success of the enterprise is based on a secret process or formula. In others, general knowledge of profit margins, lease agreements, or other operative information might injure the competitive position of the firm. The sole proprietorship offers the best possibility that such information will not become known to others, particularly when the one person who knows these secrets is also the owner of the business.

8 / Ease of dissolution. Although it may not be as easy to dissolve a sole proprietorship as it is to form one, there are no legal complications and the procedure may be very simple. For example, a building contractor who has completed a construction project decides that it would be better for him to accept a job offer as a carpenter. Assuming that he has paid for the materials and labor used as a contractor, this decision is all that is needed to wind up his business as a sole proprietor.

■ Disadvantages of the Sole Proprietorship

Although the advantages of a sole proprietorship are more numerous than are the disadvantages, any one of the objections to this type of business ownership may outweigh all of the favorable factors. Before deciding that the sole proprietorship is the best form of business ownership, consideration should be given to the following possible disadvantages.

1. Unlimited liability	4. Lack of opportunities for
2. Limitation on size	employees
3. Difficulties of management	5. Lack of continuity

1 / Unlimited liability. *Unlimited liability* refers to the availability of a person's wealth beyond the amount invested in a business to satisfy the claims of creditors of the business. For a sole proprietorship it means that practically everything an individual owns is subject to liquidation for the purpose of paying business debts. Every year thousands of sole proprietorships discontinue operations either voluntarily or because of failure. In each case creditors expect to collect the amounts owed them either from the business itself or from the nonbusiness assets of the owner of the firm.

2 / Limitation on size. The investment in a sole proprietorship is limited to the amount one person can raise by investing his own estate, by borrowing, or by a combination of the two. If the business to be organized or expanded requires a substantial amount of capital, it may well be that the individual will find it necessary to choose another form of organization.

It has been estimated that the amount of capital required to build and equip a plant to produce steel efficiently is not less than $20 million. Obviously, few individuals could form a sole proprietorship in the iron and steel industry. The problem may be just as acute for a much smaller business. A man who desires to open a job-printing shop discovers that he needs at least $12,000, but he can raise only $7,000 of this amount.

Or, assuming that he is already in business on a modest scale, he finds that he would earn two or three time as much as his present profits if he could buy $10,000 worth of additional equipment. If the minimum amount of capital needed is beyond the resources of an individual, the sole proprietorship form of ownership cannot be used.

3 / Difficulties of management. Since a sole proprietorship is ordinarily a small business, the owner often assumes the responsibility for managing such diverse tasks as purchasing, merchandising, extending credit, financing, and employing personnel. He may be unusually capable of handling some of these functions but unable to perform others. For example, a retail store with a large volume of business went into bankruptcy because the owner was so generous with extension of credit and was so poorly qualified to collect accounts that finally there was not sufficient money left to pay current bills.

4 / Lack of opportunity for employees. If an employee of a sole proprietorship proves to be an unusually able man, he may not be content to work indefinitely for the owner. Even though he is well paid, including a generous bonus based on profits, he may not be satisfied with a continuing status of merely an employee. If the owner wishes to retain his services, it may be necessary to form a partnership or a corporation in order to extend to this individual an opportunity to become a part owner of the business. Otherwise the employee may quit and, as frequently happens, start a competitive business in the same locality.

5 / Lack of continuity. The death of the proprietor terminates the life of his firm, as does his insanity, imprisonment, or bankruptcy. Furthermore, the physical inability of the owner to continue work often forces the enterprise to close its doors. One man may build up a fine business, but it is profitable only so long as he is able to run it. At his death his widow or other heirs may try to continue the business, but they frequently lack the knowledge or the ability to operate it successfully.

PARTNERSHIPS

The Uniform Partnership Act,[1] defines a *partnership* as "an association of two or more persons to carry on as co-owners a business for profit."

[1] The following ten states have not adopted the Uniform Partnership Act: Alabama, Florida, Georgia, Hawaii, Iowa, Kansas, Louisiana, Maine, Mississippi, and New Hampshire.

Such a relationship is based on an agreement, written or oral, that is both voluntary and legal. A partnership is also referred to as a "copartnership."

■ Characteristics of Partnerships

Although the typical partnership is larger than comparable sole proprietorships, most are relatively small businesses. Even though the average annual total receipts for partnerships is over $84,000, approximately two thirds of all partnerships take in less than $50,000 yearly and less than 1 percent gross more than $1,000,000. The table below shows that the classification Wholesale and Retail Trade holds first place among partnerships in contrast with sole proprietorships for which Services ranked first. Partnerships are a common ownership form for brokerage firms, local insurance agencies, and real estate brokers.

Partnership Income Tax Returns

Number, Business Receipts, and Net Profits by Industrial Divisions

INDUSTRIAL DIVISIONS	NUMBER OF RETURNS	BUSINESS RECEIPTS	NET PROFIT (LOSS)
		(THOUSANDS OF DOLLARS)	
ALL INDUSTRIAL DIVISIONS	798,534	$67,320,937	$7,857,813
Mining	15,040	912,334	(3,761)
Construction	58,164	6,804,981	594,149
Manufacturing	43,091	6,653,967	594,927
Transportation, Communication, and Sanitary Services	17,032	995,355	124,303
Wholesale and Retail Trade	267,493	36,580,084	2,198,615
Finance, Insurance, and Real Estate	229,400	4,975,893	952,454
Services	166,737	10,380,375	3,393,644
Business Not Allocable	1,577	17,948	3,482

Source: United States Treasury Department, Internal Revenue Service, *Statistics of Income—1962-1963.* Agriculture, Forestry, and Fisheries omitted.

Some of the partnerships that do business in every city, town, and village can be identified by the firm name; others cannot. Names such as Stone & Wilson or McDonald & Son usually denote a partnership, whereas the London Furniture Mart might or might not be owned and operated as a partnership. If a fictitious partnership firm name is used, such as

Wright and Wrong, some states require that a record showing the names of all partners be filed in the county office.

Of the three common forms of business ownership, partnerships are the least popular despite the sizable total of 798,534, not counting 130,-000 firms engaged in agriculture, forestry, and fisheries. There are more than seven times as many sole proprietorships, and the number of corporations exceeds 1,200,000. Within the last five years the number of partnerships has shown not only a relative decrease in an expanding economy but also a slight shrinkage in the actual number of business units operating under this ownership form.

■ Number of Partners in Partnerships

As the table below clearly shows, the vast majority of partnerships in this country consist of two persons. The average for all partnerships is almost exactly two and a half individuals, even though some partnerships include over one hundred members. Most of the larger firms, in terms of members, are in the professions such as law and public accounting. Retail stores, restaurants, and bowling alleys, if operated under the partnership form of business ownership, usually have two partners with the possibility of a third or fourth member.

Percentage Distribution of Number of Partners

	NUMBER OF PARTNERS	PERCENT
Two Partners	583,530	73.1
Three Partners	110,482	13.8
Four Partners	43,614	5.5
Five to Nine Partners	36,997	4.6
Ten or More Partners	23,911	3.0
Totals	798,534	100.0

Source: United States Treasury Department, Internal Revenue Service, *Statistics of Income—1962-1963*. Agriculture, Forestry, and Fisheries omitted.

■ The Partnership Contract

It is most desirable, although usually not necessary, that the agreement between the parties be written and signed. Such a contract, known as *articles of partnership* or "articles of copartnership," may prevent misunderstanding and ill will among the partners at a future date. An oral contract is especially unsatisfactory if profits and losses are to be divided on any basis other than equal shares because positive proof is required to overcome the presumption of equality among partners.

The common provisions of a partnership contract cover the following items:

1. The name of the firm.
2. The location and the type of business.
3. The length of life of the partnership agreement.
4. The names of the partners and the investment made by each.
5. The distribution of profits and losses.
6. A provision for salaries of partners.
7. An agreement on the amount of interest to be allowed on capital and drawing account balances.
8. A limitation on withdrawals of funds.
9. A provision for an accounting system and a fiscal year.
10. The method that will be followed in case of the withdrawal of a partner from the firm and other causes of dissolution.

The illustration on pages 77 and 78 shows how these items of information are included in formal articles of partnership.

■ Advantages of the Partnership

Partnerships and sole proprietorships are both unincorporated forms of business ownership. Consequently, they share some advantages when contrasted with corporations. A partnership, too, is easy to organize, although a lawyer should assist in drawing up the articles of partnership. The tax situation is comparable to that of a sole proprietorship even though an information return must be filed annually with the Internal Revenue Service. Freedom from governmental regulation approximates that of sole proprietorships although it is not quite as extensive due to the variety of state laws on partnerships. There are also several distinctive advantages.

1. Larger amount of capital
2. Credit standing
3. Combined judgment and managerial skills
4. Retention of valuable employees
5. Personal interest in business
6. Definite legal status

1 / Larger amount of capital. In a sole proprietorship the amount of capital is limited to the personal fortune and credit of one individual. In a partnership the capital can easily be doubled, trebled, or otherwise increased by bringing in additional owners. An inventor with little capital, for example, may locate a rich man who is willing to become a partner

Articles of Partnership

THIS CONTRACT, Made and entered into on the   second   day of   January   19   , by and between David R. Marsh and John H. Dale, each of Madison, Wisconsin.

WITNESSETH: That the said parties have this day formed a partnership for the purpose of engaging in and conducting   a laundry, pressing, and dry-cleaning business, and the doing of all things necessary and incident thereto, under the following stipulations which are made a part of this contract:

FIRST: The said partnership shall commence on the   second   day of   January   , 19   , and continue from and after said date for a period of   ten years at the pleasure of said partners; and shall be otherwise terminated by the death, bankruptcy, insolvency, or disability of either of the said parties thereto, or under the provisions for such act hereinafter set forth.

SECOND: The business shall be conducted under the firm name of   the MarDale Laundromat at   895 Porter Avenue, Madison, Wisconsin

THIRD: The investments are as follows: David R. Marsh agrees to contribute to the capital of said partnership the sum of $27,000.00 and John H. Dale the sum of $18,000.00, which shall be paid on the date of the execution of this agreement, and by the execution thereof by said partners the receipt of same is hereby acknowledged.

FOURTH: All profits and losses arising from said business are to be shared as follows: David R. Marsh, 60 percent, and John H. Dale, 40 percent.

FIFTH: Each of said partners shall devote his entire time, skill, labor, and experience to advancing and rendering profitable the interests and business of said partnership, and neither partner shall engage in any other business or occupation whatever on his individual account during the existence of said partnership without the written consent of the other partner.

SIXTH: A systematic record of all transactions is to be kept in a double-entry set of books in which shall be promptly and properly entered an account and record of all the transactions and business of the partnership. All books of account and all contracts, letters, papers, documents, and memoranda belonging to the partnership shall be open, at all times, to the examination of   either   of the partners. On   December 31   hereafter a statement of the business is to be made, the books closed, and each partner credited with the amount of the gain or charged with his share of the loss. A statement may be made at such other times as the partners agree upon.

SEVENTH: Each partner shall furnish to the other, on request, full information and account of any and all transactions and matters relating to the business of the partnership, within his knowledge.

EIGHTH: All moneys received by, or paid to, said partnership shall be daily deposited in the First National Bank, Madison, Wisconsin,   except a small change account used in the operations of said business not to exceed $ 25.00   , or in such other bank as said partners may mutually agree upon. All disbursements of partnership moneys in excess of $ 5.00   shall be made by check on said partnership bank account. Checks for amounts drawn on partnership accounts may be drawn by   either   of said partners.

NINTH: No partner shall at any time sign the firm name, or his own name, or pledge the firm's credit, or his own individual credit, in any manner as surety or guarantor on any paper, bill, bond, note, or draft or other obligation whatsoever. Neither shall he assign, pledge, or mortgage any of the partnership property, or his interest therein, or do anything or permit any act whereby the firm's money, interest, or property, or his interest therein, may be liable to seizure, attachment, or execution.

TENTH: Each partner shall promptly pay his individual debts and liabilities and shall at all times indemnify and save harmless the partnership property therefrom.

Articles of Partnership (Page 1)

ELEVENTH: Each partner is to have a salary of $ 600.00 per month, the same to be withdrawn at such time or times as he may elect. Neither partner is to withdraw from the business an amount in excess of his salary without the written consent of the other. Interest at the rate of 6 percent per annum shall be allowed on the amount of investment each partner shall have in the business in excess of his original contribution as determined at the close of each month. Salaries and interest shall be considered expenses of doing business before arriving at net profit or net loss.

TWELFTH: The duties of each partner are defined as follows: David R. Marsh is to have general supervision of the business and have charge of the accounting records, correspondence, and credits and collections. John H. Dale is to have supervision of all machinery used within and without the business and the purchase of supplies and equipment. Each partner is to attend to such other duties as are deemed necessary for the successful operation of the business.

THIRTEENTH: One partner may, at any time, dissolve said partnership by written notice of his intention to do so, delivered or mailed to the other partner, and said partnership shall be dissolved at the expiration of sixty days after the giving of such notice.

FOURTEENTH: At the time of giving notice of dissolution of said partnership, or any other termination thereof as set out in the first stipulation above, an inventory and appraisement of all assets and property of said partnership shall be made, by three disinterested parties engaged in the same or similar business in this vicinity, to be chosen by the partners to this agreement or their legal representative, at the true value to the business thereof; and an account shall be taken of all assets and liabilities. After payment of all debts and liabilities of said partnership, the assets and property so remaining shall be divided between the partners, their heirs and assigns, in the proportion in which the capital of said partnership has been contributed by each. Provided, however, that if either of the original partners to this agreement desires to carry on the said business he shall have the first option to take over said business at the net value as calculated from the account so made and assume all operations thereunder in his own right and relieve the other partner, his heirs and assigns from all liabilities. Said option to be enforceable shall be exercised within ten days after the accounting of the partnership has been made. Each partner for himself, his heirs and assigns hereby agrees to execute all instruments necessary or proper to invest the other with the property, real, personal or mixed, so taken over by him.

FIFTEENTH: No changes, alterations, additions, modifications, or qualifications shall be made or had in the terms of this contract unless made in writing and signed by each of the partners.

IN WITNESS WHEREOF, the parties have hereunto set their hands to duplicate copies hereof, the day and year first above written.

Signed in the presence of:

George S. White

Sandra Oaks

David R. Marsh

John H. Dale

STATE OF WISCONSIN , COUNTY OF DANE , SS:

Personally appeared before me, a Notary Public within and for said State and County, the above named David R. Marsh and John H. Dale , the parties to the foregoing contract, who each acknowledged the signing thereof to be his voluntary act and deed, for the uses and purposes therein mentioned.

IN WITNESS WHEREOF, I have hereunto set my hand and seal this second day of January , 19

James R. Chalmers
Notary Public, Dane County, Wisconsin

Articles of Partnership (Page 2)

by contributing a major portion of the total capital needed to produce and market the inventor's product.

2 / Credit standing. Assuming equal size, the partnership usually enjoys the highest credit standing of the three types of business owner- *Partnership* ship. As in the case of the sole proprietorship, the personal wealth of the owners is available to satisfy business debts; and since two or more individuals are owners, creditors have good reason to believe that partnership debts will be paid in full.

3 / Combined judgment and managerial skills. The old adage that two heads are better than one is true in the case of many partnerships. Partners can consult each other about proposed actions, and a wiser course of procedure may result. Sometimes two or three men complement each other in securing maximum operating efficiency. Adams is a genius at producing precision tools, but he loses all interest in them as soon as they pass final inspection. Brown, on the other hand, is an outstanding salesman but has no interest in the problems of manufacturing. As partners, the two men are very effective, but neither would be a success as a sole proprietor.

4 / Retention of valuable employees. Changing to the partnership form of business ownership offers an opportunity for a sole proprietorship to retain the services of a valuable employee by making him a partner. It also provides the same opportunity to existing partnerships, although new articles of partnership are necessary. Legal and professional accounting firms make extensive use of the practice of admitting new partners.

5 / Personal interest in business. Since each general partner is liable for the actions of the other partners as well as his own, he is vitally concerned in every move made by the business. A sense of responsibility to those with whom he is closely associated enhances the personal interest factor. Compared to the average corporation, this advantage may be very important in the ultimate success of the firm. Only in the sole proprietorship, where little or no opportunity exists to share or delegate responsibility, does the personal interest factor have greater weight.

6 / Definite legal status. Partnerships are one of the oldest forms of business ownership. Over centuries a series of court decisions have established clear-cut answers to the questions of rights, powers, liabilities, and duties of partners. A partner should have no difficulty in securing a concise answer from a lawyer on any legal question that he might care to raise concerning the partnership.

■ Disadvantages of the partnership

Despite the many advantages of partnerships when contrasted with sole proprietorships and corporations, partnerships rank third as to frequency of use among these forms of business ownership. It appears obvious that one or more of the following disadvantages not infrequently weighs heavily against selecting the partnership as the type of business ownership.

√1. Unlimited liability of the
       partners
2. Lack of continuity

3. Managerial difficulties
√ 4. Frozen investment. *trying to get out*
5. Limitation on size *dies - partner-ship dies*

1 / Unlimited liability of the partners. The greatest disadvantage is that of unlimited liability of the partners. Each general partner is liable personally for the partnership debts. If one partner makes an unwise commitment, even against the wishes of his partners, all the partners may be liable for the loss that results. If partnership A, B, and C fails with net losses totaling $100,000, and if neither *A* nor *B* has any private resources except what he had invested in the business, the entire loss would fall on *C*, assuming that he owns assets that, when liquidated, are adequate to cover the debts.

2 / Lack of continuity. If a partner dies or withdraws from the business, the partnership is dissolved. Also, if a partner becomes insane or takes out bankruptcy papers, the business is terminated. The more persons there are in a partnership, the greater are the chances that this will occur. Frequently the remaining partners find it possible to buy out the interest of the individual who withdraws or dies, and they can reorganize the business with little outward change. If it is necessary to admit a new partner to assume the interest of the old one, however, it may not always be easy to find an individual who is satisfactory to all of the old partners and who will work in reasonable harmony with them in the operation of the business.

3 / Managerial difficulties. Although better decisions usually result from the combined judgments of two or more partners, such divided control can also cause trouble. If some partners are not active in the business, time can be lost in making contact with them. Although any partner can take an action that is legally binding on the partnership, he might be reluctant to do so on important matters. Furthermore, the friendly spirit among partners that drew them together in the first place can give way in time to distrust and enmity. If the number of partners is odd, such as three or five, the minority will be outvoted by the majority. If the number of partners is even, some written agreements provide for referral to a disinterested party in case the partners are equally divided on a proposed course of action.

4 / Frozen investment. For an individual who wishes to invest some money in a business, the partnership form may prove to be a poor choice from the viewpoint of liquidity and transferability. It is almost axiomatic that it is easy to invest in a partnership and difficult to withdraw these funds. If a partner withdraws or dies, the existing firm is dissolved. Even if the remaining partners or outsiders are willing to purchase the vacated interest, it is often extremely difficult to arrive at a fair price.

5 / Limitation on size. The advantage held by a partnership over a sole proprietorship as to availability of capital can easily become a disadvantage when contrasted with a corporation. Some businesses, such as those producing steel or making automobiles, require the investment of millions of dollars by the owners. A partnership, even if composed of several wealthy individuals, would have great difficulty in raising adequate capital for organizing a successful firm in many lines of business.

■ Limited Partnerships

In the absence of specific information to the contrary, a partnership is assumed to be a *general partnership*, that is, one in which all partners have unlimited liability. A variation of the general partnership is a *limited partnership*, which is different in that one or more partners can have limited liability as long as at least one partner has unlimited liability. Assuming one limited partner, his name must not appear in the firm name; he cannot be active in the business; and if he withdraws from the firm, it need not be dissolved.

■ Kinds of Partners

The individuals who comprise a partnership are known as *partners or copartners.* They are classified in several different ways, depending upon their extent of liability, participation in management, share of profits, and other factors.

1 / General and limited partners. A member of a general or limited partnership who has unlimited liability for the debts of the firm is a *general partner*. Usually such a partner is active in the management.

A member of a limited partnership who does not assume responsibility for the debts beyond the amount of his investment is a *limited or special partner*. This type of partner is not permitted to take an active part in the management.

2 / Secret, silent, dormant, and nominal partners. An individual who is active in the affairs of a partnership but who is not known to the public as a partner is a *secret partner*. A person who is known to the public as a partner but does not take an active part in the management is a *silent partner*. A partner who does not take an active part in the management and who is not known to the public as a partner is a *dormant or sleeping partner*.

A man who is not actually a partner but who publicly announces himself as a partner or allows others to hold him out as a partner is a *nominal partner* even though he does not share in the profits or does not have an investment in the business. Under certain circumstances courts have held that a nominal partner may obligate firm members by his acts or become liable for the debts of a partnership.

3 / Senior and junior partners. A general partner who has a substantial investment in the firm, who receives a relatively larger percentage of the profits, and who, by virtue of age and years of association with the firm, assumes a major role in the management, is a *senior partner*. A *junior partner* is the opposite of a senior partner. Normally he is a young man only recently admitted to a partner's status. He does not have very much money invested, receives only a minor share of the profits, and is not expected to assume responsibility for major decisions even though he has equal voting rights with other partners.

■ Special Types of Partnerships

In addition to limited partnerships, other variations of the general partnership have been developed. The purpose in each instance has been to overcome one or more of the disadvantages of the partnership form of business ownership.

1 / Limited partnership associations. One special type of partnership, the *limited partnership association,* has the advantage of providing limited liability for all of the partners. Other features are that ownership may be evidenced by certificates of ownership, management is usually delegated to a few partners, and the name must be followed by the word "Limited" or the abbreviation "Ltd." [2] Partly because only five states permit the formation of limited partnership associations, this is not a widely used form for business ownership in this country.

2 / Joint ventures and syndicates. Another variation on the general partnership is the *joint venture* or "joint adventure." It is formed for a single undertaking, usually of short duration. Management is frequently delegated to a partner, other partners are not supposed to act for the partnership, and the death of an owner does not terminate the business. Joint ventures were commonly organized a few centuries ago in foreign countries. A typical use was to secure capital from a considerable number of investors to finance the cost of purchasing, outfitting, and operating a sailing vessel for one round-trip voyage. It would be loaded with trading goods and sent, for example, to the East Indies for a cargo of silks, spices, and tea. If the vessel returned, the goods and ship were sold and the proceeds, frequently substantially in excess of the original investment, were distributed among the partners.

In modern usage joint ventures are frequently called *syndicates*, which, because of the purposes for which they are formed, may allow members to obtain the advantage of limited liability. A common use today is the *underwriting syndicate,* which is an association of investment banking companies formed to sell a large issue of corporation bonds or stocks. Management is in the hands of the company that forms the underwriting syndicate and each member's liability may be limited to the amount of its agreed upon participation in the total issue.

3 / Mining partnerships. Another special type of partnership that has been legalized in some of our western states is the *mining partnership*. Its special features are that management is delegated to one partner, shares of ownership are issued and can be sold without the consent of other partners, profits are distributed on the basis of the number of shares owned, and the liability of partners extends only to necessary costs of operating the mine. Mining is a risky business that may extend over a long period of

[2] Corporations organized under the laws of Canada and some countries overseas use the word "Limited" or the abbreviation "Ltd." in place of the usage in this country of the word "Corporation" or "Incorporated."

time on a continuous basis, and the mining partnership recognizes these facts in providing a partnership form that is adaptable to the peculiarities of this type of undertaking.

■ Other Unincorporated Forms of Business Ownership

In addition to special types of partnerships, a few other legal forms of business ownership are available that do not require incorporation. These include joint-stock companies, Massachusetts trusts, and unincorporated associations.

1 / Joint-stock companies. *Joint-stock companies* were important in the early development of our nation but have now been almost universally replaced by the corporation. They were formed by drawing up *articles of association,* not unlike articles of partnership, with the addition of stating the number of shares of stock to be issued and providing for an annual meeting at which the shareholders would elect a board of directors. Joint-stock companies resemble general partnerships in that all shareholders have unlimited liability. They differ in that management is delegated to a board of directors, ownership is represented by shares of stock that can be sold or transferred to others, profits are distributed on the basis of the number of shares owned, and the firm is not affected by the death of one or more shareholders.

2 / Massachusetts trusts. Unlike the other forms of business ownership described in this chapter, the *Massachusetts trust* uses an entirely different approach to organizing and operating a business. Under a trust agreement, a small number of trustees accept funds from numerous investors and issue to them certificates of beneficial interest, which are called *trust shares.* The trustees invest the funds, manage the business, and distribute profits to the holders of the trust shares. Although similar in authority to a board of directors, the trustees cannot be removed from office; but aside from being unable to vote, share owners have limited liability and other rights associated with holders of stock in a corporation.

The name "Massachusetts trust" owes its origin to an historical prohibition in Massachusetts against corporations organized to buy and sell real estate. In order to secure large amounts of capital and to provide limited liability for the investors, the trustee device was used. A Massachusetts trust is also called a business trust, a common-law trust, and a voluntary association. This form of business ownership is important today because most investment trusts, popularly called mutual funds, are organized as

Massachusetts trusts. Investors, many with limited amounts of capital, purchase trust shares and these funds, now running into billions of dollars, are invested by the trustees in stocks and bonds of numerous corporations.

3 / Unincorporated associations. An _unincorporated association_ can be formed by any number of persons or companies by drawing up and signing an agreement. It differs from other special forms of business ownership in that its purpose is always nonprofit and it exists to render a service to its members. National fraternal organizations, trade associations, and the like are frequently unincorporated associations as is the New York Stock Exchange, bank clearinghouses located in large cities, and retail credit associations. In the business world there is usually a fee to join the association, and its expenses of operation are divided among its members based on their use of the services rendered. The members elect a board of governors, or directors, or trustees, who employ personnel to run the organization. Although the members probably have unlimited liability, the nonprofit and service nature of an unincorporated association are such that this risk is negligible.

BUSINESS TERMS

(a) sole proprietorship (68), unlimited liability (72)
(b) partnership (73), articles of partnership (75)
(c) general partnership (81), limited partnership (81)
(d) partner or copartner (81)
(e) general partner (82), limited or special partner (82)
(f) secret partner (82), silent partner (82), dormant or sleeping partner (82), nominal partner (82)
(g) senior partner (82), junior partner (82)
(h) limited partnership association (83), joint venture (83)
(i) syndicate (83), underwriting syndicate (83)
(j) mining partnership (83), joint-stock company (84)
(k) articles of association (84), Massachusetts trust (84), trust shares (84)
(l) unincorporated association (85)

QUESTIONS FOR DISCUSSION AND ANALYSIS

1. Is the impact of the sole proprietor on the free enterprise system more closely related to the millions of individuals involved than it is to the number of dollars received by these firms?

2. Although business corporations are owned by individuals, do you believe that the general public is more favorably disposed toward sole proprietorships and partnerships than to the corporate form of ownership?

3. Does the average consumer, when making purchases of goods and services, know or care what form of business ownership is used by the firm he patronizes?

4. Assuming a profitable business of long standing, would you rather be employed by a sole proprietorship or a partnership than by a corporation? Why?

5. If you had adequate financial resources to start a business of your own, would you prefer to become a sole proprietor rather than to seek out a partner? Why?

6. Despite their sizable number, partnerships seem to be on the downgrade in relation to sole proprietorships and corporations. How do you account for the lack of popularity of this type of business ownership?

7. Sole proprietorships and partnerships both have the important disadvantage of unlimited liability. Why should the personal nonbusiness wealth of the owners of these forms of business ownership be available to business creditors?

8. If you were invited to join a partnership, would you be satisfied with the status of a limited partner? Would your answer be different if the firm was organized as a limited partnership association?

9. Although joint ventures were more important centuries ago than they are today, are there any present-day situations that would lend themselves to this type of business ownership in preference to other forms available?

10. Why has it seemed desirable for some types of businesses to seek a form of ownership different from the predominate categories of sole proprietorships, general and limited partnerships, and corporations?

PROBLEMS AND SHORT CASES

1. Shortly after completing his college education, John Becker secured employment as the manager of a bowling alley. Since he had become a good bowler during his high school and college days, he decided to make a vocation out of an avocation in which he had a great interest. Returning to his campus for the tenth anniversary of his class, he was impressed with the shortage of alleys and decided to investigate the possibility of owning and operating a bowling alley in the college town.

Becker had saved some money during the past ten years and felt able to invest $15,000 in a business. On investigation he found two buildings suitable for installing twelve lanes, which was the number he felt would be about the right size. One of the buildings was adjacent to the campus, but the owner wanted to sell. His price was $58,000 against which Becker found he could borrow $45,000 at 6 percent interest. The other building was approximately a mile from the campus, and it could be leased for five years at $400 a month. At either location it would be necessary to make a substantial down payment on alleys, furniture, and other necessary equipment in addition to renting automatic pinspotters. A careful estimate indicated that $11,500 would cover these costs and, in addition, $2,500 would be necessary to pay for preopening costs such as painting, signs, supplies, and promotional expenses.

When Becker's plan became known, he was approached by Ralph Lloyd, a former classmate and fraternity brother, who had been employed locally for the past six years as a bank teller. He indicated a great interest in joining Becker in the business because he was an ardent bowler and wanted to get into business for himself as an owner or part owner. He offered to match Becker's capital contribution with the understanding that he would work full time at the alley in return for an equal share in the profits. Lloyd was well and favorably known in the community.

On the basis of these facts, should John Becker go into business for himself or should he form a partnership with Ralph Lloyd? Support your recommendation with a list of the advantages and the disadvantages of each course of action and the reasons for your decision.

2. For a number of years Sally Madden and Vera Bergen were employed in Springfield, Illinois, at the same beauty parlor, where they became fast friends. A few years ago Miss Madden was married to William Rowan and moved into the old Rowan home located at 100 Church Street, near the downtown business area. Miss Bergen continued at her old job but, after careful investigation and with the consent of Mr. Rowan, she and Mrs. Rowan have decided to open a beauty parlor in the Rowan house to be called the Salver Beauty Salon.

Each partner agrees to invest $8,000 in cash. Mrs. Rowan is to receive $100 a month as rent for the portion of her home devoted to the business, a salary of $300 a month, and 40% of the profits. Miss Bergen, in addition to 60% of the profits, is to receive a salary of $400 a month. She is to be in charge of buying equipment and supplies, handling receipts and disbursements, paying bills, and keeping the books of account. Mrs. Rowan is to be in charge of appointments, advertising, promotional activities, and is to serve as receptionist.

Miss Bergen agrees to devote 40 hours each week to the business and Mrs. Rowan 30 hours. Overtime, if necessary, is to be paid for at the rate of $2 an hour. The books are to be closed on June 30 and December 31 of each year; the agreement is to run for ten years, and in the case the firm is dissolved, the net assets are to be divided in the ratio of their capital accounts at that date. Neither partner is to withdraw cash from the firm other than salaries, rent, overtime payments, and net profits without the written consent of the other.

Using the above information plus any additional assumptions you care to make that are not inconsistent with the stated facts, draw up articles of partnership for Mrs. Rowan and Miss Bergen.

3. For the past ten years Julian Bogan and Harold Tatam have operated an automobile body repair and paint business under the name of the B & T Auto Repair Shop. The partnership has been profitable, clearing about $7,500 a year for each man, and it has been the sole means of support for both families. Consequently, net income has been withdrawn regularly and the $10,000 originally contributed by each partner, which is invested in equipment and supplies, has remained relatively stationary.

The firm has been renting an old building that is barely adequate for their needs. They do not have a lease, but the owner seems content with receiving $200 each month and has not raised the rent over the past ten years. Bogan and Tatam have been aware of the possibility of a long overdue rent increase and also that no other location is now available in their community.

They discussed this situation with George Lotrick, their banker and personal friend, who expressed a willingness to build a structure designed to fit their needs on property that he owns. He estimated the cost at $45,000 and indicated that he would be willing to lease the completed building for $400 a month for a period of ten years. As an alternative to a lease, he proposed that Bogan and Tatam take him into the firm as a limited partner. In return for his investment in the building, he wished to receive one third of the net profits of the business after an allowance of $300 a month as a salary to each of the two general partners. It is estimated that taxes and insurance on the new building will average $40 a month.

Should Bogan and Tatam admit Lotrick to the B & T Auto Repair Shop as a limited partner? Give reasons for your conclusion.

SUGGESTED READINGS

Anderson, R. A., and W. A. Kumpf. *Business Law,* Seventh Edition. Cincinnati: South-Western Publishing Company, 1964. Part VII.

Broom, H. N., and J. G. Longenecker. *Small Business Management,* Second Edition. Cincinnati: South-Western Publishing Company, 1966. Part B.

Dillavou, E. R., and Others. *Principles of Business Law,* Alternate Seventh Edition. Englewood Cliffs, New Jersey: Prentice-Hall, Inc., 1964. Book Five.

Finney, H. A., and H. E. Miller. *Principles of Accounting—Introductory,* Sixth Edition. Englewood Cliffs, New Jersey: Prentice-Hall, Inc., 1963. Chapter 9.

Husband, W. H., and J. C. Dockeray. *Modern Corporation Finance,* Sixth Edition. Homewood, Illinois: Richard D. Irwin, Inc., 1966. Chapter 2.

Niswonger, C. R., and P. E. Fess. *Accounting Principles,* Ninth Edition. Cincinnati: South-Western Publishing Company, 1965. Chapter 15.

Prather, C. L. *Financing Business Firms,* Third Edition. Homewood, Illinois: Richard D. Irwin, Inc., 1966. Part I.

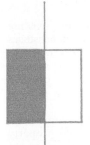

Chapter 5

CORPORATIONS

The dominant type of business ownership in the United States is the corporation. Although there are approximately five times as many sole proprietorships and two-thirds as many partnerships, corporations account for 80 percent of the total receipts of all business units and three fifths of all net profits. It is the form of ownership used for all of the private industrial, commercial, and financial giants of the business world that make a daily impact on the lives of all of us.

Although there is an element of impersonality about corporations, many are known in households throughout the land. General Motors, A. & P., U.S. Steel, G. E., and Sears, Roebuck, to name a few, are familiar abbreviations to almost all adults. Most of the products used by consumers are produced and distributed by corporations. In so doing, they employ millions of workers and have control over billions of dollars that have been invested by millions of individuals.

The high standard of living enjoyed in this country is closely related to mass production and mass consumption. The availability of large quantities of goods at prices consumers can pay is an achievement of big business units. These units, almost without exception, are corporations as no other form of business ownership lends itself to amassing the huge amounts of capital required.

Although big business and corporations go hand in hand, it would be a serious error to assume that all corporations are large. There are many corporations that are as small as or even smaller than the average sole proprietorship or partnership.

■ Nature of the Corporation

What is this form of business ownership that is so important in our economy? Probably the most famous definition of a corporation was written by Chief Justice John Marshall of the United States Supreme Court in 1819 in the case of Dartmouth College v. Woodward:

> A *corporation* is an artificial being, invisible, intangible, and existing only in contemplation of law. Being the mere creature of law, it possesses only those properties which the charter of its creation confers upon it, either expressly or as incidental to its very existence. These are such as are supposed best calculated to effect the object for which it was created. Among the most important are immortality, and, if the expression may be allowed, individuality; properties, by which a perpetual succession of many persons are considered as the same, and may act as a single individual. They enable a corporation to manage its own affairs, and to hold property without the perplexing intricacies, the hazardous and endless necessity, of perpetual conveyances for the purpose of transmitting it from hand to hand. It is chiefly for the purpose of clothing bodies of men in succession with these qualities and capacities that corporations were invented and are in use.

This definition emphasizes the fact that the corporation is a *legal entity,* which is another way of saying that the law has created an artificial being endowed with the rights, duties, and powers of a person. The definition also includes the concept of many people united into one body that does not change its identity with changes in ownership, and one that may have perpetual life.

■ The Corporate Structure

The structure of a corporation sheds further light on this form of business ownership. Its status as a legal entity stems from a *charter,* which is a document issued by a state authorizing the formation of a corporation. The owners are called *shareholders,* or stockholders. Once each year they vote the shares they own for a *board of directors,* who serve as their representatives. The directors elect the necessary *officers,* such as president, vice-president or vice-presidents, secretary, and treasurer. These men are responsible for the actual day-by-day operation of the corporation and report periodically to the board of directors. Although the full board may meet as seldom as once a year, quarterly or even monthly meetings are more common. In large corporations the board divides itself into committees, which may meet oftener than the entire board.

The chart on page 91 pictures in a simple manner the organization of the corporate form. The shareholders may be numbered in the thousands or even millions. Boards of directors usually have between nine and seventeen members although there are numerous exceptions at both ends of the scale.

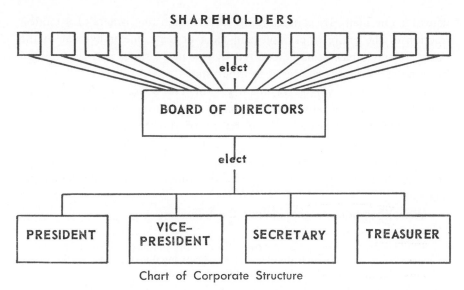

Chart of Corporate Structure

1 / Shareholders. The shareholders of a corporation have purchased shares of stock in the company; hence, they are also called stockholders. In small firms these individuals run the corporation as well as own it. In larger companies thousands of the shareholders may have purchased shares either as an investment or for speculative purposes.

Normally, each share of stock carries with it one vote. Voting by the shareholders is usually done once each year. If a shareholder can be present at the meeting, he may cast his votes in person. If, as is more likely, he cannot attend the meeting, he may send his *proxy,* which is a written authorization for someone else to cast his votes for him. Usually a majority of the voting stock outstanding must be represented at each annual meeting.

The solicitation of proxies is undertaken by the board of directors at the expense of the corporation. In corporations with a large number of shareholders this procedure usually results in board members perpetuating themselves in office or selecting their own successors. Occasionally a group of dissatisfied shareholders may attempt to solicit proxies in their behalf and against the existing board of directors. Since they must do this at their own expense, proxy battles are relatively rare when the corporation has thousands of shareholders.

A method of electing members of the board of directors that may allow a minority group of shareholders to secure representation is *cumulative voting.* Under this plan, if there are 15 directors to be elected, the owner of a single share of voting stock can cast 15 votes in any manner he chooses. For example, he can cast one vote for each of 15 men or 15 votes for one man. By concentrating their voting, the owners of a modest fraction of the entire stock issue can elect at least one individual to the board. Cumulative voting is required by law in 22 states and is permitted by some corporations chartered in other states.

In addition to voting for members of the board of directors, the shareholder votes on any amendments to the charter, on bylaws (unless this authority is delegated to the board of directors), on such broad policies as retirement or pension plans for officers and employees, on dissolution of the corporation, and frequently on the choice of the firm of certified public accountants to make the annual audit of the books and records.

Other shareholder rights include the following:

(a) To receive dividends in proportion to his holdings of stock, provided, however, that such dividends have been legally declared by the board of directors, which has sole authority to do so.

(b) To hold or to sell stock certificates registered in his name.

(c) To share pro rata in the assets that remain after the debts have been paid when a corporation is dissolved.

(d) To subscribe to additional stock offerings before such stock is made available to the general public, unless this right is waived.

(e) To inspect the books and records when good cause is shown.

2 / Board of directors. As soon as shareholders have elected a board of directors, responsibility for directing the affairs of the business rests with this body. The usual term of office is one year although some corporations have longer terms, such as three years with only one third of the board members up for election at any annual meeting. The members of the board of directors of most small corporations are usually the shareholders who own all or most of the shares of stock. The shareholders of many large corporations elect to their boards outstanding businessmen who have no other connection with the firm, as well as some officers of the company. Of seventeen directors of the General Electric Co., fifteen are "outsiders" and only two are company executives. On the other hand, only two of the fifteen directors of the Standard Oil Co. (New Jersey) provide the broader perspective associated with noncompany directors and the other thirteen are "insiders."

Within the framework of the charter that authorized the creation of the corporation, the board of directors is usually delegated the authority by the shareholders to adopt a set of *bylaws*. These specify the rules and regulations under which the board operates. Some of the important provisions in a set of bylaws cover the time and place of the shareholders' regular meetings, methods of calling special meetings of shareholders, the number of directors and their organization and remuneration, the names of the officers to be chosen by the board of directors, the duties of these officers, provisions for filling vacancies on the board, rules for the issuance and transfer of stock, provisions for publishing an annual statement and other accounting matters, and the method by which the bylaws can be amended.

Final authority for the actions of a corporation rests with the board of directors; but it customarily votes on, and usually approves, recommendations coming to it from the chief executive officer or other officials of the company. In large corporations the board rarely initiates changes in policies although it may make a choice among alternate courses of action. The individual members are not liable for actions of the board except when it does something illegal, such as declaring a dividend out of nonexistent profits.

3 / Officers. The bylaws usually specify the officers of the corporation to be elected by the board of directors. The president is normally the chief executive of the company, but some corporations delegate more power to the chairman of the board. The vice-president or vice-presidents are usually vested with specific powers. It is not uncommon to have a vice-president in charge of sales, a vice-president in charge of production, and so on.

The secretary, who is in possession of the corporate seal, signs or countersigns many corporation documents. He also attends all meetings of the shareholders and directors and keeps the minutes of these meetings. The finances of a corporation are under the supervision of a treasurer; in recent years, however, much of the responsibility for this detail has been transferred, in some corporations, to an elected officer called the controller.

■ **Separation of Ownership and Management**

Another feature of corporations, particularly the industrial, commercial, and financial giants, is the distinction between ownership and management. In the small corporation a few individuals or even one person may own all or substantially all of the outstanding shares and may be active in the business as a board member and officer. In this event the owner or owners are working for themselves in a manner comparable to sole proprietorships and partnerships. In large corporations that have many shareholders, however, it is not uncommon that no executive has any substantial stock holding in the company and that, collectively, the shares owned by all management personnel are but a small fraction of the total number outstanding. In these circumstances ownership becomes separated from management. The American Telephone and Telegraph Company with over two and a half million shareholders and no individual owning as much as 1 percent of the stock is an example.

Corporations in the United States with 300,000 or More Shareholders

NAME OF CORPORATION	NUMBER OF SHAREHOLDERS
American Telephone & Telegraph Co.	2,674,000
General Motors Corp.	1,139,000
Standard Oil Co. (New Jersey)	707,000
General Electric Co.	511,000
General Telephone & Electronics Corp.	356,000
Ford Motor Co.	338,000
United States Steel Corp.	327,000

1965 Census of Shareholders—New York Stock Exchange

The effect of divorcing ownership from management is that the executives regard the shareholders as a group who must be kept satisfied rather than as their employers. Decisions rendered take the investors into consideration on an equal but separate basis with the other employees, the firm's customers, the government, and the public. The concept of maximizing profits for the benefit of the shareholders is not as potent a factor in decision making as it is when there is no separation between management and ownership.

■ Advantages of a Corporation

The corporate form of business ownership, when compared with other types, has several important advantages. If this were not the case, corporations would not dominate our capitalistic system. Although there is some logic to the order in which these advantages are listed in the following paragraphs, it should be remembered that under a given set of circumstances any one of the factors might prove to be of maximum importance.

The principal advantages of a corporation are:

1. Limited liability of shareholders
2. Larger size
3. Transfer of ownership
4. Length of life
5. Efficiency of management
6. Ease of expansion
7. Legal entity

1 / Limited liability of shareholders. The corporate form of business organization offers the owners the advantage of *limited liability*, which means that each shareholder risks only the amount he invests in the corporation. If the company proves unprofitable and fails, creditors cannot look beyond the assets of the corporation for funds to settle their claims. If Rodney Kent decides to invest $5,000 in the Thompson Manufacturing Corporation, he knows that his risk is limited to that amount. If he owns a home or other forms of wealth, these items are not available to creditors of the Thompson Manufacturing Company.

2 / Larger size. The original size of a sole proprietorship or a partnership is limited to the amount of capital that one man or several men can provide by recourse to their own fortunes or by borrowing. The corporation, by dividing its ownership into shares of small denomination, can attract capital from thousands of individuals. If it is necessary to secure capital amounting to millions of dollars in order to organize a firm, a corporation is the only feasible form of ownership that can be used.

3 / Transfer of ownership. Ownership evidenced by stock certificates gives maximum ease of transfer. If Andrews sells his interest in a corporation to Bennett, he merely endorses his stock certificate and this change of ownership is recorded in the books of the corporation. As a general rule, corporations allow their shareholders to transfer ownership to anyone at any time; some corporations that have only a few shareholders attempt to control the ownership group by restricting transfers to the corporation itself or other remaining shareholders. Through the medium of stockbrokers and organized stock exchanges, millions of shares of stock change hands daily.

Although a corporation usually has no voice in the matter of who buys its shares of stock, it is responsible for keeping an accurate record of the shareholders. Because large corporations are subject to numerous changes in owners, some find it advantageous to hire a separate organization, usually a bank, to handle this task.

4 / Length of life. The corporation has potentialities of a permanent existence. The death or incapacity of shareholders, officers, and employees usually has little bearing on the continued existence of the business. If the business can thrive and prosper, it can remain in business indefinitely. Corporations with over one hundred years of continuous life are not uncommon. Many well-known firms, such as the Procter and Gamble Company, are included in this group.

5 / Efficiency of management. Unlike proprietorships and partnerships, the owners of a corporation do not manage it except to the extent that directors and officers are also shareholders. In the small corporation this dual role may be quite extensive on the part of management, but it is not true for medium- and large-size corporations. The corporate structure permits delegation of authority by the shareholders to the board of directors and by it to the administrative officials. Corporations frequently seek and secure the services of outstanding individuals on their boards of directors. These men give a continuity to management that is valuable. The board hires the top executives and, if these individuals do not perform efficiently, they can be replaced.

Another reason for the more efficient management of corporations stems from the attribute of size. In large corporations it is possible to delegate duties to specialists in various lines and to pay salaries high enough to attract the most competent individuals. On the payroll of such a firm may be found a purchasing agent, a sales manager, an advertising manager, a production superintendent, accountants, lawyers, and other specialists. In small firms, notably sole proprietorships and partnerships, one individual may have to perform many functions and it is unlikely that he will be equally efficient in the many diverse duties he must perform.

6 / Ease of expansion. A sole proprietor, assuming that he has tapped his resources to the limit, cannot expand without changing his form of business ownership, except to the extent that he allows profits to remain in the business. The partnership offers limited additional possibilities to the extent that one or more partners may be added to the firm. In contrast, the corporation has an almost unlimited opportunity for expansion just as long as investors are willing to purchase additional shares of stock. Furthermore, large corporations find it much easier to borrow substantial sums of money because the amounts needed are large enough to interest appropriate financial agencies in marketing the securities. In general, large corporations have attained a high degree of confidence among the members of the investing public, who are willing to purchase securities that are issued for expansion purposes.

7 / Legal entity. A corporation can sue and be sued, make contracts, and secure title to property in its own name. In this respect, the corporation is in sharp contrast to the sole proprietorship and partnership, which must use individual names in legal matters even though operating under firm names not unlike those of corporations.

◼ Disadvantages of Corporate Ownership

The corporate form of business ownership has its disadvantages as well as its advantages. Some of the more important disadvantages follow:

1. Taxation
2. Organization expenses
3. Government restrictions and reports
4. Lack of personal interest
5. Lack of secrecy
6. Relative lack of credit
7. Charter restrictions

1 / Taxation. In addition to an annual franchise tax in the state of incorporation, an annual payment is required by every state from corporations for the right to do business in that state. Similar fees are not exacted from sole proprietorships and partnerships. Furthermore, some states have levied special taxes on certain types of corporations, such as public utilities, railroads, and insurance companies.

The imposition of federal income taxes is frequently a deterrent to using the corporate form of ownership. The minimum rate on the first $25,000 of income has varied in recent years from 30 percent down to the current rate of 22 percent, and the rate on the income in excess of $25,000 has varied from 52 percent down to the current 48 percent. Then, when the corporation distributes its earnings after taxes to its shareholders, these individuals must pay personal income taxes on dividends received in excess of $100. This double taxation of earnings can be a decided disadvantage although, if a corporation has 10 or fewer shareholders, it can elect to be taxed in the same manner as a partnership. Many states also tax corporate profits.

2 / Organization expenses. Of all the various forms of business enterprise, corporations are the most expensive to organize. An incorporation fee must be paid to the state in order to receive a charter. Furthermore, stock certificates and record books must be purchased. Because of the legal nature of a corporation, it is usually advisable to engage a lawyer to assist in the organization procedures. For both large and small businesses, these costs may prove to be a real drawback.

The E. I. du Pont de Nemours & Co. is organized under the laws of Delaware with an authorized total of 4 million shares of no-par preferred stock and 60 million shares of common stock with a $5 par value.[1] Rates charged by Delaware for a certificate of incorporation are shown on the next page.

---

[1] See Chapter 18.

For each share of authorized capital stock up to
20,000 shares without par value .... ½ cent

For each share in excess of 20,000 shares and up
to 2,000,000 shares without par value ...... ¼ cent

For each share in excess of 2,000,000 shares without par value .... ⅕ cent

For each share up to 20,000 shares having par
value .... 1 cent

For each share in excess of 20,000 shares and up
to and including 200,000 shares having par
value .... ½ cent

For each share in excess of 200,000 shares having
par value .... ⅕ cent

In no case less than $10. Each one-hundred-dollar
unit of par-value stock shall be counted as one
taxable share.

The application of these rates to the par and no-par shares of the
E. I. du Pont de Nemours & Co. produces the following computation:

Preferred Stock—4,000,000 shares no-par
    20,000 shares at ½ cent each .... $ 100
    1,980,000 shares at ¼ cent each 4,950
    2,000,000 shares at ⅕ cent each .... 4,000 $ 9,050

Common Stock—60,000,000 shares $5 par
(Tax rates on par stock are based on $100 of par
value. Since it takes 20 of the above shares of $5 par
to equal one taxable share, the computation below is
on the 3,000,000 taxable shares involved.)
    20,000 taxable shares at 1 cent each   200
    180,000 taxable shares at ½ cent each   900
    2,800,000 taxable shares at ⅕ cent each 5,600   6,700

Total Cost—Preferred and Common Stocks $15,750

3 / Government restrictions and reports. Because the corporation is a
creature of the government, various departments of the state and federal
governments have the right to exercise certain restrictions and to require
certain reports. For example, a corporation cannot conduct business in a
state in which it is not registered. This registration involves the payment
of a special tax.

All types of annual and special reports, which frequently become
burdensome and costly to the corporation, must be prepared. Some

corporations, particularly public utilities, find it necessary to maintain report departments for the sole purpose of providing governmental bureaus and agencies with figures that must be furnished.

4 / Lack of personal interest. A corporation has an identity of its own. All who work for a corporation, therefore, assume the role of employees even though they may own stock in the organization. This fact sometimes results in a lack of personal interest in the success or failure of the organization. The managers draw a salary paid by the corporation; and they assume that, as long as they handle their assigned tasks efficiently, they will continue to be paid. Mistakes involving loss of profit are detrimental to the corporation but not necessarily to the managers individually. They do not feel that the loss affects them personally as they would in the case of a sole proprietorship or a partnership. The efforts of firms to sell stock to their employees have been motivated, in some instances, by a desire to mitigate the effects of this disadvantage of the corporate form of business ownership.

5 / Lack of secrecy. A corporation is duty bound to make an annual report to each shareholder. If it has only a few shareholders, these reports ordinarily do not become available to outsiders. When a considerable number of shareholders are involved, however, the annual reports become public property. Generally, such figures as sales volume, gross profit, net profit, total assets, and other financial matters are furnished in some detail. Furthermore, payments to each director and to each of the three highest paid officers of the corporation whose aggregate remuneration during the year exceeded $30,000 are detailed in the proxy statement. Other corporations, sometimes keen rivals, have an opportunity to examine the financial details of all companies that find it necessary to disclose this information.

6 / Relative lack of credit. In may seem strange that corporations do not enjoy higher credit ratings than proprietorships and partnerships, but size for size this is true. Creditors of a $25,000 corporation can look only to the assets of the organization for any debts incurred whereas a $25,000 proprietorship or partnership offers the additional security of the private fortunes of the owners.

7 / Charter restrictions. A sole proprietor can change his business almost at will. A corporation, on the other hand, must state the business it intends to pursue at the time of applying for a charter. Unless the charter of a corporation is amended, the company may not engage in any type of business not covered by the original permit.

Some states grant charters with a wide latitude in permissible corporate activities. Nevertheless, an unanticipated opportunity may suddenly present itself that cannot be seized because the type of business involved is not within the scope of the charter.

■ Organizing a Corporation

After weighing the advantages and the disadvantages, if the decision is to form a corporation, it will be necessary to secure a charter from one of the 50 states. The federal government charters national banks, federal credit unions and savings and loan associations, a few government corporations, and some scientific and educational organizations; but all industrial and commercial corporations are organized under the laws of a state.

Although incorporation laws in the several states vary in detail, they follow a general pattern. The first step necessary is to secure an application form, usually from the secretary of state of the state in which the corporation is to be formed. This form provides spaces for the name of the corporation, the names of the principal shareholders, the number and the types of shares of capital stock, the place of business, the type of business, and so forth.

When the application form is available, it is filled out, with special care given to fulfilling all specific requirements. Most states require at least three shareholders. Also, the minimum amount of capital for a business corporation is at least $500; frequently, the smallest permitted amount is $1,000.

After the requirements have been met, the completed papers with the requisite *incorporation fee* are forwarded to the state capitol. This charge varies with the number of shares of stock that the proposed corporation wishes to be permitted to issue, but a minimum fee of from $10 to $25 is customary.

The selection of the state in which to file incorporation papers depends on a number of factors. Usually, if a corporation plans to concentrate its activities within one state, it will be advantageous to secure its charter from that state. If its operations will be conducted in all fifty states, the choice may hinge on the cost of the incorporation fee, the lack of charter restrictions, and the amount of the continuing franchise tax. A *franchise tax* is an annual levy by a state on corporations it has chartered granting permission to continue in business for another year.

■ Classification of Corporations

Corporations may be classified in several ways:

1. Private and governmental corporations
2. Profit and nonprofit corporations
3. Stock and nonstock corporations
4. Domestic, foreign, and alien corporations
5. Close and open corporations
6. Industrial classifications

1 / Private and governmental corporations. A *private corporation* is one chartered, owned, and operated by individuals either for the profit of its owners or for social, charitable, or educational purposes. The vast majority of corporations are private in nature, and by far the larger number are organized with the intent of making a profit. A *governmental corporation* is one organized by the federal government, a state, a city, or some other political subdivision. Examples of governmental corporations are incorporated cities, municipally owned water companies, state universities, and such agencies of the federal government as the Commodity Credit Corporation. Governmental corporations are sometimes referred to as public corporations but, unless this meaning is made clear, there may be confusion with private corporations owned by the general public.

The Communications Satellite Corporation is an interesting mixture of a private and governmental corporation. The ownership is private, but the Corporation was authorized by the Congress and three members of the board of directors are appointed by the President. Of the remaining twelve board members, six are elected by the companies owning stock and six by the individual shareholders.

2 / Profit and nonprofit corporations. A *profit corporation* is a privately owned business, using the corporate form, that operates to make profits for its shareholders. The vast majority of all corporations in the United States are of this type. A *nonprofit corporation* is somewhat of a misnomer in that its receipts may exceed its disbursements but a distribution is never made to its owners, and any income that may result from its operations is used to further the purposes for which it was organized. Governmental as well as social, charitable, religious, and educational corporations are examples of this clasification.

3 / Stock and nonstock corporations. Business corporations issue *stock certificates*, representing shares of ownership, which provide a basis for distributing the profits to the shareholders. In general, governmental corporations, and also private corporations not organized to make profits for their members, do not issue stock. Examples of such private corporations are churches, hospitals, and schools.

4 / Domestic, foreign, and alien corporations. A corporation is usually organized under the laws of one state. In that state the business is regarded as a *domestic corporation*; but in every other state in which it may operate, it is considered a *foreign corporation*. For example, the United States Steel Corporation, which is organized under the laws of New Jersey, is considered a domestic corporation in that state; but in Pennsylvania, where it has numerous offices and factories, it is a foreign corporation.

A company doing business within the United States that has been organized in another country, such as Canada, Mexico, England, or The Netherlands, is known in the United States as an *alien corporation*.

5 / Close and open corporations. If the stock of a corporation is not available for purchase by outsiders, it is a *close corporation*. Usually it is owned by only a few shareholders, most of whom are probably active in the management. Family corporations and corporations that have been formed by converting sole proprietorships or partnerships into the corporate form are typical of the close classification.

If the stock of a corporation is available for purchase by anyone having sufficient funds, it is an *open corporation*. Most of the large corporations are open, and shares can be purchased through the agency of a stockbroker. Within recent years many close corporations, needing funds for expansion or for other reasons, have "gone public," that is, have made shares available to investors. As previously mentioned, this has given rise to the use of the term "public corporation" for what is, more accurately, an open corporation.

6 / Industrial classifications. Private, profit-making, business corporations may be classified in several ways. Moody's Manuals, which include a description of almost every corporation in the United States, as well as those in foreign countries, are issued in four volumes. These are headed Industrials; Transportation; Public Utilities; and Banks, Insurance, Real Estate, and Investment Trusts. The Industrials volume is further subdivided into aviation, chemical, petroleum, tobacco, and many other categories.

The Internal Revenue Service of the United States Treasury Department classifies corporations into several major industrial divisions. The table below shows these groups, the number of income tax returns filed by each, the total receipts, and the net profits. Since all business corporations must file returns regardless of whether or not any profits have been realized, the figures in the table reflect an accurate picture of the number and financial success of corporations operating in each classification.

Corporation Income Tax Returns

Number, Business Receipts, and Net Profits by Industrial Divisions

INDUSTRIAL DIVISIONS	NUMBER OF RETURNS	BUSINESS RECEIPTS	NET PROFIT (LOSS)
			(THOUSANDS OF DOLLARS)
ALL INDUSTRIAL DIVISIONS..	1,245,912	$889,142,468	$49,445,084
Mining	13,539	11,955,257	793,601
Construction	90,604	40,311,096	617,156
Manufacturing	183,149	399,659,829	25,350,966
Transportation, Communication, Electric, Gas, and Sanitary Services	52,701	71,091,979	8,010,628
Wholesale and Retail Trade .	388,852	293,118,648	5,172,405
Finance, Insurance, and Real Estate	359,229	46,294,993	8,680,895
Services	150,082	26,607,539	833,141
Business Not Allocable	7,756	103,127	(13,708)

Source: United States Treasury Department, Internal Revenue Service, *Statistics of Income—1962-1963*. Agriculture, Forestry, and Fisheries omitted.

■ Other Incorporated Forms of Business Ownership

In addition to corporations, there are two other incorporated forms of business ownership—cooperatives and mutual companies. Both of these forms play an important part in the particular segment of business activity where used and, in one instance, mutual life insurance companies, the form dominates the industry. Within each category there are such substantial variations in one regard or another. The following discussion will describe agricultural and consumer cooperatives, credit unions, mutual companies, and savings and loan associations.

1 / **Cooperatives.** *Cooperatives,* or *co-ops* as they are commonly called, are incorporated under the laws of a state. They are to be distinguished from corporations in the following respects:

1. Each cooperative unit is owned by the user-members of the group.
2. Each member has only one vote regardless of the number of shares of stock that he owns.
3. There is a limitation on the amount of stock that each member may own.
4. The capital for the enterprise is subscribed only by the members.
5. Interest is paid on the investment of each member-shareholder.
6. Dividends are paid on a patronage basis, in proportion to the amount of goods that each member has bought or sold through the co-op. These are referred to as *patronage dividends*.

Cooperatives have all of the advantages of corporations although the requirement of ownership by user-members limits the size and ease of expansion. They also have a tax advantage in that patronage dividends are considered a refund of overpayments rather than a distribution of profits, and the federal government provides financial assistance not available to profit-seeking corporations. In agricultural co-ops, members are frequently intensely loyal to their firm and support the business with zeal and enthusiasm.

On the other hand, cooperatives lack the profit-making incentive common to other forms of ownership, which appears to be a serious handicap. Also, there is an unfortunate tendency to rely on volunteers, e. g., members of the board of directors customarily are not paid for their services, and the salary scales for employees are frequently on the low side.

The most extensive use of co-ops is in the field of agriculture. Farm products that are marketed through farmer cooperatives include citrus fruits, butter, potatoes, milk, prunes, apricots, wool, grains of all kinds, livestock, eggs, poultry, and rice. Such well-known brands as Sunkist oranges and Sun Maid raisins are the property of *producer cooperative associations* engaged in the marketing of these products grown by their many members. There are more than 7,000 producer cooperative associations in the United States with annual sales in excess of $8 billion. In addition to producer co-ops, there are approximately the same number of farmer-owned *buying cooperatives* whose purchases of seeds, gasoline, farm machinery, etc., total about $3 billion annually.

Although *consumer co-ops,* which are user-owned retail outlets of goods and services, have long been a dominant factor in such countries as Denmark and Sweden, their influence in the United States has been relatively minor, particularly in the retailing of consumer goods. Aided by the Rural Electrification Administration, a federal agency, the sales of electricity by consumer cooperatives has grown, and rural telephone co-ops have also increased, again with federal financial aid. In other retail areas the cooperative movement has failed to generate any enthusiasm among our general public.

2 / Credit unions. *Credit unions* are cooperatives organized to accept savings from members and to loan these funds to other members. They differ from farmer and consumer co-ops in that they have the option of receiving a charter from the federal government as well as a state; members can invest in as many shares as they wish, which usually cost $5 to $10 each; and earnings are distributed on the basis of the investment of each member in the credit union. All users are members as borrowers must purchase at least one share of stock, and each credit union restricts its activities to a homogeneous group such as the employees of a corporation or members of a labor union. There are approximately 22,000 credit unions in this country with 16,000,000 members. Assets amount to $9 billion and loans outstanding are $7 billion.

3 / Mutual companies. *Mutual companies* receive a charter from a state, but their owners are the users of the service that they render. The primary use of mutual companies is in the field of life insurance and, in a limited number of states, savings banks. The purchaser of a policy from a mutual life insurance company is automatically a member as is the person who deposits money in a mutual savings bank. Each mutual company has a board of directors that tends to be self-perpetuating as members are usually not sent a proxy and rarely exercise their right to vote. Of the $150 billion in assets of life insurance companies, mutual companies own about 70 percent as opposed to the 30 percent controlled by stock companies. Mutual savings banks have approximately $44 billion in deposits, representing about 11 percent of all savings of individuals.

Since mutual companies do not issue stock, obviously there are no shareholders. Otherwise, they have all of the advantages of corporations. They also have some tax advantages as, for example, dividends on life insurance policies are considered a partial refund of premiums paid by the policyholder. Mutual savings banks can insure their accounts with an agency of the federal government and can borrow funds from the federal home loan bank system. The disadvantage of the lack of the powerful incentive inherent in a profit-seeking business form has not seemed to affect the efficiency or aggressiveness of mutual companies.

4 / Savings and loan associations. *Savings and loan associations* may be organized on a basis similar to mutual companies with the important difference that they can secure either a state or a federal charter. Of the approximately 6,500 associations in the United States, 88 percent are organized on a mutual basis as opposed to 12 percent that are stock companies. The primary purpose of savings and loan associations is to accept deposits from savers and to lend these funds to borrowers to build homes. Both savers and borrowers are members of nonstock associations, which are managed by a board of directors and staff. Members vote each year for the board members on the basis of the number of paid-up shares they own.

Of all financial institutions, savings and loan associations rank third in size exceeded only by commercial banks and life insurance companies. Total assets exceed $107 billion contributed, in large measure, by some 37 million individual savers. Advantages are similar to mutual savings banks, and the desire of management to pay competitive dividends to depositors has led to efficiency of operation for most associations.

BUSINESS TERMS

(a) corporation (90), legal entity (90), charter (90)
(b) shareholders (90), board of directors (90), officers (90)
(c) proxy (91), cumulative voting (91)
(d) bylaws (92)
(e) limited liability (95)
(f) incorporation fee (100), franchise tax (100)
(g) private corporation (101), governmental corporation (101)
(h) profit corporation (101), nonprofit corporation (101)
(i) stock certificate (101)
(j) domestic corporation (102), foreign corporation (102), alien corporation (102)
(k) close corporation (102), open corporation (102)
(l) cooperatives or co-ops (104), patronage dividends (104)
(m) producer cooperative association (104), buying cooperative (104), consumer co-ops (104)
(n) credit union (105), mutual company (105), savings and loan association (106)

QUESTIONS FOR DISCUSSION AND ANALYSIS

1. Why should corporations not be required to nominate at least twice as many candidates for the board of directors as there are vacancies and thus allow shareholders a choice when they vote at each annual meeting?
2. Does the separation of ownership and management in large corporations work to the detriment of the shareholders of the company? Why?

3. How do you account for the fact that over 20 million individuals own stock in corporations?
4. Is there any connection between the ease of transfer of ownership in a corporation and limited liability of shareholders? Explain.
5. Would a $100,000 corporation be likely to have a more efficient management than a $100,000 partnership? Why?
6. Do the advantages of corporations over sole proprietorships and partnerships mean that the latter forms of business ownership will become less and less a factor in the overall business scene? Explain.
7. Is the double taxation of corporate dividends either fair or equitable? Explain.
8. Why do some journalists, politicians, and professional reformers decry the modern corporation?
9. Can you give any reasons why consumer cooperatives have not been particularly successful in the United States?
10. What explanations can be given for the successful competition of stock companies with mutual companies engaged in the same types of business?

PROBLEMS AND SHORT CASES

1. A group of investors decide to incorporate the Lectronic Manufacturing Corp. with an authorized capital stock of 3,000,000 shares of preferred stock with a par value of $10 a share, and 6,000,000 shares of no-par-value common stock. Ohio and Delaware have been suggested as logical states in which to file incorporation papers. The cost of obtaining a charter may prove to be a vital factor in the choice between the two states.

    Compute (a) the amount of the incorporation fee in Ohio, (b) the amount of the incorporation fee in Delaware (see page 98), and (c) the amount of savings one state offers over the other.

    Incorporation fees for Ohio are as follows:

First, 1,000 shares	10 cents a share
1,001 to 10,000 shares	5 cents a share
10,001 to 50,000 shares	2 cents a share
50,001 to 100,000 shares	1 cent a share
100,001 to 500,000 shares	½ cent a share
Over 500,000 shares	¼ cent a share

2. Using the information on page 103, compute (a) the percent of total number of returns for each division to the number of returns for all industrial divisions, and (b) the percent of business receipts for each division to the total business receipts for all industrial divisions. List each set of percentages in descending order.

    What conclusions can be drawn from these computations?

3. In 1950 James Young went into business for himself manufacturing transparent plastic paperweights. At first he installed the single machine he had designed in his basement, but the business prospered

and is now housed in a rented factory building. His sales volume increased from $15,000 in 1950 to $632,000 in the past year, and he now employs 32 men and women in his factory and office. One of these is the plant manager, another is the office manager, and a third is the sales manager.

Young has two sons, who are 16 and 14, and a 12-year-old daughter. He is devoted to his family but also to his business. It has provided him with a substantial annual income, and he has been able to live well and still make personal investments outside of his business that now have a value of $420,000. At the moment the firm has adequate cash resources for current needs and no bank or mortgage debt. Young's lease on the factory building expires this year, but it can be renewed for five years at a 50 percent increase in monthly rentals or the building can be purchased for $100,000.

A lawyer who has handled Young's legal work has suggested that it might be wise for him to incorporate the business. Each of the three managers has expressed an interest in buying into the firm, and several local businessmen have told Young to let them know "if he ever decided to form a corporation."

On the basis of this information, answer these questions: (a) What are the arguments in favor of and against incorporation of this business? (b) Would you advise Mr. Young to incorporate his business?

SUGGESTED READINGS

Anderson, R. A., and W. A. Kumpf. *Business Law,* Seventh Edition. Cincinnati: South-Western Publishing Company, 1964. Part VIII.

Broom, H. N., and J. G. Longenecker. *Small Business Management,* Second Edition. Cincinnati: South-Western Publishing Company, 1966. Part B.

Dillavou, E. R., and Others. *Principles of Business Law,* Alternate Seventh Edition. Englewood Cliffs, New Jersey: Prentice-Hall, Inc., 1964. Book Five.

Finney, H. A., and H. E. Miller. *Principles of Accounting—Introductory,* Sixth Edition. Englewood Cliffs, New Jersey: Prentice-Hall, Inc., 1963. Chapters 9-10.

Husband, W. H., and J. C. Dockeray. *Modern Corporation Finance,* Sixth Edition. Homewood, Illinois: Richard D. Irwin, Inc., 1966. Chapters 3 and 4.

Niswonger, C. R., and P. E. Fess. *Accounting Principles,* Ninth Edition. Cincinnati: South-Western Publishing Company, 1965. Chapters 16-19.

Prather, C. L. *Financing Business Firms,* Third Edition. Homewood, Illinois: Richard D. Irwin, Inc., 1966. Part I.

Chapter 6

MANAGEMENT AND ORGANIZATION

Management may be said to include all the personnel of a business whose duties include the making of decisions affecting their firms' affairs, and of assuming the responsibility both for the implementation of these decisions and for the results that flow from them. Theirs is the responsibility of making certain, or trying to, that their firms' objectives are attained, whether they be profits, market share, growth, quality of product or service, community prestige, or any combination of these. Management endeavors to reach its goals through the use of organization.

Organization means that management endeavors to achieve its objectives by directing the efforts of the people under its supervision. This procedure is a necessity in small and large companies and regardless of whether the firm is a sole proprietorship, a partnership, or a corporation. While the success of a company may be attributed to many causes, the skill with which management directs its organization is one of the major factors in the end result. This chapter is concerned with business management and the organization through which it attempts to achieve its objectives. The structure and functions of each will be described, followed by a brief discussion of some of the recent developments in management theory, a subject that has been receiving an increasing measure of attention and study from researchers, teachers, and practitioners.

MANAGEMENT

The responsibility of management is that of coordinating, integrating, and controlling the personnel, equipment, material, processes, and finances of the company so that the objectives of the owners will be achieved. In a small firm one or a very few persons, usually the owners, may constitute the management, while in larger companies a much greater number of persons may be required. As noted in Chapter 5, there has been a trend toward the separation of ownership and management in medium-size to large corporations.

■ Levels of Management

Medium- and large-sized companies have three levels of management: (1) top management, (2) middle management, and (3) operating (or operative) management. *Top management* includes the president; the general manager; vice-presidents in charge of production, sales, purchasing, personnel, and finance; and the treasurer. The term *administrative management* is sometimes used in referring to top management. *Middle management* is composed of department managers, branch office and plant managers, and production superintendents. *Operating management* is made up of plant supervisors and foremen and the heads of subdivisions of the larger departments. These are the members of the management team whose major task is the immediate supervision of the workers themselves.

■ Decision Making

Possibly the foremost responsibilty of management at all levels, but especially top management, is the making of decisions. It permeates all functions of management. In accord with the broad operational policies set forth by the board of directors, top managements are daily confronted with the necessity of deciding on courses of action that will best achieve the goals to which their companies are dedicated. In many, if not most, instances, the decisions involve the making of choices between two or more alternative courses of action. And at the top echelon of management, from which the basic procedural orders for the companies' operations emanate, correct decisions may be vital to the continued success of the firms or even their survival. Farther down the managerial ladder, there is usually a decrease in the number and quality of alternatives available to the managers involved; but the importance of correct decisions at these levels is, nevertheless, essential to the well-being of the companies.

The ability to make correct decisions in business has long been recognized as a prime attribute of successful management, but until comparatively recently there has been little apparent need for inquiry into the decision-making process. However, with the growth of large corporations, with their vast resources in the areas of finance, productive capacity, and manpower, and the increased tempo of competition, the possible consequences of unwise decisions, both on the companies involved and on the economy generally, have served to focus the attention of students of business on the methods by which decisions are made, in so far as these can be discovered.

The steps included in decision making have been known for quite some time. They are: (1) the recognition of the problem involved, (2) its definition and analysis into its essential parts, (3) the attempt to establish two or more alternative solutions and to evaluate them comparatively, (4) the selection of the solution believed the most favorable, and (5) the adoption of this solution and the implementation of it through the issuing of the necessary orders. These steps may have been taken in a few moments by an executive, or they may have required a much longer time, depending on the complexity and importance of the problems at hand.

In the past few years a number of things have come into being that have brought the decision-making process into a sharper focus. From the purely mechanical side, the rapid and extensive development of high-speed computers and data processing procedures have added immeasurably to the quantity of information available to the executive, thereby enabling him to base his decisions on far greater amounts of relevant data than previously. In addition to this, social and behavioral scientists have become aware that decision making by management is not only an economic activity dependent on accurate data, but it reaches also into the fields of sociology, psychology, anthropology, mathematics, philosophy, and political science. From each of these fields of knowledge have come theories and concepts which, it is hoped, will aid management in making its decisions and bring about results that will be beneficial, not only to the firms involved but also to the society of which they are a part. Those who have been active in this area are hoping to develop a general theory of decision making that will synthesize the contributions from the various disciplines into a valid and useful whole. At present this appears to be a development of some future time. It is believed, however, that the results of both correct and incorrect decisions are of sufficient consequence to warrant continued research in this area.

The question may well be raised regarding the extent to which these new theories and concepts are being communicated to and used by management. A definitive answer to this question is not presently possible, but there is some evidence that management is aware of the growing importance of correct decision making and is receptive to some degree to any suggestion from whatever source that may be of assistance in fulfilling the rigorous responsibilities of this area.

■ **Functions of Management**

The functions of the management of a business enterprise include (1) planning and policy making, (2) organization and operation, and (3) control. The first of these, planning and policy making, is primarily the responsibility of the owners, the partners, the board of directors, or the elected officers, that is, top management. Although certain types of problems of organization and operation, as well as control, are also a concern of top management, many of these problems are somewhat routine and come under the supervision of executives at a lower level of authority, that is, middle and operating management.

1 / Planning and policy making. As indicated above, planning and policy making concerns top management more than it does management at lower levels of authority. Any organizational structure that does not free these individuals from routine tasks, leaving ample time for this important function, is not accomplishing its purpose.

A few illustrations of planning and policy making may indicate the type of decisions that should be reached by top management.

(a) Assuming that the demand for a product is beyond the capacity of a manufacturing plant, the problem arises as to whether to meet the demand and, if the decision is in the affirmative, how to produce more. Perhaps a new plant can be purchased or built, or the problem may be solved by installing a two- or three-shift operation.

(b) What should be done in case a union makes demands that management is unwilling to grant? Should a compromise be reached or will it be more satisfactory to maintain a firm stand even if doing so results in a strike?

(c) Within a few years a bond issue is going to mature. Will the company have enough cash on hand to pay this debt, or should steps be taken to secure funds from other sources to repay the original obligation?

2 / Organization and operation. Once plans have been made and policies determined, the job of carrying these out becomes one of organization and operation. If a firm is running smoothly, it may seem to an outsider that the whole process is relatively simple. Goods are shipped on time because they have been made and stored in advance of receiving an order and because packaging and transportation facilities of the right type and kind are available when needed. Actually, all of this smooth flow could not have been accomplished without an efficient organization operating under competent managerial supervision.

3 / Control. At all levels of management there must be control, all the way from knowing how much money the firm is making or losing to knowing the number of parts of a particular size and shape that are on hand. A proper organizational structure allows for the delegation of authority for control to individuals at various levels of management, depending upon the importance or type of the factor involved. Top management should not be concerned with the problem of whether a minimum of 100 or 200 one-horsepower motors should be kept on hand, but it is concerned with the total dollars tied up in the parts inventory.

Many firms have introduced data-processing units (computers) that have provided their managerial personnel with up-to-date, comprehensive information on current operations. This has greatly increased their ability to make intelligent decisions in the control phase of their functions.

Two control problems frequently arise in large businesses that are not present in smaller organizations. One of these is that of *absentee management*, a condition that exists when executives of a large corporation have their offices in one city whereas their operating divisions are scattered throughout the country. Absentee management requires the delegation of substantial authority to the men in the field, and considerable reliance must be placed on reports and occasional plant visits.

Another problem of a large firm is whether to operate on the basis of a centralized management or a decentralized management. This issue arises when a firm's operations are physically dispersed, such as the large chain-store organizations and many others that have plants and offices located in different parts of the country. Here the question refers to the measure of authority that is to be delegated to the field executives and how much is to be retained by the home office management. For example, in a firm embracing the philosophy of *decentralized management* the branch offices might be permitted to handle their own personnel problems, to set quotas for their salesmen, to make local adjustments, and to conduct dealer relations. In a company that follows the practice of *centralized management*, these matters would be reserved for the home office. Examples have been known of two competing firms, each apparently successful, which have followed different, conflicting policies.

■ The Issue of Divisionalization

In many very large companies, frequently with diversified product lines, the concept of decentralization has been extended to the point where each product line becomes the basis of a more or less semiautonomous division. In such a situation the responsibility for designing, producing, and selling its product line and of making a profit is given to the division management. This situation is known as *divisionalization*. The General Motors Corporation and the E. I. du Pont de Nemours and Company have been pioneers in this philosophy of management. Among other companies that follow this practice are the General Electric Company, IBM, and Continental Can Company. The rationale behind this practice is that these firms have become too large and their product lines too varied for a centralized management to supervise satisfactorily, so that each division acts almost as though it were an independent company. This is particularly true in the case of General Motors, where genuine competition exists between the top-priced lines of Chevrolet and the lower priced lines of Pontiac. The same situation prevails between the corporation's higher priced cars. Where divisionalization exists, each division has its own producing and selling departments, as well as its ancillary services such as personnel and accounting.

All large companies, however, do not look with favor on divisionalization. Probably the most recent example of this attitude is the United States Steel Corporation which, in January, 1964, did away with seven of its steel-making divisions and established in their stead two large manufacturing and sales departments that took over the activities of the former divisions. The term applied to this procedure is known as *functionalization* or the adopting of a functional type of control structure. With this sort of arrangement, a firm's physical operations may be dispersed, but the managerial control for all of its different operations is centralized; that is, a single sales force sells all of its different products and the manufacturing plants are directed from the home office. When the firm is not physically decentralized but is organized according to its basic activities, such as production, marketing, finance, purchasing, and personnel, each of these departments is regarded as a functional area, but it reports to and is supervised by higher levels of authority and responsibility.

Such an arrangement is also known as a *functional organization*, with the focus of responsibility centering on the president. In a large company, this concentration of responsibility may overburden the chief executive with supervisory duties, leaving him too little time for creative thinking and acting. It also tends to create a shortage of potential managers because of the centralizing of authority at the top. This latter situation has been recognized by the managements of many firms who have sought to discover and implement various procedures to overcome it.

The use of the term "functional" may be somewhat confusing to beginning students of business because the same term is used with quite a different meaning, as will be explained on page 122.

ORGANIZATION

For small businesses, such as an independently owned hardware store, the details of organization for purposes of management are comparatively simple. The owner, who is usually the manager, employs a few persons to sell, to keep the stock in order, to make such deliveries as are necessary, and to keep the store clean. The owner usually buys the merchandise, handles the office work, assigns duties to his employees, establishes the policies of the company, and directs the operation of the entire business. There is little need for a complex organization in a firm of this size and the owner-manager has few problems in this area.

If the organization is somewhat larger or if it has expanded over the years, the problem of a satisfactory organization arises. If the business is a sole proprietorship, the owner must delegate some authority and responsibility. In a partnership the segregation of functions, a factor in creating an internal structure, is often recognized in the articles of partnership by stating the duties of each partner. This separation of authority and responsibility works out even more naturally in a corporation if the board of directors elects such officers as a vice-president in charge of sales, a vice-president in charge of manufacturing, and a treasurer. These provisions are merely the beginnings of a plan for the organization of a firm, however, and need to be expanded to include all employees.

■ Importance of Organizational Structure

An *organizational structure* is a framework within which management can adequately control, supervise, delegate, and fix responsibilities, and synchronize the work done by divisions, departments, and individuals. It is a plan by which a large business can attain the same efficiency as, or greater efficiency than, a small business run effectively by one person. It should not be created or allowed to grow in a haphazard manner. Only by building a planned organizational structure, taking into account all pertinent factors applicable, can a business achieve maximum operating efficiency. In highly competitive areas, proper organization may prove to be the necessary advantage one firm has over another.

An organizational structure also plays an important part in improving and maintaining employee morale. Just as a college football team cannot measure up to its capabilities unless eleven men are playing as a unit, no firm can operate smoothly unless employees "pull together." The familiar phrase *esprit de corps*, as applied to industry, means that loyal employees are working harmoniously along side of, and in cooperation with, each other. They are eager to promote the welfare of the firm, and its continuing success is a matter of personal pride to each individual.

Although it is true that the payment of good wages is an important part of employee morale, loyalty and the urge to do a good job cannot be bought by money alone. An organizational structure that allows each worker to know what he is supposed to do, to whom he is responsible, and the part he plays in the overall picture may prove to be more important than the size of the pay check that he receives. The concept of management as leaders rather than bosses, if sincerely practiced, may be of significant assistance in gaining and retaining the loyalty of the workers.

■ Factors in Organization Planning

Fundamentally, an internal organization structure must be designed to enable the management to exercise control of activities at all operating levels. As a necessary adjunct, authority to exercise such control must be delegated.

Before formalizing an organizational structure, several factors require consideration.

1. Classification of business activities
2. Departmentalization
3. Delegation of authority
4. Subdivisions of supervisory authority
5. Clearly defined duties
6. Flexibility
7. Communication

1 / Classification of business activities. The major activities of a manufacturing concern are production, marketing, finance, and accounting and statistical controls. Nonmanufacturing enterprises omit production from their scope of operations. These classifications may well provide the starting point for the construction of an organization plan, although two or more functions may be combined under one executive or in a department. An illustration of such a grouping is found in the common practice of designating a financial officer who is also in charge of accounting and statistical controls.

2 / Departmentalization. *Departmentalization* is the practice of subdividing both people and functions into groups within an organization. Several terms are applied to this policy, such as departments, divisions, branches, and sections. The extent to which this is done depends on the size of the firm, the complexity of its operations, the diversity of its product line, and the span of its geographic range. For example, a company that had been manufacturing parts for the automobile industry

"Deep Water" - Beau Brummels

secured an order from the federal government to produce parts for guided missiles. In view of the additional personnel and manufacturing facilities required and because of the basic differences between automotive and missile parts, the firm established two separate production departments to take care of their old and new business.

3 / Delegation of authority. While it is true that the final authority for all decisions rests with the top man or men in any organization plan, it is not possible to allow every decision to reach up to the owner, president, or board of directors. If an employee is to be fired for insubordination, it may well be that this should be the prerogative of his foreman. Every employee who is placed in charge of the work of others expects to be held responsible for his productivity on the job and must be allowed to exercise some measure of authority over his subordinates.

Authority and responsibilty naturally go together and should be clearly understood by every person in a supervisory capacity. There should also be a distribution of authority so that no one man has so many decisions to make that he cannot discharge his duties promptly and, at the same time, with good judgment based on careful consideration of the facts. If an appeal is to be permitted, there should be no question about this possibility and to whom the dispute would be referred.

4 / Subdivisions of supervisory authority. In preparing an organization plan, it is necessary to decide the extent to which duties are to be subdivided and the proper sequence of authority. In a small firm, the treasurer may be the chief accountant, auditor, controller, and credit manager, whereas a larger organization would have department heads for each of these divisions. Even in a large firm, however, the type of work and the skill of the workers would play an important part. If a machine shop employed only highly skilled workers, the chances would be that each would know his job so well that very little supervision would be needed. In this case, a single foreman might have a large number of employees under him without the need for any intermediate supervision. The same situation would be true if a large number of unskilled workers were hired to do a simple task requiring very little direction. On the other hand, if it were necessary to hire untrained help to perform tasks requiring a fair amount of skill, no single supervisor could direct the work of more than a few people.

The problem of the optimum number of persons that can be efficiently supervised has been receiving increased attention in many firms. It has been divided into two parts: (1) the number of subordinate executives that a top executive can effectively control, called the *span of executive control*; and (2) the number of operatives, such as salesmen, clerks, or production workers, that a subordinate executive can effectively handle, which has been termed the *unit of supervision*. Studies in these two areas indicate that the proper number in each type is dependent upon the complexity of the situations involved as well as upon the skill and experience of the personnel concerned. These two latter factors apply to supervisors as well as workers.

5 / Clearly defined duties. The job every employee is expected to do should be clearly defined to the point that it is different from that expected of others and does not overlap duties assigned to other workers. Unless this is done, there is bound to be friction among employees at all levels. If it is the job of the repair department to keep all machines in good operating order, the foreman in the production department should not be blamed for a slowdown in production based on mechanical breakdowns. On the other hand, if it is the duty of the foreman to see that his machines are kept in operating condition, there should be no doubt as to where this responsibility lies.

6 / Flexibility. Any organization plan that unduly hampers the ability of the employee to express his individuality and initiative robs the organization of one of the most valuable assets of our type of economic society. A certain amount of regimentation is desirable but, when it stifles the worker to the place where he is just a cog in a machine, the firm loses rather than gains. There will always be exceptions to every plan, and some executives spend much of their time handling variations from the routine that has been established. Even though a foreman may have the right to dismiss an employee from his department, that man might be a valuable employee under a different boss or in another line of work.

7 / Communication. Business executives have become increasingly aware of the importance of adequate channels of communications in internal organization. The term "communication," as used in this sense, means that there should be facilities for an uninterrupted flow of orders, instructions, questions, responses, explanations, ideas, and suggestions between top management and the rest of the organization. This flow should be a two-way facility, from management to employees and from employees to management. Aside from the customary orders and instructions concerning the normal routine of operations, management frequently wishes to explain some of its policy decisions, or to give information about the company's products, finances, plans for expansion, and personnel changes. By so doing, management hopes to bring about a better understanding among its workers of the salient facts concerning the company. Employees, on the other hand, often have ideas for saving time, labor, and materials. They may have grievances of one kind or another that should reach the ears of the management. In planning the details of an organization, therefore, provision should be made for the creation and maintenance of a good two-way communication system. The communication from the lower to the higher echelons of an organization, especially with respect to information concerning the results of orders previously issued by top management, is known as a *feedback*. Further reference to this practice occurs in Chapter 15.

◼ The Organization Chart

A common practice in companies of any considerable size, is the construction of a formal *organization chart,* an example of which appears on page 120. While this chart does not customarily spell out the duties and responsibilities of each position, it serves to indicate the areas of authority within a company. If, as is occasionally found, the names of the executives and department heads are included, this implies the need for revision when promotions, transfers, resignations, or other changes occur. The failure of some firms to make the necessary changes in order to keep the information up to date has occasioned criticism of the organization chart practice.

◼ Types of Organization Structures

After a consideration of the principles involved in forming an organization structure, the next step is to decide upon the type that is best suited to a particular situation. Only two basic organization forms are in common use today, the line and the line-and-staff. The line organization is found mainly in small firms, while large concerns customarily follow the line-and-staff pattern. A third form, called the functional organization by its originator, F. W. Taylor, served as a theoretical transition between the line and the line-and-staff. The committee organization, a fourth form, is never found alone but always as a suborganizational grouping in either line or line-and-staff types. The four types of organization structures are as follows:

1. Line organization
2. Taylor's functional organization
3. Line-and-staff organization
4. Committee organization

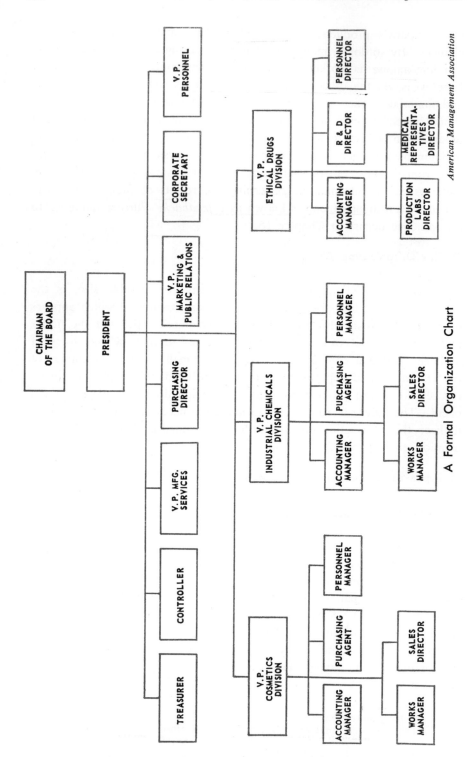

A Formal Organization Chart

American Management Association

1 / **Line organization.** A *line organization* is one in which there is a direct flow of authority from the top executive to the rank-and-file employee, usually through several lesser executives at various managerial levels. It is sometimes called the military type because each person has someone immediately over him. Although modern armies have become too complex to rely exclusively on a line organization, they still use the direct chain of command.

The chart below shows an illustration of a line organization applied to business. There are many advantages inherent in this form. It is simple and easy to understand. Responsibility is clearly defined and each worker, regardless of his rank, reports to but one individual. This makes discipline easy. Decisions can usually be rendered quickly, and executives must produce or be replaced. As long as each employee carries out the orders of his immediate superior, he is relatively free from criticism, which makes for harmonious working conditions.

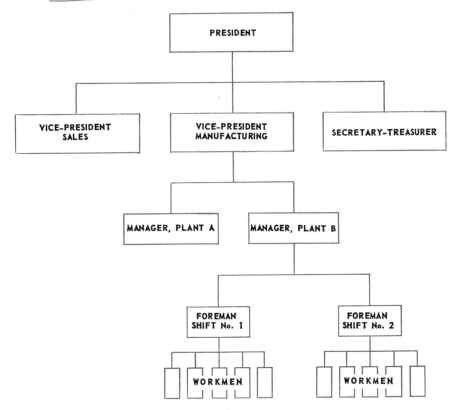

Line Organization for Plant B of a Manufacturing Corporation

The details of the organizational structure for the sales department, the secretary-treasurer's office, and plant A have been omitted.

There are, however, many disadvantages to the line type of organization. Each supervisor needs to be a master of many diverse angles to his job. He should be able to handle his men, keep the machines running, invent new processes, recommend pay increases, and train new employees. Frequently he may be outstanding at one or two of his numerous responsibilities and very poor at others. The line organization also has the disadvantage of placing so much final authority and direction at the top that the individual concerned, instead of devoting his attention to working out important matters of policy and general practices, finds most of his time devoted to reading reports and rendering decisions on operating problems. Coordination of the different "lines" is difficult to achieve, particularly in a complex, large-scale industry.

2 / Taylor's functional organization. *Taylor's functional organization* is a transitional form between the line and the line-and-staff types. It is so designated here to differentiate it from the functional type described on page 114. It was originated by F. W. Taylor in the 1880's to remedy the great weakness of the line form, the concentration of too many duties in a single supervisor. Taylor divided each foreman's job into its basic

Divided control & authority

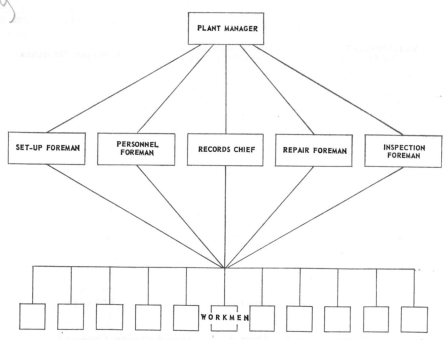

Functional Organization for a Manufacturing Operation

Note that each workman is responsible to five foremen.

components and established a functional foreman with authority over each of these divisions. Taylor's functional organization in its pure form carries the use of specialists to the extreme in that there is no single line of authority but rather multiple lines of authority affecting each employee. Every worker is responsible to someone of higher rank for each important specific part of his job. The foreman in charge of setting up a job on a machine supervises all workers to this extent. Another foreman may be in charge of personnel, and all workers report to him concerning problems of wages, hours, and shifts. The man in charge of accounting tells each worker what he shall do regarding filling out timecards and other job cost records. Likewise, the repair foreman handles the problems of damage to machinery and tools for an entire factory.

The principal objection to Taylor's functional type of organization is that workers have more than one boss at the same level. Even though each boss directs only a specific part of the employee's work, friction and overlapping are bound to develop. Disciplinary problems are difficult to handle. Divided control is more likely to retard production than to speed it up. In actual practice firms have found that a line-and-staff organization can secure the advantages claimed for Taylor's functional type without acquiring its inherent disadvantages. Consequently, this functional form is rarely, if ever, found in intelligently managed companies.

3 / Line-and-staff organization. The *line-and-staff organization* is the next logical step beyond the functional concept. It eliminates the problem of requiring each supervisor to be highly competent in each phase of his job while preserving the advantage of giving each worker, at any level, a single boss. This is accomplished by using specialists, but by giving them staff or advisory status instead of actual line authority, as in Taylor's functional form. For example, a personnel department will study all salary and wage problems throughout a factory. This does not mean that the foreman is not consulted regarding personnel problems nor that he loses any authority, but advice is available from experts in that particular field. An engineering department will work on new processes and new designs and methods of handling the raw materials. Again, the foreman will probably be consulted and may contribute ideas, but he is not primarily responsible for this important function of the business.

The chart on page 124 shows a line-and-staff organization plan. Note that foremen are not responsible to more than one supervisor, but that specialists are available for specific problems. There is no overlapping of control. The Army in World War II was essentially a line-and-staff organization in that extensive use was made of specialists in all lines who

"Darkness, darkness" —

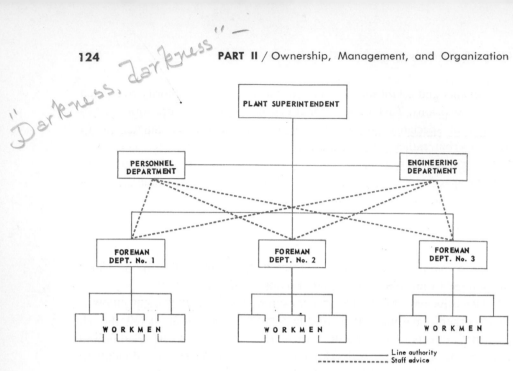

**Line-and-Staff Organization for the Manufacturing Operation
of a Small Business**

Staff functions in this business are performed by the personnel and
engineering departments.

were attached to the various units, for example, psychologists with every
branch of the service.

The many advantages of the line-and-staff plan have made it the most
popular form of business organization. It introduces a note of flexibility
into the rigid form of the line organization. The use of specialists can be
incorporated without departing far enough from the line plan of organization to lose the important advantages already enumerated. It incorporates
the principles of division of labor without losing the important combination of authority and responsibility.

On the other hand, the so-called advice given by staff employees may
be construed as demands, which can lead to divided authority or serious
friction. In some cases, the foremen and supervisors may try to shift
responsibility to staff employees for actions taken on their advice, which
do not prove successful. Also, department managers, superintendents, and
others in managerial positions may cease to give thought and attention to
some of their duties that can be referred to staff members for advice and
a recommendation.

(a) LINE DEPARTMENTS. The key to the determination of which
are line and which are staff departments is the relationship that any given

department has to the basic objectives of a company. In manufacturing firms, the production and sales departments are customarily regarded as having line status, as the goal of the companies is to make and sell things at a profit. In retail and wholesale firms, both buying and selling are essential to the firms' purposes and are considered as line departments or functions. In some companies, where research is an important aspect of their activities, this department may be classified as line.

(b) STAFF DEPARTMENTS. While there is a measure of difference of opinion among authorities as to the designation of certain departments as line or staff, the concensus of opinion would probably classify those departments that exist mainly for advisory and service purposes as staff functions. Among these would be personnel, public relations, and finance.

It should be understood that the foregoing classification is based on the relationship of these departments to the company as a whole. Within all departments, whether basically line or staff, certain positions are regarded as line if there is any authority vested in them. Thus, the head of the personnel department is a line executive within that department. He is the superior of the other employees in the department, but he has a staff job in relation to the firm itself.

4 / Committee organization. The *committee organization* type is one in which a formally constituted group drawn from those associated with a firm replaces an individual at any or all supervisory levels. Although here itemized as a separate type of organizational structure, it is rarely used except as a modification of one of the types already described. Most frequently this plan is incorporated into a line-and-staff organization with a committee that replaces a staff officer or that provides additional advisory functions.

Much is to be said for incorporating committees into an organization structure. If nothing else, the committee form allows several people to have an influence in making a decision that will probably affect their work, and the understanding of the background makes for a more enthusiastic acceptance of the new policy. The old adage that two heads are better than one is probably true; and the ultimate report of a committee, combining the judgment of several individuals, is likely to be better than one man's opinion. Furthermore, decisions reached by committees are less personal.

Committee organization has its drawbacks, too. It is usually a slow method of arriving at a decision, and sometimes important matters are held up by committees. Time is spent on argument rather than action.

Frequently committee decisions are compromises when the only hope of success would be vigorous prosecution of one viewpoint or the other. Also, the chances of securing action on a committee report are less than when one executive is interested in seeing his own ideas placed into operation. A somewhat different criticism of committees is that this organization form may usurp the decision-making functions of executives.

■ Toward a Management-Organization Theory

Since management, in the making of decisions, must implement these decisions through persons within an organization, the line of demarcation between what is management theory and what is organization theory is very thin. Why and how management does, or should, act depends greatly on the nature and functioning of the organization. For this reason, recent studies by social and behavioral scientists seeking a general theory of management, or of organization, will be considered as a unit.

1 / **Historical background.** In the early years of the 20th century, management was regarded simply as the instrument by which companies were directed toward the avowed goal of maximized profit. This point of view was implemented by the doctrines and practices of Frederick W. Taylor, whose early experiments in motion and time study [1] provided the basis for a philosophy of management—that of reducing costs in order to increase profits. This was in accord with the theories of economics, particularly the economics of the firm, and was largely mechanistic in quality.

The recognition of the oversimplified assumptions concerning the motivations of workers and the failure to achieve unified goal-directed behavior within an organization lead to the view that the firm was a social entity, with responsibilities not only to the shareholders or owners but also to the workers and to society in general. The famous Hawthorne Studies at Western Electric Company opened the view that management is largely the art of effective human relations. Leadership rather than autocratic control was to be desired. The aims and ambitions of workers should be considered by management along with the profit showing of their companies.

Such contributions of the social and behavioral sciences have been numerous but have not always been in complete agreement. There has not been a meeting of the minds of the champions of the various disciplines,

---

[1] Motion and time study is described in some detail in Chapter 14, page 306.

although some progress has been made toward a greater degree of mutual understanding. Notice, however, should be taken of the research activity of a large number of scholars in this field, the eventual results of whose efforts may be the emergence of a unified theory that may be helpful to business in its attempt to solve its management or organizational problems.

2 / Theories of organization. Historically, three theories of organization have had some influence on management thought and practice: (1) the classical doctrine, which is concerned with the makeup of formal organization; (2) the neo-classical theory, which has been interested principally in the human relations aspect of organizations; and (3) modern organization theory, which conceives of organization as a system and centers around the idea of systems analysis.

Systems analysis, basically, is the recognition of the effect of a change in any one part of the system on all of the other ingredients of the system. It recognizes the interrelation of all component elements of a system. In this instance, a firm is regarded as a system. According to this approach, there are five segments to a system: the individual, the formal organization, the informal organization, status and role patterns, and the physical environment.

The formal organization is the interrelated pattern of jobs in the system or firm. The informal organization consists of groups of people in firms whose grouping does not appear as such in the formal organization. These are people who may or may not be in the same departments but, due to their being located near each other in a plant or office and performing similar tasks even though they have dissimilar occupational interests, tend to form small groups, who communicate with each other and exert a subtle influence on the organization of the firms for whom they work. For example, executives in the sales and production departments might belong to the same golf clubs and discuss the firm's problems on the course.

Status and role patterns refer to the demands made by different jobs on the role perceptions of the individuals involved. *Status* derives from the manner in which one's superiors, equals, and subordinates regard the position occupied. *Role* refers to the duties and obligations implicit in a job. This means that positions are important for the role they confer on the holder. Authority, according to modern theory, must be earned by the individuals involved in order to be effective. The physical environment concept embraces the influence that the surroundings of the job site have on the employees.

Communication is essential to any organization, and the actual operation of an organization is the result of fusing "personalization" and "socialization"—the balancing of personal, individual goals with those of the enterprise.

PROFESSIONAL ASSOCIATIONS IN MANAGEMENT

The American Management Association, established in 1922, is an educational organization devoted to increasing the effectiveness of individuals in management. Its membership includes not only executives from industry and commerce but also members of the professions and representatives from governmental, retail, financial, and service organizations. The Association sponsors meetings in all areas of management. Several books, reports, and periodicals are published by the Association.

The Society for Advancement of Management, established in 1936, is a professional society of management people in business, government, and education. The Society promotes conferences dealing with management topics on both a national and a local scale. It also has a number of student chapters in colleges and universities.

BUSINESS TERMS

(a) management (109), organization (109)
(b) top management (110), administrative management (110), middle management (110), operating management (110)
(c) absentee management (113), decentralized management (113), centralized management (113)
(d) divisionalization (114), functionalization (114), functional organization (114)
(e) organizational structure (115), esprit de corps (115)
(f) departmentalization (116)
(g) span of executive control (118), unit of supervision (118)
(h) feedback (119)
(i) organization chart (119)
(j) line organization (121), Taylor's functional organization (122), line-and-staff organization (123), committee organization (125)
(k) systems analysis (127), status (127), role (127)

QUESTIONS FOR DISCUSSION AND ANALYSIS

1. Why is it possible for competing companies to adopt conflicting forms of field organization, one having centralized management and another decentralized management?
2. Many, if not most, small companies do not have organization charts. Do you think it would be advantageous to them if they did? Explain.

3. Would you expect that computers would ever take over decision making in business, as has been occasionally suggested? Discuss.

4. Would you regard a board of directors as an example of the committee type of organization? Why?

5. Some observers of business trends have predicted that the growth of computerization would bring about a decline in the importance of middle management. Discuss.

6. Do you think that there will ever be a universally accepted and applicable theory of management? Why?

7. What explanation can you give for the circumstance that some large, diversified companies are divisionalized while others are functionalized?

8. Some students of business feel that there should be more democracy in business organizations. Do you agree? Explain.

9. In what ways do business organizations differ from other types of organizations?

10. Would the average factory worker be concerned with whether he was working in a line or a line-and-staff organization? Explain.

PROBLEMS AND SHORT CASES

1. The Jennings Company, Inc., manufactures a varied line of chemicals that are sold to many different industries. It has several plants located throughout the country and sales offices in all of the large cities. Since the time of its founding, in 1906, the managerial policy of the company has been that of centralization, which worked out satisfactorily during the first twenty years of its existence. With a steady growth in the extent of its product line and a concomitant increase in sales, however, the management experienced more and more difficulty in maintaining the centralized management policy. Finally, after an extended period of discussion, it was decided that this practice would be abandoned and that a greater amount of authority and responsibility would be given to the branch plant managers and the field sales managers. What areas of authority might be shifted to the field, and which ones should be retained by the home office?

2. Using the current catalog of your school as a source of information, construct an organization chart of the institution.

3. The Crocker Corporation is a medium-size company that manufactures a line of men's shirts, underwear, pajamas, and socks. It is not the largest firm in the field, but it is one of the oldest. Founded around fifty years ago as a partnership, it was incorporated about thirty years ago when one of the partners died and its name was changed from Crocker and Fels to the Crocker Corporation, bearing the name of the surviving partner, who purchased the entire interest of the Fels family. Mr. Crocker was an energetic and dominating executive with very positive ideas of how the business should be conducted. For example, he continued to operate the sales division out of the home office, even though the company's products were sold

in department stores, men's furnishings stores, and variety stores throughout the country. His competitors all had established branch offices to service the trade, but Mr. Crocker turned down the suggestion of his sales manager that the Crocker Corporation follow the same practice. In the manufacturing part of the business, Mr. Crocker continued the use of machinery and equipment that his competitors had long since replaced with more modern facilities. One of the results of this was that the company's production costs were substantially above those of its competitors, which resulted in Crocker's prices being out of line, with a gradual falling off of sales.

Despite all of this, Mr. Crocker refused to change his policies. One of the results of this situation was that the morale of the personnel suffered, and many of his key men left the company. Mr. Crocker's son, who had entered the business after finishing college, was greatly worried over the condition of the company, but he was unable to convince his father that the firm's policies should change. While on a hunting trip, however, Mr. Crocker accidentally fell out of a canoe and was drowned. The control of the company passed to the son. He has asked you to suggest what steps should be taken to rehabilitate the company and put it back into competition again.

You are to write a brief paper embodying your suggestions to the son, taking into consideration the present condition of the company with regard to personnel, equipment, organization, and so on. The firm is in good financial condition despite its sales decline.

SUGGESTED READINGS

Applewhite, P. B. *Organizational Behavior.* Englewood Cliffs, New Jersey: Prentice-Hall, Inc., 1965.

Dale, E., and E. Dale Associates. *Management Theory and Practice.* New York: McGraw-Hill Book Company, Inc., 1965.

George, C. S., Jr. *Management in Industry,* Second Edition. Englewood Cliffs, New Jersey: Prentice-Hall, Inc., 1964.

Greenwood, W. T. *Management and Organizational Behavior Theories— An Interdisciplinary Approach.* Cincinnati: South-Western Publishing Company, 1965.

Moore, F. G. *Management: Organization and Practice.* New York: Harper & Row, 1964.

Newman, W. H., and J. P. Logan. *Business Policies and Central Management,* Fifth Edition. Cincinnati: South-Western Publishing Company, 1965.

Magazines: *Management Review* (American Management Association), *The Management Record* (National Industrial Conference Board), *Administrative Management* (Geyer-McAllister Publications), *Journal of the Academy of Management, Business Management.*

Part III

MARKETING

CHAPTER

7   Marketing—Its Nature and Scope

8   Wholesaling and Retailing

9   Prices and Pricing

10 Advertising Problems

11 International Aspects of Business

PROLOGUE TO PART III

MARKETING

The chapters in this part are devoted to a discussion of that sector of our economy which distributes the goods and services that we produce to those who need or want them. Its importance in the field of business has become enhanced through the shift in emphasis from production to distribution that has taken place during the past two decades.

Chapter 7 is concerned with the nature of the marketing process and sets forth such basic factors as types of goods, channels of distribution, the marketing functions, sales organizations, and the role of the consumer. Chapter 8 describes the important fields of wholesaling and retailing.

Chapter 9 takes up the role of price in marketing, both from the standpoint of economists and of those responsible for establishing prices for goods and services. Price legislation and governmental action are considered here, along with the price policies of firms.

Chapter 10 presents the types of advertising media and their characteristics. The advertising agency is considered along with the current criticisms of advertising.

Chapter 11 deals with business in its international aspects, with attention to the rapidly emerging multinational corporations. Tariffs, foreign exchange, and the role of government in this area are discussed together with such recent developments as the European Common Market and the Alliance for Progress.

Chapter 7

MARKETING—ITS NATURE AND SCOPE

Marketing is one of the major segments of the economy of this country. Through this area of economic activity goods and services flow from producers to consumers, thereby completing the basic mission of our economic system, that of satisfying the needs and wants of our people. This is a twofold task: (1) discovering what goods and services consumers need and want, and (2) providing these items for them in the places where they are, at the times that they want them, and at prices that they are able and willing to pay. And as with every other part of economic activity, this mission must be accomplished at a profit to the entrepreneurs who are engaged in it. Freedom of choice is one of the basic ingredients of capitalism, and the organization and operation of marketing are such that consumers are able to avail themselves of this privilege of choice from among the many types of goods and services that are offered to them.

■ The Changed Emphasis in Marketing

In recent years there has been a shift in emphasis, among firms producing goods intended for use by consumers, from the manufacturing to the marketing phases of their operations. With the onset of the industrial revolution in the mid-18th century, there came into being productive facilities that permitted the manufacture of greater quantities of goods and at lower prices than had previously been possible. This condition focused the attention of businessmen on the technological aspects of manufacturing and relegated marketing to a comparatively minor role. This situation remained about the same until the depression of the 1930's, when the problem of disposing of the goods that the productive facilities of the country were capable of making brought about a basic change in the thinking of many forward-looking manufacturers. From being absorbed with the problem of how to make more and more goods, they turned to the question of whether the goods that they had been producing were what consumers really wanted. Attempts were made to discover consumers' desires, and, where possible, to redesign their products in greater conformity to their findings.

After the interruption to this movement by World War II, the quest was resumed by many producers of consumer goods; and in the early 1950's, this trend became known as the *consumer-oriented management* or *total marketing concept*. This involved reversal of the marketing philosophies of many manufacturers. Whereas formerly it had been considered as the job of marketing to sell those things that production decided to make, now it became the duty of marketing to discover what consumers wanted and to inform production of its findings so that these goods could be made. It was then the province of marketing, through advertising, sales promotion, and personal selling to inform consumers of the availability of the goods and to urge them to purchase. Marketing thus assumed the vital burden of finding out what consumers wanted, a formidable task in many instances, and one which many companies have found quite difficult to accomplish. However, an increasing number of manufacturers of consumer goods have adopted this method of operation with its increased scope and responsibility for their marketing divisions. The manufacturers of industrial and commercial goods have required no such shift in marketing philosophy because their close contacts with customers has long provided them with accurate and dependable information concerning needed goods.

■ Scope and Cost of Marketing

In a country as large and as populous as the United States, with the highest standard of living that the world has ever known, a marketing system broad enough to provide for the distribution of the goods and the services desired by its people must necessarily be vast and intricate. Over 1.7 million retail stores have approximately 8.4 million employees, and some 300,000 wholesale businesses employ over 3 million people. In addition, manufacturers of goods of all sorts utilize an unknown, but very large, number of salesmen to promote their products to industrial and commercial users as well as to wholesale and retail establishments.

As might be expected, a marketing system of this magnitude is quite costly. Approximately 50 percent of the dollar value of the retail prices that consumers pay for goods represents the marketing cost. Opinions

differ as to whether or not this cost is too high. Under competitive conditions, it is reasonable to assume that sellers at all levels are striving to
lower all of their costs, including those incurred in marketing. It is conceivable that under some authoritarian economic (and probably political)
system goods could be distributed more cheaply; but it is doubtful if the
same opportunity for buyer choice and real satisfaction could be realized
under such a plan as is generally true with our present marketing
arrangement.

■ Approaches to the Study of Marketing

There are four basic approaches to the study of marketing: (1) the
commodity approach, which identifies and defines the goods concerned;
(2) the functional approach, which considers the tasks that are performed
in this field; (3) the managerial approach, which deals with the steps
taken by marketing management to achieve its objectives; and (4) the
institutional approach, which examines the different types of firms that
are found in the field of marketing. In this chapter the commodity, functional, and managerial approaches will be discussed. In the following
chapter, the institutional approach will be presented. In order that all
references to them in this chapter may be clear, however, it should be
understood that wholesalers and retailers are called *marketing institutions*
or *middlemen*.

■ Basic Types of Economic Goods

The commodity approach to the field of marketing involves a study
of the basic types of economic goods. To facilitate the study of this
aspect of marketing, goods are divided into the following three classes:

1. Industrial goods
2. Commercial goods
3. Consumer goods

1 / **Industrial goods.** *Industrial goods* are destined for use by industry
in the production of commercial goods, consumer goods, or other industrial goods. Examples of industrial goods are machinery, tools, raw
materials, fabricated materials, and supplies. The important point in this
connection is the immediate destination of the goods at the time that the
characterization is made. In most instances this is relatively simple; iron
ore, for example, could hardly be other than in the industrial goods
category, as its customary destination is the blast furnace where it is made

into pig iron. In some cases, however, this destination is not so obvious. An automobile tire, for instance, as it emerges from the last productive operation in a tire factory, may be either an industrial or a consumer good. If it is slated for shipment to an automobile factory, there to become a part of the assembly of an automobile, it is an industrial good. On the other hand, if it is to be sent to a tire dealer, eventually to be sold to some car owner to replace one of his worn tires, it is a consumer good.

2 / Commercial goods. *Commercial goods*, which are included by some writers in the class of industrial goods, consist of many items that are not intended for use in the fabrication of other goods but which are destined for use in business in the form in which they are purchased. In this category are cash registers, office machines and equipment, store fixtures, stationery and supplies, filing cabinets, and office furniture. Certain of these goods may be classified also as consumer goods, depending upon their immediate destination. Typewriters bought for home use are an example.

3 / Consumer goods. *Consumer goods* are destined for use by the individual ultimate consumer in such form that they can be used by him without further commercial processing. From the standpoint of the typical consumer, consumer goods may be further classified as (a) convenience goods, (b) shopping goods, and (c) specialty goods.

(a) CONVENIENCE GOODS. These are goods that consumers like to be able to purchase conveniently, immediately, and with a minimum of effort. They are not bought until needed and, when needed, their purchase is not long deferred. They include such items as cigarettes, popular-priced candies, newspapers, chewing gum, and many grocery products. *Convenience goods* are relatively low in price and are usually branded; they are purchased by both men and women; they are found in most types of stores. Certain convenience goods that are purchased on the spur of the moment are called *impulse merchandise*.

(b) SHOPPING GOODS. These are goods in the purchase of which the consumer desires to compare the offerings of competing stores on various bases, such as price, quality, and style. In this classification are included many goods of the type usually found in the downtown department stores, such as women's clothing, furniture, dress goods, and millinery. *Shopping goods* are frequently unbranded; but if they do bear brands, consumers are not interested in them. For example, most curtains and draperies are branded, but consumers appear to pay little attention to this fact when shopping for them. They are concerned with materials, style, and design. Shopping goods are bought more frequently by women than by men and are found customarily in the medium-price range.

(c) SPECIALTY GOODS. The consumer is willing to go to considerable effort to secure *specialty goods*, for which a brand preference usually exists. Examples of goods of this class are automobiles, men's clothing and shoes, high-priced watches, and electrical appliances. Specialty goods are always branded. They are bought more frequently by men than by women. There are, of course, individual differences of opinion between consumers concerning the same article, one regarding it as a specialty good and another as a shopping good. The classification given above, however, is made on the basis of the purchasing habits of the average consumer.

■ Marketing Functions

In the marketing of industrial, commercial, and consumer goods, certain inescapable tasks must be performed. These tasks are called *marketing functions.* It is through their performance by the marketing institutions involved that the costs of marketing arise and competitive advantage is gained by those firms who are able to achieve greater efficiency and lower expenses in the execution of these tasks. Although there are some differences of opinion among marketing authorities as to which activities to include in this group of functions, the following list is generally accepted: buying, selling, transportation, storage, standardization, finance, risk taking, and the providing of market information.

1. Buying
2. Selling
3. Transportation
4. Storage
5. Standardization
6. Market finance
7. Market risk
8. Market information

1 / Buying. Buying involves the selection of the kind of goods to be bought and the determination of the quality desired as well as the proper quantity needed for the specified purpose. The buyer also must select the sources of the goods that he wants. In many business houses buying procedures are established to take care of the details of routine purchasing and to make certain that all purchase orders are executed in a uniform fashion. Among firms that handle consumer goods, an increasing degree of consideration is given to the purchase of goods for which consumers have a preference.

2 / Selling. An important characteristic of a capitalistic economy is *speculative production,* the manufacture of goods before orders for them are received. Manufacturers produce the things that they think consumers will want and then try to sell them. For example, toy manufacturers produce their entire line of Christmas products months before the holiday selling season opens. They hope that consumers will like and buy the things they have made. Although speculative production does not apply to all types of goods, since some goods are made to order, it is characteristic of a great many lines; and it involves the necessity of finding a market for the speculatively produced goods if the manufacturers are to continue to be in business.

Wholesalers and retailers customarily maintain stocks of goods from which their customers may make their purchases. They, likewise, usually engage in selling to assure the steady outgo of their wares.

Selling can be conveniently divided into three parts: (a) personal selling; (b) advertising, which has been called impersonal selling; and (c) sales promotion, which includes those activities that supplement personal selling and advertising.

(a) PERSONAL SELLING. Selling involves a wide variety of tasks, which vary in importance with the nature of the business concerned. These include discovering potential customers, acquainting them with available goods, and endeavoring to persuade them to purchase the goods. Some selling is educational in its character, having as its principal objective the dissemination of facts concerning certain products, particularly new ones, while other types of sales effort are purely competitive, aiming to accomplish the sale of goods in competition with other similar products.

While there is no accurate information available on the subject, most personal selling, where salesmen call on prospects, is directed to business buyers, such as purchasing agents and wholesale and retail buyers. Personal solicitation of consumers is mainly confined to the fields of insurance and a few items such as Fuller brushes and Avon and Beauty Counselors cosmetics. There is also a considerable measure of telephone solicitation, the effectiveness of which is unknown. The reasons for the absence of personal selling to consumers are the increasing reluctance of housewives to admit strangers into their homes and the fact that most men are at work during the day and their wives do not wish to assume the responsibility for the purchase of expensive items, such as appliances, aluminum storm doors and screens, porch enclosures, and central air conditioning. To manufacturers of such merchandise, the problem of contacting potential buyers is probably met with advertising in most instances.

Retail selling is noteworthy in that it induces customers to come to the stores, whereas most other types of selling seek out customers wherever they may be located.

Self-service stores—in the areas of food, drugs, and variety-store merchandise, where consumers make their selections without the assistance of salespeople—have experienced a notable growth in recent years. Here, however, the selling is merely transferred from personal selling to mass display. In the absence of salespeople, the task of acquainting consumers with the availability of goods and of their appealing characteristics has had to be assumed, in a large part, by advertising.

(b) ADVERTISING. Advertising employs many media, such as newspapers, magazines, direct mail, billboards, radio, television, and catalogs. For the preparation of certain types of advertising, notably that of manufacturers of nationally known products, specialized groups, known as *advertising agencies,* are employed. They prepare much of the advertising to be found in magazines, such as the *Saturday Evening Post* and *Life,* and on radio and television. Most other advertising, particularly that of a local character, is created by the staffs of the companies concerned.

(c) SALES PROMOTION. *Sales promotion* includes those activities which assist in the sale and advertising of goods. Among these promotional procedures are the preparation of catalogs, sales manuals, and displays; the enlisting of dealer cooperation for the display and sale of goods; and the promoting of sampling campaigns, contests, and many other similar items. In many firms sales-promotion departments have been established to supervise these operations, while in others they are divided between the sales and the advertising departments.

3 / Transportation. Goods must be transported, in most instances, from the places where they are produced to the places where they will be consumed. Transportation has a dual duty to perform—goods must be taken to the places where they are wanted when they are wanted. In the language of the economists, the former involves the creation of *place utility,* whereas the latter is spoken of as providing *time utility.*

The transportation function involves the use of railroads, waterways, motor trucks, pipelines, and airplanes. The needs of the market, plus the competition between these various agencies, have resulted in the development of many specialized services, such as fast-freight and motor-truck schedules known to the trade as "hot shot" runs, refrigerated cars and trucks, and *store-door delivery.* By means of this last service, trucks owned by a railroad pick up goods at the factory and transport them to the railroad terminals, where the goods are loaded into freight cars; then, after the arrival of the goods in the destination city, they are taken by truck to the place of business of the company that purchased the goods.

4 / Storage. Storage is another essential marketing function. In many lines of business, goods are produced considerably in advance of the time of sale and, consequently, they must be stored for varying periods of time. The manufacturer, the wholesaler, and the retailer all store goods to some extent; hence all of them perform the storage function.

An important development of recent years that has had a profound effect on certain aspects of the storage function is the availability of frozen foods of many kinds. This process requires that all marketing institutions handling these goods provide adequate facilities for keeping them in a frozen state until they are purchased by consumers. Manufacturers, wholesalers, and retailers have had to install special containers where the requisite cold temperatures can be maintained. The freight cars and trucks used to transport these foods must likewise keep similarly low temperatures. At the consumer level, there has been a notably large sale of home freezers and of refrigerators with special compartments for storing frozen foods. One result of this development has been that many foods, such as strawberries, peaches, and raspberries, that could formerly be obtained only during the relatively short growing and ripening season because of their extreme perishability, are now available the year round in frozen form.

Goods may be stored in warehouses with or without any special equipment for air conditioning. The most common type of air conditioning is temperature control; in this type the temperature may range from that in rooms that are merely "cool" to that in rooms where subfreezing temperatures are maintained.

Although many business firms have the facilities for storing their own goods, others use the facilities of public storage warehouse companies. Many of these issue warehouse receipts to the storers as evidence of their receipt of and custody over the stored goods. These receipts may be taken to a bank, and a loan may be obtained by the storer, for which the warehouse receipts are deposited as collateral. Then, before the storer or any customer of his can withdraw the goods from storage, the loan must be repaid to the bank in order to obtain the warehouse receipt, for the warehouse company will not release the goods until the receipt is surrendered.

A variant of this procedure, which is called *field warehousing*, consists of the storing of the goods on the premises of the manufacturer or the distributor, with the warehouse company assuming custody. A space is fenced off for storing the goods, and a custodian is employed to look after the goods and to tend to their proper receipt and release. In this instance the warehouse goes to the goods, so to speak, instead of the goods going to the warehouse. Substantial savings in handling, transportation, and storage charges may result from field warehousing.

5 / Standardization. The development and maintenance of standards is of value in helping buyers and sellers to transact business in an intelligent and helpful manner. There may be standards of quantity, such as weights and measures, and container and can sizes, or standards of quality, which are concerned with such differences in goods as grade, substance, wearability, and serviceability.

In the realm of canned and frozen fruits and vegetables, the development of intelligible standards of quality as guides to consumers in their purchasing has taken two forms. The first of these forms involves the determination of specific grades of canned goods and the utilization of such symbols as *A, B,* or *C,* which are placed on the labels. This practice is known as *grade labeling.* A canner who wishes to designate his goods as *U. S. Grade A, B,* or *C* may do so by utilizing the Continuous Inspection Service of the United States Department of Agriculture. The accompanying label illustrates the use of this service by a canner. The second system, which de-

Packed under continuous inspection of the U. S. Department of Agriculture.

GRADE B (EXTRA STANDARD) EARLY VARIETY PEAS
This means that they meet the following standards:
1. Reasonably tender.
2. Reasonably uniform in color and size.
3. Surrounded by liquor which may be somewhat cloudy.
4. Reasonably free from skins, broken peas and other defects.
5. Must possess a good pea flavor.

GENERAL DESCRIPTION
Type . . . . Early Variety
Size . . . . No. 4 Sieve
Size of Can . . . . No. 2
Contents . . . . 1 lb. 4 oz.
Servings . . . . 4 to 5
Cups . . . . Approx. 2¼

A Grade and Descriptive Label

scribes the contents on the labels, is called *descriptive* or *informative labeling.* Most of the large canners and many of the smaller ones use this procedure. Since the sale of frozen fruits and vegetables has increased markedly in recent years, many packers of these foods have adopted a combination of grade and descriptive labeling for their products. The Great Atlantic and Pacific Tea Company has long followed this latter practice.

6 / Market finance. Handling of any economic good in a capitalistic system calls for a method of financing. If the goods are paid for immediately, the buyer must provide the necessary funds, which may be either his own or those that he has borrowed. If payment is postponed, the seller extends credit to the buyer for a period of time and thus temporarily assumes the burden of financing the transaction. Since a great many sales are made on credit, this phase of the financing function is of considerable importance. Manufacturers extend credit to wholesalers, wholesalers to retailers, and retailers to consumers.

In many instances the selling institutions are able to perform this function without recourse to outside financing agencies. It frequently happens, however, that such assistance is required because of the limited financial resources of the sellers. Banks and finance companies are employed for the purpose of providing the funds. Their methods of operation are explained in Chapter 19.

7 / Market risk. The mere act of owning goods carries with it the inescapable burden of assuming certain risks in connection with them. These risks arise from the following possibilities:

1. The goods may be damaged or destroyed in some manner.
2. They may deteriorate and become unsalable or useless, or their usefulness or salability may be impaired to some extent.
3. They may be stolen.
4. The price may move unfavorably.
5. The goods may be rendered obsolete by new inventions or by style influences.

When goods are sold on credit, the seller assumes a risk even though he no longer owns the goods because the buyer may not pay what he owes.

8 / Market information. If the businessman hopes to achieve success in the face of the rugged competition that is characteristic of many fields, he must have market information upon which to base his decisions. This information covers such topics as prices, the extent of the market, location of the market, consumer preferences, the character of the demand, and conditions of supply.

The many sources of market information include reports of government agencies, trade papers, commodity exchanges, bureaus of business research, private research organizations, and the firm's own records. Every marketing institution is a source of market information, and every marketing executive or entrepreneur must provide himself with a certain amount of market news in order to operate his business intelligently.

◼ The Manufacturers' Sales Organization

Rather wide differences exist in the organizational details of manufacturers' sales organizations. These differences depend principally on the geographic extent of their sales operations, and on the character and complexity of their lines of goods. Many producers sell only in the areas surrounding their factories, while others operate on a region- or country-wide basis. Some produce rather simple lines, consisting of one or a few items; others have much wider offerings, sometimes dozens of articles that may or may not be closely related. Obviously there will be differences in the sales organizational details of each of these various types of producers. The organization chart below, however, is typical of producers who make a varied line of goods and sell them over a broad area.

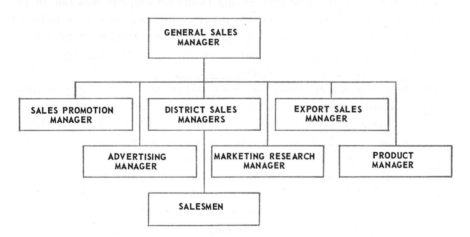

Organization Chart for a Manufacturer's Sales Organization

1 / The sales manager. The key man in any sales organization is the sales manager. Sometimes he is known as Director of Sales or as Vice-President in Charge of Sales. When a firm has a number of subsidiary sales offices, the title General Sales Manager is frequently employed to designate the top sales executive in the company. The heads of the smaller sales offices are known as branch, regional, zone, state, or city sales managers in accordance with the designation of the sales territories of which they are in charge. In instances where subsidiary sales groups are based on products rather than on territories, the subordinate sales executives may be known as sales managers for product *A, B,* or *C.*

The sales manager of a company is responsible for all aspects of the firm's sales activities. Either he or those under his direction must hire, train, control, and, where necessary, discharge salesmen. His responsibilities also include the establishment of sales territories, salesmen's routes, quotas, methods of salesmen's stimulation and compensation, and the control of sales expenses. Marketing research and the determination of the products to be sold come under his authority. This is particularly true with regard to the addition of new products to a line or the elimination of old ones. It is becoming increasingly common for the sales manager to have general supervision over the advertising and sales promotion departments.

2 / The product manager. In the marketing organizations of some large producers of consumer goods with extensive product lines, usually bearing different brand names, a number of junior executives are known as *product managers*. The Procter and Gamble Company was one of the first to establish these positions, but many other companies have followed suit. The function of a product manager is to concentrate on all aspects of the promotion of a single brand of his employer's product line, including its selling, advertising, display, sales promotion, and profit. And, according to a recent survey, in many companies his authority is quite limited, being confined to attempts to secure for his brand, through persuasion, the active cooperation of the different sections of the marketing division. It would be wise in a company with a large number of different products, however, to give the product managers the responsibility of securing the maximum marketing effort for each brand, rather than concentrating in the sales or marketing manager the sole responsibility for the promotion of them all. What needs to be worked out is an effective balance of authority and responsibility in those companies where the performance of the product managers has been something less than satisfactory.

3 / The marketing manager. An interesting development of recent years is the emergence of a number of new titles—Marketing Manager, Director of Marketing, and Vice-President of Marketing being the most common. These new titles imply the recognition of the philosophy of the total marketing concept and its implementation through the enlarging of the scope and responsibility of the marketing departments. The eventual extent of the authority of the marketing manager is not clear; but in one of the largest companies in the country it involves not only a supervision of the marketing program but also authority in such fields as product research and development and production scheduling, areas traditionally the responsibility of the engineering and production departments.

Whether or not this departure from established practices marks the beginning of a trend cannot be foretold at this time. It appears, however, to be a recognition of one of the basic truths in marketing, namely, that the most successful companies are those whose goods come the closest to being what consumers want; and, furthermore, that the marketing division, being nearest to consumers, is the one to determine what items should be made and to estimate the quantity that can be sold.

■ Channels of Distribution

The routes that goods take in their progress from producers to consumers are known as *channels of distribution*. These channels vary according to the nature of the goods, the market, the character of the demand, and the competition between sellers. The channels of distribution for consumer goods differ somewhat from those for industrial and commercial goods, mainly in that, with rare exceptions, the latter two types of goods are not sold through retailers. The pattern for consumer goods is presented first.

1 / **Channels of distribution for consumer goods.** The most direct channel of distribution for consumer goods is found where the producer sells directly to the consumer. This channel is used by many house-to-house selling firms, such as Fuller Brush and Avon Products, and by some producers who distribute by mail order, such as the New Process Company.

Producer ───────→ Consumer

In another channel producers sell to retailers, who in turn sell to consumers. This channel represents the path taken by goods handled by department stores and chain stores.

Producer ───────→ Retailer ───────→ Consumer

A third channel is utilized where the wholesaler enters the picture between the producer and the retailer. This is the traditionally characteristic method whereby goods have been distributed in this country. It is still the prevalent system for goods that reach the consumer through the small independent retailer, such as a grocer, a druggist, a hardware dealer, and a clothing specialty shop.

Producer ───────→ Wholesaler ───────→ Retailer ───────→ Consumer

A producer may adopt any one or more of these channels in his endeavors to have his goods reach the final consumers in as large quantities as possible. Many producers sell direct to the chains and larger independent stores, and at the same time utilize wholesalers to reach the smaller independent retailers. The channel of distribution pattern then would be like the following:

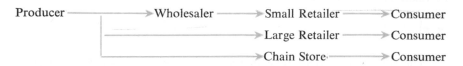

Producer ——————→Wholesaler ————→Small Retailer ————→Consumer
                                     ————————→Large Retailer ————→Consumer
                                     ————————→Chain Store ————————→Consumer

A variant on this type of distribution channel is found where producers sell directly to city retailers, regardless of their size, but utilize wholesalers to reach small town and country retail stores. The channel pattern is as follows:

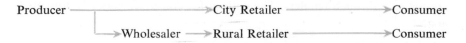

Producer ——————————→City Retailer ——————————→Consumer
        └——→Wholesaler ——→Rural Retailer ——————————→Consumer

2 / Channels for industrial and commercial goods. The major difference between the channels of distribution for industrial and commercial goods and those for consumer goods lies in the fact that, as a general rule, there are no retailers in the former scheme. The two channels found in the industrial and commercial field are:

1.) Producer ——————————————→Industrial or Commercial Consumer
2) Producer ——————→Wholesaler ————→Industrial or Commercial Consumer

The first of these two channel patterns may include producers' branch offices with or without stocks of goods for delivery to customers.

With all types of goods, there are instances where a class of wholesalers known as agents and brokers is utilized. This occurs where the characteristics of either the sellers or the buyers are such that the former find it more profitable to employ agents and brokers than to use their own salesmen. Under these circumstances in the case of consumer goods, sales are made to wholesalers or to retailers, but not to individual consumers.

The problems that arise in connection with the choosing of channels of distribution and of examining them for possible changes as occasions arise are among the most important that producers are called upon to solve.

■ Marketing Research

Marketing research is the scientific study of problems that arise in the field of marketing. It is not regarded as a marketing function, although the findings of some marketing research projects may be utilized as segments of the marketing information function. It involves inquiry into selling and buying methods, advertising, the location of markets, consumer buying habits and motives, and many other topics. Since marketing research is a comparatively recent development, many questions of techniques, methods, and objectives remain to be answered fully. Specialists in marketing research are either independent operators or are in the employ of advertising agencies and/or firms with large marketing problems. Much marketing research is also carried on in collegiate schools of business.

Marketing research involves four steps: (1) the formulation of pertinent questions about the subject of the research, (2) the collection of facts about the subject, (3) the analysis of these facts, and (4) the presentation of conclusions or a proposed plan of action based upon the analysis. This is the so-called scientific method that aims to secure the truth concerning the questions brought before it.

Some of the more pressing questions to which marketing research endeavors to find the answers are: What is the market for a new product? What do users think about the products that they now use? Why do they buy certain merchandise and refuse to buy certain other goods? Where are the users of a given product situated? What is their income status, age, education, and so on? Do they buy goods because they hear them advertised on the radio or television? Which of two or more proposed advertising campaigns will have the greatest appeal to consumers? At what prices will consumers buy the largest number of any given item?

The list is practically endless, and the answers that are obtained may not be valid a few weeks or months later. Techniques of investigation to meet these widely differing problems are equally varied. It is through the operation of marketing research that the manufacturers of consumer goods who have embraced the concept of consumer-oriented management, mentioned earlier in this chapter, try to discover the wants of consumers, and, obviously, their success or failure in this endeavor will measure the extent to which this idea can contribute to their profitable operation.

■ Marketing Strategy

The intensified competition of today, so characteristic of nearly all lines of business, has presented marketing managers with the necessity of developing effective marketing strategies with which to maintain their present shares of the market and, hopefully, to increase them. Along with this responsibility has gone that of preserving or improving their profit positions. They must endeavor to secure the greatest amount of revenue for the least amount of expenditure. The actions taken by marketing managers consist of various manipulations of the *marketing mix,* which includes all of those elements in the marketing area that are subject to control. These are the following: (1) the product mix; (2) the distribution mix; (3) the communications mix; (4) the service mix; and (5) the logistics mix.[1]

The *product mix* is the adjustment of the product line so that the market is best served. The *distribution mix* is that choice of channels of distribution which is most economical and best attuned to the market. Another aspect is the determination of the nature of the distributive pattern: (a) intensive—the use of all possible retail outlets; (b) selective—the restriction to a few retail outlets in each sales area; (c) exclusive—the use of only one retail outlet in each sales district. The *communications mix* involves the employment of the elements of personal selling, advertising, and sales promotion in such proportions as to achieve the optimum return to the company. The *service mix* means the determination of service and guaranty policies so as to produce the desired customer satisfaction. The *logistics mix* is concerned with the physical distribution of goods; it involves the selection of storage and transportation facilities in such a combination that the merchandise is moved from producer to purchaser at the lowest cost consistent with the purchaser's demand for service.

■ Marketing and Computers

While the impact of computers on marketing has been somewhat less than on some other areas of business, there is increasing evidence that electronic data processing is making appreciable progress in this field. Some of the applications of this new tool are daily reports of inventories and sales of chain and department stores; the handling of incoming orders in many different industries and their dispatch to branch plants or warehouses for filling, thereby shortening the time between the receipt of the order and its shipment; the managing of production, warehousing, and shipping by major food manufacturers; and the building of mathematical models to simulate the results of proposed marketing programs.

[1] For a further treatment of this concept, see Thomas A. Staudt and D. A. Taylor, *A Managerial Introduction to Marketing* (Englewood Cliffs, New Jersey: Prentice-Hall, Inc., 1965), pp. 34-35.

marketing
product mix
mix :

▦ The Consumer

Marketing authorities recognize three types of consumers, (1) the industrial consumer, (2) the commercial consumer, and (3) the individual or ultimate consumer.

1 / Industrial and 2 / Commercial consumers. _Industrial consumers_ are identified as business institutions that purchase goods, usually industrial goods, for use in their business operations. Manufacturing industries, mines, and the construction industry are among the kinds of businesses that are customarily included in the industrial consumer classification. _Commercial consumers_ include hotels, offices, banks, schools, hospitals, and theaters.

3 / The ultimate consumer. Broadly speaking, an economic system exists primarily for the purpose of satisfying the needs and wants of the ultimate consumer. This is particularly true of capitalism, under which consumers have practically complete freedom of choice in their selection of goods. They can accept or reject the offerings of producers in accordance with their judgments as to whether the goods will or will not satisfy their desires. It would appear, therefore, that those producers whose goods most nearly conform to the wants of the consumers will meet with the greatest measure of success in the competition for the consumers' favor. With this in mind, it would seem as if one certain way of a producer's assuring his success would be to ascertain what consumers want and then to make his goods in accord with his findings.

At this point the first important problem comes into the picture; namely, that it has proved difficult for sellers to find out what consumers want. This is not to imply that consumers do not have very decided preferences about the details of the goods that they want. The power of discrimination, however, operates only in the presence of competing offerings of goods. This means that the seller who asks consumers what they would like, in regard to the details of the commodities that they will buy at some future date, will receive unsatisfactory answers because the element of competition is missing. If he produces his goods and offers them for sale to consumers in competition with those of other makers, however, he will discover quite quickly and definitely whether or not he has made something that they will buy.

The consumers' inability to decide what they want in advance of its being offered to them for purchase has been recognized by producers for many years. As a result, two broad policies have emerged that have governed manufacturers in their determination of the essential details of the goods that they make. The first of these policies has been that of endeavoring to discover, by research or experimentation, some indication of the basic preferences of consumers; then fabricating the goods as nearly as possible in consonance with these imputed wishes; and, by advertising or personal selling, informing the customers of what has been done. The General Motors Corporation has long followed this procedure, trying to discover consumers' automotive preferences through their Customers' Research Staff.

The second policy, probably followed by a majority of manufacturers, involves the making of the goods that the producers believe the public will desire. Not much, if any, research is done. The producer then endeavors to sell the public on the idea that the goods are exactly what consumers want. Adherents of this policy have tried to justify it on the basis of the acknowledged difficulty of securing trustworthy information regarding their preferences from consumers. On the whole, this procedure has probably operated to benefit consumers, and the goods produced under it have generally been satisfactory.

◼ Aids to Consumer Buying

Buyers of industrial and commercial goods and those who purchase consumer goods for wholesalers and retailers have long been recognized as a quasi-professional procurement group with a thorough knowledge of the goods that they require and the sources from which they may be bought. By way of contrast, there is considerable evidence that many consumers lack the buying skill and discriminative judgment that should be theirs if they are to receive the greatest value for the money that they pay for goods and services.

Some businessmen and many of the more economically minded consumers who have recognized this lack of buying skill have endeavored to make available to consumers certain aids that are helpful in remedying this situation. Consumers' Research and Consumers Union were established some years ago by consumer groups for the purpose of testing consumer goods and of publishing their findings for the benefit of subscribers to their services.

A number of prominent retail organizations have undertaken to make merchandise information more readily available for consumers. Among these are Macy's; Sears, Roebuck and Company; Montgomery Ward and Company; and Marshall Field and Company. Many stores provide their salespeople with information about the goods that they handle, which they, in turn, can pass on to consumers. This is called *specification selling.*

So-called *seals of approval,* emanating from such organizations as *Good Housekeeping* magazine, the Underwriters' Laboratories, the American Medical Association, and the American Dental Association, are intended to identify goods that are outstanding.

The question naturally arises, to what extent do consumers take advantage of these aids to better buying? A definite answer is not possible because of the paucity of available data on the subject. The combined circulation of the publications of Consumers' Research and Consumers Union is placed at around 1,000,000 annually, with a readership estimated at better than three persons a copy. The extent to which these readers are influenced in their actual buying is unknown. Department store executives, in commenting on the attitude of consumers toward specification selling, have indicated that they appear to evince little interest in such information. The effect of the various seals of approval on consumer buying habits is likewise unknown, but there is little evidence to suggest that it is of much consequence. There is a pervasive belief among manufacturers and distributors of consumer goods that consumers would benefit the entire economic system were they to become better informed about the goods which they buy.

The Paradox of Capitalism

A capitalistic system functions and produces the things that consumers want only if producers see the possibility of profits in undertaking to make them. Thus we have the apparent paradox of an economic system, set up to satisfy consumers' wants, being motivated only by the profit-seeking of the producers. At various times certain economists have suggested that the system could be operated without profit to producers—"production for use, not for profit." It is difficult to see how this could be done in a civilization as complex as ours where production involves large investments in capital goods with the attendant risks.

At this point, brief mention should be made of the fact that consumers' freedom of choice is limited by the amount of their disposable income. Through the taxes which are imposed by government at all levels, the income of most consumers is decreased; hence their ability to exercise complete freedom of choice is thereby abridged. And as government purchases roads, schools, space vehicles, and many other things with the taxpayers' money, it might be said that consumers, by extension, voluntarily limit their own purchasing power to permit government to act in their behalf. This they do through the higher taxes that are voted by their elected representatives.

PROFESSIONAL ASSOCIATION IN MARKETING

The American Marketing Association was established in 1937 for "the advancement of the science of marketing." Its membership includes marketing teachers and businessmen who are prominent in all phases of marketing. There are local chapters of the Association throughout the United States and Canada. Several regional conferences are held each year with a general meeting for the academic members. The Association publishes the *Journal of Marketing,* a quarterly, and many occasional publications of interest to its members. It has recently issued a Marketing Research Code of Ethics. It has promoted the formation of student marketing clubs in many colleges and universities.

BUSINESS TERMS

(a) marketing (133), consumer-oriented management or total marketing concept (134)
(b) marketing institutions or middlemen (135)
(c) industrial goods (135); commercial goods (136)
(d) consumer goods (136); convenience goods (136), impulse merchandise (136), shopping goods (136), specialty goods (137)
(e) marketing functions (137)
(f) speculative production (138), advertising agency (139), sales promotion (139)
(g) place utility (139), time utility (139)
(h) store-door delivery (139); field warehousing (140)
(i) grade labeling (141), descriptive or informative labeling (141)
(j) product manager (144)
(k) channels of distribution (145)
(l) marketing research (147)
(m) marketing mix (148), product mix (148), distribution mix (148), communications mix (148), service mix (148), logistics mix (148)
(n) industrial consumers (149), commercial consumers (149)
(o) specification selling (150); seals of approval (151)

QUESTIONS FOR DISCUSSION AND ANALYSIS

1. Do you think that the consumer-oriented management concept is a philosophy applicable to all types of consumer goods? Explain.
2. Name several articles that might be regarded as impulse merchandise.
3. Why do consumers generally pay little attention to the brands on shopping goods?
4. Specialty goods are usually distributed either on an exclusive or a restricted basis. Why should this be so?
5. A prominent marketing personality once said, "Nothing happens until somebody makes a sale." How can this statement be reconciled to the idea of speculative production?

6. What types of products are adaptable to field warehousing?
7. How can a product manager be held responsible for the profit on a product if he has no control of the cost of manufacture?
8. Explain your concept of the term "product mix." What factors should enter into the consideration of the product mix?
9. Why are consumers not more interested in becoming better informed about the goods that they buy?
10. Consumers perform, perhaps unwittingly, some of the marketing functions. Which ones are they?

PROBLEMS AND SHORT CASES

1. Assume that you have been employed by a company that manufactures a rather wide line of food products, such as breakfast foods, canned fruits and vegetables, canned luncheon meats, and canned fish. Each product group is marketed under a different brand name, but the company's name appears in inconspicuous small print on all labels. The company is not sure of the extent to which its corporate identity is known to the public. Desiring to increase its product line and to secure greater sales volume thereby, the company is considering adding frozen fruits and vegetables. The executives are uncertain as to whether they should market the frozen products under a new brand name or whether they should use one that is borne by one of their present lines, such as the canned fruits and vegetables.

   You have been employed by the company to aid them in discovering the answers to their questions. Outline the procedures that you believe they should follow, and design a questionnaire that will produce the information which they require.

2. The Freeman Products Company is an old-line manufacturer of medium-priced living room, dining room, and porch furniture for the home. The company is well known in the furniture trade and to the department stores and furniture stores through whom it has traditionally sold its merchandise. Recently the sales manager of Freeman was approached by a buyer representing Sears, Roebuck and Company, who asked if he would be interested in making furniture for their retail stores and mail-order trade. The Sears man agreed to a scale of purchase prices that would yield a satisfactory margin to the Freeman Company, but the sales manager was concerned about the effect on the firm's present customers if it should sell to Sears also, with whom many of them are competitive.

   You are asked to analyze this situation and to advise the Freeman sales manager as to the proper course of action that he should take. Give your reasons.

3. The Collingwood Manufacturing Co. produces a line of domestic lighting equipment, such as floor, table, and bedside lamps, and household lighting fixtures. The company has been in business since shortly after World War I, and at one time it was regarded as one of the leaders in the field from the standpoint of sales volume. Donald

Holmes, the president of the firm, rose to his present position through the production division, where he was also the principal designer of the company's products. Since becoming president, in 1939, he has continued to direct the designing of the lamps and fixtures in addition to his duties as the executive head of the company. During the past few years, the company's sales have been declining, and in the opinion of the sales manager, John Hoff, this is due to the refusal of Holmes, who is now in his 60's, to permit the introduction of new and more modern designs in the firm's lines. The continued decrease in sales has come to the attention of the board of directors who, after discussion with Holmes, have decided to promote him to chairman of the board, a largely honorary position, and elect Hoff to the presidency.

Propose a course of action to Hoff that will provide the company with reliable information regarding the reasons for the decline in sales and will result in bringing the company's lamp and fixture designs into greater favor with the consuming public.

SUGGESTED READINGS

Alderson, W., and M. H. Halbert. *Marketing and Society*. Englewood Cliffs, New Jersey: Prentice-Hall, Inc., 1966.

Buskirk, R. H. *Principles of Marketing: The Management View,* Revised Edition. New York: Holt, Rinehart and Winston, Inc., 1966.

Converse, P. D., H. W. Huegy, and R. V. Mitchell. *Elements of Marketing,* Seventh Edition. Englewood Cliffs, New Jersey: Prentice-Hall, Inc., 1965.

Davis, K. R. *Marketing Management,* Second Edition. New York: The Ronald Press Co., 1966.

Kirkpatrick, C. A. *Salesmanship: Helping Prospects Buy*, Fourth Edition. Cincinnati: South-Western Publishing Company, 1966.

Otteson, S. F., and Others. *Marketing: The Firm's Viewpoint*. New York: The Macmillan Company, 1964.

Phillips, C. F., and D. J. Duncan. *Marketing: Principles and Methods,* Fifth Edition. Homewood, Illinois: Richard D. Irwin, Inc., 1964.

Taylor, W. J., and R. T. Shaw. *Marketing: An Integrated, Analytical Approach*. Cincinnati: South-Western Publishing Company, 1961.

Magazines: *Journal of Marketing, Industrial Marketing, Printers' Ink, Sales Management, Consumer Bulletin, Consumer Reports.*

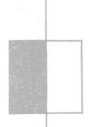

Chapter 8

WHOLESALING AND RETAILING

For marketing to fulfill its mission of supplying the wants and needs of consumers, goods must move through the channels of distribution. This involves the performance of some or all of the marketing functions by the sales organizations of the manufacturers, and by the different types of wholesalers and retailers. In this chapter the characteristics of these middlemen will be described and the special problems of each presented.

WHOLESALING

Wholesaling includes all of the marketing functions and activities that involve the sale of goods where the purpose for making the purchase is a business or profit motive. This obviously does not include sales to individual consumers. This broad segment of marketing embraces all of the following types of transactions.

Sales to retailers.
Sales to wholesalers.
Sales to manufacturers, railroads, mines, and other producers.
Sales to hotels and restaurants.
Sales of building supplies and equipment to building contractors.
All of the operations of functional middlemen, such as brokers, selling agents, and others, who facilitate the movement of goods from sellers to buyers, without taking title to them in the process.
Sales of supplies and equipment to beauty salons and barber shops.
All sales of farm products to other than the final consumers.

The discussion of wholesaling in this chapter will be concerned primarily with sales to retailers and to other wholesalers.

The following table presents a summary of the number and sales volume of the major types of wholesalers as classified by the United States Census of Business for 1963.

Number and Sales Volume of Selected Types of Wholesalers in the United States, 1963

TYPE OF OPERATION	NUMBER OF ESTABLISHMENTS	SALES VOLUME (THOUSANDS OF DOLLARS)
Merchant Wholesalers	208,997	$157,391,769
Wholesale Merchants	194,121	135,856,642
Importers	5,754	9,243,336
Exporters	2,664	8,281,884
Wagon, Truck Distributors .	5,825	1,010,107
Terminal Grain Elevators ..	633	2,999,800
Merchandise Agents, Brokers .	25,313	53,245,009
Manufacturers' Agents	11,189	10,941,319
Merchandise Brokers	5,083	13,854,546
Commission Merchants	3,416	9,524,003
Selling Agents	2,574	8,292,429
Auction Companies	1,894	5,140,616
Export Agents	544	2,178,910
Import Agents	393	2,112,040
Purchasing Agents, Resident Buyers	220	1,201,146

Source: 1963 Census of Business, Bureau of the Census.

■ Merchant Wholesalers

Merchant wholesalers are wholesale establishments that buy and sell merchandise on their own account; that is, they take title to the goods which they handle. The more important wholesalers in this group are:

1. Wholesale merchants
2. Importers and exporters
3. Wagon, truck distributors

In addition to these three groups, there are wholesalers in the industrial goods field who are known as *industrial distributors*; they operate in the fields of industrial equipment, machinery, and parts. *Specialty wholesalers* carry limited or short lines in the areas in which they operate. Thus in the grocery field, this type would confine itself to coffee or canned goods, or to a few other lines.

1 / Wholesale merchants. *Wholesale merchants* are the regular or full-service wholesalers who exist in many lines of business. They sell goods principally to retailers. They buy and sell merchandise on their own account; carry stocks in their places of business; assemble in large lots and redistribute in smaller quantities, usually through salesmen; extend credit to customers; make deliveries; and render advice to the trade. Among the types of merchandise handled by wholesale merchants are groceries, drugs, hardware, and dry goods. The term *jobber*, which still persists in a few lines of business and which had at one time a special significance, is now regarded as being synonymous with wholesale merchant.

2 / Importers and exporters. *Importers and exporters,* as the names imply, are wholesale merchants who buy and sell, respectively, in the foreign market.

3 / Wagon, truck distributors. *Wagon, truck distributors* make sales and deliveries to retailers from stocks that they carry in their trucks. They are found principally in the grocery field. They carry a limited assortment of merchandise, consisting of nationally advertised goods and fast-moving perishable items. Their practice is to sell for cash and in original packages. Examples of wagon distributors are those wholesalers who deliver tobacco products, soft drinks, milk, and bread to grocery stores and supermarkets.

■ **Merchandise Agents and Brokers**

The outstanding characteristic of this group of wholesalers is that they do not take title to (become the legal owners of) the goods with which they deal. They are in business for themselves and negotiate purchases and sales in domestic and international trade in behalf of principals who do take title to the goods. They may or may not take possession of the goods involved. An additional important function that many of them perform is the furnishing of marketing information. Such wholesalers commonly receive their remuneration in the form of commissions or fees. The term *functional middlemen* has been frequently used as a group designation for this type of wholesaler. The more important wholesalers in this classification are:

1. Manufacturers' agents
2. Merchandise brokers
3. Commission merchants
4. Selling agents
5. Auction companies

1 / Manufacturers' agents. *Manufacturers' agents* are middlemen who sell part of the output of certain manufacturers on an extended contractual basis. They are limited in respect to territory and to prices and terms of sale. Their principal duty is to sell goods in accordance with the desires of their clients, although they may also warehouse some of the merchandise. They usually represent two or more producers whose goods are noncompetitive in nature. Manufacturers' agents are prominent in the fields of machinery, industrial equipment and supplies, dry goods, men's and women's clothing, furniture and house furnishings, and groceries. In some lines of business the term "manufacturers' representative" is coming into common usage in the place of manufacturers' agent.

2 / Merchandise Brokers. *Merchandise brokers* are wholesale agent middlemen whose task is to negotiate transactions between sellers and buyers without having direct physical control of the goods. They may represent either a seller or a buyer in any given transaction, but not both. They conclude purchases or sales in the name of their principals. Their powers of determining prices or terms of sale are usually limited by their principals.

The term "broker" is also commonly applied to those individuals and institutions that are active in the investment field. The term is also found in real estate and personnel placement. The merchandise broker, however, is the only one who is regarded as a marketing institution.

3 / Commission merchants. *Commission merchants* are agent middlemen who transact business in their own names on a commission basis and who have direct physical control over the goods consigned to them. They operate in the fields of groceries, livestock, cotton, and grain.

4 / Selling agents. *Selling agents* are independent business enterprises operating on a commission basis, whose principal function is to sell the entire output of a given line of goods for one or more manufacturers with whom they maintain continuous contractual relationships. They are found in such fields as textiles, coal, metals, and food. They have full authority with regard to prices and terms of sale.

5 / Auction companies. *Auction companies* sell at wholesale by the auction method. Sales are conducted under definite rules and are usually made to the highest bidder. They operate in the tobacco, livestock, and fresh fruit and vegetable fields. Auction companies represent sellers of goods.

■ **Wholesale Services**

Wholesaling performs a necessary marketing service in our competitive, profit-motivated economy, the cost of which is broadly equated to the economic values that it creates. A large number of producers, located in many different areas, must move their products to industrial and commercial consumers and to numerous retailers, who are also widely scattered. In the years immediately following the close of World War I, there was a fairly widespread belief that wholesalers were an unnecessary part of the marketing structure, whose elimination would result in lower prices to consumers. The fact that wholesaling has continued as a vital part of our distributive system is a strong indication of its value.

1 / **Services rendered by wholesalers to manufacturers.** The services rendered to manufacturers by wholesalers are: (a) contact retailers, (b) store for manufacturers, (c) assume credit burdens, and (d) other services.

Because the operational scope of most wholesalers is strictly local in character, they are able to establish an intensive contact with retailers and, frequently, at a lower cost to the manufacturers than the latter would incur if their own salesmen called on the retailers.

Wholesalers in many lines maintain large stocks of goods from which they make deliveries to their retail customers. By this practice they perform a storage function that the manufacturers would otherwise have to undertake. This permits the manufacturers to routinize their productive processes and usually to lower their production, as well as their storage, costs.

If a manufacturer sells direct to retailers on any basis other than a purely local one, he must establish a system of credit administration that may be very extensive and costly. When wholesalers are used, they invariably assume this burden, which enables the producers to reduce the task of extending credit to that of a few, usually well-rated wholesale houses.

Wholesalers render to manufacturers still other services. Among these may be the granting of financial assistance to producers who happen to be in temporary need of funds, as well as interpreting local needs to manufacturers and thereby assisting them to fabricate their goods so as to make them more salable than would otherwise be the case.

2 / **Services rendered by wholesalers to retailers.** The following services are rendered to retailers by wholesalers: (a) simplify buying problems, (b) prompt delivery, (c) storage service, (d) credit facilities, and (e) merchandising aids.

A retail store usually stocks goods that are manufactured in many different parts of the country, if not of the world. If these goods were not assembled locally by wholesalers, retailers would need to devote much of their time either to traveling extensively to contact producers or to interviewing manufacturers' salesmen who would be calling on them. In either instance, they would have to take much time out from their normal storekeeping duties. Wholesalers assume most of these tasks and thereby simplify the retailers' buying problems.

Wholesalers are able to give retailers prompt delivery service. Because of their nearness to their customers, wholesalers are able to give them much more rapid delivery service than retailers could normally expect from manufacturers. This service enables retailers to maintain balanced stocks and not run short of needed merchandise.   •

By maintaining large stocks of goods from which retailers may draw when needed, wholesalers absorb a part of the retailers' storage burdens. If retailers bought direct from manufacturers, they would need to store the goods themselves, which would require larger storage facilities and tie up greater amounts of capital in inventory.

Wholesalers grant credit to retailers. The fact that many wholesalers operate solely in a fairly small market area permits them to offer credit to their customers on a basis that would be difficult, if not impossible, for the retailers to secure from the producers. This service may be exceedingly valuable to retailers who find themselves temporarily short of funds.

Wholesalers offer merchandising aids to their customers. Salesmen for wholesalers are frequently able to help their retailer customers by making suggestions to improve their displays, selling techniques, accounting procedures, and so on. Some go so far as to prepare and distribute sample advertising insertions, store layouts, and accounting books. Not many manufacturers could duplicate these services.

■ Bypassing Wholesalers

Despite the services that wholesalers render to both manufacturers and retailers, many manufacturers and retailers have undertaken to bypass the wholesalers by dealing directly with each other. Instances of this are to be found in the buying practices of department stores, chain stores, and mail-order houses, and in the selling policies of many producers who deal with these types of retailers, as well as those who maintain sales offices, with or without stocks, in various parts of the country. This means that these institutions must perform the storage, financing, market risk, buying, and selling functions that would otherwise be done by wholesalers.

A variant on this practice by manufacturers is where the producers sell direct to retailers located in large urban areas, while using wholesalers in all other cases, as is shown in the second diagram on page 146.

1 / Why manufacturers bypass wholesalers. Manufacturers sometimes bypass wholesalers in distributing their goods for three reasons. (a) They believe that by calling directly on the retailers who handle their products they are able to secure better control of the retail market and thus prevent their competitors from obtaining too large a share of the available business. (b) They feel the need for stronger promotional effort than wholesalers, who may be carrying many other manufacturers' goods, are able to give them. (c) In many instances they are forced to sell direct in order to meet competition.

2 / Why retailers bypass wholesalers. Likewise, there are three main reasons why retailers sometimes take the initiative in buying direct from manufacturers. (a) The principal reason is that they can frequently secure lower prices by taking over some of the wholesalers' functions and dealing directly with the producers. (b) In the handling of women's apparel, the sudden style changes, to which this type of merchandise is subject, make the time element of great importance and impel retailers to deal directly with the producers, particularly if they feature "style firsts" in their communities. (c) Retailers may buy direct from manufacturers because their competitors follow this practice and are able to undersell them unless they follow suit.

■ Does Direct Selling Lower Costs?

In order to answer this question accurately, it would be necessary to make rather detailed studies of the distribution costs of a large number of different lines of merchandise, a procedure that is not in order in a book such as this. It is possible, however, to observe what happens when goods are sold direct and to draw certain rather general conclusions from this examination.

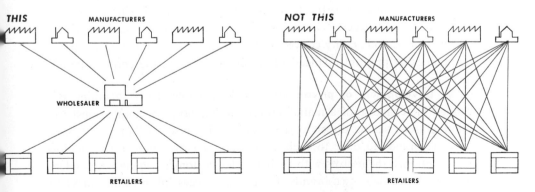

THIS   MANUFACTURERS   NOT THIS   MANUFACTURERS

WHOLESALER

RETAILERS   RETAILERS

The movement of goods in the marketing channels involves the performance of some or all of the marketing functions by the institutions handling the merchandise; and it is in the performance of these functions that marketing costs arise. When the wholesaler in any line of merchandise is bypassed, the marketing functions incidental to the movement of the merchandise, which would usually be taken care of by the wholesaler, are taken over by the manufacturer and/or the retailer. If these two are able to perform the functions only as cheaply as the wholesaler, then the saving will be largely in the elimination of the wholesaler's profit. If they are more efficient than the wholesaler, there may be additional savings; likewise, if they are less competent than the wholesaler, the savings may be reduced, even to the point where they may vanish and extra costs may arise. Comparative cost data are not available for alternate distribution channels, but the fact that direct selling has persisted in many areas appears to indicate that it is cheaper for both sellers and buyers than the utilization of wholesalers.

■ How Wholesalers Have Reacted

The wholesalers have not been unaware of the tendency for retailers to bypass them, nor have they sat idly by while it has progressed. In a number of ways they have endeavored to combat this trend, with varying degrees of success.

1. Increased efficiency
2. Development of private brands
3. Formation of voluntary chains

1 / Increased efficiency. By a careful examination of their costs, through better selection and training of their employees, and particularly through a revision of their methods of storage and handling orders, many wholesalers have succeeded in reducing their own distributive expenses. A form of automation in the food and drug wholesale business involves the use of fork-lift trucks, continuous chain conveyors, mechanical driverless tow trucks, and gravity conveyors, all of which are guided by electrical computers that preprint invoices and assist in selecting the goods ordered.

2 / Development of private brands. If a wholesaler is handling the branded merchandise of a manufacturer, he has no protection against the manufacturer's selling direct to the retailers, because the latter still have the same brands to offer to their customers. To overcome this situation and to entrench themselves with their retailer customers, many wholesalers have developed their own brands. If they are successful in selling these to retailers and if they are accepted by consumers, the wholesalers are in the enviable situation of controlling the distribution of these brands, which no manufacturer can take away from them.

3 / **Formation of voluntary chains.** By associating a number of retailers on a voluntary chain basis, many wholesalers have been able to become firmly established in their communities and to be virtually immune from the possibility of being eliminated through the actions of either the manufacturers or the retailers, or both.

■ Research in Wholesaling

Such research as has been reported in the field of wholesaling has been mainly in the area of logistics. Attempts have been made to streamline the handling of orders at the warehouses. This has been accomplished through the use of computer-managed inventory control and mechanical devices for filling orders and transporting goods to delivery platforms. The results sought by these actions involve cost-cutting, reduction of inventories, prompter delivery of orders, and better service to customers.

RETAILING

Retailing is that segment of marketing where the products of the consumer goods industry are purchased by the ultimate consumers for their own personal use or that of their families. It is the point in the channel of distribution where the offerings of manufacturers of consumer goods are accepted or rejected. It is where the validity of the total marketing concept is either proved or disproved.

The marketing institutions that operate in this field are retailers. Their contribution to the economic life of the nation arises through their creation of place, time, and possession utilities; that is, they bring the goods to places that are convenient for consumers to purchase, at the times that they want them, and they provide the facilities by which consumers may secure possession of the goods of their choice.

Retailing is a dynamic field—a scene of intense competition, of daring innovations, and of rapid change. It features dramatic sales promotion and advertising in which only those store types whose goods, locations, service, and operational methods are in line with changing trends can hope to survive the rigors of competition. Stores that have followed long-established, previously successful policies of location, layout, customer service, and merchandise selections are finding that their very existence is being threatened by competitors whose new methods of operation appear

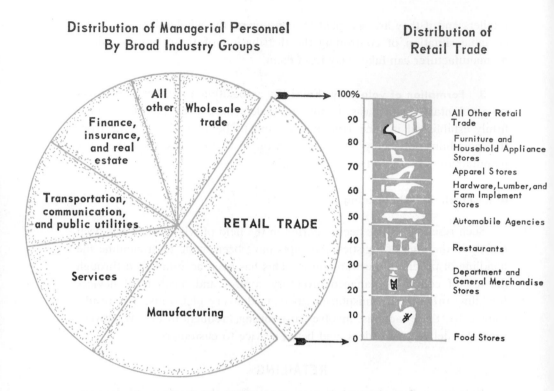

Distribution of Managerial Personnel By Broad Industry Groups

Distribution of Retail Trade

Retailing and Management
Retail trade is the largest area of employment for managers.

to hold an almost irresistible attraction for many consumers. The dynamism portrayed by this situation has given rise to the term *scrambled retailing,* which is illustrative of the unsettled conditions in this economic area.

One of the major causes of this acute competitive situation is the dramatic rise in the population of the country and the concomitant growth of the suburban areas of most of our large cities. Accompanying this factor has been the increase in the number of automobiles in use, with the resulting need for more parking facilities, both in the downtown sections and in the suburbs, and the ensuing traffic congestion that is a feature of all metropolitan areas to a greater or lesser degree.

As shown on the chart above, retailing is the largest area of employment for managers. The requirements for managerial success in retailing include considerable retail experience, keen merchandise judgment, an intuitive understanding of customer preferences, a sense of showmanship, bargaining ability for trading with suppliers, a knowledge of the latest developments in retail accounting, and, of course, the ability to direct the personnel of the store. Coupled with this should be a good measure of physical stamina and a recognition that retailing is practically a way of life, at least to the successful retail manager.

The table below shows the ten largest merchandising firms in the United States in 1965, with their invested capital and net profit as a percentage of it. The notable differences between the invested capital of food and nonfood stores is of interest.

The Ten Largest Merchandising Firms
Ranked by Sales, 1965

Rank	Company	Sales ($000)	Invested Capital ($000)	Net Profit as % of Invested Capital
1	Sears, Roebuck	6,390,000	2,179,082	14.8
2	Great Atlantic & Pacific .	5,118,978	592,615	8.8
3	Safeway Stores	2,939,043	346,139	13.9
4	Kroger	2,555,109	244,958	12.8
5	J. C. Penney	2,289,209	436,974	18.1
6	Montgomery Ward	1,748,360	656,733	3.6
7	F. W. Woolworth	1,443,322	627,184	11.6
8	Federated Dept. Stores ..	1,330,737	453,771	15.5
9	Acme Markets	1,200,750	158,479	6.6
10	National Tea	1,161,948	126,659	8.9

Reprinted from the July 15, 1966, *Fortune Directory* by special permission: © 1966, Time, Inc.

■ Retailers Classified by Types of Operation

Retailers are classified by their locations, such as downtown or neighborhood; by the types of goods handled, such as food, drugs, shoes, and hardware; by the types of operation; and on the basis of ownership. This chapter will deal with the last two categories.

When the operation of retailers forms the basis for classification, the various types are as follows:

1. General stores
2. Department stores
3. Specialty stores
4. Single-line stores
5. Specialty shops

6. Supermarkets
7. Discount houses
8. Limited-price variety stores
9. Other types of retailers

1 / General stores. The earliest type of retail outlet in this country was probably the *general store.* In the early years of our history, it was found in villages or at country crossroads as the only retailing institution in the community. It carried a broad range of goods, from food and clothing to farm implements, feed, and seeds; and it frequently housed the post office. A few are still to be found in the more sparsely settled areas.

2 / Department stores. *Department stores* are large establishments located in downtown shopping areas of cities. They handle a wide range of goods, including clothing, furniture, housewares, floor coverings, toys, millinery, lamps, draperies, yard goods, and small wares such as notions, cosmetics, and handkerchiefs.

Department stores stress the service side of their business. Free delivery, liberal credit, the acceptance of telephone and mail orders, gift wrapping, the privilege of almost unlimited return of purchased merchandise, rest rooms, nurseries for infants and children, and restaurants are among the inducements held out to their customers.

These stores may be independently owned, or they may be units of chains. At this level of retailing there is practically no difference in the operating practices and merchandising policies of chains and independents.

Most department stores buy direct from the manufacturers. They, as well as the specialty stores, utilize resident buying offices, which will be discussed in Chapter 13, quite extensively in various aspects of their purchasing operations.

Department stores rely on newspaper and direct-mail advertising, together with elaborate window and floor displays, to inform their customers of the availability of their merchandise and to attract them into their stores. Highly skilled advertising and display personnel direct these activities. Among the more prominent department stores in this country are Macy's and Lord & Taylor in New York, Hudson's in Detroit, Marshall Field in Chicago, and Bullock's in Los Angeles.

(a) BRANCH DEPARTMENT STORES. The trend for downtown department stores to establish branch stores in the suburbs of our large cities, which began in the early 1930's, has accelerated greatly in recent years. Examples of this development are to be found in the suburbs of many cities, such as New York, Boston, Philadelphia, Cleveland, Chicago, and Los Angeles. Frequently these branch stores are located in or near suburban shopping centers; and in some instances the sponsoring stores have established controlled shopping centers, incorporating their branches as the focal points in these enterprises.

Since the onset of this branch-store movement, there has been considerable speculation as to whether it might eventually replace the downtown shopping center. The migration of city population to the suburbs, the increase in the volume of automobile traffic, and the parking difficulties that confront consumers who wish to patronize the downtown stores, have all been factors that have tended to contribute to this speculation. In many cities, however, countermeasures have been undertaken, such as the erection of parking garages or the provision of large parking lots, together with free bus transportation to and from these facilities.

(b) SEARS' AND WARD'S STORES. The department stores operated by Sears, Roebuck and Co., and Montgomery Ward and Co., the country's two largest mail-order houses, constitute an important segment of retailing. In most instances, the Sears stores have been located in the larger cities, usually some distance from the downtown shopping centers, and have featured large parking lots for their customers. By contrast, the Ward stores have usually been located in the smaller cities and, where possible, in the main shopping districts of these towns. Unlike the department stores with which they compete, these stores carry very few nationally advertised manufacturers' brands of merchandise but confine their offerings mainly to goods bearing their own brands.

3 / **Specialty stores.** A *specialty store* might be defined as a department store minus the merchandise customarily known as home furnishings, such as housewares, furniture, floor coverings, electrical appliances, toys, china, and glassware. It is directly competitive with department stores. Specialty stores tend to confine their apparel offerings to women's wear and accessories, but some of them specialize in men's apparel and accessories, such as sporting goods and luggage. The buying, advertising, and service policies of these stores are identical with those of department stores. Several large specialty stores have formed a buying group, known as the Specialty Stores Association, which maintains a buying office in New York City. Specialty stores are both independent and chain owned.

4 / **Single-line stores.** The *single-line store* is the small store, independently owned, that carries a single line of merchandise, such as food, hardware, drugs, millinery, or men's furnishings. In the interest of consistency, gasoline filling stations, automobile dealers, flower shops, tire and accessory stores, furniture stores, appliance stores, jewelry stores, antique and gift shops, and restaurants should be included in this category; but many of their operating procedures and problems are different. Chain stores handling the same kinds of goods are excluded because many of their merchandising methods are different from those of the independents.

The typical single-line stores are to be found everywhere, in the down-town and the neighborhood areas and in the newly developed suburban shopping centers. The more or less isolated stores, located at or near street intersections in residential areas, are frequently of this type. They offer free delivery, extend credit to their customers, and accept telephone orders. A trend in the grocery field among these stores in recent years is the growth of the cash-and-carry system as well as that of self-service.

Single-line stores range in size from those that are literally holes in the wall to fairly large establishments with modern fixtures, adequate lighting, and general attractiveness. These stores customarily buy the bulk of their goods through wholesalers, although some of the larger ones deal directly with the manufacturers. Their advertising is usually limited, except in small towns, as they customarily cannot afford to use the metropolitan daily newspapers. In villages and suburban communities where weekly newspapers are published, many single-line stores have been able to utilize these advertising media advantageously.

5 / Specialty shops. A *specialty shop* is a store, often a member of a chain, that confines itself to a small segment of the merchandise in any single category, usually in the apparel field. Stores of this type handle dresses, or millinery, or shoes, and sometimes a combination of apparel items, such as hosiery, handbags, and shoes, or millinery and neckwear. Specialty shops are to be found in all retail areas, in the downtown as well as the neighborhood business communities and suburban shopping centers.

The buying practices of specialty shops vary according to sales volume. Those with larger sales tend to buy direct, while the smaller stores buy through wholesalers. They rely heavily on window displays to attract cus-tomers, as only the largest shops can afford to use newspaper advertising.

6 / Supermarkets. Despite the fact that supermarkets have become predominant in the grocery field, there is no generally accepted definition for this type of retail outlet. A composite of the definitions of several trade periodicals in this field would describe a *supermarket* as a depart-mentized food store, with most departments on a self-service basis, having a minimum sales volume ranging from $375,000 to $1,000,000 a year.

Although supermarkets originated in the 1930's, their period of great-est growth dates from around the end of World War II, and they have come to be preeminent in the food field. They are both chain and independently owned. In the case of the chains, large numbers of their smaller, counter-service grocery units have been closed. An interesting aspect of supermarket development has been the progressive addition of a large number of nonfood items. Among these are toilet goods, proprietary drugs, hosiery, magazines, records, kitchen utensils, small tools, glassware, hardware, and dinnerware.

In some parts of the country, small, self-service grocery stores are called *superettes,* a term that is intended to indicate their relationship to supermarkets. In many instances these superettes are former service stores that have been converted to self-service.

The success of the supermarkets has caused many students of retailing to speculate regarding the extent to which self-service will be adopted in nonfood fields. Already over 600 drugstores in this country, as well as a considerable number of variety and small department stores, are on a more or less total self-service basis.

7 / Discount houses. An important post-World War II development has been the growth of discount houses. Owned by both chains and independent operators, the *discount houses* have offered merchandise at substantially lower prices than their competitors, many of whom are department and appliance stores. They have based their low prices on a curtailment of service and, in recent years, by securing a growing volume of sales on a relatively constant expense, thereby permitting them to operate on a smaller markup than their older competitors. These stores have often specialized in electrical appliances, television and radio receivers, furniture, floor coverings, power mowers, sporting goods, and air conditioners.

Discount houses buy their goods through wholesalers in some instances and directly from the manufacturers in others. They usually sell strictly for cash and offer delivery service only on major appliances, such as stoves or refrigerators. A recent development in this field has been the appearance of discount drugstores in many cities. Customarily operating on a self-service basis, these stores feature fast-selling drug and cosmetic items at prices markedly below those of the independent drugstores and some of the chains.

In recent years there has been a pronounced trend in the discount-house field toward the broadening of their merchandise offerings. Many have been adding apparel lines to their traditional hard lines of merchandise and are thus moving in the direction of becoming full-fledged department stores.

A number of discount houses sell only to consumers who have purchased memberships. These are called *closed-door discount houses.* Members are frequently selected from more or less cohesive groups, such as government employees or labor unions, and only they are permitted to buy in those stores. Merchandise offerings parallel those of department stores. These stores are frequently known by abbreviations such as FAME, GEM, or GEX, which indicates the nature of their membership. For example, GEX stands for Government Employees Exchange. Since the prices of these stores approximate those of department stores and regular discount houses, the reason why consumers will pay membership fees to secure their goods is not entirely clear.

A relatively recent development in the discount field has been the addition of food departments by discounters in many parts of the country. In retaliation for this move, several of the large food chain operators have opened *discount supermarkets*, stores with lower prices based on curtailed advertising, elimination of trading stamps, elaborate inventories, and check-cashing services. Frequently these new stores bear different names from those of the parent companies, for example, the National Tea Company has opened a number of Big D stores.

8 / Limited-price variety stores. In 1879 F. W. Woolworth established the first store of this type, which became known as 5-and-10-cent stores because of the original limitation on the prices of goods carried. More recently the price lines of these stores have been advanced, with some goods priced as high as $25 or more. As a result, the original designation is no longer applicable, and in its place the term *limited-price variety stores* is a more accurate description and is in accord with the usage of the trade, if not of the public. Examples of this type, in addition to the F. W. Woolworth Company, are the S. S. Kresge & Company and the J. J. Newberry Company. The chains do about 90 percent of the business in this field, and a rather large group of independents obtain the rest. It is anticipated, however, that the independent group will increase its share of the business in the future.

Variety stores handle a wide array of merchandise from small wares, toys, housewares, candy, toiletries, stationery, electric appliances and bulbs, and light hardware, mostly in the low-price ranges, to table and floor lamps, furniture, and apparel items in the medium-price fields. Historically these stores have been on a cash-and-carry basis, but during the past few years, several of them have made charge accounts available to qualified customers.

The buying practices of the independent variety stores customarily involve the use of wholesalers, whereas all of the chains buy direct from the manufacturers. At least one group of independents, the Ben Franklin Stores with around 2500 units, affiliated with City Products Corporation, a wholesaler, operates as a voluntary chain.

9 / Other types of retailers. A number of other, somewhat less important, types of retailers deserve brief mention.

(a) HOUSE-TO-HOUSE SELLING. *House-to-house selling* is used to distribute such commodities as cosmetics, brushes, hosiery, vacuum cleaners, apparel, magazines, and greeting cards. Among the companies that are prominent in this field are Avon Products, the Fuller Brush Company, and the Real Silk Hosiery Mills. One of the principal deterrents to the success of house-to-house selling, aside from the prejudice against it on the part of many housewives, is the so-called "Green River Ordinance," so named because it originated in Green River, Wyoming. Such a local law has been enacted in many small communities to hamper or restrict the activities of itinerant house-to-house peddlers. Ordinances of this type ordinarily involve the payment of a fee to secure a permit to call at the local homes. These ordinances were originated by local merchants and enacted at their request in order to prevent competition between them and the house-to-house salesmen. The United States Supreme Court has upheld the constitutionality of the Green River Ordinance of Alexandria, Louisiana. A *huckster* is a house-to-house salesman who differs from other house-to-house salesmen in that (a) he carries his stock of goods with him and makes deliveries on the spot and (b) he calls repeatedly on the same customers, frequently every working day of the week, and comes to be well known to them. Hucksters are customarily residents in the cities where they operate. Huckstering includes the fields of bread and fresh fruits and vegetables. eggs

(b) MAIL-ORDER HOUSES. *Mail-order houses* sell and deliver goods by mail, making use of catalogs, newspaper advertising, and direct mail to attract customers. They offer a very wide variety of goods such as food, electrical appliances, plumbing supplies, tools, and clothing. There are a large number of mail-order houses but most of them are comparatively small businesses. Only a few, principally Sears, Roebuck and Company; Montgomery Ward and Company; and Spiegel, Inc. are of outstanding size.

(c) SERVICE RETAILERS. *Service retailers* sell services rather than goods, in most instances. Many service retailers possess professional skills that comprise their stock in trade, while others maintain facilities for processing their customers' belongings. Included in this category of retailers are dry cleaning shops, barbershops, beauty salons, reducing salons, bowling alleys, shoe repair and shoe shining places, automobile and bicycle repair shops, and radio and television repair centers.

(d) VENDING MACHINES. Although *vending machines* date back to the 1880's, their recent growth has been phenomenal. In a recent year the National Automatic Merchandising Association released the following statistics regarding their operations: Sales of over $3.2 billion were achieved in such commodities as cigarettes, bottled drinks, candy, coffee and hot beverages, soft drinks in cups, milk, ice cream, cigars, and gum. Some four million machines are involved in this volume of business.

A few department stores have been experimenting with vending machines to promote the sales of small items, such as packaged hosiery, cosmetics, handkerchiefs, and costume jewelry. Among the latest developments to aid vending-machine customers are change-making machines, some of which are capable of providing change for a dollar bill.

■ Retailers Classified on the Basis of Ownership

On the basis of ownership, retailers are classified as independents or as members of a chain.

1 / Independents. *Independents* include most stores that are individually, and usually locally, owned—principally small stores, such as grocery, drug, shoe, and variety stores. Although the members of voluntary chains are technically independents, they are excluded from this discussion because of their merchandising practices, which will be described later.

The typical independent retail store is a small operation, usually managed by the owner or owners. It is rarely incorporated;[1] sole proprietorships and partnerships predominate. These stores are usually rather inadequately financed, and many of them are never very far from insolvency. As a general rule they buy through wholesalers and do little advertising. Their selling efforts could hardly be called aggressive. Their accounting methods are often most rudimentary. Their profits are low if, indeed, many of them ever realize any profits at all. Many of them are conducted inefficiently and at a high cost. In every community, however, there are capable independents, whose methods are up-to-date and whose profits reflect their ability. Many small store operators employ accountants who visit their stores once or twice a month and assume complete responsibility for the store's accounting, even to the point of making out the monthly bills for the customers and of paying the store's invoices from their suppliers.

---

[1] For several years one of the authors taught classes made up of independent retailers. Of the 150 or more members of these classes, less than half a dozen had incorporated their businesses.

2 / **Chain stores.** There is a notable lack of agreement among governmental and retailing authorities as to the minimum number of stores that should constitute a *chain*. The Census of Business avoids the term "chain," using instead *multiunit organization*, and applies this designation to "two or more stores in the same general kind of business operated by the same firm." *Food Topics*, a grocery trade journal, defines food chains as organizations operating "four or more" stores, while the *Progressive Grocer* establishes eleven stores as the minimum number. These variations have existed for a number of years and complicate, to some extent, the determination of the number of stores, their total sales, and their share of the market.

The term *corporate chain* is commonly used to distinguish this type of operation from the voluntary chain. This group also includes manufacturer-controlled retail stores and leased departments, which are found mainly in department and specialty stores. Chain stores operate in the fields of groceries and drugs; in variety, apparel, automobile accessories, shoes, tobacco, and department stores; and in filling stations.

The chain method of operation is of importance as it furnishes the key to the truth of the claim that chain store prices are lower than those of independents. In this discussion department store chains are excluded, as they do not follow the customary pattern of chain operation.

■ Chain Store Policies

The distinctive nature of chain stores is indicated by the policies that are generally followed in connection with each of the following:

1. Buying
2. Warehousing
3. Merchandising policies
4. Chain advertising
5. Merchandise specials
6. Operational policies

1 / **Buying.** Chain systems customarily practice central buying; that is, all of the merchandise for the stores is purchased at some central office rather than by the individual store managers. This policy results in the purchase of large quantities of merchandise and, as a result, the chains obtain quantity discounts and carload freight rates, both of which effect savings in merchandise costs.

Chains also buy direct from the manufacturers, instead of through wholesalers, thereby saving at least the wholesaler's profit. They may do some manufacturing of the goods they sell. Buying committees, which will be discussed in Chapter 13, are of importance in chain groups that operate supermarkets.

2 / Warehousing. The grocery and drug chains maintain warehouses to which nearly all of their merchandise is shipped and from which it is distributed to the stores as needed. Because of their control over the stores, the chains are in a position to plan their buying, warehousing, and delivering so as to incur the lowest possible costs in this overall procurement operation.

3 / Merchandising policies. Chain retail merchandising policies are designed to bring about reduced store operating costs, which can be reflected in competitively lower prices. Among the principal merchandising policies are the following:

> Sales for cash only.[2]
> No delivery service.
> Telephone orders not accepted.
> Only fast-moving items carried.
> Vigorous exploitation of private-branded merchandise.
> Ruthless marking down of old or slow-moving merchandise.

4 / Chain advertising. Chain store groups that are located in cities of any size have a distinct advantage over their independent competitors, with the exception of voluntary chains, in that they are able to utilize the daily papers as effective and inexpensive advertising media. A single insertion, identified with the chain, serves as an advertisement for each store in the chain, and the cost per store is relatively low. The copy for the newspapers—as well as for store posters, signs, and other forms of advertising—is customarily prepared at the central offices. This results in uniformity and low cost.

5 / Merchandise specials. It has long been the practice of chain stores to select certain items from their stock, reduce their prices somewhat, and feature them in their advertising for the purpose not only of selling these items, but also of attracting customers who will buy other full-priced goods. In certain instances the depth of the price reduction and the prominence of the goods affected have brought into being the term *loss leaders,* which are those specials where the prices are so low as to give rise to the suspicion that they are being offered at or near their cost to the stores. These are almost always goods that are nationally known, both as to their quality and their customary prices. The fair and unfair trade laws, noted on page 176, have discouraged this practice somewhat.

---

[2] As previously noted, certain variety chains are now extending credit to their customers.

6 / Operational policies. The careful selection and training of personnel are outstanding characteristics of chain store operation. Many firms have formal training courses for their employees, particularly those that are designated for promotion to executive positions within the stores or the central offices.

Retail accounting has been brought to a high state of development in the chain systems. With all stores subject to the same accounting procedures, the chain management has a very effective tool to detect weaknesses and remedy them.

Many chains maintain real estate departments, staffed by experts in this field who endeavor to secure the best leasehold terms for their stores, check on the adequacy of present or prospective sites, assume responsibility for the remodeling or moving of stores, and generally seek to operate this phase of the business as efficiently as possible.

▣ Voluntary Chains

There are two types of *voluntary chains*—those sponsored by independent wholesalers, and those promoted by groups of cooperating retailers, who customarily establish and own the wholesale houses that serve them. The former group is more important than the latter as far as numbers are concerned. Their merchandising policies and practices, which are practically identical, are as follows:

1. Through the wholesale houses, they buy collectively and thereby secure quantity discounts and carload freight rates. This is perhaps the greatest advantage that voluntary chains have over the unaffiliated independents.
2. They develop and push group private brands, which they control and on which they sometimes make larger unit profits than on nationally advertised manufacturers' branded goods.
3. They advertise collectively, employing a common layout identified with their group. Because of the number of stores involved, they are able to use the daily papers at a very low cost per store. This is a second important advantage that voluntary chains have over the independents not thus associated.
4. They feature weekly specials in direct imitation of the regular chains.
5. They adopt standard store fronts and, as far as possible, standard interior layouts.
6. They adopt standard accounting methods and record keeping.
7. The latest developments in retailing are noted by the members or the wholesalers, and information concerning them is disseminated to all of the stores.

The strength of the voluntary chains has been in the cooperative spirit of the members and, by the same token, their principal weakness has been the lack of positive control within the group. Nevertheless the voluntary chain system has permitted thousands of retailers to achieve many of the savings of chain operation while still maintaining a large measure of their independence. It has likewise made better storekeepers of many of them. Voluntary chains are found mainly in the fields of groceries, variety goods, and automobile accessories.

■ Antichain Laws

In the years during which the chain stores were experiencing their greatest growth, there was a concerted movement among wholesalers and independent retailers to prevent this growth from reaching a point where the chains would endanger the existence of the independents. This movement took the form of a number of laws, both federal and state, that were sponsored by the independent group. In the main, these laws were designed to prevent the chains from selling at lower prices than independent stores.

The chain-store tax laws, in effect in 12 states, impose special tax burdens on the chains in order to increase their expenses. The so-called fair-trade laws, presently in effect in 27 states, together with the McGuire Act, a federal statute, are designed to prevent the chains from cutting prices on certain branded items. Unfair-trade laws, which are operative in 28 states and which specify minimum markups for retailers, are also intended to curb chain price cutting. The Robinson-Patman Act, a federal law, forbids many of the practices whereby the chains formerly secured price concessions from their vendors.

■ Trading Stamps

The trading stamp idea is quite old, having originated in 1891; but during the past few years it has grown to a most astonishing volume, with somewhere between $25 and $30 billion of retail sales being covered by stamps in a recent year. It is estimated that over 80 percent of American families save *trading stamps*, which are issued by some 370 stamp companies—on the usual basis of one stamp for each 10 cents of purchase value—and that redemptions of around $540 million at retail prices occur annually.

■ The Retailing Revolution

The kaleidoscopic changes that have been taking place in the field of retailing during the past few years have caused some observers to call it the *retailing revolution*. Underlying this phenomenon is a basic change in the distribution of consumer goods. The traditional merchandise lines of many stores have been altered and augmented, sometimes by competition and often by the innovations of the retailers. One phase in this change has been the great increase in nonfood items carried by the supermarkets and, because of competition, by many smaller food stores. The discount house has brought about changes that extend throughout the general merchandise field. Not only are the discount houses in many instances approaching the status of department stores, but also many department stores have endeavored to copy to some extent the price and merchandising policies of the discounters. E. J. Korvette, Inc., one of the pioneer discount houses, has taken over the former building of W. & J. Sloan, a prestige furniture store on Fifth Avenue in New York City for many years. The F. W. Woolworth Company has a chain of 16 department stores. J. C. Penney, for years a leading merchandiser of clothing and other soft goods and a limited line of home furnishings, has greatly broadened its lines by adding appliances, sporting goods, tires, and auto accessories. The S. S. Kresge Company, an old-line variety store chain, has moved into the large variety-department store field, as well as into discounting through some 65 K-Mart discount centers.

The discount houses, in turn, are broadening the area of their merchandise offerings, adding larger assortments of men's and women's apparel and, in several instances, operating full-scale supermarkets as adjuncts to their other lines. The Walgreen Company, one of the country's largest drug chains, has acquired several small department stores that it plans to operate as discount houses. The list grows, and the lines of demarcation between department stores and discount houses appear to be becoming more indistinct as each invades the other's merchandise offerings and policies.

The question naturally arises as to how this change affects consumers. Apparently they like it, since it permits them to make more of their purchases under one roof and at competitive prices. Some observers have wondered about the effect on the "carriage trade" of the department stores, whose merchandising policies have been keyed to such customers, venturing into the discount field and losing thereby, presumably, much of the "store image" that had been carefully cultivated for nearly one hundred years in some cases. This poses a sociological problem the answer to which is not completely clear; but there is a suggestion that the carriage trade has been gradually disappearing over the years, and that its place has been taken by well-to-do groups of consumers to whom merchandise values and lower prices are of greater import than the prestige gained by trading at a store with an old-established name. There is certainly abundant evidence that the managers of the stores think so. This is not to imply that prestige is a lost merchandise asset. There are still many people of means who patronize men's and women's specialty stores and shops, such as Bonwit Teller, Milgrim, Franklin Simon, and Best & Company, and many locally owned prestige stores in our large cities. There does still exist a measure of label-conscious vanity among both men and women. The question that concerns retailers in this merchandise area is whether or not the number of these consumers is on the increase or the decline.

■ Research in Retailing

The term "research" is not too frequently found in the field of retailing, but what might be called *experimental innovation* abounds. Retail managers have been constantly engaged in this sort of experimentation in such areas as the introduction of new products, store layout, suburban branches, mail-order catalogs, credit and billing procedures, and many others. The adoption of electronic data processing by department, variety, and chain stores has proceeded rapidly in the past few years and has provided these stores with valuable information upon which to base their operational decisions. From the volume and extent of this experimentation, the conclusion emerges that those stores whose executives do not follow this trend may find their sales and profits declining in such a manner as to suggest doubt as to their survival.

BUSINESS TERMS

(a) wholesaling (155)
(b) merchant wholesaler (156); industrial distributor (156), specialty wholesaler (156)
(c) wholesale merchant (156), jobber (157), importer (157), exporter (157), wagon, truck distributor (157)
(d) functional middlemen (157); manufacturers' agent (157), merchandise broker (158), commission merchant (158), selling agent (158), auction company (158)
(e) retailing (163), scrambled retailing (164)
(f) general store (165), department store (166), specialty store (167), single-line store (167), specialty shop (168)
(g) supermarket (168), superette (169)
(h) discount house (169), closed-door discount house (169), discount supermarket (170)
(i) limited-price variety store (170)
(j) house-to-house selling (171), huckster (171)
(k) mail-order house (171), service retailer (171), vending machine (172)

(l) independents (172)
(m) chain (173), multiunit organization (173), corporate chain (173), voluntary chain (175)
(n) loss leader (174)
(o) trading stamps (176)
(p) retailing revolution (177)
(q) experimental innovation (178)

QUESTIONS FOR DISCUSSION AND ANALYSIS

1. Why are there so many different channels of distribution?
2. As shown in the diagram on page 146, some producers of consumer goods use wholesalers to reach the small retailers, but they sell direct to large retailers and chains. Do you think that this practice discriminates against the smaller retailers? Explain.
3. Do you believe that the elimination of wholesalers in consumer-goods lines would necessarily result in lower prices to consumers? Why?
4. Despite the growth of supermarket chains, food wholesalers have been able to maintain their places in the grocery business. How do you account for this?
5. How do you explain the striking growth of nonfood items in supermarkets?
6. Do you believe that chain store tax laws, designed to increase the chains' operating costs, are in the best interests of consumers? Why?
7. A few department stores have installed vending machines to promote the sales of certain small items. In some instances this experiment has been quite successful; in others it has failed. What reasons can you advance for these differing results?
8. Many of the leading variety store chains have been moving into the discount department store field. Do you believe that this indicates the eventual disappearance of the variety store as it has been known for many years? Explain.
9. How is it possible for two supermarkets to remain competitive if one gives trading stamps and the other does not?
10. Do you think that department stores, with long-established names, can successfully change to self-service? Why?

PROBLEMS AND SHORT CASES

1. The Brookins Company has developed and patented a combination glass and aluminum screening unit for enclosing porches. Unlike jalousies, with which it will be competitive, it operates by sliding two glass panels that can be raised and lowered for ventilation. The screen section is outside the glass and is fixed in place. The enclosure units come in several standard widths, which can be combined to fit almost any size porch. The prices vary with the dimensions of the porches involved, but they average somewhat less than those of competing porch enclosures. The company's name is unknown to the trade and to the public. It is fairly adequately financed, but not so

as to permit of any advertising other than descripitve folders or pamphlets.

You are to prepare a distributive plan for this company that will indicate the distribution channels that should be used for this product and the types of wholesalers and retailers who should handle it.

2. The management of a department store, with a downtown unit where it originated and four suburban branches, is faced with the problem of deciding whether to continue to operate as it has, or to abandon its downtown store and concentrate on building up its sales volume from its present suburban stores and on opening more stores as conditions seem propitious. Since its suburban stores were opened a few years ago, the company's sales have increased, but its profits have declined. Moreover, the sales of the downtown store have shown a decrease for the past year, while its expenses have remained more or less constant.

You are asked to analyze this situation and to advise the store management as to the proper course of action, taking into account such factors as appear to you to be pertinent.

3. The Newsom Company, a long-established, high-prestige department store in one of the large cities, is concerned over the competition that it has been receiving from the discount houses in the area. In addition to its downtown store, this firm maintains four branch stores in the outlying suburban shopping centers. It has always stressed the quality of its merchandise and the reputation and reliability of its organization. The discount-house competition has become of such severity that the store management is seriously considering establishing its own discount operation as a means of preserving its sales and profit position. Among the questions that confront the management is whether they should enter the discount field; if so, whether the discount operation should be conducted in their present stores or in different locations; and whether the name of the Newsom Company should or should not be identified with the projected discount stores.

Advise the company on these points, giving your reasons.

SUGGESTED READINGS

Beckman, T. N., N. H. Engle, and R. D. Buzzell. *Wholesaling,* Third Edition. New York: The Ronald Press Company, 1959.

Davidson, W. R., and A. F. Doody. *Retailing Management,* Third Edition. New York: The Ronald Press Company, 1966.

Hill, R. M. *Wholesaling Management: Text and Cases.* Homewood, Illinois: Richard D. Irwin, Inc., 1963.

Staudt, T. A., and D. A. Taylor. *A Managerial Introduction to Marketing.* Englewood Cliffs, New Jersey: Prentice-Hall, Inc., 1965. Chapters 13, 14, and 15.

Magazines: *Journal of Retailing* (New York University).

Chapter 9

PRICES AND PRICING

The basic purpose of an economic system is to provide the facilities and procedures by which people can secure for themselves the goods and services that they regard as essential to their standard of living. From the earliest recorded times, individuals grew or made those articles for which they had some special aptitude and exchanged them with others. Under this procedure, it became necessary for the value of one man's goods to be expressed in terms of those of another, a system known as *barter*. This was essentially a cumbersome method, calling not only for a man with certain products to find another who needed his goods, but also one with goods that he required. Furthermore, a bargaining process usually ensued to establish acceptable exchange values for the different products involved. When at some later time the concept and use of money came into being, it became possible to express the values of all goods in this one medium of exchange, which greatly facilitated the purchase and sale of goods. These values are known as *prices,* the subject with which this chapter is concerned. The pricing system is quite universal, at least in those nations whose economies have advanced beyond the barter stage, and greatly facilitates trade in and between these countries.

■ Approaches to Price Determination

As noted in Chapter 1, there are several bases for competition, with price probably being the most important. It is therefore desirable that attention be given at the outset of this discussion to the methods by which prices are determined. In the majority of instances, prices are established in business by sellers, who take into account a number of factors. Three basic methods are followed by sellers in setting their prices. These methods are as follows:

(1) With known unit costs of production, distribution, and overhead, the seller adds a desired profit and compares the resultant figure with the prices of competition. Depending upon the nature of the product and the rigor of its competition, he then determines whether he must meet competition, price his product below it, or, in a fortunate circumstance, above his competitors' prices.

When a seller, usually a producer, establishes his prices at a predetermined level, he is following a policy of *administered prices*. This predetermined level is usually that used by competitors so that price competition will be de-emphasized in his appeal for sales. Some marketing authorities refer to administered pricing as "judgment pricing."

(2) In a situation where competition sets the price above which the product may not be sold, the seller works backward from that price to the permissible unit cost and then determines whether or not the available margin is sufficient to enable him to operate profitably. This procedure could result in a decision not to make the product in question, if the apparently available profit is unsatisfactory. As a possible alternative course, the seller may endeavor to secure lower prices from his suppliers in order to bring his costs down to a level that will permit him to compete in the market.

(3) When a firm has two or more products with a common source and with individual unit costs difficult to determine, the pricing procedure involves the attempt to secure a satisfactory profit from the pricing of the separate products, which may or may not involve a close relationship between the prices and the presumed costs of each item. This is what is known as a *joint cost* situation and is found in the petroleum, lumber, and livestock industries. For example, a butcher buys a side of beef at so many cents per pound; but in pricing the different cuts, such as porterhouse, sirloin, and round, he takes into account their relative appeal to consumers and prices them accordingly. He endeavors to set his price per cut so as to realize a satisfactory profit on each side of beef that he handles.

At the consumer level, with such exceptions as auctions, sales of antiques, objets d'art, or casual sales, the prices are set by the sellers. A *casual sale* is one that is outside the province of organized business, such as the sale of an old lawn mower by one person to his neighbor. At other than the consumer level, it is not uncommon for would-be buyers to specify the prices above which they are unable or unwilling to go. Professional buyers, such as purchasing agents and chain and department store buyers, customarily endeavor to secure the lowest available prices through a bargaining process with their suppliers.

▨ Price Determining Factors

Those individuals in sellers' organizations who have the authority to set the prices that are asked for the products to be sold may take one or more of the following factors into account:

1. Markup percentage
2. Price lines
3. Suggested prices
4. Price leadership
5. What the traffic will bear

6. Demand elasticity
7. Monopoly price
8. Monopolistic competition
9. Wage and price guideposts
10. Legislation

1 / Markup percentage. At all levels of business, but particularly at wholesale and retail, it is customary for sellers to arrive at their prices through the use of markup percentages. These markups are expressed as percentages either of cost or of selling prices.[1]

RETAIL PRICE MARKUP TABLE

How to Use This Table. Find the desired markup percentage based on selling price in the column at the left. Multiply the cost of the article by the corresponding percentage in the column at the right. Add this amount to the cost in order to determine the selling price.

DESIRED MARKUP PERCENTAGE (BASED ON SALES PRICE)	EQUIVALENT PERCENTAGE OF COST	DESIRED MARKUP PERCENTAGE (BASED ON SALES PRICE)	EQUIVALENT PERCENTAGE OF COST
5.0%	5.3%	20.0%	25.0%
6.0	6.4	25.0	33.3
7.0	7.5	30.0	42.9
8.0	8.7	33.3	50.0
9.0	10.0	35.0	53.9
10.0	11.1	37.5	60.0
12.5	14.3	40.0	66.7
15.0	17.7	42.8	75.0
16.7	20.0	50.0	100.0

There are two methods of using markup as a means of setting prices. One involves the use of a markup table as shown above. The other requires the use of one or more of the basic formulas shown on page 184.

[1] In the retail field there is a sharp divergence of practice in this regard. Some stores use the markup on cost, while others figure it on the retail price. Most large stores and the chains follow the retail method, whereas smaller stores adhere to the cost, and older, method. Leading retail authorities are in agreement that the retail method is the more advanced and useful of the two, although it is a trifle more difficult to apply. The advantages of the retail method lie in obviating the need for placing two sets of figures on the price tag, the selling price in dollars and cents and the cost in code; in facilitating the operating of the retail method of inventory; and in placing the markup percentage in the same terms or base as the gross margin and expense percentages, which are always expressed in terms of retail.

Formulas for Markup Calculations

(A) Cost + markup = Retail

(B) Cost = Retail − markup

(C) Markup = Retail − cost

(D) $\dfrac{\text{Markup}}{\text{Retail}}$ = Markup expressed as a percent of retail.

(E) $\dfrac{\text{Markup}}{\text{Cost}}$ = Markup expressed as a percent of cost.

If a seller wishes to translate markup as a percent of retail into a percent of cost, or vice versa, the following two formulas are useful:

(F) $\dfrac{\text{Markup as a percent of retail}}{100\% - \text{markup as a percent of retail}}$ = Markup as a percent of cost.

(G) $\dfrac{\text{Markup as a percent of cost}}{100\% + \text{markup as a percent of cost}}$ = Markup as a percent of retail.

(H) In whatever terms (cost or retail) a markup is expressed, that is the 100%. For example, if markup is 25% of retail, retail is the 100%.

(I) If a given number is expressed as more or less than 100%, the 100% is obtained by dividing the given number by the given percent. For example, if $12 is 40% of retail, 100% (or retail) is $12 ÷ 40% (.40) = $30.

A markup is supposed to cover the cost of handling the article to be priced, a portion of the firm's expenses, and a certain amount of profit. Because of the difficulty of establishing these costs accurately for individual articles, like items are grouped into classes for which costs can be discovered, and the average or group markup to establish the retail price for a single item is used. Thus, in a store using the retail price markup method and having established an average markup of 50 percent for a given merchandise group, the person setting the price for an article in the group that costs $5 per unit would arrive at $10 as the selling price of a unit, through reference to the appropriate columns in the table.

Or, if he were using the formula method:

$5 (Cost) + 50% (Markup) = 100% (Retail)

$5 = 100% − 50% or 50%

$5 ÷ .50 = $10 Retail

If this store were using the cost markup method, however, and wished to secure a retail price that would involve a markup of 50% on cost, the resulting price would be $7.50.

$5 (Cost or 100%) + 50% of Cost ($2.50) = $7.50 Retail

2 / Price lines. *Price lines* consist of a series of predetermined prices that are the only ones at which merchandise is offered for sale. For example, goods in a certain department might be offered only at $1.95, $3.95, and $5.95. No intermediate prices, such as $2.50, $3.25, or $5, would be used.

When a retailer wishes to establish price lines where they have not been used before, it is customary for him to list all of the prices that he has been using and to note the sales at each price for a period of time, say six months. He then selects those prices at which the largest number of merchandise units have been sold and discards the others, marking the goods at these rejected prices up or down to the new price lines, as the case may be.

3 / Suggested prices. Manufacturers sometimes print suggested retail prices on the containers of their products. Retailers may or may not adhere to these prices when they determine their own resale prices. Cut-rate stores frequently make a practice of pricing these goods below the prices suggested by the producers with a view to effecting a favorable price comparison. In some instances these prices are established by manufacturers who wish to maintain them under the fair trade laws.

4 / Price leadership. In any business field there may be certain acknowledged leaders who apparently set their prices without too much regard for the other members of the trade but whose price moves are rather quickly followed by their competitors. To a considerable extent the United States Steel Corporation in the steel business and the various Standard Oil companies in the field of gasoline and oil have been price leaders. The reasons for this price leadership are usually prestige, size, aggressiveness, and prominence.

Some writers have expressed the opinion that price leadership is effective only when prices are being raised, and that the action of nonprice leaders in cutting their prices will necessitate similar price reductions by the supposed leader.

5 / What the traffic will bear. Although this phrase has a rather unpleasant sound since it implies excessively high profits, it is nevertheless a rather widely used indicator of the upper limits to the prices that may be set by sellers. A seller who knows his market is aware of the price limits above which he cannot go and retain his customers. These limits cut across many of the other factors that enter into his price-determining procedures. "What the traffic will bear" reflects the attitude of the user of a product toward its value to him. Thus a special instrument that will aid a surgeon in performing a difficult operation might be worth $100 to him, even though it might cost only $15 to produce.

6 / Demand elasticity. This term refers to the effect that a change in the price for an item has on the quantity demanded. If changing the price of an article produces a significant alteration in the quantity demanded, it has *demand elasticity* or an *elastic demand*. Likewise, if a price change does not bring about a significant difference in the quantity demanded, the article has *inelasticity of demand*. The assumption is, of course, that the quantity demanded will move in the opposite direction from price. Examples of goods with demand elasticity are the items advertised as week-end specials by grocery stores, such as breakfast foods. The classic example of demand inelasticity is salt; regardless of the price of salt, people use a fixed amount.

As used by many economists, the demand elasticity concept embraces the idea of an actual change in the total demand for a product. There is, however, another aspect of this subject that is reflected in the action of consumers who switch from brand *A* of a product to brand *B* when the price of the latter is lowered. In such a circumstance the total demand for the basic product remains unchanged, but the sales of brand *B* have increased at the expense of brand *A*. This is known as *cross elasticity of demand*. Although it is probable that most retailers have never heard of these terms, they are usually quite aware of the items whose sales can be increased through price cutting and act accordingly. The weekly specials of supermarkets embody this type of selective price cutting and are illustrative of price competition at the retail level.

7 / Monopoly price. The presence of a monopoly implies the complete control of the price by the monopolist and the absence of competition. In the business world at large, there are very few pure monopolies. Those that do exist, such as the public utilities in most localities, are subject to governmental regulation to the extent that their freedom to set their prices is greatly, if not completely, curtailed. With this type of monopoly this discussion is concerned only to the extent of pointing out that prices are established or changed only with the consent of some governmental regulatory commission.

8 / Monopolistic competition. When two or more sellers of goods that satisfy the same needs or wants strive to persuade the same groups of buyers to purchase their wares, competition is said to exist. This applies to all levels of economic activity, manufacturers, wholesalers, and retailers. In the case of certain agricultural products, and possibly a few others, the fact that there is little, if any, difference between the products of different producers, places competition very largely on a strictly price basis. This situation is probably as close to the economists' concept of pure competition as is to be found in our economic system. With most other products, however, the producers are able to differentiate their products to a greater or less extent and escape the rigors of pure price competition.

The term *monopolistic competition* [2] describes competition between firms that have differentiated their products and have secured thereby certain aspects of monopoly, but which must still compete with each other for the favor of the buyers. These monopolistic characteristics may be those of location, of ingredients, of processes protected by patents, or even of trade names. For example, Ford, Chevrolet, and Plymouth engage in a spirited competitive battle in the low-priced car field. The Ford Motor Company, however, has a monopoly on the name Ford as applied to motor cars as, in turn, do the other two firms in the case of the names of their automobiles. Each maker also has a monopoly on certain features of design and construction. Thus the development of brand names and of minor differences between products are regarded as evidences of monopolistic competition in practice. Examples of this practice are to be found also in such commodity areas as cigarettes, liquid refreshments, soaps, men's clothing, and television receiving sets.

The seller who enjoys some aspects of monopoly must always remember, however, that there are very few commodities for which there are no substitutes; and if he raises his prices too high, he may cause his customers to turn to other products that may serve the same purpose.

9 / Wage and price guideposts. In the Annual Report of the Council of Economic Advisers, transmitted to the Congress in January, 1962, it was suggested, in the interest of price stability, that *wage and price guideposts* be informally established, to which future wage and price movements would presumably conform.

The general guide for noninflationary wage behavior was that the rate of increase in wage rates (including fringe benefits) in each industry be equal to the trend rate of overall productivity (output per man-hour)

---

[2] This discussion is an amplification of the topic "imperfect competition" mentioned on page 13 in Chapter 1.

increase. General acceptance of this guide would maintain stability of labor cost per unit of output for the economy as a whole—though not, of course, for individual industries. The general guide for noninflationary price behavior calls for price reduction if the industry's rate of productivity increase exceeds the overall rate, for this would mean declining unit labor costs; it calls for an appropriate increase in price if the opposite relationship prevails; and it calls for stable prices if the two rates of productivity increase are equal.[3] The overall rate of productivity increase is presently calculated at 3.2 percent. Thus a firm whose productivity increase was 3.2 percent could not raise its prices without contributing to an inflationary situation. The guidepost concept encountered considerable opposition, particularly in the area of wages. Further reference to this aspect of the guideposts will be made in Chapter 16.

10 / Legislation. In a number of instances legislation affects prices, directly or indirectly. In most cases, the purpose of these laws has been to raise prices, although the price-control plan that was in effect during the periods of World War II and the Korean War was intended to prevent prices from rising under the stress of the unbalanced supply-demand situation brought about by these conflicts. To the extent that goods to be priced come within the influence of these enactments, the seller must be governed by them when establishing his prices.

▨ State Price Legislation

The actions of the various states in regard to price legislation fall into two categories: (1) *fair trade laws,* which legalize resale price maintenance, and (2) *unfair trade laws* (with some variations on this title), which endeavor to establish minimum price levels below which goods cannot be sold.

1 / Fair trade laws. The manufacturer of a branded product may wish to prevent wholesalers and/or retailers from establishing a price on it that is lower than the price at which the manufacturer wishes it sold. For example, a producer of a branded tooth paste might wish retailers to sell it at 50 cents, whereas the retailers might prefer to price it at 39 cents.

Until the mid-1930's, there were only two methods by which a producer could control the prices at which his products were offered to the public. One of these methods was for the manufacturer to sell on consignment, whereby the producer retained title to the goods even though

---

[3] *Economic Report of the President Together with the Annual Report of the Council of Economic Advisers.* 1962.

they were actually on the retailers' shelves. General Electric light bulbs have long been handled on this basis. This method was far too costly for most manufacturers, as it involved a very large capital investment in stock in the dealers' stores.

The second method was through the execution of contracts with dealers in which the retailers agreed to maintain the prices stipulated by the manufacturer. There was, however, no compulsion in this method, as dealers were free to refuse to sign the contracts and the producer's only recourse consisted of refusal to sell to uncooperative dealers.

Acting under the authority of the various state fair trade laws, passed in most states in the 1930's, producers can execute contracts with retailers specifying the prices below which their products may not be sold. Through the *nonsigner clause* each contract becomes binding on all other retailers in the state, including those who may not have signed the contract, when due notice of its existence was given to them. The McGuire Act, a federal statute enacted in 1952, legalizes these contracts where the producers are located in different states from the retailers. The legality of the nonsigner clause in interstate commerce is uncertain, but several state courts have recently declared it to be a violation of their respective constitutions.

In Virginia in 1958 and in Ohio in 1959 a new type of fair trade law appeared that was designed to avoid the possible illegality of the nonsigner clause. Under these laws, signed contracts are unnecessary for the producers to maintain their prices. All that is required is that the manufacturers formally notify wholesalers and/or retailers of the prices that they wish maintained, and acceptance of the goods by the middlemen carries with it agreement to maintain the prices. The highest courts in both states have declared these laws constitutional. In 1965 North Dakota amended its Fair Trade Act to bring it into line with those of Virginia and Ohio.

Fair trade contracts have been executed for drugs, cosmetics, jewelry, silverware, tobacco, electrical appliances, some foods, and other items.

In the opinion of the proponents of so-called fair trade, the purpose of the laws is to prevent price cutters from putting their competitors out of business by their tactics. Opponents, however, assert that its purpose is to put an end to competition on the items affected and to raise prices to consumers needlessly. These two points of view, which have been argued at length, appear completely irreconcilable.

2 / Unfair trade laws. Unfair trade laws, operative in 28 states under such diverse titles as unfair trade practices act, unfair sales act, unfair practices act, unfair sales practices act, and fair sales act, have a common theme. Under them, sellers—producers, wholesalers, and retailers—are forbidden to sell goods at less than their cost plus, in many states, certain specified percentage markups. These laws, like the fair trade laws, are designed to prevent price cutting and have sometimes been called "anti-loss-leader" laws, since the form of price cutting against which they were ostensibly enacted has been the loss leader. Unlike the fair trade laws, however, which affect only goods bearing a producer's brand and then only if the manufacturer wishes the price maintained, the unfair trade laws apply to all products, branded or not.

Several states have similar laws applicable to specific commodities, such as cigarettes, dairy products, gasoline, bakery products, and alcoholic beverages.

■ Price Policies

Another group of items affect the setting of prices by sellers. These items, called price policies, might be regarded as the basic, underlying philosophies that sellers follow. They determine the general framework around which each seller fits his pricing structure.

The more common price policies are:

1. Low prices
2. High prices
3. Stable prices
4. Odd prices
5. Delivered prices
6. One price versus varying price
7. Discount policy

1 / Low prices. Some sellers follow the plan of having low prices for their goods. A well-known Eastern grocery chain uses the slogan "We sell for less," and the price setters in this organization are instructed to price their wares at the lowest prices consistent with the company's operating expenses and profit philosophy. From the time of their first appearance, low prices have been the principal sales appeal of the discount houses.

2 / High prices. This policy is embraced by numerous department and specialty stores, dealers in fancy groceries, and manufacturers of quality goods. In most shopping centers one or more stores carry merchandise much the same as that of their neighbors, but whose prices are noticeably higher than those of the others. In some instances these prices represent better merchandise; in others they reflect a desire to secure a higher profit per unit.

3 / Stable prices. Many, if not most, sellers follow their merchandising and operating costs rather closely in pricing their goods. Thus, when these costs go up or down, prices likewise go up or down. Opposed to this policy is the philosophy of stable prices, whereby a price, once established, tends to remain constant for long periods of time regardless of the fluctuations of the costs of the goods or of the expenses of the sellers involved. Examples of this policy are to be found in chewing gum, Coca Cola, and where the retail prices are printed on the packages.

4 / Odd prices. One school of merchandising thought holds with the idea that $2.95 is a more appealing price than $3, that 19 cents will sell more goods than 20 cents, and $99.95 is more effective than $100. The underlying theory of this policy is that $1.98 makes the prospective buyer think of $1 plus some cents, rather than of a price slightly less than $2. That this concept is widely held is apparent from an inspection of the price lines of many stores of all types. A price of 32.9 cents per gallon instead of 33 cents, commonly found in many gas stations, is an example of this policy.

5 / Delivered prices. Some manufacturers adopt the policy of establishing their prices on what is called a "delivered basis." This means that the price quoted to the seller is *f.o.b.* (free on board) *destination*. It includes all transportation costs and is the price that he must pay to take delivery of the goods at his receiving dock or the freight terminal in his city.

Opposed to this plan is the practice of quoting *f.o.b. shipping point* (or factory), that is, the seller will place the goods on a common carrier at the factory loading dock and all further transportation charges are to be paid by the buyer over and above the quoted price. The pricing of automobiles is an example of this latter policy. Some sellers located in the eastern part of the country take account of transportation costs by advertising "prices slightly higher west of the Mississippi River."

6 / One price versus varying price. Most retail pricing is of the "one price" variety, that is, the established price applies to all comers and is not subject to "higgling" by individual customers. At other sales levels, however, this policy does not always hold true. Although some manufacturers and wholesalers follow it rather rigidly, many others may lower their prices from time to time in favor of particular purchasers. This flexibility of price may come about because of the superior bargaining skill of certain buyers or because of the size of their purchases.

A varying price policy has the effect of enabling large buyers to secure lower prices than their smaller competitors. To prevent this practice from placing small buyers at too great a disadvantage, the Robinson-Patman Act of 1936 was passed by the Congress. This Act, which was in the form of an amendment to Section 2 of the Clayton Act, prohibited sellers engaged in interstate commerce from discriminating in price or terms of sale between purchasers of goods of like grade and quality; it prohibited the payment of brokerage or commissions where the recipient of the fee is subject to the control of the party to a transaction other than the one making the payment—so-called *false brokerage*; and it forbade sellers to grant advertising allowances or other services unless these concessions were available to all purchasers on "proportionately equal terms."

Although it is doubtful if this Act has forced many companies to adopt a strictly one-price policy, it has definitely limited the bases on which a varying price policy can be practiced and has served to place large and small buyers more nearly on an equal footing in the price phases of their purchasing.

7 / Discount policy. Sellers who elect to pursue a varying price policy have two principal methods by which they may put this plan into effect: (1) through simple price concessions and (2) by means of a discount policy. An example of the first method is the lowering of a price of $1.50 per unit to $1.35 A *discount* may be defined as a reduction in price made by a seller to a buyer on one or more of the following bases.

(a) TRADE DISCOUNTS. A *trade discount*, which is based on the list price of the product, recognizes the different functions performed by wholesalers and retailers. For example, if the list price, which is frequently the price charged the retail customer, is $45 and the trade discount is 33⅓ percent, the wholesaler's price to the retailer is $30.

When a *chain of discounts* is granted by the seller to the buyer, the list price is followed by several trade discounts, which are customarily applied in turn to an ever-lessening figure. For example, an invoice for $100; less 40%, 10%, and 5%, would be figured as follows: $100 — $40 (40% of $100) = $60; $60 — $6 (10% of $60) = $54; $54 — $2.70 (5% of $54) = $51.30, which is the net amount paid by the buyer. This method is used by sellers who desire to discriminate legitimately between their customers by granting or withholding one or more of the discounts in the chain. It also permits them to change their prices by adding or subtracting a discount, without the necessity of reprinting their price lists each time such a price change becomes necessary.

(b) QUANTITY DISCOUNTS. A *quantity discount* is offered by some sellers as a reward to buyers who order in large quantities. Presumably the large sales under this policy save the vendors storage, packing, and perhaps transportation charges. Quantity discounts may either be cumulative or noncumulative in character. Cumulative quantity discounts permit buyers to utilize two or more separate purchases in the computation of the quantities to which discounts may apply, whereas the noncumulative type is applicable only to single purchases. Thus, if a seller offered a 10 percent quantity discount for orders of 100 units or more, with the cumulative type the buyer would qualify with purchases of 25, 35, 25, and 15 units each, whereas with the noncumulative he would be obliged to purchase at least 100 units in a single order. Noncumulative quantity discounts are permissible under the Robinson-Patman Act provided the seller bases the discount on some demonstrable savings that were achieved because of the quantities of goods involved in a sale.

(c) CASH DISCOUNTS. A *cash discount* differs somewhat from the foregoing group in that it is given neither as a reward for large purchases nor in recognition of differences in functions performed. It is simply an inducement offered by the seller to encourage the buyer to pay his bill within a short time after the goods have been delivered. The cash discount takes many forms, the most common of which is 2/10, net/30; that is, if the invoice is paid within 10 days after its date, the buyer may deduct 2 percent of the amount of the invoice in making his remittance; and if the buyer elects not to pay the bill within the 10 days, he has 20 additional days in which to pay the full amount before the invoice becomes overdue. In some lines of business, notably apparel, cash discount rates run up as high as 6 percent and 8 percent. Unlike some of the other discount types, cash discounts are usually available to all the customers of a seller.

None of the above discounts is usually available to ultimate consumers, except in those instances where public utilities permit cash discounts if their bills are paid by a specified due date.

▣ Markdowns

A type of formal price reduction that differs somewhat from a discount is the *markdown*. In this instance, for any one of several reasons, sellers, usually retailers, reduce the price of an item either on a temporary or permanent basis. The most common types of markdowns and the reasons for them follow: (1) promotional, which are designed to attract customers for a brief period of time, after which the price is marked up to its original level; (2) competitive, which are made to meet the lower price of a competitor and which may or may not be permanent; (3) clearance, the objective of which is to rid the stock of the merchandise affected; (4) employee discounts, which customarily involve the giving of lower prices to the store's employees; (5) breakage, which reduces the value of damaged merchandise, often to zero. In the interest of accurate accounting for a store's operations, intelligent managerial operating methods require that all markdowns including, when necessary, the full sales price of articles broken or stolen, be recorded.

■ Price in Relation to Supply and Demand

For a competitive situation, economists have advanced several theories to explain how the price of any given commodity is set, the movement of prices, and why the price level is where it is at any one time. The *equilibrium theory of prices,* which probably has the largest number of adherents among economists, assumes that two forces operate in the field of price—supply and demand. These forces bring about a price at which the quantity demanded by buyers equals the quantity that sellers are willing to supply. Some of the units of the commodity that are necessary to make up this quantity are produced by those whose costs of production are so high that they make little or no profit, but who decide, nevertheless, to remain in business.

The theory further assumes that if the current price for a commodity is found to be above the theoretical equilibrium point, two things will happen, both of which will force the price downward: (a) the higher price will discourage would-be buyers, thereby reducing the quantity demanded; and (b) the opportunity for profits afforded by the higher price will attract new producers into the field, whose added products will increase the quantity supplied. The effect of this reduced demand and increased supply will be to reduce the price, probably below the equilibrium point. When this takes place, the results are the reverse of the condition just described: (a) the lowered price attracts buyers, increasing the quantity demanded; and (b) the diminished profits, which then occur, force some high-cost producers to leave the field, thereby reducing the quantity supplied. This brings about an upward movement of price toward the equilibrium point.

The chart on page 195 portrays a graphic representation of the operation of the equilibrium theory. Curve *D-D'* represents the quantities of the product that could be sold at the various price levels. Curve *S-S'* represents the quantities that sellers would be willing to supply at the different price levels. Point *P,* their intersection, portrays the point of equilibrium where demand and supply are equal.

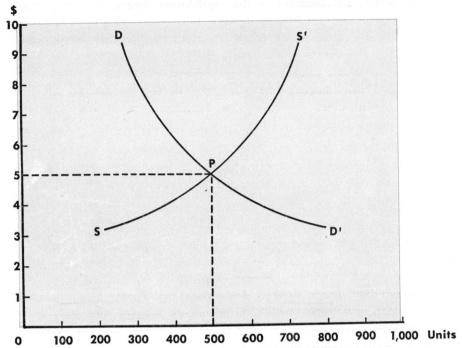

At a price of $5, 500 units would be demanded, and supply and demand would be in equilibrium.

1 / Assumptions in the equilibrium theory. The equilibrium theory is probably the explanation most widely accepted by economists of what takes place in a competitive price situation and is based on the following assumptions:

(a) COMPLETE HOMOGENEITY OF PRODUCT. According to this assumption, there is no difference between one producer's product of any given commodity and another producer's product of that same commodity.

(b) PURCHASES ONLY ON THE BASIS OF PRICE. According to this assumption, buyers do not purchase because of whim, caprice, or prejudice, but solely on the basis of the lowest price offered.

(c) COMPLETE KNOWLEDGE OF MARKET CONDITIONS. These conditions include a knowledge of supply, demand, and price on the part of both buyers and sellers.

(d) ABSOLUTE FREEDOM OF COMPETITION. Pure competition assumes the presence of the three preceding conditions.

2 / Factors not included in the equilibrium theory. Certain circumstances that are to be found in business today are excluded by the equilibrium theory. Some of the more important of these are listed below:

(a) OTHER FACTORS INFLUENCING PURCHASES. Factors other than price that influence purchases include quality, service, vendors' prestige, and chance.

(b) MONOPOLIES AND QUASI MONOPOLIES. Although there are comparatively few pure monopolies in our economic system, many firms enjoy certain aspects of monopoly because of location, control of sources of raw material, and rights protected by patent, copyright, and trademark laws.

(c) PRICE-FIXING BY PRIVATE AGREEMENTS. Private agreements may be illegal, but they sometimes remain in force for long periods of time before they are detected.

(d) BRAND INFLUENCES. These cause many consumers to demand the products of certain manufacturers merely because they have come to prefer these brands without much regard to the value of competing brands. Thus a housewife may insist on a certain soap, tooth paste, or hair shampoo because advertising has convinced her that they are the only satisfactory products on the market.

(c) THE ONE-PRICE SYSTEM. The *one-price system* prevails in most retail stores where the price of an article is determined by the storekeeper, is customarily displayed on or near the goods, and is not subject to bargaining by the customers. Customers must either pay the established price or go without the article.

(f) CONSUMER INDIFFERENCE. This indifference is manifested by the failure of consumers to give heed to informative labeling or advertising, to employ rational buying motives when making purchases, or to bother to inform themselves concerning the prices of competing stores on certain identical items. It is a fairly common practice for two or more competing stores to offer eggs of the same grade at different prices, and for some consumers to buy the high-priced ones.

■ Concepts of Supply and Demand

Despite the factors that are excluded from the equilibrium price theory, it sets forth the basic elements in competitive pricing. In the absence of restraining factors, such as wartime price controls or governmentally supported prices for certain agricultural products, prices tend to rise when demand exceeds supply, and to fall when the reverse is true. In the industrial goods field, and in consumer goods at other than the retail level, considerable bargaining takes place before sales are consummated.

At the retail level, however, the long-established one-price system probably has tended to prevent the demand side of the demand-supply equation from being as effective as it is at other sales levels. It is true, as a general rule, that raising the prices of many articles at retail will result in fewer units of the goods being sold. There are many exceptions to this situation, however, and so many other factors than price that influence consumers in their buying that the weight of demand in the price-determining process at the retail sales level is considerably less than in wholesale transactions. For example, the influence that advertising exerts on consumers in endeavoring to convince them of the advantages of one brand of goods over competing brands is undoubtedly a factor in inducing them to pay more for certain products than they might if advertising were not present in the picture. Brand loyalty on the part of consumers also appears to blind them to the possibility that lower-priced items of approximately the same value are available in the market.

The term *cost-price relationship* has appeared with increasing frequency in the trade and public press and occasionally in the halls of Congress. While often used by sellers in a rebuttal to the charge that their prices are too high, it has served to emphasize a well-known economic axiom, namely, that if overall costs are increased without a corresponding increase in productivity, the result will be an increase in unit costs. This, in turn, will bring about either an increase in the unit price or a decrease in the unit profit. In endeavoring to justify their increased prices, many sellers have claimed that their costs, especially their labor costs, have increased more rapidly than has their productivity. The labor unions have sought to combat these statements in various ways, which have included a criticism of the sellers' methods of determining productivity.

1 / Elements affecting prices sought by sellers. When a seller undertakes to establish the price at which he hopes to sell his wares, he takes the following elements into account:

(a) COST OF THE GOODS. If the seller is a manufacturer, his costs will include not only the costs of manufacture, both direct and overhead, but also his cost of selling. If the seller is a wholesaler or a retailer, he will consider how much he paid for the goods originally, together with his costs of doing business.

(b) PROFIT PHILOSOPHY. Sellers tend to embrace one of two profit philosophies. Either they seek a high profit per unit of goods sold, with relatively higher prices and with a presumed restricted sales volume, or they accept a lower unit profit, with comparatively low prices and an implied high volume of sales. There are, of course, a large number of possible gradations of position between these two extremes.

(c) SELLER'S ATTITUDE TOWARD COMPETITION. At all levels of trade, but particularly at retail, some sellers pay little attention to the prices of their competitors and rely on other appeals to sell their goods. Certain department and specialty stores are adherents of this pricing philosophy. On the other hand, some sellers will not be undersold by their competitors on identical or similar merchandise. A third type follows the practice of always being below the prices of its competitors.

(d) GENERAL OR LOCAL BUSINESS CONDITIONS. A factor that must always influence a seller in determining his price is the state of general or local business conditions, whether good or bad. This is a complicated matter that cannot be expounded here; but the effect, as far as price-setting is concerned, is that during bad times a seller will set his prices with greater regard for competition and, perhaps, at figures that include lower unit profits than during good times.

2 / Elements involved in the prices buyers are willing to pay. Buyers approach their prospective purchase transactions with rather definite ideas as to how much they are willing to pay and often with sharply defined upper limits beyond which they will refuse to go. The factors that influence the buyers in arriving at these conclusions with regard to the prices that they will pay are:

(a) CONSUMER'S PERSONAL ECONOMIC STATUS. Constantly underlying the attitude of every consumer toward prices is his personal economic status. In other words, the poor man's outlook toward a purchase transaction is different from that of a well-to-do or a rich man.

A variant on this concept is the consumer's appraisal of his future economic status, his beliefs regarding the probable permanence of his job and, for an older person, whether or not he expects to receive a pension upon retirement. Thus the consumer's attitude is conditioned not only by present but also by possible future conditions.

(b) CONSUMER'S SUBJECTIVE VALUE REACTIONS. In every consumer's mind, when he decides to make a purchase, is the idea that any given item of merchandise is worth just so much to him. The value thus approximated may or may not bear a close relationship to the price being asked for that item. If it is close, the purchase will probably be made; if it is not, the consumer may refrain from buying at the time.

(c) EFFECT OF ADVERTISING OR SALES EFFORTS OF SELLERS. Advertising and the sales efforts of sellers tend to create in the mind of the consumer an uncritical attitude toward prices. Consumer preference is created for certain brand names on a wide variety of bases, such as service, prestige, and pride of ownership. The result is that the consumer approaches the purchase of these goods with price as a secondary consideration.

(d) BUYER'S KNOWLEDGE OF HIS RESALE MARKET. This factor and the one following (condition of the supply market) apply principally to the buyer who purchases goods for resale, either in their present state or altered in some way. Examples of such buyers include the wholesale or retail buyers who buy apparel for resale to their respective customers, and the industrial purchasing agents who buy steel sheets, for example, to be formed and fabricated into automobile bodies.

In instances such as these, the buyers usually have rather clear ideas concerning the prices that their customers will pay for the goods that they are about to purchase or make. Hence their attitudes toward the prices that they are willing to pay are customarily well formulated and frequently committed to writing in advance of the buying situation. Industrial purchasing agents are often not permitted to pay more than certain prices for the items that they buy.

(e) CONDITION OF THE SUPPLY MARKET. This factor applies to the prices that buyers will offer with the same force that it applies to prices that sellers seek. When supplies are short, prices tend to rise and, when the market is oversupplied, they tend to fall. This is also true of the consumer market.

■ Nonprice Competition

At the retail level of distribution, particularly, sellers often stress some factors other than that of price in their appeals for consumer purchase of their products. Substituted for price are style, satisfaction, durability, prestige, taste, service, reliability, and many others. This is known as *nonprice competition.* Where fair trade or unfair practices laws are in force, the establishing of floors below which prices may not go more or less automatically de-emphasizes prices as a competitive weapon and turns the consumer's attention to some other aspect of competition. Some critics of nonprice competition believe that it results in a watered-down competitive situation, while advocates of the practice feel that it places competition on a higher plane than price and directs the consumer's attention to all of the satisfaction-producing aspects of competing goods.

■ Price Developments

The chart below illustrates the trend of consumer prices since 1958. With the price level of 1957-59 taken as 100, the changes since then indicate the gradual upward movement of consumer prices of all items and show the preponderant influence of services on this trend. During this same period, wholesale prices maintained a much greater degree of stability.

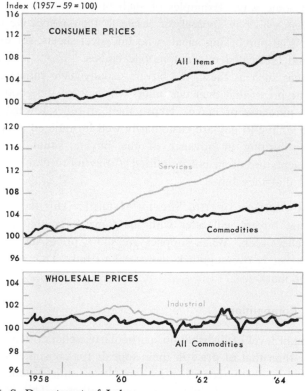

Source: U. S. Department of Labor.

Price Developments

BUSINESS TERMS

(a) barter (181), prices (181)
(b) administered prices (182); joint cost (182); casual sale (182)
(c) price lines (185)
(d) demand elasticity or elastic demand (186), inelasticity of demand (186), cross elasticity of demand (186)
(e) monopolistic competition (187)
(f) wage and price guideposts (187)
(g) fair trade laws (188), unfair trade laws (188), nonsigner clause (189)
(h) f.o.b. destination (191), f.o.b. shipping point (191)
(i) false brokerage (192)
(j) discount (192), trade discount (192), chain of discounts (192), quantity discount (193), cash discount (193)
(k) markdown (193)
(l) equilibrium theory of prices (194), one-price system (196)
(m) cost-price relationship (197)
(n) nonprice competition (199)

QUESTIONS FOR DISCUSSION AND ANALYSIS

1. Do you think that capitalism would have evolved in this country without a price system? Explain.
2. Some critics of business methods believe that administered pricing indicates that price competition is absent. Do you agree? Support your stand.
3. Do you believe that a manufacturer could consistently follow the practice of placing falsely high prices on his goods so as to permit retailers to appear to cut them, as has been alleged? Discuss.
4. Do you think that the presence of price leadership in an industry is indicative of price collusion among the producers? Explain.
5. Is the degree of demand elasticity for a product subject to accurate measurement? Why?
6. How would you define the public interest in regard to the pricing of products?
7. Do you believe that the main purpose of the fair trade laws is to raise prices to consumers? Discuss.
8. Should retailers be prohibited from cutting prices on such items as cigarettes, wines, liquors, and gasoline? Why?
9. Do you believe that odd prices sell more goods than would be sold at the next higher price lines, e.g., $1.95 vs. $2? Explain.
10. Do you think that the one-price system prevalent at the retail level causes generally higher prices for customers than if it did not exist? Why?

PROBLEMS AND SHORT CASES

1. (a) A department store buys $800 worth of merchandise, terms 6/10, net 30. The invoice is dated August 19 and is paid on August 28. How much is remitted to the seller?

   (b) A retailer buys some merchandise for $750, with trade discounts of 35%, 15%, and 5%. How much do the goods cost him?

2. Using the formulas on page 184 that are applicable, compute the answers to the following markup problems:

   (a) Markup on cost 25%, cost $8; find retail.

   (b) Markup on cost 40%, retail $4.20; find cost.

   (c) Markup on retail 30%, cost $6.30; find retail.

   (d) Markup on retail 45%, retail $20; find cost.

3. Justin and Knowles, Inc., is a long-established producer of machinery and equipment that is used in a number of different industries. The company is practically unknown to the public. Recently it has acquired a patent that covers the manufacture of a power lawn mower, which can be converted into an instrument for removing snow from sidewalks and driveways. The key to this new product is a solar-powered battery that derives its power from exposure to sunlight. Aside from this feature the mower is about the same as a gasoline or or electric-powered machine. From its research the company believes that its solar-powered mower can be offered on the market at a price competitive with other types of power mowers. The problem facing the company is whether to price its product competitively, which would allow wholesalers and retailers markups equivalent to those received on other mowers, or to set its price somewhat higher, so that the higher markup available will induce dealers to push the product. The company is also considering the advisability of placing its mower under fair trade, in order to avoid any price cutting with resulting lowering of dealers' profit margins.

   Advise the company on the pricing problems in these two areas, giving reasons for your conclusions.

SUGGESTED READINGS

Converse, P. D., and Others. *Elements of Marketing,* Seventh Edition. Englewood Cliffs, New Jersey: Prentice-Hall, Inc., 1965. Chapters 10, 11, and 28.

Davis, K. R. *Marketing Management,* Second Edition. New York: The Ronald Press Co., 1966. Chapters 18 and 19.

Hailstones, T. J., and J. H. Dodd. *Economics: An Analysis of Principles and Policies,* Fifth Edition. Cincinnati: South-Western Publishing Company, 1965. Chapters 6, 7, and 12.

Harper, D. V. *Price Policy and Procedure.* New York: Harcourt, Brace & World, Inc., 1966.

Chapter 10

ADVERTISING PROBLEMS

The Definitions Committee of the American Marketing Association defines *advertising* as "any paid form of nonpersonal presentation and promotion of ideas, goods, or services by an identified sponsor." Another definition, which reflects some of the latest thinking in this area, is "advertising is constructive communication with consumers." This latter definition embraces the concept that advertisers should endeavor to make a purposeful contact with consumers. This circumstance is mutually beneficial in that consumers are informed of the availability of goods for which they have a need and the advertisers secure a profit through providing these goods. It also assumes that the advertising appears in the right media, with the right appeals, at the right times, at the right prices, for the consumers whose needs will be best satisfied by the goods involved. Advertising has been called "the voice of business," which is an appropriate characterization, for it is the means by which firms inform the public of the excellence and desirability of their products, and also set forth their positions on matters dealing with economics, politics, or public relations.

◼ The Relationship of Advertising to Selling

Under our capitalistic system, when goods have been produced, they move into the channels of distribution and thence to the industrial or ultimate consumers through the selling process; that is, those who have goods to sell endeavor to locate possible buyers, to inform them of the availability of these wares, and to persuade them to buy. There are two elements in the sales process: personal selling, in which salesmen participate, and advertising, which has been called impersonal selling.

Manufacturers and wholesalers customarily send out salesmen to contact their prospective customers—industrial buyers, wholesalers, or retailers. As a means of assisting their salesmen, they may advertise to acquaint buyers with their goods and to augment the efforts of their sales representatives.

As a general rule, retailers depend mainly on advertising to secure their customers. Hence, retail advertising must not only tell consumers about the merchandise that the stores have for sale, but it must also impel them to visit the stores and seek out the goods that have been advertised.

The phenomenal expansion in recent years of self-service in food, drug, and variety-store retailing has emphasized the selling aspects of advertising in these commodity areas. The absence of salespeople, among whose duties has been that of suggesting items of merchandise to customers, has placed the burden of arousing interest in goods on advertising and, within the limits of available store space, particularly on the medium of store display. The advertising of self-service stores and of the manufacturers of the goods sold in them has been affected to a considerable degree by this circumstance.

■ Types of Advertising

The two basic types of advertising are commodity and institutional. *Commodity advertising* is designed to sell one or more definite, identified commodities, and usually it describes and extols their good qualities or satisfaction-giving features, or their prices.

Within the general category of commodity advertising are several subtypes. (1) *Primary advertising* is intended to stimulate an interest in and a desire for a certain class of goods, particularly some new type of product that has just come on the market, or in which the public has yet to manifest any appreciable interest. The advertising of color TV receivers has been of this kind. (2) *Selective advertising* is supposed to impel consumers toward the purchase of a particular brand of goods, such as a Ford Mustang or a pair of Nettleton shoes. It is quite common to find primary and selective advertising in the same advertisement. (3) *Mass advertising* is advertising that appeals to a cross section of the populace. (4) *Class advertising*, on the other hand, is directed at special groups of people, such as newly married couples, golfers, or college students. (5) *Publicity* is information about a product that is supplied to the advertising media, usually newspapers or magazines, by the producer, which the publisher may or may not use. It usually appears in editorial or news form and frequently does not include the name of the maker. Publicity is not paid for by the manufacturer of the goods.

A type of commodity advertising that cuts across the first four types just mentioned is known as *name advertising*. This type occurs where the nature of the product, its ingredients, the manner in which it is used, the product benefits to be expected, or the fact that it is very well known to the public suggests the desirability of advertising its name, with non-technical copy, often in an attractive setting. Name advertising is commonly employed for cigarettes, soft drinks, aspirin, alcoholic beverages, and cosmetics.

Institutional advertising is created for the purpose of getting some message across to the public, which may or may not be closely related to the sale of any particular merchandise. By means of institutional advertising a firm may announce a change in location, the adoption of a new policy, the acquirement of a new line of goods, or anything else that might be of general interest to their customers. Institutional advertising is sometimes referred to as nonproduct advertising.

Another form of institutional advertising exists when several advertisers issue a joint advertisement for the benefit of all of them. Advertisements of this sort may be devoted to trying to sell goods or merely to promoting ideas. The advertisements of the Association of American Railroads, the American Gas Association, and the American Institute of Laundering are examples of group institutional advertising.

■ Types of Advertising Media

Of paramount importance to advertisers is the selection of the media that will carry their advertising. The term *media*, which is commonly used in the advertising world, refers to the different types of vehicles or devices by which advertising reaches its audience. These include the following:

1. Newspapers
2. Magazines
3. Radio
4. Television
5. Direct mail
6. Outdoor
7. Transportation
8. Business papers
9. Other media

In the discussion of media types that follows, four of the bases of comparison that will be utilized require some preliminary explanation. They are: (a) *geographic selectivity,* which refers to the ability of a medium to deliver the advertiser's message to a particular geographic area, such as a designated city or metropolitan community; (b) *interest selectivity,* which means the capacity of a medium to deliver the advertiser's message more or less exclusively to groups of consumers who would presumably be interested in the product being advertised, such as homeowners for room air conditioners or farmers for tractors; (c) *flexibility*, which refers to the ability of the advertiser to change his message, if need be, a relatively short time before the advertisement is to appear; and (d) the *identity of the audience*, which means the extent to which the names, addresses, and pertinent characteristics are known to the media.

The following table presents a list of the 10 leading national advertisers in 1965. The media included are magazines, network television, spot television, network radio, spot radio, newspapers, farm publications, business publications, and outdoor.

Top Ten National Advertisers of 1965 in Major Media

1. Procter & Gamble Co.	$177,640,876
2. General Motors Corp.	148,003,459
3. Bristol-Myers Co.	100,228,408
4. General Foods Corp.	88,821,685
5. Ford Motor Co.	88,495,005
6. Colgate-Palmolive Co.	82,042,178
7. Chrysler Corp.	72,273,322
8. R. J. Reynolds Tobacco Co.	69,825,109
9. American Home Products Corp.	69,478,212
10. Lever Bros. Co.	66,600,269

Reprinted with permission from *Advertising Age,* June 27, 1966. Copyright 1966 by *Advertising Age.*

1 / Newspapers. The daily and, in smaller communities, weekly newspapers are exceedingly useful media for certain kinds of advertising. They have a high circulation, relative to the number of people who might see them, and their readers are usually concentrated in a comparatively small area.

Newspapers are especially effective in carrying the advertisements of local merchants who wish to reach all parts of the cities concerned. Department stores, specialty stores, and food and drug chains commonly use newspapers to good advantage. In large cities, however, small stores whose patronage is limited to customers from surrounding residential areas usually find the cost of metropolitan newspaper advertising too great and the coverage too extensive. Community newspapers, usually published weekly, are used quite frequently by these small stores.

National advertisers find newspapers an excellent way to secure local coverage and to tie in their messages with the sales efforts of their dealers in the community.

Newspapers are quite selective from a geographical standpoint because through them it is possible for an advertiser to pin-point his advertising to the metropolitan areas that he wishes to reach. From the standpoint of interest selectivity or ability to reach special groups, newspapers reach all economic and social levels of the people and have a general, rather than a special, appeal. Most papers, however, contain specially edited sections, such as sports, the women's page, school news, and church notices, which may help the advertiser with a message for consumers interested in such topics.

A favorable characteristic of newspaper advertising is its flexibility or timeliness. In most cases, changes in advertising copy can be made up to within a few hours of the time the paper goes to press. This permits advertisers to follow national or local events, the weather, or changes in their own internal situations with great speed. It is even possible in times of great urgency to alter advertising insertions between editions.

With the daily newspapers, a substantial portion of their readers are known through their home-delivery lists. Somewhat less is known about those who purchase their papers at newsstands or vending machines. Many daily papers maintain research departments that endeavor to classify their known readers on the bases of income, education, religion, age, and many other characteristics that are useful for advertisers to know.

2 / Magazines. Since America has a large number of magazine readers, magazines constitute a very important advertising medium for many classes of advertisers. For the advertisers with nationwide distribution, the fact that most magazines have countrywide coverage makes these media singularly advantageous. For advertisers with a more limited geographic distribution of their goods, regional editions of many magazines provide access to these smaller markets, without requiring them to pay for circulation in the areas where their products are not sold. Among the magazines of general editorial interest, *Life, Look,* and *Reader's Digest* offer regional editions; while the *Saturday Evening Post,* under its *Select-a-Market* scheme, permits an advertiser to direct his advertising to those areas where his product is for sale.

As regards interest selectivity, the general editorial group, including those just mentioned, reach groups of rather divergent interests and are, therefore, effective media for products with a wide appeal. Most others, however, are consciously directed toward readers who are included in rather specifically defined interest groups. In this class of magazines are those appealing to farmers, women, young people, homemakers, and the various trade journals. Magazines in the last group circulate only within the trades affected, such as groceries, drugs, and metals.

Magazine advertising is not flexible, in that the lapse of time between the deadlines for advertising copy and the public appearance of the issues is so great as to incur the risk that the themes of the insertions may be out of date by the time they reach the readers. Many magazine publishers require that the completed copy for advertisements be submitted from four to six weeks before the time that they will reach the newsstands or the homes of subscribers. This situation makes it rather difficult for national advertisers to tie up their advertising with unscheduled but important events, such as international crises, unseasonal weather, or sudden changes in the economic life of the nation.

As with newspapers, magazines have their subscription lists, which are classified according to the pertinent factors involved and which reveal important information for advertisers.

3 / Radio. Established as a major medium for advertising in the late 1920's, radio maintained a very satisfactory position among competing media until the advent of television in the immediate post-World War II years. Since then, it has suffered to some extent. This has been particularly true of network radio. Local or *spot radio*, on the other hand, has held up remarkably well and appears to be capable of continuing as a profitable advertising medium both for station owners and advertisers. Its effectiveness, however, appears to be greater during the daylight hours than at night when television commands the larger audience.

Radio is an excellent medium for territorial selectivity because an advertiser can select just those stations that broadcast into the areas that he wishes to reach. For any radio station, the outer limits of its listening audience can be determined quite accurately. This may differ somewhat at night from the daytime, but research has defined the territorial coverage for most stations in a rather convincing fashion.

Interest selectivity, on the other hand, is somewhat less certain because the make-up of the listener group for any one program cannot be ascertained with any great degree of accuracy. Advertisers customarily assume that listeners of various types will be attracted to programs that offer entertainment of the sort that will appeal to them—for example, sports broadcasts for men. There is always the possibility, however, that the people to whom their programs are directed may be listening to other radio stations or may not even have their radios turned on. This makes for considerable uncertainty in determining the character and extent of the audience for any one program. In recent years, the adoption of FM (frequency modulation) radio transmission, which features a minimum of background noise or static, by an increasing number of stations that feature principally music, has apparently resulted in attracting a large number of music-loving listeners.

Radio advertising is exceedingly flexible because it is possible to effect changes in the copy even while a program is in progress, if such a thing should become necessary. This permits advertisers to capitalize to the fullest possible extent on sudden events to which they may wish to tie in their messages.

Except for such information as might be secured through research into radio listening and letters to the stations, relatively little is known about the identity of the listening audience. This is especially true with regard to those who listen to their car radios, since no satisfactory method has been devised to contact them.

Radio is a form of advertising that relies on sound to deliver its story. Unlike many of the other media, where the printed message may be accessible for varying lengths of time with the chance that it will be seen more than once and thus acquire the advantage of repetition, the *radio commercial*, as it is called in the trade, must be heard when it is spoken or sung, or it is forever lost. Furthermore, if a listener is tuned in to one program, he can hear none of the others that are broadcast at the same time, and they are lost to him forever unless he learns of them from others. In an attempt to overcome this situation, the so-called *spot announcement* has come into being, whereby short, frequently recorded commercials are given on many different stations in the time between programs. These announcements also occur during *station breaks*, which are for the purpose of permitting the stations to identify themselves. These same conditions and practices apply to television.

4 / Television. This medium, the newest one in advertising, has assumed a most important place. While still behind newspapers in percentage of total advertising, it has passed direct mail, magazines, and radio. The combination of the spoken word and the visual presentation of products and their benefits, which television offers, has been most intriguing and alluring to many advertisers. The extension of color TV and the further usage of ultra-high frequency program transmission and reception should add to the stature of television as an advertising medium.

Two factors have arisen, however, that could conceivably affect the willingness of advertisers to use television. The first is the very high cost of television programs, which tends to discourage advertisers with limited budgets. The second is the uncertainty of a reliable pattern of consumer use of television receiving sets. Unlike radio, which requires only part of the listeners' attention, television demands that viewers concentrate solely upon it; they must cease all or most other activities at the time. The weight of accumulated evidence appears to indicate that viewers will scan the program announcements quite carefully and select only those programs that appeal to them, leaving their sets turned off the rest of the time. There is some doubt, however, in the minds of many advertisers regarding the exposure of viewers to the commercial announcements. There is evidence that many viewers do not remain in their chairs during these intervals, but take advantage of these breaks to perform various household chores, such as preparing snacks and liquid refreshments, returning to their viewing at the conclusion of the commercials.

The matters of geographic and interest selectivity, flexibility, and identity of the audience are essentially the same for television as for radio.

5 / Direct mail. This widely used advertising medium takes on a number of different forms. Postcards, letters, catalogs, folders, and booklets are commonly used. Direct mail can be used by any advertiser, large or small, because of the wide variability of its coverage. Mail may be sent to a few prospects in a single neighborhood or to millions of persons located in all parts of the country.

The basis of all direct-mail advertising is the mailing list. Lists may be compiled from a variety of sources and may be classified almost endlessly. It is most important that the lists be assembled with the utmost care and that they be kept up to date. Through the manipulation of the list, direct-mail advertising can be made extremely selective, regarding both geographical location and consumer interests. Depending somewhat upon the elaborateness of the copy, this medium can be changed rather quickly in accordance with important events; and of course any copy can be changed or discarded entirely up to the time that the mailing is effected. Audience identity is a function of the care and accuracy with which the mailing lists are compiled and kept current.

6 / Outdoor advertising. This medium—utilizing either paper posters, painted bulletins, or electrically illuminated displays—is one of the older forms of advertising. It is available to almost any type of business, from the largest to the smallest, through the utilization of a large number of posters down to a single one. Outdoor advertising is directed at people who are outside of their homes or offices and are presumably bound on some sort of errand, business or social. Many, if not most of these people, will be riding in automobiles; therefore, the time that each reader is exposed to the advertising is necessarily brief. For this reason, the amount of subject matter that can be placed on a poster is limited. The most satisfactory results are achieved with trade names, slogans, and pictures of the products in use. Certain very elaborate and costly displays, known as *spectaculars*, may command sufficient attention to permit the use of relatively long advertising messages. The size of spectaculars and their intricacy, brilliant illumination, and location enable them to attract large audiences of passers-by. Examples of spectaculars are to be found in most large cities; Times Square in New York City is specially notable in this regard.

Outdoor advertising is quite selective, particularly in terms of geographic coverage. The ability of an advertiser to reach any locality that he wishes is limited largely by the availability of sites. As far as interest selectivity is concerned, outdoor advertising is effective only insofar as particular groups are located near, or pass by, the places where the advertising is displayed. The Traffic Audit Bureau, a research organization, conducts traffic counts at selected billboard sites to evaluate the passing auto traffic both qualitatively and quantitatively.

The flexibility of outdoor advertising is determined by the time required to reprint or repaint those displays that are out of date. Since this may take several days or weeks, there is always the chance that some event may take place which will make the selling theme obsolete. Because of the nature of this medium, name advertising is predominant.

The Highway Beautification Act of 1965 provides for control of outdoor advertising in areas adjacent to the Interstate Highway System and the primary system, which includes state roads and streets that receive federal aid for their construction and maintenance. The basic purpose of this legislation is to limit the number, lighting, and spacing of advertising within 660 feet of the nearest edge adjacent to the highway systems.

7 / **Transportation advertising.** In street cars, buses, subways, and commuters' railroad cars, *car cards* are used where they may be seen by people on their way to and from work and on shopping trips. Transportation advertising is used for all types of advertisers—national, regional, or local. By a judicious selection of the routes to be employed, even small merchants who draw their trade from single communities in the large cities have been able to utilize this medium advantageously. Transportation advertising is selective only to the extent that it reaches the riders in a given locality or with similar interests. Its flexibility approximates that of outdoor advertising.

8 / Business papers.   The term *business papers* is applied to a considerable number of trade, industrial, and professional magazines and newspapers that circulate only among businessmen and that are useful in advertising industrial or business goods and services.   Prominent among business papers are *American Machinest, Metalworking Manufacturing, Aviation Week & Space Technology, Chemical Engineering, Coal Age, Factory, Industrial Distribution, National Petroleum News,* and *Textile World.*

9 / Other media.   Other advertising media include store displays, packages, sampling, catalogs, and advertising specialities.

All stores feature merchandise displays to some extent, ranging from the artistically appealing show windows and interior displays of department and specialty stores to the crudely assembled piles of unassorted goods to be seen in some of the smaller neighborhood shops.   Many manufacturers provide store displays for their dealers, often requiring their salesmen to set them up to assure their being used.

Most manufacturers utilize the exterior of the packages in which their goods are enclosed for brief advertising messages.   They may use inserts, describing and praising their wares.   Labels are also used to carry short selling messages.   The use of packages and store displays is called *point-of-purchase advertising.*

Another form of advertising that has been used with some effectiveness is merchandise sampling.   Crews of distributors go from house to house, leaving either small samples of the products being advertised or coupons that can be redeemed at the local stores.   Sometimes a combination of these two methods is used.   In most instances, sampling is confined to food, candy, and detergents.

Catalogs are rather widely used in advertising industrial or business goods.   In fact, many producers of these items confine their advertising efforts to this type of medium.   Two outstanding examples of catalog advertisers are the mail-order catalogs of Sears, Roebuck and Company and Montgomery Ward and Company, which have long been published on a semiannual basis by these two firms.   As a general rule, however, sellers of consumer goods use catalogs to a lesser extent than do those of industrial goods.

Advertising specialties consist of a large number of different items that are useful in carrying an advertiser's name or a brief sales message. Among these are calendars, match folders, ash trays, bottle openers, pencils, ballpoint pens, key tags, blotters, coin purses, emery boards, and rulers.

■ Volume of Advertising

The table below presents an authoritative estimate of the advertising volume for 1965. A completely accurate statement of the dollar volume of advertising in this country cannot be secured, however, because of the lack of reliable data concerning such advertising types as circulars, small newspapers, and some kinds of direct mail. The table is adequate, however, for the purpose of observing the relative standing of the various media that are used.

Dollar Volume of Advertising in the United States
by Medium in 1965
(Millions of Dollars)

MEDIUM	DOLLAR VOLUME	PERCENT OF TOTAL
Newspapers	$ 4,456.5	29.2
Magazines	1,198.8	7.9
Television	2,522.0	16.6
Radio	890.0	5.8
Farm Magazines (Regional)	33.5	0.2
Direct Mail	2,324.0	15.2
Business Papers	671.0	4.4
Outdoor	180.0	1.2
Transit	32.9	0.2
Miscellaneous	2,946.3	19.3
Total	$15,255.0	100.0

Reprinted from *Printers' Ink,* August 12, 1966. Copyright 1966 by Printers' Ink Publishing Corp.

■ Is Advertising Effective?

Without doubt, advertising is effective, that is, it helps to sell goods. The answer to the question, however, is not so simple as that. It resolves itself into weighing the effectiveness of one medium against another, of one type of television program compared with another, of one advertising theme against another, and many other equally pertinent questions.

To discover the answers to some of these problems, the practice of testing advertising effectiveness has developed. Many methods of testing are in common usage, each peculiarly suited to the medium employed or the appeal to be weighed.

TESTS

1. Consumer pretest
2. Inquiry test

3. Sales test
4. Readership reports

1 / The consumer pretest. The customary procedure of the *consumer pretest* consists of selecting a group of consumers to whom are submitted samples of advertising copy that have not been released for publication, for the purpose of selecting the one that appeals to them the most. They may be asked to rank the advertisements in terms of attractiveness, attention getting, or persuasion. The consumers may be contacted through personal interviews or by mail. This method is useful for prejudging the effectiveness of different advertisements but not that of competing media. This procedure is also identified by the terms "consumer jury" or "consumer panel."

2 / The inquiry test. The *inquiry test* consists of devising a procedure whereby those who are exposed to the advertisements to be tested are induced to make inquiry concerning the advertised merchandise. Then the inquiries are counted, and the advertisement with the greatest number of responses is regarded as the most effective.

The readers of such advertisements in newspapers or magazines, for example, may be encouraged to reply by the use of coupons, keyed to reveal the media from whence they came or the advertisements of which they were a part; or they may be offered some sort of a reward, such as a sample of the advertised merchandise or a souvenir.

A follow-up on the effectiveness of the inquiry test is to relate the number of inquiries to the number of sales resulting from each advertisement. This is sometimes rather difficult to do; but where it is possible, it provides a good check on the test itself. For a test to be satisfactory, there should be a close correlation between the number of inquiries received and the sales that followed as the result of each advertisement.

3 / The sales test. The procedure in the *sales test* is to select two cities, as nearly alike as possible, and run new advertising in one while not advertising in the other. The sales that occur in both areas during the test period can then be compared for the purpose of judging the effectiveness of the advertising. There are a number of variations on the sales test, such as running one set of advertisements in one area and a different set in the other. Care must be taken to choose cities that are similar, and an examination should be made of the chosen areas during the test to make certain that no external factors enter the picture to destroy the validity of the comparison.

4 / Readership reports. A form of testing that has attained considerable prominence is the Readership Reports published by Daniel Starch and Staff, an organization of consultants in marketing research. The procedure is to seek out readers of certain magazines and newspapers and endeavor to discover the extent to which they paid attention to the advertisements in these media. The results are in the form of "noted," which means that the reader recalled seeing the advertisement; "seen-associated," which shows that the reader associated the advertisement with the advertiser; and "read most," which indicates that the interviewee read over 50 percent of the advertisement.

■ Testing Radio and Television Advertising

One of the major problems in connection with testing the effectiveness of radio and television advertising is to discover who is listening to the programs. The presence of a radio or television receiving set in a home does not tell whether or not the instrument is turned on or, if it is, to what station it is tuned.

Various methods have been devised to attempt to answer these questions, one of which involves the use of the telephone. Batteries of telephone operators are employed to call homes at random during the broadcasting time, and to endeavor to discover if the radio or television sets are turned on and, if so, the stations to which they are tuned. This test is known as the *coincidental method*.

Probably the best known testing method, and certainly the most controversial, is the Nielsen *Audimeter*. This is a mechanical device that is installed in the home near the radio or television set to which it is attached and which records on a tape the times when the set is turned on and to what station or channel. Each tape must be replaced every two weeks and returned to the A. C. Nielsen Company for analysis. The fate of many prominent television programs hangs on the evidence revealed by the Audimeter. The controversial aspect of this method arises through criticism of the quality and quantity of the homes where the Audimeter is installed. Some 1,100 households, where Audimeters are placed, are regarded by Nielsen as an adequate and accurate sample of the television viewing public of the country. Many people in the television business have questioned both the quantity and the quality of this sample.

■ The Advertising Agency

The *advertising agency* is a specialized institution that assists businessmen in all phases of their advertising effort. Advertising agencies were originally space sellers for the media, but they now help to create advertising for business firms that seek their services.

An advertising agency is equipped to undertake all phases of the preparation and execution of advertising for its clients. It handles the complete advertising campaign, which includes writing copy, creating art work, and selecting and making contracts with the media. Formerly the agencies were active in the production of network television shows, but recently the networks have taken over most of this area. Such secondary activities as product and market research, designing of packages and labels, and consultation on marketing matters generally are among the services of the larger agencies.

The chart shown below shows the organization of a typical advertising agency, on the basis of the functions performed.

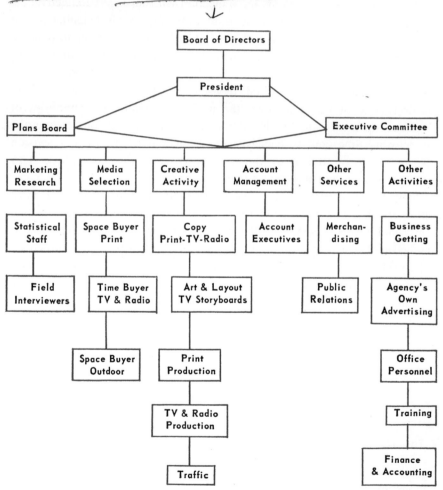

American Association of Advertising Agencies
A Typical Advertising Agency Organization Chart by Functions

Practically all national magazine and newspaper advertising is produced by agencies, whose specialized talents enable them to perform these functions better than the advertisers could themselves. Agencies are used by almost all firms that advertise on a large scale with the exception of department stores, most of whom maintain their own advertising staffs.

Oddly enough, the principal method by which the agencies are compensated dates back to the period when they operated as space brokers for the publishers. Under this system they are paid a 15% commission by the media on the basis of the space or time cost of the advertising placed by them in behalf of their clients, the advertisers. For example, assume that an agency, acting for a client, buys space in a magazine that costs $30,000. The magazine bills the agency for $30,000, less the 15% commission of $4,500, or a net of $25,500. The agency, in turn, bills the client for the full $30,000, and when this is paid by the client, deducts the $4,500 and remits the $25,500 to the magazine. Agencies regularly report their _billings_ to the trade press for statistical purposes.

Other, less important, forms of advertising agency compensation are service charges and fees. Service charges include the cost of materials and services, which are purchased by the agencies from outside sources. These include art work, photography, engravings, and related services. Fees are used frequently to cover agency services, such as research and sales promotion, where there are no advertisements created and inserted from which commissions could be received from the media.

The following table shows the total billings of the 10 top agencies in the United States in 1964 and also on a domestic and international basis.

Ten Top Advertising Agencies in the United States

AGENCY	TOTAL BILLINGS	DOMESTIC	INTERNATIONAL
	(Millions of Dollars)		
1. J. Walter Thompson Co.	$530.1	$351.5	$178.6
2. McCann-Erickson, Inc.	420.0	270.0	150.0
3. Young & Rubicam	372.7	306.1	66.6
4. Batten, Barton, Durstine & Osborne	304.4	292.7	11.7
5. Ted Bates & Co.	237.5	180.4	57.1
6. Foote, Cone & Belding	233.0	186.0	47.0
7. Leo Burnett Co.	188.6	184.7	3.9
8. Ogilvy & Mather International ...	156.4	94.4	62.0
9. Doyle Dane Bernbach	148.9	139.1	9.8
10. Benton & Bowles	140.2	130.2	10.0

"Hey Joe" — Jimmy hendrix

KINK underground

■ The Advertising Manager

In large concerns the advertising manager is one of the major executives. Quite commonly he reports to the sales manager. Where the company utilizes the services of an advertising agency, the advertising manager customarily selects it and acts as the point of contact between it and his employer. He interprets his firm's objectives to the agency, accepts or rejects the copy that is prepared by it, and handles the budgetary details. He supervises whatever other advertising activities the agency does not handle, such as research, publicity releases, and the preparation of visual sales material, easels, portfolios, and slide films for use by the firm's salesmen.

Where a firm does not use an agency, the advertising manager has charge of the preparation and insertion of the advertising, in addition to the other duties just noted.

■ Advertising in the Small Business

There are thousands of small businesses, manufacturers, wholesalers, and particularly retailers with restricted markets and even more restricted advertising budgets. For most of these businessmen, an advertising agency is out of the question; consequently, they must prepare their own copy and find a medium to carry it.

For the small manufacturer, there are trade journals in which can be placed a modest advertisement that will reach the eyes of prospective customers. He may also use direct mail. Dealer display pieces are often helpful in promoting his sales, too, if he can afford them.

The small wholesaler faces a different type of problem. His customers are probably confined to the city where he is located, and very few trade journals have so small a circulation. He must rely on direct mail and augment this with broadsides, which can be enclosed with the merchandise when it is delivered to customers. *Broadsides, dodgers,* or *throw-aways* are printed sheets containing advertising matter that can be distributed by hand to prospective customers. They are frequently printed on colored paper of a cheap grade and are thrown away by customers immediately after being read.

Small retailers usually confine their advertising activities to window and interior displays. For those who wish to go beyond this, there is direct mail if they can secure good lists and the facilities for duplicating their copy. Broadsides are often circulated in this manner. They may also find the local community newspaper, if one is published, of value.

Many small retailers have found the use of spot radio an effective and relatively inexpensive method of broadcasting their advertisements.

■ Criticisms of Advertising

Advertising in general and individual advertisements have long been the targets of adverse criticism. Some of the expressions of disapproval have been actually criticisms of business itself and many of its practices. Among these have been claims that much advertising is merely competitive; that it stresses minor differences in products which serve the same purpose and are essentially the same; that it causes consumers to want—and presumably to purchase—goods that they would not desire if they were not exposed to the advertising; and that it is designed to create demand for products. In answer to these criticisms it should be noted that competition is a fundamental principle of capitalism; that product differentiation [1] is a method by which producers of homogeneous products endeavor to make their goods appear slightly different from those of their competitors; and that, in many instances, consumers would not know of the existence and availability of many products if they were not advertised.

In the criticism that advertising creates demand, it must be admitted that many, if not most, advertisers believe that demand creation is one of the main functions of advertising. A demand for a commodity cannot exist without a knowledge of the availability of the commodity on the part of potential users. But demand must be more than mere knowledge of the existence of a commodity; it must involve the desire for it on the part of prospective purchasers.

It is very difficult for consumers to make their wishes known to the producers in such manner as to serve as a guide for production schedules. In order to avoid the stalemate that might otherwise theoretically follow this situation, it is only natural that manufacturers should make what they think the public wants and then try to convince consumers that they should buy the advertised goods. There is obviously the possibility that the goods produced and promoted may be of little value to consumers, but this seems to be a risk inherent in a situation where the buyers are practically inarticulate. It seems, therefore, that the demand-creation concept is a perfectly defensible philosophy, considering the inability of buyers to make known their wants in advance.

Other criticisms are: (1) that advertising makes the goods advertised cost more than would be the case if they were not advertised; (2) that

---

[1] See Chapter 1, page 13.

others are in poor taste or offensive to the public; and (3) that many advertisements are false or misleading. These criticisms will be examined in turn.

1 / Does advertising make goods cost more? Advertising is a selling cost and, like all other costs, must be covered by the selling price of the advertised article. One might say, then, that anything that increases the cost of an item increases its price. This is, however, an oversimplification of the cost-price relationship, which needs to be examined more closely.

There are two types of costs—direct and indirect. *Direct costs* are those that can be directly allocated to the production of a commodity, such as materials and labor. *Indirect costs* are those that cannot be directly allocated, such as occupancy expenses, superintendence, power, and administrative costs. Roughly speaking, the total direct and indirect costs divided by the number of items produced will give the cost per item.

A peculiarity of indirect costs is that they tend to remain fixed over wide ranges of output. It is conceivable that the total indirect cost of producing an item would be the same whether the production were 100 or 1,000. It is obvious, then, that the indirect cost per unit would be much less for 1,000 units than for 100 or even 500.

Advertising is generally regarded as an indirect cost and, if the result of advertising a commodity is to increase its sales greatly, it is entirely possible that this sales increase may be of sufficient magnitude to bring about a decrease in unit costs that more than offsets the increase in total cost due to the advertising expense. If this is true, then the lowered unit cost would permit the producer to lower his price, which might give him a competitive advantage in selling his product.

It may be stated, then, that (a) when advertising results in increased sales, (b) when these increased sales result in lowered unit costs, and (c) when the lowered unit costs result in lowered prices, advertising not only does not increase the price of goods but actually decreases it. There are probably many instances where all of these conditions are not present, in which cases it may be said that advertising either increases the prices of goods or at least does not decrease them.

2 / Is advertising in poor taste? The only possible answer to this criticism must necessarily be equivocal. That there have been occasional advertisements which have violated the accepted standards of good taste is undeniable, although there is reason to believe that these have been few and far between. That the majority of advertisements conform to these standards is likewise certain. There have been those advertisements that are offensive to some people, while perfectly acceptable to others. Under the pressure of competition, it is entirely possible that some creators of advertising have exceeded the bounds of good taste for some segments of the public. Advertising agency executives, however, are aware of this possibility and generally endeavor to prevent the appearance of any advertisements that might provoke displeasure. Some instances of name advertising, particularly on radio and television, may appear to be inane, but they are not necessarily in poor taste.

3 / Are many advertisements false or misleading? Among the criticisms of advertising, none has been more cogent than those that have flayed the prevalence of untruth in its messages. This does not mean all advertising is untrue, for such is not the case; but it does mean that too many advertisements have contained statements or claims that were not strictly true.   !

It is practically impossible to define untruthfulness to the satisfaction of all concerned. The advertiser who proclaims that his product is the best in the world may believe that it is, but what of his competitor who makes the same statement about his product? Obviously they both cannot be right. In fact both products may be inferior to any number of others. This sort of thing, which is quite common, is called harmless *trade puffery*. It merely amounts to a certain amount of public breast-beating.

Untruthfulness in advertising assumes many forms, among which are false testimonials, exaggerations, false claims, misrepresentation, false or near-false labeling, and the use of confusing terminology. It is a sad commentary on the gullibility of many consumers that they can be misled by such frauds. Another unfortunate aspect is that it tends to undermine public confidence in all advertising, to the detriment of those advertisers who follow the policy of checking their copy carefully to make certain that it contains nothing but the truth. There are many such firms, and they are keenly aware of the transgressions of their less ethical competitors.

■ Ensuring Truth in Advertising

There is no single method of ensuring that a certain amount of untruth will not appear in the advertising of the country as long as a system of free private enterprise continues. It is furthermore probable that we will never be able to purify our advertising copy to the complete satisfaction of everyone.

A number of steps designed to protect the public and ethical business leaders from some of the more flagrant and harmful types of false advertising have been taken.

1. Industry self-regulation
2. Action by media
3. Better Business Bureaus
4. The federal government
5. *Printers' Ink* statutes

These and other methods have gone far to clean up the advertising picture, which is unquestionably on a far higher plane than it was a few years ago.

1 / Industry self-regulation. A great many business houses enforce strict codes of ethics upon themselves in order to make certain that their advertising is as strictly in accord with the truth as human watchfulness can assure.

Recognizing that false or misleading advertising reflects unfavorably on all members of the trade, some industries have endeavored to establish the machinery for self-regulation. The Proprietary Association, made up of manufacturers of pharmaceutical preparations and patent medicines, is a good example. By means of argument and moral suasion, they have endeavored to prevent some of the members of the trade from continuing advertising that was manifestly false.

A number of industries have cooperated with the Federal Trade Commission in setting up Trade Practice Rules which, among other things, may prohibit false advertising, misbranding, and deception on the part of its members. Among the groups whose Trade Practice Rules include strong condemnation of false or deceptive advertising are the Tobacco Smoking Pipe and Cigar and Cigarette Holder Industry, the Cosmetic and Toilet Preparations Industry, and the Fountain Pen and Mechanical Pencil Industry. The television networks undertake to censor certain types of medical advertising that refer to bodily functions not normally a part of polite conversation.

The major difficulty with self-regulation is that it is entirely a voluntary matter. There is no method of compelling recalcitrant members of the trade to hew to the straight and narrow path if they wish to break away from it. This method, therefore, democratic and desirable as it is, can be only partly successful.

2 / Action by media. Nearly all media have certain minimum ethical standards to which all advertising must conform in order to be acceptable for publication. They recognize that false advertisements reflect not only on the advertisers but also on the media in which they appear. Many publishers also feel a moral obligation toward those advertisers whose copy is on the level and with whom unethical advertising would be unfair competition.

3 / Better Business Bureaus. *Better Business Bureaus,* which are well known for their activities to protect consumers, were originally established by businessmen for the purpose of protecting themselves from the unfair competition of the less ethical members of the community and were only incidentally protectors of consumers. The critical examination of all local advertising, particularly that of retailers, has long been foremost among the duties of these bureaus. Their weapons have been twofold—publicity for the offending firms and recourse to the federal courts when false advertising was sent through the mails. Many Better Business Bureau offices maintain service departments that will advise consumers concerning complaints made against specific advertisers. The extent to which this service is utilized has not been disclosed.

4 / The federal government. The two principal agencies for the combating of fraudulent advertising are the Federal Trade Commission and the Food and Drug Administration. The Federal Trade Commission Act of 1914 established the Commission and gave it authority to prevent the use of unfair methods of competition in interstate commerce. In 1938 the Wheeler-Lea Act (an amendment to the Federal Trade Commission Act) added to the duties of the Commission by giving it authority to prevent "unfair or deceptive acts or practices in commerce."

Following the passage of the Wheeler-Lea Amendment (which prohibited the false advertising of food, drugs, cosmetics, and therapeutic devices), the Federal Trade Commission maintains a Bureau of Deceptive Practices which scrutinizes the advertising of newspapers, magazines, catalogs, and radio and television broadcasts to detect false or misleading advertising in these fields. The Commission is thus enabled to investigate instances of alleged or suspected false advertising and to issue cease and desist orders when the advertising is found to be in violation of the Federal Trade Commission Act. The Commission also has the task of enforcing the following labeling laws: Wool Products Labeling Act, Fur Products Labeling Act, Flammable Fabrics Act, and the Textile Products Identification Act.

The Federal Food, Drug, and Cosmetic Act of 1938 strengthened the hands of the Food and Drug Administration in its dealing with false labeling of "foods, drugs, devices, and cosmetics." Both this agency and the Federal Trade Commission have been diligent in their efforts to suppress false advertising.

5 / Printers' Ink statutes. In 1911, *Printers' Ink*, a leading marketing trade periodical, set forth a model statute that was designed to aid in eliminating dishonest advertising. Persons interested in truthful advertising undertook the task of inducing state legislatures to adopt laws embracing its principles. As a result, 43 states have passed laws based on the *Printers' Ink* pattern. These laws, of course, are confined in their application solely to intrastate advertising, and their value has been lessened in some instances by poor enforcement. They do indicate, however, an awareness of the need for corrective action in this area.

■ The Advertising Council

In 1941 a group of individuals representing national advertisers, advertising agencies, and the major media founded *The Advertising Council,* dedicated to the idea that advertising could and should be used in the public interest as it had been in the private interest. During World War II this organization undertook the task of publicizing the many activities that the country required for the successful prosecution of the war effort. After the war the Council promoted such things as the need for better schools, accident prevention, ownership of U. S. savings bonds, prevention of forest fires, and many other worthwhile causes. In this way the leaders of the advertising field are endeavoring to implement the concept that advertising is a potent force for social good in this country.

BUSINESS TERMS

(a) advertising (203)
(b) commodity advertising (204), institutional advertising (205)
(c) primary advertising (204), selective advertising (204), mass advertising (204), class advertising (204), publicity (204), name advertising (205), institutional advertising (205)
(d) media (205)
(e) geographic selectivity (205), interest selectivity (205), flexibility (206), identity of the audience (206)
(f) spot radio (208), radio commercial (209), spot announcement (209), station breaks (209)
(g) spectacular (211)
(h) car cards (211)
(i) business papers (212)
(j) point-of-purchase advertising (212), advertising specialty (212)

(k) consumer pretest (214), inquiry test (214), sales test (214)
(l) coincidental method (215), Audimeter (215)
(m) advertising agency (215), billings (217)
(n) broadside, dodger, or throw-away (218)
(o) direct cost (220), indirect cost (220)
(p) trade puffery (221)
(q) Better Business Bureau (223), Advertising Council (224)

QUESTIONS FOR DISCUSSION AND ANALYSIS

1. Some critics of big business have said that the ability of such firms as General Motors and Procter and Gamble to advertise extensively gives them an unfair advantage over their smaller competitors and tends to create monopolies. Do you agree with this point of view? Defend your answer.

2. Do you think that name advertising, including such items as singing commercials, actually sells goods? If you do, explain how. If you do not, would you advise the advertisers to abandon this type of advertising? Why?

3. A prominent economist has stated that all advertising is waste and should be prohibited. Do you agree? Explain.

4. A criticism of advertising that is heard occasionally, particularly from labor union representatives, is that the newspapers, being mainly dependent on advertising revenue for their income, give their editorials a pro-business slant. Do you think that this is true? Explain.

5. Can you think of any method by which the radio listening habits of automobile occupants could be accurately discovered? Discuss.

6. What do you think would be the effect on the sales volume of such products as beer, cigarettes, or soft drinks if their advertising volume were cut in half? Explain.

7. Evaluate the advertising effectiveness of broadsides, either as distributed in the stores or mailed to "occupant" at specified addresses.

8. Do you think that the Federal Trade Commission should have the authority to promulgate compulsory standards of good taste in advertising? Why?

9. Do you think that "harmless trade puffery," as it is called, deceives any substantial number of people? Why?

10. It has been estimated that the average person is exposed, via all media, to approximately 1,200 advertisements daily. Do you think that this situation, if fairly accurate, might result in a growth of consumer indifference, if not antipathy, toward advertising? Explain.

PROBLEMS AND SHORT CASES

1. Many advertisers change agencies frequently. Every issue of *Printers' Ink* and *Advertising Age* lists these changes. From the agencies' side, there are occasional instances where an agency "resigns" an account

or terminates its relations with an advertiser. Some advertisers have a policy of changing agencies every few years, while there are others whose connections with their agencies are of many years standing.

Referring to the files of the two periodicals mentioned, prepare a report stating the causes of these differing policies.

2. There is a constant volume of institutional advertising appearing in magazines and newspapers. Collect a portfolio of a least ten such items, and write a report indicating the objective of each advertisement and your opinion of its probable effectiveness.

3. The controversy over advertising agency compensation, while of many years standing, has been attracting more attention among both the agencies and advertisers in recent years. The critics of the historic 15% commission system feel that it is an arbitrary plan which may have been satisfactory when the agencies acted as space salesmen for the media, but that today it no longer correctly reflects the value of the services rendered by the agencies to the advertisers. Furthermore, the complaint has been heard that the commission system tempts agencies to recommend more advertising than their clients require. Agency spokesmen have stoutly denied this allegation with the statement that this would be a stupid policy inasmuch as advertisers judge the effectiveness of advertising by the resultant sales, and unless more sales followed the increased advertising, the agency would be blamed. Those who uphold the 15% commission system frequently claim that no other method would be as satisfactory.

Consult back files of *Business Week, Printers' Ink,* and *Advertising Age* in your library, and write a brief report on the merits of this controversy.

SUGGESTED READINGS

Caples, J. *Tested Advertising Methods,* Revised Edition. New York: Harper & Row, 1961.

Crawford, J. W. *Advertising,* Second Edition. Boston: Allyn & Bacon, Inc., 1965.

Dirksen, C. J., and A. Kroeger. *Advertising Principles and Problems,* Revised Edition. Homewood, Illinois: Richard D. Irwin, Inc., 1964.

Hepner, H. W. *Advertising—Creative Communication With Consumers,* Fourth Edition. New York: McGraw-Hill Book Company, Inc., 1964.

Kirkpatrick, C. A. *Advertising: Mass Communication in Marketing,* Second Edition. Boston: Houghton Mifflin Company, 1964.

Kleppner, O. *Advertising Procedure,* Fifth Edition. Englewood Cliffs, New Jersey: Prentice-Hall, Inc., 1966.

Sandage, C. H., and V. Fryburger. *Advertising Theory and Practice,* Sixth Edition. Homewood, Illinois: Richard D. Irwin, Inc., 1963.

Magazines: *Advertising Age, Printers' Ink.*

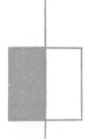

Chapter 11

INTERNATIONAL ASPECTS OF BUSINESS

Although the major emphasis in this text is on the policies and procedures of business firms in the United States in their contacts with each other, it should be recognized that no small part of the total volume of business transacted by these companies is the result of their sales to and purchases from firms located in other lands. There are three aspects of this phase of business: (1) international trade; (2) international marketing; and (3) international business. It is the purpose of this chapter to discuss these terms, beginning with the economic and governmental aspects of international trade. This will be followed by a brief account of international marketing, an area of increasing interest to businessmen. Then the relatively recent concept of international business will be examined as it affects the international aspects of business.

INTERNATIONAL TRADE

International trade is the buying and selling of goods and services between the business firms of the various countries of the world and the payments that are made for them. Strictly speaking, international transactions between private citizens of the countries involved should be included in this category also, but because of their relative infrequency they are usually disregarded.

As nations grew in economic resources, businessmen with goods to sell over and above the quantities their own countries could absorb undertook to find markets for their wares in other lands. Thus was born the practice of international trade, a process that has grown until today trade between the nations of the world has assumed impressive proportions. It is through the operation of international trade that the products of one country are made available to the other nations of the world. The discussion here will concentrate on the role of the United States in this area.

227

■ **Reasons for International Trade**

The reasons for international trade may be classified as:

1. Business reasons
2. Economic reasons
3. Political reasons

1 / Business reasons for international trade. Businesses in this country import goods from abroad because: (a) the goods either are not available in this country or, if available, are not in sufficient supply for our purposes; (b) the prices are lower than for similar goods produced domestically; and (c) by so doing, the importing firms are more certain of a foreign market for their products—the firms from whom they buy in other lands may be willing, in turn, to purchase their goods.

American firms endeavor to sell their products in foreign countries: (a) to increase the total volume of their sales, possibly to the point where their production rate may approach the optimum volume; (b) because of less competition, either from United States or foreign sellers; (c) to level off seasonal sales fluctuations, particularly through sales to those countries located south of the equator whose seasons are the direct opposite of ours; and (d) because of a demand for their goods in other countries.

2 / Economic reasons for international trade. The two economic reasons for the development of international trade are called (a) the theory of absolute advantage and (b) the theory of comparative advantage. They are useful as a means of indicating the underlying economic bases for the development of international trade and its persistence in the face of formidable obstacles.

(a) THEORY OF ABSOLUTE ADVANTAGE. There are two aspects to the *theory of absolute advantage*. A few countries possess, through pure chance, certain goods that cannot be obtained elsewhere. Natural diamonds in South Africa and emeralds in Columbia are two examples. Under these circumstances trade will take place between these countries and any others who need or desire these goods.

Trade will also occur in instances where, although several nations are capable of producing the same goods, certain countries are able to produce them more cheaply. As a result, they become the sources of supply for these items and sell them to other countries because of their cost advantage. The areas in which countries may have this aspect of absolute advantage might be skilled or unskilled labor, patented processes, managerial know-how, climate, or abundance of raw materials. Here the theory holds that countries will concentrate their productive efforts on the goods in the manufacture of which they have an absolute cost advantage and abstain from the production of goods in which they are at an absolute disadvantage. The surpluses of some goods thus produced and the need for other goods thus created bring about the movement of goods in the channels of international trade as each nation tries to sell the goods that it makes and to buy the goods that other nations make, both on the presumed basis of absolute advantage. Two examples of this aspect of the theory of absolute advantage are the manufacture of linen cloth in Ireland and the growing of bananas in Costa Rica.

(b) THEORY OF COMPARATIVE ADVANTAGE. The *theory of comparative advantage* assumes that trade will take place between nations that are capable of producing the same products, but where certain nations have a comparative advantage in the production of certain products in comparison with other products. For example, even though Country *A* may have lower costs than Country *B* in the production of, say, twelve different products, it will tend to concentrate on the production of those items, perhaps four, in which its comparative cost advantages are the greatest, leaving the production of the remaining eight to Country *B*. Under these circumstances Country *A* might import the remaining eight products from Country *B*.

In the more highly developed industrial nations of the world the trend has been definitely away from following the theory of comparative advantage, at least regarding the products of a mechanized economy. The trend has been toward the manufacture of everything that would come into this general category and to employ trade barriers, usually tariffs, to equalize the cost differences on goods coming from countries that are able to produce them at less cost. It is, of course, obvious that the extension of this trend would have the effect of lessening the volume of trade between countries. Later in this chapter we shall note some of the more recent steps that have been taken by various nations to reverse this trend and to increase the volume of international trade in some parts of the world.

3 / **Political reasons for international trade.** Many people feel that the greatest possible volume of world trade between nations is desirable as an important step in the direction of world peace. Countries that have extensive business dealings with each other are presumed to be on a more friendly basis than those whose contacts are few in number or virtually nonexistent. Except for the nations in the communist bloc, the

volume of trade between the United States and most of the other countries of the world has been growing since the end of World War II. No small part of the trade with the nations of Western Europe has been motivated by the attempt to strengthen their economies as a bulwark against the encroachment of communism.

■ Extent of Our International Trade

Our international trade varies quite measurably from year to year, depending upon a number of factors, including trade barriers, price levels, the state of the economy in various nations, international trade agreements, and the presence or absence of war anywhere in the world. The basic trend of both exports and imports of merchandise, however, has been upward as is indicated by the chart below.

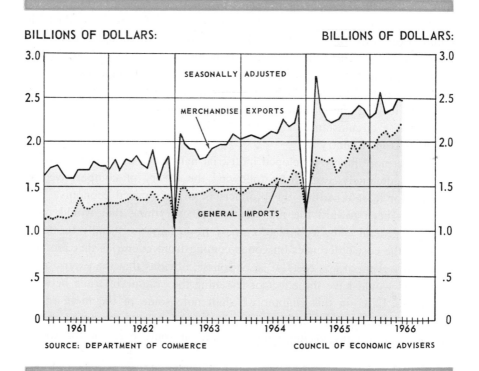

BILLIONS OF DOLLARS: BILLIONS OF DOLLARS:

SEASONALLY ADJUSTED

MERCHANDISE EXPORTS

GENERAL IMPORTS

SOURCE: DEPARTMENT OF COMMERCE   COUNCIL OF ECONOMIC ADVISERS

Merchandise Exports and Imports

The bar chart on page 231 shows the United States trade with major world areas for 1963 and 1964, in dollar volume and for basic commodity groups.

Composition of United States Trade With
Major World Areas Annual 1963 and Annual 1964

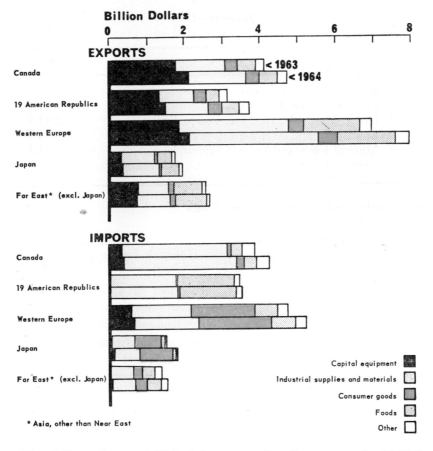

The dollar volume of United States merchandise exports in 1965 by major commodity groups is shown in the following table:

Exports—1965
(Millions of Dollars)

COMMODITY GROUP	EXPORTS
1. Machinery and Transport Equipment	$10,015.7
2. Food and Live Animals	4,003.8
3. Manufactured Goods	3,257.8
4. Crude Materials, Inedible, except Fuels	2,855.6
5. Chemicals	2,401.8
6. Mineral Fuels and Related Materials	946.5

The dollar volume of imports by the leading commodity groups for 1965 is listed below:

Imports—1965
(Millions of Dollars)

COMMODITY GROUP	IMPORTS
1. Manufactured Materials	$5,555.9
2. Food and Live Animals	3,459.6
3. Crude Materials, Inedible, except Fuels	3,033.9
4. Machinery and Transport Equipment	2,946.8
5. Mineral Fuels and Related Materials	2,222,4
6. Chemicals	781.3

■ Characteristics of International Trade

International trade has several characteristics in common with domestic trade. The goods and services offered must have the power to satisfy human wants; there must be people somewhere who want them and are able and willing to pay for them; there must be a commonly accepted and trusted medium of exchange in which values may be expressed or quoted; and the goods and services offered must be quoted at prices that will both find ready buyers for the entire amounts that are for sale and yield reasonable profits to the sellers. Sales effort is likewise required, both to bring the goods to the attention of prospective buyers and to effect their sale.

It is with the characteristics of international trade that are unlike those of domestic trade, however, that this discussion is principally concerned.

1. Language differences
2. Different monetary standards
3. Trade barriers
4. Transportation costs

Other differences, such as customs, habits, legal systems, governmental attitudes toward business, and political systems in the various countries, also serve to differentiate international from domestic trade.

1 / **Language differences.** Except for trade between countries speaking a common tongue, language differences must be overcome. These affect the necessary correspondence, the creation of advertising, and the labeling and marking of the goods. To take care of this situation, some firms employ foreign-language speaking correspondents and interpreters. Translation services are available from a number of sources, such as the larger

chambers of commerce, the Pan-American Union, and international trade clubs.

The post-World War II years have witnessed the gradual spread of English as an acceptable common business language in many areas of the world, notably in parts of Western Europe and Latin America.

2 / Different monetary standards. Every nation has its own peculiar currency—the dollar in this country and Canada, the yen in Japan, the drachma in Greece, the peso in Mexico, the guilder in The Netherlands, and the lira in Italy. This situation requires not only a mechanism whereby the seller may be paid in his own currency while the buyer makes payment in his, but also a method whereby each of these national currencies may be expressed or valued in terms of every other one. At one time gold served as a common denominator for all currencies; but for several years the so-called gold standard has been nonexistent, and this fact has greatly complicated the problem. The possible fluctuation in these relative values does not help to simplify this situation.

3 / Trade barriers. All countries, for one reason or another, interpose barriers that tend to restrict the free flow of goods across their borders. These barriers apply, in most cases, only to imports or goods moving into these countries. They consist of tariffs, quotas, exchange restrictions, barter arrangements, and occasionally, absolute prohibitions to the import of certain commodities.

4 / Transportation costs. A factor in which international trade differs from domestic trade, mainly in degree, is that of transportation costs. Although it may cost less to ship goods from Boston to Quebec than from Seattle to Miami, in general the transportation costs incident to international trade are considerably higher than those incurred in moving goods within this country.

■ **Nationalism and Its Effect**

International trade is or should be a two-way arrangement, that is, a country should buy as well as sell goods and services. Although it is to be expected that exports and imports will not balance out evenly in every instance and that the differences will be settled through payments of gold or in some other acceptable fashion, it is an economic fallacy to assume that a country can always sell more than it buys and receive the difference in gold. Yet this is exactly what the growth of economic nationalism has tended to bring about. Great emphasis has been placed on the export of goods to other countries, but the notion that imports should play a prominent part in the economy of the nation has been decried and barriers have been erected in the path of the free inflow of goods.

The concept of a nation's relationship to world trade as being purely that of a seller is one that dates back to the mercantilists in England. The mercantilists believed that the country's prosperity, as far as international trade was concerned, depended on exporting merchandise and importing only gold as payment for the exports.

This philosophy has been further emphasized by the phraseology employed to describe our country's position as a buyer or a seller in world trade. The term *favorable balance of trade* has been used to describe the situation when our exports exceeded our imports, and *unfavorable balance of trade* has been employed when imports exceeded exports. Furthermore, the balance of trade idea embraced purely "visible" or merchandise items, such as machinery, shoes, and typewriters, and ignored the "invisible" items, such as loans to foreign countries, payments for insurance abroad, or money spent by tourists. The use of these terms has been most unfortunate in that it has appeared to portray a situation of advantage or disadvantage that was not necessarily or even usually true.

The idea that a nation should be economically self-sufficient, as far as the United States is concerned, received considerable impetus during World War II because the early enemy conquests cut off our supply of many essential raw materials, such as rubber and quinine, necessitating our searching for substitutes or doing without until the enemy was defeated. Many business and political leaders hold to the belief that, as far as possible, we should never permit ourselves to be caught in this position again. The implementation of this conclusion would result in our endeavoring to produce a number of commodities that can be grown or produced much more cheaply abroad. This may be regarded as a purely defensive measure, but it is bound to have an adverse effect on the extension of our international trade, particularly our imports. The increasing world tensions of the past few years, however, will doubtless place the matter of national safety well ahead of the notion of the general desirability of extended world trade, at least in the thinking of many people in this country.

■ Historical Role of Our Government

Our government has always felt compelled, for one reason or another, to exercise its influence in the field of international trade. Generally, this

exports exceed imports favorable balance so trade

has been done in a genuine and sincere effort to safeguard and promote the interests of the citizens in their international transactions, on the ground that individually they were not strong enough, or could not afford, to do this for themselves.

These activities of the government have manifested themselves in a myriad of ways. Merchant fleets have been subsidized or built with public funds. The diplomatic, and particularly the consular, services of the government seek to assist international traders in establishing and extending their commercial activities by advising them concerning international governmental regulations. Commercial treaties with general and specific agreements concerning the rights and the obligations of the signatory countries have been concluded.

One of the oldest, and formerly most controversial, aspects of the intrusion of government into international trade is in the levying and administering of tariffs on imports. This subject is of sufficient importance to warrant a rather thorough discussion, particularly as it is through the manipulation of tariff schedules that foreign-made goods are encouraged or discouraged from entering the country.

■ Types of Tariffs

A *tariff* is a system of duties levied against goods being imported into the country. There are two types of tariffs, (1) the revenue tariff and (2) the protective tariff.

1 / Tariff for revenue only. A *tariff for revenue only* is designed principally to raise revenue for the government and is not designed primarily to discourage imports. Revenue rates are usually relatively low, since the lower they are, the greater the quantity of imports and hence the larger the amount of revenue.

2 / Protective tariff. The purpose of a *protective tariff* is to keep out of the country goods that would otherwise undersell domestic goods of the same or similar kind—goods in the production of which other nations have a comparative advantage. To understand the meaning and implications of the protective tariff, it is necessary to inquire into the arguments that have been advanced in its behalf and to examine their validity to some extent.

(a) THE MILITARY ARGUMENT. This argument holds that all industries vital to the national defense should be kept alive through tariff protection if necessary. It has been proposed that, when this needs to be done, subsidies be employed, perhaps even from the outset, and that the costs be properly labeled as those of national defense.

(b) THE HOME-INDUSTRY ARGUMENT. This argument holds that, if foreign goods are kept out of the country, domestic manufacturers will enjoy a larger home market than would otherwise be the case. The argument has been used by business interests that have been interested more in protecting their own existence from foreign competition than in promoting American industry generally. With high tariffs to keep out foreign competition, individual firms thus protected are able to get higher prices for their products than if tariffs were lower. High-cost producers, who might be forced out of business if subjected to the competition of efficient foreign producers, are enabled to continue to operate while thus protected.

(c) THE INFANT-INDUSTRY ARGUMENT. The tenor of this argument is that young, struggling industries in this country should be protected from competition from foreign producers until they have had a chance to get well established. There is a certain amount of merit to this thesis, provided that the protection is continued only until the infant has attained competitive maturity. The difficulty arises in determining how long this protection is needed and when it should be discarded. Furthermore, each industry might require a different period of time to mature. Administratively, this part of the problem is extremely difficult.

(d) THE WAGES ARGUMENT. The theme of this argument is that, by excluding foreign goods made by lower-paid labor, goods made by higher-paid domestic labor can be sold in this country, thereby serving to maintain or raise domestic wages. There are several aspects to the consideration of the wages argument. First, by keeping out goods made by lower-paid labor of other countries, the prices of competing American goods may be raised to American buyers, thus leaving them less money with which to buy other goods. Second, in the years since World War II, there has been remarkable economic growth in many parts of the free world. In many instances this has been the result of financial assistance rendered by the United States, coupled with instruction in modern managerial techniques given by representatives of American industrial companies. This industrial growth has resulted in higher standards of living for the people of these countries. And while it is true that their wage scales are still substantially below those of this country, their productivity is growing and, in addition to their being able to offer goods to our buyers, in some cases for less than they can be purchased here, these nations offer a challenging market for the producers in this country.

(e) THE FAVORABLE-BALANCE-OF-TRADE ARGUMENT. The measure of the prosperity of a country, as far as its international trade is concerned, is not to be found in its export or import position, but rather in the effect that its international trade has on the standard of living of its people. If a people can import certain goods at prices lower than the cost of making those goods themselves, they should do so and concentrate their productive efforts on making other goods that they can produce more cheaply than other countries can and sell these goods abroad. However, the problem of convincing business and labor leaders of this truism is a difficult one.

■ Types of Tariff Duties

There are three types of tariff duties: specific, ad valorem, and compound. The rates affecting all commodities are set forth in the tariff acts.

Specific duties are amounts levied at so much per unit, or pound, or ton, of the commodities affected. For example, the specific duty on butter is 7 cents per pound and that on champagne and all other sparkling wines is $1.50 per gallon.

Ad valorem duties consist of levies based on some aspect of the value of the goods in question. For example, the ad valorem duty on hides is 4 percent of their value.

Compound duties involve both specific and ad valorem levies. For example, ethylene glycol (antifreeze) has a duty of 3 cents per pound plus 15 percent ad valorem, and men's suits, 37½ cents per pound and 21 percent ad valorem.

■ The Flexible Tariff System

Introduced in 1922 and continued up to the present, federal legislation has empowered the President of the United States to change tariff rates without reference to Congress, subject to certain restrictions or limitations. The purpose was to speed up the adjustment of rates in accord with changing conditions, as compared with the cumbersome and log-rolling methods of legislative changes in the tariff laws.

■ Foreign Exchange

Foreign exchange is concerned with the methods whereby buyers and sellers in international trade pay and receive payment for goods and services. Money is seldom shipped abroad in the settlement of international trade transactions. The typical method of settlement is by means of *bills of exchange,* which are nothing more nor less than the drafts.[1] used in domestic trade, except that they may be written in terms of francs or marks instead of dollars.

1 / Use of bills of exchange. When an exporter sells goods or renders service to a foreign importer, he draws a bill of exchange ordering the importer to pay him a stated amount of money either on sight or a specified number of days in the future. Since he ordinarily will not want to wait until it matures to cash it, he takes it to his bank and discounts it. This means that the bank gives him cash for it, less certain interest and accommodation charges. This transaction may be effected before the bill of exchange is presented to the importer if his credit standing is good; otherwise, time must be spent to send it to him for acceptance and for its return before the exporter can present it for discount.

The discounting bank, or its larger city correspondent, simply credits the bill of exchange to its account in the country where it was drawn; and when the bill becomes due, it is presented to the importer by a bank in his own country, and payment is effected and the transaction completed without any money being sent from the importer to the exporter. This same discounting bank is then in a position to sell drafts on its foreign balances to American importers who thus reimburse the bank for the money it paid to the American exporter when it discounted his original bill of exchange. Likewise the importer has funds available abroad for the payment of the amount that he owes to the exporter in that country without sending actual cash.

2 / Rates of exchange. Bills of exchange are bought and sold in a so-called foreign exchange market, which is located in the large financial centers of the United States and of the world. The prices of these bills are known as the *rates of exchange.* Before World War I, when gold could be shipped between countries, these exchange rates were kept within narrow limits because of the possible alternative of actually shipping gold in or out of the country if the price of the bills of exchange exceeded the cost of shipping the gold. At present, gold cannot be shipped, except in rare instances, hence the demand for and the supply of the bills of exchange determine their price (rate of exchange). Thus, if American exports sell a lot more to importers in India than our importers buy from India exporters, the supply of bills will exceed the demand, the rate of exchange will go down, and the exporters will be harmed as their bills will bring less in the market. Likewise, importers in all countries will be encouraged

[1] See Chapter 19, page 417.

to buy more in India by virtue of the lower price of the instruments used to pay for their purchases. In time, a balance will be reached that will bring the rate up again.

■ Recent Developments in International Trade

After World War I, particularly during the depression years of the 1930's, and again since World War II, the intrusion of all governments into the international trade picture has been noteworthy. The following are the principal events that have featured this development.

1. Export control
2. Exchange restrictions
3. The Trade Expansion Act
4. Export-Import Bank
5. The International Bank for Reconstruction and Development
6. International Monetary Fund
7. General Agreement on Tariff and Trade
8. Foreign trade zones

1 / Export control. The major purpose of export control in this country is to prevent the shipment of militarily strategic items to countries behind the Iron Curtain. The administration of export control, which in one form or another dates back to around 1940, is in the hands of the Bureau of Foreign Commerce of the United States Department of Commerce.

2 / Exchange restrictions. Following the depression of the 1930's exchange restrictions were adopted, especially by South American countries. Several modifications of this method were used, but basically it meant that exporters sold all their bills arising from selling goods abroad to their government at a fixed price. The government, in turn, decided how much exchange would be released to importers and at what price. In many cases, certain importers (of necessities) were given lower prices than others (importers of luxuries). In any event, it was possible for the government to effect any degree of favorable trade balance that it desired, regardless of the economic consequencs of such action.

3 / The Trade Expansion Act. The Trade Expansion Act of 1962 is a successor to a series of Reciprocal Trade Agreements Acts, which originated in 1934 and had been renewed periodically since then. This new law permits the President to enter into international trade agreements for a period of five years. He is specifically empowered to cut any tariff up to 50 percent. Duties may be removed in part or entirely on goods in which 80 percent of world trade is accounted for by the United States and the European Economic Community.

The Act includes provision for an *escape clause* whereby imports that are causing damage to domestic producers may be removed from the list of products upon which duties may be lowered. The President is also permitted to enter into marketing agreements with foreign countries, limiting the export of certain articles to the United States as a means of easing the impact of international competition on the producers of these goods in this country. There is also included a program of adjustment assistance to industries, firms, and worker groups who may be seriously injured or threatened with injury by increased imports resulting from concessions granted in trade agreements. This provision of the Act has been invoked only rarely thus far.

The basic purpose of the Act is to enable producers in this country to enter the European market by stimulating both exports and imports between those countries and the United States through reciprocal trade agreements.

4 / Export-Import Bank. The Export-Import Bank is a federal lending agency created by an Act of Congress in 1934 and subsequently extended from time to time. Its purpose is to help promote trade between the United States and other countries through loans to importers and exporters in this country who are unable to secure adequate financing from private agencies. Aid may also be extended to foreign governments for the purpose of helping them in the development of their resources and in their international trade.

5 / The International Bank for Reconstruction and Development. This institution was organized in 1946 for the purpose of floating foreign loans in the private capital markets of members by giving an international guarantee. This bank had an original capital of around $8 billion, of which the United States subscribed about 40 percent. This capital is kept as a reserve, and funds for loans are secured through the sale of the bank's securities to the public. Loans totaling more than $10 billion have been made to a dozen or more member nations.

6 / The International Monetary Fund. This institution began operations in 1947. Its aims are to provide the machinery for consultation and collaboration on international monetary problems; to facilitate the expansion and balanced growth of international trade; to promote stability of foreign exchange; to avoid competitive exchange depreciation; and to provide members with funds to meet temporary unfavorable trade balances.

7 / The General Agreement on Tariff and Trade. The General Agreement on Tariff and Trade, known commonly at GATT, contains a set of rules by which member governments agree to conduct their mutual international trade relations. It provides a means of reducing tariffs and other governmentally imposed barriers to international trade through negotiation. Established in 1947 at Geneva, Switzerland, 72 governments are associated with GATT. The United States participates under the authorization of the Trade Expansion Act.

8 / Foreign trade zones. In 1934 the Foreign Trade Zones Act was passed by the Congress under which it has been possible for firms in the United States to bring in foreign materials to *foreign trade zones,* where they could be processed for reexport or for sale in this country. The advantageous aspect of the foreign trade zones is that the goods from other lands involved in this procedure are not subject to tariffs, quota restrictions, or other customs regulations, unless they are later destined for import into this country. The processing may take place in the established trade zones, or, more recently, the Foreign Trade Zones Board, which administers the law, has authorized the establishment of special purpose subzones which are set up at locations away from the regular zones for the purpose of manufacturing operations. This has resulted in substantial cost savings in manufacturing goods for export. As the volume of international business grows, it is expected that there will be a commensurate increase in the use of foreign trade zones by firms who are in a position to take advantage of these facilities. For some manufacturers where the duties on manufactured parts are less than on the materials from which they are made, there is a substantial saving through the use of the zones for goods intended for use in the United States. At present there are five zones in the United States: at New York, New Orleans, San Francisco, Seattle, Toledo; and Mayaguez in Puerto Rico.

■ **Trade Activities in Europe and Latin America**

In recent years two notable occurrences in Western Europe are bound to have far-reaching effects on international trade. In 1957, the *Treaty of Rome* established the *European Economic Community* (EEC) or the *European Common Market.* Signatories to the treaty were Belgium, France, Italy, Luxembourg, the Netherlands, and Western Germany. The broad purpose of this action was to lay the foundation for the gradual merging of the economies of these nations into a huge common market, to be accomplished by a progressive lowering of their tariffs and trade import quotas.

Following the organization of the European Common Market, Austria, Britain, Denmark, Norway, Portugal, Sweden, and Switzerland formed the *European Free Trade Association* (EFTA), sometimes called the Outer Seven, to promote trade among each other, but reserving the right to trade with other nations on terms of their own, which was a contrast with the nations of the EEC. Opinions have been expressed that eventually some or all of the EFTA nations would join the EEC. The effect on international trade of the organization of these two groups must of necessity be far-reaching in the years ahead. *The Central American Common Market*, established in 1962, is made up of Costa Rica, El Salvador, Guatemala, Honduras, and Nicaragua. Its objective is to enhance the economic growth of its members and it is already reporting slow but promising growth in this area. Its progress will depend to a considerable extent on the political stability of the nations involved.

■ **Recent Action by the United States**

As a means of stimulating postwar foreign trade with the countries that suffered most in World War II, the United States undertook a broad program of foreign aid in 1948. This project was originally designed as a pump-priming operation for the affected nations in order to provide them with U. S. dollars with which they might purchase in this country the tools and materials to rehabilitate their war-torn factories and begin to produce goods for themselves. The *European Recovery Plan*, originally known as the Marshall Plan, was instituted to facilitate the recovery of certain European nations.

By 1957 the rate of growth in Europe had become such that the attention of the United States was directed elsewhere to a considerable extent, and foreign aid was made available to countries in the Near and Far East, in Africa, and particularly to Latin America. In the latter instance, the formation of the *Alliance for Progress* in 1960 signified the desire of the United States to aid the nations of Central and South America in their efforts to increase their per capita income, to achieve a more equitable distribution of their national income, and to diversify the economies of Latin American countries. The *Inter-American Development Bank* was established as an agency through which funds could be advanced to countries who qualified for aid under the Alliance for Progress.

INTERNATIONAL MARKETING

The growth in volume of the international trade of the United States, together with the competition offered by firms in other countries, has focused the attention of marketing managers of exporting companies on certain aspects of their duties that have increased in importance along with the growth of their sales in other lands. The term *international marketing* has emerged as a group description of these enhanced responsibilities. This new concept requires the recognition of differences in marketing procedures and in the legal, cultural, and economic factors in the different countries. All phases of planning and organizing for international marketing operations are covered, which include sales forecasts and market analyses; strategies of product, pricing, advertising, and selling; and the choice of channels of distribution. The *international marketing manager* must determine the characteristics of the products that can be sold in each country. He decides on whether to use salesmen from these countries or to train men from the States to handle the sales jobs. The determination of price policies, discounts, and terms of sale must be made with a full knowledge of the customs of the different nations involved. In many instances these matters require different procedures and practices from the marketing of goods in this country.

INTERNATIONAL BUSINESS

During the 1960's, there has been a notable growth of direct investments overseas by United States firms. About three-fourths of these investments have been in firms in which the equity, or ownership, of the United States companies was 95 percent or more. In 1963 the volume of direct investments abroad was $40,686 million, which was increased in 1964 to $44,344 million. In 1964 the earnings of foreign affiliates of American companies was $5.1 billion. It is anticipated that there will be a continued increase in these amounts in the years ahead.

■ The Need for American Firms to Go International

A factor in the international business picture that has become of growing importance to many firms who sell abroad is the need to adapt their operational procedures as well as their products to the peculiarities of the nations concerned. For example, the Philco-Ford Corporation, a subsidiary of the Ford Motor Company, has found it profitable to adapt its appliances to the needs of the users in Italy and to construct production facilities in that country. It looks forward also to an expansion into other countries of Europe. General Electric has acquired a 49 percent interest in Machines Bull, the leading French manufacturer of business machines. Chrysler has purchased a majority interest in Simca of France and has substantial holdings in Britain's Rootes Motors.

American firms are coming to regard their foreign operations as integral parts of the companies as a whole, not merely as stepchildren in other lands. The need for management personnel who are familiar with the customs and practices of these nations is being increasingly recognized. This is especially true in the case of firms who wish to enter the fields of Asia and Latin America.

■ Factors in the Growth of International Business

The rise of the international business concept may be attributed, with varying degrees of impact, to (1) the establishment of the European Common Market and the European Free Trade Association; (2) the increasing nationalism in many parts of the world; (3) the rising standards of living in many countries; (4) the gradual entry of some of the Eastern European Communist countries into the world economic scene; and (5) the decline of colonial empires, particularly in Africa, which holds out promise of enhanced economic activity as the governments of these emerging nations become more stable.

■ The Major Aspects of International Business

For firms that embrace the international business concept, there are several matters of considerable import. In many instances negotiations with the governments of foreign lands will be requisite to their operating in these countries. A pattern of ownership must be established—through licensing, joint ventures, or wholly owned subsidiaries. Control policies for subsidiaries or affiliates must be determined upon for such factors as the product mix, the budget, accounting procedures, and sources and uses of funds. Policies must be established determining the selection, training, transfer, and promotion of managerial personnel. In short, the foreign operations of American firms must be thoroughly integrated with the overall corporate direction of the companies concerned.

There are several items of importance upon which successful international business is dependent. Among these are the following: (a) the development of a permanent market for the producers' goods; (b) the reinvestment of the earnings in additional plant facilities, research, and development; (c) the development of products which are fitted for the markets that are sought; (d) the establishment of business practices that conform to local customs; (e) the employment of local personnel above the semiskilled category; and (f) the providing of adequate, prompt service for technical products sold.

■ Piggyback Export Sales

An international business practice of some years standing, but which has grown rapidly recently, is that of *piggyback export sales.* This is a procedure in which one producer uses its international distribution facilities to sell the products of another company along with its own. Among the more prominent firms that engage in this practice are the General Electric, Merck, Borg-Warner, and General Tire and Rubber companies. The benefits ascribed to this practice include the giving of more things to sell to foreign distributors; the broadening of product lines of the carrier companies providing the base for piggyback sales; and the bolstering of faltering sales abroad. While there are a number of different practices in this field, in most instances the carrier company buys the product that it is going to sell from its domestic producer and sells it either under its own name or that of the manufacturer.

■ The Future of International Business

Assuming that there will not be a World War III, it would seem reasonable to anticipate that the concept of international business would continue to grow. As more and more United States firms become involved in international activity, it is expected that business will assume an ever greater international character. International operations will be handled on a vice-presidential level or higher, with more attention being given to this area by corporate executives. That there may be some deterring factors as the international economic situation develops is to be expected. Credit restrictions, exchange controls, rising tariff walls, and requirements that all or part of the goods offered for sale in some countries must be produced there, are circumstances to challenge the skill and resourcefulness of American businessmen.

■ Multinational Business

The term *multinational business* is applied to a growing number of firms whose home bases are in the United States, but whose operations extend to many parts of the free world. Among these companies are the Caterpillar Tractor Company, International Telegraph and Telephone Company, Standard Oil Company (New Jersey), National Cash Register Company, Colgate-Palmolive Company, H. J. Heinz Company, and F. W. Woolworth Company. Such firms do not regard their overseas operations as mere adjuncts to their business in this country. Instead, they conceive of their organizations as multinational corporations, companies that may be located and incorporated in many foreign lands, but which are managed from their home offices in this country. It should be noted, however, that the multinational company is not solely an American institution. A large number of firms based in other lands conduct similarly widespread but centrally directed operations.

The advantages that are derived from the multinational philosophy of management and organization include the availability of managerial know-how for the direction of overseas plants and offices; the interchangeability of both personnel and products between the different countries involved; and the development of groups of managerial personnel.

Two possible disadvantages are evident. One is the difficulty of securing personnel who are capable of assuming managerial responsibilities in these far-flung companies. The other is the rising tide of nationalism evident in many countries today, of which the potentiality of the European Common Market in this respect is perhaps the most serious. For the first problem, steps are being taken to arouse an interest in this field on the part of eligible personnel both here and abroad. The problem of nationalism is a much more difficult one.

BUSINESS TERMS

(a) international trade (227)
(b) theory of absolute advantage (228), theory of comparative advantage (229)
(c) favorable balance of trade (234), unfavorable balance of trade (234)
(d) tariff (235), tariff for revenue only (235), protective tariff (235)
(e) specific duties (237), ad valorem duties (237), compound duties (237)
(f) foreign exchange (237), bills of exchange (238), rates of exchange (238)
(g) escape clause (240)
(h) foreign trade zones (241)
(i) Treaty of Rome (241), European Economic Community or European Common Market (241)
(j) European Free Trade Association or Outer Seven (242), Central American Common Market (242)
(k) European Recovery Plan (242), Alliance for Progress (242), Inter-American Development Bank (242)
(l) international marketing (243), international marketing manager (243)
(m) piggyback export sales (245)
(n) multinational business (245)

QUESTIONS FOR DISCUSSION AND ANALYSIS

1. If the more highly developed industrial nations of the world are moving away from following the theory of comparative advantage, of what value is this theory? Explain.
2. Should there be a greater volume of trade with the nations in the communist bloc and this country? Why?
3. Would you expect English to eventually become the universal language in international business? Why?
4. Why are the "invisible" items in international trade not included in the balance of trade concept?
5. What would be the effect on the economies of the different nations of the world if all tariffs were to be abolished?
6. What effect might the growth of multinational companies have on the attitude of American young men toward more or less permanent positions in other countries?
7. What steps can American business take to counteract the growth of nationalism abroad?
8. Would the adoption of a common currency by all nations tend to increase the volume of international trading? Why?
9. What are the advantages and disadvantages of seeking a career in overseas business management?
10. What would be the effect on the economy of this country if we were to stop trading with other nations?

PROBLEMS AND SHORT CASES

1. There is a growing concern in many commodity areas over the price differentials between foreign-made goods and similar products made in this country. Steel from Europe and small television receivers from Japan are examples of this circumstance. As a solution for this situation, some American firms have established branch plants in Europe to take advantage of the lower wage rates there, a move that organized labor in this country has opposed. Another remedy suggested has been the raising of tariffs on the imported products to bring their prices up to those made in the United States. A third suggestion has been to find ways of lowering the costs of domestically produced goods so that their prices may be competitive with foreign products.

   You are asked to evaluate these suggested remedies and to present your conclusions as to which should be undertaken, giving your reasons.
2. The Central American Common Market (CACM) has been experiencing a fairly satisfactory growth since its inception in 1962. Exports totaled $700 million in 1964, while trade among the members amounted to $90 million. A number of factors, however, are operating to retard the continued growth of CACM, among which are the poverty and illiteracy of many of the people, the political instability

that has long been a characteristic of this area, and the lack of adequate roads, particularly in Honduras and Nicaragua.

You are to prepare a suggested program to be engaged in jointly by the Alliance for Progress and the CACM, the objective of which would be the alleviation of these obstacles to progress and the bringing about thereby of a more rapid rate of economic growth and trade. International trade periodicals in your library that deal with Latin America and the foreign trade sections of such domestic publications as *Business Week, Time*, and *U. S. News and World Report* should be helpful in the preparation of this paper.

3. The Sampson China Company is a manufacturer of vitrified dinnerware that is sold to hotels, restaurants, and private clubs. None of its products is designed for consumer purchase. It has two strong competitors in this field, but due to the excellence of its patterns and the sturdy character of the china, the company has long held a position of prominence in the industry. Since World War II, plastic dinnerware from Japan has been taking over an increasing share of the market for hotel dinnerware in this country, affecting the sales of the Sampson China Company quite unfavorably. To meet this competition, the members of the industry in this country are considering whether to try to secure higher tariffs on imported plastic dinnerware, to produce their own plastic products, or to engage in a strong sales promotional campaign designed to regain some of the market that has been lost to the Japanese products. The manufacturing processes involved in the production of plastic dinnerware are very different from those employed in making vitrified china dinnerware.

What action should the Sampson China Company and the other members of this trade take? Justify your recommendations.

SUGGESTED READINGS

Blaisdell, D. C. *International Organization*. New York: The Ronald Press Co., 1966.

Dowd, L. P. *Principles of World Business*. Boston: Allyn & Bacon, Inc., 1965.

Farmer, R. N., and B. M. Richman. *International Business: An Operational Theory*. Homewood, Illinois: Richard D. Irwin, Inc., 1966.

Kramer, R. L. *International Marketing,* Second Edition. Cincinnati: South-Western Publishing Company, 1964.

Leighton, D. S. R. *International Marketing*. New York: McGraw-Hill Book Company, Inc., 1966.

Root, F. R., and Others. *International Trade and Finance: Theory, Policy, Practice,* Second Edition. Cincinnati: South-Western Publishing Company, 1966.

Magazines: *Current History, International Affairs, American Economic Review.*

Part IV

CHAPTER

12   Location and Layout

13   Purchasing and Inventory Control

14   Production Problems

PROLOGUE TO PART IV

OPERATIONAL FACTORS

The chapters in this part set forth the underlying principles and practices in the operations necessary to the establishing of places of business, and the procuring, handling, and manufacture of goods.

In Chapter 12 are described the problems and procedures involved when firms undertake to locate their places of business and to plan the details of their interiors. Included are all of the common types of organizations, such as factories, wholesale establishments, retail stores, and offices, with a presentation and analysis of the determining factors that influence management's decisions in these areas.

Chapter 13 deals with the practices and policies involved in the acquisition of goods by firms of all kinds and the procedures commonly followed in accounting for their presence and assuring their safekeeping until they are sold. Included in this discussion are the activities of manufacturers, wholesalers, and retailers.

Chapter 14 takes up the more common types of production problems and processes. The rapidly emerging roles of automation and computers in this area are presented. The development of the concept of scientific management is discussed, as is the organization for production management and control and the methods by which accuracy in manufacture is achieved.

Chapter 12

LOCATION AND LAYOUT

The two problems of location and layout—where business firms are to be situated and the nature of the arrangement of their offices, stores, warehouses, or factories—must be met and solved by all types of enterprises. This is true whether they be manufacturers, wholesalers, retailers, financial institutions such as banks, or service industries such as hotels, motels, laundries, or dry cleaning establishments. These problems arise not only at the time a firm is being organized, but also when, because of various reasons such as growth, changing markets, or sources of supply, it is desirable to change the location or layout. The same circumstances arise when a firm decides to establish branch plants or offices or to enlarge its present quarters.

Management should be aware of the importance of correctly solving these problems because the eventual success or failure of the firm may well be determined by its decisions concerning them. This is especially true with regard to the question of location, but only somewhat less so with layout.

PLANT LOCATION

In these days of intense competition, the difference between a favorable and an unfavorable competitive position may well depend upon the factor of proper location. Competition frequently manifests itself through the instrumentality of prices, which in turn are based on costs. A good location may contribute heavily toward a favorable cost position, whereas a poor location may have just the opposite effect. The relative permanence of any location and the difficulties attendant upon any attempt to move make it imperative that every possible step be taken to ensure the selection of the best available place.

In recent years many firms that had formerly been able to achieve satisfactory profits have discovered that their profit margins were declining, even in the face of greatly augmented sales volume and markedly higher prices. Inquiry into the possible cause of this condition frequently revealed that these companies were operating at a competitive cost disadvantage due solely to their geographical locations. While the locations were comparatively favorable at the time that the plants were established, they were later subjected to influences that brought about changes unfavorable to these localities. The companies were faced, therefore, with the problem of deciding whether to remain and endeavor to overcome their cost handicaps by achieving economies in other aspects of their operations, or to seek more favorable locations. In such cases the expense of establishing new plants and of moving machinery must be considered.

Plant Location, a Threefold Problem

The location problem for manufacturing plants has three important aspects. Management must consider, first, the section of the country where it wishes to place its producing facility; second, the particular city, town, or village that seems most desirable; and third, the availability of sites that appear to be acceptable, not only for present needs but also for any foreseeable expansion. The growth that many firms have experienced over the past two decades or more has brought with it, in many instances, the necessity for increasing their productive capacity. Where sufficient land has been available at their present sites, the problem has been relatively easy to solve. In other cases, the companies concerned have been forced to find other localities, which has involved the necessity of moving all or part of their productive facilities, with the attendant expense, which might have been avoided if their original sites had been adequate for the needed expansion. The subject of site adequacy will be discussed again briefly later in this chapter.

Production Factors Involved in Plant Location

A number of elements are involved in the determination of the location of a manufacturing facility. One group of these items, which can be classified as production factors because they are primarily related to one or more of the production problems, includes the following:

1. Raw materials
2. Labor
3. Power
4. Fuel
5. Water
6. Transportation
7. Climate

1 / **Raw materials.** The raw materials for an industry may consist of either or both of the following types: (1) unprocessed substances fresh from the earth, such as agricultural products and petroleum; and (2) semifinished goods, such as chemicals, bearings, and tanned leather, which are the end products of other industries but must be either further processed or assembled with other articles before they are ready for sale to their final consumers. The lower cost of transporting these items as raw materials as compared to that of transporting the finished products is frequently a determining factor in the placing of factories that must use them.

If the raw materials are perishable, the plants that utilize these types of goods are usually located in the agricultural districts where they are grown, as is the case in the processing of fast-frozen fruits and vegetables, and frozen fruit juice concentrates.

The raw materials question, like the others in the problem of plant location, is often one of relative costs, which need to be kept at the lowest possible level in the formidable competition that characterizes many lines of business today.

There are times when the sources of the necessary raw materials are so varied and widespread and the cost situation is so complicated that no clear-cut advantage appears to attach to locating the plant near any one of them. In such instances some other factor, such as nearness to markets or to labor, will probably be decisive.

2 / **Labor.** In determining the location for a factory, the management must study the question of the available labor supply in each community under consideration. If the company requires skilled workers, it would be foolish for it to establish its plant in a place where there is a shortage of this type of operator. If its processes require special skills that are to be found only where there are plants of a similar character, then the decision is a comparatively simple and obvious one. A firm seeking to manufacture automobile tires, for example, would find a concentration of skilled rubber workers in Akron, Ohio. On the other hand, if unskilled labor can perform satisfactorily the production tasks, the company will have a broader field from which to choose and can contemplate the setting up of its plant in those neighborhoods where unskilled workers abound.

In recent years the rapid extension of automation has pointed up some significant aspects of the labor factor. While the introduction of automated processes has frequently resulted in the displacement of unskilled and semiskilled workers, it has also brought about the need for rather highly skilled operators who can set up, operate, and, when necessary, repair the machinery. Due to the comparative newness of automation, many firms have been required to offer special training in these areas to the best workers available. However, consideration must be given to the cost of retraining workers whose former skills have been rendered obsolete through the development of automated processes. In one instance, a firm built its plant in an area where a large number of such workers were available. But the time and money involved in training the workers to become productive in the new skills were so great that it strained the resources of the company to the extent that it was forced to shut down and liquidate.

Other things being equal, there is a tendency for firms in many lines of business to gravitate away from districts where high wage rates prevail to those where labor costs are lower. The classic example of this point is to be found in the migration of large portions of the textile industry from New England to the South, although other considerations, such as the proximity of raw materials, were involved. On several occasions the National Labor Relation Board,[1] which has jurisdiction in such cases, has ruled that a unionized plant that either had moved to a lower wage location or was contemplating such action, might be in violation of its labor contract; and in at least one case the company was required to return to its original location.

In recent years *geographic wage rate differentials* (differences in wage rates between one geographic section and another) have tended to diminish. Whereas at one time differentials of as much as 50 percent were not uncommon, today these have shrunk to from 10 percent to 20 percent, with the probability that they will vanish almost entirely. Labor legislation, particularly the federal Fair Labor Standards Act, and the activities of the unions have been responsible to a large extent for this situation.

Another factor that has been of considerable moment is that of the presence or absence of labor unions. This element, like the matter of wage rate differentials, is undergoing a change; and the time may not be far distant when manufacturers will find it extremely difficult to discover communities where unions are absent. State labor laws, such as workmen's compensation acts or laws restricting the hours of labor of women or minors, constitute another factor that might influence the decision in favor of states that are lenient in this respect.

3 / Power. Relatively cheap sources of power are necessities to businesses that utilize large quantities of this service in their productive processes. Within this category are many plants manufacturing chemicals

[1] See Chapter 17 for a further discussion of the National Labor Relations Board.

and abrasives. The cheap power may be the result of a natural resource, such as Niagara Falls, or it may come from large central stations that are found in many parts of the country. The TVA (Tennessee Valley Authority) is a good example of a man-made power source. The plant of the Atomic Energy Commission at Oak Ridge, Tennessee, is located where it can take advantage of TVA power. The Norris Dam and the other dams in this project produce large quantities of power.

An alternative to the purchase of power is for a company to produce its own. This involves the construction and operation of a powerhouse, which entails not only a heavy investment in plant and equipment but also rather high fixed charges that continue even if the factory is idle for an extended period of time. For this reason many concerns prefer to purchase their power rather than to produce it themselves. They are interested, therefore, in those communities that can offer them cheap power.

4 / Fuel. In those industries where fuel is a major item of expense, proximity to low-cost sources may be one of the determining factors in the choice of a factory location. Regions that can provide large resources of oil, natural gas, or coal are in a position to offer important advantages to these industries. One of the principal reasons why the steel industry is not located at the ore sites in Minnesota, South America, or around Hudson Bay is the absence of coal in those areas. It is possible that the development of atomic energy as a source of fuel may lessen the dependence of manufacturers on regions where fuels are available.

5 / Water. Certain types of manufacturing plants require large quantities of water. For example, approximately 50,000 gallons of water are required in the manufacture of a ton of steel. In some localities the purity of the water supply is important. Among these are factories producing chemicals, paper, and rayon. Localities where the water supply is sparse or where the available water is unduly hard would be less well regarded than those areas where abundant quantities are to be found and where the softness of the water would obviate the necessity for installing expensive water softening equipment. In some parts of the United States the water table has been reported to be dropping, due both to abnormal lack of rainfall and to the increased water requirements of the factories in these areas. This condition has prompted manufacturers who are affected by the water shortage to seek new locations. The apparently increasing degree of pollution of many of the rivers of the country, due to population growth and to greater industrialization in the affected areas, has served to complicate the problem of securing pure water. Current efforts to convert ocean water into fresh water may alter existing shortages in some areas.

An additional consideration relates to the presence of adequate drainage facilities, particularly in areas where the possibilities of seasonal flooding of nearby rivers is a hazard to be encountered. In many communities, action has been taken by local governmental authorities to lessen the dangers from flooding and of water pollution. One of the more ambitious projects along this line involves the cooperative efforts of the several states that border on Lake Erie in an attempt to lessen the degree of its pollution and to remove the causes.

6 / Transportation. The transportation factor involves costs, speed, and the selection of a particular carrier from among those that are available in a given locality. If the products concerned, such as lumber and cement, can be moved by water, the problem may take on quite a different aspect than if that form of transportation is not available. The expansion of the country's network of highways, which has greatly facilitated the development of truck transportation, has served to widen the markets for companies that are able to ship their products in this manner.

The significance of freight rates as one of the elements in the transportation picture is something to which the management of a concern looking for a place to locate should give close attention. A recent study of five possible locations for a manufacturing plant disclosed the fact that between the best and the poorest locations considered, there would have been a variation of over $400,000 a year in the annual freight bill of the concern. A number of freight rate increases have materially altered the relative desirability of different communities. This circumstance is of interest not only to managements seeking locations for new or branch plants, but also to those whose present factories are situated in places that have suffered because of the changes in the freight-rate structure. The important point is that a factory should avoid locations where it would be at a disadvantage as compared with its competitors in regard to transportation. The proximity of any given site to a railroad is frequently the deciding factor in the selection of a specific location in a desirable community.

The major methods of transportation are (a) railroads, (b) motor trucks, (c) waterways, (d) pipelines, and (e) airplanes.

(a) RAILROADS. The railroads handle the largest part of the transportation in this country, embracing a total trackage of some 390,-

000 miles, and carrying between 2 and 3 billion tons of freight each year. Railroad rates are generally expressed in rates per 100 pounds or per ton from the point of origin to the destination. A distinction is made in the rates applicable to goods shipped in carload lots (*CL*) and those shipped in less than carload lots (*LCL*). LCL rates are generally between 15 and 30 percent higher than those for carload shipments.

(b) MOTOR TRUCKS. For relatively short hauls, up to 300 miles, motor trucks compete with railroads. They are of particular importance for communities with infrequent or no railroad service. Their rates vary from levels lower than those applied by the railroads to those measurably higher. In many parts of the country, a combination truck and rail service, known as *piggyback freight*, is available. In this instance, goods are loaded on trucks which, in turn, are driven up onto special railroad flat cars. These cars are then made a part of a train moving in the direction of the trucks' destinations, frequently overnight. Later at a predetermined point, the trucks are driven off the cars and proceed under their own power to the points to which the goods are consigned.

(c) WATERWAYS. The waterways of the country—rivers, the Great Lakes, and the coastwise routes—are of considerable importance in the movement of certain kinds of freight, such as goods of large bulk and low value, of which coal, grain, oil, lumber, sugar, and cotton are examples. Water transportation is the cheapest but also the slowest method of moving goods. The Great Lakes are important to the movement of iron ore, grain, and coal. The rivers are used to move cotton, coal, and building materials. Coastwise shipping is useful for oil, cotton, lumber, and coal. The St. Lawrence Seaway has increased the international trading facilities of Great Lakes ports. Water transportation also affords a type of service called *fishyback freight,* similar to the piggyback freight of the railroads, in which trucks can be driven onto ships and transported to points nearer their destinations.

(d) PIPELINES. A network of around 160,000 miles of pipelines is used to transport crude petroleum and natural gas. If the cost of building a pipeline is to be justified, there must be continuous processing of the material transported at each end of the line. For this reason, companies owning the pipelines consider them to be extensions of their productive facilities rather than as transportation devices. While pipelines have the disadvantages of governmental regulation and inflexible routes, they have a distinct cost advantage over transportation by railroad or motor carrier.

(e) AIRPLANES. Air transportation is noteworthy for its speed, its advantage in long-distance hauling, its relatively high cost, and the fact that its cargoes must consist of items of relatively small bulk and high value, or quick perishability, although more recent developments would seem to indicate that quite large commodities can be flown to their destinations. Many of the major airlines of the country offer air-freight service to and from the bigger cities, utilizing large jet aircraft.

7 / Climate. In certain industries the nature of the climate—temperature and humidity—is a factor that assumes considerable importance. The manufacturer of shoes, for example, prefers a moist climate because he does not wish the leather that he uses to dry out rapidly. The manufacturer of airplanes seeks a climate that makes possible the year-round testing of his finished product.

Recent developments in air conditioning have tended to lessen the importance of the climate factor. At one time New England was considered the most desirable section of the nation in which to locate a textile industry. Now that it is possible to control the humidity of the air in a factory by mechanical means, New England does not have this same advantage over certain other sections of the country.

A factor in the recent migration of many plants to the South and Far West is that in these sections of the country, with their relatively short seasons of cold weather, heating costs are appreciably less than in northern climes.

■ Other Factors Involved in Plant Location

Production factors are not the only ones considered when a decision is made concerning the location of a plant. Other factors involved include:

1. Markets
2. Location of competitors
3. Special characteristics of
   the business
4. Room for expansion

5. Local inducements
6. Chance
7. Land and building costs
8. Human factors

1 / Markets. In many lines of business it is vital to the success of the enterprise that the factory be located close to the markets for the products. Examples include producers of oil-well equipment, who are usually located near the oil fields; makers of automotive parts, who are to be found in lower Michigan near the manufacturers of automobiles; and producers of folding boxes, who are ordinarily located in the same cities as their customers. Nearness of factory to appropriate markets is essential where rapid delivery to customers is important, where the product is relatively perishable, and where frequent factory service is necessary. In these instances the factory or, in some cases, branch plants should be situated comparatively close to the markets for the goods produced. The element of transportation costs naturally enters the location decision with regard to proximity to markets, the lower cost locations in this respect being preferable, provided there is no important sacrifice of speed of delivery.

2 / Location of competitors. Some lines of business have centered around certain localities. Examples are the automobile industry, the majority of whose members have their main plants in or near Detroit, Michigan; the steel industry around Pittsburgh, Birmingham, and Gary; and cotton textiles in the Southeast. Originally there may or may not have been some logical reason, such as nearness to raw materials or power, that accounted for the selection of their localities by the industries concerned. Regardless of these factors, however, it is sometimes greatly to the advantage of a concern contemplating the establishing of a new factory, or the removal of an old one, to be situated in or close to the center of the industry. Frequently there are accessory businesses nearby; the offices of the trade associations may be located there; or the labor supply may be peculiarly well suited to the type of business. In any event, when a recognized center for manufacturers of a given type has been established, there is a tendency for newcomers to be attracted to the same locality.

3 / Special characteristics of the business. The manufacture of some lines of goods takes place under conditions that involve special problems of location. Plants where explosives are made are customarily placed far from other factories or places of human habitation. Chemical plants sometimes emit unpleasant or harmful odors that cause them likewise to be placed in isolated spots. The same may be true of industries where large quantities of refuse are inescapable results of the manufacturing processes.

The plant of the Corn Products Refining Company, built to process milo maize and placed in an isolated section of Corpus Christi, Texas, near the Gulf of Mexico, is an interesting example of the need for a special location on account of the peculiar characteristics of the production process. The manufacture of this product involves potential danger from explosions and acid fumes. Hence the plant was placed where the breezes from the Gulf could carry away the fumes and far enough from the populated portion of the city itself to obviate the possibility of danger from a blast.

4 / Room for expansion. As previously noted, the adequacy of any site for anticipated future expansion is receiving increasing attention from managements. The term *site saturation* is used to describe a condition where a given location offers little, if any, opportunity for future expansion. Alert managements endeavor to avoid placing their plants where site saturation may be indicated at some future time. Likewise, a firm whose present location may be so limited as to suggest that this condition could occur in the not too distant future would be well advised to consider moving to a larger site before this time arrives.

5 / Local inducements. There are times when the foregoing factors are of no particular consequence and when the choice between two or more acceptable communities may be determined by certain local considerations. Some of these are low taxes, even postponement of taxes for a period of time in some instances, free or cheap land, available sites, low rentals, favorable banking connections, and good living conditions. The chambers of commerce of most cities are very active in endeavoring to attract factories to their localities, and competition between these places sometimes produces some enticing offers to interested industrialists.

With the ever-increasing attention that management has been giving to the well-being of its employees, the availability of such civic benefits as good schools, housing, hospitals, shopping centers, recreational facilities, and libraries is sometimes given considerable weight in the final choice of a location.

A matter of growing importance is the availability of a local airport that will serve executive airplanes. With the increase in the number of firms with branch offices and plants in different parts of the country, adequate facilities for handling air traffic of this nature constitute a strong point in favor of those communities thus equipped.

6 / Chance. A realistic view of the factors affecting the choice of a plant location must recognize that many communities are selected on the basis of chance to some extent. This does not mean that a coin is tossed or that dice are thrown, but rather that the irrationality of human conduct in many instances brings about decisions in this matter that have little, if any, foundation in reasoned conclusions based on a careful evaluation of all of the factors concerned. In a great many instances a company is located where it is merely because the founders or owners happened to live there. Likewise, when a move is contemplated or a branch plant is projected, the selection may be based on the personal prejudices of certain officers or on other wholly illogical grounds. This method is not recommended as a scientific procedure, but it would be useless to deny its existence.

7 / Land and building costs. Although there is frequently little difference in land prices and building costs, the marked advance in these items in certain sections of the country during recent years has directed management's attention to these costs as possible deciding factors in the choice between two or more sites under consideration.

8 / Human factors. An item that can be of some consequence when the location of a plant is under consideration is known as human factors. It refers to the general attitude of the people in a community, particularly toward new industries and the personnel associated with them. This is an intangible factor, often difficult to evaluate in advance of the actual locating of a plant; but it can sometimes be sensed through observation and such contacts with the people of the different areas as may be achieved during the survey of the eligible sites.

■ **Site Selection Procedure**

The actual determination of a location for a factory may be made by top management, sometimes assisted by engineering firms who are skilled in the methods of site selection. Flying over prospective sites by helicopter is recommended as a method of permitting a comprehensive view of the terrain involved, which might be difficult from the ground. Regardless of actual steps taken, such of the preceding factors as are pertinent should be carefully considered before a final decision is made.

LOCATION OF OTHER TYPES OF BUSINESSES

The factors that make up the location problems of nonmanufacturing businesses are fairly simple since they are largely local in character. For these concerns the question of location usually resolves itself into that of determining upon the section of a city or its suburbs where they wish to go. There are exceptions, of course, as in the case of a wholesaler who wishes to extend his market into other parts of the country or of the chain store organization that desires to broaden its scope along the same lines.

The notable growth of the suburbs that surround most of the large cities of this country has created location problems of considerable magnitude for all types of nonmanufacturing firms.

For the purpose of clarity and simplicity, the nonmanufacturing companies are divided into wholesalers, retailers, and service establishments, and their location problems are considered separately.

■ Location of Wholesalers

Wholesalers who are contemplating establishing warehouses or moving from their present quarters must consider the following points: nearness to retail stores, to a railroad siding, and to the wholesale district; and available sites.

With the establishing in the past few years of suburban shopping centers on the peripheries of metropolitan areas, wholesalers have been forced largely to disregard the factor of nearness to their customers. In smaller cities, without such developments, proximity to most of their customers is still of some consequence.

It is frequently desirable for a wholesaler to be located on a railroad siding, as this reduces the handling and transportation costs on incoming goods.

Firms engaged in some lines, such as wholesale fresh fruits and vegetables, should be situated in or close to the wholesale district specializing in their wares. In other lines this proximity is not a matter of any consequence. In many cities, however, drug, hardware, clothing, and paper wholesalers tend to be grouped together.

In any case the number and the location of available sites are limiting factors in the determination of a wholesaler's business address.

■ Location of Retailers

Manufacturers and wholesalers go to their customers through representatives or salesmen, but the customers of retailers come to them. Consequently, retail stores must be readily available to their patrons. A store that is unfavorably situated in this regard may lose out competitively even though its merchandise is excellent, its prices are attractive, and the management is entirely capable.

Of paramount importance to a retailer seeking a location for his store is the matter of available sites. If he wishes to enter a certain community that has no vacant stores, he is prevented from achieving his objective until more store buildings are constructed or until one of the present stores moves or leaves the field.

The following factors must be considered:

1. Nature of customer traffic
2. Character of neighbor- hood
3. Availability of adequate parking space
4. Nearness to a trading center
5. Nearness to competitors
6. Rental or sale price
7. Downtown vs. suburbs

1 / Nature of customer traffic. A retailer who is appraising the merits of a prospective location should give some thought to the character and amount of the pedestrian traffic that passes the store because it is from these passers-by that many of the store's customers will come. This factor has assumed considerable importance in recent years. Chain store executives conduct qualitative and quantitative traffic counts near the places where they contemplate establishing stores. A retailer who expects to stock his store with women's wear will hardly choose a location where the traffic consists chiefly of men.

2 / Character of neighborhood. A retailer should study carefully the characteristics of the neighborhood that he is considering. This applies with particular emphasis to any changes for better or for worse that may be noticeable or in prospect. In various parts of the country trading centers have declined because the character of the neighborhood has changed. This is frequently the result of the advance of slum areas in cities, because a factory has been closed, or sometimes because a change in city zoning laws has permitted factories to enter an area, with a consequent lowering of the economic level of the surrounding residential district. Retailers who are so unfortunate as to be caught in such circumstances may experience the failure of their enterprises.

3 / Availability of adequate parking space. The need for adequate parking space for customers' cars has been increasingly recognized by retailers operating in the suburban shopping centers of the larger cities. The speed with which the stores in these projects have been rented and the relative absence of vacancies attest to the importance of parking.

4 / Nearness to a trading center. Stores tend to be grouped together into what are known as *trading centers*. Examples of these are the downtown shopping centers, the neighborhood trading centers, and the "automobile rows" of many large cities, as well as those that have appeared in recent years on the outskirts of many metropolitan centers. To these centers the customers come to make their purchases. A store

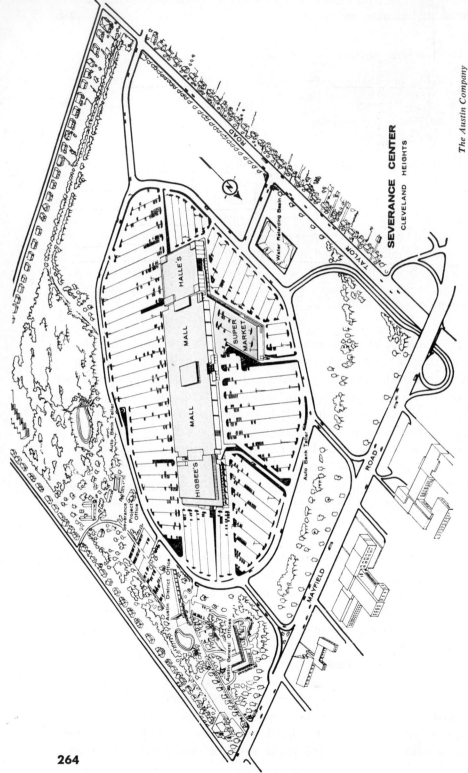

SEVERANCE CENTER
CLEVELAND HEIGHTS

The Austin Company

An Innovation in Shopping Centers

In this type of shopping center all or most of the stores are under one roof, with a central mall, sometimes covered and air-conditioned. The parking areas surround the shopping center.

located near the heart of a trading center will thus have a certain advantage over one that is situated on the outskirts of the center. Hence it is advisable for a retailer to note the position of any available vacancies with respect to the trading centers of which they may be parts. Delicatessen stores, which are open evenings and on Sundays, may be able to disregard this factor to some degree.

In the so-called *controlled shopping centers,* a recent development in the trading-center field, the owners of these projects frequently determine, in advance of giving leases, the number of stores of each type that will be permitted on the premises. Thus, in any one center there may be only two grocery stores, two drugstores, two apparel stores, and so on. The purpose of this restriction is to afford the tenants a reasonable chance of profitable business by preventing too great a concentration of competing stores.

The sketch on page 264 shows one of the latest developments in controlled shopping centers. Here all of the stores are under one roof and may be entered from a central, air-conditioned mall. The parking areas surround the shopping center.

5 / Nearness to competitors. Progressive retailers, particularly those handling shopping goods, try to secure locations as close to their competitors as possible. They do so on the assumption that this proximity will bring the consumers who visit their competitors into their stores also. This factor is closely related to the trading-center idea.

6 / Rental or sale price. Usually a fairly close relationship exists between the rental or sale price of a location and its relative desirability as a site for a store. Competition between retailers who wish to rent or to buy and between landlords who wish to lease or to sell their properties tends to bring about a parity in rentals or selling prices for locations of equal desirability. In occasional instances, however, outside influences may enter the picture and disrupt this condition. The need for settling an estate, new store building projects, or other things of this nature may enable a retailer to make unusually favorable arrangements concerning the rental or purchase price of his new location. Alert retailers are always on the lookout for such situations.

7 / Downtown vs. suburbs. As noted in Chapter 8, the growth of suburban shopping centers has brought about the question of the desirability, perhaps even the eventual survival, of the downtown retail areas. The answer to this question is still far in the future and will be a local situation in every instance, depending upon the geography of the cities involved, the character of the public transportation, the access routes available, the parking facilities, and other factors. The problem presented to retailers already located downtown is that of deciding whether to move to suburban sites, to establish branches there, or to remain in their present locations. For those who plan to open new stores, the desirability of downtown versus the suburbs must be determined, a decision fraught with considerable risk. And for retailers who favor the suburban locations, there is the problem of selecting the one or more communities in which to establish their stores.

■ Location of Service Establishments and Offices

Service establishments, such as garages and service stations, restaurants, laundries and dry cleaning shops, beauty parlors, and barber shops, also have location problems. To a very considerable extent the factors that affect the choice of the location of retail stores apply to this category of enterprises.

For gasoline service stations, restaurants, and motels, the growth of the interstate freeway system has presented new locational opportunities. While these facilities are not permitted on the freeways, many of them have been established near the exits, with signs visible from the freeways indicating their presence.

The problems of office location are rather simple. Downtown business offices are dependent for their locations on the availability of vacant space in office buildings and its adequacy for their needs. Factory offices are usually located on the factory sites. In many of the larger cities, firms whose offices had been located in the downtown areas have been moving to the suburbs. Among the principal reasons for this has been the growing traffic congestion in and around these cities, which has made going to and from work quite difficult for the personnel of these companies, particularly for those who live in suburban communities. By moving out of the central city areas, the problems of traffic congestion and parking have been largely alleviated.

LAYOUT

Business firms must solve problems of layout as well as those of location. The types of layout problems depend upon the nature of the business, that is, whether it is a manufacturing company, a retail store, or an office.

■ **Plant Layout**

The purpose of plant layout is to bring about the best obtainable combination of plant and equipment from the standpoint of the highest standards of production and the lowest unit cost. The more important factors that must be taken into account by plant executives at the time the matter of plant layout comes up for consideration are the following:

1. Type of manufacturing process
2. Manufacturing policy
3. Type of product
4. Amount of labor required
5. Volume of work
6. Internal transportation
7. Need for flexibility

1 / Type of manufacturing process. The two principal types of manufacturing process are the intermittent and the continuous. The difference between the two is to be found mainly in the length of the period of time during which labor and equipment are applied continuously to the materials being processed. In the case of the *intermittent process* these periods are relatively brief. With the *continuous process* they are much longer, often being of several months' duration.

In many lines of production, such as in the manufacture of electrical appliances and typewriters, it is both possible and feasible to interrupt the flow of production at regular or irregular intervals. In the steel, glass, and synthetic fiber industries, on the other hand, it is essential that certain of the manufacturing processes be continued day and night, Sundays and holidays, if the products are to be suitable for later fabrication and losses through product spoilage are to be avoided.

2 / Manufacturing policy. Closely allied to the foregoing factor is that of manufacturing policy since it determines whether the company is to produce to order or for stock. When a firm follows a policy of *production to order,* it makes an item only after it has received a customer's order. This situation is quite common where a company makes goods to the buyer's specifications, as in a custom machine shop or a retail lumber yard. *Production for stock,* however, is undertaken before orders are received and when a company's product is more or less standardized, as in the manufacture of many electrical appliances and men's clothing. Manufacturing policy is determined to some extent by the nature of the products; for example, road-building machinery, which is usually designed especially for the job, is rarely made up for stock. Shirt makers, however, may keep a sizable inventory of finished goods on hand for rapid delivery to their customers.

3 / Type of product. The manufacturing policies of some companies call for the fabrication of products almost in their entirety, while others call for the purchase of nearly all of the component parts from outside makers and the performance of only the assembly operations. A good example of the former policy is the Ford Motor Company, which has always made a very large portion of the parts entering into the Ford products. Some manufacturers of room air conditioners exemplify the latter practice. Companies that embrace the first of these policies have problems of layout that are quite different from those to be met by concerns that follow the second course of action.

4 / Amount of labor required. The quantity of labor that the manufacturing operation requires, in relation to machines, tools, benches, and other equipment and tools, is likewise pertinent to the question of layout. Concerns that require considerable hand labor, such as tool makers, will seek the solution of their layout problems along lines different from those of firms with a low ratio of labor to machinery, such as in machine shops. For those firms whose manufacturing processes have been automated to any extent, the layout problems may be quite extensive.

5 / Volume of work. The amount of work that will normally be progressing through a plant will have an important bearing on the number of machines and men required to handle it and the consequent physical setup of the plant.

6 / Internal transportation. Intrafactory transportation of parts and materials is costly. A well-planned layout, having due regard for the materials-handling equipment on hand or available, will reduce this cost to a minimum. In recent years this factor has been receiving an increasing amount of attention from engineers and builders who have recognized the cost-saving aspects of layouts where crosshauling is reduced to a minimum and where the straight-line pattern of moving goods can be employed most fully.

The layout shown on page 269 is an excellent example of the straight-line production layout. The incoming materials (sometimes known as *inputs*) enter at the right, and the finished products (*outputs*) leave the plant at the left after going through the requisite manufacturing processes.

7 / Need for flexibility. Underlying all other considerations in the matter of layout is the basic need for flexibility and changeability in any plan that might be adopted. The attempt should be made to foresee any

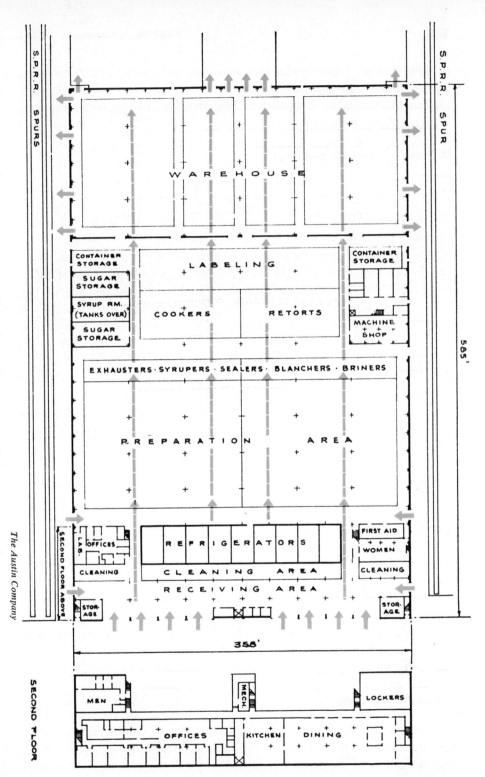

The Austin Company

585'

S.P.R.R. SPURS

S.P.R.R. SPUR

WAREHOUSE

CONTAINER STORAGE

SUGAR STORAGE

SYRUP RM. (TANKS OVER)

SUGAR STORAGE

LABELING

COOKERS

RETORTS

CONTAINER STORAGE

MACHINE SHOP

EXHAUSTERS · SYRUPERS · SEALERS · BLANCHERS · BRINERS

P. R E P A R A T I O N   A R E A

SECOND FLOOR ABOVE

LAB.

OFFICES

CLEANING

STOR-AGE

REFRIGERATORS

CLEANING   AREA

RECEIVING   AREA

FIRST AID

WOMEN

CLEANING

STOR-AGE

358'

SECOND FLOOR

MEN

MECH.

LOCKERS

OFFICES

KITCHEN

DINING

possible future circumstances that may call for changes in the layout. Although this obviously cannot be done with a very great degree of exactitude, any effort expended in this direction should result in time-saving and troublesaving.

■ Types of Factory Buildings

Most factory buildings in this country can be classified as single, or flat-roof, and multistory types. The *flat-roof type* is widely used in many different industries, among which are those that produce sewing machines, electrical precision instruments, aircraft, and saws.

Designers of factory buildings have lately been given increasing attention to planning structures in which there is positive control of light, ventilation, temperature, humidity, and sound, quite independent of the natural sources of these elements. Many of these plants have few windows and rely entirely on artificial controls. This is undoubtedly one of the most outstanding plant-construction developments of recent years.

The multistory type is useful where the ground space available is limited and when materials may be moved through gravity conveyor systems. It is used in the rayon and coffee-roasting fields, for example. One disadvantage of this type is lack of flexibility. Natural illumination is possible only when the floor space is greatly restricted in size. For several years engineers and architects who plan factory buildings have strongly favored the flat-roof, single-story structure as being more economical than the other types where the production processes permit of its use.

■ Wholesale Layout

The problems that wholesalers must solve in their layouts are concerned mainly with the most economical movement of the goods from the receiving docks to the storage bins, and thence, as orders are received and processed, to the shipping platforms for delivery to the firms' customers. Attaining efficient procedures in wholesale operations has involved a multiplicity of materials-handling equipment, such as overhead conveyors, chutes, tracks for small trucks, and roller conveyors.

■ Retail-Store Layout

The current trend toward the modernization of retail stores, together with the increase in the factor of self-service, makes layout a problem of intense interest to the student of business. As in the case of plant layout, several factors must be taken into consideration when the store owners or executives are contemplating the establishment of a new store or the remodeling of an old one. These factors are:

1. Type of merchandise
2. Type of service
3. Characteristics of customer traffic
4. Method of moving customers
5. Lighting
6. Ventilation and heating
7. Store service requirements
8. Customer parking

1 / Type of merchandise. The nature of the merchandise is basic in the consideration of mercantile layout. The handling and sale of groceries, drugs, hardware, wearing apparel, and furniture, to mention only a very few of the many different types of goods sold at retail, give rise to problems of layout peculiar to the particular goods concerned. Furniture, for example, requires a large amount of space for the proper display of the various pieces and suites. Wearing apparel, on the other hand, can be hung on racks but requires mirrors and individual dressing rooms.

2 / Type of service. The trend to self-service (sometimes called self-selection) in the food, drug, and variety fields has brought a number of novel and interesting developments. For this type of operation wide aisles and easily accessible shelving or tiered tables are required. Space must also be provided for cart storage, checkout counters, and, in many instances, facilities whereby customers' purchases may be placed in their cars as they drive up to the "pick-up" station.

The growth in the production and sale of frozen foods has brought with it the need for a greater number of refrigerated cases to store and display these goods. Another recent development in some of the more modern self-service grocery stores involves the cutting, weighing, and packaging of meat prior to its being offered for sale to consumers. This presale preparation takes place in the store's backroom, and the various packaged cuts are displayed in cold counters that have been specially designed for this purpose. The location of these new types of counters, with respect to the flow of traffic through the store, becomes a major problem of layout for the self-service type of store.

Opposed to this type of store is the older, service kind, in which clerks "wait on" the customers and procure for them the desired goods. Here counters of various lengths are required, and the layout is quite different from that of the self-service store. Among the operators of both service and self-service stores there appears to be little agreement as to the best patterns of layout.

3 / Characteristics of customer traffic. In many types of service stores the flow of customer traffic has an important bearing upon the location of the goods. The fact that customers tend to turn to the right upon entering the store is of importance in the placing of certain goods, such as impulse merchandise, on the right side of the store, where they will be exposed to the greatest amount of traffic. Impulse merchandise is frequently bought as the result of customers' spur-of-the-moment decisions, which are stimulated by attractive displays that call merchandise to their attention. Examples include such varied types of products as candies, men's neckwear, tobacco products, inexpensive or costume jewelry, novelties, toilet goods, and ladies' purses.

The owners of some self-service grocery stores have planned the layouts of their aisles in such a manner that customers are required to proceed to the rear of the stores in order to gain access to most of the merchandise displays and to the check-out counters. The purpose of this sort of layout is to force customers to pass a large part of the goods on sale before leaving. The belief is that in this manner customers will be exposed to a greater variety of goods, and presumably will buy more.

4 / Method of moving customers. If goods are offered for sale on more than one floor, as in department and specialty stores, there arises the question of the means of affording customers access to the upper levels. Stairs, elevators, and escalators are commonly used for this purpose. The selection of the types to be used and their location provide one of the major layout problems that store executives must solve.

5 / Lighting. The sources of illumination, either natural or artificial, are important elements in determining where goods and fixtures shall be placed. Displays should be adequately lighted so that customers may be attracted to the merchandise and be able to inspect it. In this, as in many of the other items in mercantile layout, the comfort and the convenience of customers are given paramount consideration.

6 / Ventilation and heating. In planning the layout of a store, provision must be made for the placing of the heating and ventilating apparatus. With the great increase in the use of air conditioning in stores of many kinds, the locating of the required ducts and vents has become a problem calling for careful consideration.

7 / Store service requirements. In addition to the foregoing factors, which are principally concerned with those phases of store operation that have to do with customers, there are several others that might be termed "store service requirements." Some of these concern the provision of adequate and correct space and facilities for receiving, marking, and storing merchandise, and for wrapping and packing it for delivery after it is sold. Added to these are the requirements for office space and rest rooms.

8 / **Customer parking.** Some of the suburban branch department stores have endeavored to aid in solving their customers' parking problems by providing space on their roofs for this purpose. Ramps lead up from the street level, and easy access to the stores is provided through conveniently located penthouse type structures that house stairways or elevators.

■ Office or Commercial Layout

The third major type of layout to be considered is that of office layout, or commercial layout as it is sometimes called. The items to be considered in this connection are quite different from those discussed in plant and mercantile layout. Goods are not fabricated in an office, and the convenience of customers need not be considered in the same way. The problems of office layout are related primarily to the efficient performance of clerical work. They include the following factors:

(1) The course of the flow of paper work governs, to a considerable extent, the layout of the office. Insofar as possible, the work should move uninterruptedly through the various departments, following as straight a line as conditions will permit. This factor affects not only the placing of departments, but also the locating of desks, files, and other equipment within the departments.

(2) The need for private offices for executives and department heads will have an important bearing on the office layout.

(3) The number of business machines used and the amount of disturbance that they make will determine whether they are to be placed in the general office or given an enclosure of their own. Certain types of tabulating and accounting machinery produce a din that makes it necessary to place them in a separate, more or less soundproof room.

(4) Light, heat, ventilation, and air conditioning must be kept in mind in planning the office layout, since they will weigh heavily among the items that affect the efficiency of the office employees.

(5) In many instances provision must be made for the reception of visitors whose business requires them to call at the office. In some of

the newer offices rather elaborate facilities are to be found for this purpose, such as waiting and conference rooms.

The fairly widespread introduction of data processing equipment and computers in the past few years has brought about the need for revamping office layout in many firms.

■ Layout Procedures

Before actually proceeding to arrange the machinery, fixtures, or furniture in any layout situation, it is customary for those in charge of the job to set forth their ideas in miniature. They utilize for this purpose a large sheet of paper and small paper, cardboard, or even metal pieces that represent the essential furniture or fixtures. These miniature items are sometimes referred to as *templates*. On the paper the outlines of the available rooms with all doors, windows, heating and lighting outlets, and other permanent parts of the building are drawn to scale. On this sheet are placed the pieces, likewise carefully made to scale, in the locations that the real fixtures will probably occupy. In this manner it is possible, to some extent, to foresee the finished layout and to judge its probable effectiveness. Any adjustments to the layout plan that may appear to be needed can be made in miniature, and the results of these changes may be noted before the actual placing of the fixtures is begun. Thus there emerges from this process a much more satisfactory final layout scheme than would probably be the case if this step were omitted.

BUSINESS TERMS

(a) geographic wage rate differentials (254)
(b) CL (257), LCL (257)
(c) piggyback freight (257), fishyback freight (257)
(d) site saturation (260)
(e) trading centers (263), controlled shopping centers (265)
(f) intermittent process (267), continuous process (267)
(g) production to order (267), production for stock (267)
(h) inputs (268), outputs (268)
(i) flat-roof type (270)
(j) templates (274)

QUESTIONS FOR DISCUSSION AND ANALYSIS

1. Where the available locations for a new factory all seem to be equally advantageous, what factors might be determinative in the final selection by management?

2. Many metropolitan areas have set aside large tracts of land for what are known as industrial parks, anticipating that a considerable number of new factories will locate there. What arguments can you think of as favorable to a plant selecting a site in one of these parks? What unfavorable ones?

3. Do you think that the eventual disappearance of geographic wage differentials will retard the movement of factories from the North to the South? Why? *shoe industry can move to south, may slow it down somewhat* *argue either way*

4. Do you agree with the decision of the National Labor Relations Board, mentioned in this chapter, that ordered a firm which had moved to a lower wage area to return to its original location? Why?

5. Do you think that the probable increased use of automation in factories will have any effect on the location decisions of plants that adopt this method of production? Explain.

6. In many cities the movement of population to the suburbs has left a considerable acreage of land in the central cities that is either vacant or has become a slum area. Do you think that the vacant spaces should be rezoned for industrial production? Why?

7. It is common practice in many supermarkets to establish a "fast checkout," where customers with fewer than eight or ten items may go to avoid the waiting in line that is common when there is no such facility. Other supermarkets do not provide such a checkout. Which of these conflicting practices is preferable? Why?

8. Should a department store branch be established in a shopping center where a competing department store already has a branch, or should it be placed where no such competition is present? Explain.

9. Do you know of any plants in which chance was probably the determining factor in their locations? If so, name them and give reasons for your opinion.

10. With the continuing spread of suburbs in areas ever farther away from the central cities, would you anticipate that there would be a growth of branch wholesale houses to serve the retailers in the new suburban areas? Explain.

PROBLEMS AND SHORT CASES

1. Firms that are considering the establishment of branch plants frequently find that their basic location choices are between vacant areas in large cities and similar vacancies in small cities in rural areas. You are to assume that the decision to locate a branch plant in one or the other of these contrasting localities has been made your responsibility.

   Prepare a short paper setting forth the reasons for and against each of these location types and giving your recommendation as to the action that should be taken. You may make any assumptions that you wish regarding the production processes, types of labor required, transportation, or any other pertinent factors.

2. Since the first suburban branch department store was established in 1930, the prediction has frequently been made that eventually the

downtown shopping areas of our large cities will disappear and that
all surviving department stores will consist of outlets located in the
suburbs. Over 30 years have passed since the trend to suburban
branches began; and the downtown areas continue to survive, although
in New York, Boston, and Cleveland, there have been instances of
department stores closing their downtown outlets, and in most large
cities the branch store movement has been growing.

Prepare a paper setting forth your own opinion in this matter.
Give your reasons.

3. The F. C. Taylor Company, one of the leading manufacturers of
electronic equipment widely used in industry, with plants located in
many different parts of the country, has long had its general offices
located in an old office building in a suburb of New York City. The
growth of the company during the past few years, which has required
the employment of additional office personnel and also the installation of data processing equipment, has forced the management to lease
space in various other office buildings in its present community to
provide adequate space for its office employees and computers. Over
the years this arrangement has proved to be both costly and unwieldy and the management is contemplating a move that will concentrate the personnel and the office hardware in a single location.
Two alternatives are being considered. One possibility is for the
company to move into one of the newer office buildings that have
been erected in New York City; the other is to purchase land nearer
one of the expressways and construct a building of its own.

Make a list of the advantages and disadvantages inherent in both
of these moves and give your opinion of the more favorable action
that the company should take.

SUGGESTED READINGS

Armine, H. T., and Others. *Manufacturing Organization and Management,*
Second Edition. Englewood Cliffs, New Jersey: Prentice-Hall, Inc.,
1966. Chapters 4 and 10.

Broom, H. N. *Production Management.* Homewood, Illinois: Richard D.
Irwin, Inc., 1962. Chapter 9.

Broom, H. N., and J. G. Longenecker. *Small Business Management,*
Second Edition. Cincinnati: South-Western Publishing Company,
1966. Part B.

Davidson, W. R., and A. F. Doody. *Retailing Management,* Third Edition. New York: The Ronald Press Co., 1966. Part II.

Lasser, J. K. *How to Run a Small Business,* Third Edition. New York:
McGraw-Hill Book Company, Inc., 1963. Part I.

Moore, F. G. *Manufacturing Management,* Fourth Edition. Homewood,
Illinois: Richard D. Irwin, Inc., 1965. Chapters 11, 12, and 13.

Neuner, J. J. W., and B. L. Keeling. *Administrative Office Management,*
Fifth Edition. Cincinnati: South-Western Publishing Company, 1966.
Part II.

Chapter 13

PURCHASING AND INVENTORY CONTROL

At the producers' level, the acquiring of goods is termed *purchasing*. At the wholesale and retail levels, the term *buying* predominates. *Inventory control* (or *stock control*) is the term used to describe the procedures and methods involved in taking care of the goods at all three levels. The purpose of this chapter is to discuss the problems of purchasing and inventory control as they affect producers of all goods, consumer and industrial, and the distributors of consumer goods. In the field of manufacturing, these goods are frequently called *materials*; in wholesaling and retailing, the term *merchandise* is in common usage.

■ Importance of Purchasing and Inventory Control

Consumers buy things for their own use, not for resale, and the determining factors in the choice of goods are frequently of an emotional rather than a rational nature. With business buyers, however, the element of profit (or loss) that is inevitably present, tends to emphasize the rational aspects of any purchase transaction. Producers buy goods that are to be fabricated into products for which they believe there is a market. These products may be purchased by other producers for further processing, or by wholesalers or retailers for eventual sale to ultimate consumers. Since consumers are free to choose between different types of goods in making their purchases, it becomes essential that business buyers at the wholesale and retail levels, who deal in goods that are destined for consumer use, be adept both in judging consumers' preferences and in estimating the quantities that they will buy. Manufacturers of consumer goods must likewise strive to guage the wants of consumers, but this is usually the function of the marketing officials or of the engineers rather than that of the purchasing department. The same situation regarding the role of

277

purchasing and the purchasing department prevails in the manufacture of industrial and commercial goods.

During the time that goods are in the possession of a business, a tie-up of capital is involved, capital upon which the company wishes to make a profit. It is therefore requisite that these goods should be properly handled, stored, and accounted for during the time that the firm has them in its possession. Proper storage and handling facilities and inventory control routines are necessary to safeguard the valuable investments that are represented in the inventories of goods. Thus purchasing involves the securing of the right goods and inventory control protects and accounts for them after they are bought.

A major aim of inventory (stock) control is to achieve the correct balance between the quantity of stock on hand and the current requirements of the business.

■ Types of Goods

The goods involved in purchasing and inventory control can be divided into two broad groups: (1) those purchased infrequently and on a nonrepetitive basis, such as machinery, office equipment, lighting fixtures, store counters, and cash registers; and (2) those bought more often on a repetitive basis, such as raw materials, semifinished goods, and finished goods, which may be either industrial or consumer goods. With the first group there is no problem of stock control because these items become part of the fixtures of the companies using them and are replaced only as they wear out or become obsolete. The second group, however, presents problems both of purchase and of inventory control. Such goods must not only be bought, but they must also be subjected to control procedures while they are on hand in order to make certain that they go to their proper destinations in the production process or within the warehouse or store and to prevent their being lost.

PURCHASE OF MATERIALS

Before the production of goods can proceed in a plant, the materials that make up the product must be purchased and brought into the factory. The requisite machinery, tools, transportation equipment, and other manufacturing facilities must also be present. These, however, are more a part of the construction and layout picture than of production. For this discussion it is assumed that these facilities have been provided and that what is needed is to acquire the materials from which the finished products will be made. The function of the purchasing division is to assume the responsibility for seeing that this need is taken care of. Chronologically, purchasing might be regarded as the first step in production. Materials must be purchased before they can be processed.

■ Purchasing Department

That part of the organization of a manufacturing firm that has the task of procuring the required materials for production is known as the *purchasing department*. The head of the purchasing department is usually called the *purchasing agent*. In small plants the purchasing agent and a clerk or two may comprise the purchasing department, while in larger establishments there may be a specialized group of buyers working under the supervision of a purchasing agent, who may bear the title of General Purchasing Agent or, occasionally, Vice-President in Charge of Purchases.

■ Organization and Status of the Department

The accompanying chart indicates the position of the purchasing department in a company of average size and shows the internal organization of the department. There is some variation in the status of purchasing departments. In many concerns the purchasing department has a separate status equivalent to sales, production, and finance. This situation is the

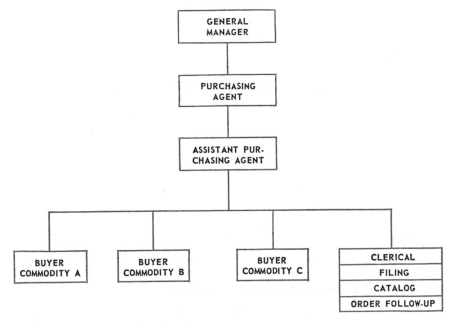

Organization Chart of a Purchasing Department

result of a growing recognition of the importance of the purchasing function and of the need for according it appropriate organizational standing.

In companies in which purchasing is not a separate entity, it may be placed under the production manager or in the treasurer's department. In very small firms the job of purchasing agent may be a part-time activity handled by one of the executives of the firm in addition to his other duties.

The division of the purchasing work is customarily on the basis of classes of materials rather than according to the use of the materials within the plant. Thus one man might be given authority for the buying of textiles only, rather than all the material needs of the shop. He would thus become an expert in textiles.

In some companies the receiving and material stores departments are placed under the purchasing agent as a part of the purchasing department, while in other companies these units are placed under the production manager. When they are part of the purchasing department, control routines can be established to effectuate the naturally close connection between purchasing, receiving, and storage. When they are under the production manager, interdepartmental liaison must be established so that the production division can work closely with purchasing.

Although the chart shown on page 279 portrays the basic organizational design of the purchasing function, such as might be found in a small-to-medium-size company, in many large firms a much greater number of buyers may be employed, depending upon the variety and breadth of the types of materials required.

■ Centralization versus Decentralization of Purchasing Function

Many firms have widely separated plants, which brings up the question of whether the purchasing department should be centralized at the home office or decentralized and located in the field at the different branches. There is no single solution to this policy question, as there are arguments favoring both practices. For centralized buying, there is the fact of larger purchases, with frequently lower prices or larger discounts. For decentralized purchasing, the purchases would be smaller in quantity, but with possibly faster delivery, more favorable relations with local suppliers, and better inventory balance.

■ Extent of Purchasing Department's Authority

Although there is no question about the authority of the purchasing department to adopt procedures for the placing of orders, there are instances where the actual determination of the goods to be bought resides with the executives who will be responsible for their use in the plant or office. For example, the decision to purchase automated machine tools might well be that of the production manager, who would be accountable for the results obtained through their use. Or the selection of data processing equipment might be made by the controller or the chief statistician. These and other similar instances do not imply the downgrading of the purchasing department, but rather that those responsible for the use of certain items are given the right to choose the types or makes which they prefer. Situations of this sort have tended to increase in number with the growing complexity of the equipment used in business. Except for circumstances such as these, the purchasing department usually has the authority to buy most items bought on a repetitive basis.

■ The Prime Objectives of Purchasing

Every department in a business has certain prime objectives toward the attainment of which the departmental executives and personnel should constantly strive. In the case of a purchasing department four such goals can be stated quite succinctly. They are: (1) buying the proper products for the purpose required; (2) having the materials available at the time that they are needed; (3) securing the proper amount as required; and (4) paying the right price. To the extent that any purchasing department approaches the attainment of these objectives, it will be fulfilling its mission for its employer.

■ Steps in Ordering and Receiving Goods

The steps leading to the purchase and receipt of certain materials are:

1. Establishing specifications
2. Initiating the buying procedure
3. Investigating the supply market
4. Starting purchasing negotiations
5. Placing and following up the order
6. Receiving the goods

1 / **Establishing specifications.** Before the purchasing department can procure the needed goods, their descriptive details or *specifications* must be available. Industrial purchasing conforms almost entirely to specifications that are established by the purchasers. These specifications originate, usually not with the purchasing department, but customarily with the engineering staff. In setting up specifications, scientific accuracy is desirable in order that the purchasing department may purchase materials

that will do the job required of them but that are not too good for the task at hand. It is uneconomical to buy a certain grade of material when a lower and cheaper grade will give satisfactory service.

Many industrial goods have industry-wide standards that are commonly recognized and accepted by all users. Nuts, bolts, screws, washers, steel bars, raw cotton, lumber, and many other finished or semifinished goods come into this category. In specifying these items, the engineering department merely indicates to the purchasing department the industry grades desired.

2 / Initiating the buying procedure. In those plants where products do not vary greatly over long production runs and where the process involves repetitive manufacturing processes, the need for materials is revealed in the stock room. Records are established there that will call for the issuance of a purchase requisition when the stock of any item gets down to or below the predetermined minimum. The *purchase requisition* serves two purposes: (a) it sets forth the necessary details and specifications to guide the purchasing department in buying; and (b) it serves as a warning that the stock of the item in question has reached a point where a reorder is required at once to prevent a production delay.

3 / Investigating the supply market. Before the purchasing agent is ready to place orders for requisitioned items, he must investigate the supply market for these commodities. He must know all the suppliers, whether producers or industrial distributors, their products, their prices, the quality of their wares, their terms and discounts, their reputations in the trade, their reliability to deliver goods when promised, and anything else that will enable him to perform his buying function more intelligently and to the advantage of his firm.

4 / Starting purchasing negotiations. In the case of certain standardized products that are bought frequently, or in those instances in which the wanted items have been purchased before on a satisfactory basis, the order may be placed as soon as the requisition is received. This is particularly true if the price tends to remain stable over long periods of time.

In the case of goods for which the price is not stabilized, or when the company has never made a similar purchase before, or when industry standards are not available, the purchasing agent may send *letters of inquiry* to several suppliers, stating the company's needs and inviting the suppliers to submit bids or to call and demonstrate their products. Following this, there may be a series of conferences between the suppliers' representatives and the purchasing agent, who may call in the engineer or the plant superintendent to aid him in deciding on the best source of supply for the needed item.

5 / Placing and following up the order. The practice of most companies is to execute a formal *purchase order*, specifying carefully all the facts pertaining to the transaction, such as an exact description of the goods wanted, the unit prices, the quantities desired, the delivery dates, the discount terms, shipping instructions, billing instructions, and an identifying order number.

In order to make certain that all orders will be delivered on time, many concerns install and operate an order follow-up system, which is designed to keep the purchasing agent informed regarding the status of all outstanding orders. Through frequent contacts with suppliers, the follow-up man endeavors to make certain that there are no delays in the receipt of goods for which orders have been placed.

6 / Receiving the goods. When the goods arrive, they are checked against the copy of the order by the receiving clerk to make certain that all of the provisions of the purchase order have been met. With certain types of goods it is desirable to institute an inspection routine to check on the quality of the shipment. If the shipment is correct in quantity, quality, and price, the goods are sent to stock, and the vendor's invoice is certified for payment. If there are any discrepancies between the order and the shipment, the purchasing department should be notified so that the shipper can be contacted and the error remedied. Pending rectification of the error, the goods may be held in the receiving room. Or, if the difference is one of quantity and the vendor is one of the firm's regular suppliers, the goods may be put in stock pending later adjustment.

■ **Purchasing Policies**

Some of the policies that govern the purchasing department may originate in that department and be decided by the purchasing agent, while others may arise in other parts of the plant and require that the executive heads of the company confer and establish the policies to be followed.

1. Buying versus manufacturing
2. Hand-to-mouth buying versus forward buying
3. Speculative purchasing
4. Contract purchasing
5. Reciprocal buying
6. Sealed bids
7. Buying ethics

1 / Buying versus manufacturing. The decision as to whether to purchase a certain part required in fabricating a firm's product or to manufacture it is obviously one that transcends the scope of the purchasing department and becomes a matter of company policy. For example, a manufacturer of washing machines must decide whether to purchase electric motors for his products or to make them. The part that the purchasing department plays in formulating such a rule is to furnish the company executives with sufficient information concerning the supply market for the item in question so that they may make a wise decision. The purchasing department should be constantly alert to any changes in the supply market that might influence the company heads to change their minds.

2 / Hand-to-mouth buying versus forward buying. The basic difference between hand-to-mouth and forward buying lies in the size and frequency of purchase. If a firm follows a policy of *hand-to-mouth buying*, it orders smaller amounts at more frequent intervals. On the other hand, *forward buying* involves orders for larger amounts issued less frequently. There is no sharp line of demarcation between the two; but purchasing departments tend to follow one or the other, depending upon the price aspect of the market. If prices tend to fluctuate rather unpredictably at frequent intervals, hand-to-mouth buying will probably govern the purchasing in order to minimize the risk of loss through inventory depreciation. On the other hand, if prices tend to be relatively stable over long periods of time, the company may be willing to commit itself to larger purchases at each ordering period, with longer intervals between orders.

Another factor that warrants consideration by many companies is the amount of capital tied up in their inventories of materials and parts. In recent years the concept of frequent turnover of inventories—with consequent savings in storage space required, a minimizing of risk of spoilage and damage, and the release of capital for other uses—has gained a number of adherents. Theirs is the philosophy of hand-to-mouth buying, the making of more frequent purchases of smaller amounts of materials. These firms have found, in many instances, that the savings that they are able to effect through this policy more than offset the additional purchasing, transportation, and receiving expenses, which are usually inescapable concomitants of hand-to-mouth buying. There is doubtless a point beyond which this policy cannot profitably be carried, when order sizes become so small and orders so frequent that the added costs more than offset the savings. Each company must determine this point for itself in the light of its own experience.

3 / Speculative purchasing. In contrast to the buying that arises directly from the current need for certain items, there is *speculative* or *market purchasing*. This means that the purchasing department, believing that prices of certain items are going to rise appreciably in the near future, places orders for them in quantities in excess of their usual amounts. This is done to take advantage of the anticipated price rise. If the amount ordered and the terms of buying bear little relationship to the current needs of the company, the speculative nature of the transaction is apparent. It is probable, in many if not most companies, that the purchasing agent would be required to secure authorization from top management before making a speculative purchase. Furthermore, the materials involved would, of necessity, have to be products that the company uses regularly in its manufacturing process.

The principal danger in speculative purchasing, apart from the amount of capital it ties up, lies in the possibility of an unforeseen price drop, which may not only wipe out the anticipated advantage that inspires this policy, but also entail a severe loss if the price decline is sufficiently far-reaching. Many businessmen believe that the proper function of a purchasing department is to buy materials to the best advantage at the time they are needed, and not to engage in extraordinary purchasing except where necessary to protect the company's supply against possible future shortages. An alert purchasing agent, however, constantly studies price trends and, if he thinks he discerns price increases in the immediate future, the temptation to try to take advantage of the situation may be overwhelming. If he guesses correctly, his company may benefit and his own prestige may be greatly enhanced.

4 / Contract purchasing. *Contract purchasing* is the policy of a company entering into contracts with its suppliers covering the purchase of certain materials, the delivery of which will be effected over long periods of time. There are two reasons for this practice—to protect the supply and to take advantage of low prices prevailing at the time the contracts are executed. Under some circumstances, where the vendor might have little control over his costs of raw material or labor, the price might not be guaranteed for a long period of time. However, the buyer would be assured of a source of supply and regular shipments.

5 / Reciprocal buying. *Reciprocal buying* means buying from customers or, stated somewhat more explicitly, favoring customers over prospective vendors who are not customers when purchase orders are placed. For example, a producer of motor trucks might buy coal only from a coal company that uses its trucks for delivery. Although this practice has been universally condemned as uneconomic and wasteful, it still persists in many lines of trade. The arguments against it are that it narrows the field of suppliers with the result that the buyer pays higher prices and possibly fails to procure the exact goods that he requires. The main argument in favor of reciprocal buying is that it helps to hold customers, a rather powerful persuasive factor.

6 / Use of sealed bids. Sometimes the selection of a source of supply is made on the basis of sealed bids. When this method is used, the purchasing agent provides to prospective suppliers complete information in the way of specifications and quantities needed. The suppliers who are interested submit secret, written offers on or before a certain date, at which time the *sealed bids* are opened, the proposals are compared, and the order is given presumably to the lowest bidder. The sealed bid procedure is quite common in the procurement practices of governmental agencies, federal, state, and local, and is gaining adherents in private business and among schools and hospitals.

7 / Buying ethics. Unfortunately the field of purchasing has not been entirely free from some rather sharp practices on the part of the buyers. These practices have ranged from indiscriminate and pointless cancellations to the use of falsehoods in playing off one vendor against another. In some instances buyers favor salesmen who entertain them or give them valuable presents. Needless to say, these practices do not redound either to the credit or the long-time advantage of the perpetrators. Most firms recognize the value of ethical dealing with their suppliers as well as with their customers. The National Association of Purchasing Agents has promulgated a set of rules known as the Principles and Standards of Purchasing Practice to which its members are pledged to adhere.

■ **Value Analysis and Purchasing**

An activity that has attracted considerable attention in the past few years is known as *value analysis*. It involves a systematic appraisal and examination from time to time of products and parts for the purpose of discovering if any cost-saving changes in design, materials, or processes can be brought about. Among the participants in value analysis, along with representatives of engineering, production, and sometimes marketing, are members of the purchasing department, who can bring to bear on the problems their knowledge of suppliers' offerings and prices.

HANDLING AND CONTROL OF MATERIALS

From the moment that industrial materials arrive at the receiving platform or yards until they emerge as the completed product and are loaded for shipment to customers, they must be handled and moved from place to place in accordance with the nature of the finished product and of the materials themselves. The movement from the receiving room is frequently to stock rooms, where the materials are stored until they are needed in production. Then they must be taken to the point of the first application of the production process and thence through the manufacturing routine until the finished product is ready to be shipped or sent to storage to await future shipment.

■ Materials Management

The term *materials management* has recently appeared on the business scene. While its meaning and scope vary somewhat in different companies, it may include any or all of purchasing, warehousing and inventory control, production control, and quality control, the latter two of which are treated in Chapter 14. Through the use of computers, many firms are able to speed up the purchasing process and to keep track of all materials in the warehouse, in the production process, or on the shipping dock. Some of these companies claim to have achieved substantial savings in their inventories and in a shortening of the time required for delivery of orders to their customers. With the heightened degree of competition in many lines and the pressure against price increases, cost savings that result from materials management are most welcome. Materials management includes not just materials control but the entire concept of the manipulation of materials as an aid to greater profits for the firm.

■ Materials Control

Industrial materials are placed under a system of strict control as soon as they reach the receiving department; and they remain under it, in one form or another, until the finished product is delivered to the shipping department for transportation to a customer. *Materials control*, which takes the form of records and procedures, is designed to keep the management constantly informed of what materials and how many units of each are in the plant, and in what departments they are located. It provides a written record of the transfer of materials from one department to another and of the manufacturing processes through which the materials pass, and it serves as the authority for such movement. It is likewise important as a source of cost data for the cost accounting department.

The details of materials control procedure vary considerably from industry to industry and from company to company. The basic philosophy of the operation, however, is much the same in all concerns. When the goods are first received and placed in stock, records are made of all pertinent data. All subsequent movements of the materials, however simple or complex, are accompanied by such paper work as is necessary to inform the management of their exact location at all times. Periodic counts are made to be certain that none of the items has been lost in the production process. Whenever materials move from one place to another within the plant, records are adjusted to reflect this transfer and to fix the responsibility for their custody. Identifying tags accompany all goods to facilitate accurate checking. As a means of providing information on the number of items of each kind in the stock room, perpetual inventory records are kept. As the stock minimums are reached, purchase requisitions are made out for the purchasing department. The use of computers is rising rapidly in this area of materials control, as through their memory drums the location and quantity of each item can be stored and retrieved quickly.

■ Methods of Handling Materials

The methods used in handling materials are determined by the nature of the materials, by the layout of the factory, and by the type of product made. No small part of the cost reduction in manufacturing that has taken place in recent years has been achieved through improvements in the handling and moving of materials. In the early days of manufacture most of the moving of materials was done by hand with trucks and skids, but recent years have seen a definite swing toward mechanical conveyors. Whenever possible, gravity has been harnessed for this purpose and in many industries it supplies almost the entire motive power for handling materials. Because of the multiplicity of devices in common usage and the specialized nature of the handling problems in each industry, the various conveying methods will be merely named here. No attempt will be made to describe them or to suggest the ways in which they might be employed. Chief among these devices are overhead cranes, conveyor belts, roller conveyors, pipe lines, trucks, overhead conveyors, and forklift trucks. A fast-growing device for handling materials is the driverless tractor, which, through a pattern of slots in the floor, enables a hidden towline to move them to any location desired in the warehouse. There materials may be either loaded on the tractors or removed from them by warehouse employees using various types of mechanical equipment.

■ **Storage of Materials**

To a large extent, the storage of materials is a problem the solution to which is dependent upon the nature of the goods and the manufacturing processes to which they are subjected. Coal and iron ore are usually stored on the ground; liquids, such as chemicals, paints, and oils, are kept in tanks; small metal parts are stored in bins in stock rooms; and so on.

Stock rooms may be centralized or decentralized, depending upon the area covered by the production division and the rapidity with which the stored materials are consumed in manufacture. The basic idea back of the stock room operating policy should be that of having the materials available for production at the times they are wanted, in such quantities as to ensure unbroken operation of the production facilities, and yet not to impede free movement of the operating personnel in performing their duties.

■ **Types of Materials Stored**

There are three types of materials for which storage must be provided. (1) *Raw materials* include ores, chemicals, paper pulp, castings, forgings, and supplies, such as lubricating oils and greases. (2) *Semi-finished goods*, or "worked materials," have been subjected to certain manufacturing processes and are held in storage until they are needed for assembly into finished products. Among these are small motors, gears, lenses, carburetors, and oil filters. (3) *Finished goods* are completed items that are placed in stock to await shipment to customers.

PURCHASE AND CONTROL OF MERCHANDISE

Problems of purchasing and control are also encountered by non-manufacturing enterprises, such as wholesalers and retailers in connection with merchandise.

■ **Purchasing in Nonmanufacturing Enterprises**

The problem of purchasing in wholesale and retail businesses differs from that in manufacturing enterprises. Wholesalers and retailers buy only finished goods, and the major factor that determines which items shall be purchased is the probable salability of the goods.

1. Wholesalers' buying personnel
2. Wholesalers' buying procedures
3. Retailers' buying personnel
4. Retailers' buying procedures

1 / **Wholesalers' buying personnel.** In wholesale establishments, the persons who are responsible for the purchasing are known as *buyers*, except in small firms in which the buying function is assumed by one of the company heads. Larger concerns quite commonly employ a number of buyers, each concentrating on a group of related items. For example, in a grocery wholesale house there might be a buyer for canned and frozen goods; one for fancy groceries; one for cereals, flour, and other staples; and one for nonfood related items, such as soaps, cleansers, detergents, and paper goods. Concerns of this size frequently have a head buyer who is in charge of all buying personnel and is responsible to the top management for the operation of his department. In addition to his supervisory duties he usually does some buying for his company. Frequently his position is of vice-presidential rank.

2 / **Wholesalers' buying procedures.** Wholesale buying procedures are relatively simple and are divided into two kinds: original buying and repeat buying. In the case of original purchase, the buying of goods that have not been handled before, it is customary for the salesmen to contact the buyers and to demonstrate their wares, either in the manufacturers' showrooms or at the wholesalers' places of business. If the sale is consummated, a purchase order is made out, indicating the goods involved and such other data as prices, terms, delivery dates, and transportation methods. The purchase order forms are not essentially different from those used by industrial purchasing agents, except that the specifications cover finished goods rather than industrial materials. The initial stimulus to make the purchase may come from advertising put out by the producers, visits by salesmen, and requests from customers.

Repeat purchases (in many lines these comprise the bulk of such operations) are usually handled by mail on a routine basis. The incentive to make the purchase usually comes from the fact that the stock records indicate that the supply of the items to be purchased has fallen below the prescribed minimum requirements.

3 / **Retailers' buying personnel.** Although retail buying follows the same general pattern in all stores, there is a notable difference between the carefully determined practices of the department stores, the chain stores, and the specialty stores on the one hand, and the unorganized buying procedures of small stores on the other. In the larger stores the purchasing personnel are called buyers and customarily are in complete charge of the departments for which they buy, including responsibility for sales, stocks, and personnel. Each buyer specializes in a relatively few

closely related items and becomes quite expert in these fields. For example, in a typical department store there will be a furniture buyer, a toiletries buyer, a housefurnishings buyer, and others. Each buyer is responsible for the profitable operation of his department, and he endeavors constantly to buy the merchandise that will appeal to his customers.

Until the early 1920's, most department and specialty store buyers reported directly to the heads of their stores. Since then the position of *merchandise manager* has come into being for the purpose of securing for the store management a closer supervision over the activities of the buyers, which, of course, includes that of buying. For convenience, the various merchandise departments have customarily been separated into four groups, called divisions. They are the Main Floor, Apparel, Home Furnishings, and Basement divisions. Each division is headed by a merchandise manager whose authority extends over the buyers of the departments in his group.

Another interesting development in this sector of retailing has been the growth of *resident buying offices.* Most of these are located in New York City, with a few in Chicago, St. Louis, and other buying centers. They may be either independent operations or owned by one or more stores. Department store chains not infrequently have their own resident buying offices, as do such groups as the Associated Merchandising Corporation, which is an association of noncompeting independent department stores. Some of the services of resident buying offices are indicated by the chart on page 292. In addition, they provide office space for visiting buyers when they are in the market cities and assist them in contacting suppliers, even furnishing display rooms where salesmen for manufacturers may show their wares to buyers.

In the chain stores, other than in department store chains, the personnel are likewise known as buyers, but they are usually situated at some central buying office, which may or may not be located at a merchandise warehouse. They customarily confine their activities to buying and have no other responsibilities. The buying organization is usually set up in the same manner as in the larger wholesale establishments, with a head buyer in charge of the others, each of whom buys only certain commodities. In most instances the member stores of department store chains do not follow the orthodox chain pattern in their buying practices, but instead each store maintains a complete corps of buyers who act in the same manner as the buyers of wholly independent stores.

In small stores the proprietors usually do the buying along with their other managerial and entrepreneurial duties.

SERVICES OF A RESIDENT BUYING OFFICE

BLAKE'S FURNITURE CO.

STORE CONTRACTS FOR ANNUAL SERVICE—PAYS MONTHLY

RESIDENT BUYING OFFICE

RESIDENT-BUYING OFFICE REPRESENTS STORE AT MAIN MANUFACTURING CENTERS

Buys Merchandise For Retailer

Investigates and Reports on Market Conditions

Combined Buying Power Gets Goods at Lower Prices

Helps Retailer on General and Special Promotions

Analyzes Trends in Styles

Helps Retailer Get Credit Privileges from Manufacturer

A post-World War II development that has attained considerable stature in supermarket purchasing is the *buying committee*. This group, which is composed of the top marketing and purchasing personnel in the company concerned, is charged with the duty of determining the acceptability of new items that are offered to their stores for sale. The great increase in the number and variety of goods, both food and nonfood, which have come on the market in the postwar period and the impossibility of a supermarket buying them all is the cause of the rise of the buying committee. Where such a group operates, the individual buyers do not have the authority to approve new items, but merely to purchase those which have been previously passed by the committee. Over 90 percent of supermarkets are reported to utilize this method of appraising new products offered to them. As an additional duty, the buying committees of many chain supermarkets review the proposed promotional campaigns of manufacturers and decide whether or not their stores will cooperate with these endeavors through advertising and display.

4 / Retailers' buying procedures. In the larger stores the buyers frequently take the initiative in seeking out new goods and make regular trips to the market centers for this purpose. They customarily buy the bulk of their merchandise direct from the manufacturers and employ wholesalers only rarely. Their buying practices for original purchases are simple and involve viewing available lines of merchandise, selecting the desired items, and making out the order. The order forms are much like those already described. Repeat buying is a routine procedure, usually handled by mail. The incentive to make original purchases arises from goods seen on previous market trips, magazine advertisements, competitors' offerings, and occasionally customers' requests. The incentive for repeat buying comes from the stock cards when the on-hand figures show that the stock is below the established minimum.

In the chain stores the opposite procedure is to be found, with the salesmen going to the buyers as a general rule.

Buying in small stores may take place in the stores with the wholesalers' salesmen in attendance or in some instances at the wholesalers' warehouses. Retailers' purchase order forms for these stores are practically unknown. The orders are taken on the wholesalers' blanks. Frequently the wholesalers' salesmen enter the stores, count the retailers' stocks of the goods concerned, and make out the orders for the quantities that they believe should be purchased. This procedure, of course, applies only to repeat purchases. For original purchases the salesmen display the goods and endeavor to persuade the retailers to purchase.

In the large stores careful preparations are made by the buyers in advance of their trips to the market. *Buying plans*, which set forth in detail the types, sizes, costs, and selling prices of goods to be bought, are prepared and followed quite closely during the time when the buyer is in the market. Limits to the amount of money to be spent, as well as the approximate retail prices at which the goods will be offered, are established. In the small stores buying is done more or less on the spur of the moment when the wholesalers' salesmen appear.

■ **Inventory Control in Wholesaling and Retailing**

Department and specialty stores and the chains maintain fairly elaborate inventory control records as a guide to purchasing and to account for the merchandise that they handle. In the smaller stores such records are almost unknown and stock control is practically nonexistent.

A typical stock control record consists of a file of cards, one for each different type of goods, which provide for complete descriptions of the items and their sources, together with spaces to record the arrival of merchandise, its outward movement as the result of sales to customers, and the current balance of stock on hand. Minimums are computed for those items subject to repeat purchase for the purpose of notifying the buyers when the stock of these items is getting low. Maximums are also computed in order that the buyers may be advised of the items for which the stock on hand is running too high for the profitable operation of their departments.

Wholesalers customarily maintain these records for all of their merchandise, as do the chains. Department and specialty stores do likewise for goods for which repeat purchases are made and for some types of merchandise that move slowly and of which a reserve stock is kept in stock rooms. Many kinds of goods, such as women's apparel, toiletries, and accessories, sell so rapidly, however, that the entire stock is carried in the selling departments (*forward stock*); and only the most rudimentary stock records are kept, if indeed any are kept, on many fast-moving items.

■ Style Life Inventory Management

A new term has appeared in the area of control of retail inventories of style merchandise. This is known as *style life inventory management* (SLIM). With the aid of computers a procedure has been devised with the objective of preventing an accumulation of garments that are selling slowly, and also making certain that an adequate stock of fast selling items is always on hand.

BUSINESS TERMS

(a) purchasing or buying (277), inventory control or stock control (277)
(b) materials (277), merchandise (277)
(c) purchasing department (279), purchasing agent (279)
(d) specifications (281), purchase requisition (282), letters of inquiry (282), purchase order (283)
(e) hand-to-mouth buying (284), forward buying (284)
(f) speculative or market purchasing (285), contract purchasing (285), reciprocal buying (285), sealed bids (286)
(g) value analysis (286)
(h) materials management (287), materials control (287)
(i) raw materials (289), semifinished goods (289), finished goods (289)
(j) buyers (289), merchandise manager (291)
(k) resident buying office (291), buying committee (292), buying plans (293)
(l) forward stock (294), style life inventory management (SLIM) (294)

QUESTIONS FOR DISCUSSION AND ANALYSIS

1. In department and specialty stores, the buyers are responsible for both the purchase and the sale of the merchandise that they handle. Why are not purchasing agents in manufacturing plants also in charge of sales?
2. In what ways can computers be of assistance to purchasing agents?
3. Do you believe that the increasing complexity of the equipment used in manufacturing will reduce the status of purchasing agents to that of order clerks? Explain.
4. Do you think that materials management should be the responsibility of the purchasing agent? Why?
5. Who should have the authority of finally accepting or rejecting materials as satisfying or failing to satisfy the order specifications? Explain.
6. Should the purchasing agent be a member of top management? Why?
7. In some manufacturing plants the position of purchasing agent is of equal rank with the sales manager. In others the sales manager is of higher rank. Which of these practices is preferable? Why?
8. In what ways can the purchasing department assist in the function of value analysis?
9. Do you think that unethical purchasing practices can be eliminated? Why?
10. Do you think that purchasing departments should be responsible for disposing of the surplus material and scrap which all plants have to some degree? Why?

PROBLEMS AND SHORT CASES

1. In some plants the purchasing department has no authority over the receiving department or the stock room where materials are stored after receipt. These functions are under the supervision of the production department. In other companies, receiving and storage are in charge of the purchasing department. Prepare a list of reasons both for and against each of these practices. Select the alternative that you prefer and give the basis for your choice.
2. The advent of the buying committee, in a majority of the large supermarkets and supermarket chains, has been a source of irritation to the sales managers of many of the companies whose products are distributed through the supermarkets. These sales managers claim that the inability of their salesmen to gain access to the buying committee meetings prevents their being able to make their sales presentations for new products or to present arguments why some of their goods, currently being handled by the stores, should not be discontinued. The buying committee personnel, on the other hand, maintain that admitting salesmen to their meetings would serve merely to prolong them and would have no effect on the committee's decisions.

   You are asked to evaluate these opposing positions. Can you suggest some course of action whereby the sales managers would be more satisfied without nullifying the basic objective of the buying committee, which is that of bringing the judgment of a group to bear on the subject of the admission or rejection of goods in the shortest possible time.

3. In the past twenty years many department stores in the larger cities have established suburban branch stores. As the number of branches that each store operated has increased, a problem has come up with regard to the placing of the responsibility for buying and stock control for the branches. When the first one or two branches were established, the buyers in the downtown stores were assigned the task of buying for the branch stores also and of being accountable for their stocks. Later, as more branch stores were opened, often at some distance from the main store, it was felt that the continuance of the present buying responsibility at the main store was unwieldy and placed too great a burden on the buyers there. The alternative was to decentralize the buying function and place it with the department heads in the branches.

You are asked to examine all aspects of both buying situations and to present arguments for and against each. Which do you think would be the preferable solution?

SUGGESTED READINGS

Ammer, D. S. *Materials Management.* Homewood, Illinois: Richard D. Irwin, Inc., 1962.

Anton, G. J. *Managing an Integrated Purchasing Process.* New York: Harper & Row, 1963.

Davidson, W. R., and A. F. Doody. *Retailing Management,* Third Edition. New York: The Ronald Press Company, 1966. Part VI.

England, W. B. *Procurement: Principles and Cases,* Fourth Edition. Homewood, Illinois: Richard D. Irwin, Inc., 1962.

Heinritz, S. F., and P. Farrell. *Purchasing: Principles and Application,* Fourth Edition. Englewood Cliffs, New Jersey: Prentice-Hall, Inc., 1965.

Heskett, J. L., and Others. *Business Logistics—Management of Physical Supply and Distribution.* New York: The Ronald Press Company, 1964. Part IV.

Hodges, H. G. *Procurement: The Modern Science of Purchasing.* New York: Harper & Row, 1961.

Moore, F. G. *Manufacturing Management,* Fourth Edition. Homewood, Illinois: Richard D. Irwin, Inc., 1965. Chapters 34, 35, and 36.

Roscoe, E. S. *An Introduction to Industrial Management,* Third Edition. Homewood, Illinois: Richard D. Irwin, Inc., 1963. Chapters 11 and 12.

Westing, J. H., and I. V. Fine. *Industrial Purchasing: Buying for Industry and Budgetary Institutions,* Second Edition. New York: John Wiley & Sons, Inc., 1961.

Magazines: *Purchasing Magazine, Purchasing Week, Industrial Purchasing Agent.*

Chapter 14

Few areas of economic activity have received as much technical attention and experienced as great a measure of change during the past two decades as has production. The remarkable growth in population in this country, together with the increasing need for goods by both industry and consumers, along with the rise in demand for military hardware occasioned by the Southeast Asian conflict and the requirements of the space age, have all brought with them not only the need for more things but also for radical improvements in many production methods, materials, and control procedures. This chapter deals with the principles, processes, and methods that are used in the manufacture of goods for industrial, commercial, and individual consumers.

PRODUCTION PROCESSES

The methods by which the materials of industry are produced or manufactured into the things that industry or consumers want are known as *production processes*. The treatment of production in this chapter does not attempt to include all of the many different types of businesses that engage in production, nor should it be assumed that the production control methods outlined here are used by all producers. Many types of firms operate on such a small scale that the use of modern methods of production control would be too costly and quite unnecessary. Plumbers, furniture refinishers and upholsterers, earth movers and excavators, small machine shops, appliance repair shops, greenhouses, and similar small businesses with few employees and comparatively simple manufacturing processes have no need for the complicated control systems that are required in large-scale productive enterprises. The methods that are discussed here are those used by producers who range in size from those of moderate proportions to the industrial giants in the electrical, steel, automobile, and chemical industries.

■ **Types of Production Processes**

According to one classification, production processes are identified as shown below.

1. Extractive process
2. Analytic process

3. Fabricating process
4. Synthetic process

1 / **Extractive process.** In some industries the basic production process is one of extracting substances from the earth or the sea, known as the *extractive process*. Examples of this process are the mining of coal, iron ore, lead, gold, and silver; drilling for petroleum; and the extraction of magnesium and other chemicals from the ocean. Farming and fishing may be called extractive industries, but they are on an ownership and operating basis different from the above industries.

2 / **Analytic process.** The *analytic process* is one in which a basic substance is broken down into a number of other materials, which may or may not bear any resemblance to the parent substance. In this category are petroleum refining, meat packing, and lumber milling.

3 / **Fabricating process.** The term *fabricating process*, although used principally in the structural steel business, refers to a process that is rather widespread in industry wherein a material has its form changed to some extent by being machined, woven, cut up, pressed, finished, or treated in some other manner. It is sometimes called the *converting process*, particularly in the textile field. Examples of the fabricating process are to be found in the manufacture of clothing, shoes, certain types of furniture, nuts, and bolts.

4 / **Synthetic process.** *Synthetic process* refers to those industries in which a number of different materials are combined to form a single product. In the manufacture of steel, glass, rayon, and dinnerware the final products are quite different from the original ingredients because of physical or chemical changes. In other industries, such as in the production of automobiles, electrical appliances, radios and television receivers, where the materials are merely assembled without undergoing physical or chemical change, this process is sometimes called the *assembly process*. This is particularly true in industries employing the assembly line as a part of their manufacturing process. The automobile industry is a good example of one that uses this method. In this case the frame of the car or truck is placed on a long, slowly moving conveyor; and as it passes the various stations on the line, the different component parts—such as the motor, the transmission, the drive shaft, the rear axle, the wheels, and the body—are attached; and at the end of the process the car is driven off the line under its own power and to the final inspection that it receives before shipment to some dealer.

It is quite common to find the fabricating and synthetic processes operating in a single company. The decision of some producers to make rather than to buy some or all of the components of their products results in the combining of these two processes in these firms. Continuing with the example of the automobile manufacturers, it is common practice for them to fabricate their motors, bodies, transmissions, and other metal parts, while buying tires, batteries, and fabrics for upholstery from the makers of these products. The comparative costs of buying or producing these parts are usually the determining factor in the decisions to make or to buy them.

■ Continuous and Intermittent Processes

A second classification of production processes includes:

> 1. Continuous process
> 2. Intermittent process

1 / Continuous process. The term *continuous process* is used to describe a manufacturing situation where long periods of time may elapse before any radical changes are made in the set-up of the machinery and equipment involved, that is, most or all of the machines will perform the same operations indefinitely. The production of automobiles where model changes occur only once a year is an example of the continuous process. Another instance of continuous production is found in the steel industry where the productive facilities must be kept constantly in operation for relatively long periods of time, necessitating day and night shifts and Sunday work. In this business the furnaces must be kept hot, once they have been lit, until a shutdown is caused by a mechanical failure, lack of orders, or, occasionally, a labor dispute. If the furnaces are allowed to cool, they must usually be rebuilt before they can be used again. Thus it is evident that the term "continuous process" may include industries where production may be halted every night—a one-shift operation—and resumed the next morning, and also those where the characteristics of the production pattern require the operation to run without stopping for long periods of time, months or even years, depending on the demand for the products.

2 / Intermittent process. The term *intermittent process* involves manufacturing conditions in which the duration of each run is sufficiently short so that the machines are shut down rather frequently and retooled to produce some different product. Most so-called "job shops" come under this category. A *job shop* has certain manufacturing facilities, such as machine tools or foundry equipment, that are available to make almost anything that its customers want. What is being produced in a plant of this type at any given time is what the current customers have ordered; and it may differ radically from what will be made six months hence.

■ Standard Versus Custom Manufacture

All manufacturing is divided into two basic groups—*standard manufacture*, which includes those companies that manufacture standard articles, which are frequently originated, developed, and branded by the manufacturers; and *custom manufacture*, which refers to those companies that produce goods to their customers' specifications. Occasionally both of these types are found in the same company. The principal product is one that bears the maker's brand name but, because it does not require all of the producer's manufacturing facilities, the company keeps the factory fully employed by taking on a certain amount of custom business in addition to its own standard product.

Standard manufacture frequently involves producing for stock, as well as for immediate shipment to customers and to dealers. This may be occasioned by a seasonal selling period, even though production continues the year round, because of the need for a reserve stock from which deliveries can be made to customers who are unable or unwilling to wait for goods to be manufactured, and for the purpose of stabilizing production when the demand is irregular. This condition raises questions of securing sufficient capital to carry the inventories, of providing adequate storage space and custodial personnel, and of the risk of loss through market price declines, fire, or theft. To firms engaging in custom manufacture, these problems are not usually present, as the customers specify the quantities to be made and the firms limit their production to these amounts.

Television receiving sets, refrigerators, men's hats, toothbrushes, and toiletries are common examples of the products of standard manufacture. Custom manufacture includes the production of such commodities as made-to-measure men's clothing, machine tools designed for special jobs, counters and fixtures for retail stores, and elevators and escalators.

The automobile industry provides something of a variation on the standard manufacture policy. While there are certain fundamental features that are common to all models of a given make, such as the frame, wheels, motor, and basic body types, customers may specify such items as the color, character of upholstery, transmission type, power brakes and steering, and hi-fi equipment, which will be assembled at the factory in accordance with their individual choices. There thus emerges a combination of standard and custom manufacture for those buyers who wish to take advantage of this opportunity.

■ **Recent Developments in Production**

During World War II and the years following, the need for greater production of goods and more economical methods brought about a number of noteworthy developments in production that may conceivably rank in importance with the introduction of the assembly line shortly after the end of World War I. These include:

1. New materials
2. New processes
3. Miniaturization

4. Numerical control
5. Automation

1 / New materials. The first group of recent developments in production embraces those synthetic substances commonly called "plastics." It also includes the discovery of new alloys through the combining of various metals into compounds that possess greater strength than any of them alone and the finding of new uses for materials that have long been known to production engineers and metallurgists. The utilization of titanium alloys, cermets (metal-filled ceramic materials), beryllium, and chromium-based alloys, as well as the more recent applications of aluminum, are examples of this latter type.

2 / New processes. A considerable number of new processes, or refinements of old ones, have appeared in recent years. Among these are: the use of liquid nitrogen to fast-freeze foods at —320 F, which permits of the freezing of tomatoes, avacados, and other foods that had previously resisted freezing for commercial purposes; the pelletizing of low-grade ore that allows the mining companies to use a grade of ore for steelmaking that had been previously considered worthless; continuous casting in the steel business that eliminates many time-consuming, costly steps in the making of steel; the basic oxygen furnace, also in steel, that is replacing the open-hearth method of many years standing; and electrical discharge machining, whereby the metal is eaten away by an electric spark, which saves on expensive finishing operations.

3 / Miniaturization. Noteworthy progress has been made in the area of *miniaturization*, the development of products and production equipment on an ever-smaller scale. This has been particularly evident in the field of electronics, which has been characterized by frequent design changes in the interest of less material and less processing.

4 / Numerical control. *Numerical control, (N/C),* is a procedure by which machine tools are actuated electronically by the use of coded tapes to perform a number of predetermined tasks. In the automobile industry a dramatic development is unfolding in the shortening of the *lead time* [1] involved in the designing and developing of a new model. The lead time in the automobile field has traditionally been from 20 to 24 months. Through the use of N/C in the designing and producing of the dies for forming the various car body parts, this time has been cut dramatically. The procedure, somewhat simplified for explanation, calls for the stylist to construct a clay model of the proposed car, the contours of which are scanned by a device somewhat like a television camera, which translates these contours into computer language. The computer puts these data on a tape that can be fed into a N/C machine instructing it how to cut the body dies.

5 / Automation. The term *automation* is applied to circumstances where computers control the operation of machine tools, with the assistance of a *feedback* by which information regarding the progress of the operation is relayed back to the computer to enable it to make any adjustments or corrections that may be necessary. If the computer is capable of making the requisite adjustments in the machine without human assistance, this is known as *closed-loop control*. In a circumstance where the computer is not connected with the instruments that can make machine adjustments, it will signal for the operator to reset the machine. This is known as *open-loop control*.

Of particular interest is the trend toward the automatic or "robot" factory—one in which machinery is substituted for manpower—a condition that has been closely approximated in the manufacture of petroleum and some chemicals. In some of the newer steel rolling mills, a computer governs the speed of the steel strips, makes continual adjustments in the roll openings to keep the gauge constant, takes X-ray pictures of the moving strips, and automatically corrects any errors in the process before

---

[1] Lead time is the number of years, months, or days that are required from the time a new product or model is first planned until it is ready for sale.

the tolerances of the strip are exceeded. This is all done automatically by closed-loop control. In other factories metals are transported, machined, formed, perforated, or strengthened, in accord with the type of manufacturing processes involved. The devices that are employed for these purposes are called *servo-mechanisms*—the brains and muscles of completely automatic machine tools.

The fundamental purpose of automation, which has been called the "second industrial revolution" by some observers, is that of reducing the costs of production—and this usually means labor costs. In an era of advancing wages and a trend toward shorter working hours, managements have been forced to seek out new and effective methods of cutting costs in order to remain competitive. To the extent that automation, in the plants that have adopted it, results in lower production costs, it can be said to be an economical movement and it may be expected to increase in extent and importance as long as this objective is attained. From the standpoint of the workers who are displaced by automated processes and whose skills are no longer required, a personnel problem is involved the solution to which is presently unclear and which will be discussed in Part V.

■ Research and Production

The creation of new products and methods has come about as the result of unceasing research in these fields. Under the relentless pressure of competition, many far-sighted manufacturers have established research departments for the purpose of seeking out new products with which to invade the market and cheaper ways to produce those already in their lines. Very large sums of money are spent annually for these purposes. A few of the leaders in the field of product and production research are Procter and Gamble, General Motors, DuPont, General Electric, Dow Chemical, and Ford. The General Motors proving ground near Milford, Michigan, is the oldest, largest, and best equipped automotive testing ground in the world. Here and at two other locations, the corporation carries on extensive research and testing of its automotive products.

PRODUCTION MANAGEMENT

The management of production involves the utilization of certain techniques and methods that have become fairly well standardized. Included in these is a procedure known as scientific management, the development of which brought about a revolutionary change in managerial practices.

■ Development of Scientific Management

Frederick W. Taylor, who has been called the father of scientific management, was an engineer who in 1882 was in the employ of the Midvale Steel Company in Philadelphia. During a period of duty in the company's machine shop, he was impressed by two facts that disturbed him. One fact was that no one, workers or management, seemed to know what constituted a day's work at any of the tasks in the plant; the other was that the details of the performance of any given job were left entirely to the individual workers. The workers were presumably skilled at their various trades and, when they were assigned to a task, it was their responsibility to work out the techniques and procedures in the light of their own training and ability. Furthermore, management was generally in complete ignorance of these procedures and relied on the workers to use their best judgment and skill.

Under these circumstances, management had little means of knowing whether the workers were using the best production methods and whether they were working at their own best speeds. Furthermore, management often did not possess sufficient knowledge of the workers' trades to permit it to offer constructive suggestions or corrective criticism of those whose output appeared to be faulty. In short, management did not truly manage.

1 / **Taylor's philosophy of management.** Taylor set out to remedy this situation and to place in the hands of management sufficient information regarding the details of the workers' jobs so that (a) management would know just what a worker was supposed to do on any given job; (b) management could instruct each worker in the best way to perform each task and then make certain that these instructions were followed; (c) management could establish standards for the rate of output for every job and thus be able to determine which of the workers were turning out satisfactory work from the standpoint of quantity and quality; and (d) management could establish a wage-incentive system that would reward the diligent, ambitious workers and spur on the poorer workers to greater effort and production.

2 / **Taylor's attitude toward the workers.** Taylor's attitude was not entirely that of management. He was thinking also of the worker, particularly from the standpoint of the reward he received for his labor. Taylor felt that the ignorance on the part of management of how a worker should do his job and of what constituted a good day's work served to penalize

the better workers and failed to spur the poorer workers on to the effort of which they were capable and the enhanced earnings that would follow from their increased productivity.

Taylor's method in bringing about this change was to select the best worker he could find at any given task and to observe what that worker did when he was working at his best sustained speed. As the result of this observation, Taylor broke down each task into its component elements, timed each element separately with a stop watch, and recorded each timing carefully. When this process had been completed several times, the observations were studied and compared; and finally the one best method of performing each task was evolved. This method was committed to writing as a permanent guide to both management and labor. In these studies the workers were informed of the purposes of the project, one of which was to enable them to earn more money.

The next step was to select a good, intelligent worker and require him to follow the instructions covering the best evolved method of doing his task, even to the point of resting at certain intervals in the procedure. Over a considerable period of time there emerged from Taylor's researches a collection of standard job instructions, which, if followed faithfully by the workers after they had been given adequate preliminary instruction and coaching, almost invariably resulted in increased earnings for the workers and greater production for the company. Furthermore, the management now was in possession of the detailed information about all of the tasks under its control as well as a technique for a continuing appraisal of them and for the establishing of a work routine for any new ones.

3 / Scientific management. This new tool of management Taylor named *scientific management*.[2] The implication of the term was that scientific methods would replace the rule-of-thumb procedure which had so long characterized the presumed control of production exercised by the executives of manufacturing companies. Throughout the years since Taylor's work, alert management has refined his methods and developed new ones, as the occasion has required. The term "scientific management" is no longer in common usage; but the techniques and practices that it was coined to describe, modernized in keeping with present-day production problems, are now accepted as essential, integral parts of the implements of progressive production management.

[2] Other pioneers in the development of scientific management techniques and procedures were Henry Gantt, Frederick Halsey, Harrington Emerson, and Frank and Lillian Gilbreth.

■ **Organization of Production**

In a manufacturing company the responsibility for producing the goods that the firm makes is placed with the production division, which is composed of groups of specialists, each of whom is expert in planning, supervising, or performing one or more of the various steps in the productive procedure. The extent and complexity of the organizations involved depend on both the size of the companies concerned and the relative intricacy of the manufacturing processes required. The chart on page 307 portrays the organizational aspects of a medium-sized firm that makes a fairly simple product. It should be noted that the production control and inspection divisions, while subordinate to the production manager, are completely independent of the actual manufacturing division, the pattern of whose work they control and whose products they inspect, respectively.

■ **Motion and Time Study**

Taylor's method of studying the motions of workers as they perform their tasks and of measuring the time that these motions require has been continued under the name of *motion and time study*. In this manner management seeks to establish time standards for the performance of all productive work, which are of value in the exercise of production control. The principal purposes of motion and time study are as follows:

(a) TO DETERMINE THE BEST METHODS OF PERFORMING EACH TASK. Through breaking each job into its component elements and observing the time required to perform each element, management can determine the most efficient methods to be used.

(b) TO AID IN PLANNING PRODUCTION. When management is confronted with the task of planning production, the knowledge of the standard time required to perform each operation is of value in setting up the production schedule. This has an additional importance when the planned operations include some that have not yet been time studied. Through the study of the elements involved, for which time standards may have been previously recorded on other jobs, it is possible to arrive at approximate time standards for the new jobs that are useful in estimating the probable production time.

(c) TO CONTROL OPERATING COSTS. Through the use of time standards established through time study, comparisons can be made between the standards and the actual performances by the workers. Differ-

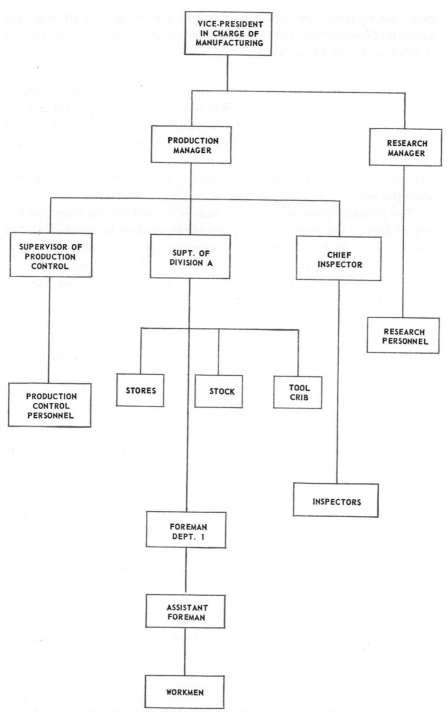

Organization Chart of a Production Department

ences can be noted, and remedial measures can be applied to bring the actual performance into line with the standard performance. Thus control of labor costs can be achieved.

1 / **Motion study.** This is the first step in analyzing a job. It consists of a careful scrutiny of all the motions that go to make up a task. Examination is made not only of the actual motions that the observed worker makes, but also of the physical conditions surrounding the job site, such as the distance from the machine to the boxes holding the incoming and outgoing work, the lighting, and anything else that may affect the job.

The principal purpose of motion study is to establish the most effective way of doing a job from the standpoint of the motions involved. A skilled observer can quickly detect waste movements that can be corrected in the interest of better performance. From this study will come a series of elemental motions that will produce the best method of doing the job. Each of these elemental motions can then be timed.

2 / **Time study.** The mechanics of time study is a rather technical process that requires considerable experience and training on the part of the observer. It is not desirable in this discussion to go beyond a brief description of the time-study procedure. The details are more properly given in specialized texts dealing with motion and time study or production management.

Equipped with a special stop watch, an observation sheet for recording data, and a special board to hold both the watch and the sheet, the observer stations himself where he can see everything that the worker does during a *job cycle*.[3] He then times each elemental motion and records on the observation sheet the findings in each instance. This goes on until a considerable number of job cycles have been completed, sometimes as many as fifty. During this time the observer notes everything that happens, all delays—from whatever cause—and all of the worker's actions, whether cyclically recurrent or not. When the observations have been completed, a time-study clerk calculates the time allowance for a unit of work by adding the periods of time required for the elemental motions that make up that unit. The standard thus determined can be

---

[3] The term job cycle refers to all of the motions necessary to the complete processing of one unit of work, for example, the drilling of a certain number of holes in a piece of steel or iron. The job cycle includes everything the operator does from the moment he turns to pick up the undrilled iron piece until he lays down the finished piece.

used as a measure of efficiency in production as well as a base for determining the worker's compensation.

3 / Micromotion study. A refinement of the time-study method is *micromotion study*, which involves the use of a motion-picture camera. Instead of an observer who watches the worker and records the times of the elemental motions, a camera captures the actions as well as the times, which are taken from a clock with a large dial that is placed in focus with the operator. The analysis of the film is made later by trained engineers. This method is of value when the operation involves a great many motions that are too rapid or complicated for the human eye to follow. Micromotion study is probably used on a limited scale because of the cost involved as compared with the gains achieved, and the relative shortage of competent observers and analysts.

The extension of automation throughout industry would certainly lessen the importance of motion and time study because of the progressive elimination of the machine operators. The degree to which this situation will affect skilled workers is uncertain at present.

PRODUCTION CONTROL

In its highest state of development, *production control* consists of a well-defined set of procedures that has as its objective the coordination of all of the elements of the productive process—men, machines, tools, and materials—into a smoothly flowing whole, which results in the fabrication of products with a minimum of interruption, in the fastest possible time, and at the lowest obtainable cost. The details of the various systems of production control differ according to the characteristics of the industries in which they are used, but the basic principles are the same. The present discussion will be limited to an examination of those fundamentals.

■ Types of Production Control

There are two types of production control: order control and flow control. *Order control* is used by manufacturing concerns that operate their plants only when they have received orders from their customers. *Flow control* is used in factories that produce for stock and are prepared to make immediate deliveries from their finished goods inventories as soon as customer orders are received. The procedures in both types are approximately the same, and it is their function either to make certain that the flow of materials through the factory is such that the promised delivery dates are met, or that the delivery to stock is so timed that a proper balance of stocks to sales may be maintained at all times.

■ Steps in Production Control

The basic steps in production control, in the order in which they occur, are:

1. Planning   3. Scheduling
2. Routing   4. Performance follow-up and control

1 / Planning. When a customer's order or a company stock order is received by the production planning department, it is broken down into its component parts. This involves a *bill of material*, which lists the finished parts, subassemblies, and assemblies that are called for by the order. This list, in turn, is broken down into those parts that are purchased in finished form from other manufacturers and the materials that are bought for fabricating and processing in the company's own factory. After reference is made to the inventories, purchase requisitions for the parts and materials needed are issued to the purchasing department, which issues purchase orders to the proper vendors.

From the engineering and production departments information is secured that indicates the number and types of machines that are required, the processing time for each part, and the tools that will be needed. From this information the production control department can determine the starting dates for processing all parts and materials so that they will arrive at the assembly at the proper time. If any tools are not available, the purchasing department is notified so that it may place orders in time to assure their being on hand when needed.

2 / Routing. *Routing* is the stage of production control which determines the route that the work will take through the shop and where and by whom the processing shall be done. It specifies the sequence of operations pertaining to a single part and also in regard to its relationship to other parts. Routing is sometimes regarded as part of the planning process.

3 / Scheduling. *Scheduling* involves the setting up of the timetables that will govern the movement of the work as it is subjected to the various fabricating processes. A *master schedule*, which indicates the number of finished products that will come off the assembly each month or week until the order is completed, is created.

Weekly departmental schedules set forth the expected production of all parts in each department for each week of the production cycle. Care is taken not to schedule work for a department in excess of that department's capacity to deliver, taking into consideration the normal contingencies that must be met, such as machine breakdown, set-up time, length of shift, and number of shifts. By *set-up time* is meant the time required to prepare the machine for a particular job. This includes adjusting the cutting tools and the machine speeds.

Load ahead schedules are made up for each department. These indicate the amount of work that lies ahead of the department until the present run is completed. The load is altered from week to week as the actual production results are achieved. The load ahead schedule is very important from the standpoint of scheduling subsequent jobs as orders are received. It prevents scheduling more work for a department than it can handle.

Another part of this operation is that of scheduling purchase requisitions so that purchase orders may be placed with a view to achieving well-balanced inventories, and of scheduling tools so that the toolroom will have the proper tools on hand when needed.

4 / Performance follow-up and control. After the preparatory steps have been completed, work orders are released and production starts. The putting into effect of the work orders and the transmission to the shop of the routing papers are called *dispatching.* Elaborate control boards are sometimes set up, utilizing various printed forms that show the progress of the work in the shop and serve as indicators of production irregularities which call for supervisory corrective action. The function of production control then becomes that of following up on all of its performance schedules to detect any significant variations from the plans, to discover and correct the causes of these variations, and to compensate for any irregularities.

Various follow-up routines are established, particularly for purchases, tools, and production. *Schedule performance reports* are issued by the production control department on the basis of parts and schedule follow-up reports received from the operating departments. These reports set forth the performance of all departments as compared to the schedules. In this way top management is kept informed of the flow of work through the shop, and it can note any deviations from the plans and fix accountability for them. *Scrap reports*, received from the inspection department, relate the number of pieces rejected and the reasons. These reports permit the production control department to notify the production department of an unusually large number of pieces scrapped so that arrangements can be made for additional production to take their places, in order to prevent shortages from occurring at some later stage with a possible consequent delay in delivery of the products to customers.

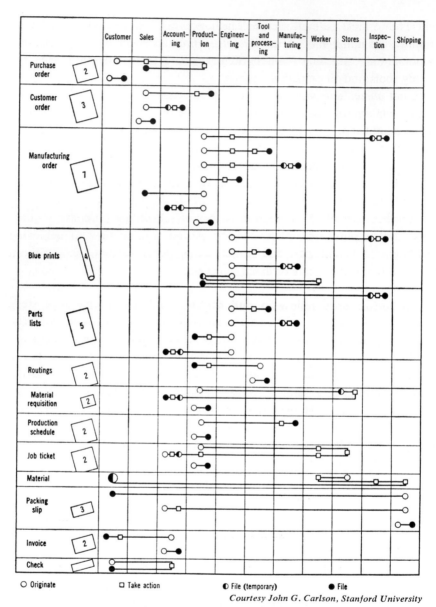

	Customer	Sales	Account-ing	Product-ion	Engineer-ing	Tool and process-ing	Manufac-turing	Worker	Stores	Inspec-tion	Shipping

Flow of Paperwork in a Production Control Procedure

As the flow of production progresses and the processed parts move to the subassemblies and to the final assembly and finally emerge as finished units, the paper work routine indicates this to the production control department and the records are marked accordingly. When the entire order is completed, the schedules are terminated, the whole project is wound up, and the records are filed for future use.

The foregoing description has been presented as if a single order were all that occupied the attention of the production control department at any one time. This is an oversimplification in many instances, as it is more likely that a large number of orders, in varying stages of completion, are running coincidentally. The principles of operation, however, are as outlined and, if followed through on each order, regardless of how many other orders the department may be processing at the same time, they will result in an intelligently controlled production situation, with a minimum of cost and a maximum utilization of productive facilities.

To an increasing degree the use of computers has been growing in the different areas of production control. In all of the steps involved in production control, it has been proven beneficial in some plants to employ these electronic devices as aids to the performance of the functions previously handled manually. The further extension of this trend will depend upon the relative costs of using computers or of continuing with the older methods.

In recent years certain statistical and mathematical techniques called operations research (see Chapter 26) have been adopted by many firms. One of these techniques, linear programming, is particularly useful in production control procedures. It has been helpful in problems involving the optimum, or lowest cost, allocation of all of the various instruments of production and production control. The development of high-speed computers has made large-scale linear programming possible.

■ Program Evaluation and Review Technique / (PERT)

Recently a new management tool called *PERT* (Program Evaluation and Review Technique) has been developed. Originated by the U. S. Navy in connection with the Polaris guided missile project in 1959, it has been adopted by a number of industries, particularly those having government contracts. Its major applications have been in the area of production control, although some of its proponents believe that it will eventually be used in other management decision-making areas. Somewhat oversimplified, the basic procedures of PERT call for careful planning of all the activities necessary for the manufacture of a desired product with particular emphasis on time, cost, and reliability, the last referring to the ability of the end product to do what it is designed to do. Then actual performance is measured against the plan, and deviations from it are remedied as production proceeds. The introduction of high-speed data processing equipment in recent years has greatly aided those managements who have undertaken PERT in their plants.

One of the interesting and beneficial aspects of PERT has been the development of the *critical path method (CPM)*. This is particularly helpful in the estimating of the length of time that will be required to complete an order for a customer. In brief, the procedure in establishing the critical path is to note the different times required for each separate productive operation and to add the times for operations that cannot be performed concurrently in order to arrive at the greatest amount of time that will be required to finish the order. In this way it becomes possible for a producer to quote reliable delivery dates to a customer, with a greater probability of being able to meet these dates than might otherwise be the case.

■ Quality Control and Inspection

In all manufacturing operations the work is produced to certain standards that must be met if the commodities in question are to meet the requirements of buyers in a satisfactory manner. These standards are usually set forth in writing for the guidance of production and inspection personnel. The function of *inspection* is to measure the extent to which these standards have been observed and to detect and reject any part of the product that is not up to the standard. The establishment of these standards and the subsequent inspection is called *quality control*.

Inspection is performed by a special department that is set up for that purpose and that is frequently under the supervision of the works manager; but only rarely are the inspectors under the control of production department foremen. The reason is that the duty of the inspectors is to "call them as they see them"; and as the rejection of material is somewhat of a reflection on the foreman in charge, a more objective determination of quality can be obtained if the foreman is not the inspector's immediate superior.

1. Time of inspection	3. Inspection devices
2. Place of inspection	4. Quantity inspected

1 / **Time of inspection.** The problem of when inspection takes place is dependent upon the complexity of the manufacturing processes concerned and the wishes of the management. Most incoming parts and materials are inspected as they arrive from the vendors. After this point the minimum inspection requirement is one made of the finished article before it is shipped to the customer. The maximum conceivable number of inspections would include an inspection after each separate operation with a 100 percent final inspection. Originating during World War II and

continuing since then, 100 percent inspection of all ordnance items has been generally required of their suppliers by the armed services.

In most cases the prevailing practice is somewhere in between these two extremes, depending upon the nature of the manufacturing processes, the tolerances permitted, and the past history of defective material and workmanship. The term *tolerance* refers to the practice of permitting a certain leeway in the measurements of manufactured parts.

2 / Place of inspection. The inspection operation may take place at one or more centralized locations to which the work is transported and where the inspection personnel are more or less specialized and completely removed from contact with the workers whose product is being examined; or it may be done at every work station. The latter method has the advantage of saving material transportation costs, but also the disadvantage of the proximity of the workers and the inspectors.

In certain complicated machining operations, the worker does his own preliminary inspection as the work progresses, but the work is checked by an inspector when the job is done. An inspection is quite common immediately after a machine has been set up for a new operation and before the production run has started.

3 / Inspection devices. A wide variety of tools and devices are used in inspection. Gauges, chemical processes, X-ray equipment, and electrical apparatus are among those commonly found. Some plug gauges are quite simple in their construction and application, while others are exceedingly complicated. Micrometer gauges are a part of the tool equipment of most machinists and are widely used in inspection work. Electrical devices are valuable in inspecting electrical apparatus, and the X-ray has recently been employed to detect flaws in castings or other materials where visual inspection methods are inadequate.

Inspection can aid in exposing weak points in the production process so that management can apply remedial measures. It can also help to build goodwill by preventing the shipment of finished products that vary from the prescribed standards.

Inspection must be conducted objectively according to a set of standards that should be sufficiently rigid to assure the satisfactory operation of the parts concerned, but flexible enough to allow for the permissible variations and tolerances within whose limits the materials are acceptable. Inspection standards should be as high as necessary, but should not be needlessly strict. The determination of these limits is the concern of the engineering department.

4 / Quantity inspected. There are three methods of meeting this problem—100 percent inspection, single-sample inspection, or multiple-sample inspection. The 100 percent method is required only in those instances where the products are of exceptionally high quality or where the accuracy of the manufacturing processes is dependent more on the skill of the operators than on that of machines. The choice between the other two methods depends on how close the tolerances are and the extent to which the productive processes are mechanized.

■ Statistical Quality Control

An inspection procedure that has been growing in usage in American industry is known as *statistical quality control.* It involves the use of certain mathematical principles that are applied through statistics and has resulted in a reduction in the number of items that need to be inspected, with a consequent saving in the cost of inspection. This new system of inspection has been extended into a quality control of manufacturing processes so that variations from acceptable standards are detected before a large number of pieces have been spoiled.

BUSINESS TERMS

(a) production processes (297); extractive process (298), analytic process (298), fabricating (converting) process (298), synthetic (assembly) process (298)

(b) continuous process (299), intermittent process (300), job shop (300)

(c) standard manufacture (300), custom manufacture (300)

(d) miniaturization (302), numerical control (N/C) (302), lead time (302)

(e) automation (302), feedback (302), closed-loop control (302), open-loop control (302), servo-mechanisms (303)

(f) scientific management (305)

(g) motion and time study (306), job cycle (308), micromotion study (309)

(h) production control (309), order control (309), flow control (309)

(i) bill of material (310)

(j) routing (310)

(k) scheduling (310); master schedule (310), weekly departmental schedules (310), set-up time (311), load ahead schedule (311)

(l) dispatching (311); schedule performance reports (311), scrap reports (311)

(m) PERT (313); critical path method (CPM) (314)

(n) inspection (314), quality control (314), tolerance (315)

(o) statistical quality control (316)

QUESTIONS FOR DISCUSSION AND ANALYSIS

1. Can you name any types of manufacturing businesses, other than those given in the text, where modern methods of production control would not be required?
2. Why is there a difference between the economists' use of the term "production" (Chapter 1) and that of business? Which is more correct in your opinion? Why?
3. Motion and time study has been applied to office workers in some companies. Would you think that this would be a logical procedure? Why?
4. Can you name any examples of custom manufacture other than those given in the text? If so, what are they?
5. What would be the effect on competition in the automobile business if the lead time in the industry could be reduced to six months?
6. Would you expect to find flow control in a job shop? Why?
7. Do you think that automation will eventually displace most unskilled workers? skilled workers? Why?
8. Would you expect that the completely automatic plant would ever come into being? Explain.
9. Should workers ever be permitted to inspect their own work? Explain.
10. In what industries would you expect to find the highest degree of automation? the lowest?

PROBLEMS AND SHORT CASES

1. A number of recent articles relate to automation, its effects on personnel, competition, and production methods both past, present, and future. Consult current and recent issues of such periodicals as *Fortune, Business Week, Dun's Review, The Wall Street Journal,* and similar publications that are in your school library and select at least five articles dealing with automation. Write a brief report to include a summary and your own commentary on each article.
2. Make a motion and time study of some simple operation. Prepare a report showing (a) the nature and purpose of the study; (b) the procedure that was followed; and (c) the findings, including your recommendations regarding the best manner in which to perform the operation and a reasonable time standard. You should indicate the elemental motions into which the overall operation was divided.

    Examples of simple operations that might be studied for this problem are: (a) inserting a new lead in an automatic pencil; (b) tying a bow tie; (c) shuffling and dealing the cards for four hands of bridge.
3. Howlett and Houston, Inc., is a medium-sized firm producing a line of standardized pumps and compressors that are used in a large number of different industries. Their sales have averaged around $5 million yearly for the past decade or so. Basically this company is more of an assembling organization than a manufacturing one, since it has long been their policy to purchase most of the component parts of their pumps and compressors and to assemble them for

delivery to their customers as orders have been received. The firms supplying these parts numbered around 50, with most of whom Howlett and Houston had done business for many years.

During the late 1950's and early 1960's the rapid advances that had been made in the technology of production had created a number of problems for this firm. They were increasingly being requested to supply pumps and compressors that differed from those which had long comprised their line. This situation had required them to seek out new sources of supply, for many of their regular vendors were unable to provide them with the parts that were needed for the types of pumps and compressors that were currently in demand. This circumstance caused them to lose occasional orders due to their inability to find suppliers who could provide them with parts in time to satisfy the delivery dates specified by their customers. Also some of the items furnished by their new resources did not come up to the standards of quality that were necessary for the more precise specifications of the present-day products, causing both delay in filling orders and an increased incidence of rejected parts. The executives of Howlett and Houston are giving a great deal of thought to adopting a policy of manufacturing all or most of the components that go to make up their products.

Write a report setting forth all of the factors that the company should take into consideration in arriving at a decision in this matter.

SUGGESTED READINGS

Buffa, E. S. *Modern Production Management,* Second Edition. New York: John Wiley & Sons, Inc., 1965.

Folts, F. E. *Introduction to Industrial Management,* Fifth Edition. New York: McGraw-Hill Book Company, Inc., 1963.

Garrett, L., and M. Silver. *Production Management Analysis.* New York: Harcourt, Brace & World, Inc., 1966.

Greene, J. H. *Production Control: Systems and Decisions.* Homewood, Illinois: Richard D. Irwin, Inc., 1965.

Hansen, B. L. *Quality Control: Theory and Application.* Englewood Cliffs, New Jersey: Prentice-Hall, Inc., 1963.

Laird, D. A., and E. C. Laird. *How to Get Along with Automation.* New York: McGraw-Hill Book Company, Inc., 1964.

Moore, F. G. *Manufacturing Management,* Fourth Edition. Homewood, Illinois: Richard D. Irwin, Inc., 1965.

Timms, H. L. *The Production Function in Business: Management Decision Systems,* Revised Edition. Homewood, Illinois: Richard D. Irwin, Inc., 1966.

Magazines: Publications of American Management Association and National Industrial Conference Board, *Factory, Factory Management and Maintenance, Industrial Quality Control, Automation.*

Part V

PERSONNEL

CHAPTER

15 Employee Selection and Training

16 Employee Compensation

17 Labor Problems and Legislation

PROLOGUE TO PART V

PERSONNEL

In Part V the major role of the personnel phase of business in our economy is recognized.

Chapter 15, Employee Selection and Training, takes up the role of the personnel department and examines the policies and procedures that are used in the selection and training of employees. The concept of industrial human relations is introduced, and its bearing on current personnel practices is weighed, particularly in reference to the achieving by management of an effective and reasonably satisfied group of workers.

Chapter 16, Employee Compensation, is concerned with the many different methods that are employed for the purpose of rewarding and compensating workers for their productive efforts. The current methods of wage determination are examined, as are also some of the economic theories of wages. Consideration is given to the relationship of wages and prices and to the growing impact of fringe benefits and pensions.

In Chapter 17, Labor Problems and Legislation, the apparent causes of labor-management friction, together with the methods whereby this conflict may be alleviated, are examined. The role of unions is stressed, and there is a discussion of the major labor laws that have been enacted for the purpose of providing solutions to some of the important problems of labor-management relations.

Chapter 15

EMPLOYEE SELECTION AND TRAINING

A responsibility that must be assumed by business firms is that of maintaining sufficient personnel in their organizations so that the purposes for which they exist may be achieved. This requires a continuous effort to find, select, and train those individuals whose skills, aptitudes, potentials, and personal preferences qualify them as employees. In the past two decades or more, the notable growth in the technological complexity in many of our industries, both in the office and in the factory, has placed increased emphasis on the problem of locating people who have the requisite skills or who are capable of acquiring them. The enhanced status of personnel departments, at least in the larger and more forward-looking firms in the country, gives evidence of the awareness by top management in these companies of the importance and complexity of the task of employee selection and training as well as that of human relations in industry.

■ Industrial Human Relations

The basic objective of industrial human relations is to find newer and better methods of understanding man and his relationship to his work, and of motivating him to ever higher standards of workmanship. Management should so organize the work that it will provide the opportunity for self-realization on the part of the workers. Included in this objective is the need for management to provide the proper leadership and an organizational environment in which the workers may find satisfaction. Communication between workers and management should be improved so that necessary changes in policies and procedures may be understood and accepted affirmatively by the work force. Worker involvement in these matters should bring about a stronger and closer identification between workers, their work, and management.

The responsibility for the implementing of this concept of industrial human relations is not the province of the personnel department alone, although it should accept a major role in this endeavor. Rather it should be the interest and duty of all managerial personnel to bring about the conditions just indicated. Furthermore, this must spring from a sincere belief in the desirability of achieving these objectives, for workers are quick to detect any artificiality on the part of management and will react unfavorably to it.

■ The Importance of Communication

A major contributing factor to the development of better personnel relations is found in the area of intracompany communication. The need for open channels of communication is coming to be recognized in a growing number of progressive firms. Communication is a three-way process—downward, upward, and horizontally. Workers should know more about managerial thinking, management should be aware of what is going on in the workers' minds, and there should be communication between those who occupy identical strata in the company's organization. There are several methods whereby this desirable communication can be achieved. Among these are: oral, face-to-face; employee newspapers and magazines; bulletin boards; handbooks; booklets; financial reports; letters from executives; and meetings.

A common practice in industry is the employee *suggestion box*, whereby workers are given the opportunity to present suggestions for improving efficiency or criticisms of company policies and practices. Many companies offer cash rewards to those workers whose contributions are of value to their employers. The establishing of open communication lines between employees and management has paid handsome dividends.

■ Nature and Background of the Problem

A threefold problem is involved here: (1) the right people must be found and the proper choice made from those available; (2) those whose skill or experience is inadequate for the jobs in question must be trained to remedy this deficiency; and (3) it is very desirable that the conditions on the job be such (industrial human relations) that there will exist among the employees an attitude—a state of mind that will be favorable to the company—which is called "morale" or "esprit de corps."

In the period prior to the emergence of the medium-to-large-size companies, these problems were much simpler to handle. Then close contact was possible between employers and employees in all phases of personnel relationships.

The emergence of larger sized concerns, with employees numbering into the hundreds of thousands, brought about changes in all aspects of personnel dealings. This involved the development of different techniques for hiring new employees, for training them, and for the whole area of employer-employee relationships. While some of the old-time informality between bosses and workers still persists in small firms, in the larger companies today the applicant for a job meets a professional personnel manager or one of his assistants; the trainee goes through a routinized training procedure under the supervision of a professional training director; the worker, in many instances, feels little loyalty to the company; and, in some cases, the officers of the company apparently feel little sense of responsibility toward him.

The growing measure of labor unrest that has characterized the last 75 years or more is probably due, to a large degree, to the gap that has developed between employers and employees. Psychologists, sociologists, economists, and social anthropologists have been asked to study this problem and to suggest ways in which their disciplines could contribute toward the establishing of better relationships between employers and employees. From their efforts and researches has emerged the concept of industrial human relations described above.

From the standpoint of the organizations of the companies involved, one of the first evidences of concern along these lines was the emergence of personnel departments and their development into positions of major importance in many firms. In these departments qualified individuals were assigned the responsibilities of hiring and training new workers, which had previously been exercised by various members of management whose expertise lay mainly in fields other than that of personnel.

■ Personnel Department

Starting many years ago as an employment office, the personnel department has gradually expanded and added to its duties until now it embraces a rather wide range of personnel matters. The director of personnel is one of the key men in the firm, sometimes with vice-presidential rank. The other employees in the department are chosen for their demonstrated interest in and ability to meet the personnel problems of present-day industry.

The many duties of the personnel department are allocated naturally into the following divisions: employment, training, personnel services,

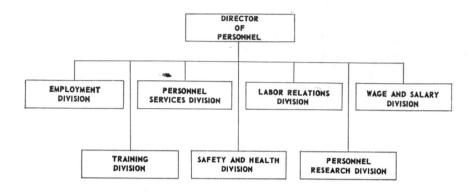

Organization Chart of the Personnel Department

safety and health, personnel research, labor relations, and wages and salaries. The first five of these divisions will be discussed in this chapter.

The labor relations division, which is sometimes called the employee representation division in firms that do not have unions, is concerned with the relationships between the employees as a group and the company. Shop committees, grievance-hearing procedures, and other matters in this area come within its jurisdiction. When a union exists in the plant or office, this division serves as the point of contact between the union and the company. The subject of labor relations is treated quite extensively in Chapter 17. The subject of wages and salaries is discussed in Chapter 16.

EMPLOYMENT DIVISION

The principal purpose of modern hiring procedures is to fill all jobs that become vacant with the best equipped and trained workers that can be found. The so-called round pegs should be fitted into the round holes, and the square pegs into the square holes. This results in a more effective labor force and a lower labor turnover. The United States Department of Labor has defined *labor turnover* as "the replacements in a working force made necessary by employees leaving the service." It is generally regarded as an index of the stability of the employee group in a business concern. Where labor turnover is high, the presumption is that all is not well personnel-wise within the plant. Conversely, where labor turnover is low, good personnel conditions are believed to exist. There may, of course, be external circumstances, such as a high rate of unemployment in an area, that might contribute to a low labor turnover rate without regard to whether or not good personnel conditions prevailed in the companies concerned.

■ Job Analysis, Description, and Specification

The first step in an intelligent approach to the problem of securing the best people for a group of jobs is to discover all of the pertinent facts relative to each job. This procedure is known as *job analysis* and involves inquiry into all the details of each position in the company that the personnel department might be called upon to fill. Nothing that pertains to or affects a job is too small to be noted and set down on the record.

Among the topics that should be covered in a job analysis are the location of the job; its duties and responsibilities; the equipment, tools, or machines used; the working conditions; the pay; the opportunities for promotion; and whether or not any training for the job is offered. It is furthermore desirable that data be gathered concerning the qualifications that are required of the prospective employee. These data can be secured from department heads or the present workers, or both. Occasionally a firm of personnel management consultants is called in if the magnitude or complexity of this work warrants this action.

The information that is gathered during the job analysis which relates strictly to the job itself is then put in writing in the *job description*. From the personnel data provided by the job analysis, the *job specification* is also prepared. This consists of a statement of the personal qualifications required of prospective employees for each type of job, such as skill, age, experience, and special aptitudes.

Armed with the job descriptions and job specifications for all positions, the employment division of the personnel department is equipped to proceed intelligently with the task of securing the best available workers for any jobs that must be filled.

■ Sources of Workers

The sources of supply for prospective employees are many and varied. The extent to which the more common ones can be utilized depends upon the nature of the business, the degree of skill required for the different jobs, and the character of the population in the area in which the plant is located. These sources include past and present employees, their friends and relatives, applications on file in the employment office, state employment agencies, private employment agencies, employment scouts, schools and colleges, trade and technical schools, classified advertising, and union headquarters and hiring halls.

Some concerns have a policy of looking first within their own organizations for workers to fill all jobs above the beginning or lowest grades. For example, the variety chains, such as the F. W. Woolworth Company

JOB TITLE: PERSONNEL CLERK

Department: Personnel   Date: March 26, 1967

Employees in Department: 12   Name: John Clark

Employees on This Job: 3

GENERAL DESCRIPTION OF THE JOB

Works under the supervision of the Employment Manager; assists in clerical routine of induction which involves interviewing new workers; performs a variety of clerical and stenographic work.

SPECIFIC DUTIES OF THE JOB

1. Interviews new workers after they have been given induction information such as hours, working conditions, services, etc. to verify personnel information and prepare records; checks information on application, statement of availability, draft, citizenship, and the like; obtains necessary information for income tax withholding, and determines classification; prepares forms for hospitalization, group insurance, and bond deductions; assigns clock number, makes up time card and badge card.

2. Calls previous employer to get reference information while applicant is being interviewed; may check references by mail after employee is hired, and occasionally records information from Dun & Bradstreet on personnel card.

3. Telephones employee's department or home after extended absence to determine when employee is expected to return, if at all; follows same procedure at end of leave of absence.

4. Handles stenographic work of Employment Manager.

5. Does miscellaneous clerical work; assigns clock numbers and makes up time cards for employees transferred between departments; keeps record of equipment loaned to employees, such as micrometers, goggles, etc.; maintains current address file of employees in service; performs other clerical duties as assigned.

6. May substitute for Receptionist for short periods; give induction information to new employees in absence of Personnel Induction Clerk, escort new workers to departments; administer tests.

Job Description

and the S. S. Kresge Company, have long adhered strictly to this policy, which is presumed to enhance the morale among their employees. Other firms are more or less indifferent regarding the sources of their new workers, endeavoring always to obtain the best available candidates regardless of other factors.

A point of some consequence from the standpoint of human relations concerns the question of whether or not the employees should be informed of vacancies in departments other than their own and be given the opportunity to apply for them if they believe themselves qualified. In some instances workers have resented not being told of positions in other departments that were filled from outside the plant. That some managements are aware of this situation is evidenced by occasional "help wanted ads," particularly for positions of some responsibility, which contain a statement to the effect that the company's employees have been informed of the advertisement.

Nepotism, or the favoring of relatives of the firm's executives or personal friends when attractive positions are open, is to be found in many companies. It frequently has a disquieting effect on the other employees. Charges are sometimes made that mediocre individuals are hired because of their family connections and that more deserving applicants are turned away.

■ Employment Procedures

Several procedures feature the employment process. Any or all of them may be used in any given instance, depending upon the policies of the companies concerned. These procedures include: (1) application blanks, (2) preliminary interview, (3) tests, (4) investigation of applicant's background, (5) physical examinations, and (6) main interview.

The order of the steps in employment procedures is frequently based on placing first the ones that may reveal the necessity of rejecting an applicant. Thus the physical examination might be placed ahead of the other steps in a company where some physical attributes were essential to the job, such as strength or unusual manual dexterity.

In recent years tests have been used as a means of determining the fitness of applicants for the jobs to which they aspire. These tests are used for the purpose of measuring (a) so-called general intelligence or mental alertness, (b) aptitude or basic talents along particular lines, and (c) ability or proficiency in given trades or skills. While there has been some criticism of the value of these tests, they are generally useful employment techniques.

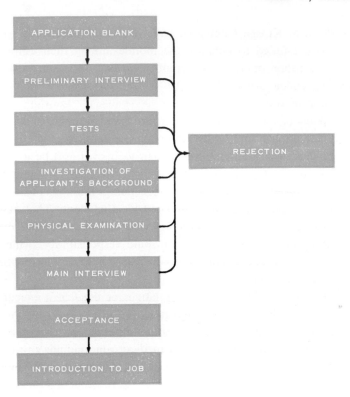

Employment Procedures

The main interview is usually the occasion when the applicant is either definitely hired or rejected. If psychological tests are administered or a physical examination is required, these usually precede the main interview. During this conversation the employment official endeavors to make a final evaluation of the applicant and to determine whether or not he should be hired. It is a crucial point in the employment procedure, and one to which personnel experts have given considerable thought and study because of the wide variations in the conclusions that may result from several different people's interviewing the same applicant. In some companies the interviewer has a prescribed form to follow, with a fixed series of questions and remarks. Others allow their interviewers a free hand in conducting their conferences, merely holding them responsible for the selection of good workers and for the rejection of poor ones.

■ Legal Restrictions on Hiring Policies

On July 2, 1965, Title VII of the *Civil Rights Act of 1964* went into effect. This section of the Act makes it illegal to hire or favor an applicant for a job over another solely on account of race. Employment cannot be denied to a woman solely for reasons of her sex. No worker can be discharged because of his color, religion, national origin, or sex. Preference in pay raises or promotions that discriminate against certain employees because of their sex or national origin is illegal. Aptitude tests can still be administered, but the employer must be sure that the tests administered are the same to all applicants. Unions and employment agencies are also forbidden to discriminate in membership or employment recommendations because of race, color, religion, national origin, or sex. This section of the Act became applicable to companies or unions with 75 or more workers in 1966; 50 or more in 1967; and 25 or more in 1968.

The *Equal Employment Opportunity Committee* of five members has been established to administer the provisions of the Act. There will probably be many points of law that must be determined by the EEOC, and eventually the courts, before the full implications of the Act become apparent. There are also 25 states that have Fair Employment Practices Codes, which have the same objectives as the federal Act.

For government contractors and subcontractors the President's Committee on Equal Employment Opportunity has the power to cancel contracts held by companies that practice discrimination in employment.

■ Postemployment Procedures

The responsibility of the Employment Division for the new worker does not cease when his name is added to the payroll. It sees that he is properly launched on his new career and checks on his progress.

1. Introduction to the job
2. Follow-ups

1 / Introduction to the job. After the applicant has been hired, he must be properly introduced to all of the details and personnel connected with the job. He must be directed to the department where he will work and be presented to his superiors and, in some instances, to his co-workers. There is a perceptible tendency in personnel circles to refer to this as *induction to the job,* using a term which probably had its origin in this respect during World War II.

The details of this introduction or induction vary with different firms. A common procedure is for a representative of the personnel division to accompany the new employee to the locale of the job and arrange for the meeting with the foreman. The latter, in turn, shows the newcomer where he will work and explains the details of the job. Many foresighted companies have found it worthwhile to make this introduction as friendly and cordial as possible in order to put the new man in a good frame of mind and to enlist his best abilities right from the start.

Certain details concerning the company and the job must be imparted to new employees so that they may understand the policies and rules of the company and fit themselves into the picture with the least friction or delay. These matters include hours of work, lunchroom facilities, attendance rules, rest periods, safety rules, locker or coatroom facilities, methods and times of wage payment, employees' organizations, recreational facilities, and medical services available. This information is usually printed in booklet form and presented to the new employee with the request that he read it and familiarize himself with its contents.

2 / Follow-ups. Some companies have a policy of periodic follow-up on new workers, the purpose of which is to discover the character of performance that they are putting forth, whether or not they are happy in their jobs, and so on. The first of these follow-ups may occur at any time within the first few days after employment and the others at more or less regular intervals thereafter, sometimes twice a year.

A few firms make an annual checkup on the performance of all of their employees. This is sometimes referred to as the *personnel audit*. The customary procedure is for a committee, consisting of representatives of top management as well as of the personnel division, to examine the records and achievements of all employees, including those in supervisory positions. As the result of their findings, the committee recommends promotions, pay changes, censure, demotion, or discharge, as the case may be. In some cases employee rating sheets are used as a means of standardizing the review procedures.

A number of companies hire firms of management engineers or of psychologists to check on the fitness of their employees for the jobs that they hold. This process is called *personal evaluation* and consists of setting up job descriptions for the various positions and then determining the competency of the incumbents for their jobs. It is only fair to state that there are rather sharp differences of opinion among businessmen concerning the value of this procedure.

Both the personnel audit and the personal evaluation require deft handling by management if the effect on human relations is to be advantageous. Resentment and antagonism on the part of employees are not uncommon in companies where management has failed to take into consideration the feelings of unrest and insecurity that these procedures may engender.

■ Employee Transfer, Promotion, and Discharge

These three personnel functions are common to all companies. If not correctly handled, they may have very unfortunate results on employer-employee relations.

1. Transfer
2. Promotion
3. Discharge

1 / Transfer. *Transfer* is the shifting of a worker from one job to another that does not involve the employment of greater skills or the assumption of additional responsibilities. Transfers take place to offset a decrease in the work load in a department; to correct a faulty placement and to give an employee work more suited to his abilities; to take care of older workers who must be assigned to lighter tasks; to transfer promising employees from jobs without opportunity for promotion; to rotate workers in dangerous or unpleasant jobs; to afford employees training in several jobs; and frequently to alleviate unfortunate personal experiences or incompatibility with supervisors or fellow workers.

Policies and rules governing transfers must be established in order that the employees affected may feel certain that they are being given fair consideration and treatment, and not merely being pushed around at someone's whim.

2 / Promotion. *Promotion* may be defined as the advancement of an employee to a job that requires greater skill and larger responsibilties with, customarily, a commensurate advance in compensation. There are many reasons for promotions, foremost among which is the need for a company to place its men in positions where their mental and physical capacities will be most useful for their employer. Other reasons include the rewarding of good performance; the retention of valuable employees; and the maintaining of the morale of the workers. It may be assumed that, whenever a promotion takes place, some of those not thus favored will be unhappy. If the advancement has come as a reward for demonstrated merit, however, and if it has been carefully considered before being announced, the effect on the other employees will be more favorable than when the opposite is the case.

A carefully thought-out promotion policy should be established. Apart from the ill effects of infrequent promotions, few circumstances will wreak more havoc with the esprit de corps of an organization than the practice of ill-advised or undeserved promotions.

Three factors should be considered when a promotion is being considered: (a) the personal and technical requirements of the job; (b) the ability of the worker under consideration to satisfy them, as compared to that of the other employees; and (c) the length of his service with the company. This latter point, which is called *seniority,* is of vital importance in its effect on other employees of the firm who regard themselves as eligible for the advancement. Where two or more individuals of approximately equal abilities are being considered for a promotion, it is usually the part of wisdom for management to select the one with the greatest seniority.

Nepotism sometimes also plays a part where promotions are concerned. If the favored persons have outstanding ability, the fact that they are related to the bosses will be a matter of passing moment, as their superiority will doubtless become quickly apparent and the wisdom of their being selected will be realized. The morale of the firm's personnel may be seriously impaired, however, if the persons concerned are less able than some of those who are passed over at times of promotions. These points must be borne in mind if the management wishes to avoid stirring up resentment among the other workers and crippling their morale. When a company establishes a policy of carefully scrutinizing every proposed promotion in these respects and then follows it consistently, the danger of unfavorable consequences is greatly diminished.

3 / Discharge. *Discharge* involves the permanent separation by the company of the employee from its service. A *layoff* differs from discharge in that it is assumed that the separation is merely temporary. Many reasons exist for the discharge of employees. One group of causes is concerned with company policies, such as the elimination by automation of the activities in which the employee has been engaged, or the presence of cyclical or competitive influences that necessitate a reduction in the work force. The other group of reasons is concerned with the employees themselves. Among these are incompetence, insubordination, laziness, and incompatibility. A recent research into the reasons for the discharge of office personnel and junior executives revealed that the inability of those discharged to get along with their fellow employees ranked at the top of the list.

Policies range from the simplest, where the mere word of a superior is sufficient to effect a discharge, to quite complex procedures that call for the referral of all proposed discharges to committees, formal statements of charges, hearings in which the prospective dischargee is given a chance to defend himself, and a final review by the personnel manager. In many companies it is the policy to endeavor to effect a transfer of the employee concerned to some other department, unless the charge is insubordination or something similar.

Regardless of the length of the procedures specified, it is customary for the management to uphold the supervision that initiated the move toward the dismissal, at least as far as the department is concerned. Even if a mistake has been made, most companies will consent to the worker's dismissal from the department if his foreman insists.

A layoff is quite different and usually results from a diminution of work, either in a particular department or in the company as a whole. It assumes reemployment as soon as conditions have become better. Within certain limits it is customary to effect layoffs in reverse order of seniority, those with the shortest period of service being the first to go.

In companies that are unionized, totally or in part, transfer, promotion, discharge, and layoff are customarily made the subjects of negotiation between the unions and the employers, with the result that the conditions affecting each action are set forth in considerable detail in the union-company contracts. Obviously where this is the case, the companies must abide by the contract provisions. In many of these contracts the matter of seniority is of first importance, at least in regard to transfer, layoff, and discharge. Frequently the union has the power to nullify the action of management if it sees fit. Whether this has contributed to better personnel relations in these companies is possibly open to some question.

TRAINING DIVISION

All new employees require a certain amount of training before they can give their best efforts to their jobs. This training is of two types: training on the job and training for the job.

■ Training on the Job

Certain types of work lend themselves to training on the job, whereby the employee learns while doing. These are usually fairly simple jobs, where the presence of unskilled workers does not seriously affect the smooth operation of the business.

The training may be given by foremen or supervisors, by experienced operators, or by special instructors employed for this purpose. In department stores the *sponsor system* is often used, whereby an older employee "sponsors" the new worker for the first few days and teaches her the details of the job. In some stores the sponsor receives the commission on the sales made by the new employee during the training period.

■ Training for the Job

This type of training is given before the new worker starts on the job. It is used where the jobs are rather complex and where inexperienced operators cannot be permitted to function without seriously interfering with the production flow.

Many firms operate so-called *company schools* to which new employees are sent after they are hired but before they are assigned to their jobs. In these schools they are given the requisite instruction for handling their jobs and they are tested for the proficiency that they acquire. These schools are staffed by special instructors who frequently devote their entire time to teaching. Obviously this sort of school is useful only where many workers are to be trained and where the training period is of more than brief duration. The Ford Motor Company has long maintained a training school of this type. In some companies the term *vestibule school* is applied to this type of training setup.

The *apprenticeship system* is one in which inexperienced workers are apprenticed to master craftsmen for a period of years, during which time they are supposed to become thoroughly grounded in their trades. This method of training is found in the building trades and, to some extent, in firms that manufacture machinery, but it is not common in other branches of industry. One of the reasons is that with the gradual change in the character of many factory jobs, whereby merely the ability to operate a specialized type of machine is required rather than the skill of an all-round machinist, the vestibule school is able to provide the requisite training in a matter of days, and the need for the prolonged period of apprenticeship no longer exists.

1 / Foremanship training. A considerable number of companies offer courses in foremanship. These are designed to enable foremen more adequately to discharge their duties as the representatives of management in closest contact with the workers. The old concept of the foreman as a rough, domineering boss, whose physique and language kept his workers in a state of constant awe, has long since been discarded. In its place has come the modern idea of the foreman as an executive whose main task is that of securing the greatest amount of production at the lowest cost. Instruction is now available in the many facets of the job, and as a result more intelligent and effective foremen are secured. In many industries, the rapid pace of technological change has brought with it a need for the retraining of foremen in the new techniques and procedures that these developments require of supervision.

Increasing attention is being given to the human relations and leadership aspects of foremanship. It seems probable that this trend will continue to grow. From this it is expected that more harmonious employee relations will emerge.

2 / Executive training. Many firms maintain training courses for selected college graduates. These are frequently designed to provide broad schooling in all phases of the business, with the expectation that the trainees will find their own places in the organization as the plans unfold. The management training course of the Jones and Laughlin Steel Corporation is an example of such a program.

Executive training at rather high levels is offered by some firms which believe that the way to be assured of good executives is to select the individuals with great care and give them thorough training, not only in the essentials of their jobs, but also in the broader aspects of economics and business practices and policies. Increased emphasis is being placed on human relations and the development of leadership, skill in writing and speaking, creativity, and analytical skills. Sometimes these courses are given on the companies' premises with instructors drawn from the firms' executives; in other cases the facilities of local educational institutions are utilized, with the tuition paid by the company. The executive programs of the Harvard, Chicago, and Columbia Graduate Schools of Business are examples of the latter type of approach to executive training.

With the increasing importance of the personnel aspect of the managerial function has come the concept of personnel relations as an overall company activity. As a result, training in the techniques of good personnel relations is offered not merely to foremen and employees of the personnel division, but also to other supervisors and to company executives at all levels. One of the methods employed for this purpose is the *psychodrama* or roleplaying. Under the guidance of a trainer from the personnel division, the trainees assume the parts of foremen and workers and act out some of their more troublesome situations. In this way the foremen come to appreciate the workers' viewpoints and are able to develop more effective methods of dealing with their subordinates than had previously been used. By including the higher executives as observers and actors in the psychodrama, their interest on these matters can be aroused and their thinking directed toward the solution of the company's personnel problems.

■ Retraining

Retraining employees whose jobs have been discontinued has always been a problem in industry to some degree. However, the advent of auto-

automation, which in some instances has involved the replacement of relatively large numbers of workers by the automated machinery, has raised to a position of considerable importance the issue of the retraining of these unfortunate individuals. As stated previously, the fundamental reason for the adoption of automation is that of achieving cost savings, usually in labor costs. This can result in the discharge of those workers whose jobs are taken over by the machines, and many companies have been reluctant to take such a drastic step. On the other hand, there is the question of how these displaced workers can be absorbed in the organizations.

In many instances the introduction of automated equipment has eliminated the need for some unskilled or semiskilled workers at the same time that it has created a need for highly skilled operatives to set up, run, and repair the new complicated machinery. The question then arises as to whether the workers whose jobs have disappeared have sufficient native ability to qualify for retraining for the more skilled positions. Furthermore, unless there is a significant increase in the company's productivity or a decrease in the unit cost of the product, it would appear that only a fraction of the workers involved could be assimilated into the higher skills, leaving the remainder with the necessity of finding employment elsewhere.

Currently the Manpower Development and Training Act (MDTA) of 1962, administered by the Bureau of Apprenticeship and Training of the U. S. Department of Labor, provides occupational training and pay allowances to selected unemployed workers or those whose skills have become obsolete. In many instances this training is available "on the job" in the plants where the workers are employed.

PERSONNEL SERVICES DIVISION

The idea that the duty of an employer should include something other than paying good wages and providing a safe place to work has made notable headway in the past few decades. Progressive companies have come to recognize that *personnel services,* as this area of activity is known, if offered as a concomitant of acceptable wage rates and not as a substitute, are a potent force in bringing about a happier and more contented employee group, lessening labor turnover, and increasing the productive effectiveness of the personnel. It is through the many functions of this division that the attempt is made to bring about better human relations.

■ Types of Personnel Services

The list of personnel service activities is a long one. Eating facilities, rest rooms, and locker rooms are found in many plants and large stores.

Recreational opportunities take the form of football, baseball, and bowling teams sponsored by the firms. Some plants provide handball, volley ball, and tennis courts, with the necessary equipment for the workers. Legal advice and assistance is sometimes made available to employees through the company's legal department. Many concerns encourage the establishment of credit unions. Employee savings plans help the workers put aside a part of their earnings. For all but the first three items of the foregoing group, the personnel services division customarily offers to assist the employees only if they wish to engage in these activities.

Group insurance and hospitalization plans have been common for several years. Retirement and disability plans, which are financed either by the employers alone or jointly by them and the employees, have become increasingly frequent. Since 1949, when certain unions in the automobile and steel industries won pensions financed entirely by the employers, public interest has been increasingly focused on this aspect of personnel relations. The advent of social security in 1935 has given added emphasis to the problem of taking care of superannuated workers.

■ **Employee Counseling Service**

A comparatively recent development in the field of personnel services is that of employee counseling. This usually involves the employment of professional psychologists whose services are made available without charge to those employees who wish assistance in the solution of their problems. In addition to their work along these lines, the psychologists devote a considerable part of their time to the devising and perfecting of tests to be used in screening applicants for employment. They may also assist in any other aspects of the hiring procedure where their professional training and experience are valuable.

A subject in which the managements of a growing number of firms have become interested in the past few years is the retirement plans of their older employees. Not only is provision made for pensions, but attempts are being made to prepare their workers for the forthcoming change in their status through counseling, suggesting hobbies, and otherwise trying to help them to effect the transition in as smooth a manner as possible. One company is experimenting with the idea of setting up a preretirement period of several months, during which the eligible employees gradually taper off their hours of work at the rate of one additional free day each month until finally they stop working altogether. As yet the results of this test are inconclusive, but it is indicative of some of the thinking that is taking place in this area of personnel relations.

SAFETY AND HEALTH DIVISION

■ Employee Safety

The promotion of employee safety has made rapid strides, not merely as a humanitarian measure, but also because many firms have discovered that the prevention of industrial accidents is desirable as an aid to a continued high rate of production. This movement is manifested through the installation of safety devices of all kinds on dangerous machinery and through the dissemination of safety information to workers. In this latter activity, safety clubs, literature, posters, and contests are enlisted for the purpose of making employees safety-conscious. An added incentive for employers to stress the safety theme is the presence, in almost all states, of workmen's compensation acts which, while they vary somewhat from state to state, generally increase the cost to a company that has a bad accident record and, conversely, reward a concern that is able to reduce the number of its accidents by lowering its required contributions.

■ Employee Health

A few companies have quite adequate medical and dental facilities available to their employees; others have nurses on hand, with physicians available on call; but the majority of businesses, particularly small ones, have little or nothing along this line.

Where industrial medical attention is provided for the workers, it is intended to supplement rather than to supplant the outside medical care that they receive from their family physicians. First-aid treatment of injuries is of prime importance, and all other treatment is secondary. Many companies treat colds, headaches, and other ailments, and are thus able to provide a service that their employees might not otherwise enjoy, in addition to lowering the absentee rate--in most instances. The dental services offered by a few concerns are supposed to be used solely for the treatment of emergency cases and probably follow this policy fairly closely.

Many companies offer periodic physical examinations to their employees as a means of helping to maintain their health. These are valuable to both employers and workers. In this way employers can detect physical defects of which the individuals are often unaware and suggest remedial measures before the trouble has progressed too far. A common requirement is that all persons who have been absent because of illness or injury report to the medical department for examination before returning to work.

In recent years the more far-seeing companies have recognized a condition among their employees that is known as *industrial fatigue*. It results from too long application to the job. It produces diminished perceptive faculties and a proneness to accidents. Long hours, overtime, and Sunday work, with insufficient rest, bring about industrial fatigue. Poor working conditions; faulty lighting, heating, or ventilation; and excessive monotony in the job are all contributing factors. Occasionally industrial fatigue appears as the result of the placement of individuals in jobs for which they are definitely unfitted.

The remedy for this condition is found in its causes. Shorter hours, rest periods, better working conditions, and, for the persons wrongly placed, transfer to more congenial work are the best methods of combating industrial fatigue. As a part of the growing interest in human relations in industry, some firms have been exploring the possibility of helping workers to gain a sense of accomplishment in their work as a further means of combating industrial fatigue.

PERSONNEL RESEARCH DIVISION

In those companies that maintain a personnel research division within the personnel department organization, it is customary for this group to be concerned with such matters as records and reports; statistical analyses of personnel records; the publication of manuals for the guidance of the department; the systems and procedures followed by or prescribed for the department; and the administration of personnel audits and evaluations. An activity which has been growing for some time is that of maintaining personnel records in computers. Prior to this development, all such facts were kept in personnel data folders, a practice that did not lend itself to a rapid retrieval of information regarding the employees of a company. With this new practice, such data as name, age, social security number, work experience, salary level, skills, and other pertinent characteristics can be recorded in the computer, permitting a speedy disclosure to personnel officers of a wide variety of specifications concerning the work force. This is especially valuable when management wishes to locate individuals in the company whose records, skills, and other characteristics would suggest their promotability to better jobs. A start has been made toward the recording of the results of researches in the behavioral sciences with the hope that further progress in this field will aid management in appraising the probability of success in their new jobs of the individuals whose other attributes appear favorable.

A few companies have developed a computerized file of prospective employees, which enables them to locate individuals not in the employ of the firms whose abilities have become needed. Among the companies that have embraced the use of computers for the storing of personnel information are Ford Motor Company, International Business Machines Corporation, Standard Oil Company (N. J.), and General Electric Company.

Another innovation in this field is that of research among employees in an attempt to discover worker attitudes toward the various aspects of their jobs, and particularly toward their employers. The General Motors Corporation has established its Employee Research to undertake this activity; this department endeavors to sound out employee thinking by questionnaires and by inviting the workers to submit written comments about their jobs. Other firms have employed outside research agencies to secure the same information, sometimes utilizing the group interview technique, in which a group of workers is invited to talk things over with representatives of the agency. One of the purposes of these researches is to provide better means of communication between workers and management, particularly in the upward flow of ideas, suggestions, and criticisms.

PROFESSIONAL ASSOCIATIONS IN PERSONNEL

The American Society for Personnel Administration (ASPA) was organized in 1949 for the purpose of striving for higher standards of performance in every phase of personnel administration, and to provide a central, national clearinghouse for authoritative data and information in this field. The ASPA has promulgated a code of ethics to guide its members. It holds annual conferences, regional institutes, and personnel workshops to further its aims. It publishes a bimonthly journal for its members. A number of local chapters are affiliated with ASPA.

The American Personnel and Guidance Association, Inc. (APGA) is dedicated to the improvement of standards of guidance and personnel work. Founded in 1952, it brings together in strong professional unity several guidance and personnel associations whose histories extend back to the beginnings of the organized guidance movement early in this century. The APGA publishes the *Personnel and Guidance Journal* nine times a year. A set of ethical standards was adopted in 1961. Over 90 local chapters, known as branches, exist in the United States and Europe. The association promotes meetings for the exchange of professional experience.

BUSINESS TERMS

(a) suggestion box (322)
(b) labor turnover (324)
(c) job analysis (325), job description (325), job specification (325)
(d) nepotism (327)
(e) Civil Rights Act of 1964 (328), Equal Employment Opportunity Committee (329)

(f) induction to the job (329)
(g) personnel audit (330), personal evaluation (330)
(h) transfer (331), promotion (331), seniority (332)
(i) discharge (332), layoff (332)
(j) sponsor system (333)
(k) company school (334), vestibule school (334), apprenticeship system (334)
(l) psychodrama (335)
(m) personnel services (336)
(n) industrial fatigue (338)

QUESTIONS FOR DISCUSSION AND ANALYSIS

1. Should a company follow a policy of always promoting from within its organization? Explain.
2. A few firms adhere to the policy of not hiring two members of the same family. What reasons can you think of in favor of this practice?
3. Do you believe that a firm should base its employment policies solely on the results of tests? Why?
4. Should a firm ask an applicant for references from his former employers? Discuss.
5. Do you think that the current intensified interest in industrial human relations will bring about more amicable relationships between employers and employees? Why?
6. How can a company overcome the adverse employee reaction to a policy of nepotism?
7. Do you approve of the policy, prevalent in some companies, of transferring employees from department to department in an attempt to find places where they will fit before discharging them except for cause?
8. Should the federal government assume the responsibility and expense of retraining workers whose present skills are no longer required in industry? Explain.
9. Does the procedure of the psychodrama appeal to you as one that would bring about an understanding of the point of view of one's superior? Explain.
10. Do you think that the sources of industrial fatigue should include a worker's concept of his job? Why?

PROBLEMS AND SHORT CASES

1. Prepare a job description for a position with which you are familiar or for which you can secure the necessary information. Also prepare a job specification for this position.
2. The response to the MDTA of unemployed workers and those whose skills have become obsolete has been rather disappointing, despite the fact that the federal government offers to pay allowances to participants and, in some instances, to provide travel and living expenses to those who are required to leave their homes to secure this training.

You are asked to suggest reasons for this rather meager response to the government's efforts on behalf of the unfortunate workers.

3. The Granite State Office Furniture Company produces a line of wooden desks, tables, and chairs for use in offices of all types. The firm is about 75 years old; and while it was originally a family business, the control passed to certain key executives some ten years ago through their purchase of the stock previously held by the Wilson family, who had decided to give up the ownership of the company. Recently the Granite State Company was approached by the owners of the Model Corporation with a suggestion that the two firms be merged. The Model Corporation is a successful manufacturer of filing equipment and of metal office furniture, whose sales volume and position in the industry is distinctly superior to that of the Granite State Company.

As the merger negotiations progressed, it became apparent that the workers in the Granite State plant would be retained because of their experience in woodworking, but that the Granite sales force would no longer be needed, nor would most of the executives of the smaller firm. The latter group comprised most of the owners of Granite. As individuals, they were interested in the rather generous cash offer that the Model Corporation presented, but they also wanted to retain their connection with the merged company. The Model Corporation, on the other hand, felt that the expense of retaining these men over a long period of time would not be economical.

You have been called in as a business consultant to suggest a plan by which the Model Corporation can absorb the Granite State firm, as both desire, but which will satisfy the latter company's officers. Outline your plans in detail, giving the reasons for your recommendations.

SUGGESTED READINGS

Chruden, H. J., and A. W. Sherman, Jr. *Personnel Management,* Second Edition. Cincinnati: South-Western Publishing Company, 1963.

Gellerman, S. W. *The Management of Human Relations.* New York: Harper & Row, 1966.

Guion, R. *Personnel Testing.* New York: McGraw-Hill Book Company, Inc., 1965.

Heneman, H. G., Jr., and D. Yoder. *Labor Economics,* Second Edition. Cincinnati: South-Western Publishing Company, 1965. Part IV.

Owen, W. V., and H. V. Finston. *Industrial Relations—Management, Labor, and Society.* New York: Appleton-Century-Crofts, Inc., 1964.

Pfiffner, J. M., and M. Fels. *The Supervision of Personnel: Human Relations in the Management of Men,* Third Edition. Englewood Cliffs, New Jersey: Prentice-Hall, Inc., 1964.

Magazines: Publications of American Management Association, National Industrial Conference Board, and Bureau of National Affairs; *Personnel, Personnel Administration, Personnel Journal,* and *Personnel and Guidance Journal.*

Chapter 16

EMPLOYEE COMPENSATION

In a capitalistic economic system several methods of compensation accrue to those who are involved in its production phase, which reward them for their participation, and, hopefully, encourage their continued activity in this area. For the entrepreneur, this takes the form of profits; for the shareholder who invests his capital, dividends may be expected; for those who lend money to enterprise, the return is that of interest; for the property owners, there is rent; and for employees the combined reward and stimulus is that of employee compensation, customarily referred to as wages. The term "wages" is in more common usage than "employee compensation" and it will be used in most instances in this chapter in the interest of brevity. It is an all-inclusive term and embraces not only the remuneration received by workers in stores, factories, offices, banks, and all other forms of economic endeavor, but also the salaries of executives and managers, and the commissions paid to salesmen. As mentioned later in this chapter, certain patterns of wage payment are designed to serve as stimuli for workers to exert extra efforts on their jobs.

In most cases the wages that employees receive constitute their sole income. There thus emerges the concept of wages as the source of purchasing power—the means by which the goods and services produced by our economic system are bought by those who need them. An additional concept would equate the wages received by an individual to the value of the productive effort that he exerts. Wages, then, play a dual role in our economy. They comprise the prices that are paid by entrepreneurs for the human effort that is put to use in the creation of goods and services and at the same time provide the means by which these products are taken off the market. The relationship and importance of employee compensation to the total national income is graphically portrayed in the chart on page 43.

■ Variation of Wages Among Individuals

Wages paid to different individuals, or more correctly, for different jobs, vary widely. An elevator operator receives a small fraction of the pay of a corporation president; a day laborer gets much less than a good salesman; a filing clerk receives less than does an expert typist; and so on, through a long and diversified category of jobs. Why should this be so, and is there any justification for such wide variations?

1. Supply and demand
2. Competition
3. Other factors

1 / **Supply and demand.** Two basic reasons account for this divergent wage phenomenon. The first of these is a matter of supply and demand. Many people, whose capacities are limited or who find themselves in situations where the opportunity to develop their latent capacities is limited, are able to do work only approximating that of common laborers. The ratio of these workers to the number of jobs available is high; hence it is usually not necessary for management to pay high wages in order to secure as many workers of this type as it needs. As the scale of job complexities and as the level of personal skills required to fill them rises, increasingly fewer individuals are qualified to fill them; therefore, they are paid higher and higher wages. For high executive posts, comparatively few persons have the requisite qualifications; hence, they are able to command very large salaries.

2 / **Competition.** The second reason for the variation in wages is a corollary of the first and is based on the fact that the instruments of production compete with each other on a cost basis for employment in the productive process. There is not only intergroup competition (labor competing with capital, man versus a machine) but also intragroup rivalry (laborers competing against laborers, executives against other executives).

Not only must a large number of laborers compete among themselves for the available jobs, but laborers, as a group, must compete against machines which can do the same things that they can do, and frequently can do them more cheaply. This situation tends to keep laborers' wages at a relatively low level. By the same token, not only are there comparatively few executives to compete among themselves, but also there is practically no competition offered by land or capital. Hence the remuneration of executives is relatively high. This same analysis can be made for all grades of jobs.

3 / **Other factors.** Among individuals performing the same types of work, wage differentials may be based on certain personal or geographic factors. One of these factors is seniority in the department, where the wage rates are based on length of service. Differences in the capabilities of the workers may also be reflected in varying rates of pay, the more skilled receiving the greater stipends. A situation of this sort serves a dual purpose —it acts as a reward for the better workers and as a stimulus to the poorer ones to improve their performance. Sometimes pay variations are due to the differing bargaining abilities of the employees when they were applying for their jobs; the better bargainers start out at higher levels than their co-workers who are less skilled at negotiating such matters. The warmer climate in the South, with a presumed lower cost of living, has often been advanced as a reason for wage differentials between the South and the North.

Historically it has long been common for wage differentials to be found between men and women performing the same work, and this condition persists in many work areas. In 1963 the Equal Pay Act, an amendment to the Fair Labor Standards Act of 1938, was passed by Congress under which women must receive equal pay with men if their jobs are substantially the same and have the same working conditions. This Act became effective in June, 1964, and affects industries whose products enter interstate commerce. A number of states have similar laws that apply to specified industries. Certain types of positions, such as executives and professional workers, are exempt.

The unions have generally tended to disapprove of different rates of pay by the same firm for the same work, except where this reflects seniority. Their philosophy of "equal pay for equal work" assumes that the quality of work done by all workers will be the same, which is not always so. Such thinking tends to deaden the ambition of the better workers without providing any stimulus to the poorer ones.

■ Variations of Wages Between Industries

As shown in the chart on the following page, there are substantial differences in average hourly and weekly earnings between durable goods and nondurable goods industries. The explanation for this would appear to be found in the greater degree of skill required in the durable goods field, coupled with strong union pressure; whereas for the nondurable goods area the presence of a large number of women operatives and the location of many of the plants in the southern part of the country are probably accountable.

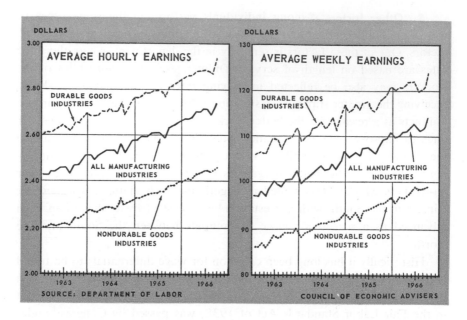

Average Hourly and Weekly Earnings of Selected Industries

■ Economic Theories of Wages

Despite the fact that economists have theorized for many years on the manner in which wages and wage levels ‘are determined, none of these theories is a complete and satisfactory explanation of the wage situation today. Many economists are still searching for new theories that will explain the current wage situation more adequately than has been done thus far. Because of this situation, only three currently recognized economic wage theories are presented here. They do not explain the entire wage picture, but they account for certain segments of it.

          1. Marginal productivity theory
          2. Bargaining theory
          3. Standard-of-living theory

1 / Marginal productivity theory. This rather complicated theory introduces two concepts: marginal productivity and marginal revenue. *Marginal productivity* is the value (selling price) of the goods produced by the last (or marginal) worker hired by a firm. *Marginal revenue* is the amount of increase in the total revenue (income) of a firm that results from the sale of one additional unit of output. The marginal productivity theory says that, under conditions of pure competition, an entrepreneur, whose objective is *maximization of profit* (securing the greatest possible profit), will continue to hire additional workers until the point is reached where the value of the marginal product of the last worker hired just equals the wages paid to the last (or marginal) worker. Furthermore, the wages of all workers of the same ability in the firm will be determined by that paid to the marginal worker and the number of workers employed will be established at the point where their cost (wages) and marginal revenue are equal. Presented in another way, the point at which the wage of the marginal worker and the marginal revenue coincide will designate both the wage level of the workers and the number to be employed.

The major drawbacks to this theory are the almost total absence of pure competition in our economy and the great difficulty in accurately determining the productivity of the marginal worker under conditions generally present in business today. It appears reasonable to assume, however, that an entrepreneur would not continue to hire workers beyond the point where the return from the output of the marginal worker is less than the wages paid him. A further difficulty is found in the suggestion of some writers in economics that entrepreneurs do not always maximize their profits but, instead, endeavor to increase their sales volumes or merely to maintain their competitive position in the industry.

2 / **Bargaining theory.** Many observers of the economic scene favor the bargaining theory of wages. The *bargaining theory* assumes that wages are set in more or less of a labor market place as the result of a bargaining process between labor, as sellers, and management, as buyers, and that the relative bargaining strengths of these two factors determine the wages to be paid. This theory has the virtue of describing an actual procedure in that it portrays the collective bargaining process with a fair degree of fidelity. As this practice spreads in industry, as now seems quite probable, the pertinency of the theory will become even greater.

To assume, however, that an individual applicant seeking a job with an employer, particularly a large corporation, engages in a bargaining process, is to take an entirely unrealistic view. This statement is true, even though one aspect of the bargaining theory assumes that there are lower limits, below which the workers are unwilling to go, and upper limits to the employers' offerings. The fact of the matter is that most jobs carry price tags, so to speak, or at least have a range of wage rates that are set by the employers on a take-it-or-leave-it basis. When there is a range, the employing officials are usually allowed to use their judgment, but they are rarely permitted to go above the upper limits.

The bargaining theory is a satisfactory explanation of one segment of the wage-determining process, but it is inadequate as far as the rest of the picture is concerned. It fails to explain high wages in unorganized industries or fields. It overlooks the relative productive value of skilled and unskilled workers, and does not explain the variations in wages between workers of equal skills in identical jobs. In plants where unions exist but where all workers are not required to join the union (the open shop [1]), the nonunion workers may receive the same benefits as the union members, frequently to keep them from joining the union. Also, in many plants senior workers receive automatic wage increases.

3 / **Standard-of-living theory.** The *standard-of-living theory*, which is a comparatively recent development in wage theories, finds its roots in a rather pervasive belief that wages should be at least high enough to ensure workers a reasonable standard of living. The presumption upon which this theory is based is that all employers should pay wages high enough so that their employees may enjoy not only the necessities of life (food, clothing, and shelter) but also education for their children, adequate medical and dental care, and possibly savings.

This theory is obviously concerned only with the lower level of wages and seeks to establish a humanitarian, rather than an economic, basis for such minima. It is therefore not to be considered as an overall wage-fixing theory. The apparent assumption with regard to firms that cannot afford to pay such minimum rates is that they must either find ways of so doing or go out of business as socially undesirable. The concept of standard-of-living wages is at the root of minimum wage legislation.

■ **Minimum Wage Legislation**

The *Fair Labor Standards Act,* known as the Wage and Hours Act of 1938, was the first of a series of federal enactments designed to place a floor under the wages of labor and a ceiling on the number of hours of work per week for workers in private industry whose products enter interstate commerce. The philosophy behind the concept of minimum wages and maximum hours was that low wages constituted unfair competition and were detrimental to the health, efficiency, and general well-being of workers. Originally the minimum wage was 25 cents per hour and the maximum workweek, over which time and one-half rates had to be paid, was 44 hours, but this was soon reduced to 40 hours. Through several amendments, the minimum rate has been advanced to $1.40 an hour, effective February 1, 1967, and to $1.60 an hour, effective February 1, 1968, for the types of employment covered prior to February 1, 1967.

---

[1] The open shop is further defined on page 370.

Coverage has been extended to laundry and dry cleaning enterprises; construction enterprises; hospitals, nursing homes, and most schools. Hotels, motels, restaurants, retail and service enterprises, and gasoline service stations with sales above certain stated minima are included. Federal government hospitals are excluded. Under certain specified circumstances, the minimum wage law is applicable to farm labor. In addition to the federal legislation, 32 states have minimum wage laws applicable mainly to women and children in selected industries.

The argument in favor of these laws is that employers should be compelled to pay employees the minimum wage rates requisite for a fair standard of living. The labor unions have been particularly active in bringing pressure on the Congress and the state legislatures to enact such legislation and to raise the minimum standard. Opposed to this argument have been the claims of many economists that these laws do not benefit those whom they are ostensibly designed to help, namely, the unskilled. Rather than benefit by the establishing of legal wage minima, they maintain, the effect has been to place their wage rates above those that they were capable of earning, with the result that they have been forced into the ranks of the unemployed.

■ Factors Actually Determining Wages

The shortcomings of all wage theories, both old and new, arise from the attempt that each makes to explain the whole wage-determining process, which tends to oversimplify an exceedingly complex situation. A large number of different factors enter the wage-determining picture, and their relative weight in any situation varies with the peculiar conditions present in each instance. These wage-determining factors include the following:

> Demand for the various classes of labor.
> Wage philosophy of the employers.
> Stage of the business cycle—prosperity or recession.
> Profit situation in the various businesses.
> Degree of skill required.
> Prevailing wage rates in the community.
> Wage rates paid by other communities.
> Degree of organization among the workers.
> Bargaining skill of the workers' organizations.
> Cost of living in the community.
> Supply of the various classes of labor.
> Relative mobility of labor.
> Relative disagreeableness or attractiveness of the work.
> Social desirability of the jobs.

■ Wage Guideposts

As noted on page 187, in January, 1962, the Council of Economic Advisers, suggested that *wage and price guideposts* be informally established to promote price stability. The reaction of labor leaders to this suggestion has been one of undisguised hostility and indifference. They have maintained that the 3.2 percent rate of annual productivity gain is far too low, and also that the profits of business are high enough to call for much greater wage increases.

■ Money Wages Versus Real Wages

An important distinction should be made between money wages and real wages. *Money wages* are, as the term implies, the actual dollars and cents that workers receive from their employers as payment for services rendered. *Real wages* are the goods and services that the money wages will buy at any given time. This means that real wages are dependent on the current price level as well as on the existing wage level. If money wages are high and the price level is relatively low, real wages are higher than if the price level were to be raised several points. In view of the fact that the value of money lies in the goods and services that it will buy, the test of the adequacy of any given wage level is in the real wage concept.

In order to portray correctly the real wage situation at any one time, the United States Department of Labor and other organizations publish wage data for various industries. In such data the wage rates are expressed in terms of some arbitrarily selected prior period rather than in terms of their current dollar values. By examining these data, it is possible to determine how the workers are faring as compared to their status in the reference period.

A great many workers and labor leaders appear to be entirely unaware of the importance of real wages. They struggle to secure higher money wages, quite without regard for the fact that, in many instances, their increased wages may result in higher prices for the things that they buy. Furthermore, they may do practically nothing to bring about a lowering of the price level, even though this might result in their being able to buy more goods and services on their present incomes than they could buy were they to secure the "raises" that they seek. Labor is "money wage" minded, whereas it needs to turn its attention more to the real wages aspect of its income problem.

The reasons for the failure of the "real wages" concept to be more widely adopted by workers and their leaders seem to be: (1) it is difficult to compute real wages on a basis that would be meaningful to individuals; (2) little, if any, instruction is offered in our schools that fosters a recognition of real wages; (3) labor leaders can bargain for visible money gains for their adherents, whereas a gain in real wages would be most difficult, if not impossible, to measure and report to their followers; and (4) the public, by and large, is money-minded rather than value-minded, a long-time attitude that shows no sign of changing.

■ Wages as a Cost of Production

The wages paid to workers in a capitalistic system constitute one of the costs of production. Thus, if the degree of productivity of the workers remains the same, a wage increase becomes at once a cost increase and must result either in a narrowing of the profit margin or in a price increase. Among the sources of conflict between management and the representatives of organized labor in recent years has been the question of whether wage increases should be absorbed out of profits or be translated into price rises.

In many cases, however, wage increases accompanied by increased productivity on the workers' part do not result in cost increases but bring about unit cost decreases, which may permit prices to be lowered. In many, if not most, cases, however, this increased productivity has come about not because the employees are working any harder or longer hours, but through the introduction of more efficient machinery, thereby permitting the same number of workers to produce more units. When cost-cutting machines are introduced into industry, it is often possible to increase wages and to reduce unit costs at the same time. In a certain sense the workers are rewarded for the savings that are effected by the machines. As this process may bring about a more careful and effective operation of the machines by the workers, with continued lowered costs while maintaining a fair volume of profits, the consequent possible price reductions will complete the favorable cycle by benefiting the buyers also. The extent to which this actually occurs is, of course, unknown.

■ Wages and Prices

Increasing the prices of many commodities reduces the demand for them. This is the effect if the demand is elastic, that is, if the demand drops significantly as the price goes up. If prices are increased too greatly, the demand will fall to the point where the goods are said to be "priced out of the market." This means that the prices are so high that the sale of these items is practically stopped.

This principle has two applications. The first application refers to the inescapable fact that wages are the prices paid for labor and that, if they are too high relative to the workers' productivity, management may be forced to switch to some other instrument of production, such as capital in the form of machinery that replaces labor. Labor, in this case, will have priced itself out of the market. Automation, in its present state of development, may be an example of this situation. A somewhat similar condition exists with regard to foreign-made products whose lower prices reflect the lower wage rates prevailing in other countries.

The second application of this principle is found in those situations in which increased wages have forced the management to raise its prices to the point where sales have experienced a significant decline. Although the product may not be forced off the market, a falling off in sales may result in actually lowered money wages for the workers whose demands for wage increases started the unfortunate chain of events. While many things, such as union contracts or adherence to federal or state wage laws, may prevent an employer in a situation such as this from lowering the wages of the workers, they may be subject to layoffs that will have the effect of reducing their take-home pay.

The operation of this same demand elasticity can be seen where, although wages may have been increased, the combined efforts of management and labor have brought about lowered unit costs and, hence, lower prices. In a case like this, the increase in demand results in greater sales and, not infrequently, in the creation of new jobs for workers to supply this augmented demand.

■ Higher Wages, Fewer Hours

The preceding statements apply with equal force to the matter of increasing wages and decreasing hours at the same time. When this takes place, (1) the productivity of the workers may be increased with unit production costs remaining constant; (2) under the same conditions, these costs may decline; (3) the workers' productivity may be lowered with a consequent increase in unit costs. Under the first two circumstances prices may remain constant or be reduced. In the third instance these higher unit costs must either be absorbed out of profits or be translated into higher prices, which may reduce sales. There are no other alternatives to these possibilities.

Many industries have been able to reduce hours and increase wages through the introduction of modern production methods that increased the workers' productivity. Sometimes the reduction of workers' fatigue through

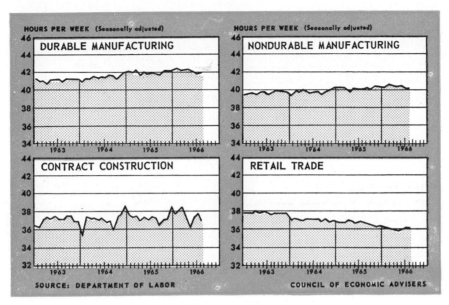

HOURS PER WEEK (Seasonally adjusted)

DURABLE MANUFACTURING

NONDURABLE MANUFACTURING

CONTRACT CONSTRUCTION

RETAIL TRADE

SOURCE: DEPARTMENT OF LABOR

COUNCIL OF ECONOMIC ADVISERS

Weekly Hours of Work

shortening the working hours has had a favorable effect on the rate of production. In other instances, motion and time study has resulted in increased worker efficiency so that production costs were not increased by curtailing the hours of daily or weekly labor and increasing wages. The chart above portrays the average weekly hours of work in four economic areas.

■ Wage Incentives

The purpose of *wage incentives* is to induce workers at all levels to put forth greater productive efforts for which a cash reward is paid. The installation of a wage-incentive system in a company is a task that requires a high degree of skill, judgment, tact, and knowledge of the productive processes that are employed. Experience seems to indicate the desirability of "tailoring" each system to the plant in which it is to operate. The confidence of the workers must be gained, and they must understand thoroughly just how the system works. In unionized plants employees who are union representatives, known as *union stewards* or *shop stewards,* are brought into the operation and their approval secured.

Incentive plans can be used for office workers, salesmen, and even for executives. In each instance they must be fitted with care to the job to be done, and close attention should be paid to equalizing the extra reward to be paid with the additional effort required by the worker to secure it. The basic characteristics of a good incentive plan are: (1) it should provide a reward to the workers for the exercise of a reasonable measure of effort and attention, without creating a harmful physical or mental state on their part; (2) the production goals per worker should be reasonably attainable by the average employee affected; and (3) the added wage costs to the company should be at least balanced by the lowered production costs. A poor incentive plan would be lacking in one or more of these characteristics. A good incentive plan can do much to improve the productivity and morale of an organization, whereas a poor one can have a devastating effect on the personnel.

In an attempt to overcome some of the disadvantages of individual incentive plans, a number of companies have instituted *group incentive plans,* which include all or most of the plants' employees. In some of these plans, representatives of the workers meet with management to discuss wage rates, machine speeds, and other details of shop practice. In several instances reports of these group efforts indicate quite favorable results from the standpoint of increased productivity, lower unit labor costs, improvement in product quality, reduction in scrap, and enhanced employee morale. Some observers believe that the extension of automation will bring about the replacement of individual wage incentives with group incentive plans.

■ Methods of Wage Payment

The most common of the different methods of making wage payments to workers are:

1. Straight salary	4. Bonus payments
2. Time wages	5. Piece-rate payment
3. Shift premium	6. Commission payment

1 / Straight salary. A straight salary, which is the simplest form of wage payment, may be expressed in terms of a stated amount per day, week, month, or year. Straight-salary plans may or may not provide for deductions for absence or tardiness according to the policies of the companies using them. There is little in this system other than the possibility of a salary increase to serve as an incentive to an employee to exert extra effort on the job.

2 / Time wages. In this system payment is made on the basis of stated rates per hour or per day worked, without regard to quantity or quality of output. If a worker's hourly rate is $2.25 and he works 8 hours, he receives a total wage of $18. Under the Fair Labor Standards Act employers must pay time and one half for overtime. Many contracts negotiated with management by labor unions also provide double time for work on Sundays and on holidays. It is customary for the regular working hours to be indicated either on a daily or a weekly basis. Except for the overtime feature and the possibility that markedly substandard work may involve discharge, there is nothing of the wage incentive in this system.

3 / Shift premium. A variant of time wages occurs when a higher rate is paid to workers on the afternoon and night (graveyard) shifts. This system is known as the *shift premium plan*. Appearing during World War II when additional rewards were required to induce employees to work on these two shifts, the system has continued in some industries.

4 / Bonus payments. A mild form of incentive wages is found in the bonus payments that many firms make to their employees. These bonuses, which are frequently paid on a yearly basis, are customarily related to length of service rather than to output. They are used in banks, offices, stores, and other establishments where a record of each individual's production would be difficult, if not pointless, to maintain. They are incentives to employees to stay with the company but have little other value. Executive bonuses, which are sometimes related to the profitableness of the company, may take on the nature of incentives.

A notable example of a bonus plan that does have an incentive effect on the employees is that of the Lincoln Electric Company of Cleveland, Ohio. Since 1934, all of the company's personnel have participated in year-end bonuses which, in many cases, have equaled or exceeded the annual wages of the individual workers. The base for the bonuses is the company's success for each year, and the distribution to the employees is in accordance with an evaluation procedure that measures the worker's worth to the company.

5 / Piece-rate payment. The piece-rate payment plan involves payment at a stated rate per piece produced. Thus, if the piece rate for a given part is $.005 and a worker produces 2,500 pieces in a day, he receives $12.50 for his efforts. In many plants each worker has a day (or hour) rate that becomes effective whenever he is not working on piece work. This allows for time consumed in setting up the machine, sharpening tools, machine breakdown, power failure, waiting for stock, and so on. Usually these plants guarantee their workers their day rate of pay as minimum wages. This is customarily well below what they can earn on piece work.

It is through piece-rate systems that wage incentives are usually established. A large number of such systems have been in force during the past several years, all of them varying slightly from the others but all designed to induce additional effort on the worker's part and to reward him for it. Most of them establish a standard task that the worker must perform before he can begin to reap the additional remuneration that the system holds out. Another point of similarity has to do with the problem of whether the worker should receive all of the earnings from the incentive or whether part should go to the worker and part to the foremen.

6 / Commission payment. The *commission payment* type of wage payment is confined to salesmen and is, in effect, a piece-rate system. The salesman's remuneration is a commission that is paid for each unit of product that he sells. The commission may be either a certain sum of money per unit, or it may be a percentage of the value of the item sold.

Since some companies pay only on a commission basis, a salesman who fails to sell anything during any given period receives no pay for that time. Other companies pay a basic salary plus commissions. A number of firms give their salesmen drawing accounts, which are chargeable against commissions earned. For example, a salesman who has a drawing account of $100 a week might, during a 4-week period, earn $600 in commissions. A common method of handling this situation is to pay the salesman his $100 weekly for the first three weeks and then at the end of the fourth week to pay him $100 plus $200 ($600 commissions minus $400 drawings) or a total of $300.

If, however, his commissions for the four weeks are less than $400, say $350, he would receive only $50 at the end of the fourth week. A number of firms utilize a *guaranteed drawing account*. This operates in the same manner as the regular drawing account except that at the end of a stipulated period, such as four weeks, if a salesman's commissions are less than the total of his drawings, the debt is canceled and he starts with a clean slate. Thus a guaranteed drawing account is quite similar to a salary.

■ Profit Sharing

An incentive payment that has had some vogue in this country is the distribution of some fraction of a firm's profits to its employees without requiring them to purchase stock. This is called *profit sharing*. It may be accomplished either through cash payments or through distribution of company stock. The purposes of profit sharing include inducements for greater production, lower labor turnover, economy in worker use of materials and supplies, loyalty to the company, and resistance to pressure for unionization.

Profits are distributed according to some predetermined pattern. They frequently recognize length of service, both in the matter of the amounts paid to individuals and in the requirement of a certain minimum period of employment as a prerequisite to participation in the distribution. It should be recognized that profit sharing is an expense of doing business and is really a bonus based on the size of the profits.

Some firms feel that the effects of profit sharing have been most beneficial, while others have indicated their sentiments by discontinuing the plan. The critics say that the whole idea is unsound as it violates the fundamental purpose of profits, that is, to reward the shareholders for the risk that they are willing to take in investing their money in the company; and they point out that the employees have no financial stake in the company's success other than that of continued income if it succeeds or discharge if it fails.

A profit-sharing scheme assumes the presence of profits available for distribution, which may not be realized in times of poor business or depression, or when it seems the part of wisdom to plow a large part of the earnings back into the business. The effect on the workers of the failure of the company to continue to distribute the profit bonuses is said to be distinctly unfavorable and to more than offset any benefits that previous distributions may have afforded.

The Merrill Manufacturing Corporation of Merrill, Wisconsin, has had a cash profit-sharing plan since 1949 that is reported to be quite successful. Through the operation of an arithmetical formula, a certain percentage of the company's yearly profits are distributed quarterly to all employees, except officers, who have been in the continuous employ of the company for three months or more. The workers are kept informed of the profit-sharing plan through their foremen and an annual meeting. A careful check is kept on quality control, and the employees responsible for a spoiled material are informed about it. Suggestions for improvements in operations are invited by the management. A series of interviews with the employees by an outside agency indicated that the workers like the profit-sharing program, both because of the checks that they receive and because they understand how the plan operates.

■ The Guaranteed Annual Wage

The concept of the *guaranteed annual wage,* an idea that has been gaining considerable attention for several years, is that the employer agrees to pay eligible workers (usually with one or two years' service) a certain guaranteed wage every week of the year or for 48 weeks, regardless of sales volume or the stage of the business cycle. The best-known plans are probably those of the Procter and Gamble Company, which manufactures soap and detergents; George A. Hormel & Company, which produces meat products; and the Nunn-Bush Shoe Company. The plans of these concerns date back before World War II. Their products are consumer goods that are sold at relatively low prices and with a considerable measure of stability in their sales volume. This means that there is a minimum of time when the plants are shut down or are working part time.

The big stumbling block to the widespread adoption of the guaranteed annual wage is the professed (and probably actual) inability of many employers to continue to pay wages when sales are low or nonexistent. Certain unions, however, have stated their intention to press for guaranteed annual wages from their employers, and in 1955 the United Auto Workers negotiated a contract with the Ford Motor Company that has been regarded as a step in this direction. The Ford contract, which has provided the pattern for similar agreements in more than 100 companies, is actually for *supplementary unemployment benefits,* commonly known as SUB. While there is considerable difference in detail among these agreements, the basic pattern is that the employer will make payments to laid-off eligible employees, which, when combined with unemployment compensation from the state, will not exceed 65 percent of the employees' take-home pay for the first 4 weeks of unemployment and up to 60 percent of such pay for the next 22 weeks. Eligibility is based on length of service. The total time during which payments are made varies from 26 to 52 weeks. The operation of these plans requires changes in state laws or rulings by state attorneys-general that will permit workers to receive both unemployment compensation and SUB in full amount at the same time. Several states have acted to permit this. The funds from which the employers make the SUB payments are built up by contributions made by the companies on the basis of from 3 cents to 5 cents per employee for each hour worked. If the funds go below certain specified levels, the payments may be reduced or even suspended.

It may be expected that the unions will continue to bring pressure toward a genuine guaranteed annual wage.

■ Pensions

The practice of employers' providing old-age pensions for their employees dates back into the 1800's; but since the passage of the federal

Social Security Act in 1935, there has been a vast increase in the extent of such coverage. This has been particularly true in plants where the unions have contracts. Some pension plans are financed entirely by employers and others by joint contributions to the funds by both employers and employees. In either case a labor expense is involved for the companies concerned.

The details of these plans vary considerably. It seems probable, however, that either through the extension of federal social security, the growth of company financed projects, or perhaps both, pensions will become a fixed part of the employee remuneration picture in this country. The growth of pensions has been a potent instrument in the betterment of human relations in the companies that have adopted it, as it goes a long way toward satisfying workers' desire for economic security.

There has been some agitation, by union leaders, for what is called *portable pensions.* Under a plan of this sort, a worker with pension benefits accrued could take them with him to a new job. Workers in a plant that is closed down would receive the benefits due them at the time of its closing. At present the legal and financial problems involved appear quite formidable, but with the growing strength of many union groups, portable pensions may become a bargaining issue in future labor-management negotiations.

As a means of providing jobs for younger men, and also of enabling an employer to discontinue certain jobs, *early retirement* has become a provision of many retirement plans. This permits employees to retire at an earlier than normal age, and still receive their pensions. The United Automobile Workers union has negotiated an early retirement agreement with many companies that permits workers with 10 years service to retire at 60 and receive double the retirement benefit until they reach 65, after which they revert to their normal pension rates but become eligible for social security.

■ Fringe Benefits

During World War II and the years following, a group of so-called *fringe benefits* have come into being, as additions to workers' direct wage payments. Among these are health, accident, and life insurance, and hospital and surgical care with the cost paid wholly or in part by the employers; paid vacations and holidays; paid time off for voting; rest periods; *severance pay,* which is sometimes given an employee upon the termination of his employment over and above any unpaid wages due him; payment for work tools; and payment for work clothing.

■ Wage and Salary Administration

The overall control of all phases of employee compensation is a management function known as *wage and salary administration.* Its purpose is to provide adequate compensation for all employees, and as such it has an important influence on the existence of satisfactory employee human relations. The broad determination of wage and salary principles in any organization is a top management prerogative, but carrying out the details of wage and salary administration is entrusted to various divisions of different companies, among which are the industrial relations division, industrial engineering department, the treasurer or controller, and the personnel department.

In the setting of wage rates, a process known as *job evaluation* takes place, in which each job is rated on the basis of the necessary skill, experience, responsibility, and working conditions. From this procedure the wage rate for each job in a plant is computed. Commonly this is the function of the wage and salary administration.

BUSINESS TERMS

(a) marginal productivity (346), marginal revenue (346), maximization of profit (346)
(b) bargaining theory (347)
(c) standard of living theory (348)
(d) Fair Labor Standards Act (348)
(e) wage and price guideposts (350)
(f) money wages (350), real wages (350)
(g) wage incentive (353), group incentive plan (354)
(h) union steward or shop steward (353)
(i) shift premium plan (355), commission payment (356), guaranteed drawing account (356)
(j) profit sharing (356)
(k) guaranteed annual wage (357), supplementary unemployment benefits (358)
(l) portable pensions (359), early retirement (359)
(m) fringe benefits (359), severance pay (359)
(n) wage and salary administration (360), job evaluation (360)

QUESTIONS FOR DISCUSSION AND ANALYSIS

1. Why should women who hold executive and professional positions be exempted from the Equal Pay Act?
2. Recently a few observers of consumer actions indicate that they believe that people are becoming more "real wage" minded. Do you think this signifies a trend for the future? Why?

3. Would you expect a single unified theory of wages to emerge in the course of time? Explain.
4. Should the money value of fringe benefits be taken into consideration when an employer is bargaining with a union over the subject of wage rate increases? Why?
5. Would you expect the gaps between the average hourly and weekly earnings of durable and nondurable goods industries to narrow or widen with the passage of time? Why?
6. Do wages come out of profits or do profits come out of wages? Discuss.
7. Union leaders claim that workers should share in the benefits of increased productivity that have been brought about through the introduction of machinery. Do you agree? Why?
8. How can the management of a company tell whether its incentive plan is a good one or not?
9. Why do some companies have satisfactory experience with profit-sharing while others do not?
10. Should workers who move from one company to another be able to take the accumulated pension benefits with them? What difficulties might arise if this condition were to become common practice?

PROBLEMS AND SHORT CASES

1. In 1960, the Brown Manufacturing Company decided to expand its sales force and hired a number of recent college graduates, paying them $375 a month plus expenses. By the time 1966 came around, these men were averaging $500 to $550 a month plus expenses. At this time the company decided to further increase its sales force and approached a number of colleges to recruit these men. Somewhat to their surprise, the recruiters discovered that they had to offer around $500 a month plus expenses to attract desirable prospective salesmen. But if the company offered this much, it meant that the new recruits would be paid as much as the salesmen with six years experience.

   You are asked to discuss this situation and to suggest steps that might be taken to alleviate it.
2. The topic of minimum wage legislation, which has been so prominent in congressional circles recently, has created a considerable controversy between those who favor the minimum wage and those who are opposed to it. The issues involved cover the question of whether the minimum wage increases the incomes of those whom it is ostensibly intended to benefit or merely prevents the unskilled from securing employment. There is also the question regarding the employer who is unable to pay the minimum wage to his workers, and, more recently, the point of whether farm workers should be covered by this legislation.

   Consult periodicals and newspaper articles in your school library and write a report covering this controversy, indicating your views on the subject and substantiating them.

3. The Dave Lee Company, Inc., has just been formed for the purpose of manufacturing and selling a new all-purpose detergent that is useful for washing dishes, clothes, kitchen floors, and automobiles, and every other cleaning job including personal use by individuals. The company officials believe that it will have a very large market once it has been introduced to the public. The company plans a city-by-city expansion of its selling territory, moving from one place to another as soon as an acceptable density of distribution has been achieved. Local advertising consists of newspaper ads and house-to-house distribution of samples with coupons offering a 10-cent per bottle saving on subsequent purchases. When national distribution has been achieved, advertising is planned for magazines and possibly television.

The company wishes to hire a group of salesmen for each community that they enter, whose first duty will be that of persuading supermarket operators and druggists to stock the new product—a creative selling job. Once the detergent has received public approval, however, the salesmen's job will consist merely of making routine calls to take orders, in no sense a creative selling job. The problem facing the company is how to structure the compensation plan for their salesmen so that they will be adequately rewarded for their creative efforts in introducing the product and at the same time not overpaid when their jobs become largely routine.

Prepare a written report suggesting a solution to this compensation problem. Give reasons for your suggestions.

SUGGESTED READINGS

Brennan, C. W. *Wage Administration: Plans, Practices, and Principles,* Revised Edition. Homewood, Illinois: Richard D. Irwin, Inc., 1963.

Chruden, H. J., and A. W. Sherman, Jr. *Personnel Management,* Second Edition. Cincinnati: South-Western Publishing Company, 1963. Part VI.

Gardner, B. B., and D. C. Moore. *Human Relations in Industry,* Fourth Edition. Homewood, Illinois: Richard D. Irwin, Inc., 1964. Chapter 15.

Heneman, H. G., Jr., and D. Yoder. *Labor Economics,* Second Edition. Cincinnati: South-Western Publishing Company, 1965. Parts V and VI.

Kindall, A. F. *Personnel Administration: Principles and Cases,* Revised Edition. Homewood, Illinois: Richard D. Irwin, Inc., 1964. Part V.

Lanham, E. *Administration of Wages and Salaries.* New York: Harper & Row, 1963.

Moore, F. G. *Manufacturing Management,* Fourth Edition. Homewood, Illinois: Richard D. Irwin, Inc., 1965. Chapters 24 and 25.

Pigors, P., and C. A. Myers. *Personnel Administration,* Fifth Edition. New York: McGraw-Hill Book Company, Inc., 1965.

Chapter 17

LABOR PROBLEMS AND LEGISLATION

While technically "labor" encompasses the entirety of the human element in business, management as well as those in lower levels of the organization, in the discussion here labor will be identified as a group term for human beings who must work for a living in subordinate positions and who have certain goals in life that they aspire to attain through the jobs which they hold. Without indicating any order of precedence, the goals of individual workers are: (1) an increase in their standards of living, which usually means higher wages; (2) security, the removal of fear of the loss of jobs; (3) a feeling of creativity in their jobs, a sense of doing something worthwhile; (4) a feeling that they are important parts of the companies that employ them; and (5) a sense of dignity in their jobs, however lowly they may be in the economic scale.

The fact that in the past, and to some extent at present, many workers appear to believe that these goals are not being achieved, nor even recognized as such by management, has given rise to resentment and antagonism on the workers' part which, to a large extent, are the sources of the problems of labor-management relationships that have become more and more acute over the years. These problems in turn have led to legislation designed originally to strengthen the hands of labor in dealing with management and later to remedy some of the situations that have followed upon the enhanced power of labor.

LABOR PROBLEMS

In many industries and companies, frictions of various kinds have led labor and management [1] into a state of mutual antagonism. To some

---

[1] Management, in the sense that the term is used here, refers to the policy-making group in any company regardless of its identity with the owners.

observers, these irritations have been the result of the attitudes and actions of management, including its failure to recognize and to be sympathetic with the goals of the workers, rather than any behavior on labor's part. Labor's reaction to these stimuli, however, is what has aroused resentment on the part of management. Regardless of the real source of these animosities, there is no question about their existence.

■ Sources of Annoyance to Labor

Prominent among the contributions made by management to labor-management friction are those listed below:

1. Management's preoccupation with profits
2. Management's concept of labor as a cost of production
3. Management's impersonality and arbitrariness
4. The incomprehensibility to labor of many common business methods
5. Management's ignoring of workers' goals

1 / Management's preoccupation with profits. This, in the final analysis, is in line with management's main job, that of securing profits for the owners. A firm belief exists among many workers, however, that all business is extremely profitable and that most companies could easily pay higher wages without seriously impairing their profit positions. This belief, coupled with the conviction held by a large segment of labor that the purpose of business is to provide jobs rather than to make profits for the owners, accounts for labor's irritation at management's predominant profit consciousness.

Workers do not appear to realize that a business which is not profitable will sooner or later cease to exist, and the jobs that it provides will disappear. One of the social responsibilities that business has to the community which it serves is to maintain a profit position that reasonably guarantees its continued existence.

2 / Management's concept of labor as a cost of production. This concept is the result of the emphasis that many owners of businesses have placed on profits, which, in turn, has forced management to do its utmost to reduce costs. The development of modern cost accounting methods has pointed up the cost phase of the labor picture. Thus some managers see labor, not as a group of human beings, but as a cost of production. The fact that the introduction of automated machinery has resulted, in some companies, in the displacement of workers has served to convince them of management's attitude in this respect. Competitively, management must subject its costs to the closest scrutiny as one of the prices of survival.

3 / **Management's impersonality and arbitrariness.** In its dealings with labor, management has too often manifested an impersonality and arbitrariness that has antagonized workers, in many instances needlessly. Men have been hired, transferred, and discharged in a manner that has admitted of no argument and has given the impression that management had little regard for the workers' feelings. The growth of the concept of human relations in business, plus the strength of the unions in many areas, has served to blunt the force of this source of irritation to labor.

4 / **The incomprehensibility to labor of many common business methods.** Many of the everyday business procedures, particularly accounting and financial practices and those by which the payment of various jobs is computed, have long been a source of distrust on the part of the workers. The failure of management to educate the workers in the meaning and purpose of managerial procedures has served merely to aggravate labor's suspicion of these methods. Another factor is the apparent lack of understanding by labor of the role of profits in capitalistic enterprise.

5 / **Management's ignoring of workers' goals.** Although some enlightened managements are aware of the goals of their workers, many are not—a circumstance that is both irritating and frustrating to labor. And even where managements are sympathetic with their workers' aims, circumstances frequently prevent them from doing much to implement this understanding. Such factors as the pressure of competition that may set a ceiling on wages, the basic repetitive nature of many mass-production jobs that denies to the workers much sense of creativity, and the risks inherent in many enterprises that prevent management from guaranteeing security to their employees are hindrances to management's desires to assist their workers in the fulfillment of their objectives. In what is probably a declining number of instances, management feels that there exists an inherent conflict between the needs of production and the needs of people as workers. There are also some managers who are convinced that workers are basically lazy and have a congenital dislike for work.

■ **Reaction of Labor**

These management attitudes and actions have served to create resentment and distrust on the part of labor. This situation has made a large segment of labor receptive to the proposals of union organizers. Here they have found folks who talk their language and appear to have their interests at heart, who will listen to their troubles and try to do something about them. The workers have long since discovered the futility of trying to accomplish any betterment of their condition singlehandedly and now are confronted with the possibility of bringing this about through joint action. It is small wonder that labor organizations have grown in numbers and in strength, particularly during a period which has seen a phenomenal growth in the size and power of many industrial and commercial companies.

There is evidence to indicate that a sympathetic, more understanding attitude on the part of management would have retained the loyalty of the workers and made the task of the union organizers immeasurably more difficult. This statement is made because a great many workers feel an almost instinctive loyalty toward any organization of which they are a part. This is most noticeable in the case of new, young workers, who usually approach their first jobs with an enthusiasm and a desire to excel that would augur well for their employers if they would recognize and encourage it. Instead, management often appears more or less indifferent to this priceless offering and, as a result, this loyalty quickly subsides and is replaced by a sullen distrust and resentment. Workers in this frame of mind are quite favorably disposed toward the overtures of union organizers. Oddly enough, the so-called *white-collar workers*—those who work in offices and in engineering jobs—while they may experience some of the same reactions toward management as the *blue-collar* (or factory) *workers,* are much less receptive toward union membership than those who work in shops and factories. The reason for this appears to be in the attitudes of the white-collar groups, who regard themselves as being more individualistic, aggressive, and closer to management in their thinking.

■ Sources of Annoyance to Management

Certain aspects of labor's reaction to management's attitudes and actions have, in turn, caused considerable annoyance to management. The following are the more common sources of this irritation:

1. Loss of workers' loyalty
2. Weakening of management's authority
3. Belligerence of labor leaders

1 / Loss of workers' loyalty. When workers join unions, they are under considerable pressure from the union leaders to transfer their loyalty from their employers to the unions. This situation usually comes as a distressing discovery to management.

2 / Weakening of management's authority. A subject commonly covered by union-management contracts is the transfer and discharge of workers. Before the advent of the union, management's authority in this regard was practically absolute; but when a plant is unionized, the agreement of the union frequently must be secured before a worker can be transferred, discharged, or made the object of disciplinary action. This obviously dilutes management's authority, often to the dismay of the executive personnel involved. Since this situation is well known by the workers, some of them will assume a defiant attitude when their work or conduct is questioned by their superiors. In many such instances union representatives feel duty-bound to take the part of the offenders even though they realize that the latter may be at fault. No small part of the reason for this latter action lies in the political nature of the union leaders' jobs. They are regarded by the union membership as champions of the workers by whom they are elected, and their continued occupancy of their jobs may well be jeopardized if the members come to think that they are siding with management too frequently.

3 / Belligerence of labor leaders. Although many leaders in organized labor are noted for their courtesy and reasonableness, unfortunately some labor representatives assume a markedly belligerent attitude when dealing with employers or when speaking for public consumption. Management's reaction to this display of pugnacity is, in many instances, similarly contentious, with the result that there is apt to be more heat than light generated when the representatives of labor and management meet.

■ Other Reasons for the Growth of Labor Organizations

Several other factors have helped advance the growth of labor organizations. These factors are: (1) through organization, workers are placed in a much stronger position when dealing with management on matters of wages, hours of work, seniority, and working conditions than when they act as individuals; and (2) especially in large companies, the workers, through their organizations, are able to elect their own representatives to deal with management, whereas the very size of the firms is such that it would be virtually impossible for the individual worker to do this for himself.

■ Emergence of Unions as Preferred Labor Organizations

While some companies have had satisfactory experience with *shop committees* that meet with management to solve day-to-day problems, over the past 30 years or more unions have come increasingly to be preferred by workers who wish to be organized. Among the reasons for this preference are: (1) the recognition by many workers that only completely independent organizations can be certain of being free from possible domination by management; (2) the fact that the company-dominated union was outlawed by the National Labor Relations Act of 1935; (3) the availability in the unions of able and experienced negotiators whose skill in dealing with management assures the workers of a good chance that their requests will be granted; and (4) the aggressiveness and salesmanship of union organizers who have been successful in many fields in persuading the workers that their best interests would be served by joining the unions.

Union Membership, 1956-64

Year	Total Members	Percent of Nonfarm-Workers Belonging to Unions
1956	17,490,000	33.4%
1957	17,369,000	32.8
1958	17,029,000	33.2
1959	17,117,000	32.1
1960	17,049,000	31.5
1961	16,303,000	30.2
1962	16,586,000	29.9
1963	16,559,000	29.2
1964	16,841,000	28.9

Source: U. S. Labor Department

Emphasis is placed on the last of the reasons just enumerated because organizing the nonunion workers has come to be an ever-increasing goal of organized labor. Teams of experienced organizers are continually being sent to try to convince the employees of unorganized companies of the benefits of union membership. Achieving the largest possible number of dues-paying members is obviously one of the major objectives of the unions.

■ Union Objectives

The aims of organized labor are both political and economic. The political aspects of union activity, which appeared with the passage of the National Labor Relations Act of 1935 and have expanded to a marked degree in the past decade, include lobbying activities designed to secure the passage of favorable legislation and the rejection of unfavorable proposed laws in Congress and the state legislatures. Efforts have been made to "bring out the labor vote" for the purpose of electing so-called "friendly" candidates for public office and defeating "unfriendly" ones.

The economic, and historically older, group of objectives, the purpose of which is to benefit the workers and to strengthen the unions, include the following:

1. Higher wages and shorter hours
2. Seniority provisions
3. Union security or recognition
4. Checkoff
5. Restriction of output and job retention
6. Fringe benefits

1 / Higher wages and shorter hours. Foremost among the aims of unions are the raising of wages and the shortening of the number of hours of work. Any betterment in these factors is immediately recognized. In the long, slow movement toward higher wages and shorter hours since the early days of the Industrial Revolution, the unions have played a notable role.

2 / Seniority provisions. Many agreements contain seniority provisions that specify the rights and privileges of employees from the standpoint of length of service. These provisions are concerned mainly with layoffs, rehiring, transfers, and promotions. Obviously this objective disregards individual ability, loyalty, and ambition.

3 / Union security. With *union security* employers admit the right of employees to choose their own representatives and agree to recognize the chosen union as the sole bargaining agent for the workers, or at least that portion of the workers who want the union. The items that follow indicate the ways in which unions have sought security.

Under the *closed shop* the employer agrees to hire only persons who are union members, and all employees must remain members in good standing during their term of employment with the company. The Labor Management Relations Act of 1947, usually called the Taft-Hartley Act, outlawed the closed shop. It still exists in some industries, notably construction, printing, and maritime industries. The reason for this apparently illegal practice is that many workers in these industries get their jobs through *union hiring halls.* Employers who need qualified help contact the local union business agent, who sends out workers who are registered in the hiring halls as being available.

A *union shop* differs from a closed shop in that the employer may hire nonunion workers, but they must join the union after a prescribed period and remain in good standing as a requirement of continued employment. Most employers have been opposed to both the closed and the union shop. In their stead employers have preferred the *open shop* in which, at least theoretically, both union and nonunion workers may be employed. Labor leaders, on the other hand, have been most violently opposed to the open shop. Right-to-work laws place a ban on the union shop in several of the states.

In the *agency shop* all employees for whom the union, the *bargaining unit,* negotiates are required to pay dues to the union, but they do not have to join it. The agency shop is legal except where the states forbid it, which they have the right to do. Thus the agency shop is legal in Indiana but illegal in Florida. The agency shop was devised by the unions to circumvent state right-to-work laws.

Under a *maintenance-of-membership* arrangement, a worker need not belong to a union in order to obtain a job, nor must he join it in order to retain his job. If he is a member of the union at the time that the maintenance-of-membership shop becomes effective, however, or if he joins after that date, he must maintain his membership in good standing for the life of the existing contract as a requirement of continued employment.

In a *preferential shop* the employer agrees to give preference to union members in hiring and in layoffs. Thus union workers, if available, are hired before nonunion workers, and they are retained until the last when layoffs are necessary. The Taft-Hartley Act outlaws the preferential shop as well as the closed shop.

In some situations where not all employees are members of the union, the contract includes a provision by which the union is recognized as the sole or exclusive bargaining agent for all employees. Such a provision is characteristic of approximately one fifth of existing agreements. In some areas of public employment the union is recognized as representing only those employees who are members of the union. The employer deals with nonmembers on an individual basis.

4 / Checkoff. The term *checkoff* is applied to the collection of union dues by the employer through payroll deductions. Provisions for this collection are contained in the agreement executed between the union and management.

5 / Restriction of output and job retention. One of the economic aims of unions, which may or may not be admitted by labor leaders, is some form of restriction on the amount of work that will be turned out daily.

The union thinking back of this action is to preserve jobs, on the theory that there is only so much work to be done and that it should be so parceled out that all the present employees retain their jobs. The contract requirement stating that certain jobs be continued after management believes they are no longer needed is known as *featherbedding,* a practice that the employing companies have been trying for years to eliminate.

6 / Fringe benefits. In the past two decades or more, the unions have also sought and secured such fringe benefits as pensions, employee insurance, hospitalization, and many other items of advantage to their members.

■ Effects of These Aims

The economic effect of higher wages and shorter hours was discussed in Chapter 16. The effect of the other objectives—particularly the union shop, and the closed shop if it should again be legalized by subsequent legislation—is to move toward a monopoly of labor, wherein it is conceivable that one would have to join and remain a member of a union as a prerequisite to holding and possibly to getting a job. The first of these conditions exists in many fields of industry and is spreading to others. It tightens the hold of labor leaders over the rank and file, and it probably forces into the unions many persons who would not choose to join of their own free will.

Furthermore, the attainment of these objectives puts an exceedingly powerful club into the hands of the labor leaders, who have in some instances shown little reluctance to use it, without the slightest regard for the effects on the communities where the impact between labor and management takes place. It is doubtful that the best interests of the people of this country are to be served by permitting such a condition either to develop or to continue. It is interesting to note that abuses of monopoly power by business have been curbed through the Sherman Antitrust Act, the Clayton Act, and the vigilance of the antitrust division of the United States Department of Justice. Organized labor, on the other hand, was exempted from the antitrust laws by the Clayton Act of 1914.

■ Industrial Strife

In many instances organized labor has been able to achieve its objectives through the process of negotiating (or bargaining) with management. Perhaps unfortunately, however, there have been a large number of cases where labor and management have been unable to settle their differences on a peaceful basis and have had to resort to more strenuous practices.

1 / Labor's methods. A *strike* is a temporary refusal by employees to continue their work until their demands have been granted by management. The term *walkout* is used as a synonym for strike.

Usually the workers on strike remain away from the plant, but there have been two types of strikes in which they remain in the plant. These are the *sitdown strike,* in which the workers appear at their posts but refuse to perform their appointed tasks or to leave the premises until their demands are met; and the *slowdown strike* where the workers continue to work but at a markedly reduced tempo so that production is curtailed but not completely halted. The sitdown strike has been declared illegal by the courts in some states and has almost disappeared.

In a *jurisdictional strike* the union tries to force the employer to recognize it instead of another union for certain stated types of work. Under the Taft-Hartley Act most jurisdictional strikes are unfair labor practices and, as such, are prohibited. A *wildcat* or *outlaw strike* occurs when a group of workers go on strike without the official consent of the officers of the union or in violation of the terms of the contract. The *sympathy strike* is found where a group of workers go on strike because of sympathy with another group who are also on strike. The sympathy strikers usually have no grievance against their own employers but strike as a part of the union strategy to help the original striking group.

It is probable that, in many cases, strikes are settled without all of labor's demands being granted by the employers. It is not at all uncommon for the labor leaders to be willing to compromise on some of their demands as a part of a strike settlement.

Picketing consists of posting one or more persons at the entrance to the struck plant for the purpose of dissuading or preventing persons from entering the plant and of informing the public that a strike is in progress. *Mass picketing* occurs when a large number of pickets assemble at the entrances to a struck plant and forcibly prevent persons who may wish to go to work from crossing the picket lines. This is mob rule and has generally been frowned on by the courts.

Soldiering on the job occurs when one or more workers deliberately reduce the pace of their work, for the purpose of impeding production in the plants where they work. If this takes place on an organized basis, it is called a *slowdown strike.* The workers in this instance do not stop working, they merely slow down the tempo of their operations. *Sabotage* occurs when workers maliciously cripple or destroy the productive equipment of the plants where they work. This is illegal and is not prevalent at present.

A *boycott* takes place when union members refuse to purchase products from companies whose employees are on strike or where some condition prevails to which the union is opposed. This type of boycott is called a *primary boycott*. A *secondary boycott* exists when workers apply these tactics against a secondary handler, who offers for sale the goods of a struck or a nonunion plant. The Taft-Hartley Act prohibits certain types of secondary boycotts.

2 / Management's methods. These methods have consisted mainly of the lockout, the blacklist, and the injunction.

A *lockout* consists of an employer's refusal to permit workers to enter the plant to go to work. This usually takes place because the employer resents some action on the part of the workers. At other times lockouts have occurred for the purpose of denying union organizers access to the plants to prevent their holding organizing meetings.

A *blacklist* is a secret list of union organizers and members that is compiled by employers' associations and circulated among the members for the purpose of denying employment to the listed persons. Blacklisting is regarded as an unfair labor practice under a ruling of the National Labor Relations Board.

An *injunction* is a court order, secured by the employer, that aims to restrain the unions from interfering with the production of a plant in some manner, usually at the time of a strike. At one time, injunctions were issued against almost all forms of strike activity, but in recent years they have been restricted to mass picketing, acts of violence, or damage to the employer's property.

A *yellow-dog contract* is an agreement signed by workers, usually as a condition of securing jobs, whereby they promise not to join a union while working for their employers. The Norris-LaGuardia Act outlawed this type of contract.

Strike insurance funds have been established in the newspaper and air transport industries and in the railroads from which any member of these groups can receive payments during a strike. Contributions are made by all members on a self-insurance basis. The purpose of this action is to strengthen the managements of struck firms and to enable them to hold out for long periods of time in the event of strikes. The unions, naturally, are bitterly opposed to strike insurance, although they have long had similar funds to aid strikers.

STRUCTURAL ORGANIZATION
OF THE
AMERICAN FEDERATION OF LABOR AND CONGRESS OF INDUSTRIAL ORGANIZATIONS

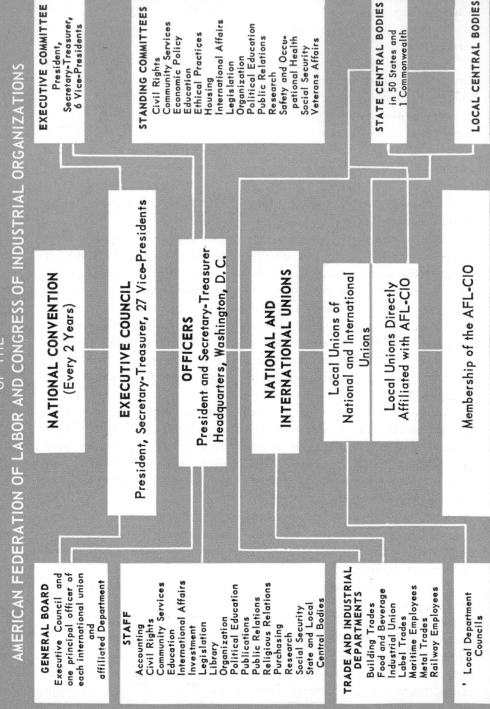

EXECUTIVE COMMITTEE
President,
Secretary-Treasurer,
6 Vice-Presidents

STANDING COMMITTEES
Civil Rights
Community Services
Economic Policy
Education
Ethical Practices
Housing
International Affairs
Legislation
Organization
Political Education
Public Relations
Research
Safety and Occu-
pational Health
Social Security
Veterans Affairs

STATE CENTRAL BODIES
in 50 States and
1 Commonwealth

LOCAL CENTRAL BODIES

NATIONAL CONVENTION
(Every 2 Years)

EXECUTIVE COUNCIL
President, Secretary-Treasurer, 27 Vice-Presidents

OFFICERS
President and Secretary-Treasurer
Headquarters, Washington, D. C.

**NATIONAL AND
INTERNATIONAL UNIONS**

Local Unions of
National and International
Unions

Local Unions Directly
Affiliated with AFL-CIO

Membership of the AFL-CIO

GENERAL BOARD
Executive Council and
one principal officer of
each international union
and
affiliated Department

STAFF
Accounting
Civil Rights
Community Services
Education
International Affairs
Investment
Legislation
Library
Organization
Political Education
Publications
Public Relations
Religious Relations
Purchasing
Research
Social Security
State and Local
Central Bodies

**TRADE AND INDUSTRIAL
DEPARTMENTS**
Building Trades
Food and Beverage
Industrial Union
Label Trades
Maritime Employees
Metal Trades
Railway Employees

' Local Department
Councils

■ Types of Unions

The two basic types of unions in this country are the craft union and the industrial union. *Craft unions* are organized according to crafts or trades, such as painters, plumbers, machinists, and teamsters. *Industrial unions* are organized according to industries, such as steel workers, clothing workers, and automobile workers.

Historically, unionism in this country developed on the trade or craft basis, and only since 1935 has industrial unionism made much headway. The years since then, however, have witnessed a profound trend toward the industrial union; and even the craft unions are now admitting to membership some of the unskilled and semiskilled workers in plants where formerly only the skilled workers could qualify.

At present there is one large formal union group in this country, The American Federation of Labor—Congress of Industrial Organizations, commonly known as the AFL-CIO. There are also a number of independent unions that are not affiliated with the AFL-CIO.

1 / Structure of the AFL-CIO. The organizational structure of the AFL-CIO consists of an Executive Council that includes the president, the secretary-treasurer, and 27 vice-presidents who are elected at the biennial convention and who govern the AFL-CIO between conventions. This group meets at least three times a year. The Executive Committee is made up of the president, the secretary-treasurer, and six vice-presidents chosen by the Executive Council. Its function is to advise and consult with the president and the secretary-treasurer on policy matters; it meets bimonthly. The General Board consists of Executive Council members and one officer of each affiliated union and trade and industrial departments. This group meets at least once a year.

There are six trade and industrial departments—the Building and Construction Trades, Industrial Union, Maritime Union, Metal Trades, Railroad Employees, and Union Label and Service Trades—which work closely with the appropriate member unions.

The field organization of the AFL-CIO consists of the various state federations, 134 local central bodies, 129 national and international unions, and 56 federal labor unions and local industrial unions, which are not affiliated with any of the national or international unions.

The affiliated national and international unions are more or less autonomous, being subject only to suspension or expulsion from the AFL-CIO by vote of the biennial convention. The unaffiliated unions are directly attached to the AFL-CIO and are under its control.

The general structural organization of the American Federation of Labor—Congress of Industrial Organizations is shown in the chart on page 374.

2 / Independent unions. The independent union picture is a somewhat confused one, due to the actions of the AFL and CIO, prior to their merger, in expelling the International Longshoreman's Organization by the AFL and the Office and Professional Workers; Public Workers; Food, Tobacco, and Agricultural Workers; United Electrical Workers; and Farm Equipment Workers, by the CIO. Since the merger, the AFL-CIO has expelled the International Brotherhood of Teamsters, the Bakery and Confectionery Workers, and the Laundry Workers International Union. Whether any or all of these unions will become affiliated with the AFL-CIO in the future is unpredictable.

Among the other prominent independent unions are the United Mine Workers, the Order of Railway Conductors, and the Brotherhood of Locomotive Engineers. Of the other independent unions that are scattered over a wide variety of occupations, some are confined to a single plant; others are federations of many local units. Included in this latter classification are federal employees, postal employees, marine firemen, foundry and metal workers, and watch workers.

■ Collective Versus Individual Bargaining

When a company becomes unionized, collective bargaining is substituted for individual bargaining, and the union becomes the bargaining agent for its members and, in some instances, for some or all of the non-union employees. It might be noted that in many, if not most cases, the office workers are not included in the bargaining unit. In *collective bargaining* the representatives of labor bargain with management over wages, hours, and other terms and conditions of employment, whereas in individual bargaining each individual bargains with the management on these matters. The power of collective bargaining lies in the saying "in union there is strength." When labor's representatives sit down around the conference table with management, they are in a much stronger position to secure their demands if they have all of the workers in the plant behind them than if each man represents only himself. The power behind the threat of a strike of all the workers is vastly greater than the possibility that a few individuals may quit if they are not given what they want.

For this reason collective bargaining is one of the major methods by which unions endeavor to achieve their objectives. It permits the unions to employ skilled negotiators in their bargaining activities, something that no individual could hope to do. It is through this process that labor is coming to have a voice in the operation of industry.

The collective bargaining agreement between a company and a union usually establishes procedures by which the union representatives in the shop can bring employee grievances to management's attention at any time. Likewise management may consult with the union on subjects that concern both parties. Also the necessity for the interpretation of clauses in the agreement calls for more or less continuous contacts between union and management.

The main drawback to collective bargaining is that it tends to level out differences in income among workers doing the same tasks. It also acts as a deterrent to ambitious workers who might be able to advance through their own superior efforts or abilities. The lot of most workers under collective bargaining is probably better, however, than it would be without this process, and an exceptional worker can usually find ways of making his presence felt and of receiving a reward commensurate with his value.

■ Methods of Settling Labor Disputes

Inasmuch as labor disputes are regarded as such only if management and labor are completely unable to agree on the points in question, the methods for settling them must of necessity involve the intervention of some outside agency or person, who may or may not represent some phase of government.

1. Mediation
2. Arbitration
3. Compulsory investigation

1 / Mediation. In *mediation* a third party tenders his good offices to both sides in an attempt to bring them to a point of common agreement. This is done without coercion and purely on the basis of helpfulness and the disinterestedness of an impartial third party. The term conciliation is frequently used synonymously with mediation. In a strict sense *conciliation* means that the mediator reviews the proposals put forth by both parties, whereas mediation implies that the mediator also offers his own proposals.

The Federal Mediation and Conciliation Service, created in 1947, was established for the purpose of providing means whereby the good offices of a government agency could be made available to the parties of a labor dispute should they care to take advantage of them. Neither disputant is required to accept its offer of assistance or to abide by its suggestions for solution of a dispute.

2 / **Arbitration.** Arbitration involves the submission by labor and management of the issue at stake to an individual arbitrator or, more commonly, a board. Usually each side has one representative on an arbitration board and a third party, someone acceptable to both disputants, is chosen as chairman. He may be a public official or someone in the community who has a reputation for fairness and impartial judgment. Once both parties agree to submit the dispute, the decision becomes binding, morally if not legally. This method of settling labor problems is known as *voluntary arbitration.* It is included as a possible procedure in some contracts between companies and labor unions. *Compulsory arbitration,* whereby both labor and management are required to submit to arbitration upon failure to settle their differences by other means, has made very little headway in this country, except in a few states and cities where employees of nonprofit hospitals, public utilities, and police and fire departments are prohibited by the law from striking and must submit their grievances to binding arbitration.

In a few cases, mainly in public utilities, impartial umpires have been appointed to whom all unsolved disputes are submitted for settlement. Their decisions are usually binding on both parties.

3 / **Compulsory investigation.** Either through legislation or by contract agreement, threatened strikes that may imperil public health and safety are postponed for varying lengths of time while impartial third parties investigate the disputes and make reports on their findings, which may or may not include recommendations for settlement. This is known as *compulsory investigation and delay.*

■ **Prospects for Labor Peace**

Will the time come when strife will disappear from this area of economic activity and, in its stead, will come an era of peaceful relationships? In most companies, unionized or not, the relations between management and the workers present the appearance of harmony as far as strikes, lockouts, and the like are concerned. And it is probable that, aside from the inevitable frictions that are bound to develop when people work together, the employees and their bosses get along fairly well. Why, then, does trouble periodically break out in certain well-unionized industries year after year?

> Is it because the conditions of employment are more onerous, or the pay scales lower, or the employer attitudes tougher in these fields than in most others?

Is there anything inherent in the character of the work in these industries that prompts the periodic eruptions that attract so much attention?

Is it possible that the personal ambitions of the labor leaders, in their attempts to gain prominence in the labor field, cause them to feel that they must continuously produce "rabbits out of a hat" —gain ever greater concessions from the employers regardless of dislocations that are often attendant upon the satisfying of these demands?

Is the answer to our labor problems to be found in an ever greater spread of unionism, the election of legislators "friendly" to labor, and the attempted subjugation of the public welfare to the demands of the unions?

These questions are difficult to answer. The present trend toward the extension of unionism is probably an inevitable consequence of prevailing conditions and has doubtless served to remedy some circumstances that could not have been altered by any other means. But, if there is ever to be any measure of industrial peace in this country, it will come about, not as the result of the mutual antagonisms of the representatives of both sides, but because labor and management can come to recognize the basic identity of their aims and aspirations. Each must bring to the bargaining table a respect for the other's opinions, viewpoints, and responsibilities. This condition is to be found now in many companies where management and labor meet to solve their various problems in an atmosphere of mutual confidence and trust and where each side realizes that the gaining of a temporary unfair advantage over the other can only lead to trouble. It is perhaps unfortunate, but probably inevitable, that the subject of labor-management relations has become so prominent in the political scene, thereby infusing an element of questionable relevance.

LABOR LEGISLATION

In the attempts that have been made by both labor and management to secure and retain advantages in their dealings with each other, legislation has come to play an increasingly important role. For some years the representatives of organized labor have striven to secure legislation favorable to their aims. At the same time employers have endeavored to retain the advantage that they had early in this century. The history of the more important labor laws since the early 1930's reflects the relative success with which these two parties have pursued their respective objectives at both the national and the state levels.

It is noteworthy that labor unions, over the years, have emerged from being purely economic organizations to ones which have strong political overtones. Many, if not most, national and international unions maintain lobbyists in Washington and in some of the state capitals whose function is to persuade legislators to vote favorably on measures that labor desires and against those to which it is opposed. The *Committee on Political Education,* commonly referred to as *COPE,* representing the AFL-CIO takes a very active part in the endeavor to secure prolabor legislation.

In the sections which follow, the laws that have had the most marked effect on management-labor relations are listed, and their more important provisions are set forth. In the main, the discussion will concern federal legislation, with the state laws occupying a secondary position, largely because of the variations in their provisions and their limited scope.

■ The National Labor Relations Act

In 1935 Congress passed the National Labor Relations Act, commonly known as the Wagner Act because of the sponsorship of Senator Wagner of New York. The purpose of this law was to help workers organize into unions that were completely free from employer domination and to secure recognition for these unions from their employers. A National Labor Relations Board, consisting of three members who were not to be affiliated with either labor or industry, was established to administer its provisions.

These provisions included a list of five so-called "unfair labor practices" in which employers were forbidden to engage. These were (1) to interfere with, restrain, or coerce employees in their collective bargaining or self-organizing activities; (2) to dominate or interfere with the formation or administration of any labor organization or to contribute financially to its support; (3) to discriminate in conditions of employment against employees for the purpose of encouraging or discouraging membership in any labor organization; (4) to discharge or otherwise discriminate against an employee because he has filed or given testimony under the Act; and (5) to refuse to bargain collectively with the chosen representatives of his employees. The Act did not recognize any unfair practices on the part of the unions, in which it differed from subsequent legislation in this area.

Employees were given the right to self-organization; to form, join, or assist labor organizations; to bargain collectively through representatives of their own choosing; and to engage in concerted activities for the purpose of collective bargaining or other mutual aid or protection.

The Board was empowered to prevent employers from engaging in any of the listed unfair labor practices and also to conduct elections among employees in order to determine the representatives who should bargain collectively for them with the employers. The Act also provided that representatives designated for collective bargaining by the majority of the employees in a plant should be the exclusive representatives of all the employees in the plant in matters of wages, hours of work, and other conditions of employment.

The Board was given the power to investigate instances where there appeared to be evidence of unfair labor practices by employers, together with the authorization to issue cease and desist orders where necessary.

After the validation of the Act by the Supreme Court in 1937, the unionization of large segments of American industry proceeded rapidly. The so-called company union, insofar as it was company dominated and financed, underwent a change that resulted in divorcing it from the control of the company. Many completely independent unions exist, not affiliated with any outside labor groups, whose membership is confined to the employees of the companies where they are to be found. They are actually company unions but not under the influence of the employers.

From 1935 until 1947, except for the period of World War II when certain steps were taken in the area of labor relations to meet war conditions, the National Labor Relations Act remained in force without change, and organized labor never functioned under more favorable legal auspices than during those years.

■ The Labor Management Relations Act

As time went on, many observers felt that the Wagner Act had gone too far in trying to remedy a situation that had been more favorable to management than to labor. Accordingly, the Labor Management Relations (Taft-Hartley) Act was enacted in 1947. At first vetoed by the President, it was subsequently passed over his veto.

According to its preamble, this was "an act to amend the National Labor Relations Act, to provide additional facilities for the mediation of labor disputes affecting commerce, to equalize legal responsibilities of labor organizations and employers, and for other purposes." Under its terms all of the provisions of the National Labor Relations Act that were not amended or repealed remained in force. Some of its more important provisions follow.

1. The National Labor Relations Board
2. Unfair labor practices
3. Other provisions

1 / The National Labor Relations Board. The Board was increased from three to five members. The position of General Counsel of the Board with rather wide powers was created. In addition to having general supervisory authority over the board's attorneys, he has charge of the investigation and prosecution of all unfair labor practices. At the same time the Board itself no longer prosecutes cases of this sort that come before it, but merely hands down decisions regarding them.

2 / Unfair labor practices. The employer unfair labor practices listed in the National Labor Relations Act are continued in force except that it is no longer considered an unfair practice for the employer to express his opinion on the issues of a labor dispute provided "such expression contains no threat of reprisal or force or promise of benefit." This same clause applies to unions.

A notable feature of the new Act is that it contains a list of unfair labor practices in which the unions are forbidden to engage. These are: (1) a union may not coerce employees into joining a union (except in the case of a union shop) nor employers in the selection of their representatives for collective bargaining or handling of employee grievances; (2) it may not try to force employers to discriminate against an employee (such as through discharge) except in the case of a union shop where the employee has not paid his union dues and initiation fee; (3) if a union has been certified as the bargaining agent for the employees, it cannot refuse to bargain collectively with the employer; (4) it is not permitted to engage in secondary boycotts or jurisdictional strikes, or to force assignment of certain work to certain unions; (5) the union may not charge excessive fees under union shop agreements; (6) it may not require an employer to pay for work that is not performed.

3 / Other provisions. The closed shop is outlawed and certain restrictions are established regarding the union shop. Unions may be sued for breach of contract and for damages resulting from strikes, jurisdictional disputes, or secondary boycotts. The National Labor Relations Board may seek injunctions to prevent unions or employers from engaging in unfair labor practices. When, in the opinion of the President, an actual or threatened strike or lockout imperils the national health or safety, he may seek an injunction to postpone the action for 80 days, during which time attempts are to be made to effect a settlement of the dispute. Employers are not required to recognize or bargain with supervisors' or foremen's unions. Unions must file financial reports and copies of their rules and regulations annually with the Secretary of Labor, and the officers must certify that they are not connected with the Communist Party in any way, as prerequisites to the acquisition of any statutory rights under the Act, such as petitioning the Board for an election and asking for an investigation of employer unfair practices. Unions, together with employers, are forbidden to make contributions to national political campaigns or candidates. Government employees are forbidden to strike. Of particular interest is that section of the Taft-Hartley Act (14b) which permits states to pass legislation forbidding the union shop. Further reference to this appears in the section under State Labor Legislation.

▓ The Labor-Management Reporting and Disclosure Act of 1959

This law was enacted as a result of the revelations of the McClellan Committee in regard to racketeering and financial irresponsibility in certain unions and as a result of pressure from the public. Every union must file a detailed annual financial report with the Secretary of Labor and make the information in it available to members; disclosure of the financial and "conflict of interest" activities of union leaders is required; theft or embezzlement of union funds is made a crime; union officers must be bonded by American companies; new regulations are established for the election of union officers; the NLRB is permitted to refuse jurisdiction over certain types of cases; *organizational picketing* (where a union places pickets outside a firm it is unsuccessfully trying to organize) is prohibited; certain aspects of secondary boycotts are eliminated; and the non-Communist affidavit clause of the Taft-Hartley Act is eliminated. Employers and labor-relations consultants must also report annually to the Secretary of Labor on all payments made or received to influence employees on labor matters.

▓ Other Federal Legislation

Numerous other federal laws affect labor, some of which have been mentioned earlier in this chapter. Two interesting laws worthy of mention are the Byrnes Antistrikebreaker Act that prohibits the interstate shipment of strikebreakers and the Lea Act that lifted restrictions the musicians' union had placed on broadcasting school orchestras and bands. Because railroad workers have always been considered as employed in interstate commerce, much labor legislation concerning them has been separate but comparable to that applying to workers generally.

Also, the Walsh-Healey Act of 1936 requires all employers who sell goods to the federal government to an aggregate value of over $10,000 to compensate their employees at the prevailing wage rates and to observe certain standard conditions concerning hours of work, safety, and sanitary surroundings, etc.

■ State Labor Legislation

In addition to federal labor legislation, laws affecting many phases
of the labor situation have been enacted by several states. Among these
are laws outlawing the closed shop; banning strikes by public employees
and employees of public utilities; forbidding jurisdictional, sitdown, and
sympathy strikes; and prohibiting compulsory unionism. Incidentally, the
Taft-Hartley Act permits states to outlaw the closed shop, the union shop,
maintenance of membership, and preferential hiring; and it does not
authorize any of these conditions in states where laws prohibiting them
are in force. In the opinion of many students of the field of labor legislation, including many labor leaders, state laws are frequently harsher on
labor in their provisions than are federal laws. This applies particularly
to the so-called *right-to-work laws,* which stipulate that no one shall be
required to join a union to secure or to retain a job.

The repeal of the right-to-work laws or the prevention of their being
enacted by state legislatures has become a major objective of organized
labor, as has also the repeal of section 14b of the Taft-Hartley Act.

BUSINESS TERMS

(a) white-collar worker (366), blue-collar worker (366)
(b) shop committee (367)
(c) union security (369); closed shop (369), union hiring hall (369),
      union shop (369), open shop (370), agency shop (370), bargaining
      unit (370), maintenance-of-membership (370), preferential shop
      (370)
(d) checkoff (370), featherbedding (371)
(e) strike or walkout (372); sitdown strike (372), slowdown strike
      (372), jurisdictional strike (372), wildcat or outlaw strike (372),
      sympathy strike (372)
(f) picketing (372), mass picketing (372)
(g) soldiering on the job (372), sabotage (372)
(h) boycott (373); primary boycott (373), secondary boycott (373)
(i) lockout (373), blacklist (373), injunction (373), yellow-dog con-
      tract (373)
(j) strike insurance fund (373)
(k) craft union (375), industrial union (375)
(l) AFL-CIO (375)
(m) collective bargaining (376)
(n) mediation (377), conciliation (377), voluntary arbitration (378),
      compulsory arbitration (378)
(o) compulsory investigation and delay (378)
(p) Committee on Political Education (380)
(q) organizational picketing (383)
(r) right-to-work laws (384)

QUESTIONS FOR DISCUSSION AND ANALYSIS

1. Do you believe that unions should be subject to the antitrust laws? Why?
2. How can management reduce the impact of the various sources of annoyance to labor?
3. In a competitive capitalist economic system can management avoid regarding labor as a cost of production? Explain.
4. How would you suggest that management should proceed if it decided to instruct workers in the role of profits in a capitalist economy?
5. Do you think that the increasing political activity of the unions is a desirable development? Why?
6. Do you think, as the labor leaders do, that section 14b of the Taft-Hartley Act should be repealed? Why?
7. Should the states be permitted to enact labor legislation that is contrary to the federal laws? Explain.
8. It has been stated that if the checkoff were to be abolished, the unions would decline rapidly in membership and power. Do you agree? Explain.
9. Do you believe that employers should not be permitted to establish strike insurance, as the unions claim? Why?
10. Should strikes be permitted in public-utility industries? Why?

PROBLEMS AND SHORT CASES

1. For many years the General Electric Company has adhered to the bargaining philosophy of making one firm offer to the unions and refusing to deviate from it as the bargaining sessions proceeded. This has been called Boulwareism after the man who instituted this practice some years ago. The company maintains that this is a fair practice, based on a careful study of all pertinent factors at the time. The unions, on the other hand, claim that this line of action violates the basic give-and-take concept of bargaining and have tried to persuade G. E. to change it.

    Consult current and back issues of such periodicals as *Business Week* and write a report, stating your opinion of this controversy and giving your reasons.

2. The past few years have witnessed a number of strikes of newspaper employees, one of the outstanding aspects of which has been the length of time that these work stoppages continue. In Cleveland, Detroit, New York City, and Boston these strikes continued for several months, resulting, in most instances, in a complete absence of newspapers in the affected communities.

    You are to consult the *Readers Guide to Periodical Literature,* and any newspaper files that your library carries, and to write a report showing the reasons for these long walkouts and also your opinion of the public-interest aspect of a stoppage of such sources of information as the newspapers. Give reasons for your conclusions.

3. A problem facing labor leaders at this time is the result of high employment, good wages, and the rapid extension of fringe benefits in the past few years. The nub of this problem is the apparent growing apathy on the part of union members toward any militant posture by the unions toward business. This does not mean that the members are not interested in economic betterment, but rather that they appear to have reached a state of mind where they would prefer to enjoy the benefits which they have achieved rather than to assume a more aggressive stand toward their employers. Certain labor leaders have been trying to arouse member enthusiasm for such issues as integration, the abolition of poverty, the minimum wage, job security for all, and other public questions.

Write a paper expressing your opinion on this development, its probable effect on the strength of the labor movement, and any remedies that you can suggest to rekindle the crusading spirit which was once so prominent in the labor movement. Reference to recent issues of *Business Week* should be of assistance in preparing your paper.

SUGGESTED READINGS

Bloom, G. F., and H. R. Northrup. *Economics of Labor Relations,* Fifth Edition. Homewood, Illinois: Richard D. Irwin, Inc., 1965.

Chamberlain, N. W., and J. W. Kuhn. *Collective Bargaining,* Second Edition. New York: McGraw-Hill Book Company, Inc. 1966.

Chruden, H. J., and A. W. Sherman, Jr. *Personnel Management,* Second Edition. Cincinnati: South-Western Publishing Company, 1963. Part V.

Henderson, J. A., and Others. *Creative Collective Bargaining: Meeting Today's Challenges to Labor-Management Relations.* Englewood Cliffs, New Jersey: Prentice-Hall, Inc., 1965.

Heneman, H. G., Jr., and D. Yoder. *Labor Economics,* Second Edition. Cincinnati: South-Western Publishing Company, 1965.

Hutchinson, J. G. *Management Under Strike Conditions.* New York: Holt, Rinehart & Winston, Inc., 1964.

Mabry, B. D. *Labor Relations and Collective Bargaining.* New York: The Ronald Press Company, 1966.

Maher, J. E. *Labor and the Economy.* Boston: Allyn & Bacon, Inc., 1965.

Northrup, H. R., and G. F. Bloom. *Government and Labor: The Role of Government in Union-Management Relations.* Homewood, Illinois: Richard D. Irwin, Inc., 1963.

Owen, W. V., and H. V. Finston. *Industrial Relations—Management, Labor and Society.* New York: Appleton-Century-Crofts, Inc., 1964.

Taft, P. *Organized Labor in American History.* New York: Harper & Row, 1964.

Magazines: *Monthly Labor Review, Industrial and Labor Relations Review, The American Federationist.*

Part VI

FINANCE

CHAPTER

18   Long-Term Financing

19   Short-Term Financing

20   Security Exchanges and Financial News

21   Risks and Insurance

22   Financial Problems and Policies

PROLOGUE TO PART VI

FINANCE

The major functions of business can be divided into production, distribution, finance, and control. Part VI endeavors to explain the financial aspects of business and why good financial management is so necessary to the successful operation of all business enterprises.

Chapters 18 and 19 discuss the various sources of funds for business divided between those appropriate for long-term and for short-term needs. In addition to analyzing the methods used to raise funds for varying lengths of time, the institutions that specialize in the long-term and short-term capital markets are described and their services to business are explained.

The distinctive roles played by two other major types of financial institutions—security exchanges and insurance companies—are analyzed and interpreted in Chapters 20 and 21. The chapter on security exchanges also describes the vast amount of information available and useful to financial managers. The chapter on insurance stresses the risks of conducting business and the extent and methods by which these risks can be reduced.

This part closes with Chapter 22, which presents some of the common financial problems that face most business units as well as various financial policies that may be adopted. With the preceding four chapters serving, in part, as background material, attention is devoted to decision making in the financial area based on an intelligent appraisal of the facts in each situation.

Chapter 18

LONG-TERM FINANCING

Businesses of all types and sizes have financial needs and requirements. Almost every business unit finds it necessary to own such items as buildings, equipment, and inventories, plus having an adequate supply of cash on hand. These are called *assets*. When firms first begin business, they must raise enough funds, or *capital*, which is one common use of this term, to purchase the necessary assets. Later, if they wish to expand or, for example, to buy out a competitor, these firms may again be seeking capital to accomplish the desired goal.

■ Types of Capital

There are two major types of assets: fixed and current. *Fixed assets* consist of real estate, machinery and equipment, and other tangible items that have a useful life of from one to many years. Money invested in these is called *fixed capital*. *Current assets* include cash, receivables (amounts due from customers, for example), and inventories. There is a continuous flow of current assets in the direction of cash as inventories are sold and receivables are collected. Because of this constant movement, current assets are also called *circulating capital*.

The distinction between the two types of capital is important because long-term financing is appropriate for acquiring fixed capital, whereas short-term financing is better suited to satisfying circulating capital needs except for a minimum permanent supply that must be maintained year in and year out. The purchase of land and buildings, for example, should be financed with funds secured from the owners of the business or from lenders who do not expect to be repaid for a number of years. On the other hand, it is usually satisfactory for a business to borrow money from a bank on a 60-day note to purchase merchandise that will be sold in less than 60 days because the receipts from the sale of these goods will provide the cash with which to repay the loan.

This chapter will deal primarily with *long-term financing*, which includes funds secured from owners as well as from loans that mature in several years, usually ten or more. It will discuss alternate sources of such funds, the financial instruments appropriate to different methods of raising capital, and the financial institutions that specialize in assisting in long-term financing. Chapter 19 will present a similar treatment covering short-term financing, which covers loans with a maturity of one year or less. Occasionally, some financing requirements fall in the time span between one and ten years, an area known as *intermediate credit*, but such needs are relatively infrequent and are usually handled as extensions of short-term financing.

■ Long-Term Noncorporate Financing

The major source of long-term financing for sole proprietorships and partnerships is *equity capital*, the funds invested by the owners. This fact, in part, accounts for the small size of most unincorporated businesses, and it is responsible for the conversion of many growing proprietorships and partnerships into corporations. Unless one or more owners are very wealthy and are willing to place their fortunes into one business, funds available for long-term financing are likely to be limited in amount.

Equity capital is not, however, the sole source of long-term funds for unincorporated businesses. *Debt capital*, which is that provided by borrowing, offers some possibilities. If the fixed assets owned or to be acquired include land and buildings, the property can be mortgaged for around two thirds to three fourths of its value. Although repayment of a note secured by such a mortgage on a monthly basis is common, the loan usually does not mature in less than twelve years and frequently runs for twenty to thirty years.

Another possibility for securing some debt capital occurs when the assets of the firm include equipment of the type frequently found in manufacturing operations. A portion of the buying price can be borrowed by signing a note and pledging the equipment as collateral for the loan. This kind of mortgage, except for a shorter maturity date, does not differ substantially from a real-estate loan. In both instances a major disadvantage is the need to make periodic payments at a time when the firm may be struggling to earn a profit. "Starting a business on a shoestring," which is an expression used to denote a high ratio of debt capital to equity capital, is extremely risky.

The lack of financial resources for small businesses, which includes most unincorporated firms, has been a concern of the federal government. The Small Business Administration, a federal agency created in 1953, has the authority to loan up to $250,000 to a firm unable to secure funds elsewhere. The SBA, as it is known, may also participate with a bank in making funds available and makes loans to privately owned investment companies organized to finance small businesses. Because loans made from or with the assistance of the SBA can run for as long as 10 years, unincorporated businesses now have an additional source of long-term financing.

■ Long-Term Corporate Financing

All of the sources of debt capital for long-term financing that have been described as available to noncorporate businesses, including SBA aid, are also available to and used by corporations, particularly those that are relatively small. Larger corporations are much more likely to satisfy their fixed-capital needs by selling bonds and stocks, frequently to the general public. The ability to market both types of securities is basically the reason for the larger size of corporate firms. Not all corporations issue bonds although some secure over one half of their total capital from this source. All corporations do issue stock since stock represents ownership, and there must be shareholders who own the corporation.

Because both bonds and stocks are issued in a variety of forms, and because they are of such importance in the business world, they will be described in some detail. Although very different, since bonds represent debt capital and stock in any form is equity capital, collectively they are the reason why corporations have been able to satisfy their needs for billions of dollars in capital funds.

BONDS	STOCKS
1. Represent debt of issuing corporation.	1. Represent ownership in corporation.
2. Must be repaid at some future date.	2. No obligation to repay although sometimes stock is retired.
3. Definite rate of interest due at stated intervals.	3. Unless and until dividends are declared, no return is due stockholders even though preferred stock may state a specific rate of return.
4. Interest on bonds is an expense of doing business.	4. Dividends are a distribution of profits.

BONDS

A *bond* is a type of security that is a debt of the issuing corporation that matures at a stated future date and on which interest is paid annually or semiannually. All bonds issued by private companies contain some common features. In addition, there are many special provisions, one or more of which may apply to a particular issue.

■ General Features of Bonds

Considerations applying to all bond issues sold by industries, railroads, public utilities, and financial enterprises are:

1. Provision for trustee
2. Denomination of bonds
3. Maturity dates
4. Registered versus coupon bonds

1 / Provision for trustee. Bonds, which represent a debt of the issuing corporation, are usually held by a large number of investors. These investors may be widely scattered over the country and may not be acquainted with each other. They need someone to act in their behalf and to safeguard their interests. Such a person is known as a *trustee* and is chosen by the corporation at the time the bond issue is sold. Modern practice usually calls for a trust company or large bank to serve in the capacity of trustee.

The duties of the trustee are included in the agreement under which the bonds are issued. This legal document is called the *indenture*. Under it the trustee certifies that the bonds are genuine, holds any collateral that may be used as security for the issue, and collects money from the corporation to pay the interest and also the principal. In addition to these specific duties, the trustee undertakes, in behalf of the bondholders, to make sure that all provisions of the indenture are carefully followed during the lifetime of the issue.

2 / Denomination of bonds. Most industrial, railroad, financial, and public utility bonds are issued in units of $1,000. Sometimes the denominations of part of the issue will run higher, such as $5,000, $10,000, and $50,000 units, or may be printed in lower amounts, usually $500 or even down to the $100 level. If bonds have a face value of less than $500, they are frequently referred to as *baby bonds*. Despite these varying denominations, the price of a bond is quoted in terms of a ratio to 100, such as 101½. This quotation means that a $1,000 bond would cost $1,015.

Because of the promotional efforts of the federal government, including the possibility of purchase under a payroll deduction plan, many individuals are more familiar with United States savings bonds than they are with corporation bonds. Although the federal government issues many types of bonds, the average saver purchases Series E savings bonds, which are available in units as small as a $25 maturity value. A distinctive characteristic of this series is the method used to compensate the lender for the use of his money. Instead of paying interest semiannually, as is customary, these bonds are sold at a discount and, if held for 7 years, interest amounting to 4.15 percent is earned on the cost price. The bonds are sold at $18.75 or multiples thereof, and mature at $25 or proportionally higher amounts. Securities that pay interest in this fashion are known as *accumulation bonds*.

3 / Maturity dates. Because bonds are a debt, they must be repaid at some future date. The length of time between the issue and repayment varies considerably, but practically all bonds will run for at least 10 years and may not mature for as long as 100 years. As an instrument of long-term financing, a period shorter than 10 years would hardly be satisfactory. Common lives of bond issues are 20, 30, and 40 years.

4 / Registered versus coupon bonds. A *fully registered bond* shows the name of the owner on the face of the security; a record of the owner is kept by the issuing corporation; and interest checks are mailed to the holder. A *coupon bond* shows no evidence of the owner; the corporation does not know who holds it; and interest is paid to the party who presents the dated coupons which are clipped from the bond.

The advantage of a registered bond is that the owner is protected against loss in case it is stolen. The coupon bond, which is a bearer instrument, is usually assumed to belong to the person who has it in his possession. The disadvantage of a registered bond is that title cannot pass unless the owner indorses the bond to a purchaser and this fact is recorded on the books of the issuing corporation. The coupon bond is easier to sell and is more satisfactory to deposit with a bank as security for a loan. Corporations floating a large issue may sell both types of bonds.

In some instances a coupon bond is registered as to principal only. Interest is collected by the coupon method as in the case of the ordinary bearer bond, but the owner is protected by registration against loss by theft as to the principal sum. This is known as *partial registration*.

Corporation Bond

The coupons at the right provide for semiannual interest payments of $13.75. The original of the bond illustrated had 60 coupons of this type attached to it.

■ Special Features of Bonds

Practically every bond issue is different in some respect from one issued by another company or from another series that is sold by the same organization. The names by which bond issues are advertised and sold frequently contain a descriptive phrase indicating the inclusion of one or more of the following special features:

1. Security
2. Method of repayment
3. Callable or redeemable bonds
4. Convertible bonds

1 / Security. Since bonds are a debt of the corporation, investors usually expect some type of security as protection in case the issuing party finds it impossible to live up to the terms of payment of interest or principal. Bonds usually run for a long period of time, and a corporation that is prosperous today may fall on evil times before the maturity date of the issue. Some of the common types of security offered to bondholders are described briefly in the following paragraphs.

(a) Real Estate Mortgages as Security. The most common type of security for a bond issue is a mortgage on real estate, which can be foreclosed by the trustee acting for the bondholders. Such bonds are called *real estate mortgage bonds*.

Mortgage bonds have an almost endless variety of special features such as first-mortgage bonds that rank ahead of second-mortgage bonds, and the inclusion of an *after-acquired clause* that has the effect of adding properties built or purchased subsequent to the sale of the issue to the real estate originally mortgaged. If the entire issue is sold at one time, it is known as a *closed-end issue* as opposed to an *open-end issue* that permits the sale of additional bonds at a later date under the original mortgage.

(b) Chattel Mortgages as Security. If a mortgage on movable items, such as machinery and equipment, is used as security for bonds, the securities are known as *chattel mortgage bonds*. When used by railroads to purchase engines, freight cars, and passenger coaches, they are known as *equipment trust certificates*. Such bonds command a strong market because, in case of default, the trustee could easily sell the mortgaged equipment to another railroad.

(c) Stocks and Bonds as Security. Stocks and bonds of various other companies that are owned by the corporation desiring to borrow funds from the investing public are frequently used as security for a bond issue. The securities are deposited with a trustee who, under the terms of the indenture, can sell them for the benefit of the bondholders in case of default on either interest or principal payments. Such bonds are called *collateral trust bonds*. If the pledged stocks and bonds are issues of good companies and have a value in excess of the amount of the bonds sold, collateral trust bonds are an attractive investment.

(d) Excellent Credit Rating as Security. Occasionally a firm is so strong that it does not feel the need for stating any security behind the issue except the general excellent credit standing of the corporation. In this case the bonds are called *debenture bonds*. The Standard Oil Company of New Jersey has outstanding a $150 million issue of 25-year, 2¾-percent, debenture bonds due in 1974. All United States Government bonds are of the debenture type.

2 / **Method of repayment.** Prospective investors would like to be sure that, when their bonds mature, the company will be financially able to pay back the money borrowed. Consequently, the plan by which this objective is to be attained is announced at the time the securities are sold. If the total issue runs into millions of dollars, the problem of repayment might be a very grave one.

There are two common methods of repayment, which result in liquidating the debt. One is to issue bonds that mature in different years so that the impact of the full amount will not be felt at a given date. Such bonds are known as *serial bonds*. For example, a 20-year $1 million issue might run for 10 years without any bonds maturing. At the end of the eleventh year and annually thereafter during the life of the bonds, $100,000 worth mature as specified when the bonds were first sold.

Another method of repayment is the establishment of a sinking fund. Under this plan, the issuing corporation deposits annually with the trustee an amount of money that, at the expiration of the bond issue, will equal the amount due. Using the same size of issue as that in the preceding illustration, the corporation might deposit $50,000 a year with a trustee. At the end of 20 years, assumed as the life of the bonds, the deposits would amount to the face value of the total issue. Actually, the size of the annual deposits could be smaller because of interest earnings on the funds in the hands of the trustee. Such bonds are known as *sinking-fund bonds*.

Some corporations, particularly railroads and public utilities, that always have a large number of bonds outstanding, do not expect to liquidate the debt other than by retiring one issue with the proceeds received from another. When bonds are sold for this purpose, the word *refunding* is added to the description.

3 / Callable or redeemable bonds. Although bonds must be retired when they mature, it may be desirable for the debtor corporation to liquidate the debt at an earlier date. To make this possible, a clause is frequently inserted in the indenture providing that the bonds can be called at the option of the issuer, usually at a premium. The exact amount at which the bonds can be redeemed is known as the *call price*. Bonds that have this feature are known as *callable* or *redeemable bonds*.

In years of a declining interest rate, the privilege of repaying a bond issue prior to maturity is exercised. For example, a company issued $10 million worth of bonds in 1948, which were to run for 40 years, and carried an interest rate of 6 percent. Later, this corporation believes it can sell a new issue at 5 percent at par. Assuming that it will cost $1,050 to redeem a $1,000 bond, because of the premium provision on early redemption, the saving in interest in the long run will more than offset this added cost. In five years the interest saving will amount to $50, and after that an annual saving of $10 will be in effect on each $1,000 bond outstanding.

4 / Convertible bonds. Bonds, as an investment, appeal to insurance companies, savings banks, and individuals who desire a stated rate of return coupled with a high degree of safety. In order to attract buyers who desire some speculative possibilities as well, some bond indentures provide for the exchange of bonds into common stock at the option of the holder during the life of the bond issue. These are known as *convertible bonds.*

A typical convertible feature would allow the holder of a $1,000 bond to exchange this security for 25 shares of common stock. If, at the time the bond issue is sold, the shares are selling for $30 each, the conversion privilege is of no value. If the stock advances to $50 per share, the bond will rise in value to approximately $1,250; but the dividend on 25 shares may well exceed the fixed yield on the bond. If a considerable portion of the bond issue is converted, the corporation has solved a large part of its redemption problem.

■ Bond Premium or Discount

If the corporation selling a bond issue is highly regarded by investors, or if the bond market is favorable, or if the interest rate offered is higher than prevailing rates on comparable bonds, an issue may be sold for more than its face value. The amount by which the price exceeds the stated value is called a *bond premium.* If a bond with a face value of $1,000 is sold for $1,062.50, the $62.50 is the amount of the premium. If conditions are the reverse of those indicated above, a $1,000 bond may be sold for $987.50 and, in this case, the $12.50 reduction from the face value is known as the *bond discount.*

PREFERRED STOCKS

Preferred stocks represent shares of ownership, the certificates show a stated rate of return that, when paid, is known as a dividend, and the stock does not have a maturity date. Because of the stated dividend rate and other possible features, such as convertibility, some investors feel that preferred stocks occupy a middle ground between bonds and common stocks. Legally there is no justification for this viewpoint as preferred stocks are a form of ownership rather than debt. Furthermore, although a preferred stock shows a rate of return, such as 6 percent, even this dividend is not owed until so declared by the board of directors. Also, unlike bonds, the authority to issue preferred stock must be obtained from the state in which it is incorporated. The number of shares to be authorized and a brief description of the type or types of preferred stock that may be issued are contained in the original application for a charter or might, at a later date, be the subject of a charter amendment. A more detailed statement of general and specific features, as described below, is printed on the face of each preferred stock certificate.

■ General Features of Preferred Stocks

All preferred stocks have a preference as to dividends, and they are either cumulative or noncumulative, participating or nonparticipating, voting or nonvoting, and par or no-par.

1. Preference as to dividends
2. Cumulative or noncumulative
3. Participating or nonparticipating
4. Voting or nonvoting
5. Par or no-par

1 / Preference as to dividends. The very name "preferred stock" indicates that this type of stock must have a preference over another type. Without exception, preferred shareholders receive dividends before common shareholders. If a company has some earnings but not enough to warrant declaring dividends on both preferred and common stocks, the preferred stocks will be favored. The board of directors of a corporation has the right to *pass the dividend,* which means that the dividend that might be expected by the preferred shareholders is not declared. It would not be legal, then, to declare a dividend on the common stock.

2 / Cumulative or noncumulative. Dividends on preferred stock are usually declared on a quarterly basis although some companies pay on a semiannual or annual basis. If a dividend is passed by the board of directors, the question arises as to whether the amount is forever lost to the preferred shareholders. If the stock is *cumulative preferred stock,* the dividends omitted in previous periods must be declared before any action can be taken leading to a distribution of profits to the common shareholders. If the stock is *noncumulative preferred stock,* such omissions need not be taken into consideration at a later date.

For example, assume that a corporation has outstanding a 5 percent, preferred stock issue of $1,000,000. In 1967 the company just about breaks even financially, and the board of directors decides to pass the dividend on the preferred stock. In 1968 the corporation earns $100,000, and the board votes dividends equal to this amount of profit. If the preferred stock is noncumulative, $50,000 will be paid to these shareholders and the common shareholders will receive the same amount. If the preferred stock is cumulative, the entire $100,000 will be paid to the preferred shareholders because they are entitled to $50,000 for 1967 plus $50,000 for 1968.

3 / Participating or nonparticipating. Preferred stocks have an established dividend rate. For example, an issue may state that the return shall be $6 a year per share. When the firm is particularly successful, however, the preferred shareholders will be limited to an annual return of the amount stated unless the stock is participating. In other words, *participating preferred stock* allows the owners to share in excess earnings, whereas *nonparticipating preferred stock* limits the annual dividends to the amount stated at the time of issue.

If a company has outstanding 1,000 shares of preferred stock on which the established dividend rate is $5 and 1,000 shares of common stock, and has earnings of $25,000 available for dividends, the distribution of this amount will vary between the two stockholding groups depending on whether the preferred is participating or nonparticipating. If the latter, $5,000 will be paid to the preferred shareholders and $20,000 to the common shareholders. If the preferred stock is participating to the fullest extent possible, $5,000 will be paid to holders of preferred stock as a prior claim on earnings and the common shareholders will next benefit by a like sum. This leaves $15,000, which would be distributed equally on all shares outstanding. This would result in a total payment of $12.50 on each share of stock, whether it be preferred or common. Sometimes preferred stocks that are participating do not share in excess earnings until after the common shareholders have received a larger payment per share than the stated rate on the preferred stock.

4 / Voting or nonvoting. Common law holds that, since stock is ownership, all stock is entitled to vote. In the case of preferred stocks this privilege is frequently removed or restricted by the contract under which it is issued. It is a right that is sacrificed in return for securing other favored treatment.

If preferred stock does not have regular voting power, that is, one vote for each share, it may be given voting privileges on special matters, such as when a bond issue is proposed that might jeopardize the favored position of the preferred shareholders. An even more common provision is the extension of voting rights when a stated number of quarterly preferred dividends have been passed by the board of directors.

5 / Par or no-par. Almost all preferred stocks are issued with a stated value printed on the face of the certificate, which is known as its *par value.* If no stated value is so indicated, it is known as *no-par stock.* The fundamental distinction is whether the stock certificate does or does not carry a printed monetary value.

Historically, all stocks had a par value that the public, to its sorrow, frequently confused with market value. In order to combat this type of fraud, state legislatures authorized corporations to issue no-par stock. For accounting purposes the board of directors sometimes assigns an arbitrary stated value to each share of no-par stock, but such an action does not change its status. As far as owners are concerned, there is practically no choice between par and no-par stocks.

When the preferred stock has a par value, for example $100 a share, the dividend rate is given as a percent, such as 5 percent. Also, the stock may be sold at a premium or discount, above or below par, as in the case of bonds. If the stock has no face value, the dividend rate must be stated in terms of dollars, such as a $5 preferred stock.

◼ Special Features of Preferred Stocks

There are fewer varieties of preferred stocks than there are of bonds. Nevertheless, special features are incorporated into the agreement or contract under which authority is granted for the sale of this type of security. These include provisions for redemption, conversion, and special preferences. Other features may arise also as a result of having dividends guaranteed by another corporation or of issuing another series of preferred stock.

1. Callable or redeemable
2. Convertible preferred stock
3. Preference as to assets
4. Series issues

1 / Callable or redeemable. A feature of many preferred stocks, which is similar to a common provision in bond issues, is the inclusion of a call price at which preferred stocks may be redeemed at the option of the issuing corporation. If no such feature is included in the original agreement, there is no legal right by which a corporation can call in any outstanding preferred stock. The only possibility in this case is to buy the shares on the open market; but, if some owners refuse to sell, these shares will remain outstanding as long as the corporation is in existence.

2 / Convertible preferred stock. Although preferred stocks are more subject to market fluctuations in price than are bonds, they represent a more conservative investment than do common stocks. In order to enhance their attractiveness to investors, a clause providing for conversion into common stocks may be included in the preferred stock contract. If a preferred stock selling for $100 a share is convertible into four shares of common stock, and the common stock is quoted at $22 a share, there is no value to the conversion privilege. Should the selling price of the common stock rise beyond $25, the preferred stock will increase in value. At some point the holder might decide to convert if he did not object to owning common stock and if the yield on four shares of common was higher than the income from one share of preferred.

3 / Preference as to assets. Most preferred stocks have a prior claim on assets in case it is necessary to dissolve the corporation. This means that preferred stockholders will be paid the amount due them before any distribution is made to common stockholders.

In case a corporation is liquidated, the first task is to sell all of the assets. Cash received must be used to pay off all liabilities, including all bond issues, before giving any consideration to the ownership group represented by preferred and common stocks. At this stage the preferred stockholders are in an advantageous position if their stock is preferred as to assets for otherwise they would share equally with the common stockholders in any distribution that could be made.

4 / Series issues. Some corporations have more than one issue of preferred stock outstanding. Because each issue was originally sold on different dates involving varying market conditions, the stated rate of return is different for each series. Otherwise, the various issues are almost always on an equal footing. Series issues of preferred stocks are more widely used by public utility and railroad companies than by industrial corporations.

COMMON STOCKS *- long-term security*

Common stocks are long-term securities that represent ownership in its basic form at the lowest or residual level. They are the least complicated of all long-term securities. No dividend rate is ever stated. Except as noted below, voting rights are not restricted. Common stock cannot be convertible because conversion rights always provide for an exchange into a lower level security. Also, dividends on common stocks are not cumulative, as there would be no point to such a provision. If it is pos-sible to make up dividends not declared in former years, the procedure is to pay a large dividend in the current year.

In exactly the same manner as preferred stocks, common stocks may have a par value printed on the face of the certificate, or the stock may be of the no-par variety. A majority of common stocks are no-par, whereas most preferred stocks are of the par-value type. If the common stock does have a par value, it is likely to be $1, $5, $10, or $25 while many preferred stocks have par values of $100.

In order to retain control of voting rights and, at the same time, avoid the restrictions of preferred stocks, some corporations issue more than one class of common stock. The main distinction between Class A stock and Class B stock, which are the names usually given to different issues of common stock, pertains to voting privileges. One class votes, the other does not. Usually the Class B retains the exclusive right to vote, although, in some instances, the Class A votes and the Class B does not. A provision rarely included is a difference in dividend rates or dividend preferences. In this event, Class A stock assumes many of the character-istics of a preferred issue.

Recently several corporations with two classes of common stock have switched to one type. It appears that Class A and Class B common stocks may soon disappear from the financial scene.

FINANCIAL INSTITUTIONS—LONG-TERM CAPITAL

The high degree of specialization characteristic of our capitalistic sys-tem, already observed in production and distribution, also extends to the area of finance. The many and diverse monetary needs of the business community are so complex that no single financial institution attempts to perform more than a limited number of functions. Some of these institutions operate primarily in the short-term capital field while others specialize in providing business firms with assistance in solving their long-term financing problems. In this latter category investment banking com-panies provide direct aid to corporations wishing to sell bonds and stocks to the public, while several other types of financial institutions play an important but indirect role in the long-term capital area.

■ Investment Banking Companies

The primary function of *investment banking companies* is to market securities for corporations that have long-term capital needs. Such bank-ing companies are sometimes called "security houses" and this title describes, in part, their operations. The "merchandise" they purchase for subsequent sale to investors consists of bonds, preferred stocks, and common stocks of old and new companies.

If the Stoddard Manufacturing Co. decides to construct a new factory building and equip it with the necessary machinery, the Company may need additional capital funds. If a decision is reached to obtain the funds needed, estimated at $50 million, from an issue of mortgage bonds, the problem of selling these securities to the public would loom as almost insurmountable to a company unfamiliar with this field of finance. An investment banking company can be contacted and, if it agrees to market the bonds, the entire problem is solved as far as the manufacturing company is concerned.

The investment banking company would make an investigation of the Stoddard Manufacturing Co. prior to making a commitment regarding the proposed bond issue. If reports received from engineers, accountants, and other-experts were favorable, the investment banking company would then enter into negotiations to underwrite the bond issue. This means that an offer would be made to the Stoddard Manufacturing Co. to buy the bonds. An acceptance would result in immediate access to the cash needed. The price that the investment banking company would be willing to pay would depend on the amount that it anticipates can be realized from the sale of the bonds. If its experts conclude that the bonds can be sold at par, the bank might pay $49,600,000 for the issue. The discount of $400,000, which would represent the gross profit to the bank, is called the *spread*.

If the issue is not too large in relation to the size of the investment banking company, the institution may handle the entire transaction through its central office and branches. If the issue is too large for one firm, or if the risk is too great, several other investment banking companies may be invited to participate in the financing as a syndicate. Some investment banking companies specialize in organizing syndicates and in wholesaling blocks of securities to smaller dealers located in various cities. Other investment banking companies operate many retail outlets and employ large numbers of salesmen. The well-known firm of Merrill Lynch, Pierce, Fenner & Smith, Inc. is in the latter class.

■ Other Financial Institutions for Long-Term Capital

The financial institutions listed at the top of page 404 are essential elements in the overall long-term capital picture even though their assistance to corporations is, normally, more indirect than that provided by investment banking companies.

1. Brokerage firms   4. Insurance companies
2. Trust companies   5. Savings and loan associations
3. Investment companies   6. Savings banks

1 / Brokerage firms. A broker buys and sells for others, and charges a commission for this service. Brokers operate in many fields, including investment securities in which they play an important part. In the financial field it is very common for a group of brokers to form a *brokerage firm*, which not only buys and sells stocks and bonds for their customers, but also assists in financing these transactions.

Some brokerage firms or houses function as investment banking companies on occasion, and some investment banking companies also do a brokerage business. In the main, the activity of the brokerage firm is to buy and sell securities that have been issued. They may be issues that are sold on organized exchanges, or stocks and bonds that have not been accepted for trading by a stock exchange. Those in the latter group are known as *unlisted securities,* and they are traded in the *over-the-counter market.* A brokerage firm makes contacts with individuals who wish to buy unlisted securities and with others who wish to sell. The price the prospective purchaser is willing to pay is called the *bid price,* as opposed to the *asked price* of the present owner. If either party meets the price of the other, a transaction takes place.

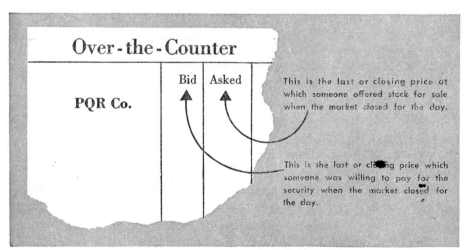

Over-the-Counter

| | Bid | Asked |
| PQR Co. | ↑ | ↑ |

This is the last or closing price at which someone offered stock for sale when the market closed for the day.

This is the last or closing price which someone was willing to pay for the security when the market closed for the day.

Hayden, Stone, Inc.

2 / Trust companies. *Trust companies* are financial institutions that specialize in assuming the capacity of trustee for business firms and individuals. In today's financial world most trust companies also operate as commercial or savings banks, and the majority of large commercial banks maintain a trust department. Consequently, the functions of a trust company are frequently carried out by a department of a larger financial institution.

The major portion of a trust company's business consists of the management of estates and of serving as a trustee under the provisions of a will. In this connection funds turned over to the trust company are invested in such securities as bonds, preferred stocks, and common stocks. Under the *prudent-man rule*, which has been adopted by most states, the trustee can purchase securities that a careful investor would buy for his own account. In some instances specific securities are purchased for an estate, but a majority of the states now permit the use of a *common trust fund* by which the funds from several estates are combined for the purchase of securities.

As explained on page 392, a trust company function of particular interest to business is that of serving as trustee of a bond issue. The indenture under which bonds are issued always provides that there shall be a trustee to act for the bondholders in such a manner as to protect their best interests. Under the Trust Indenture Act of 1939, a federal law, the trustee for a bond issue must take an aggressive position in behalf of the bondholders.

Another financial service rendered many businesses by trust companies is that of acting as registrar and transfer agent for stock issues. In the role of *registrar*, the trust company guarantees to the investing public that the various issues of stock that may be outstanding are accurately stated and within the limits established by the charter. The duties of *transfer agent* involve recording changes in ownership following each sale of stock. For large businesses with thousands of outstanding shares of stock, which are traded daily on stock exchanges, the service of a transfer agent is necessary and important.

Still another function rendered business by a trust company is serving as a special depository for important papers that are not to be delivered until certain terms are met. For example, the Dodge Construction Company agrees to build a factory addition for the E-Z Tool Company provided this company will sell a bond issue in order to raise the necessary funds. The contract for building may be placed in the hands of the trust company to be delivered to the E-Z Tool Company when it completes the agreement to sell the necessary bonds. The legal term *in escrow* is used for such papers while they are in the hands of the trust company.

Other services of trust companies include writing and mailing dividend checks, serving as the trustee for employee profit-sharing funds, investing funds contributed for pensions, and exchanging corporation securities under a refinancing program.

3 / Investment companies. *Investment companies* sell shares to individual investors and use the capital raised in this manner to purchase securities in other companies. Investment companies are also called *investment trusts* and, even more popularly, *mutual funds*. The holdings, called the *portfolio*, of some investment companies are diversified among bonds, preferred stocks, and common stocks; while others buy only common stocks in one industry, such as chemicals or electronics. In any event, investment companies provide the individual with limited funds the opportunity to own, indirectly, an interest in many companies.

Investment companies, by channeling the savings of thousands of individuals into the security markets, have become an important factor in the long-term capital field. One of the largest of the more than four hundred companies is the Massachusetts Investors Trust with assets of over $1 billion in common stocks. Other investment companies, such as the Eaton and Howard Balanced Fund, hold bonds and preferred stocks as well as common stocks.

Investment companies are regulated under the provisions of the Wagner-Lea Act, a law passed by Congress in 1940 and known officially as the Investment Company Act. Each company must register with the Securities and Exchange Commission, as must investment counselors and advisory services under the Investment Advisers Act, a companion piece of legislation. No investment trust can be organized with a capital of less than $100,000, the management must be selected by the shareholders, funds cannot be invested in other investment trusts or affiliated companies, and the types of securities that the investment trust can issue are subject to restrictions.

4 / Insurance companies. Organizations that insure individuals and businesses against many types of risks are known as *insurance companies*. They are an important source of long-term capital for corporations that choose to issue bonds. In recent years they have become large holders of mortgages on business and residential properties. The cash received by insurance companies from premiums paid by policyholders normally exceeds the payments on claims and other business expenditures, which leaves a balance to invest. Life insurance companies are the largest holders of industrial and government bonds.

The types of securities that insurance companies can purchase are regulated by the several states. Companies must secure a license to sell in the state, and they are subject to an annual audit by the state commissioner or superintendent of insurance. Other regulatory features concern rates, policy forms, and methods of settling claims. Although most insurance is sold in interstate commerce, the McCarran Act, passed by Congress in 1945, allows the states to supervise the activities of companies that do business within their borders.

'5 / **Savings and loan associations.** *Savings and loan associations,* or *building and loan associations* as they are known in some areas, are formed for two major purposes: (a) to loan money for the purchase of homes and business properties and (b) to enable individuals to invest funds with comparative safety at yields usually higher than available in savings accounts with banks. Their form of organization and ownership was described in Chapter 5. A first mortgage on property is almost universally required as security for a loan, and the interest rate charged on the unpaid balance is usually about 6 percent. Although savings and loan associations specialize in making mortgage loans on residences, included in the more than $90 billion of credit extended are loans on office buildings, apartment houses, and other structures used for business purposes.

Membership in the Federal Deposit Savings and Loan Association is required for federally chartered associations and is available to those holding state charters. This federal agency, which was created in 1934, insures accounts in eligible savings and loan associations up to $15,000. Savings and loan associations may also join the Federal Home Loan Bank System, a federal agency organized for the purpose of extending credit to its member mortgage-lending institutions.

6 / **Savings banks.** Except in states that permit mutual savings banks, the common situation is to find a savings department in a commercial bank. *Savings banks* accept deposits from savers on which an announced rate of interest is paid. These funds are then invested in mortgages, bonds, and other securities permitted by law. Interest earned on these investments provides earnings that make possible the payment of interest on savings accounts. Many individuals find a savings account a convenient way of accumulating funds. Christmas savings clubs are featured by many savings banks and departments of commercial banks.

Membership in the Federal Deposit Insurance Corporation is available to savings banks as well as commercial banks. This organization, created in 1933 by the federal government, insures deposits up to $15,000 in any one bank in any one name. An individual can obtain insurance on all of his savings by patronizing more than one savings bank or department.

PROFESSIONAL ASSOCIATION IN FINANCE

Organized in 1940, the American Finance Association's membership includes professors in universities, financial economists, bankers, treasurers, analysts, and other individuals interested in financial problems. It publishes a quarterly magazine, the *Journal of Finance,* which is available to students at a special rate. Approved finance or economics clubs at universities may obtain a charter of affiliation. A national convention is held each year in late December.

BUSINESS TERMS

(a) assets (389), capital (389)

(b) fixed assets (389), fixed capital (389), current assets (389), circulating capital (389)

(c) long-term financing (390); intermediate credit (390)

(d) equity capital (390), debt capital (390)

(e) bond (392), trustee (392), indenture (392)

(f) baby bond (392), accumulation bond (393), fully registered bond (393), coupon bond (393), partial registration (393)

(g) real estate mortgage bond (395), after-acquired clause (395), closed-end issue (395), open-end issue (395)

(h) chattel mortgage bond (395), equipment trust certificate (395)

(i) collateral trust bond (395), debenture bond (395)

(j) serial bond (396), sinking-fund bonds (396), refunding (bond issue) (396)

(k) call price (396), callable or redeemable bond (396), convertible bond (397)

(l) bond premium (397), bond discount (397)

(m) preferred stock (397); cumulative preferred stock (398), noncumulative preferred stock (398), participating preferred stock (399), nonparticipating preferred stock (399)

(n) pass the dividend (398)

(o) par value (400), no-par stock (400)

(p) common stock (401)

(q) investment banking companies (402); spread (403)

(r) brokerage firm (404)

(s) unlisted securities (404), over-the-counter market (404)

(t) bid price (404), asked price (404)

(u) trust company (404); prudent-man rule (405), common trust fund (405)

(v) registrar (405), transfer agent (405), in escrow (405)

(w) investment company or investment trust (406), mutual funds (406), portfolio (406) holdings

(x) insurance company (406)

(y) savings and loan association or building and loan association (407), savings bank (407)

QUESTIONS FOR DISCUSSION AND ANALYSIS

1. Why has the federal government been concerned with the long-term financing problems of unincorporated businesses?
2. Would it always be desirable to finance the fixed capital needs of a firm with either all or a high proportion of equity capital?
3. Why should a trustee be needed for a bond issue but not for issues of preferred and common stocks?
4. Considering the success the federal government has had with its series "E" bonds, why have private corporations not sold accumulation bonds?
5. Assuming other factors equal, what provisions in a bond issue would make it most attractive to prospective purchasers?
6. What features that might be included in a preferred stock issue would make it most attractive to prospective investors?
7. Why are common stocks the most popular security purchased by the over twenty million institutional and individual investors in this country?
8. Considering that financial institutions deal primarily with a single commodity, why should not a single institution be prepared to handle all of the monetary needs of a business firm?
9. Why should the federal government create and operate agencies to insure accounts in savings and loan associations and in savings banks?
10. If a real estate firm wished to borrow money to build an apartment house, what financial institutions might be interested in loaning the necessary funds, and what factors would influence the firm in making its selection?

PROBLEMS AND SHORT CASES

1. The Reynolds–Standard Steel Corp. has outstanding a $50,000,000 issue of 6 percent first-mortgage bonds that were sold 20 years ago and which mature in 20 years from today. The bonds are callable at 104 ($1,040 for each $1,000 bond). At this time it appears that a 20-year refunding issue can be sold at par ($1,000 for each $1,000 bond) at an interest rate of 5½ percent.

    Compute the amount of saving over the remaining life of the bond issue if the Reynolds–Standard Steel Corp. refinances its debt capital on the above basis. The interest payment due at the end of the twentieth year has just been paid.

2. The capital structure of the Janver Manufacturing Co. consists of the following:

    Preferred stock—100,000 shares, par value $100 per share,
    6%, cumulative, nonparticipating.

    Common stock—500,000 shares, no-par.

    Through 1966 dividends were paid on both classes of stock, but net profits after taxes were only $310,000 in 1967 and the board of directors passed the dividends. In 1968 the profits increased to $440,000 and the board declared a dividend of $4 a share on the preferred stock. In 1969 profits increased sharply to $1,800,000 and the board of directors wishes to resume dividend payments on the common stock.

Show calculations to determine the maximum per share dollar distribution available to the common stockholders in 1969, assuming distribution of all profits earned in 1967, 1968, and 1969.

3. A group of five businessmen have decided to form a corporation to be called Amusement Enterprises, Inc. Living in a community that has had very limited recreational facilities, these men came to the conclusion that the population of the area was more than adequate to support an amusement park. They have taken an option on 160 acres of land located a half mile from the city limits and only a quarter of a mile from an exit on an interstate highway.

Their plans for the area include a large swimming pool, a dance hall, a roller coaster and other rides, concession stands, and a midget car racetrack. The total cost of the entire project, including land, access roads, and parking lot, has been carefully estimated at $9,800,000. The promoters feel that they should raise $10,000,000 in order to proceed with construction.

Publicity about the project, which has been widespread due to an article in a financial paper, has aroused considerable interest on the part of various financial institutions and investors. It would appear that there would be no difficulty in marketing mortgage bonds, preferred stock, and common stock. Each of the five incorporators is in a position to invest $300,000 of his own money in the corporation.

On the basis of the information given, present a financial plan for Amusement Enterprises, Inc. and indicate the financial institution or institutions you would use. Justify the type, amount, and terms of each security selected and the institution or institutions selected to assist you in selling these securities.

SUGGESTED READINGS

Cohen, J. B., and S. M. Robbins. *The Financial Manager: Basic Aspects of Financial Administration.* New York: Harper & Row, 1966. Part IV.

Dauten, C. A., and M. Welshans. *Principles of Finance,* Second Edition. Cincinnati: South-Western Publishing Company, 1964. Part 2.

Husband, W. H., and J. C. Dockeray. *Modern Corporate Finance,* Sixth Edition. Homewood, Illinois: Richard D. Irwin, Inc., 1966. Part II.

Johnson, R. W. *Financial Management,* Third Edition. Boston: Allyn and Bacon, Inc., 1966. Part V.

Prather, C. L. *Financing Business Firms,* Third Edition. Homewood, Illinois: Richard D. Irwin, Inc., 1966. Part V.

Weston, J. F., and E. F. Brigham. *Managerial Finance,* Revised Edition. New York: Holt, Rinehart, and Winston, Inc., 1966. Part V.

Magazines: *Journal of Finance, Commercial and Financial Chronicle.*

Vanilla Fudge

Chapter 19

Circulating capital, or current assets, as defined in the previous chapter, consists of cash and those assets that will be converted into cash through the usual operations of a business within a year. The funds necessary to acquire a minimum supply of circulating capital should come from the same sources as for fixed capital requirements. Most firms, for example, maintain at least a modest balance in their checking account and an inventory of goods on hand to sell. Over and above these basic needs, however, practically every business unit secures some of its circulating capital from short-term financing sources.

The area of *short-term financing* consists of obligations, or debts as they are usually called, that have a maturity date of less than one year. Typical debts include amounts owed to suppliers of goods purchased from them on credit terms, to banks and other financial institutions that have made short-term loans to the firm, and other types of payables. These are called *current liabilities*. The difference between the total current assets and the total current liabilities is called *working capital*. This amount represents the total circulating capital that has been obtained from long-term financing sources.

The management of working capital, a task usually assigned to the treasurer or controller, is extremely important to the success of a firm. It is inefficient to have too much cash on hand, but it is also hazardous not to have enough to pay wages, salaries, and outstanding bills when they are due. Too large an inventory is expensive, but not having enough can lose production time or sales. Money borrowed, except on trade credit terms, involves an interest cost. The job of management is to have the right amount and types of current assets on hand at all times and to provide these at the least possible cost, which generally involves the use of short-term debt.

411

■ Advantages of Short-Term Financing

The use of short-term financing is advantageous to a firm for several reasons: (1) seasonal needs can be met more efficiently, (2) acquiring a good credit reputation may prove helpful, (3) growth can be financed without constant resort to long-term sources, and (4) the total cost of financing may well be less.

1 / Seasonal needs. The sales made by many businesses are uneven over the months of the year. Department stores, for example, have peak sales between Thanksgiving and Christmas. Merchandise to be sold during this period is purchased no later than September or October, and the suppliers expect to be paid long before the customers buy the goods. By borrowing for 60 or 90 days, the firm is able to pay promptly, often taking advantage of cash discounts offered. By the close of the year the receipts from sales have usually provided the cash necessary to repay the loan.

2 / Credit rating. Most business concerns buy the equipment, supplies, and goods needed by ordering from a supplier with the intent of paying after delivery has been made. If bills are met promptly, the firm acquires a good credit rating. Then, if an emergency arises in the future that precludes prompt payment, the supplier will usually be willing to carry the customer beyond a due date if past experience has been favorable.

3 / Growth requirements. Although starting a business or acquiring an existing firm normally creates a demand for capital at a specific date, growth is usually gradual. Since resort to long-term financing is not done on a day-by-day basis, financing a steady increase in size is accomplished more efficiently by use of short-term financing. As loans mount in total, management will decide at some point to secure debt or equity capital on a long-term basis to repay the short-term obligations.

4 / Lower cost. To the extent that current assets in use are represented by amounts owed to suppliers, there is no cost to this portion of the total capital. If funds have been borrowed, the rate may well be higher than could be secured on a long-term commitment, but the time factor reduces the cost. If funds are needed for only 60 days in a year, it is less expensive to borrow for this length of time even at a higher rate than to pay a lower rate of interest for an entire year on a long-term obligation or to pay dividends on more shares of stock.

SHORT-TERM OBLIGATIONS

In order to meet short-term financing needs, business firms assume one or more of several types of obligations. These debts may be owed to trade creditors or to institutional and individual lenders. Practically all businesses, large and small, make regular use of at least one and, frequently, more than one of these sources of short-term funds. It would be unusual to find a firm that does not owe a supplier for goods bought on credit terms, and borrowing from a commercial bank on one or more occasions during a year is a common business practice.

■ Types of Short-Term Obligations

Short-term obligations may take several forms with open-book accounts and notes payable in favor of a commercial bank being by far the most common. An examination of the various types of these obligations will clarify the distinctions among them and indicate their appropriate uses.

1. Open-book accounts
2. Notes payable *most common*
3. Commercial drafts
4. Bank acceptances
5. Commercial paper

1 / Open-book accounts. When a manufacturer, wholesaler, or retailer buys materials, equipment, supplies, and merchandise from a supplier with the implied obligation to pay the invoice at a later date, an *open-book account* is entered on the books of both companies involved. Somewhere between 85 and 90 percent of all business transactions in the United States involving the sale and purchase of goods use an open-book account. Although not usually thought of as a loan, the net effect is that the seller is financing the buyer for the period of time between the receipt of the goods and the payment of the bill rendered. Between retailers and consumers the term *charge accounts* replaces open-book accounts.

The smooth flow of business transactions in this country could not be maintained without the use of open-book accounts. The manufacturer buys raw materials on credit terms, converts them into finished goods, and sells them to wholesalers on open account. The wholesaler sells the merchandise to retailers without requiring immediate payment, and the retailer may do likewise in his sale to the consumer. When consumers pay for their purchases, the cash received by the retailer permits him to pay the wholesaler who, in turn, can pay the manufacturer. Although the manufacturer, wholesaler, and retailer may have paid for the specific goods sold the ultimate consumer from their supplies of permanent working capital, the receipt of cash all along the line permits payments for goods still in the distribution channels.

(a) LENGTH OF CREDIT TERMS. Because of the added amount of time needed by those farther back in the flow of goods from maker to user, credit terms granted to manufacturers are usually longer than those extended to the wholesaler, and so on to the retailer and consumer. For example, raw materials may be sold to the manufacturers on credit terms of 90 days, the manufacturer may extend 60 days credit to the wholesaler, the wholesaler may allow the retailer 30 days, and the retailer expects his regular charge accounts to be paid once a month, which means credit from 1 to 30 days. Actually, credit terms vary by industries and by different suppliers. Granting more liberal credit terms may be one of the elements of competition.

Frequently the maximum length of the credit terms is not used because the seller allows the purchaser a cash discount. As described in Chapter 9, if an invoice carries the terms 2/10, net 30, the buyer can deduct 2 percent if he pays within 10 days after the date of the invoice. Although the payment of an open-book account within a cash-discount period 'shortens the duration of the use of this source of short-term financing, the saving is so substantial that many firms have a policy of taking advantage of every cash discount offered.

Actually, if the terms of an invoice dated, for example, June 15, are 2/10, net 30, the debtor firm has the option of paying the invoice price less 2 percent on or before June 25 or of waiting 20 more days to pay the full sum. This means that 2 percent is earned for the 20-day interval, which amounts to 36 percent a year as shown below:

$$
\begin{array}{rl}
20 \text{ days } / \quad 360 & \text{interest days in a year} \\
\overline{\quad 18} & \text{intervals of 20 days in an} \\
& \text{interest year} \\
\times \quad 2\% & \text{savings for each 20 days} \\
\overline{\quad 36\%} & \text{annual interest earned}
\end{array}
$$

Each different cash-discount allowance changes the interest-earned rate; but regardless of the rate of cash discount, money can usually be borrowed at a lower cost. Firms that receive the cash earlier may also be able to take advantage of cash discounts, which is one of the reasons they can afford to offer such generous terms.

(b) CREDIT INFORMATION. Most established businesses have a proven reputation for prompt payment of their accounts, and sellers are willing to ship goods to them on an open-book account basis. New firms

[handwritten in top margin: maker - pays note / payee - note is drawn in favor of this individ.]

do not have this advantage and, in some instances, older firms are not acquainted with the credit reputations of new customers. In these circumstances the firms wishing to secure the credit usually furnish the names of their banks and invite correspondence to verify the financial responsibility of the organization. In order to facilitate this type of credit investigation, the name of the bank may appear on the letterhead of the newly organized or unknown firm.

There are also credit-rating agencies to whom a supplier can turn in order to check on the desirability of shipping goods on open account. Of these, Dun & Bradstreet, Inc. is outstanding. This is a nationwide mercantile credit-rating agency that lists thousands of large and small business organizations in its publications. Subscribers to its *Reference Book* can determine the credit standing of any one of approximately three million prospective customers on a moment's notice. At the retail level credit-rating agencies are available in most large cities. The retailers in a community, particularly the large department stores, support an organization that maintains records on the thousands of individuals who have charge accounts at member stores.

2 / Notes payable. Next to the use of open-book accounts as a source of short-term debt capital is the use of notes that are payable to commercial banks or to individuals or firms. A *promissory note*, which is a note payable on the part of the issuing party, is a written instrument in which the maker promises to pay to the party named a definite sum of money at a determinable future date. The *maker* is the signer of the note and eventually becomes the one who pays the note. The bank or individual or company in whose favor the note is drawn is the *payee*. Most promissory notes bear interest at a rate that is stated on the face of the instrument. As used in short-term financing, most notes have a maturity date of from one to six months.

$900 00/100   ALLENTOWN, PA. *October 15*, 19____

Six months ____ after date ____ *I* ____ promise to pay to

the order of *Merchants National Bank*

At the **MERCHANTS NATIONAL BANK** of Allentown, Pa.

Nine hundred and no/100 _____ dollars

and interest at *5* %

No. *27*   Due *April 15,* ____   *John C. Parker*

Promissory Note

The promissory note in the illustration carries the words "pay to the order of" before the name of the payee. Either this phrase or the words "or bearer" following the name of the payee make it possible for that individual or firm to pass the note on to another party by signing on the reverse side of the instrument. This signature is known as an *indorsement*, and the ability to pass the note from hand to hand qualifies it as a *negotiable instrument*. Most notes are designed to be negotiable, although banks usually hold them until maturity.

If a note is given by the buyer to a seller for merchandise or equipment purchased, the interest and the face value of the note are both due at maturity. In this case the note may be a substitute for an open-book account. The advantages to the payee of the note are that he has a written promise to pay on the part of the maker of the note, the amount involved and the time of payment are clearly stated, and he may receive interest in addition to the principal. Furthermore, if he so desires, he can raise cash on the note by discounting it at his bank. This procedure, however, merely changes the nature of his current assets; it does not increase total working capital.

(a) BUSINESS LOANS FROM THE BANK. If a firm wishes to borrow $25,000 from a bank for 90 days or 3 months, it will sign a note payable to the bank for this amount and insert the rate of interest the bank agrees to charge. Assuming that this rate was 6 percent, the total cost of borrowing $25,000 for one fourth of a year would be $375. The bank may subtract this amount from the face of the note, in which case the proceeds would be $24,625 instead of $25,000. Interest deducted in advance by a bank is known as *bank discount*.

(b) DISCOUNTING CUSTOMERS' NOTES. If a business has received a note from a customer and does not wish to wait until maturity to receive the cash, it can discount the note at its bank by indorsing it. The bank now has two sources of repayment as this *double-name paper* becomes an obligation of the indorser as well as of the maker. Discounting this kind of paper involves a more complicated calculation than the procedure outlined when a borrower signs his own note at a bank. It is necessary to (1) compute the interest on the note, (2) add this interest to the principal to arrive at the full maturity value, (3) find the maturity date, (4) determine the number of days in the discount period, (5) calculate the interest for this discount period on the maturity value at the discount rate, and (6) subtract this discount from the maturity value to arrive at the proceeds.

If the Reliable Furniture Company has given the Redwood Manufacturing Corporation a $900, 6 percent, 2-month note on August 1 and the Redwood Manufacturing Corporation discounts it at its bank on August 14 at 7 percent, the computation to determine the amount of the proceeds is as follows:

(1) $900 $\times$ $\frac{2}{12}$ $\times$ $\frac{6}{100}$ = $9.

(2) $900 + $9 = $909.

(3) Two months after August 1 is October 1.

(4) August 14 to October 1 = 48 days.

(5) $909 $\times$ $\frac{48}{360}$ $\times$ $\frac{7}{100}$ = $8.48.

(6) $909 — $8.48 = $900.52.

(c) INSTALLMENT PURCHASES OF EQUIPMENT. Notes are also used in connection with purchases of machinery and equipment on an installment basis. Although the bulk of installment buying is done by consumers, businesses may purchase such items as delivery trucks, drill presses, and other forms of heavy machinery on an installment basis. This involves a down payment and the signing of a series of notes due each month for the entire credit period, which may stretch over as much time as three years. The seller may hold the notes or, if he wishes, sell them to a finance company interested in purchasing obligations of this type. To the extent that the notes mature in more than one year, the financing enters the intermediate rather than short-term credit area.

3 / Commercial drafts. A *commercial draft* is a credit instrument not unlike a promissory note except that it comes into being upon the initiative of the person who is to receive the money. A *drawer*, usually the business firm that originates the draft, sends it to a *drawee*, the person who is obligated to the drawer, or to his bank. The drawee, if he accepts the draft, writes his name across the face of the instrument. Commercial drafts may be *time drafts*, in which case the drawer will indicate the length of time on the face of the draft, or they may be *sight drafts*. In the latter event the drawee pays upon presentation of the draft. A time draft that arises in connection with a shipment of merchandise is known as a *trade acceptance*.

Commercial drafts are sometimes used to attempt to collect an overdue open-book account. The firm to whom the money is owed draws on the delinquent debtor with the hope that the draft will be accepted. More frequently commercial drafts arise in connection with sales to businesses that do not have an established or satisfactory credit rating. When a manufacturer or wholesaler receives an order from an unknown firm, an attempt is made to determine the financial responsibility of the would-be customer. If the firm is not listed in Dun & Bradstreet, a request can be made for a special report from this organization or from any one of several other credit reporting services. If the investigation indicates a doubtful credit standing, a sale can be made by use of a commercial draft.

The procedure is to make a shipment by freight on a cash-on-delivery basis, which involves the use of a sight draft. The shipper secures a receipt called an *order bill of lading* from the railroad company when the goods are delivered for shipment. When this document is used, the railroad agent at the destination cannot release the goods until the order bill of lading is presented. The shipper attaches a sight draft to the order bill of lading and mails both papers to the bank of the purchaser of the goods. In order to secure delivery of the shipment, the purchaser must accept the sight draft by paying it. The order bill of lading is then given to him, and he can secure the goods from the railroad company.

4 / Bank acceptances. *Bank acceptances* provide a method of borrowing from a bank that has the advantage of securing only those funds actually needed and at the time of need. For example, the Foss Manufacturing Company wishes to purchase some raw materials and, before ordering, arranges with its bank to accept drafts drawn against the bank for the goods to be purchased. The bank issues statements to the effect that it will accept the drafts, which are known as *letters of credit*. The Foss Manufacturing Company then sends the letters of credit to the producers of the raw materials with instructions to send the bills of lading to the bank and to draw on the bank for the purchase price.

When the materials arrive, the bank accepts the drafts and, in return for the bills of lading, the purchasing company signs a note in favor of the bank and also a financing statement. A *financing statement*, as prescribed by the Uniform Commercial Code, describes the property that is pledged as security for a loan. By filing the financing statement with the secretary of state or at a county courthouse, or at both locations, other creditors are placed on notice that although a firm has title to and possession of certain assets, there is a lien against them in favor of the lending company.

In the case of the Foss Manufacturing Company, it is expected that the raw materials will be converted into finished goods but that, before they are sold, the Company will pay the note owed to the bank. If it is unable to do so, other raw materials may be substituted for those originally pledged or, if the bank prefers, it has the right to sell the finished goods to satisfy its claims.

Although this procedure may appear very complicated, in actual operation the use of bank acceptances is relatively simple. They can be used when the credit standing of the buyer is unknown to the seller, which is especially true in international-trade transactions. By substituting the unquestioned ability of a bank to pay the draft for a company with only local credit standing, a business transaction is completed that otherwise might not have been consummated.

5 / Commercial paper. In the financial world, *commercial paper* refers to unsecured promissory notes that well-known corporations sell on the open market. They are issued in large units, such as $2,500 up to $10,000, amounting in the aggregate to a substantial sum, run for from two to six months, and are sold to commercial paper houses who, in turn, sell them to other financial institutions. To those who can make use of this method of securing short-term funds, the advantages of commercial paper are that money can be borrowed at a lower rate of interest than would be charged by a bank, and the borrower can secure more funds than most banks would be willing or able to lend.

■ Security for Short-Term Loans

The more widely used sources of short-term funds rarely involve providing any type of security for the loan. An open-book account, almost by definition, is an implied promise to pay in accordance with the credit terms. Bank loans for a month or two are normally unsecured. In both instances the ability of the firm to repay the amount borrowed and its reputation for prompt settlement were considered when credit was extended. The lender rightly assumes that the past performance of the borrower will be continued in the immediate future.

When a sole proprietorship, or any individual, is granted a bank loan solely on his own signature, it is known as a *character loan*. In some instances, because there may be some doubt about the ability of the individual to repay the loan either from business income or his personal assets, the bank may ask the would-be borrower to secure a third party, in whom it has confidence, to sign the note. If this individual signs on the face of the note along with the maker, he is known as a *comaker* or *cosigner*. If he indorses the note on the back, he is known as an *accommodation indorser*. The only difference between the two types of guarantee is that cosigners are equally liable along with the maker for the note whereas an accommodation indorser is not required to pay until after the maker has defaulted on his obligation.

In some instances firms engaged in short-term financing are either required to pledge assets as security for the loan or do so because they may then benefit from a lower interest cost. The common types of assets that are used in this manner are:

1. Accounts receivable
2. Inventories
3. Movable property
4. Fixed assets

1 / Accounts receivable. Commercial banks, commercial finance companies, and factors [1] will loan short-term funds to a business with the pledge of open-book accounts owed to the firm (called accounts receivable) as security for the loan. The usual procedure involves the allocation of all or a selected number of the accounts to the lending agency and receiving in return a loan of from 75 to 80 percent of their total value. The borrower promises to forward all cash received from these customers until such time as the loan plus interest has been repaid.

Under the circumstances outlined, the debtor of the borrowing firm is not aware that his account has been pledged as security for a loan. This is known as a *nonnotification plan* and is almost universally followed when such a loan is obtained from a commercial bank or commercial finance company. Because some business concerns borrow on their accounts receivable only as a last resort, there is an implied element of financial weakness in a firm that must secure short-term funds by this method. Such knowledge on the part of the customer could prove detrimental to future business relationships, although as such loans become more and more frequent, this objection may well disappear from the current business scene.

Another method of borrowing using accounts receivable as security is to sell the accounts, which is the method used when a factoring company is involved. This procedure requires that the debtor be informed of the sale so that payments on account will be made to the new owner of the receivables. This is known as a *notification plan*; and where trade custom has made it a common practice, the implication of financial weakness is virtually eliminated. It has long been customary in the textile field to sell accounts and, in recent years, this custom has been spreading to such industries as furniture, paper, furs, and a few others.

2 / Inventories. There are two common methods of borrowing by using goods owned as security for a loan. One involves loss of physical

[1] See page 428.

movable property - most widely used forms

possession and use of the raw materials or merchandise pledged while the other permits possession and processing of the security.

When goods are stored in a warehouse owned by an independent warehousing company, known as a *bonded public warehouse*, the owner of the goods receives a *warehouse receipt*. Usually such receipts specify that the goods will be released to the person who rented the space, or to his order or the bearer, upon payment of the storage charges. This wording makes warehouse receipts negotiable and allows firms to pledge the goods owned as collateral for a loan, which is usually secured from a commercial bank. For example, the Crescent Candy Company purchases one hundred tons of sugar, which is sold on terms of 2/10, net 30. The shipment arrives and is stored in a bonded public warehouse. The warehouse receipt is indorsed in favor of the firm's bank, thus serving as collateral for a promissory note. The cash received from the bank allows the candy company to pay the invoice within the discount period. When the note is due, the borrower will have to pay it or sacrifice the right to have the warehouse receipt returned. In the latter event the bank will sell the sugar to other users in order to avoid loss on the defaulted note.

In some instances the physical possession of and the ability to convert inventories into salable merchandise are essential to the firm's operations. This situation gives rise to the use of a financing statement as described in the discussion of bank acceptances.

"LAY LADY LAY" - B.D.

3 / Movable property. The most widely used form of security for short-term loans is movable property such as automobiles and trucks, equipment, supplies, and even livestock, if ownership of animals is involved in the business. Actually, the most extensive use of this type of security for a loan results from financing consumer purchases of durable goods on an installment basis. Whereas businesses may also purchase cars and trucks, machinery, and other similar items with payments scheduled on a monthly basis, business loans made with movable property used as security are sometimes repayable at a single maturity date.

The procedure used for obtaining a loan secured by movable property involves signing a note, which specifies the terms of repayment, and also a financing statement of the type described on page 418. The seller of the goods pledged can repossess the article or articles if payments are not made in accordance with the terms of the loan. For example, the Acme Auto Sales Company sells a delivery truck to Chris Jensen, who operates a grocery store. Mr. Jensen makes a down payment of $600 on the $4,200 purchase price and signs a note and financing statement agreeing to pay $200 a month for the next eighteen months. In case these payments are not made as scheduled, the Acme Auto Sales Company can repossess the truck.

An interesting exception to the need for filing a financing statement occurs in the case of automobiles, trucks, mobile homes, and other items for which a certificate of title is issued. Since the owner cannot sell the pledged property without delivering this certificate, the lending agency protects itself by retaining possession of it until the loan is paid.

Prior to the adoption of the Uniform Commercial Code, the credit sale of movable property frequently involved the use of a chattel mortgage or a conditional bill of sale. When a *chattel mortgage* was used, title passed to the purchaser immediately, but the seller retained a lien on the movable property until payment was made in full in a manner comparable to the use of a financing statement. If a *conditional bill of sale* was used, title remained with the seller until the buyer completed his payments. These methods of providing security for short-term loans are still legal if other conditions of a secured transaction as defined in the Code are satisfied.

4 / Fixed assets. While it is true that fixed assets are commonly used as security for long-term loans, some may be appropriate for short-term financing. If the firm owns securities such as government bonds or bonds and stocks of other companies, these may be turned over to a bank as security for a loan. If the need for funds is of short duration, it might be preferable to borrow against assets of this type rather than to sell them in order to raise the cash needed. Another asset that can be used as collateral is the cash surrender value of life insurance policies that may be carried on the lives of partners or executives of a company. A loan can be secured from the insurance company, or a bank would be willing to accept an assignment of the cash value as security for a promissory note. Banks will frequently make such loans at a lower rate of interest since there is no chance of loss as long as the cash value of the policies exceeds the amount of the loan and interest.

Cost of Short-Term Financing

Sound financial management dictates that short-term funds should be secured at the lowest possible cost. The least expensive method of borrowing is the open-book account. Whereas some retailers add an interest charge of 1 percent a month on unpaid monthly balances on customer charge accounts, interest on open-book accounts, even when overdue, is a rarity. On interest-bearing obligations, rates vary from approximately 5 to 7 percent per annum, with lower charges applying to commercial paper and to loans involving little or no risk to the lender.

(handwritten margin notes: commercial bank - direct value to every business unit. *(most imp. in short-term financing)* Sales finance co. imp. only to certain types of firms 423)*

In computing costs, business firms as well as consumers need to be aware of the difference between nominal and effective rates of interest. The *nominal rate of interest* is the one stated on the instrument used in connection with the loan, while the *effective rate of interest* is the true interest cost. Bank discount and the not uncommon requirement that a business obtaining a loan from a commercial bank must maintain a checking account balance equivalent to, for example, 20 percent of the loan, are examples of the higher cost of the effective rate since the interest is based on a larger total than usable funds. More commonly, the effective rate on loans repayable on an installment basis, e.g., most automobile financing, is almost double the nominal rate due to calculating interest on the full amount of the loan for the entire borrowing period despite the gradual reduction in the size of the loan.

The lack of understanding on the part of the public between nominal and effective rates of interest has become a matter of concern to federal legislators. "Truth in lending" bills have been introduced in the Congress that would require an accurate statement of effective rates regardless of the announced nominal rate. Despite opposition from some financial institutions, there seems to be a growing sentiment in favor of passing federal legislation requiring disclosure of the true cost of borrowing.

■ Consumer Finance

The availability and use by customers of various types of consumer finance have a direct bearing on the short-term financing needs of a business. Consequently, it is important that the businessman have an understanding of the problems, costs, and effects on his business if he elects to market his goods or services on other than a cash basis. For example, firms selling automobiles, furniture, kitchen appliances, and other durable goods on an installment basis almost universally sell the notes received from the buyers to a bank or sales finance company for cash, which reduces their need for short-term funds from other sources.

FINANCIAL INSTITUTIONS—SHORT-TERM CAPITAL

Several financial institutions assist businesses either directly or indirectly with their short-term capital problems. One of these, the commercial bank, is of direct value to practically every business unit while others, such as a sales finance company, are important to only certain types of firms. Still other institutions are of indirect value to businesses in that they provide loans to individuals who may then be able to pay their business debts. Since the commercial bank is the most important financial commercial bank — best known, financial instit.

institution in the short-term capital field, its operations will be examined in some detail.

■ Commercial Banks

A *commercial bank* is a financial institution that accepts deposits against which checks are drawn, loans money, and renders several other services. It is the best known of all financial institutions and the one with which businesses have the most frequent and recurring contacts. The relations between a banker and the owners and managers of businesses are usually close and also helpful and friendly. The services a commercial bank renders to businesses can be summarized as follows:

1. Checking accounts
2. Bank drafts and checks
3. Short-term loans
4. Foreign exchange
5. Other functions

1 / Checking accounts. From the viewpoint of the business community, the chief function of a commercial bank is to accept money for deposit and to pay out these funds on order of the depositor by means of checks. A *check* is a negotiable instrument signed by the bank customer directing that the amount of money specified be paid by the bank to the payee or his order. With the exception of cash sales at the retail level, checks are used for the settlement of practically all business transactions.

After a check has been written but before it has been cleared by the bank on which it was drawn, it is possible to *stop payment* on the check by notifying the bank. This is not done unless a good reason for the procedure exists, such as discovering that a person obtained the payment under false pretenses. Payment cannot be stopped on certified checks, however, because they represent a liability of the bank. A *certified check* is one that a bank charges against the proper account at the same time that the check is stamped as "certified."

Many banks make a service charge for maintaining checking accounts if the business allows its daily balances to fall below a minimum figure adequate to compensate for the cost of handling its volume of deposits and checks. A charge is made for each deposit or check with an off-setting credit of interest on the lowest balance shown during a month. For personal accounts the same plan is followed, or the individual may purchase a book of 20 checks for $2 or more.

2 / Bank drafts, cashier's checks, and traveler's checks. If payment is to be made by check to a business located some distance away, this business might be reluctant about accepting a check from a small unknown firm. In order to avoid delays that might otherwise occur, the depositor can give his bank a check for the amount, and the bank will write a *bank draft*. This draft is really a check of the bank drawn on another larger bank. This is possible because the bank has on deposit certain amounts with the other bank. The big city bank is known as the *correspondent bank* in relation to the local institution.

For local transactions, usually confined to large cities, the bank may provide the depositor with a *cashier's check*, which differs from a bank draft in that it is drawn on the bank that issues it instead of a correspondent bank.

As a substitute for cashier's checks, some banks provide personal money orders. These are drawn on the bank issuing them; but, unlike cashier's checks, the user has a carbon copy indicating the date, amount, and the name of the debtor to whom he mails or delivers the money order.

When an officer or salesman takes a business trip and does not wish to carry large sums of money, *traveler's checks* may provide the most satisfactory solution to this problem. These are retailed to customers by most banks, who purchase them from The American Express Company or from a few other suppliers, notably the National City Bank of New York and the Bank of America in California. Traveler's checks are issued in convenient denominations, such as $10, $20, and larger figures. At the time of purchase, the user signs his name to each check and must sign again when the check is cashed. This identification through comparison of signatures permits traveler's checks to be cashed in most parts of the world.

3 / Short-term loans. Commercial banks are a common source of short-term funds for businesses. Many firms negotiate loans one or more times each year. As noted previously in this chapter, the notes may be secured or unsecured, may or may not be discounted, and normally are repaid in one lump sum at their maturity. Outstanding commercial loans in excess of $60 billion provide some idea of the importance of commercial banks in the short-term capital field.

Some business firms, anticipating that they may need to borrow at some indefinite future time, submit detailed information to their banks covering such items as financial statements, names of officers and directors, and certain details about their operations. If an investigation of these facts seems to warrant making a loan, the firm will be notified that the bank has granted a *line of credit* for a specified amount such as $25,000 or $500,000. The obvious advantage in having established a line of credit is the advance knowledge of how much can be borrowed quickly at any time the need arises.

4 / Foreign exchange. If a firm engages in foreign business, it faces the problem of making payments in foreign currencies or receiving payments involving, for example, pounds sterling in place of dollars. The bank is willing to handle the conversion of United States dollars into the proper amount of foreign currency, or of foreign currency into United States dollars.

5 / Other functions of commercial banks. In addition to the functions described above, commercial banks maintain savings departments; rent safe deposit boxes for the storing of valuable business papers; render business and investment advice; collect notes, drafts, and bond coupons; serve as a source of credit information; and may even assist in preparing payroll envelopes for employees. In recent years several banks have installed electronic data computing equipment that, for an hourly fee, is available for use by their customers.

■ **Regulation of Commercial Banks**

Commercial banks are regulated by the federal government or by the state, depending, in part, on whether they are national or state banks. Actually, the federal government plays the more important part because many state banks as well as all national banks belong to the Federal Reserve System and to the Federal Deposit Insurance Corporation and must follow procedures prescribed by these agencies. Other regulations are administered by the comptroller of the currency for national banks and by state bank examiners for state banks.

Of primary importance to depositors is the fact that all banks are examined periodically by federal or state auditors who make a careful study of the financial condition of the bank and report any irregularities to the proper governmental officials. These examiners make unannounced visits so that the officers and employees do not have a chance to cover up any discrepancies or errors of poor judgment. Any irregularities that are discovered by the examiners must be corrected promptly or action will be taken against the bank by the proper federal or state banking officials.

The Federal Reserve System is a powerful, independent, federal agency that has considerable influence on commercial banking. There are twelve federal reserve banks distributed geographically over the United States, and these banks have branches, such as the Pittsburgh and Cincinnati branches of the Cleveland Federal Reserve Bank. Member banks obtain from the federal reserve bank the currency that they pay out, and they are permitted to discount certain notes and drafts that they have accepted from their customers, in much the same manner as the original transactions. These notes and drafts, as well as bills of exchange and banker's acceptances, are known as *eligible paper*, and the rate of interest charged for discounting eligible paper is known as the *rediscount rate*.

One of the important functions of a federal reserve bank is clearing interdistrict and intradistrict checks for its members. If a check that is drawn on a bank in San Francisco is deposited in a Chicago bank, it must be sent to the bank in California for collection. This process is known as *clearing a check* and is handled by the two district federal reserve banks involved, the one in Chicago and the one in San Francisco. Or, if a check is received by a bank in San Antonio, Texas, drawn on a bank in Houston, Texas, it will be cleared by the Dallas Federal Reserve Bank as both of the other cities are located in the Dallas district.

Of numerous regulations emanating from the Federal Reserve System and other governmental agencies, two are of particular concern to businesses. One of these is the restriction on the amount that may be loaned to any one firm to 10 percent of the total of the capital stock and undivided profits of the lending bank. Another is a prohibition against paying interest on *demand deposits*, or checking accounts as they are usually known.

■ Other Financial Institutions for Short-Term Capital

The following financial institutions also specialize in assisting businesses with their short-term financial problems. Some of these make loans to business units while others are active in the field of consumer finance.

1. Commercial finance companies
2. Factoring companies
3. Sales finance companies
4. Commercial paper houses
5. Consumer finance institutions

1 / **Commercial finance companies.** Although commercial banks make short-term loans to business with accounts receivable or inventories pledged as collateral, such loans are more commonly secured from commercial finance companies. This is particularly true when receivables are involved. A nonnotification arrangement, by which the borrower's customers are not notified of the plan, is customary. A *commercial finance company* is a financial institution operating on a local or national basis

that makes loans to business by discounting accounts receivable or by taking chattel mortgages on inventories or machinery.

In addition to a large number of small commercial finance companies, two operate on a national basis. These well-known companies are the Commercial Credit Company and the Commercial Investors Trust Financial Corporation. Interest charges on loans made are relatively high, usually between 10 and 15 percent. The money loaned by commercial finance companies is secured in part from the owners of the companies, and the balance is borrowed by issuing bonds or securing short-term loans from commercial banks.

2 / Factoring companies. *Factoring companies,* or *factors* as they are more commonly called, specialize in making loans to business based on accounts receivable. They differ from commercial finance companies in that they purchase the accounts receivable and are responsible for collecting the amounts due. Consequently, a notification plan is universal. Interest charges on loans are reasonable but, in addition, a fee or commission is assessed. Originating in the textile field, factoring has spread in recent years to many other types of business.

3 / Sales finance companies. *Sales finance companies* purchase installment sales contracts from the dealers who have sold the merchandise to the consumer. In this respect they differ from other types of loan companies that make loans directly to consumers repayable on an installment basis. Such companies are organized under the laws of a state, but several operate on a national scale.

The principle upon which sales finance companies operate is relatively simple. Aside from a small amount of cash received from the owners, funds are obtained by borrowing. Because the credit standing of the company is usually excellent, funds are secured at a low rate of interest. Installment contract paper is then purchased from businessmen who do not care to or cannot afford to handle their own sales financing. Gross earnings on these contracts should equal or exceed 12 percent in order to cover expenses, losses, and the cost of the money borrowed.

The largest number of sales finance companies operate in the automobile field, and the dollar volume of the business of all such organizations is greatest in installment contracts written to cover the sale of new and used cars. Over one half of all new cars and two thirds of all used cars sold are financed, and practically all of these contracts are sold to sales finance companies or other financial institutions. Three companies operate on a national scale: the General Motors Acceptance Corporation and two others that also engage in commercial financing, the Commercial Credit Company and C. I. T. Financial Corporation. In addition to these three giants numerous smaller companies are local in character or operate in one or more states.

Regulation has been undertaken by several states including, in some instances, a maximum limit on finance charges. Generally the legislation has taken the direction of full disclosure of all charges so that the consumer knows how much he is paying for the different elements of cost in his contract, such as interest, insurance, and finance charges. The Federal Trade Commission has also issued some trade practice rules on the retail installment sales financing of motor vehicles.

4 / Commercial paper houses. Firms that issue commercial paper, described on page 419, would have a problem of distribution were it not for the existence of *commercial paper houses.* These organizations specialize in handling such notes either buying them outright or selling them on a commission basis. Commercial paper houses employ salesmen who retail commercial paper to commercial banks, investors, and other purchasers interested in this type of investment. They serve a useful purpose not only to the issuing firm but also to their customers in providing to them a diversified list of high-grade short-term paper.

5 / Consumer finance institutions. The major types of institutions, other than commercial banks, that make loans to consumers are consumer finance companies, industrial banks, and credit unions. Other than the possibility that a sole proprietor or member of a partnership might seek a personal loan to increase his investment in his business, consumer finance institutions are valuable to business only by way of providing customers with funds to purchase goods, to settle accounts, or to maintain installment payments.

Consumer finance companies, also called *small loan companies* and *personal finance companies,* specialize in making cash loans of from $100 to $500 on single- or double-name paper although larger loans are also available, particularly if security is offered. Some companies are local and others, such as the Household Finance Corporation, operate in many cities. Loan repayments are almost universally on a weekly or monthly basis. In most states consumer finance companies are subject to regulation by a Uniform Small Loan Law that provides for licenses and a rate limit of from 2½ to 3 percent a month on the unpaid balance of the loan.

A third major type of consumer finance institutions, credit unions, received attention in Chapter 5 as an example of a form of cooperative.

Many credit unions require a membership fee, which may be as low as 25 cents. The usual interest rate charged borrowers is 1 percent a month on the unpaid balance, loans generally do not exceed $300, and security may or may not be required.

ORGANIZATION FOR FINANCIAL MANAGEMENT

The person in charge of a financial department is usually the treasurer although his title may be that of vice-president—finance or controller. This individual is directly responsible to the president of the company, and under him he may have a staff of assistants who head up various functions. The chief financial officer may make some decisions on his own, in others he may seek support from the president, and some matters must be referred to the board of directors. For example, declaring divi-dends, authorizing a bond issue, or selling shares of stock would be decisions reached by the board based, usually, on recommendations received from the treasurer. On the other hand, many decisions must and should be made by the chief financial officer. Short-term borrowing, the investment of idle funds, credit and collection policies, types and amounts of insurance, and the internal control of cash are examples of financial matters under the jurisdiction of the treasurer.

BUSINESS TERMS

(a) short-term financing (411)
✓(b) current liabilities (411); working capital (411)
(c) open-book account (413), charge account (413)
(d) promissory note (415); maker (415), payee (415)
(e) indorsement (416); negotiable instrument (416)
✓(f) bank discount (416); double-name paper (416)
(g) commercial draft (417), drawer (417), drawee (417)
(h) time draft (417), sight draft (417), trade acceptance (417), order bill of lading (418)
(i) bank acceptance (418), letter of credit (418), financing statement (418)
(j) commercial paper (419)
(k) character loan (419)
(l) comaker or cosigner (419), accommodation indorser (419)
(m) nonnotification plan (420), notification plan (420)
(n) bonded public warehouse (421), warehouse receipt (421)
✓(o) chattel mortgage (422), conditional bill of sale (422)
(p) nominal rate of interest (423), effective rate of interest (423)
(q) commercial bank (424), check (424), stop payment (424)
(r) certified check (424), bank draft (425), correspondent bank (425)
(s) cashier's check (425), traveler's check (425), line of credit (425)

(t) ˙eligible paper (427), rediscount rate (427)
(u) clearing a check (427), demand deposits (427)
(v) commercial finance company (427), factoring company or factor (428)
(w) sales finance company (428), commercial paper house (429)
(x) consumer finance company or small loan company (429), personal finance company (429)

QUESTIONS FOR DISCUSSION AND ANALYSIS

1. Why would it be inefficient for a firm to maintain a cash position that would always be in excess of any reasonable expectation of need?
2. There is a definite element of trust in an open-book account. What problems would arise if this confidence disappeared and businesses had to conduct their affairs without using open-book accounts?
3. Are there any justifiable reasons why a firm would not take advantage of every cash discount offered to it?
4. If a customer does not pay his open-book account and refuses to issue a note in payment of his debt, would he be likely to accept a draft drawn on him? Why?
5. When a third party signs a note as-a comaker or an accommodation indorser, is there a high degree of chance that he will end up paying the note? Why?
6. If security is required for a short-term loan, what type or types would the borrower prefer to offer? What type or types would the lender prefer?
7. Do you believe that most borrowers, particularly consumers, are aware of the effective rate of interest they pay?
8. Considering the number of services that a commercial bank renders to businesses, many of them without charge, how can these banks make a profit?
9. The majority of the sales of some firms, e.g., automobile dealers, involve installment notes. What problems would these firms have if they did not sell these notes to a sales finance company or some other financial institution?
10. If you need to borrow a small amount of money, e.g., $100, what type of financial institution would you prefer to patronize? Why?

PROBLEMS AND SHORT CASES

1. The Winther Manufacturing Co. purchased raw materials at an invoice price of $9,600. Terms allowed were 2/10, net 30, but the firm does not have the cash available to take advantage of the discount. The commercial bank with which the Winther firm does business is willing to make a loan for any amount up to $20,000 for 20 days at 6 percent, but it requires that the borrower maintain a balance of 20 percent of the loan in its checking account.
    Show calculations to indicate the net saving if the minimum necessary amount is borrowed to take advantage of the cash discount.

2. The Kent Corporation received a note for $18,000 from the Henry & Lampson Co. on June 10 bearing interest at 6 percent and maturing in three months. On June 30 the Kent Corporation discounted this note at its bank at a 7 percent rate.

Show calculations to determine the proceeds to the Kent Corporation on the discount date.

3. The Wood Manufacturing Co. has been considering the desirability of trading in all of its lathes for new models of the same type of machines. The total cost to make the trade will be $600,000, an amount that exceeds by $480,000 the amount of cash that can be spared from current operating needs.

It is estimated that the new machines will save their cost in about two years. The maker of the machines will extend 30-day credit terms, which is about the length of time it will take to install the new machines. At the end of 30 days the seller would expect to be paid in full or is willing to accept $120,000 in cash and a series of 6 percent $20,000 notes, one due at the end of each month for 24 months. The commercial bank patronized by the Wood Manufacturing Co. has indicated its willingness to loan $480,000 for 6 months at 5¾ percent; and it has given every assurance that, if $120,000 is paid on the note at maturity, the balance can be extended for 6 months, and so on until the note is retired.

Assuming that the Wood Manufacturing Co. decides to purchase the new machines, what source of short-term financing seems most appropriate? Justify your decision by indicating the factors that influenced your conclusion. Would it be desirable for the Wood Manufacturing Co. to investigate other sources of short-term funds?

SUGGESTED READINGS

Brandt, L. K. *Business Finance: A Management Approach.* Englewood Cliffs, New Jersey: Prentice-Hall, Inc., 1965. Part IV.

Cohen, J. B., and S. M. Robbins. *The Financial Manager: Basic Aspects of Financial Administration.* New York: Harper & Row, Publishers, 1966. Part III.

Dauten, C. A., and M. Welshans. *Principles of Finance,* Second Edition. Cincinnati: South-Western Publishing Company, 1964. Part 2.

Johnson, R. W. *Financial Management,* Third Edition. Boston: Allyn and Bacon, Inc., 1966. Part IV.

Prather, C. L. *Money and Banking,* Eighth Edition. Homewood, Illinois: Richard D. Irwin, Inc., 1965. Part II.

Walker, E. W. *Essentials of Financial Management.* Englewood Cliffs, New Jersey: Prentice-Hall, Inc., 1965. Chapter 12.

Weston, J. F., and E. F. Brigham. *Managerial Finance,* Revised Edition. New York: Holt, Rinehart and Winston, Inc., 1966. Part IV.

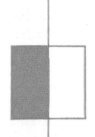

Chapter 20

SECURITY EXCHANGES AND FINANCIAL NEWS

Every working day millions of shares of stock change hands on and off security exchanges. Current stock prices are of considerable interest to businessmen, investors, speculators, and a substantial segment of the general public. The ups and downs of the stock market reflect the optimistic and pessimistic views of buyers and sellers of shares and constitute an important barometer of current and anticipated business conditions.

The widespread interest in the stock market is reflected in the space devoted by almost all daily papers to reporting sales and prices, and TV and radio stations include similar information in their news broadcasts. Metropolitan newspapers usually print full details concerning transactions on the New York Stock Exchange, and some carry news about stocks traded on other exchanges or in the over-the-counter market. In addition, other financial news is printed in the same section as that devoted to stock prices. Events affecting the finances of individual corporations, such as contract awards, new security issues, and dividend declarations, are promptly reported. Items of general interest to the financial world as, for example, changes in interest rates or government financing, are considered newsworthy.

This chapter will examine security exchanges in some detail because an understanding of them is necessary for an appreciation of the important role they play in the financial world. In addition to an explanation of their primary function—making a market for listed stocks and bonds— attention will be given to the extensive state and federal regulation of security sales. Further details about stock and bond quotations and averages will be provided along with mention of other types of financial news. Emphasis will be placed on the interpretation and use of such information by the business world.

SECURITY EXCHANGES

A *security exchange*, commonly called a stock exchange, is an organization that provides facilities for its members to buy and sell securities. It is usually organized as an unincorporated association, a type of business ownership that was described in Chapter 4. Membership fees are charged, and dues or assessments cover the expenses of operation. The members elect a board of governors who, in turn, elect officers, including a president. The officers employ the necessary personnel to operate the exchange.

The most famous and largest of the security exchanges, the New York Stock Exchange, has a limited membership of 1,375. The members are individuals, many of them partners in brokerage firms. A membership is called a *seat*, and it can be sold if the prospective purchaser has been approved by the Board of Governors of the Exchange. The price on these seats has been as low as $17,000 and as high as $625,000 within the present century, although recently the range has been between $150,000 and $250,000.

The stocks and bonds that have been approved for trading by security exchanges are *listed securities*. The New York Stock Exchange lists approximately 1,500 stocks and 1,100 bond issues, and transactions in more than 1,250 different stocks are completed daily. The American Stock Exchange in New York and the Midwest Stock Exchange in Chicago are two other fairly large security exchanges.

It should be noted that the stock of many publicly held corporations is not listed on any exchange either because the company does not qualify for this privilege or because it prefers not to meet the necessary requirements. The New York Stock Exchange, for example, will not grant an application for listing unless the corporation, in addition to securing approval from the Securities and Exchange Commission, meets the following standards: (a) the company must have 1,000,000 shares outstanding of which 700,000 must be publicly held; (b) there must be at least 2,000 shareholders of whom 1,700 must each own at least 100 shares; (c) annual earnings should exceed $2 million before taxes; and (d) the common stock publicly held must have a minimum market value of $12 million.

■ Operation of Security Exchanges

A description of the operation of security exchanges, insofar as the general public is concerned, will clarify the usefulness of this type of financial institution. The chief function is to provide a convenient means by which individuals and organizations can buy or sell stocks of well-known corporate enterprises. A security exchange is not a source of capital to the corporation that has its stocks and bonds listed. These securities have already been sold, usually through investment banks; and subsequent sales that take place on a stock exchange are between such diverse security holders as individuals, corporations, banks, insurance companies, pension funds, investment trusts, churches, hospitals, trust funds, and endowment funds.

For every buyer there must be a seller. The statement that "everybody is buying stocks" merely means that the demand is greater than the supply, with a resultant increase in prices. When an investor thinks a stock is going up in price, he would not be able to buy if a security holder did not believe it was a good time to sell or had to dispose of his holdings for other reasons. Conversely, even in a severely depressed market there is always a buyer if the seller is willing to accept his offering price.

1 / **Trading procedures.** An order to buy stocks on an exchange, regardless of the residence of the potential investor, is routed to the trading floor. Here it is given to a member of the exchange, usually a partner in the same brokerage firm patronized by the buyer.

On the floor of the exchange there are a number of *trading posts* at which a specified list of stocks are bought and sold. If the order placed by the investor is for 100 shares of common stock of United States Steel Corporation, the member locates the post and makes an offer to buy under the terms specified. This might be "at the market"—the current price at which the stock is being sold—in which case the order would probably be filled immediately because someone is always ready to sell if his offering price is accepted. If a limited order is given, such as $50 a share, and the stock is selling at $55 a share, the member leaves the order with another broker who spends most of his time at one post and is known as a *specialist* because he concentrates his attention on a limited number of securities. The specialist makes a memorandum of the order and, if at a later time in the day or at a later date an offer is made to sell U. S. Steel shares at $50, he executes the order.

Trading is conducted in *round-lots* that normally are 100-share units. If the order is for 25 shares, it is placed by the member with an *odd-lot broker* who makes a specialty of handling such orders, for which he receives a special commission. By grouping several odd-lot orders he may be able to buy one or more round lots, which are distributed to the several purchasers, or he may purchase the additional shares for his own account.

(a) A Sample Transaction. Mr. Jordan, who lives in a suburban area near St. Louis, has decided to buy 25 shares of International Harvester Company common stock. One of his neighbors is Mr. Samuels, a stockbroker employed by a large brokerage firm with offices in many cities including downtown St. Louis. Mr. Jordan, after reaching Mr. Samuels by telephone, places an order to buy at 46, and this purchase request is immediately teletyped to the New York office of the brokerage firm. From there it is telephoned to the floor of the New York Stock Exchange (on which IHC is listed) and delivered to a partner on the trading floor.

This member goes to the post at which IHC is sold and, because the order is for only 25 shares and the trading unit is 100 shares, he turns the buy order over to an odd-lot specialist operating at that post. At this particular moment IHC has dipped to 45½, so the odd-lot specialist buys 100 shares and allocates 25 to the exchange member with whom we are concerned. This man reports back to his New York office that the stock has been bought, the teletype carries the news to St. Louis, and Mr. Samuels notifies Mr. Jordan that his order has been executed. A seller rather than a buyer of IHC stock will have gone through a similar process.

The machinery for buying or selling stocks is well established, and transactions are completed in a relatively short time. A buyer or a seller in a broker's office in a large city can expect to complete a transaction within one or two minutes if he is willing to do business at market quotations.

GIS	J	GT	PA
$57\frac{3}{4}$	$3s64\frac{3}{8}$	$3,000s46\frac{3}{8}$	44

This illustration shows a small segment of ticker tape. Each stock has an abbreviation, which may or may not be easily recognizable. Below the symbol is the sales price for 100 shares or, in the case of sales up to 1,000 shares, the number of hundreds is indicated. For large sales the exact quantity is shown. The letter "s" separates the size of the sale from the sales price when more than a single round-lot is involved. The reading of the tape shown is as follows:

100 shares of General Mills, Inc. common at 57¾
300 shares of Standard Oil Co. of New Jersey common at 64⅜
3,000 shares of Goodyear Tire & Rubber Co. common at 46⅜
100 shares of Pennsylvania Railroad Co. common at 44

(b) Stock Quotations. How did Mr. Jordan decide on a buying price of $46 a share? He may have been following the daily reports in his newspaper, or his stockbroker may have recommended the stock as a good buy at this price. If he had been in the St. Louis office of the brokerage firm that executed the order, he could have watched the *ticker tape*. This is a transparent tape that is projected on a screen so that actual sales .transactions on the large exchanges can be seen within a few seconds of the time of the sale. More recently, many large investment brokers have also installed the Ultronic Stockmaster or the Quotron. These are electronic devices placed on the desks of account executives that will provide almost instantaneous information about stocks and their price quotations.

2 / Cost of trading. The customer of a brokerage firm pays a commission for the service rendered. Commissions charged by members of the New York Stock Exchange, which are shown on the next page for round-lot and odd-lot purchases and sales, are typical of charges made on other exchanges. As an example, if a customer buys or sells 100 shares of stock that has a market price of $30 a share, the commission will amount to $34 ($19 plus ½ percent of $3,000).

Odd-lot brokers receive 12½ cents a share commission on stocks selling below $40 a share and 25 cents a share commission on stocks selling for $40 and above per share. If a purchase order is entered at a fixed price, such as $35 a share, it will not be executed by the odd-lot broker until the market drops to 34⅞.

In addition to commissions, both the federal government and the state of New York levy a tax on the transfer of shares, which is paid by the seller. The federal tax is a Security and Exchange Commission fee of 1 cent for each $500 of the market price or fraction thereof. This fee is withheld by the broker from the proceeds that are due the seller of the stock. New York rates are as follows:

Shares selling under $5	1¼ ¢ per share
Shares selling between $5 and $10	2½ ¢ per share
Shares selling between $10 and $20	3¾ ¢ per share .
Shares selling for over $20	5¢ per share

3 / Investors and speculators. An *investor* is one who buys securities with the idea of holding them on a more or less permanent basis. In every market there are also *speculators* who hope to make a profit by buying and selling within a few weeks, days, or within the trading hours of a single day. Speculators who buy stocks in anticipation of a rise in price are known as *bulls*; and those who sell, expecting the market to go down in the days or weeks ahead, are known as *bears*.

As illogical as it may seem, a bear frequently sells stocks he does not own. This market operation is known as *selling short*. He sells today

New York Stock Exchange
Commission Charges on Stocks

MONEY INVOLVED	PERCENT OF MONEY INVOLVED	MINIMUM COMMISSION PER TRANSACTION	
		PLUS STATED AMOUNT	
		FOR 100 SHARES	LESS THAN 100 SHARES
$100 to $399*	2%	$ 3	$ 1
$400 to $2,399	1%	7	5
$2,400 to $4,999	1/2%	19	17
$5,000 and above	1/10%	39	37

* Minimum commission $6

If money involved is under $100, the minimum commission is as mutually agreed. Top minimum is $75 per transaction, or $1.50 per share (subject to $6 minimum). For transactions in excess of 100 shares, each 100 shares or fraction thereof is considered separately.

expecting to buy, or cover his short sale as the process is called, within a relatively short time after the market goes down to a point where he can make a profit. Of course, if the market does not go down, he suffers a loss. Because he must deliver stock to the purchaser, he borrows it from a broker who has it available. In return for the use of the cash proceeds from the sale, the broker usually loans the stock without charge. This stock may be shares owned by the brokerage firm or, more likely, shares that it is holding in its name for the benefit of one of its customers.

Another possibility for a speculator to enhance his profits is to buy stocks on a margin. If a buyer can *margin* his account with a broker up to 50 percent, it means that he needs to have only one half as much money as his purchase calls for. If a speculator has $1,000, he can buy either 100 shares of a stock selling at $10 or 200 shares at the same price by borrowing the extra $1,000 from his broker. In case the stock rises to $15, he can sell for a profit of $500 in one case and $1,000 in the other, minus commissions and taxes and, in the latter instance, interest on the money borrowed. On the other hand, if the stock declines in value, the broker will call for an additional deposit to protect himself against loss. If the margin trader cannot put up additional funds, his broker will sell the stock no later than when the price drops to $5 in order to protect the loan, and the speculator's original $1,000 deposit will be lost.

Beginning in 1954, members of the New York Stock Exchange launched a venture designed to induce more investors to purchase stocks by offering a payment plan similar to that used for installment sales. Individuals select the stock or stocks they wish to own and pay for these by making regular monthly or quarterly deposits with their broker of an amount as low as $40 a quarter or as high as $999 a month. The Monthly Investors Plan, or *MIP* as it is sometimes called, allows an individual to channel regular savings into the ownership of corporation stocks. Over 125,000 persons have taken advantage of this opportunity, and the number seems to be growing each year.

■ Value of Security Exchanges

Security exchanges render an extremely valuable service in the field of finance. The maintenance of a free market, with prices established at all times by the forces of supply and demand, make listed securities more useful than unlisted stocks and bonds. They can be used as collateral at a bank for a loan or as the security for collateral trust bonds. New issues of the companies involved are easier for investment banks to sell. Estates are easier to appraise to the extent that they contain listed securities. Even the speculator is valuable since his frequent purchases and sales help to maintain an active market. Furthermore, by providing a channel through which millions of individuals invest their savings in long-term securities, the stock exchanges make possible, indirectly, the growth of hundreds of corporations.

■ Regulation of Sales of Securities

In the early part of the twentieth century less than a half million people owned corporate stocks and bonds, and no effective regulations covered security sales. The doctrine of *caveat emptor*—let the buyer beware—held full sway. Unscrupulous promoters sold shares of stock in ventures having scant, if any, hope of success, and the public was the victim of many security swindles. A group of men would organize a corporation and peddle stock to a so-called "sucker list." Widows, preachers, doctors, dentists, school teachers, and other individuals who might be expected to having savings available for investment were considered the best prospects. Literature describing the golden opportunities of an oil company or a mining company with an invitation to subscribe to the stock would be mailed to these persons. Telephone calls and personal solicitations would follow. After the promoters had worked a territory for all of the cash possible, they would disappear from their impressive office quarters and, usually, the shareholders would not hear from them again. An aroused public finally demanded legislation to curb these swindles, and eventually both the states and the federal government enacted appropriate laws as listed at the top of page 440:

1. State regulation
2. Federal Securities Act of 1933
3. Federal Securities Exchange Act of 1934

1 / State regulation of security sales. Although in 1909 the United States Post Office had secured the passage of a law that made it a criminal offense to use the mails to defraud, this legislation did not prevent crooked security salesmen from operating in various cities and communities. In 1911 Kansas passed a law regulating stock sales in that state. At the time it was under consideration, a member of the legislature remarked that some promoters would sell stock in the "blue sky" itself. Today, the laws regulating security sales that have been passed in all states except Nevada are known as *blue-sky laws.*

These blue-sky laws frequently cover such items as (a) required registration of new security issues with an appropriate state official; (b) an annual license for dealers, brokers, and salesmen; and (c) a provision for prosecuting individuals charged with fraud in connection with the sale of stocks and bonds. Unfortunately, state regulation provides little or no control over interstate sales, a situation that the federal government had recognized as early as 1920 when it gave the Interstate Commerce Commission jurisdiction over the sale of railroad securities. Need for further controls was apparent, and since 1933 the federal government has played a dominant role in blue-sky legislation.

2 / Federal Securities Act of 1933. The Securities Act of 1933 was predicated on the belief that potential investors had the right to know all pertinent facts about a company issuing new securities and that the officers, accountants, engineers, and lawyers providing such information should be held legally liable for supplying such facts. It has been called the "information law" because full disclosure of pertinent financial facts is the major requirement of the Act. This is accomplished by (a) requiring the filing of a *registration statement,* which contains extensive details about the company and the proposed issue of securities, and (b) the preparation of a condensed version of this statement, called a *prospectus,* that must be furnished to each prospective purchaser of the stocks or bonds offered for sale.

Since 1934 the enforcement of this law has been under the jurisdiction of the Securities and Exchange Commission. The Commission is given twenty days after the registration statement is on file to issue a *stop order* if it believes the proposed offering should not be made to the general public. Even though a stop order is not issued, the Commission does not guarantee the correctness of the information supplied and can request the Department of Justice to institute criminal proceedings if, at a later date, the law seems to have been violated.

Some security issues are exempt from registration. These include all forms of government securities, railroad issues subject to the ICC, and stocks and bonds of cooperatives and nonprofit institutions. Also, sales not involving the use of mails or interstate commerce are exempt, as well as those in which there has been no public offering. In recent years, many issues have been sold at private sale for the express purpose of avoiding registration under this law.

3 / Federal Securities Exchange Act of 1934. Although the 1933 law was and is still effective, further legislation was passed less than a year later extending the regulatory jurisdiction of the federal government. The Securities Exchange Act of 1934, in addition to establishing the Securities and Exchange Commission, provided for three major reforms. These reforms were (a) registration of all corporations whose stocks were listed on exchanges, (b) regulation of national stock exchanges, and (c) credit restrictions through control of margin requirements for stock purchases.

(a) COMPANY REGISTRATION. Every corporation whose stock was listed on one of the national exchanges was required to file a registration statement with the Securities and Exchange Commission. Furthermore, it was specified that this statement must be kept up to date by the filing of annual reports. Whether or not a company is in the process of selling new securities, an investor is able to find out the same type of information that formerly was available only when new securities were to be sold.

(b) NATIONAL STOCK EXCHANGES. Practically all of the security exchanges, including the large ones previously mentioned, were classified as national and placed under the jurisdiction of the Commission. Although each had adopted certain trading rules, self-regulation had not prevented abuses by professional traders at the expense of the investing public. The "insiders" had been able to manipulate stock prices for their own profit with losses going to a gullible public who swallowed rumors and purchased shares at unjustified higher and higher prices. The legitimate functions of security exchanges were being abused and, due to the interstate nature of most transactions, regulation by a federal agency seemed to be the only available solution. Currently the Securities and Exchange Commission employs a competent staff to watch the sales on

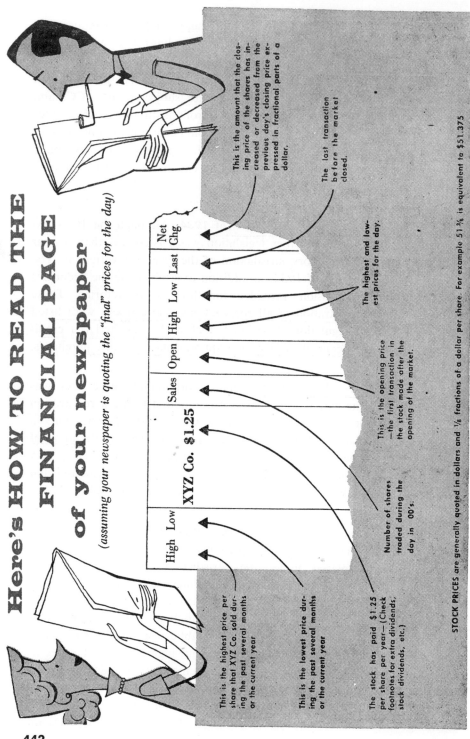

Here's HOW TO READ THE FINANCIAL PAGE of your newspaper

(assuming your newspaper is quoting the "final" prices for the day)

High	Low		Sales	Open	High	Low	Last	Net Chg
XYZ Co. $1.25								

This is the highest price per share that XYZ Co. sold during the past several months or the current year

This is the lowest price during the past several months or the current year

The stock has paid $1.25 per share per year—(Check footnotes for extra dividends, stock dividends, etc.)

Number of shares traded during the day in 00's.

This is the opening price —the first transaction in the stock made after the opening of the market.

This is the amount that the closing price of the shares has increased or decreased from the previous day's closing price expressed in fractional parts of a dollar.

The last transaction before the market closed.

The highest and lowest prices for the day.

STOCK PRICES are generally quoted in dollars and ⅛ fractions of a dollar per share. For example 51 ⅜ is equivalent to $51.375

Hayden, Stone, Inc.

national exchanges and to investigate those that might either be illegal or give rise to unfair trading.

(c) MARGIN REQUIREMENTS. A third purpose of the Securities Exchange Act of 1934 was to restrict the amount of credit that would be available for financing the purchase of stocks. Control over this feature was placed in the hands of the Federal Reserve Board, which governs the federal reserve banks. This Board determines the extent to which a purchaser can margin his account and also limits the amount of loans that can be made by a member bank or by a broker for the purpose of financing stock purchases. During the years the law has been in effect the margin requirement has been placed as high as 100 percent, which means the equivalent of outright cash purchases, and as low as 50 percent.

(d) OTHER PROVISIONS. Further provisions of the law and subsequent amendments relate to regulation of over-the-counter markets and the control of exchange members and corporate officers. Trading in the over-the-counter markets is regulated in a manner comparable to that of securities dealt in on the organized exchanges, in order to close this possible loophole in the whole picture. Exchange members must indicate whether they are operating for their own accounts or as brokers, and also whether they are floor traders, odd-lot dealers, or specialists. Each classification must conform to certain rules and regulations laid down by the Commission. A corporate officer who owns 10 percent or more of the stock of a company that is listed on a national exchange must list his holdings with the Commission, must not sell the company's securities on a "short" basis, and any profits made by him through the purchase and sale of securities of the corporation that are completed in a period of less than six months must be paid to the company.

Although the security laws passed in 1933 and 1934 have not worked out perfectly, the general results have been favorable. Millions of small investors now have fairly adequate protection against losses due to outright misrepresentation or fraud on the part of the promoters or others who offer the securities for sale.

FINANCIAL NEWS

As mentioned earlier in this chapter, radio and TV stations include financial items in their news broadcasts and practically all daily newspapers have a financial section that is widely read by businessmen. In addition to the generous coverage of financial news in metropolitan newspapers, magazines including *Business Week, U. S. News and World*

Report, Time, and *Newsweek* publish a number of articles on financial events. Even more slanted to news of interest to the financial community are such papers as the *Wall Street Journal* and such magazines as *Fortune, Barron's,* the *Commercial and Financial Chronicle, Forbes,* and *Dun's Review and Modern Industry.*

The use of computers by financial analysts and reporters has made available information about corporations and industries that would have been impossible to compile a few years ago. So much information is printed in newspapers and magazines that reading and interpreting financial news requires selection and, above all, understanding. The remainder of this chapter will examine and comment on the more widely read items that provide useful information to businessmen. These will be divided into three classifications: stocks, bonds, and other financial news items.

■ Stocks

Without much question, more people turn to the financial pages of newspapers to check the stock market than for any other reason. They may be interested in stocks they own or plan to purchase, or in the stock of the company for which they work. Corporate officials watch movements in the stocks of their competitors as well as their own company. Bankers, loan officers, statisticians, and many others including government officials are interested in the performance of individual stocks as well as the market generally. For example, a commercial bank may hold shares of stock as collateral for a loan, or the board of directors of a corporation may have to reach a decision on raising additional capital by selling additional shares of its stock.

1 / **Stock quotations.** A summary of transactions is prepared for publication after each day's trading on an exchange. Stocks are itemized alphabetically and for each the following facts are provided: high and low for the current year; abbreviated name of corporation; the kind of stock (if stock is a preferred issue, the letters "pf" are shown, otherwise the listing is common stock); the annual dividend rate or other information about the dividend; sales in round-lots for the day; the price per share at the opening of the market; the high and the low for the day; the closing price; and the net change between the closing price for the day and that of the previous day on which the stock was traded.

Prices per share are quoted in eighths, quarters, or one half. For convenience of printing, a few papers use decimals, but these are parts of eight rather than parts of ten. For example, a quotation of 23.7 is the same as 23⅞ or $23.875. As a footnote to the quotations, the meaning of the small letters shown in many cases after the corporate name and dividend is explained. These are frequently very important as, for example, if a stock is purchased "xd," the previous owner will receive the current dividend check.

2 / **Stock averages.** The general trend of stock quotations is shown in the daily movement of market averages for all stocks, which are further subdivided into industrials, railroads, and utilities. Two widely known *stock averages* are the Dow–Jones Averages and the Standard & Poor's Index. The Dow–Jones Averages are based on 30 industrial, 20 railroad, and 15 utility stocks whereas the Standard & Poor's Index uses 425 industrials, 25 rails, and 50 utilities. In each case the movement of the averages has been plotted day by day for many years.

Because the above averages, and others that have been compiled, are based on a limited number of stocks, many interested parties complained that they did not truly reflect market changes. In order to eliminate this criticism, the New York Stock Exchange since July, 1966, has issued an index of all of its more than 1,250 stocks. These are also subdivided into four groups—industrial, transportation, utility, and finance. All five of these indexes were assigned a base of 50.00 as of December 31, 1965, which was an approximation of the dollar average of all stocks on that date.

Of considerable interest to many investors is a report made every half hour during the trading session and at the close of the day that shows the rise or fall in the average price of New York Stock Exchange common stocks expressed in dollars and cents. For example, the market report at the close of the day might state that stocks gained, on the average, 28 cents a share. The extensive calculations necessary to produce this average promptly became practical after the Exchange had installed its computer.

3 / **Over-the-counter markets.** In addition to the stocks that are listed on one or more of the national exchanges, shares of stock in approximately 40,000 corporations can be bought and sold through brokers on the over-the-counter market. The stocks so traded are frequently those of smaller corporations; or if larger companies are represented, such corporations do not wish to have their stocks listed or, for one reason or another, cannot qualify under the listing rules established by the various exchanges.

The over-the-counter market, described briefly on page 404, is actually the name given to all trading activities that do not take place on an organized exchange.

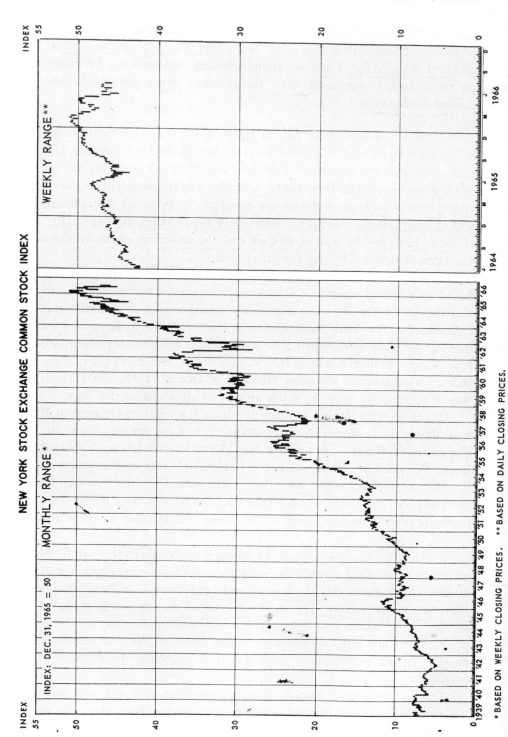

NEW YORK STOCK EXCHANGE COMMON STOCK INDEX

INDEX: DEC. 31, 1965 = 50

MONTHLY RANGE *

WEEKLY RANGE **

*BASED ON WEEKLY CLOSING PRICES.   **BASED ON DAILY CLOSING PRICES.

Through a reporting service of the National Association of Securities Dealers, Inc., the bid and asked prices on thousands of unlisted stocks and bonds are reported daily. These are made available to the public at the offices of the member brokers and quotations on many of the more active issues are also published in the financial pages of newspapers and magazines. Although public attention is more often directed to the stocks sold on the national exchanges, a vast majority of all purchases and sales of stock take place on the over-the-counter markets.

■ Bonds

Bond issues are traded on national exchanges and in over-the-counter markets. Those that are listed are bought and sold daily, and reports of these transactions are printed in the financial pages of newspapers and in financial magazines. By following the ups and downs of the bond market, a businessman can determine the cost of borrowing long-term funds and can obtain an idea of the general availability of credit.

1 / **Bond quotations.** Although many similarities exist between stock and bond quotations, there are some important differences. For one, separate listings are provided for different types of bonds, such as domestic corporation bonds, foreign bonds, and United States Government bonds. Another difference is that bond prices are quoted in relationship to 100 regardless of the denomination of the bonds, which is usually $1,000. A bond selling for 91½ would cost $915 to purchase, and one selling for 134¼ would cost $1,342.50. The trading-unit variation in bonds is ⅛ except for government securities, which are quoted in 32nds. In order to simplify printing, a government bond is quoted at, for example, 95.24 ($95\,24/32$), which means that the price is $957.50.

The high and low for the year and for the day are shown as well as the last sale price and the net change from the previous day's trading. Opening prices are not shown. In place of information about the dividend, an abbreviated description of each issue shows the interest rate and maturity date and, when appropriate, reference is made to any special features such as, for example, *cv* meaning that the bond is convertible into common stock.

A corporation may have more bond issues outstanding than it has varieties of stock issues. Each separate bond issue demands a separate listing because the prices may vary for the different types and maturities. Another important fact is that the buyer of bonds pays accrued interest from the date of the last interest payment up to his purchase date in addition to the quoted price. He will, of course, recover this added amount when he receives his first interest payment which will cover six months since most bonds pay interest on a semiannual basis.

2 / Bond averages. In a manner somewhat similar to stocks, *bond averages* are computed daily. The best known, the Dow–Jones Bond Averages, show a composite average of 40 selected bonds and also averages of 10 Higher Grade Rails, 10 Second Grade Rails, 10 Public Utilities, and 10 Industrials. Other bond averages include those computed by *The New York Times*, which are grouped into railroad, public utility, industrial, and foreign classifications in addition to a composite average.

For the average businessman or investor, these averages present information that is more useful than individual quotations in that they reflect the general condition of the bond market. If a corporation is debating whether to sell more stock or to issue bonds in order to raise additional capital, the appropriate bond averages may well help in making an intelligent decision.

■ News Items

In addition to details on stocks and bonds, many other items of financial information are included in news stories. Some appear on the front pages of newspapers, such as indictments for violating the antitrust laws, but the majority are concentrated in financial magazines or the financial section of newspapers. They cover a wide range of topics, but it is possible to classify the majority of news items under the following headings:

1. Corporate news	4. Government news
2. Money and credit	3. Commodity prices
5. International news	

1 / Corporate news. Many of the actions of corporations, such as expansion plans, mergers proposed, promotions of key personnel, and actions taken by boards of directors, are newsworthy. The following list of stories taken from a single issue of a financial newspaper gives some idea of the scope and the variety of corporate news.

Reports of sales and earnings	Personnel changes
Dividend news	Court orders
Stock-split proposals	New products to be marketed
Sales of subsidiaries	New corporations organized
Backlogs of orders	

2 / Money and credit. Since a major proportion of business transactions involve credit and because most business firms borrow money for one purpose or another, the market for money and credit plays an important part in many business decisions. The cost of credit as reflected in interest rates for short-term and long-term borrowing, the rediscount rate of the federal reserve banks, and many other factors, including spending by the federal government, all play a part in determining the financial climate at any given time.

The reader of financial news can easily follow the cost of borrowing long-term funds by noting the effective interest rate of various types of securities offered to the public. This information is contained in news releases and advertisements of the syndicate handling the offering. Changes in short-term interest rates and in the rediscount rate of the Federal Reserve System are reported regularly.

3 / Commodity prices. The cost of raw materials is a vital element in the production of most manufactured goods and, in many instances, prices are established daily on a commodity exchange.[1] Firms that use agricultural products such as wheat, corn, and soybeans can determine not only the current cost of their materials but also the trend in prices by day-to-day reference to financial news. Livestock prices are also reported daily as are prices for feeds, eggs, dairy products, candy ingredients, fats and oils, hides, potatoes, onions, and several other commodities. Metals such as copper, tin, lead, and zinc are traded on exchanges centered chiefly in New York with the London Metal Exchange a world center for these raw materials.

Trading in grain, metals, and some other commodities on commodity exchanges can be on a cash (*spot market*) basis, or contracts can be purchased or sold for delivery in the future at a specified price. Both markets are of great interest to those manufacturers whose raw materials are bought and sold on commodity exchanges. The trend or the upward and downward movement of cash or futures prices can be followed by reference to the Dow-Jones Spot Commodity Price Index and the Dow-Jones Commodity Futures Index.

4 / Government news. Because government has such a marked effect on business, many actions taken by federal, state, or local governments have financial implications. Foremost among these are changes in tax rates or decisions of tax courts that affect business. Other news items are

---

[1] See Chapter 21, page 456.

concerned with issues of government securities, investigations by governmental agencies, and budget news, particularly of the federal government.

An illustration of an action by a state and one of the federal government will emphasize the importance of government news on business. Recently the state of New York considered raising the rates on the transfer of securities traded within the state whereupon the New York Stock Exchange threatened to move its operations to another state. On July 1, 1966, the federal program known as medicare became effective, which had a profound effect on insurance companies as well as hospitals. There is no question but that government news, particularly that coming out of Washington, D. C., may have an important bearing on the financial health of specific businesses, industries, or the economy as a whole.

5 / International news. Now that the jet age has reduced the size of our globe, happenings in foreign countries have a greater effect on domestic conditions. The ability of foreign countries to purchase our goods, as reflected in overseas prosperity and currency exchange rates, is important financially to all firms that do an export business. News of trade agreements made between the United States and foreign governments, or among foreign countries such as those that comprise the Common Market, may have an effect on the prosperity of a company or an entire industry.

BUSINESS TERMS

(a) security exchange (434), seat (434), listed securities (434)
(b) trading post (435), specialist (435)
(c) round lots (435), odd-lot broker (435)
(d) ticker tape (437)
(e) investor (437), speculator (437)
(f) bulls (437), bears (437)
(g) selling short (437), margin (438), MIP (439)
(h) caveat emptor (439)
(i) blue-sky laws (440)
(j) registration statement (440), prospectus (440), stop order (440)
(k) stock average (445), bond averages (448)
(l) spot market (449)

QUESTIONS FOR DISCUSSION AND ANALYSIS

1. Do you believe that the wide coverage given financial news, particularly the stock market, is justified by the news value of such items?
2. If you headed a corporation that could obtain a listing on a security exchange, would you make an application? What advantages would accrue to your company?
3. Brokerage firms in such lines of business as food or real estate are not allowed to charge a fee to both a buyer and a seller in the same

transaction. Why should stock brokerage firms be permitted to charge commissions to both buyers and sellers who patronize their firms?

4. Is there any justification for permitting speculators to operate on security exchanges?

5. It would be possible to prohibit selling short. Would such a regulation be advantageous to the investing public?

6. Why should the public be given more protection when buying securities than it is when making many other types of purchases?

7. If you planned to make an investment in a new security and were furnished with a prospectus, would you read it? Discuss.

8. Why do stock and bond averages not include all issues traded? Would they not be more valuable if they did?

9. How do you explain the fact that more shares of stock change hands on the over-the-counter market than on organized exchanges?

10. Can you give some examples of governmental acts at the local, state, and national levels that would have a bearing on a specific business, an industry, and on business in general?

PROBLEMS AND SHORT CASES

1. (a) Refer to a current newspaper and report the high, low, and closing prices of the following stocks that are listed on the New York Stock Exchange:

> Consolidated Edison Co., Preferred
> Firestone Tire & Rubber Co., Common
> General Electric Co., Common
> New York Central Railroad Co., Common
> Standard Oil Co. of New Jersey, Common

(b) Following the same procedure, report the closing prices for the following bonds:

> Bethlehem Steel Co. 4½'s due in 1990
> Douglass Aircraft 5's due in 1978
> Pennsylvania R. R. 4¼'s due in 1984
> Standard Oil Co. of Indiana 4½'s due in 1983
> Western Union 5¼'s due in 1987

2. Trustees for the Haven Foundation, a nonprofit enterprise, received a cash bequest that was promptly invested in the following list of common stocks. Compute the amount spent by the trustees, including commissions paid.

SHARES	COMPANY	PRICE PAID
200	American Telephone & Telegraph Co.	62
50	E. I. duPont de Nemours & Co.	205½
100	General Foods Corp.	76⅝
100	Texaco, Inc.	72¾
100	United States Steel Corp.	45

3. Raymond Fry, an investment counselor, received a visit from Harold Henderson who was a personal friend but, as a retired farmer with extensive land holdings, had never been interested in securities. Henderson explained to Fry that he was tired of government controls over agriculture and had decided to sell his farms. He believed that, after taxes, he would have about $600,000 in cash to invest and wanted Fry to give him some advice.

Henderson, although 70 years of age, is in good health as is his wife. They have three children, all of whom are married. His farms have been his sole source of income, and he wishes to invest his $600,000 in securities that will yield an annual income of between $25,000 and $30,000. Although Henderson admits that he does not know anything about bonds, preferred stocks, or common stocks, he has heard of the New York Stock Exchange and wants to own the kind of securities traded on this exchange so that he can get a daily report on them in the newspapers. Furthermore, he fears that, without the chore of managing his farms, he may be bored. Spending some time each day checking on his securities may be interesting and possibly profitable as well.

What advice should Fry give to Henderson? Your recommendations on investments can be either general or specific.

SUGGESTED READINGS

Bellemore, D. H. *Investments: Principles, Practices, and Analysis,* Second Edition. Cincinnati: South-Western Publishing Company, 1962.

Bowyer, J. W., Jr. *Investment Analysis and Management,* Third Edition. Homewood, Illinois: Richard D. Irwin, Inc., 1966.

Clendenin, J. C. *Introduction to Investments,* Fourth Edition. New York: McGraw-Hill Book Company, 1965.

Eiteman, W. J., C. A. Dice, and D. K. Eiteman. *The Stock Market,* Fourth Edition. New York: McGraw-Hill Book Company, 1965.

Lefllar, G. L., and L. C. Farwell. *The Stock Market,* Third Edition. New York: The Ronald Press Company, 1963.

Prime, J. H. *Investment Analysis,* Fourth Edition. Englewood Cliffs, New Jersey: Prentice-Hall, Inc., 1967.

Sauvain, H. C. *Investment Management,* Third Edition. Englewood Cliffs, New Jersey: Prentice-Hall, Inc., 1967.

Magazines: *Forbes, Barron's, Magazine of Wall Street.*

Chapter 21

RISKS AND INSURANCE

In a capitalistic system, as noted in the first chapter, risk is an inescapable characteristic of private enterprise. To some degree, the assumption of risks on the part of entrepreneurs is a justification for the profits they frequently earn. *Risk,* which may be defined as exposure to losses or injuries, is an ever-present hazard to the successful operation of a business. Damage from fire, water, or wind; the untimely death of a key executive; price changes; and even shifts in the whims and fancies of customers are just a few of the unexpected possibilities that can cause business losses.

The burden of some types of risks can be shifted, either wholly or in part, to businesses organized for such purposes. Other types of risks cannot be passed on and must be assumed by the owners and managers of business units. Together, the hazards of risks that can only be shifted in part and those that cannot be shifted at all constitute as much of a burden as most businesses care to bear. Consequently, sound management usually dictates that, when possible, use be made of companies which, for a fee, will relieve the firm of all insurable risks.

Businesses organized for the express purpose of assuming certain types of risks are known as *insurance companies*. By a process called *underwriting,* the insurance company enters into an agreement with a business to reimburse it for losses of specific types. In return for a payment, known as a *premium,* the insured business receives a printed document, called an *insurance policy,* that specifies the terms of the insurance contract.

This chapter will examine the various types of risks to which most businesses are exposed, indicating some that must be absorbed as opposed to others against which insurance can be carried. Considerable attention will then be devoted to the various insurance coverages carried by large

453

major risk - cannot operate at a profit

and small firms in their efforts to protect themselves against losses. Since most of the policies that businesses purchase are also available to individuals, an understanding of insurance will prove personally beneficial even though the emphasis in this chapter will be on business applications.

■ Types of Business Risks

The major risk facing any business enterprise is the ever-present possibility that it cannot be operated at a profit. If the income from sales or services is inadequate to meet necessary expenses, losses result. If these continue for any length of time, sooner or later the business will have to discontinue operations. Thousands of businesses fail each year with resultant losses to the owners and, frequently, to creditors as well. The possibility that a business, old or new, may not be able to survive in our competitive economy is inherent in a capitalistic system.

Other internal risks include, for example, losses from fire, theft, product liability, and injuries to employees. These are all insurable and most firms find it worthwhile to purchase appropriate insurance policies despite the sizable premiums involved. The total cost of insurance premiums becomes an expense of doing business that enters into a firm's costs and is a factor in the prices it charges for goods or services.

Most of the types of risks that are not insurable are external rather than internal. The individual business frequently has little or no control over a course of events that may prove disastrous to it. Some of the more common categories of risks that must be assumed are as follows:

1. Development of new products
2. Changes in distribution methods
3. Fluctuations in prices
4. Changes in laws

1 / Development of new products that replace the old. The classic example of the firm that continued to manufacture buggy whips after the advent of the automobile or the horseless carriage, as it was called, points up the nature of this hazard to an established business. At the present time the application of atomic energy to industrial uses, notably the generation of electric power, concerns the management of several businesses. The recent decision of the TVA to build a nuclear-powered generating plant in the very heart of the coal-mining area is a severe blow to the latter industry.

2 / Changes in distribution methods. The comparatively recent development of chain stores, supermarkets, and shopping centers has had an impact on the small, independently owned stores. Many have been forced to close their doors.

3 / Fluctuations in prices and price levels. If raw materials are an important element in the cost of a finished product, a sharp increase in their cost may cause losses to a firm that is committed to sell at a fixed price. Or, as happened in the thirties when prices dropped to depression levels, many businesses were operated at a loss as costs did not shrink in proportion to sales prices.

4 / Changes in laws. When changes are made in tariffs that permit increased imports of competitive goods, the local firm may find itself unable to price its products above its costs. Likewise, when a city, a town, a county, or a state votes to prohibit liquor sales, taverns, night clubs, and restaurants in that area may be forced out of business.

■ Protection Against Risks

Sound business management is one of the best antidotes against losses. Businesses compete with each other and the efficient ones survive. A well-managed firm using modern equipment and methods has a much better chance of success than does a company with outmoded techniques of manufacturing and selling. Such a firm protects itself against the risk of obsolete products or methods of distribution by a generous allocation of funds for research and development. It installs safety devices on its machines, builds fireproof or fire-resistant buildings, installs sprinkler systems, and conducts safety programs among its employees. Capital may be conserved by leasing space and equipment or by subcontracting a portion of its manufacturing requirements until such time as equity capital is available.

Excellent management also recognizes that protection against many of the types of risks already mentioned can best be secured by purchasing insurance policies. There are, however, two situations worthy of mention that do not involve insurance companies. One of these may apply to large organizations that own so many factories, warehouses, stores, trucks, and other supplies and equipment scattered throughout the country that normal losses will cost less than insurance premiums. Rebuilding, for example, a section of a warehouse following fire damage may well be much less expensive than paying for full fire protection on two or three hundred buildings valued at millions of dollars. This method of protection against risks is called *self-insurance,* which should involve annual deposits into a special fund from which losses can be paid.

Insurance - most common method of
protection against risks
highly specialized

For firms that use raw materials traded on commodity exchanges, protection can be secured against price changes while the materials are being processed. A *commodity exchange* is a trading center, not unlike a security exchange, on which such products as wheat, corn, soybeans, oats, coffee, sugar, and cotton are bought and sold. The largest and best known commodity exchanges are the Chicago Board of Trade, the Kansas City Board of Trade, and the New York Cotton Exchange. On these exchanges it is possible to buy or sell a contract for future delivery of any of the commodities listed. A manufacturer of flour, for example, will buy wheat for processing and sell a *futures contract* for the same number of bushels to be delivered when the flour is ready for the market. At that time it buys a contract for delivery of wheat to the original buyer of the futures contract. If the price of wheat has gone up or down, the gain or loss on the futures transaction will be offset by a larger or smaller profit on the flour. The sale of a futures contract on a commodity exchange to protect a legitimate manufacturing profit on the later sale of the finished product is called *hedging*.

Despite the above exceptions, insurance remains by far the most common method of protection against risks. Consequently, after an examination of the characteristics of insurable risks, attention will be given to organizations that write insurance coverages and to the various types of policies that are useful in the business world.

■ **Characteristics of Insurable Risks**

The characteristics of a risk that can be shifted to a company formed for this purpose are as follows:

(1) The annual loss must be predictable. The number of people who will die each year or the number of houses that will burn each year can be predicted with amazing accuracy.

(2) The risk must be spread over a wide geographical area. A fire insurance company could not afford to insure all the houses in one city only. A disastrous fire such as occurred in Chicago in 1871 would bankrupt the company.

(3) Risks must be selected. No company can afford to insure only people who are seriously ill, have heart trouble, or make their living testing new airplanes.

(4) The risks must be numerous enough as a group to make the law of averages work. Insuring one life for a small annual premium could not be done on a scientific basis, but insuring the lives of 100,000 people can.

How does a policy insuring the hands of a piano player for $100,000 or the nose of a movie actor for a fabulous sum fit into the classification of insurable risks? The answer is that such policies are not written except by Lloyds of London, an organization that is not an insurance company but rather an association through which members offer to underwrite hazards of all types. Marine insurance, which falls within the classification of insurable risks, forms the bulk, though not the spectacular portion, of the underwriting business of Lloyds.

■ Insurance Underwriters

Insurance is a highly specialized business, and each underwriter handles only certain classifications of risks. In the private sector, there are two major types of company ownership—stock companies and mutual companies, both of which were explained in Chapter 5. In the life insurance field mutual companies predominate, and the reverse situation is true for property and casualty insurance companies. In one area, hospital costs and surgical fees, nonprofit Blue Cross and Blue Shield corporations play a dominant role.

Both states and the federal government are also in the insurance picture, sometimes in competition with private enterprise. All states participate in a nationwide plan of unemployment insurance, and some states operate retirement plans for state employees and underwrite workmen's compensation insurance. The federal government insures parcel post packages, deposits of banks and of savings and loan associations, and through the Old-Age, Survivors, and Disability Insurance System, better known as Social Security, has embarked on an extensive program of payment to retired or disabled workers or their surviving dependents. At times, it has made low-cost life insurance available to members of the armed services. The Federal Housing Administration insures private lending agencies against loss on FHA approved loans made to buy, build, or remodel homes.

Beginning on July 1, 1966, the federal government embarked on a program of health insurance for individuals 65 years of age or older. As a feature of Medicare, all individuals 65 years of age or older are entitled to hospitalization, extended care, home health, and out-patient hospital diagnostic benefits. If these persons elect to pay $3 a month, which is matched by the federal government, they receive medical insurance that, after a $50 deductible amount for each year, will pay 80 percent of doctor's, home health, and other medical services. Excluded from coverage are such items as eyeglasses and patent medicines.

■ Types of Insurance Coverages

The types of insurance policies available to businesses and individuals are numerous and varied. The major classifications are (1) property and casualty insurance and (2) life insurance. This division is in line with the sales outlets of insurance companies. Individuals or firms engaged in the business of selling insurance are customarily either general insurance agents or life insurance agents. A general insurance agency handles all types of property and casualty insurance and represents a number of different companies, including competing concerns in the same underwriting field. The agency may represent a life insurance company too, but it does not stress this area of its business. The life insurance agent normally sells policies on a commission basis for only one company.

Further evidence of these two classifications is found in the professional designations, CLU and CPCU, that are granted to individuals who qualify for and pass certain examinations. The initials *CLU* stand for Chartered Life Underwriter and the abbreviation *CPCU* designates a Chartered Property and Casualty Underwriter.

The remainder of this chapter will discuss first some of the more common types of property and casualty insurance, such as fire, automobile, theft, accident and health, marine, and fidelity and surety bonds as well as other coverages falling within this classification. This discussion will be followed by a description of the different types and uses of life insurance policies.

PROPERTY AND CASUALTY INSURANCE

Specialization on the part of underwriting companies indicates four major classifications of property and casualty insurance. These are:

1. Fire insurance
2. Casualty insurance
3. Marine insurance
4. Fidelity and surety bonds

Within recent years the dividing line among these classifications has been disappearing as policies have become more and more comprehensive in their coverages. For example, automobile insurance is a form of casualty insurance, but practically all such policies cover damage that may be caused by fire.

■ Fire Insurance

One of the common risks against which insurance is carried is that of fire. Homes, apartment houses, store buildings, factories, and almost every type of building can be insured against loss resulting from fire. The same thing is true of the contents, whether it be furniture, merchandise, machinery, or supplies of any type and description. Policies are sold on a one-, three-, or five-year basis as a general rule. Longer term policies are less expensive; a three-year policy costs 2.7 times the annual rate, and a five-year policy, 4.4 times the one-year premium.

Premium rates are relatively low but vary considerably in different geographical areas and among types of construction. For example, cities are graded on such items as water supply, fire alarms, building laws, and the efficiency of the fire department. Within the city the location of a building is important as it may stand between two old buildings or at some distance from other structures. If the construction is considered fireproof, the rate will be lower than on frame buildings. The lowest rates are in the neighborhood of 10 cents for each $100 of coverage, and more hazardous risks may cost $2 for each $100.

1 / Coinsurance clauses. Fire damage to industrial property resulting in complete destruction of the property insured is rare. If it were permissible to buy an insurance policy for one third or one half of the total value of the property owned, the annual saving in insurance premiums would probably offset a fire loss in excess of this coverage. Insur-

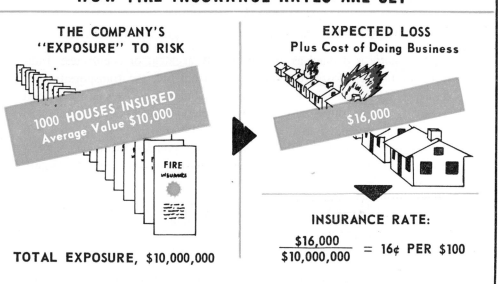

HOW FIRE INSURANCE RATES ARE SET

THE COMPANY'S "EXPOSURE" TO RISK

1000 HOUSES INSURED
Average Value $10,000

FIRE INSURANCE

TOTAL EXPOSURE, $10,000,000

EXPECTED LOSS
Plus Cost of Doing Business

$16,000

INSURANCE RATE:

$$\frac{\$16,000}{\$10,000,000} = 16¢ \text{ PER } \$100$$

Institute of Life Insurance

ance companies protect themselves against this reduced premium income by inserting in the policy what is known as a *coinsurance clause,* which requires that the insured buy coverage up to a stipulated percent of the value of the property, usually 80 percent, or assume a proportion of each fire loss. In most states residence property is not subject to coinsurance clause restrictions.

If a factory is properly valued at $100,000 but is insured against fire for only $50,000, the risk is only partially covered because the minimum insurance for full protection against partial losses is 80 percent or $80,000. If a fire occurs with a total damage of $20,000, the insurance company will pay $50,000/$80,000 or ⅝ of the loss. This means a payment of $12,500 even though the loss was $20,000.

2 / Allied coverages. By the addition to a fire insurance policy of a special agreement, known as a *rider* or *endorsement,* the insuring company will cover such losses as wind or water damage. Within recent years a fire and extended coverage policy has proved very popular. This type of policy, in addition to fire coverage, includes protection against windstorm, cyclone, tornado, hail, explosion, riot, aircraft, smoke, and vehicle damage. For individuals, a comprehensive dwelling or so-called homeowners policy is available that covers casualty losses as well as damage to the property. This type of policy is in line with a general trend to incorporate more and more types of coverages in a single comprehensive insurance contract.

■ Casualty Insurance

A *casualty* is defined as an unfortunate accident or occurrence. Individual or business losses that may result from fire, the transportation of goods, or death fall within this definition, but these losses are classified separately for insurance purposes. All other types of risks that qualify as casualties are included in the broad category of *casualty insurance.* No attempt will be made to itemize all of the policies available, but an examination of the most common types will clarify the area of casualty insurance.

1. Automobile insurance
2. Theft insurance
3. Accident and health insurance
4. Workmen's compensation
5. Public liability insurance
6. Miscellaneous casualty coverages

1 / Automobile insurance. The usual types of automobile coverage include fire and theft, bodily injury liability, property damage, and collision insurance. If the policy covers fire and theft, the amount paid the insured in case of total loss is the value of the car at the date of the fire or theft. Within recent years automobile insurance companies have offered *comprehensive coverage*, which is a contract that covers practically all damage to the insured's automobile, including fire and theft, except that resulting from collision and upset. For example, claims have been paid for accidental damage to upholstery and for windshields broken by flying stones.

Bodily injury liability insurance will pay the policyholder's legal liability for injury to one person or to a group. If a driver hits a pedestrian or causes injury to persons in another car, the insurance company will pay damages up to the amount of coverage carried. A common policy fixes a maximum of $5,000 for liability resulting from the death or disability of one person, and $10,000 for similar reasons to more than one person. This type of policy is frequently identified by the fraction 5/10. Higher maximum coverages than 5/10 can be obtained in amounts such as 10/20 or 20/40 by paying a higher premium.

A *medical payments endorsement* can be purchased that will pay hospital and doctor bills up to a specified maximum for each occupant of the insured's car who is injured in an accident, including the policyholder. In many states legislation that relieves the driver of a car from liability for injury to his passengers arising from an accident has been enacted. Such "guest laws," as they are termed, were passed to prevent friendly suits against the car owner with the knowledge that the insurance company would finance the settlement.

Property damage liability insurance is stated at a single amount, such as $5,000. If the insured car damages another car, or runs into a house, or damages any property not belonging to the insured, the insurance company will settle the claim up to the amount of the policy. It will not pay anything for damages to the policyholder's car unless *collision* or *upset insurance* is carried. This type of coverage protects the car owner against any damage to his automobile resulting from an accident, but it is relatively expensive unless he purchases collision insurance with a deductible allowance, such as $50 or $100. In this event the insurance company pays for damages that are in excess of the stipulated deductible amount. Many drivers do not carry collision insurance because of the relatively high cost, although cars purchased on the installment plan are so covered in order to protect the finance company.

Many states have passed financial responsibility laws. These usually provide that the driver of a car at fault in an accident must show evidence that he has assumed his financial obligation in order to merit his

[handwritten note: residence burglary = most common / accident & health = oldest form]

continued right to operate his automobile. Ownership of an insurance policy covering bodily injury and property damage liability is the preferable method of demonstrating financial responsibility.

2 / Theft insurance. The most common types of theft insurance are burglary and robbery. The former covers the unlawful taking of property within premises closed for business, and evidence of forcible entry must be visible. The latter covers the unlawful taking of property from another person.

Although residence burglary insurance is the most common type written, the businessman is more interested in other forms. These include mercantile open stock, business safe, office burglary and robbery, and paymaster protection. Small retailers can obtain a comprehensive storekeepers' burglary and robbery policy that will cover safe and mercantile open stock burglary; damage to money, securities, merchandise, or equipment caused by burglary or robbery; theft of money or securities from a residence or night depository; kidnapping an employee to gain entrance; and robbery inside or outside the business premises. Pilferage of merchandise from a store during open hours is not covered by burglary insurance because the requirement of visible evidence of breaking or entering is lacking.

3 / Accident and health insurance. The oldest form of casualty insurance is accident and health insurance. In case of an accident, which may occur at any place and at any time, the policyholder will receive weekly payments; certain medical expenses will be taken care of; and, if the accident results in a serious disability or loss of life, a specified sum is paid. For example, if the insured loses a hand in an automobile accident, he may draw weekly payments for 100 weeks, or the policy may specify a lump sum payment such as $2,500.

Broadly speaking, health insurance covers all expenditures necessary because of loss of health not resulting from an accident, including loss of income. One policy may cover physician's services, surgical fees, hospital charges, and income payments; or, as is frequently true, more than one policy is involved. For example, as noted earlier in this chapter, the federal government and Blue Cross and Blue Shield organizations play an important role in paying costs connected with hospitalization. A recent popular addition to health insurance is a major medical policy that pays all costs up to a specified maximum, such as $10,000, that are in excess of a deductible amount, frequently $300, incurred in connection with a single accident or illness.

Ferre Grignard - vangaurd records
"THE GYPSY - "Gordon Lightfoot

Many employers have taken out group accident and health insurance covering their employees. Such policies frequently pay as high as two thirds of the regular salary of the employee, in addition to medical expenses, for a period of 26 weeks. Sometimes, the employer pays the cost of the policy; in other cases, the employee contributes all or a share of the cost under a payroll deduction plan.

4 / Workmen's compensation. Almost all states have passed laws making it compulsory for employers to purchase workmen's compensation insurance. Certain classes of workers, notably farm and domestic laborers, are exempted, and a certain minimum number of employees is usually stated. In some states, the workmen's compensation insurance is a monopoly of the state; in others, private insurance companies compete with state funds; and in still others, private insurance companies handle the business unless the employing company is large enough to warrant approval for self-insurance. The rates are assessed against the payroll, and they vary with the hazard of the industry.

The purpose of *workmen's compensation insurance* is to guarantee medical expenses and salary payments to workers who are injured on the job unless it can be shown that the employee's injury or death was willful or caused by intoxication. The usual practice is to specify weekly benefits. These are set at a fraction of the regular wage, such as one half or two thirds, in order to discourage those who might prefer to draw benefits rather than work. A waiting period of from a few days to two weeks is also a common provision of many laws. This means that no benefits can be drawn until the expiration of the waiting period, which eliminates claims for minor accidents. In case of death, weekly payments are made to the dependents of the deceased for a specified period, frequently eight years.

5 / Public liability insurance. A great many manufacturers, retailers, service industries, entertainment centers, building operators, and even homeowners, buy a public liability insurance policy. The purpose is to protect the policyholder against claims that may be made by the public from real or fancied injuries received while using the facilities or products of the business. For example, the manufacturer of candy bars might be sued by an individual who claimed damage to his dental bridgework caused by a stone in a candy bar. This type of coverage is known as *products liability insurance.*

Most public liability policies are concerned with injuries that are received on the premises of the insured. Building operators are subject to elevator accident risks, people fall down steps in darkened movie theaters, and visitors to industrial plants may be hit by a moving crane. In each case there may be a claim against the property owner because he can be held responsible for conditions that permit the accident. Although liability insurance covering each specific type of risk is available, most businesses purchase a comprehensive general liability policy.

6 / Miscellaneous casualty coverages. The number of types of insurance coverage that can be secured from casualty companies is almost endless. Additional common types, which are practically self-explanatory, include plate glass insurance, steam boiler insurance, power plant insurance, use and occupancy losses following shutdowns as a result of a fire, and power interruption insurance.

■ Marine Insurance

Two general types of marine insurance are ocean marine and inland marine. Both are transportation insurance and, despite the connotation of the word "marine," inland marine insurance need not involve shipment by water.

1 / Ocean marine insurance. The oldest form of insurance is that on ships of all types as well as their cargoes. An *ocean marine insurance* contract covers practically all perils of shipments on the high seas, including all degrees of loss from injury to the vessel and contents up to a complete loss of both as a result of sinking. Fire insurance is included as a part of the policy.

2 / Inland marine insurance. A typical *inland marine insurance* policy provides protection against loss on movable goods while being transported by rail, truck, airplane, inland and coastwise steamers, and barges. Such a policy covers a variety of risks, such as hazards of water and land transport, fire, and theft. Of interest to many businessmen is a form of inland marine insurance designed to cover shipments of merchandise by parcel post. One method is to buy a coupon book that provides insurance tickets to be inserted in each parcel shipped; another is a blanket policy that covers all parcel post shipments. Either method is less expensive and less bothersome than insuring each package at the post office.

A type of inland marine insurance that has become quite popular in recent years is the *personal property floater*. This policy provides protection of personal property from all hazards wherever located—in the home, in transit, or abroad. It is a comprehensive type of coverage that includes fire and theft protection as well as other risks. Under such a policy the personal effects of a student attending college away from home can be covered in transit or while at his college residence, as well as clothes mailed back and forth in laundry bags.

■ Fidelity and Surety Bonds

Fidelity and surety companies specialize in guaranteeing policyholders that other individuals, corporations, and agents with whom the insured may have business relations are reliable. In many cases losses might result from such connections, and the business firm is not in a position to investigate the character or financial responsibility of each of the persons or corporations involved. The only way that the company can protect itself against such losses is by carrying the proper insurance protection. In fact, members of a board of directors occupying a position of trust may find themselves personally liable for losses if employees are not properly bonded.

Fidelity bonds are usually written to cover an employee occupying a position of trust in which he has jurisdiction over funds. The employer is guaranteed against loss caused by the dishonesty of such employees, and the insurance company will reimburse the policyholder for losses up to the amount specified in the policy. Coverages may be individual, or group, or may name positions. For example, a business firm may secure a fidelity bond on specifically named employees for such varying amounts as the funds to which each has access. Or, the company may secure a policy covering a group of employees in a particular department. Still another possibility is to purchase a policy in which positions and the amounts of coverage are specified, such as treasurer—$50,000. Whoever is hired for a specified task is bonded for the stated amount.

Surety bonds are written to protect the insured against loss from the nonperformance of a contract or the nonperformance of any agreed-upon act or business transaction. A building contractor, for example, might be required to furnish a surety bond that he will erect a factory according to specifications and within the allowed time interval.

LIFE INSURANCE

As in the case of other forms of insurance, life insurance is based on the law of averages. No one can predict whether a particular individual will die during any given year, but the number of persons living at the beginning of a year who will die within twelve months can be computed within narrow margins. The annual premium on a life insurance policy is related to statistics covering deaths as compiled by actuaries. An *actuary* is an individual employed by an insurance company who is an expert at computing risks and the size of insurance premiums necessary to the profitable operation of his company. Although insurance companies rely on more than one table, many states require the use of a mortality schedule compiled by the National Association of Insurance Commissioners, an organization of state insurance commissioners. In 1958 this body adopted the Commissioners Standard Ordinary Mortality Table, which is shown on page 467.

Note that the *CSO 1958 Mortality Table,* as it is called, covers the life history of ten million people beginning at birth and continuing to the age of 99. For each year there is shown the number living at the beginning of the year, the number who will die during the year, and the death rate per 1,000 for that year. For example, at the age of 18 a total of 9,698,230 young men and women will be living out of the original group of 10 million. During the year 16,390 will die, which is a death rate of 1.69 per 1,000.

Life insurance has a number of applications to business, although it is true that most policies are purchased by individuals for the protection of their families. Businesses have discovered that carrying a policy on an important executive or financing a retirement plan through a life insurance policy may prove to be a wise expenditure of funds. A life insurance policy covering all employees is very popular today as a fringe benefit, which may have been negotiated by a labor union.

■ Types of Life Insurance Policies

Before discussing specific applications of insurance policies to business uses, it is important to have some understanding of the four basic types of policies available, each of which has its place in business.

1. Term life insurance
2. Straight life insurance
3. Limited-payment life insurance
4. Endowment life insurance

1 / Term life insurance. *Term life insurance* bears a similarity to fire insurance in that the insurance company is obligated to pay only if a loss (death in this case) occurs within the time limit covered by the policy. If the insured is living at the end of the specified term, all premiums paid are the property of the insurance company and the policy automatically expires. If term life insurance policies were written on an annual basis,

Commissioners 1958 Standard Ordinary
Mortality Table

Age	Number Living	Deaths Each Year	Death Rate per 1,000	Age	Number Living	Deaths Each Year	Death Rate per 1,000
0	10,000,000	70,800	7.08	50	8,762,306	72,902	8.32
1	9,929,200	17,475	1.76	51	8,689,404	79,160	9.11
2	9,911,725	15,066	1.52	52	8,610,244	85,758	9.96
3	9,896,659	14,449	1.46	53	8,524,486	92,832	10.89
4	9,882,210	13,835	1.40	54	8,431,654	100,337	11.90
5	9,868,375	13,322	1.35	55	8,331,317	108,307	13.00
6	9,855,053	12,812	1.30	56	8,223,010	116,849	14.21
7	9,842,241	12,401	1.26	57	8,106,161	125,970	15.54
8	9,829,840	12,091	1.23	58	7,980,191	135,663	17.00
9	9,817,749	11,879	1.21	59	7,844,528	145,830	18.59
10	9,805,870	11,865	1.21	60	7,698,698	156,592	20.34
11	9,794,005	12,047	1.23	61	7,542,106	167,736	22.24
12	9,781,958	12,325	1.26	62	7,374,370	179,271	24.31
13	9,769,633	12,896	1.32	63	7,195,099	191,174	26.57
14	9,756,737	13,562	1.39	64	7,003,925	203,394	29.04
15	9,743,175	14,225	1.46	65	6,800,531	215,917	31.75
16	9,728,950	14,983	1.54	66	6,584,614	228,749	34.74
17	9,713,967	15,737	1.62	67	6,355,865	241,777	38.04
18	9,698,230	16,390	1.69	68	6,114,088	254,835	41.68
19	9,681,840	16,846	1.74	69	5,859,253	267,241	45.61
20	9,664,994	17,300	1.79	70	5,592,012	278,426	49.79
21	9,647,694	17,655	1.83	71	5,313,586	287,731	54.15
22	9,630,039	17,912	1.86	72	5,025,855	294,766	58.65
23	9,612,127	18,167	1.89	73	4,731,089	299,289	63.26
24	9,593,960	18,324	1.91	74	4,431,800	301,894	68.12
25	9,575,636	18,481	1.93	75	4,129,906	303,011	73.37
26	9,557,155	18,732	1.96	76	3,826,895	303,014	79.18
27	9,538,423	18,981	1.99	77	3,523,881	301,997	85.70
28	9,519,442	19,324	2.03	78	3,221,884	299,829	93.06
29	9,500,118	19,760	2.08	79	2,922,055	295,683	101.19
30	9,480,358	20,193	2.13	80	2,626,372	288,848	109.98
31	9,460,165	20,718	2.19	81	2,337,524	278,983	119.35
32	9,439,447	21,239	2.25	82	2,058,541	265,902	129.17
33	9,418,208	21,850	2.32	83	1,792,639	249,858	139.38
34	9,396,358	22,551	2.40	84	1,542,781	231,433	150.01
35	9,373,807	23,528	2.51	85	1,311,348	211,311	161.14
36	9,350,279	24,685	2.64	86	1,100,037	190,108	172.82
37	9,325,594	26,112	2.80	87	909,929	168,455	185.13
38	9,299,482	27,991	3.01	88	741,474	146,997	198.25
39	9,271,491	30,132	3.25	89	594,477	126,303	212.46
40	9,241,359	32,622	3.53	90	468,174	106,809	228.14
41	9,208,737	35,362	3.84	91	361,365	88,813	245.77
42	9,173,375	38,253	4.17	92	272,552	72,480	265.93
43	9,135,122	41,382	4.53	93	200,072	57,881	289.30
44	9,093,740	44,741	4.92	94	142,191	45,026	316.66
45	9,048,999	48,412	5.35	95	97,165	34,128	351.24
46	9,000,587	52,473	5.83	96	63,037	25,250	400.56
47	8,948,114	56,910	6.36	97	37,787	18,456	488.42
48	8,891,204	61,794	6.95	98	19,331	12,916	668.15
49	8,829,410	67,104	7.60	99	6,415	6,415	1,000.00

the CSO 1958 Table can be used to compute a basic cost. Referring to the figures shown above, if all of the 9,698,230 eighteen-year-old men and women were insured for $1,000 for one year, the insurance company would pay out during the year $16,390,000 to the *beneficiaries* (the persons who receive the face value of a policy) of the 16,390 individuals who would die during the year. This means that, if a premium payment of $1.69 were made for each policy, the insurance company would have just enough money to meet the necessary outlay. The actual premium would, of course, need to be higher for several reasons, including meeting the expenses of doing business. Note that the costs of term insurance computed on this basis would increase year by year amounting to $3.53 per $1,000 at age 40 and increasing to $20.34 at age 60.

Individuals who buy term insurance usually prefer a *level-term contract,* that is, one that does not require a larger premium payment each year. Examples are 5-year, 10-year, and 20-year term insurance. These policies are usually renewable up to the age of 65 without the necessity of the policyholder providing evidence of his insurability. Group life insurance, which will be discussed later in this chapter, is written on a one-year basis.

The chief advantage of term life insurance is its low cost. More protection can be purchased for a given premium payment than is available under any other type of life insurance policy. Since most term policies are convertible into more permanent forms of life insurance, they are especially attractive to young persons faced with family and home responsibilities.

2 / Straight life insurance. The most popular form of life insurance is *straight life.* The premium, which remains constant throughout the life of the insured, varies with the age at which the coverage is purchased; and the policy combines a plan of protection and savings. The advantage of a straight life policy is that maximum protection can be attained for the lowest premium, with the single exception of term insurance. Disadvantages include the fact that the insured must die before full payment is made on the policy and also that premiums may be due in years after earning capacity has ceased. If a man retires at 65, he must still continue to pay premiums.

The reason that straight life premium rates are higher than those charged for term insurance is that each payment contains an element of savings as well as the amount necessary to buy protection. These savings remain with the life insurance company, unless the policy is canceled, and provide what is known as the *cash surrender value* of the insurance con-

Guess Who- "Love and a yellow Rose"

tract. If the policyholder lives a number of years, the cash value increases to a sizable amount in relationship to the face value.

3 / **Limited payment life insurance.** The differences between *limited-payment life insurance* and straight life insurance are that premiums on limited-payment policies are due for only a stated number of years, the annual payments are larger, and the cash surrender values are higher. The most common period of time is twenty years, although any number of years can be selected. The advantage of this type of policy is that the individual is able to eliminate the drain of premium payments extending over a lifetime and can concentrate his expenditures for life insurance within the period of his maximum earning capacity. The chief disadvantage is that more protection could have been secured for the same annual outlay if straight life had been selected. As in the case of straight life, the insurance company pays the face value of the policy only upon the death of the insured.

4 / **Endowment life insurance.** *Endowment life insurance* is similar to limited-payment insurance with the exception that it emphasizes the savings element in a contract over the protective features. The annual premium is larger than for straight or limited-payment life, and consequently the cash surrender value of the policy increases at a faster rate. At the expiration of a stated number of years, which may be an even figure such as 30 or the number of years before the insured reaches 65, the cash value of the policy equals its face. If, at the age of 30, a man takes out a $1,000 endowment policy running for 30 years, he has automatically created an estate of $1,000 by the time he is 60. If he dies within this period, the insurance company will pay the face of the policy. If, however, he lives to the age of 60, the company will pay him the face of the policy at that time, or he may elect to receive annual payments.

The following premiums of an insurance company for selected ages indicate the relative costs of the different types of policies described per $1,000 of coverages for policies of from $10,000 to $25,000.

Age	5-Year Renewable Term	Straight Life	Twenty-Pay Life	20-Year Endowment
20	$ 4.88	$15.21	$26.71	$47.96
30	5.41	20.00	32.29	48.58
40	7.90	27.85	40.12	50.86
50	15.20	41.09	51.74	57.05

■ Business Uses of Life Insurance

Life insurance can be and is used by sole proprietorships, partnerships, and corporations. Some of the more common adaptations of policies to business uses are described below:

1. Group life insurance
2. Credit life insurance

3. Insurance on owners or executives
4. Retirement and pension plans

1 / Group life insurance. The most extensive use of life insurance by business in recent years has centered about *group life insurance*, which is simply a policy covering each employee of a single firm for a sum such as $5,000, or the amount may vary with different categories of ·employees. Such insurance is usually written on a one-year renewable term plan. It is distinctive in that no medical examination is required. This is possible because of the number, as well as the composition, of the group covered. Most employers do not hire workers who are not physically fit, and most of them are in a relatively healthy age bracket.

The employer usually pays at least a portion of the premium, which really constitutes a bonus to the employee. Rates are lower than for any form of an individual policy because the premiums are paid by the company in one check, which greatly reduces collection costs; there are no medical examination fees; and commission rates are lower than on other types. The $306 billion in group term insurance outstanding at the end of 1965 provides some idea of the extensive use business makes of this form of life insurance.

2 / Credit life insurance. The extensive purchase of goods on the installment plan and the use of short-term borrowing by consumers has made credit life insurance the fastest-growing form of life insurance. *Credit life insurance* guarantees repayment of amounts due on installment contracts or personal loans in case the debtor dies. It has assumed one of the risks of consumer financing, both for the lender and the borrower.

Banks, finance companies, credit unions, and retailers are the chief purchasers of credit life insurance. It is written on a one-year basis, and the amount applicable to a borrower decreases as he reduces his debt. Practically all credit life insurance is written on a group basis, although individual policies are available. The extensive use of credit life insurance has resulted in outstanding policies in excess of $40 billion.

Credit life insurance should not be confused with *credit insurance*, which is a type of policy available to a firm insuring it against unusually

3 common methods of insuring pensions
1. deposit administration plan
2. paid-up annuity benefit
3. trust plan (life insurance)

high losses resulting from the extension of credit on open-book or charge accounts. Normal losses are absorbed by the company, but amounts in excess of a stated sum are reimbursed by the insurance company.

3 / Insurance on owners or executives. If a sole proprietor dies, his business may have to be sold to pay funeral and administration expenses, and taxes. An adequate term life insurance policy payable to his estate can avoid the necessity for a sale, and his business can be continued by his widow, son, or other heirs. A straight, limited-payment, or endowment policy might be preferable, since any one of these types could be used during the lifetime of the owner as a support for his credit standing, as collateral for a bank loan, and as a basis for a retirement plan.

When a partner dies, the partnership must be dissolved; but the question remains as to who will buy the deceased's interest in the firm. A term life insurance contract payable to the surviving partner or partners can provide a fund with which to buy this interest and avoid the necessity of taking in a new partner. If it is assumed that the partner is to retire at a given age, an endowment policy maturing at the agreed retirement age guarantees that funds will be available to buy out his interest.

Some corporations have found that their profitability is closely connected to the abilities and contacts of one or two key executives. Carrying an insurance policy on their lives, payable to the corporation, can provide a cushion to absorb the reduction in earning power that might result from the death of one of these individuals. These funds could well carry the company through the months necessary to hire and train an adequate replacement.

4 / Retirement and pension plans. Firms interested in providing a continuing income to retired employees above and beyond the benefits from the federal social security system can finance such a program through insurance companies. Currently, some 7 million employees are covered by insured pension plans and the number is growing rapidly each year.

There are three commonly used methods of insuring pensions. The most widely favored by business is a so-called deposit administration plan in which a single fund is established with an insurance company that covers all employees. As each employee retires, money is withdrawn from the fund to purchase an annuity for him. Another popular method involves the purchase each year of a paid-up annuity benefit for each employee. Smaller firms frequently make use of a pension trust plan, which requires the purchase of a life insurance policy for each covered employee.

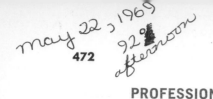

PROFESSIONAL ASSOCIATION IN INSURANCE

The American Risk and Insurance Association is devoted to furthering the science of risk and insurance through education, research, literature, and communications. Founded in 1932 as the American Association of University Teachers of Insurance, the Association now has 1,500 members drawn from academic institutions and the insurance business in all parts of the world. It holds an annual meeting, has a Commission on Insurance Terminology, and supports research. A major activity is the publication of a quarterly magazine *Journal of Risk and Insurance*. A special student membership rate includes a subscription to the Journal.

BUSINESS TERMS

(a) risk (453), insurance company (453), underwriting (453)
(b) premium (453), insurance policy (453)
(c) self-insurance (455)
(d) commodity exchange (456), futures contract (456), hedging (456)
(e) CLU (458), CPCU (458)
(f) coinsurance clause (460), rider or endorsement (460)
(g) casualty (460), casualty insurance (460)
(h) comprehensive coverage (461), bodily injury liability insurance (461), medical payments endorsement (461), property damage liability insurance (461), collision or upset insurance (461)
(i) workmen's compensation insurance (463)
(j) products liability insurance (463)
(k) ocean marine insurance (464), inland marine insurance (464), personal property floater (464)
(l) fidelity bond (465), surety bond (465)
(m) actuary (466), CSO 1958 Mortality Table (466)
(n) term life insurance (466), beneficiary (468), level-term contract (468)
(o) straight life insurance (468), cash surrender value (468)
(p) limited-payment life insurance (469), endowment life insurance (469)
(q) group life insurance (470), credit life insurance (470), credit insurance (470)

QUESTIONS FOR DISCUSSION AND ANALYSIS

1. What are some of the risks, both internal and external, that a business must assume in addition to the ones mentioned in the text? Give specific examples.
2. Can you name any consumer products on the market today that have substantially replaced products in general use at the turn of this century?
3. The federal government and most states do not insure the properties they own. Is this an example of self-insurance?

4. What are some of the common characteristics of commodities traded on commodity exchanges?
5. Why should the states and the federal government conduct insurance programs? Which ones are in competition with private enterprise?
6. What are some of the reasons a fire insurance policy on a business property frequently contains a coinsurance clause whereas it rarely does on residential property?
7. If a business firm owns and operates a fleet of 100 trucks, what types of automobile insurance, if any, should it carry?
8. Although business losses from pilferage run into millions of dollars annually, insurance is not written covering thievery of this type. Why is this so?
9. All property and casualty insurance is sold on a term basis. Why has this practice not been universally followed in the life insurance field?
10. What reasons can be given for the extensive use of group life insurance by employers?

PROBLEMS AND SHORT CASES

1. A business property is appraised as being worth $1,000,000. Assuming that the owner takes out a fire insurance policy with an 80% coinsurance clause, how much insurance can be collected in each of the following situations?

	FIRE LOSS	INSURANCE COVERAGE
(a)	$ 200,000	$400,000
(b)	400,000	500,000
(c)	600,000	600,000
(d)	800,000	700,000
(e)	1,000,000	800,000

2. Assume that the average age of 1,000 employees is 30 and that a company wishes to purchase a $10,000 group life insurance policy for each worker on a one-year basis. If the insurance company needs a 20 percent margin on total premiums to cover its costs with a reasonable margin of safety, what would be the premium cost of this policy? Refer to the Commissioners 1958 Standard Ordinary Mortality Table shown on page 467 to compute your answer.
3. The Townsend Corporation employs 2,000 factory and office workers at a central location in a midwest city. Its sales over the past five years have averaged $25,000,000, its profits before taxes $2,500,000, and it regularly pays $1 in dividends on the 600,000 shares of common stock outstanding. Although the corporation is now publicly owned, Adam Townsend, the founder of the firm, is Chairman of the Board of Directors, and his son Karl is the President. There has never been a labor union in the corporation due, in part, to the

attitude of Adam Townsend and partly because the workers have always been paid a higher hourly rate than has prevailed in the community.

Karl Townsend has proposed to his father that the company should further its good employee relations by providing some types of insurance, either on a contributory or noncontributory basis. Specific types of insurance under discussion are as follows:

Group Life—$5,000 with higher benefits for managers and executives drawing higher salaries.

Health and Accident

Pension Plan—to be financed with life insurance companies

Blue Cross

Blue Shield

It is estimated that the annual cost per employee of the various types of insurance will be as follows:

Group Life	$ 50
Health and Accident	75
Pension Plan	200
Blue Cross	100
Blue Shield	30

On the basis of the above facts, what action should the Townsend Corporation take in regard to an insurance program for its employees?

SUGGESTED READINGS

Greene, M. R. *Risk and Insurance.* Cincinnati: South-Western Publishing Company, 1962.

Gregg, D. W., Editor. *Life and Health Insurance Handbook,* Second Edition. Homewood, Illinois: Richard D. Irwin, Inc., 1964.

Huebner, S. S., and K. Black, Jr. *Life Insurance,* Sixth Edition. New York: Appleton-Century-Crofts, 1964.

Life Insurance Fact Book. New York: Institute of Life Insurance, 1966.

Magee, J. H., and D. L. Bickelhaupt. *General Insurance,* Seventh Edition. Homewood, Illinois: Richard D. Irwin, Inc., 1964.

Mehr, R. J., and E. Cammack. *Principles of Insurance,* Fourth Edition. Homewood, Illinois: Richard D. Irwin, Inc., 1966.

Riegel, R., and J. S. Miller. *Insurance Principles and Practices,* Fifth Edition. Englewood Cliffs, New Jersey: Prentice-Hall, Inc., 1966.

Magazine: *Journal of Risk and Insurance.*

20 pages

Chapter 22

FINANCIAL PROBLEMS AND POLICIES

In our highly competitive economic system, sound financial management is as important to a business as making or buying goods and selling them at a profit. Those responsible for a firm's finances face many problems and must formulate many policies. For example, what steps should be taken if the manufacturing division wishes to buy new equipment costing far more than available cash? Should the firm meet payrolls weekly, semimonthly, or monthly? Should cash discounts on sales be offered and, if so, at what rate? What proportion of net earnings should be distributed to the shareholders? The solution to these and a host of similar problems and the adoption of financial policies most suitable to the health and growth of a business are matters requiring excellent judgment, which is frequently exercised at a top management level.

Although space does not permit an examination of every financial decision that must be reached, this chapter will discuss some of the more important problems and policies. These will include the capital structure of a firm and the related problems of a choice and sale of securities, the refinancing of outstanding issues, policies on the distribution of earnings, and the current vogue for combinations and consolidations. Attention will also be devoted to procedures available to salvage or to liquidate firms that are in serious financial trouble.

■ Capital Structure

As noted in previous chapters, there are two sources of securing funds at the time a firm is organized. One source is the owner or owners of the business, and the other source is its creditors. Within this framework, equity capital can come from different classes of investors, and debt capital can be either short-term or long-term.

475

Individuals who go into business as sole proprietors or as members of a partnership should invest a substantial proportion of the funds needed by the business, preferably 70 to 80 percent. Rather than to borrow heavily, they should turn to some of the numerous methods available to reduce the funds needed to launch the enterprise. Land and buildings can be rented rather than purchased. Equipment can be secured on lease arrangements and, currently, leasing companies are willing to provide all types of equipment needed. If delivery or hauling is involved, these services can be secured under contract arrangements. If the business is manufacturing, parts can be purchased rather than produced and sub-contracting offers additional possibilities for conserving capital.

Corporations, particularly those classed as small businesses, can be placed in the same category as sole proprietorships and partnerships as to a desirable capital structure. Ability to borrow should be reserved for possible emergencies, and a generous ratio between equity and debt capital is most desirable. For larger firms, with the ability to market various types of securities, more alternatives may be available; but a conservative capital structure is sound for large as well as small corporations.

In addition to starting a business with a sound capital structure, many of the same problems may arise if a decision is reached to expand the size of the firm. The owners may invest additional funds, or the existing debt structure may be expanded. Another possibility available to a going concern is to retain all or a substantial portion of the yearly profits. These earnings belong to the owners; but if they are not paid out, the net effect is to increase the investment of the owners in the firm. Unless all of the cash generated from profits is used to reduce debt, expansion will take place although, most likely, at a slower rate than if additional capital were secured.

▨ Security Selection Factors

Assuming that capital is to be raised, either to start or to expand an enterprise, several factors must be considered in arriving at a choice as to the sources of these funds. Although the following discussion centers about corporations large enough to have access to alternate sources of capital, some of the items mentioned apply with equal force to small firms, both incorporated and unincorporated.

1. Debt or equity capital	4. Market conditions
2. Taxes	5. Stability of earnings
3. Voting control	6. Rate of earnings

1 / Debt or equity capital. As explained in Chapter 18, if bonds are issued, the amount involved becomes a debt of the corporation, which involves repayment at some future date. If stock is issued, there is no problem of repayment. For bonds, interest must be paid and, in the case of mortgage bonds, there is the danger of foreclosure if interest and principal payments are not maintained on schedule. On the other hand, more stock means sharing the expected profits with more owners.

2 / Taxes. Interest on bonds is a business expense and is allowable as a deduction in computing net earnings for purposes of income taxes. Dividends are not a business expense and under present laws do not decrease earnings, but rather they are a distribution of profits. Also, taxes on total stock outstanding are assessed by the state in which the corporation is organized. From the viewpoint of reducing taxes, raising funds by selling bonds is to be preferred over the sale of stock.

3 / Voting control. In deciding whether to issue stocks or bonds, a corporation must consider the problem of voting power. Bondholders are not owners and rarely assume any voting rights. Although the voting rights of preferred shareholders are sometimes restricted, the general rule is that all shareholders are entitled to vote. Unless the existing shareholders buy new issues in proportion to their former holdings, voting control may pass to new investors in the firm.

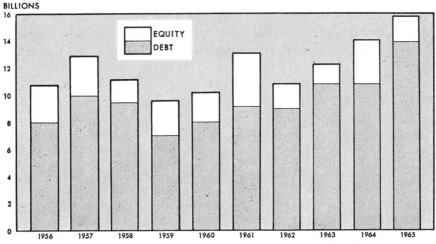

Securities and Exchange Commission

Corporate Security Offerings

4 / Market conditions. If the sale of securities is to be made to the general public, market conditions may be an important factor. When business conditions are prosperous, most investors prefer common stocks. They are interested in the high return possible as well as a hedge against inflation. When business is depressed, the more sure return on preferred stocks and bonds is of greater interest. The willingness of investors to purchase the type of security offered can be more important than any other factor under certain market conditions, while at other times it is only a minor consideration.

5 / Stability of earnings. The total funds that can safely be secured from bonds varies directly with the stability of the earnings. A corporation that has stable earnings year in and year out can best afford to sell bonds. Such a concern can finance yearly interest payments and yearly deposits into a sinking fund for the retirement of the issue. A firm with highly fluctuating profits, on the other hand, can pay interest one year with ease and yet be seriously handicapped by this fixed charge in the next year.

This factor, together with a large investment in fixed assets available for mortgaging, explains why public utilities, such as gas and electric companies, frequently secure one half to two thirds of their total capital from bond issues. These firms are permitted by law to earn a fair return on their total investment, and consumers use about as much gas and electricity in one year as another. On the other hand, a firm that manufactures a luxury item is likely to have high profits one year and low profits another. Unless the amount of the bond issue outstanding is small in proportion to total capital, the financial burdens imposed by fixed interest charges and sinking-fund payments might cause the company to fail.

6 / Rate of earnings. If a firm expects that it can earn 10 percent on new capital employed in the business and can borrow money from bond-holders at 5 percent, the difference of 5 percent will be available for the shareholders. The rate of 5 percent on the bonds is fixed and has no relationship to the profits that may be earned on the money contributed by this class of investors. The principle of borrowing money at a lower rate than the rate of expected earnings on these funds, with a resulting excess available to shareholders, is called *trading on the equity*.

For example, if a corporation has $100,000 in assets acquired from the sale of common stock, and if this company earns 10 percent on these assets, it has $10,000 in profits available for distribution to the owners.

The corporation now decides to double its size and secures an additional $100,000 by selling bonds with a 5 percent interest rate. If profits remain at 10 percent of assets, there will be $20,000 in earnings before bond interest is paid and $15,000 available to the owners after the interest payment. Without any additional investment on their part, the owners can share in an additional $5,000 profit.

Trading on the equity is a sound business principle, but it becomes increasingly risky as the percentage of borrowed capital increases in proportion to the total assets. A corporation can secure comparable advantages for its common shareholders by issuing nonparticipating preferred stock bearing a lower stated rate of return than the expected rate of earnings on its assets. Companies that have either bonds or non-participating preferred stock outstanding and that earn a higher rate on the assets acquired with the proceeds of these issues than the cost of the capital obtained have what is known as a *leverage factor*. The common stock of leverage companies is more speculative than that of companies with no senior securities outstanding.

A recent emphasis in financial management is the *cost-of-capital concept*. The cost to secure new capital is balanced against the rate of earnings expected from the assets to be purchased. If the cost of capital is higher than estimated earnings from the new facilities, those responsible for financial decisions will bring in a negative recommendation on the proposal.

■ Methods of Selling Securities

After a decision has been reached as to the securities to be sold, the next question involves the sales method to be used. If bonds are to be issued, there is not much question but that an investment bank, or possibly an insurance company, will be contacted. If a new corporation is being formed and it is decided to sell stocks, unless the company is relatively small, once again an investment bank would be the most logical choice to underwrite the securities. For local, relatively small companies, the promoters may have enough friends, relatives, and wealthy acquaintances to market the stock among these individuals.

If a corporation already in existence decides to expand by selling additional shares of stock, the law usually requires that the existing shareholders have the first opportunity to buy the issue unless these shareholders vote to waive this privilege. Only by this protection can a shareholder be sure that his percentage of ownership will not be diluted. This would be very important to an individual owning voting control of the corporation.

The legal right of a shareholder to subscribe to new issues of stock in proportion to his holding of old stock is known as his *privileged subscription* or *preemptive right*.

If shareholders have not agreed to waive their preemptive right in a new stock issue, the corporation mails each one a certificate, called a *subscription warrant*, that indicates the number of rights to which he is entitled. One *right* is allotted to each share of old stock, and it customarily takes more than one right to purchase a share of the new stock. For example, a corporation with 500,000 shares of common stock outstanding may decide to sell an additional 100,000 shares. In this event it would take 5 rights to have the privilege of purchasing one share of the new stock. The holder of 100 shares of the old stock would receive a subscription warrant entitling him to use his 100 rights to purchase 20 shares of the new issue.

In order to make it desirable for the old shareholder to exercise his subscription warrant or to sell it to someone else, it is customary to offer him the opportunity to buy new shares for somewhat less than the current market price of the old shares. This differential makes it profitable for a nonshareholder to buy rights from those who do not wish to exercise them in their own behalf. If the stock referred to above is selling for $150 a share and the holder of 5 rights can purchase a share for $140, each right would sell for slightly less than $2. If a shareholder has only 4 rights, he will have to buy another or sell the ones he has, for fractional shares are not issued. If the stock involved is listed, rights are sold on national exchanges. In any event, the corporation or its agent will usually buy and sell rights for its shareholders.

Within recent years practically all large corporations have requested their shareholders to vote to waive their preemptive right on a stated number of shares in order to install a stock option plan. A *stock option* is a privilege granted to certain key executives to purchase stock of the company under certain specified conditions as to time and price. It has been heralded as an important device to attract and keep young executives of outstanding ability. If a vice-president, for example, is given an option to purchase 10,000 shares of the company's stock at a time when it is selling for $8 a share, and the market price subsequently advances to $58 a share, the executive has a paper profit of a half million dollars.

■ Refinancing Programs

The financial structure of a business is subject to constant change, particularly as regards circulating capital. The amount owed on open account and to banks may rise and fall month by month as changes take place in inventory accumulations, collections on account, the payment of dividends, and other similar receipts and expenditures. Fixed capital is more likely to change slowly unless new securities are sold. Retained earnings do increase the amount of equity capital, and payments on bond issues do reduce the amount of debt capital; but these shifts are usually relatively minor compared to the total value of all assets.

Occasionally a corporation may decide to make substantial changes in its capital structure even though no expansion is contemplated. The original plan may have proved to be faulty or market conditions may now be ripe for issuing some types of securities that were not previously in public favor. Some of the more common refinancing plans are as follows:

1. Bonds for bonds
2. Stocks for bonds
3. Stock for stock
4. Long-term for short-term financing
5. Spin-offs

1 / Bonds for bonds. The indenture of a majority of bond issues includes a provision that the bonds may be called or redeemed prior to maturity at the option of the corporation. Usually a premium must be paid, which varies with the length of time the bonds have been outstanding. For example, a 40-year bond issue may not be callable for 10 years; then it may be redeemable at 110 percent of par for the next 10 years, and then at 105 for the remaining life of the issue.

Since issuing bonds for bonds does not change the financial structure of a firm, it might seem that there would be no point in refinancing on this basis. Actually, there are two occasions when replacing old bonds with a new bond issue would be pertinent. The more common situation is the opportunity to replace a high-interest bond issue with one carrying a lower interest rate. The saving in the annual interest cost may well equal the bond premium in two or three years and, aside from the expense of exchanging or selling the new bonds, the reduced expense will prove to be a profitable move over the life of the issue. Another occasion when bonds might replace bonds arises when an old issue matures and no provision has been made for its retirement. The proceeds from a refunding issue are used to pay off the old bonds and the corporation's financial structure remains intact. The debt of the federal government is very largely managed in this manner; and some corporations, notably railroads, follow this practice.

2 / Stocks for bonds. A number of bond issues outstanding are convertible into common stock and, if the conversion feature is both worthwhile and has an expiration date, there is a possibility that this shift will take place almost automatically. Usually, however, when a shift from debt capital to equity capital is contemplated, the bonds outstanding are redeemed with the proceeds from a stock issue. The procedure is quite simple. The corporation sells preferred stock or common stock for cash by methods previously described. If necessary, the charter can be amended to provide for additional shares, or authority may have been granted originally for more stock than is presently outstanding. The money received is used to redeem the bonds either at maturity or earlier, if the bonds are callable and the company exercises its call privilege.

3 / Stock for stock. Corporations with preferred stock outstanding usually have a clause in the contract under which this class of stock was issued that allows for its redemption. This provision may be similar to those incorporated in a callable bond, or it may state a single premium at which the stock can be called at any time at the option of the corporation. For example, a $100 preferred stock may have a redemption price of $110 that remains constant throughout the life of this stock.

The purposes of redeeming a preferred stock issue are to refinance with a new issue carrying a lower dividend rate or to eliminate this class of stock. If a corporation has outstanding a sizable issue of 7 percent preferred stock, the company may decide to replace this stock with an issue of 5 percent preferred. The change will increase common stock dividend possibilities, assuming that the preferred stock is nonparticipating. Or, the corporation may decide that the market is strong for common stocks and that now would be a good time to eliminate the preferred class. The advantage in this shift would be to remove a security senior to the common stock so that, if more capital is needed at a later date when the market is strong for preferred stocks, the way would be open for such an issue.

4 / Long-term for short-term financing. Some refinancing plans are undertaken to convert, on a relatively permanent basis, all or a portion of the short-term debt into long-term securities. A corporation may find that its cash balance does not improve to a point where the short-term indebtedness can be liquidated out of current receipts at any time during the year either because the original financial plan was faulty or because the firm has expanded. As a result, the problem of paying these debts presents a constant source of financial difficulty, usually met by other short-term borrowing. A more satisfactory solution is to sell bonds or stock and to reduce the short-term debt to a manageable size.

5 / Spin-offs. Within recent years a new type of refinancing plan has been used by corporations that wish to divest themselves of a segment of their businesses. The unwanted assets are transferred to a new corporation in exchange for stock, which is then distributed to the shareholders of the original corporation. This procedure is known as a *spin-off*. An advantage that may be gained, in addition to eliminating a business not compatible with the firm's main objectives, is a reduction in corporate taxes because the rate on the first $25,000 of net income is substantially lower than on profits in excess of this amount.

■ Distribution of Earnings Policies

Another financial problem faced by all business enterprises requires a decision regarding the distribution of earnings. In the case of sole proprietorships and partnerships, the owners usually pay themselves a modest salary if they are actively engaged in the operation of the business. This amount probably covers their normal living costs. Any withdrawal beyond a salary allowance may or may not be prudent, depending upon the size of the profits and the extent to which borrowed capital is used. Some partnership agreements place restrictions on amounts a partner may withdraw without the written consent of all partners.

In some instances sole proprietors or partners have no personal need for withdrawing any of the profits. The question then arises as to whether

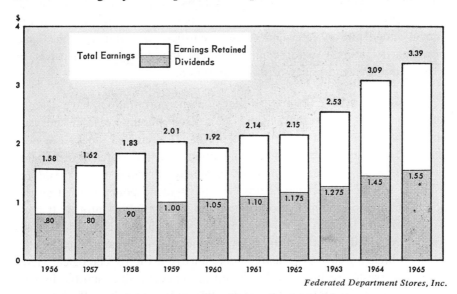

Federated Department Stores, Inc.

Per Share Earnings Retained and Dividends Paid by One Firm
(Dollars)

better use of these funds would be in the business or in outside investments. If they are left in the business, the firm automatically will grow in size after debts have been liquidated. If they are withdrawn, the firm will not expand, which may be desirable in view of location, available volume of sales, or nature of the business. The chances are that the profits could be used either in or out of the business, and the policy of withdrawing all or a part calls for good judgment on the part of the owners.

The dividend policies of corporations are of more importance because thousands of shareholders may be affected. Dividends represent a distribution of earnings by a corporation to its shareholders. If a company has not earned a profit and has no retained earnings from former years to distribute, or if the board of directors feels that it is unwise to declare a dividend, the owners will receive no income from their investment. The majority of successful corporations, particularly those whose securities are listed on an exchange, do pay dividends regularly. These may be paid in cash, stock, or securities or scrip, with cash dividends accounting for four fifths of all types.

1. Cash dividends
2. Stock dividends
3. Securities or scrip dividends

1 / Cash dividends. Customarily, dividend-paying corporations, or their agents, mail checks to their shareholders on a quarterly basis. In the case of preferred stocks, the amount paid per share is one fourth of the annual stated rate of return for these securities, assuming that the issue is nonparticipating. As for common stock, the distribution depends in part on the dividend policy of the corporation.

(a) REGULAR DIVIDEND POLICY. Some corporations have a reputation for paying quarterly dividends of a fixed amount, year in and year out, without regard for their current profits. If preferred stocks are outstanding, they are probably nonparticipating, and the stated rate is paid. In a somewhat comparable manner, a steady dividend rate is paid on common stocks. A variation of this type of dividend policy is used by the board of directors of many corporations in years of high profits. It consists of the declaration of the regular dividend plus a so-called "extra," frequently added to the last quarterly payment of the year. Actually, this means a higher yield to the shareholder, but from the psychological viewpoint the investor realizes that he should not expect a like sum the following year unless operations are again unusually profitable. If the extra dividend is sizable, the declaration may be termed *cutting a melon.*

(b) VARIABLE DIVIDEND POLICY. A variable dividend policy is the exact opposite of a steady yield in that in some years no dividends may be declared and in others the amount paid out may be a handsome return on the investment. If operations are not profitable, no distribution is made even though the corporation could do so legally and with no damage to its financial structure. On the other hand, if profits are large, dividend payments are generous. In some instances, every dollar earned in a given year is distributed to the shareholders that year.

(c) CONSERVATIVE DIVIDEND POLICY. A modification of the variable dividend policy is the plan of declaring a certain percent of earnings in the form of dividends and retaining the rest as a reinvestment of earnings. The board of directors might decide that one half to two thirds of the earnings should be distributed each year but that the remainder should be held.

2 / Stock dividends. Although over 80 percent of all dividend payments are made in cash, some companies either substitute stock dividends for cash distributions or supplement the cash dividend with shares of stock. The rate may be low, such as a 3 or 5 percent stock dividend, or as high as 50 or 100 percent. For example, if a firm declares a 10 percent stock dividend, each shareholder will receive one new share for each ten already owned. Unlike distributions in cash, stock dividends do not constitute taxable income to the shareholders unless these individuals sell the shares received. The main reason for stock dividends is that the corporation has urgent needs to retain the cash that would otherwise go to its owners but feels an obligation to distribute some tangible return to keep faith with those who have invested in it.

Although frequently confused with a stock dividend, a *stock split-up* is legally entirely different even though in both instances the investor receives additional shares of stock. A stock dividend is a distribution of profits earned in the current or prior years in the form of stock rather than cash. A stock split-up consists of dividing the common stock outstanding into additional units such as a two-for-one or three-for-one split. It merely increases the number of shares representing the amount of capital raised by selling common stock. For example, common stock may originally have been sold at $100 a share. Assuming no change in its market value, a two-for-one split would give each shareholder twice as many shares but the value of each would be $50.

3 / Securities or scrip dividends. If a corporation owns stock in another company, it can distribute these securities as a dividend to its shareholders. In the early 60's, the E. I. duPont de Nemours & Company was ordered by a federal court to divest itself of the 63 million shares of General Motors Corporation stock that it owned, and it chose to distribute these to its owners as a securities dividend. Spin-offs and court orders are the major reasons for the use of this type of dividend.

On rare occasions when a corporation wishes to distribute a cash dividend but does not have an adequate balance in its checking account, it may issue a scrip dividend. A *scrip dividend* is a short-term paper somewhat similar to a note payable, which may or may not bear interest, and is usually due in a few months. Since a scrip dividend is clear evidence of a weak cash and credit position, its use is generally confined to close corporations.

■ Business Combinations

The second half of the current century has witnessed a marked trend in the growth of many corporations that have achieved a larger size by buying up or joining forces with one or more formerly independent companies. The objectives behind these combinations are usually: to obtain the economies of large-scale production, distribution, and financing; to widen sales territories; to assure a continuous supply of some needed parts or materials; and, sometimes, to lessen the competitive stress in the company's particular field. The methods used to form combinations frequently create extensive financial problems that vary with the method selected to effect the consolidation.

Since financing may be related to the types of business activities brought under one management, the different kinds of combinations will be examined briefly. If different companies doing exactly the same business activity are combined, it is a *horizontal combination*. A chain of drugstores, restaurants, motels, hotels, supermarkets, lumber yards, or department stores, if under one ownership and management, provide an illustration of this common form of combination. By contrast, a *vertical combination* joins together types of companies doing different but related activities in the production and distribution of a product. For example, the United States Steel Co. owns coal and iron ore companies, shipping lines, railroads, blast furnaces, rolling mills, and fabricating plants.

Sometimes two businesses are combined because their activities are so closely interwoven that it seems preferable to have them under one management. Such a combination is called a *complementary combination*. Meat packers have joined forces with fertilizer factories; business machine companies have bought electronic data equipment manufacturers; and in some cases the need to dispose of by-products, such as gas from coke production, makes it advantageous for two formerly separate companies to join forces. In other instances the companies combined are in allied lines, which is a *circular combination*. For example, Standard Brands, Inc., when it was formed, combined coffee, baking powder, yeast, and other diverse food products into one organization.

More recently there has been a rash of companies joining forces that have little or no logic in their association together. These are called *conglomerate mergers*. Textron, Inc., for example, has bought up companies manufacturing helicopters, eye glasses, wristwatch bands, electric band saws, outboard motors, and a host of other military, industrial, and consumer products. Recently, the American Tobacco Company bought Sunshine Biscuits, Inc.

As might be expected, financing these various types of combinations can be extremely complex, particularly if the companies concerned are sizable in their own right. Occasionally, when one large firm buys a relatively small company, it may do so for cash. In this case the financing may be no more of a problem to the buyer than would the purchase of a new piece of heavy equipment. More commonly, securities are involved as will be noted in the following examination of the three major methods used to form combinations.

1. Mergers
2. Amalgamations
3. Holding companies

1 / Mergers. When a *merger* takes place between two or more companies, the dominant one absorbs the smaller units and they disappear as separate entities. If Company *A* makes an offer to Company *B* to purchase its assets and liabilities and the offer is accepted, Company *B* ceases to exist as a separate organization, and Company *A* is then a larger concern. If the payment to Company *B* is entirely in cash, as mentioned above, the only financial problem may be to arrive at a mutually agreed upon price. If, however, the payment is to be made in bonds, preferred stock, or common stock of Company *A*, or some combination that may even involve part cash, long hours may be spent by the financial managers of both firms in arriving at an equitable settlement.

Although there is no dominant single pattern, the most widely used technique is to make payment in common stock, partially because this method is tax free to the shareholders of Company *B*. If, for example, on the date of the sale, Company *A*'s stock is selling for $40 a share and Company *B*'s shares are quoted at $60, Company *A* will issue 1½ shares of its stock for each share of Company *B* stock outstanding. Company *B* will then be dissolved and, quite possibly, be operated as a division of Company *A*. Incidentally, the shareholders of Company *B* would have to vote to accept the offer of Company *A*, but it would not be necessary to hold a special meeting of Company *A*'s shareholders as their preemptive rights do not extend to stock issued to purchase assets.

2 / Amalgamations. The difference between a merger and an *amalgamation* is that in the latter instance a new company is formed in the process of combining two or more existing organizations. If Company *A* and Company *B* decide to combine instead of merging one into the other, a new Company *C* is formed, which buys up the assets and liabilities of Companies *A* and *B*. In this case, both of the old companies disappear and a new one is born. For example, the American Motors Corporation is an amalgamation that, when it was formed in 1954, combined the Hudson Motor Car Company and the Nash–Kelvinator Corporation.

Since a new company is formed in an amalgamation, its financial structure can consist of any desirable combination of debt and equity capital. The size of the new firm will, obviously, be dictated by the amount paid for the companies forming the amalgamation. The kinds of securities issued may, however, be influenced by what the shareholders of the old companies are willing to accept. If they wish a tax-free exchange, the new company may issue only common stock for the purchase prices.

3 / Holding companies. The most popular device for combining a number of concerns is the *holding company*. In its pure form, a holding company is organized for the sole purpose of buying enough of the voting stock in other companies, called *subsidiaries*, to ensure control. Theoretically, this should be approximately 51 percent, but in actual practice some holding companies own all of the stock of their subsidiaries and in other cases much less than one half, which, under the system of management-secured proxies, is adequate for effective control. The latter situation presupposes a large number of shareholders with no rival holdings of substantial blocks of stock. Also, in actual practice, many holding companies conduct operations in their own names as well as functioning as holding companies.

It would be difficult to mention the name of a well-known corporation that is not also a holding company to some extent. The American Telephone and Telegraph Company, the Pennsylvania Railroad, the United States Steel Corporation, E. I. duPont de Nemours and Company, and a host of others are holding companies for one or more other organizations.

If a holding company is formed to buy voting stock in the open market of companies it wishes to control, it can raise the necessary capital by selling bonds, preferred stock, or common stock or some combination of these types of securities. The cash received from the sale of these securities is then used to buy voting shares in the company it wishes to control in the same manner as an individual investor would use. Sometimes, in order to obtain control, particularly if a stock is not listed, the holding company will extend to each shareholder of the independent company an offer, called a *tender*, to buy his shares at a price that is usually in excess of the current market value. It may also offer to exchange its stock for the shares of the company it wishes to control.

■ Failures and Reorganizations

Every year some businesses, including those both new and well established, meet with financial reverses. The fault may lie with the present management or may be caused by outside factors over which no control can be exercised. For example, a neighborhood grocery store that had been prosperous for many years found its profits changed to losses when a large supermarket was opened in the vicinity. Regardless of the reason or reasons, continued losses will usually weaken the financial structure of a firm to a point where some action must be taken by the owners or managers.

Under the National Bankruptcy Act, *insolvency exists whenever* the aggregate of a person's property is not, at a fair valuation, sufficient to pay his debts. Anyone who reads the financial pages of a local newspaper has probably noted that a corporation has been adjudged bankrupt, for example, with assets of $13,200 and liabilities of $64,500. An individual or a firm may also become insolvent under state laws merely because of inability to pay debts currently owing. A manufacturing firm may have assets valued at more than its liabilities but, because most of its capital is tied up in special machinery, the assets cannot be liquidated to pay accounts and notes payable that are due.

Three possibilities for salvaging or liquidating an insolvent business are as follows:

1. Creditor agreements   2. Equity receivership   3. Bankruptcy

1 / Creditor agreements. When the owner or owners of a business realize that the firm is in dire financial straits, the first step is to call a meeting of the creditors. At this time a decision can be reached as to whether to seek a solution with or without court assistance. The creditors know that if the company is adjudged bankrupt by a court, the legal costs will be high and it is most unlikely that they will receive full payment for their claims. Furthermore, a former customer who might otherwise be saved for future business, is probably lost.

If the creditors believe that the business can operate at a profit in the future, despite past reverses, they may agree to postpone the due date of their claims. Such an *extension agreement* must be signed by all creditors in order to give the plan a fair chance to work out successfully. A variation of the extension agreement is a *composition settlement*, by which the creditors accept a reduction in the amounts due them. These amounts may be paid in cash immediately, or settlement may be postponed for a few months.

In these voluntary agreements, the creditors usually elect a representative who assumes active management of the firm for a long enough period of time to guarantee that the plan will be followed. As soon as the organization is operating smoothly and successfully, the creditors' representative or committee withdraws and allows the original managers to operate without supervision.

If the creditors cannot agree to some kind of a voluntary settlement of their claims or if there seems no hope of successful operation, the only alternative is to turn to the courts for help. Such a step can be taken by the insolvent firm, or the creditors may force the issue. In either case there is a choice between an equity receivership and bankruptcy.

2 / Equity receivership. In an *equity receivership*, the court appoints a *receiver*, who operates or liquidates the company in the interests of the creditors. If it is decided to continue the firm, the results may be similar to that of a voluntary agreement on the part of the creditors with the added authority given by the law and, likewise, added costs. The chief advantage is that no single creditor can block the proceedings by refusing to become a party to the agreement. Another advantage is that the receiver reports to the court and must make an accounting for all receipts and expenditures. Furthermore, no creditor can bring suit or insist on collection of his claim as long as the receiver is in charge of the business.

If the receiver believes the better plan is to liquidate the firm, he will apply to the court for this permission and, if granted, will convert the assets into cash and pay creditors in their order of preference. Some debts may be secured by mortgages or other collateral sufficient in sales value to provide adequate funds to discharge these claims in full. Or, if the security is sold for less than the amount owed, the creditor will receive the proceeds and join the unsecured creditors for the balance due him. General creditors will usually receive only a portion of their claims, for the sale of assets under forced-sale conditions does not normally produce enough money to satisfy all claims in full.

3 / Bankruptcy. Equity receiverships may be under the jurisdiction of state courts or federal courts, depending upon whether the business is local or interstate. If a firm goes into bankruptcy, however, the proceedings will be in a federal court because the Constitution of the United States provides for a national and uniform bankruptcy law. An individual or a corporation, with certain exceptions such as banks, may go into *bankruptcy* by declaring under oath that liabilities owed exceed the value of assets owned. Or, if an act of bankruptcy is committed, such as assigning assets to a favored creditor, three other creditors (if there are more than twelve) with claims of $500 or more can file a petition asking that the firm be declared a bankrupt. Unless the business can refute the charges, the court will approve the petition.

The judge then appoints a *referee* who serves as his representative in subsequent proceedings. The referee calls a meeting of the creditors at which time they elect a representative known as a *trustee.* In most instances the trustee, with approval by the referee, liquidates the assets, pays preferred claims, and distributes the balance, if any, to the general creditors. The debtor is legally discharged from his obligations, and the creditors are given impartial treatment in accord with their legal status.

Under this procedure, a business that in some instances might have been saved is lost. The current National Bankruptcy Act recognized this problem as far as corporations are concerned by including procedures for financial reorganizations.

Reorganization plans usually involve the scaling down of amounts owed or the interest or dividend rates, with more sacrifices being taken by the common shareholders and other unsecured interests. For example, first-mortgage bondholders owning 6 percent securities might agree to accept 4 percent bonds in exchange. Second-mortgage bondholders might agree to a reduction in the interest rate and also in principal amount. Preferred shareholders might be given new preferred stock with a lower dividend rate or even common stock. Common shareholders are sometimes eliminated entirely or are given a small amount of new stock in exchange for their previous holdings. The net effect is to reduce the annual fixed charges for interest and debt retirement to the point where normal operations of the business will allow for these charges and still leave a profit margin.

PROFESSIONAL ASSOCIATION IN FINANCIAL MANAGEMENT

The Financial Executives Institute, which was established in 1931 as the Controllers Institute of America, now has a membership of more than 6,000 individuals who are primarily financial and control executives of leading business concerns. Chapters are active in many cities in the United States, Puerto Rico, and Canada. A monthly magazine, *Financial Executive,* is published by the Institute. Although the regular subscription price is $8 a year, students may subscribe for eight issues at a cost of $2. Local chapters customarily promote contacts with finance and accounting majors at universities and colleges.

BUSINESS TERMS

(a) trading on the equity (478), leverage factor (479); cost-of-capital concept (479)
(b) privileged subscription or preemptive right (480), subscription warrant (480), right (480)
(c) stock option (480)
(d) spin-off (483)
(e) cutting a melon (484); stock split-up (485); scrip dividend (486)
(f) horizontal combination (486), vertical combination (486), complementary combination (486), circular combination (487), conglomerate mergers (487)
(g) merger (487), amalgamation (488), holding company (488) subsidiaries (488), tender (489)
(h) insolvency (489); extension agreement (490), composition settlement (490)
(i) equity receivership (490), receiver (490)
(j) bankruptcy (491), referee (491), trustee (491), reorganization plans (491)

QUESTIONS FOR DISCUSSION AND ANALYSIS

1. Why is it more important for sole proprietorships, partnerships, and small corporations to rely more heavily on equity capital than it is for large corporations?
2. It has been said that when a firm retains earnings it is, in effect, requiring the owners to make an additional investment in the business. Do you agree? Discuss.
3. Can you name some types of businesses, other than public utilities, that might be expected to have stable earnings? Give reasons for your selections.
4. Does trading on the equity assume that the rate of earnings on assets will be greater than the cost of capital?

5. If a shareholder does not care to use his subscription warrant and sells his rights, what effect does this act have on his share of ownership in the corporation?

6. What is your opinion of the wide use of stock options by large corporations?

7. Would you prefer to own stock in a company that followed a regular, variable, or conservative dividend policy? Give reasons for your decision.

8. Of the various types of combinations, does any one type seem to be more justifiable from an economic viewpoint than other types?

9. What circumstances might determine whether a merger, an amalgamation, or a holding company would be the best method of combining two companies? Would your answer be different if ten companies were involved?

10. If you were a creditor of a firm in financial trouble, what would be your preference on the course of action to be taken?

PROBLEMS AND SHORT CASES

1. The Evans–Moore Manufacturing Co. has regularly averaged a 14 percent operating profit, before interest, on its $6,000,000 in total assets. The debt and equity capital is represented by $500,000 in open-book accounts, $800,000 borrowed from a commercial bank at 5½ percent interest, and $4,700,000 in common stock and retained earnings represented by 200,000 shares of common stock outstanding. The Company decides to expand by selling $1,000,000 in 5 percent bonds and $1,000,000 in 6 percent preferred stock. The bank loan is to be liquidated, but with the increased size it is expected that the amount owed on open-book accounts will increase to $700,000.

Assuming a continuation of the 14 percent return on operations and that all earnings are paid out either as interest or dividends, what dollar dividends per share were available to the common shareholders before and after the expansion? Show calculations.

2. The capital structure of the Midland Shoe Corporation consists of $4,000,000 in 6 percent first mortgage bonds and $6,000,000 in common stock with a par value of $100 a share. For several years the Corporation has been unable to show a net profit, although profits from operations before interest on bonds have averaged $200,000. Because the firm is in default on its bond interest for the past two years, it seeks relief under the National Bankruptcy Act.

A reorganization plan is agreed upon by the bondholders and shareholders. The bondholders are willing to accept $2,000,000 in 4 percent bonds and $2,480,000 in 4½ percent preferred stock for their present claims against the Corporation with the understanding that the common shareholders agree to reduce their holdings to $2,000,000 in $100 par shares.

Assuming the continuation of operating earnings of $200,000, can the Corporation meet its obligations on the bonds and preferred stock and still pay a dividend to the common shareholders? If so, how many dollars a share?

3. The capital structure of the Davis Steel Corporation shows the following:

Debenture notes, 4%, maturing in one year ..	$ 5,000,000
Mortgage bonds, 5½%, callable at 105, due in 1975	40,000,000
Preferred stock, 7%, $100 par, nonparticipating, redeemable at 110	15,000,000
Common stock, nopar, 10,00,000 shares authorized, 6,750,000 outstanding	52,000,000

The firm has been prosperous and has established a regular dividend policy of $2 a share on its common stock, which is listed on a national exchange. Recent trading in this stock has hovered around $48 a share, although the price range has fluctuated between $40 and $60 a share within the past year. The bonds and preferred stock are also listed and usually sell at a 5 percent premium above par.

The management of the Davis Steel Corporation wishes to raise enough new capital to retire the debenture notes and to buy a steamship company with which it does an extensive amount of business. The shareholders of the steamship company are willing to accept $5,000,000 in cash for their business or would be willing to exchange their ownership for 100,000 shares of the Davis Steel Corporation common stock. The reputation of the Corporation is such that it appears certain that the market will absorb any type or types of securities that it offers for sale.

Present a financial plan for the Davis Steel Corporation that will accomplish the two stated objectives. Explain why your plan is preferable to alternate methods that could be used.

SUGGESTED READINGS

Cohen, J. B., and S. M. Robbins. *The Financial Manager: Basic Aspects of Financial Administration.* New York: Harper & Row, Publishers, 1966. Parts V and VI.

Corrigan, F. J., and H. A. Ward. *Financial Management: Policies and Practices.* Boston: Houghton Mifflin Company, 1963. Part Six.

Guthmann, H. G., and H. E. Dougall. *Corporate Financial Policy.* Fourth Edition. Englewood Cliffs, New Jersey: Prentice-Hall, Inc., 1962. Parts VIII and IX.

Husband, W. H., and J. C. Dockeray. *Modern Corporate Finance,* Sixth Edition. Homewood, Illinois: Richard D. Irwin, Inc., 1966. Parts IV–VII.

Weston, J. F., and E. F. Brigham. *Managerial Finance,* Revised Edition. New York: Holt, Rinehart and Winston, Inc., 1966. Parts V–VII.

Magazines: *Financial Executive, Financial Analysts Journal.*

Part VII

QUANTITATIVE CONTROLS FOR DECISION MAKING

CHAPTER

23   **Accounting and Financial Statements** *MON.*

24   **Business Statistics**   *TUES.*

25   **Data Processing**   *WEDNES.*

26   **Budgeting and Forecasting** *Thurs.*

QUANTITATIVE CONTROLS FOR DECISION MAKING

Managers of business enterprises devote considerable time to the functions of control and planning. In discharging these important tasks, they are aided by quantitative data drawn both from internal and external sources.

Accounting and statistics, the subjects of Chapters 23 and 24 respectively, describe how dollars and quantities are collected and processed for presentation to executives and other interested parties. The accounting chapter stresses financial statements and their analysis rather than accounting techniques. The chapter on statistics explains some of the common types of statistical measurement useful to business.

Chapter 25, Data Processing, describes in relatively simple language the part that computers are playing in the business world. The widespread adoption of electronic data processing by large and small firms makes it imperative that students of business have at least a rudimentary knowledge of this relatively new "tool" as used for purposes of control and decision making. Emphasis is placed on the value of electronic data processing to a firm rather than the techniques involved in programming and operating a computer.

Decision making may involve the future, and Chapter 26, Budgets and Forecasting, describes two of the common devices by which executives plan ahead. The mechanics of preparing a budget are explained, and some methods of making forecasts are described. Emphasis is placed on the advantage these techniques have in minimizing risks.

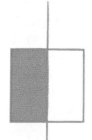

Chapter 23

ACCOUNTING AND FINANCIAL STATEMENTS

Every working day a business is likely to buy goods and supplies, make sales for cash or on credit terms, meet payrolls and incur other expenses, and deposit and withdraw money from its checking account. These are business transactions, and a suitable record must be made of each one. Even though such transactions may number in the thousands daily, they have one common characteristic, namely, all are measurable in dollars and cents. The recording of these business transactions and organizing these money figures into usable data comprise, in general, the area known as accounting.

While it is true that accounting does not, of itself, produce any profits, it is a necessity for all businesses ranging from the smallest to the largest. Many enterprises have failed either because their accounting records were inadequate or nonexistent. A firm must know its cash balance, the amounts owed and receivable, total sales, expenses classified by different categories, and its net income. Granted that these figures represent history when presented to owners and executives, the fact remains that a majority of all managerial decisions are reached only after reference to accounting data.

In addition to the owners and managers, many outsiders are interested in the facts and figures compiled by a firm's accountants. The federal government and many states collect taxes on incomes and payrolls. Commercial banks, bonding companies, and investment banks or services are very much interested in the financial picture of each firm with whom they have contacts. Creditors are vitally concerned with the financial strength of the enterprises that owe them money, and stockholders and investors rely on published financial data for knowledge about the firm in which they have an ownership interest.

■ **Types of Accountants**

In a very small firm the owner may keep such records as are maintained, he may employ a part-time accountant, or he may use an outside bookkeeping service. In large enterprises the accounting department is organized into numerous functions and each of these is headed by a specialist. As a result, industrial accountants may become known by such terms as cost accountant, tax accountant, systems accountant, internal auditor, or budget accountant. The chart below shows the organization of the accounting department of a large manufacturing concern.

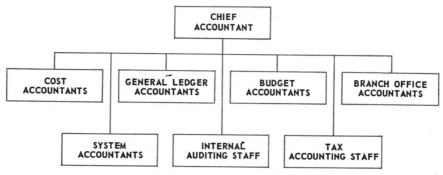

Organization Chart for an Accounting Department

In addition to the broad classification of industrial accountants, other categories are public accountants and governmental accountants. *Public accountants* are independent firms who offer their services to the public. If they have complied with the state rules governing certification, which includes passing a rigorous examination, they may designate themselves as *certified public accountants.* CPA's, as they are generally known, audit the books and perform various services for the clients who employ them. Their work is professional in nature and requires ability and integrity of a very high order. *Governmental accountants* are those employed by local, state, and national governmental units including such federal agencies as the Federal Bureau of Investigation, the Bureau of Internal Revenue, and the General Accounting Office.

■ **Accounting Procedures**

Accounting may be defined as the recording, classifying, and summarizing of business transactions, and interpreting this compiled information. In order to record transactions, the necessary information must be assembled from a number of sources. All types of business papers, such as invoices, checks, notes, contracts, payroll records, and machine tapes, provide facts and figures that are translated into entries. For example, sales made by retail stores are evidenced by sales slips and cash register tapes or dial readings.

Although some very small firms still rely on pen-and-ink records, the use of business machines, such as adding machines, cash registers, and posting and billing machines, is widespread. More recently, electronic data processing has made rapid strides in assuming not only the burden of recording business transactions but also in classifying and summarizing these more rapidly than was formerly possible. The use of punched cards, tapes, tabulators, computers, and high-speed printers has made possible a high degree of automation in the accounting department.

Without regard for the specific techniques used, which may be influenced by the types of mechanical aids employed, summarized or individual transactions are entered in some form of a *journal,* which is a book of original entry in which transactions are recorded in chronological order. From here the dollar amounts are transferred to a *ledger*, which is a book of accounts. Each account brings together all transactions affecting one item, such as cash or sales. At stated periods—monthly, quarterly, semi-annually, or annually—the ledger accounts are totaled or balanced and provide the basic information for financial statements.

The two principal statements that are prepared at the close of a stated interval of time are the balance sheet and the income statement. They are the result of, and the reason for, much of the work done by an accounting department and will be examined in some detail in this chapter. Among numerous other possible presentations of accounting data, a retained earnings statement, a cost of goods manufactured schedule, and a statement of source and application of funds are frequently compiled, and they will be discussed briefly. After these statements are available, it becomes possible to interpret them for managerial purposes; and some of the more commonly used measures will be explained and illustrated.

■ Balance Sheet

The *balance sheet* lists the assets, the liabilities, and the proprietorship interest of the owners of a business. *Assets* consist of the property owned and used in the operation of the firm, such as land, buildings, merchandise, office equipment, and cash. Some of these assets may have been acquired by buying on open account or by the use of borrowed funds secured from a bank or from the proceeds of a bond issue. Until such time as these debts are paid, creditors have a claim against the property owned by the business. The rights of these creditors in the assets of the business are known as *liabilities.* The remaining and secondary claim against the assets, which is the right of the owner or owners in the property, is the *proprietorship.*

Because all of the assets of a business are subject to claims by creditors and owners, it follows that the total value of the property owned equals the total rights of creditors and owners. For example, Arnold Richardson buys a radio business for $25,000. Of this amount he is able to invest $20,000 of his own funds and borrows the remaining $5,000 at his bank. His balance sheet after purchase shows assets, $25,000; liabilities, $5,000; and proprietorship, $20,000. This information can be expressed as an equation, as follows:

$$\text{Assets} = \text{Liabilities} + \text{Proprietorship}$$
$$\$25,000 = \$5,000 + \$20,000$$

The truism that assets equal liabilities plus proprietorship is known as the *balance sheet equation.* By transposing the liabilities, the equation can be made to read, assets minus liabilities equal proprietorship. This equation stresses the fact that a business has an entity of its own in showing the amount of its obligation to its owner. Published balance sheets most frequently use the first formula and show equal totals for assets and for liabilities and proprietorship combined.

On page 501 is shown a balance sheet for a sole proprietor, A. R. Morgan, who owns and operates a retail furniture store. Note that the balance sheet items not only have been grouped according to the three major classifications but also have been divided into subclassifications. Assets have four classifications and liabilities two.

1. Current assets
2. Plant assets
3. Investments
4. Intangible assets

5. Current liabilities
6. Long-term liabilities
7. Proprietorship

1 / Current assets. Cash and other assets that will be converted into cash or consumed within a short time are *current assets.* The maximum length of time for conversion is usually one year, and it is expected that this process will take place in the normal operations of the business. If merchandise is sold on open book account or for notes, it is reasonable to assume that the accounts receivable or notes receivable will be collected in less than one year from the date of the sale. Such items as office supplies on hand will be used within a year and insurance currently prepaid will expire in the months ahead.

MODERN FURNITURE MART
Balance Sheet
December 31, 1968

<u>Assets</u>

Current assets:
```
Cash  . . . . . . . . . . . . . . . . . . .          $ 7,200
Accounts receivable . . . . . . . . . . .  $15,400
   Less allowance for doubtful accounts .    2,800    12,600
Merchandise inventory . . . . . . . . . . . . . . .  46,350
Store supplies  . . . . . . . . . . . . . . . . . .     810
Office supplies . . . . . . . . . . . . . . . . . .     640
Prepaid insurance . . . . . . . . . . . . . . . . .     480
   Total current assets . . . . . . . . . . . . .            $ 68,080
```

Plant assets:
```
Store equipment . . . . . . . . . . . . .  $14,750
   Less accumulated depreciation  . . . .    5,900  $ 8,850
Office equipment  . . . . . . . . . . . .  $12,400
   Less accumulated depreciation  . . . .    4,960    7,440
Building  . . . . . . . . . . . . . . . .  $61,500
   Less accumulated depreciation  . . . .   12,300   49,200
Land  . . . . . . . . . . . . . . . . . . . . . .     5,000
   Total plant assets . . . . . . . . . . . . .             70,490
```

Investments:
```
Stock in Toolcraft, Inc.  . . . . . . . . . . . .            3,000
```

Intangible assets:
```
Goodwill  . . . . . . . . . . . . . . . . . . . .            2,500
```

Total assets $144,070

<u>Liabilities</u>

Current liabilities:
```
Notes payable . . . . . . . . . . . . . . . . . .   $ 6,000
Accounts payable  . . . . . . . . . . . . . . . .    14,600
Taxes payable . . . . . . . . . . . . . . . . . .     1,280
   Total current liabilities  . . . . . . . . . .            $ 21,880
```

Long-term liabilities:
```
Mortgage payable  . . . . . . . . . . . . . . . .            30,000
```

Total liabilities . . . . $ 51,880

<u>Proprietorship</u>
```
A. R. Morgan, Capital, January 1, 1968 . . . . . .  $88,440
Net income for 1968 . . . . . . . . . . .  $13,940
   Less withdrawals in 1968 . . . . . . .   10,190    3,750
A. R. Morgan, Capital, December 31, 1968 . . . . .           92,190
```

Total liabilities and proprietorship $144,070

Balance Sheet

2 / Plant assets. Assets that possess a degree of permanence extending beyond one year and which are intended for use rather than for sale are known as *plant assets* or *fixed assets*. Some assets, such as automobiles or trucks, may not last more than three to five years, while land for a building site may last forever. Although such assets are sold when they are no longer useful to the firm, they are not purchased for this purpose.

With the exception of land, plant assets deteriorate in value with use and the passage of time. Because it is desirable to show the original cost of the asset as well as its reduced value year by year, two separate figures are required. The accumulated depreciation is increased each year until it may equal the value of the asset from which it is subtracted. At that time, if the estimate of the useful life of the asset was accurate, the balance sheet value will be zero and the asset will be discarded. Scrap values are taken into account when warranted.

3 / Investments. Stocks or bonds of other organizations that are purchased with the intent to hold them for income or for other reasons are known as *investments*. It is unusual for a sole proprietorship, such as that owned by A. R. Morgan, to have investments, although many corporations acquire assets of this character in order to cement trade relationships or to secure voting control of another corporation.

4 / Intangible assets. Assets in the nature of a legal right or some other value without physical substance that have been purchased are classified as *intangible assets*. The most common of these is *goodwill*, which is the price paid for a firm over and above the net fair value of its assets over its liabilities because of the good name, trade connections, or earning capacity of an operating business. Patents purchased by a firm may be valuable for the 17 years for which they are granted by the United States Patent Office. Copyrights are another example of an intangible asset with a somewhat longer life as they are granted for 28 years and can be renewed for a like period of time.

5 / Current liabilities. Debts that are owed and payable within a short time are classified as *current liabilities*. Amounts owed to trade creditors, banks, employees, and other debts of a similar nature are common current liabilities. For example, purchases of merchandise on open book account are due in 30, 60, or 90 days depending upon the terms of the transaction. As in the case of current assets, the usual rule is that liabilities that will come due and be payable within one year after the date of the balance sheet should be included under this heading.

6 / Long-term liabilities. Long-term debts that will not be due for several years are called *long-term* or *fixed liabilities*. Money borrowed by selling bonds, long-term notes, or by assuming a mortgage payable results in liabilities classified in this section of the balance sheet. Adding the long-term liabilities to the current liabilities gives a total that represents that amount of the capital employed by a firm in its business that is classified as debt capital.

7 / Proprietorship. Net worth is a common synonym for proprietorship, which represents the equity capital portion of the financing of a firm's assets. Although the assets and the liabilities of a single proprietorship, partnership, or corporation might be identical, this would not be true of the proprietorship section. By examining the proprietorship information on a balance sheet, it is possible to determine the type of business organization as to ownership.

The proprietorship section of the balance sheet of A. R. Morgan clearly indicates a sole proprietorship. Changes that have occurred in his proprietorship interest between the beginning and end of the year have been shown, but this analysis is not absolutely necessary.

If a business firm is operating under a partnership agreement, the capital interests of the partners are shown in the proprietorship section of the balance sheet. For example, if Carter, Nelson, and Prince own and operate a business under the name of the Carter Drug Company, the proprietorship section of the balance sheet for this firm might appear as follows:

C. D. Carter, Capital	68,400
H. H. Nelson, Capital	35,250
S. R. Prince, Capital	19,800
Total proprietorship	123,450

In the case of a corporation the individual interest of each stockholder is not shown on the balance sheet even though the company may have only three or four owners. Also, although some corporations have different types of stock and retained earnings, frequently only two items are shown. One is the original investment on the part of the stockholders in the capital stock of the corporation, and the other is the sum of past earnings that have not been distributed to the owners. The capital section of the balance sheet of a small corporation might appear as follows:

Capital Stock	25,000
Retained Earnings	8,385
Total capital	33,385

■ Retained Earnings Statement

The proprietorship or capital section of a balance sheet for a corporation can become quite involved if all pertinent information is shown. Because the owners like to know the additions to and the subtractions from retained earnings that have been made during the year, a *retained earnings statement* is frequently shown in addition to the balance sheet and the income statement.

INGERSOLL STEEL CORPORATION
Retained Earnings Statement
For Year Ended December 31, 1967

Balance, January 1, 1967		$12,486,750
Net income for year		3,190,486
Total		$15,677,236
Less cash dividends:		
Preferred stock	$ 300,000	
Common stock	1,200,000	1,500,000
Balance, December 31, 1967		$14,177,236

Retained Earnings Statement

■ Income Statement

The statement that summarizes the incomes and expenses of a business for a stated period of time is the *income statement*. It shows such information as the total merchandise purchased and sold, expenses incurred, and miscellaneous sources of income. Other names given to this statement are the profit and loss statement, operating statement, income summary, and income account.

The income statement is dynamic, whereas the balance sheet is static. This means that the income statement reflects summaries of operations over a period of time such as a year, six months, a quarter, or a month, while the balance sheet is a picture of the business at a given instant of time, usually the close of business on the date of the balance sheet. Both statements are prepared at the same time, and the net income or loss shown on the income statement is reflected in the proprietorship section of the balance sheet.

On page 506 is shown an income statement for the Modern Furniture Mart, whose balance sheet has already been illustrated. Note that the income statement is divided into sections for the grouping of like items.

1. Revenue from sales
2. Cost of merchandise sold
3. Gross profit on sales
4. Operating expenses

5. Net income from operations
6. Other income and other expense

7. Net income

1 / Revenue from sales. The major source of income for most firms is the sale of merchandise, and this is the first section on the income statement. The _sales_ figure includes the amounts paid by customers and the amounts they have agreed to pay if sales have been made on account. It is a total for the year or for a shorter period of time if statements are prepared more often. From this total must be subtracted the value of the merchandise returned or reductions in price granted following complaints by the customer as to quality or quantity received. The resulting figure is called *net sales*.

2 / Cost of merchandise sold. The _cost of merchandise sold_ represents the purchase price of the merchandise that was sold by the firm during the year. The formula used for arriving at the cost figure is usually the one shown on the income statement. Merchandise on hand at the beginning of the year plus purchases, adjusted for returns and allowances and purchase discount, gives the total cost of all the merchandise that might have been sold. Subtracting the inventory figure at the end of the year from this total results in the cost of the merchandise sold.

The beginning and ending inventories are determined by a physical count of each item in stock and a valuation of these quantities. The purchases of merchandise made during the year can be secured from the ledger account in which have been posted all of the invoices covering the various shipments received. Returns and allowances follow the same pattern as indicated above for sales.

3 / Gross profit on sales. The difference found by subtracting the cost of merchandise sold from the net sales is termed the *gross profit on sales*. If there were no expenses in connection with the sales, gross profit would be the amount of net income earned. For business firms that have substantial operating expenses, the gross profit on sales must be from one

MODERN FURNITURE MART
Income Statement
For Year Ended December 31, 1968

```
Revenue from sales:
  Sales . . . . . . . . . . . . . . . . . . . . . . . . . . .   $232,400
  Less sales returns and allowances . . . . . . . . . . . .       5,100
  Net sales . . . . . . . . . . . . . . . . . . . . . . . .                $227,300
Cost of merchandise sold:
  Merchandise inventory, January 1, 1968 . . . . . . . .     $ 51,200
  Purchases . . . . . . . . . . . . . . . . . .   $152,210
  Less:  Purchases returns & allowances  $6,840
         Purchases discount . . . . . .   2,570      9,410
  Net purchases . . . . . . . . . . . . . . . .               142,800
  Merchandise available for sale . . . . . . . . .           $194,000
  Less merchandise inventory, December 31, 1968 . . . . .      46,350
    Cost of merchandise sold . . . . . . . . . . . . . . .                 147,650
Gross profit on sales . . . . . . . . . . . . . . . . . .                  $ 79,650
Operating expenses:
  Selling expenses:
    Salesmen's salaries . . . . . . . . . . . .   $ 23,900
    Advertising expense . . . . . . . . . . .       8,100
    Store supplies expense . . . . . . . . . .      1,240
    Depreciation expense--store equipment . .       1,475
    Miscellaneous selling expenses . . . . . .      2,805
      Total selling expenses . . . . . . . . . . .          $ 37,520
  General expenses:
    Office salaries . . . . . . . . . . . .      $ 12,240
    Office supplies expense . . . . . . . . .         875
    Insurance expense . . . . . . . . . . .         3,200
    Uncollectible accounts expense . . . . . .      1,230
    Taxes expense . . . . . . . . . . . . . .       3,455
    Depreciation expense--office equipment . .      1,240
    Depreciation expense--building . . . . . .      2,460
    Miscellaneous general expense . . . . . .       1,980
      Total general expenses . . . . . . . . . . . .         26,680
  Total operating expenses . . . . . . . . . . . . . . .                    64,200
Net income from operations . . . . . . . . . . . . . . . .                 $ 15,450
Other income:
  Dividends on stock . . . . . . . . . . . . . . . . . .   $     300
Other expense:
  Interest expense . . . . . . . . . . . . . . . . . . . .     1,810         1,510
Net income . . . . . . . . . . . . . . . . . . . . . . . .                 $ 13,940
```

Income Statement

third to two thirds of the total sales figure. In retail circles the gross profit on sales is known as the *gross margin* and reflects the average overall markup percentage on goods sold.

4 / Operating expenses. Payrolls for sales clerks and office employees, supplies consumed, depreciation on plant or fixed assets, advertising costs, taxes, and expired insurance are examples of *operating expenses*. All of the costs that a business firm incurs in its normal operations are grouped under this classification. Individual items are shown so that the owner or owners can note the amount spent for each purpose. If certain expenses appear too large, as brought out by comparison with previous income statements, steps can be taken to correct this situation.

Operating expenses are usually subdivided into selling expenses and general or administrative expenses. *Selling expenses* are those that are incurred as a direct result of the sales activities of the firm. Such items as salaries of sales clerks, advertising, store supplies used, depreciation on store equipment, and delivery costs are examples of selling expenses. The advantage of segregating these from general expenses is that the total for one year compared with the total for another year may be significant. If selling expenses have increased in total, it is then possible to analyze the individual items to locate the cause or causes.

Office salaries, rent, taxes, insurance, office supplies used, depreciation on buildings and office equipment, and the cost of bad debts resulting from account sales that prove uncollectible are examples of *general expenses*. They are costs connected with the general operation of the business. If an expense is difficult to allocate between the selling and general classification, such as fire insurance on merchandise inventory, it is usually assigned to the general expense classification.

5 / Net income from operations. The difference found by subtracting the total of the operating expenses from the gross profit on sales is known as the *net income from operations*. If there are no other items of income and expense, this figure is also the net income, but most businesses do have nonoperating incomes and costs. In some instances the total operating expenses may exceed the gross profit on sales. Should this occur, the difference between the two amounts would be known as the *net loss from operations*.

6 / Other income and other expense. Most firms secure some income and incur some expenses of a financial, rather than an operating, character. These are classified as *other income* and *other expense* and are added to or subtracted from the net income from operations. Other titles used for these sections are nonoperating income and expense and financial income and expense. The most common items are interest received and paid on notes, mortgages, and bonds.

7 / Net income. The final figure on an income statement and the one that represents the results of all operations of a business, both operating and nonoperating, is called the *net income* or *net loss*. It is, naturally, the most interesting single figure on an income statement. Although the amounts used in arriving at the final result are of interest to those connected with the management of the firm, others are more concerned with the amount of net income or net loss. It is the figure on which taxes are based and, for corporations, plays an important part in dividend declarations.

■ Schedule of Cost of Goods Manufactured

A. R. Morgan, as a retail furniture merchant, purchased all of the merchandise that he sold. Manufacturing firms, on the other hand, produce their goods from raw materials purchased. In this event the line titled "Purchases" in the income statement would be replaced with "Cost of Goods Manufactured, Schedule No. 1." An illustration of such a schedule is shown on page 509. Note that inventories of raw materials and of goods in the process of manufacture are shown, and that the nature of the manufacturing expenses is somewhat different from operating expenses.

■ Statement of Source and Application of Funds

A recent development in statements prepared from accounting data and published in the annual report to shareholders is the *statement of source and application of funds*. It shows the major sources of the flow of funds (additions to current assets) into the business and the uses made of such funds. It is usually prepared on the same date as that of the balance sheet, and covers the same period of time as the income statement.

Current assets (circulating capital) are constantly subject to change, and the same can be said for current liabilities. The difference between the total current assets and total current liabilities is called *working capital*. A statement of source and application of funds does not detail the increases and decreases in each current asset and current liability account, although this information is frequently shown separately. Rather, the net difference between the working capital at the beginning and end of the period under review becomes the residual figure of the statement. If more

DONOVAN MANUFACTURING CORPORATION
Schedule No. 1 - Cost of Goods Manufactured
For Year Ended December 31, 1968

Work in process inventory, January 1, 1968			$ 29,000
Raw materials:			
Inventory, January 1, 1968		$ 61,000	
Purchases	$184,900		
Less purchases returns & allowances . . .	2,500		
Net purchases		182,400	
Total cost of materials available for use		$243,400	
Less inventory, December 31, 1968		70,000	
Cost of materials placed in production		$173,400	
Direct labor		152,000	
Factory overhead:			
Indirect labor	$ 14,800		
Repairs	12,000		
Heat, light, and power	19,600		
Depreciation--machinery & equipment . . .	25,350		
Factory supplies expense	10,400		
Patents expense	7,250		
Insurance expense	3,600		
Total factory overhead		93,000	
Total manufacturing costs			418,400
Total work in process during year			$447,400
Less work in process inventory, December 31, 1968 . .			34,800
Cost of goods manufactured			$412,600

Schedule of Cost of Goods Manufactured

funds have been received than used, the working capital will have increased; and if more funds have been used than received, the working capital will be a smaller figure.

As shown in the illustration on page 510, the customary major source of funds is net income. Next in order is commonly the total of depreciation charges. These have reduced net income but did not require an outlay of cash during the current year. Other sources might include the sale of plant assets, such as unneeded land, or the receipt of cash from a bond issue. The application of funds of profitable corporations usually includes dividend payments, the purchase of plant assets, and, possibly, the reduction of long-term debt. All increases and decreases in noncurrent assets and liabilities, in the proprietorship accounts, and the net change in working capital, are likely to reflect sources and applications of funds.

Closely allied to sources and applications of funds is a relatively recent concept known as cash flow analysis. *Cash flow* consists of the net income of a firm plus all expense charges that did not require an outlay of funds

CARPENTER CORPORATION

Statement of Source and Application of Funds

For Year Ended December 31, 1967

Source:

```
Net income for year  . . . . . . . . . . . . . . $2,189,000
Depreciation charges on plant assets . . . . .      432,000
Sale of warehouse  . . . . . . . . . . . . . . .    120,000   $2,741,000
```

Application:

```
Cash dividends paid  . . . . . . . . . . . . . . $1,200,000
Purchase of equipment  . . . . . . . . . . . . .  1,108,000
Retirement of serial bonds . . . . . . . . . . .    250,000    2,558,000
```

```
Increase in working capital . . . . . . . . . .            $   183,000
```

Statement of Source and Application of Funds

minus any income that did not generate cash. For financial managers it is useful in determining the ability of the company to pay dividends, to purchase additional machinery and equipment, and to retire bonded debt without recourse to bank borrowing or the sale of additional securities. Cash flow is usually a considerably higher figure than net income and, when published on a per-share basis, may lead to shareholder dissatisfaction with the size of dividend checks.

■ Interpretation of Statements

After the balance sheet, income statement, and any other desired statements are prepared, the fourth and last step in the work of an accountant, that of interpretation, can be performed. The fact that a business may or may not have been operated at a profit is of vital concern, but this one figure fails to tell the whole story. For example, a bank may be willing to extend a loan to a firm that has a strong financial structure despite recent operating losses. Judicious use of such borrowed funds might correct conditions so that future business operations would be profitable. On the other hand, a firm may be headed for financial trouble even though operating profitably.

By means of ratios, percentages, and other devices, it is possible to analyze the financial status of a company. The directions such an analysis may take are varied and extensive. The current balance sheet offers definite possibilities in itself, and comparisons can be made with previous balance sheets and also with the balance sheets of competing companies. The same remarks apply to the income statement. Furthermore, there are a number of important relationships between the two statements. In addition, other statements and schedules prepared offer analytical possibilities in and of themselves or in conjunction with the balance sheet and income statement.

A few of the most useful and common methods of analysis are described below. These have been restricted to the statements of the Modern Furniture Mart, previously illustrated, which means that no attempt has been made to show trends, to contrast the efficiency of Morgan's firm with any of his competitors, or to rely on any data not contained in a single balance sheet and income statement.

1. Current ratio
2. Acid-test ratio
3. Working capital
4. Turnover of merchandise inventory
5. Ratio of ownership to debt
6. Rate of net income on proprietorship
7. Rate of net income on sales
8. Rate of net income on assets

1 / Current ratio. The ratio of current assets to current liabilities is the *current ratio*. It is found by dividing the current assets by the current liabilities. This ratio is very important to the owners and to short-term creditors because the current assets constitute a source of funds to pay current liabilities. An acceptable minimum ratio is usually 2 to 1, which takes into consideration the fact that current assets sometimes shrink in value whereas current liabilities do not.

Reference to the balance sheet of A. R. Morgan shows that on December 31, 1968, his current assets totaled $68,080 and his current liabilities $21,880. The calculation for his current ratio is as follows:

$$\frac{68,080}{21,880} = 3.1 \text{ to } 1$$

2 / Acid-test ratio. The *acid-test* or *quick ratio* is a refinement of the current ratio in that it determines the ability of a firm to meet its current debt on very short notice. It recognizes the fact that the conversion of merchandise inventory into cash takes more time than is true for other current assets. The formula is to divide the total cash and receivables by the current liabilities, and an acceptable minimum is 1 to 1. If the firm owns marketable securities purchased on a temporary basis, these may be added to the cash and receivables.

The balance sheet of A. R. Morgan shows that he owns cash and accounts receivable totaling $19,800 and that his current liabilities total $21,880. His acid-test ratio is computed as follows:

$$\frac{19,800}{21,880} = .9 \text{ to } 1$$

Whereas the current ratio was considerably in excess of the minimum, the above ratio falls short of the 1 to 1 requirement. This may indicate a situation that should be corrected by a more rapid turnover of the inventory; otherwise Mr. Morgan may not be able to meet maturities on his current debt.

3 / Working capital. As noted previously, the excess dollar value of the current assets over the current liabilities is the working capital of a firm. It should be large enough to absorb any possible shrinkages as inventories and receivables are converted into cash and still leave a comfortable margin to pay current liabilities as they mature. In the case of A. R. Morgan, the excess of $46,200 ($68,080–$21,880) should provide adequate protection.

4 / Turnover of merchandise inventory. A retail establishment must always be alert to "turn over" its stock of salable goods as rapidly as possible; in other words, to sell present stock before it loses its maximum value. The frequency with which this move is accomplished is called the *inventory turnover* and is a measure of efficiency.

The preferred method of determining the turnover of merchandise inventory is to divide the cost of merchandise sold by the average inventory. In the case of Mr. Morgan, only the beginning and ending inventories can be averaged because other inventory figures are not available. The information available on page 506 shows a merchandise inventory on January 1 of $51,200 and on December 31 of $46,350. These two amounts average $48,775, the cost of goods sold is shown as $147,650, and the turnover calculation is as follows:

$$\frac{147,650}{48,775} = 3.0 \text{ turns}$$

For a retail grocery store this would be a poor turnover, since from 5 to 10 turnovers each year are secured by efficient firms. Mr. Morgan, however, operates a furniture store, and the figure of 3.0 is very good. Most businesses of this type are not able to turn over their stock more than from 1 to 4 times a year.

5 / Ratio of ownership to debt. Practically every business is financed by a combination of funds secured from the owners and by borrowed capital. The ratio of ownership to debt shows the relative proportion of capital secured from the two sources. A mark of conservative financing is substantial ownership on the part of the proprietors or stockholders. This means that the ownership equity is large enough to absorb even extensive and continued losses, and there is less danger of insolvency.

The balance sheet of A. R. Morgan shows total liabilities of $51,880 and total proprietorship of $92,190. The ratio is found by dividing the ownership equity by the creditors' equity as follows:

$$\frac{92,190}{51,880} = 1.8 \text{ to } 1$$

This is a fairly conservative ratio, for Mr. Morgan has contributed almost two times as much capital as he has borrowed. Some businesses operate on a much lower ratio. As has been mentioned earlier, public utilities and railroads frequently have ratios of less than 1 to 1.

6 / Rate of net income on proprietorship. The reason an owner invests his own funds in a business is to secure a return on his investment. Because of the risks involved, this rate should be higher than if a similar amount were invested in conservative securities. Furthermore, in the case of a sole proprietorship, the net income also includes the personal service factor. Despite the fact that an owner may devote full time to his business, he does not include a salary for himself as one of his operating expenses.

Mr. Morgan's investment in his business was $88,440 at the beginning of the year and $92,190 at the end of the year. An average of these two amounts is $90,315. (It would be preferable to compute a monthly average to determine the investment throughout the year.) The net income was $13,940. This return divided by the average investment shows a yield of 15.4 percent.

$$\frac{13,940}{90,315} = .154 = 15.4\%$$

7 / Rate of net income on sales. If a business is able to sell a large volume of goods on a small investment, the net return on each dollar's worth of goods sold can be very small, perhaps as low as one cent on the dollar. This is the principle under which chain stores and supermarkets operate. If the turnover of total assets (the number of times each dollar value of assets is converted into a sales dollar in one year) is low, however, the net return on each sales dollar must be substantial if a satisfactory return is to be secured.

The net sales made by the Modern Furniture Mart in 1968 totaled $227,300, as shown on page 506, and the net income was $13,940. Since the furniture business does not lend itself to a high volume of sales on a low investment, the firm's return of 6.1 percent on its sales must be considered satisfactory.

$$\frac{13,940}{227,300} = .061 = 6.1\%$$

8 / Rate of net income on assets. In attempting to compare the cost of capital with the rate of earnings on assets purchased by borrowing or securing additional funds from owners, it is important to determine the percentage of net income, before income taxes, on the assets employed in a business. The total assets of the Modern Furniture Mart, as shown on page 501, were $144,070 on which the firm earned $13,940. The rate of net income of 9.7 percent must certainly have been in excess of the cost of any borrowed capital used as well as demonstrating a profitable use of the total capital employed in the business.

$$\frac{13,940}{144,070} = .097 = 9.7\%$$

PROFESSIONAL ASSOCIATIONS IN ACCOUNTING

The American Accounting Association is a professional society for educators, practitioners, and students of accounting. Organized in 1916 by a group of accounting teachers, it broadened its membership in 1935 and now has approximately 10,500 members of whom 2,500 are accounting professors. Students in universities are eligible for associate membership at an annual fee of $3 which includes a subscription to the *Accounting Review,* a quarterly publication of the Association. A national convention is held each year as well as regional meetings.

The National Association of Accountants, which was founded in 1919 as the National Association of Cost Accountants, has over 58,000 members organized into chapters in many cities in the United States and in Puerto Rico and Mexico City. Every month the Association publishes a 64-page technical magazine, *Management Accounting,* which is available to students at a special rate of $2 for nine months. In addition to the magazine, the Association sponsors research studies, seminars, regional meetings, and a national convention.

The American Institute of Certified Public Accountants is the national organization representing state societies, firms, and individuals who hold a certified public accountant's certificate from one of the fifty states. An annual convention is held but much of the work of the Institute is accomplished through numerous committees. It publishes books, monographs, and the *Journal of Accountancy,* a monthly magazine. Subscriptions to the *Journal* are available to students at a special rate of $4 a year, and for 50 cents additional they can receive the semiannual CPA Questions and Answers pamphlet. The Institute has approximately 60,000 members. Among its various services to the profession is the highly important one of writing and grading the examination given in all states as a part of the requirements for the designation of certified public accountant.

BUSINESS TERMS

(a) public accountant (498), certified public accountant (498), governmental accountant (498)

(b) accounting (498)

(c) journal (499), ledger (499)

(d) balance sheet (499); assets (499), liabilities (500), proprietorship (500)

(e) balance sheet equation (500)

(f) current assets (500), plant or fixed assets (502), investments (502), intangible assets (502), goodwill (502)

(g) current liabilities (502), long-term or fixed liabilities (503)

(h) retained earnings statement (504)

(i) income statement (504)

(j) sales (505), net sales (507), cost of merchandise sold (507), gross profit on sales (505), gross margin (507)

(k) operating expenses (507), selling expenses (507), general expenses (507)

(l) net income from operations (507), net loss from operations (507)

(m) other income (507), other expense (507), net income or net loss (508)

(n) statement of source and application of funds (508); working capital (508), cash flow (509)

(o) current ratio (511), acid-test or quick ratio (511), inventory turnover (512)

QUESTIONS FOR DISCUSSION AND ANALYSIS

1. Why might a business fail just because it did not keep a set of books?
2. Certified public accountants belong to a profession. Why are other areas of business not regarded as having professional status?
3. Does the total value of assets as shown on a balance sheet provide an accurate statement of the gross value of a firm?

4. Are the current and long-term liabilities as shown on a balance sheet an accurate statement of debt capital?

5. Why should not sole proprietorships and partnerships show a retained earnings amount on their balance sheets as does a corporation?

6. Why are selling and general expenses separated on an income statement?

7. Is there any information shown on a statement of source and application of funds that could not be located on balance sheets of two consecutive years? Explain.

8. What makes the cash flow figure more valuable to some financial managers than the amount of net income?

9. Of all possible ratios, percentages, and turnovers, which ones are most useful in appraising the effectiveness of top management?

10. As stated in the chapter, accounting does not produce any profits. Is it then merely a necessary evil that should be relegated to as minor a role as possible? Discuss.

PROBLEMS AND SHORT CASES

1. (a) The following account balances were taken from the books and records of the Orton Drug Store on December 31, 1968. Prepare a balance sheet using the statement for the Modern Furniture Mart, illustrated on page 501, for guidance as to form and arrangement.

Cash	$17,420	Accumulated depreciation—	
Accounts receivable	18,275	office equipment	$11,100
Allowance for doubtful accounts	1,420	Building	84,000
Merchandise inventory, 12/31/68	83,760	Accumulated depreciation— building	20,160
Store and office supplies	1,815	Land	18,000
Prepaid insurance	910	Goodwill	10,000
Store equipment	22,800	Notes payable	15,000
Accumulated depreciation—		Accounts payable	28,275
store equipment	13,680	Mortgage payable	68,400
Office equipment	18,500	Geo. W. Orton, capital (1/1/68)	96,375
		Geo. W. Orton, drawing	10,400
		Net income for 1968	31,470

(b) The following account balances were taken from the books and records of the Orton Drug Store on December 31, 1968. Prepare an income statement using the statement for the Modern Furniture Mart, illustrated on page 506, for guidance as to form and arrangement of accounts.

Sales	$315,400	Depreciation expense—	
Sales returns and		store equipment ...	$ 2,280
allowances	1,240	Office salaries	16,750
Merchandise inven-		Uncollectible accounts	
tory, 1/1/68	71,840	expense	420
Purchases	194,290	Depreciation expense—	
Purchases returns and		office equipment ...	1,850
allowances	4,150	Depreciation expense—	
Purchases discount ..	3,910	building	2,100
Merchandise inven-		Taxes expense	5,340
tory, 12/31/68 ..	83,760	Insurance expense ...	4,185
Sales salaries	42,400	Miscellaneous office	
Advertising expense .	25,190	expense	930
Store supplies expense	2,360	Interest expense	4,575

2. The following figures were taken from the statements of the New-comb Department Store, Inc. for the year ended December 31, 1968. Compute the (a) current ratio, (b) acid-test ratio, (c) working capital, (d) inventory turnover, (e) ratio of ownership to debt, (f) rate of net income on proprietorship, (g) rate of net income on sales, and (h) rate of net income on assets.

Current assets	$ 660,800	Current liabilities ..	$ 242,500
Cash and receivables	376,600	Total liabilities ...	542,500
Merchandise inven-		Capital, 1/1/68 ...	776,700
tory 1/1/68 ...	294,200	Capital, 12/31/68 .	864,800
Merchandise inven-		Net sales	2,496,400
tory 12/31/68 .	276,400	Cost of merchandise	
Total assets	1,407,300	sold	1,280,000
		Net income	176,200

3. Family Frocks, a ladies' and children's dress shop, has an excellent location in a large shopping center. The owners were approached by a competitor who wished to sell out, and they agreed to buy his stock of merchandise at what, without any question, was a very advantageous price. For $20,000 the owners of Family Frocks acquired an inventory that they estimated could be sold, at regular prices, for approximately $50,000. Terms of the sale were cash in thirty days.

The balance sheet of Family Frocks, prior to this purchase, showed the following current assets and liabilities:

Current Assets

Cash	$ 5,200
Accounts receivable	12,800
Merchandise inventory	18,000
	$36,000

Current Liabilities

Accounts payable	$ 7,600
Notes payable	8,400
	$16,000

The purchase of the competitor's stock increased the merchandise inventory to $38,000 and the accounts payable to $27,600. When the proprietors of Family Frocks approached their bank for an additional loan of $20,000, they were told that the funds would not be advanced because their current ratio was now less than 2 to 1, and the acid-test ratio was less than 1 to 1. The banker was sympathetic, agreed that the purchase was a good one, but explained that the policy of his bank would prevent a loan until the ratios were met.

Assuming no other source of credit is available, what steps must Family Frocks take in the next thirty days in order to qualify for a $20,000 bank loan?

SUGGESTED READINGS

Anderson, W. T., C. A. Moyer, and A. R. Wright. *Accounting: Basic Financial, Cost, and Control Concepts.* New York: John Wiley & Sons, Inc., 1965. Chapters 3, 14, and 19.

Finney, H. A., and H. E. Miller. *Principles of Accounting—Introductory,* Sixth Edition. Englewood Cliffs, New Jersey: Prentice-Hall, Inc., 1963. Chapters 20-23.

Foulke, R. A. *Practical Financial Statement Analysis,* Fifth Edition. New York: McGraw-Hill Book Company, 1962.

Meigs, W. B., and C. E. Johnson. *Accounting.* New York: McGraw-Hill Book Company, 1962. Chapters 1 and 28.

Moore, C. L., and R. K. Jaedicke. *Managerial Accounting,* Second Edition. Cincinnati: South-Western Publishing Company, 1967. Parts I and II.

Niswonger, C. R., and P. E. Fess. *Accounting Principles,* Ninth Edition. Cincinnati: South-Western Publishing Company, 1965. Chapters 1, 2, 27, and 28.

Pyle, W. W., and J. A. White. *Fundamental Accounting Principles,* Fourth Edition. Homewood, Illinois: Richard D. Irwin, Inc., 1966. Chapters 1-3, 24, and 26.

Seiler, R. E. *Elementary Accounting.* Columbus, Ohio: Charles E. Merrill Books, Inc., 1963. Chapters 1 and 17.

Magazines: *Accounting Review, Journal of Accountancy, N.A.A. Bulletin, Data Processing for Management, Business Automation.*

Chapter 24

BUSINESS STATISTICS

Decision making in business and executive control of operations rely heavily on information obtained from quantitative data, and it is in this area that statistics plays an important role. All facts that are capable of being expressed numerically can be specifically stated, processed, measured, analyzed, and summarized to produce meaningful results. The importance of statistics to business management has taken a sharp upward turn with the advent of electronic computers. These high-speed machines have made it possible to process larger quantities of data in greater detail than previously. Furthermore, the end results can be on an executive's desk in a matter of hours rather than days or weeks, and time is frequently an important factor in issuing corrective instructions or making a decision.

Since accounting is also based on quantitative data, it may be well to examine its relationship to the field of business statistics. One major difference is that business statistics is broader than accounting because it uses all units of measurement, whereas accounting is more or less restricted to dollars and cents. For example, if a firm sells 62,000 units for $100,000 to 3,500 customers located in 15 states, it is probable that the only fact of interest to the accountant is $100,000. To the statistician, the number of units involved, the average size of the orders from the 3,500 customers, and the dollar sales in each state may be just as important and significant as the total dollar sales.

Another difference between accounting and statistics is that accounting is restricted to internal data resulting from the profit-making transactions of the firm while statistics makes use of external data as well as internal data covering any and all measurable activities of a business. In estimating the sales potential of a consumer product in a new territory, for example, data released by the Bureau of the Census would be significant and helpful.

Or, if the external data have not been made available by some governmental or private agency, the statistician may decide to collect his own information from outside sources.

In summary, *business statistics* can be defined as the (1) collection, (2) analysis, summarization, and measurement, (3) presentation, and (4) interpretation of numerical data that are related to the problems of industry. The remainder of this chapter will deal with some of the accepted procedures involving each of these four steps and will describe some of the common statistical measurements of value to business management.

■ Collection of Data

Numerical data must be collected before they can be summarized and used. If the figures are concerned with operations of the company, without regard for outside influences, the source for these data lies within the records of the particular business. Financial statements, purchase invoices, sales reports, and payroll records can supply vital information that is subject to statistical analysis. As an illustration, a company may show an operating profit in the current year of $325,000 as contrasted with a corresponding figure of $300,000 for the preceding year. If these figures represent the output of a factory and no expansion took place during the current year, the conclusion might be reached that more efficient use was made of the production facilities or that the plant operated more hours. However, an analysis showed that 50,000 units were sold in the current year as contrasted with 60,000 in the preceding year and that the increased operating profit was due entirely to an increase in selling price. In this case, the sales manager rather than the plant superintendent may have deserved commendation.

Although internal data provide many useful figures, particularly for control at the executive level, external data are more helpful in arriving at sound solutions to many problems. If, by chance, the wanted information is available from outside agencies, its use will save time and money. More often, the statistical department of a business must secure the facts it needs by its own efforts. Three common methods are used to obtain needed original information: (1) mail surveys, involving questionnaires mailed to individuals or firms; (2) personal interviews, in which the interrogator fills out a questionnaire form; and (3) telephone calls, with answers noted on a suitable form. Each method has its advantages and disadvantages, some of which are fairly obvious. For example, for a given amount of money, more individuals can be contacted by a mail survey than by personal interviews, and unless telephone calls are restricted to one community, toll charges may prove to be prohibitive. In some instances a combination of two or all of the above methods may be preferable to relying on only one procedure.

When a questionnaire is used, it must be prepared carefully. It should not be too long, the questions must be clear and easy to answer, and, above all, questions must not be "loaded" in favor of a desired response. In a personal interview more answers can be obtained and the questions can be more complicated as the interviewer can clarify any misunderstandings. If questionnaires are mailed, only a 10 to 15 percent return can be expected if the mailing list is large or if the questionnaires are sent to individuals who do not have a vital interest in the subject. General Motors, through its Customers' Research Staff, has made extensive use of mail surveys in an attempt to find out what car owners want in the many details of their automobiles.

1 / **Sampling techniques.** Regardless of the method used to collect external data, most problems are of such a nature that a complete coverage is impracticable. For example, a department store in a community of 10,000 homes might want to know which evening or evenings customers and potential customers would prefer that it remain open. Obviously, the task of contacting every family would be difficult and expensive. This leads to a process known as *sampling*. The theory of sampling is that the characteristics of an adequate sample are representative of those of the whole (called the *universe* by statisticians) of which it is a part. Applied to the problem stated, if interviews were held with 1,000 householders, it might be reasonable to assume that the answers would be consistent with those that would be obtained if all 10,000 were contacted.

Random sampling results when each individual in the group to be surveyed has an equal chance of being included. Again referring to the above situation, if 10,000 names were typed on identical cards and these were thoroughly shuffled, the top 1,000 names would constitute a random sample. If these names were taken from a telephone book, and calls replaced interviews, the fact that all homes do not have telephone service could invalidate the results of the survey.

Most sampling for business purposes is *controlled sampling* in that an effort is made to contact a small group that is representative of the larger number about whom some information is wanted. For example, a manufacturer of pipe tobacco might like to know whether an aromatic or nonaromatic product would sell better. It is obvious that contacts should be made with men of adult ages; but there might be differences between the tastes of rural and city dwellers, high and low income groups, indoor and outdoor workers, and among different age groups. The reliability of the results of the sampling would vary with the care used in determining the composition of the sample group so that the above-mentioned, and probably other, factors would be properly balanced.

Some business firms are not large enough to maintain a market research or other type of statistical department. In this event they may find it advantageous to hire an outside agency to make special studies for them. These agencies, operating in most cities, also collect information for more extensive distribution, such as newspaper releases. Polls of public opinion, particularly those that are concerned with election results, are well known to everyone. Although somewhat discredited because of incorrect forecasts in some elections, these polls have a very low percentage of error. At the same time, incorrect forecasts point up the truth that results obtained from questionnaires and interviews must always be interpreted with great care and that the validity of results from a sampling process are always open to some question.

2 / Sources of data for business. Both internal and external data gathered by or for a firm for its use are known as *primary data.* If these facts are published or otherwise released, they are known as *secondary data* in the hands of subsequent users. Since additional handling of the figures allows more chances for errors, and time is likely to have elapsed since the data were first collected, secondary data should be used with caution. They are, nonetheless, widely used because of the enormous quantities of data available, frequently without cost, from government and private agencies.

(a) U. S. GOVERNMENT PUBLICATIONS. The federal government is outstanding in providing secondary data of value to business. Various departments, bureaus, and agencies compile and publish statistical information covering a wide variety of activities related to the economic life of the United States.

The Department of Commerce exists primarily to serve the needs of large and small businesses. Among its numerous publications are the monthly *Survey of Current Business,* the biweekly *Bulletin of Commerce, Industry Reports,* and the *Small Business Management Series.*

The Bureau of the Census is another government department that makes available important statistical material. In addition to population figures, which are basic to many surveys, this Bureau issues many other

publications, including the annual *Statistical Abstract of the United States.*
The Bureau is responsible for the Census of Business, which classifies
the channels of distribution on a geographical basis, and for the Census
of Manufactures, which presents important information covering the
various types of industries.

One of the most reliable indexes of industrial production is published
monthly by the Board of Governors of the Federal Reserve System. The
annual report of this body, as well as the bulletins issued by the individual
federal reserve banks, are helpful in the field of banking and finance.

The Bureau of Labor Statistics of the Department of Labor issues
the *Monthly Labor Review,* which gives information on price levels,
unemployment, and wages. This Bureau is responsible for a number of
indexes as well as other statistical measurements.

The Department of Agriculture, although primarily concerned with
its own field, presents in its *Agricultural Yearbook* many facts that can
be used by the businessman who is concerned with the use of raw materials
grown on the farms. Soybean acreage or production, for example, would
be of interest to a manufacturer of paints.

(b) NONGOVERNMENT SOURCES. Another valuable source of
secondary data includes publications issued by newspapers and magazines,
trade journals, trade associations, private agencies, and institutions.

In addition to newspapers and magazines, both general and specialized, that have been mentioned in previous chapters, many publications
classified as trade journals deal with one segment of industry. *Plastic
Age* and *Air Transportation* are examples of such magazines. The publications of the American Iron and Steel Institute are examples of those
issued by trade associations. Private agencies include such well-known
organizations as Moody's Investors Service and Dun and Bradstreet, Inc.
Publications issued by the Brookings Institution, the Twentieth Century
Fund, the National Industrial Conference Board, and many universities
are examples of institutional releases.

■ **Analysis, Summarization, and Measurement**

Once the data are available, whether secured from a primary or
a secondary source, or both, the figures must be processed. Sometimes
they need to be broken down into segments, and at times they are summarized into usable totals. Various types of statistical measurement can
then be applied to yield results ready for presentation and interpretation.

When thousands of individual items have been collected, the chore of summarizing the data can be simplified by various business machines. Calculators and adding machines are helpful, punched card equipment is invaluable for many situations, and, more recently, electronic computers have been added to process information at a much faster rate and with more variables. A punched card permits the coding of a great many items, which can then be tabulated by machines in a variety of ways.

An example may clarify the use of a punched card. Referring to the survey on aromatic and nonaromatic tobacco mentioned previously, each interview furnished the following information about the men: (1) Age, (2) Nationality, (3) Married or Single, (4) State of Residence, (5) Rural or City Dweller, (6) Occupation, (7) Annual Income, (8) Indoor or Outdoor Worker, (9) Pipe, Cigar, or Cigarette Smoker, (10) Occasional or Habitual Smoker, (11) Brand of Pipe Tobacco Used. The answers to these questions, punched on cards, permitted summaries and an analysis of each factor in relation to any other factor.

■ Types of Statistical Measurement

Assuming that the necessary data have been processed into usable details or summaries, the next procedure is to apply an appropriate type of measurement. Two possibilities, ratios and percentages, were illustrated in Chapter 23 in connection with the interpretation of financial statements. Both ratios and percentages are useful for data other than those secured from accounting information. For example, a firm had total sales of $1,000,000 of which $800,000 was derived in states east of the Mississippi River and $200,000 in states west of that dividing line. This fact could be expressed as a 4 to 1 ratio, or 80 percent.

In addition to ratios and percentages there are several other types of statistical measurement available and useful in specific situations. Some of the more common forms that are applied to numerical facts include averages, index numbers, correlation, and time series. Each of these will be explained, and their meaning will indicate which are peculiarly appropriate for use in connection with different types of raw data.

1. Averages
2. Index numbers
3. Correlation
4. Time series

1 / Averages. The vocabulary of most individuals includes the word "average," but different meanings are frequently involved. A parent tells his next door neighbor that his son is an "average" college student, which is his way of saying that he assumes his son's scholastic attainment is approximately equal to that of the majority of college students. On the other hand, a baseball player's batting average of .298 is based on a refined mathematical technique.

Three types of *averages,* which may be defined as measures of central tendency, are commonly calculated: the mode, the median, and the arithmetic average or mean. Each has its advantages, and one may give a much better picture of the "average" than the other in specific instances. For example, an instructor may grade an hour examination and wish to announce the average grade to his class. The size of the group is 27, and the papers, arranged numerically, show the following marks:

99	75	67
98	75	66
96	75	66
92	70	65
88	68	63
88	67	63
84	67	63
84	67	62
78	67	62

This series of grades, or numbers, is known as an *array,* which is simply a list of all of the figures to be used in a statistical computation listed in order of size. The first step in computing an average might be to condense the array by noting the number of students who earned each different grade. This is known as a *frequency distribution.*

GRADE	NUMBER OF STUDENTS
99	1
98	1
96	1
92	1
88	2
84	2
78	1
75	3
70	1
68	1
67	5
66	2
65	1
63	3
62	2

(a) MODE. Without further handling of the data, the mode and median can be determined. The *mode* is the number that occurs most frequently in any distribution. The grade received by the largest number of students is 67. This is the value that occurs the greatest number of times, by a considerable margin. Sometimes other grades might have been earned by an almost equal number of students, in which case there would be subsidiary modes. Also, each student might have received a different grade on the examination. In such a case, there would be no mode.

(b) MEDIAN. The *median* is the number in an array that divides the group in half. Referring again to the illustration, since there are 27 students in this class, the fourteenth student in the list would have 13 individuals above him and 13 below him. Counting down from the top or up from the bottom, the fourteenth grade is 68, which is the median. If a class had an even number of students, it would be necessary to calculate an arithmetic average of the two middle grades.

(c) MEAN. The *arithmetic average* or *mean* is the most common type of average employed, so much so that it is implied in most requests to furnish an average. It is the result of dividing the total of a series of numbers by the number of units making up the series. To calculate the mean for the above problem, add all of the grades received and divide by the number of students.

GRADE	NUMBER OF STUDENTS	TOTAL GRADE POINTS
99	1	99
98	1	98
96	1	96
92	1	92
88	2	176
84	2	168
78	1	78
75	3	225
70	1	70
68	1	68
67	5	335
66	2	132
65	1	65
63	3	189
62	2	124
	27	2,015

$$\frac{2,015}{27} = 74.6$$

The arithmetic average of 74.6 is the highest average of the three computed and is the result of the handful of very high grades in the series. This emphasizes a characteristic of the mean, which is that a few high or low figures have an undue influence on the result.

(d) COMPARISON OF THE THREE AVERAGES. In the example, the mode was the lowest average, and the mean the highest. Taking a different series of grades, the results might have been exactly opposite. Furthermore, if 300 or 400 grades are used, the averages normally approximate each other.

The question might well be asked, "Which method of averaging is the best to use?" In the problem given above, assuming that 70 is a passing grade, the mean of 74.6 would indicate a satisfactory result. Actually over one half of the class flunked the examination. The median is probably the best measure of central tendency to use in this case, since the mode includes such a small percentage of the entire group and the mean has been overly influenced by a few high grades. On the other hand, if a manufacturer of men's hats wanted to specialize in one size, he would want to produce an average hat size that would fit the greatest number of people, which would be the mode.

For the majority of business problems, the arithmetic average or mean is used. If hourly wage rates in a factory are $1.75, $2.00, $2.20, $2.40, and $3.00, multiplying these wage rates by the number of employees at each level and dividing total payroll by total number of employees will give a significant average hourly wage rate. There are times, however, when the computation of an average is of little or no value. For example, two grandfathers, aged 78 and 82, decided to form a partnership with their mutual 23-year-old grandson. To say that the average age of the three partners is 61 is accurate but almost meaningless.

2 / Index numbers. An *index number* is a device for measuring the change that has taken place in a group of related items in a period of time. More use is probably made of index numbers by the business world than of any other kind of statistical measurement. In order to determine whether prices paid by consumers are rising or falling, whether wholesale prices are up or down, or the relative activity in the building industry, in stock price movements, and in many similar items, index numbers are constructed. Some of these may have a direct effect on a firm as, for example, an agreement in a labor contract to adjust hourly rates of pay whenever the Consumer Price Index rises or falls an agreed-upon number of points.

Issued monthly by the Bureau of Labor Statistics of the Department of Labor, the Consumers Price Index, or CPI as it is called, measures changes in the retail prices of goods and services purchased by a typical family. It is expressed as a percentage of the average prices that prevailed in a base period, currently 1957-1959. Many other index numbers are issued by governmental and private agencies.

In order to clarify the meaning of index numbers and to illustrate their construction, a greatly simplified retail price index computation is shown below. Only three commodity items have been included instead of the 400 items used by the Bureau of Labor Statistics in preparing its Consumer Price Index. This brief illustration provides an opportunity to show the use of *relatives,* a device that permits the comparison of unlike figures. If it could be assumed that the only purchases made by an average family consisted of three items, eggs, gasoline, and cloth, and if it is desired to compare the current year with a base year, say five years earlier, the computation might appear as follows:

	BASE YEAR	CURRENT YEAR
1 dozen eggs	$ .50	$ .54
1 gallon gasoline	.30	.32
1 yard cloth	.40	.46
	$1.20	$1.32
	$1.20 = 100	$1.32 = 110

On the basis of the above calculations, this consumers' price index has risen from 100 in the base year to 110 in the current year. The fallacy in this computation is that the quantities used of the different items have not been taken into consideration. A family might purchase 50 dozen eggs in a year and 200 gallon of gasoline but buy only 25 yards of cloth. A *weighted index number* takes into account the different quantities purchased in order to reflect more accurately the movement of prices. Using the same prices that were shown above, the calculations necessary to compute the weighted index number would be as follows:

	BASE YEAR		CURRENT YEAR	
	PRICE PER UNIT	TOTAL AMOUNT	PRICE PER UNIT	TOTAL AMOUNT
50 dozen eggs	$.50	$25.00	$.54	$27.00
200 gallons gasoline ..	.30	60.00	.32	64.00
25 yards cloth	.40	10.00	.46	11.50
		$95.00		$102.50
		$95.00 = 100		$102.50 = 107.9

Whereas the unweighted index number showed an increase of 10 points, the weighted index number shows an increase of 7.9 points over the base year. It is easy to understand why index numbers covering a particular subject prepared by the statistical departments of different organizations may show considerable variation. Both the items used and the weights assigned must be determined, and two separate agencies might not agree on these factors. Another variation results from the use of a different base year or base period.

3 / Correlation. If it can be determined that there is a definite relationship between separate sets of figures, the measurement of the degree of relationship between the two variables is known as *correlation*. This statistical device can be used in forecasting when one variable can be measured earlier than the other, and it can also be used in estimating when one variable is known but the other is not.

Correlation as a forecasting device assumes a known time lag. For example, the probable total enrollment in the first grade of elementary schools should logically have a measurable degree of correlation with the birth rate. If a number of children born in any given year is higher than the number born the previous year, it is reasonable to forecast that the number of children entering the first grade six years later will be higher than the number entering in the fifth year. Several factors, such as an unforeseen high level of infant mortality or a law stating that children could not enter the first grade until they were seven years old, might invalidate the prediction. In the past, however, the two variables have shown a high degree of correlation, and the forecast is very likely to prove accurate.

Many statisticians concerned with business forecasting attempt to find series of figures that can be used to predict the level of business activity in the months or years ahead. The index of productivity in the machine tool industry is usually considered a fairly accurate forecast of business conditions in the year ahead as industry must "tool up" before it can produce. The Bureau of the Census has developed a monthly report in which it uses 30 series covering many facets including production, distribution, finance, labor, construction, and prices.

Sometimes one variable is available in accurate form but the other is not. Since every state keeps a record of all of the passenger cars it licenses, the number on the road each year is reasonably well known. If, in the past, there has been a high correlation between the gasoline sales of an oil company and the number of cars on the highways, the expected year's sales can be estimated not only by territories but even by months.

The preceding examples have assumed a functional relationship between two sets of variables, which is known as *simple correlation*. When three or more sets of data are used, the term applied is *multiple correlation*. The number of students who plan to enter college in 1978 can be predicted from the birthrate of 1960, but a more accurate estimate would result if the expected economic status of the family unit was also introduced as a factor. The number of parents who can afford to send their children to college might be more important than the number of high school graduates.

4 / Time series. Our economic system is in a constant state of change. At any given date it is possible to plot known data and to compute exactly where we are in reference to the past. Before action can be taken on the conclusions drawn from this calculation, however, conditions may have changed. Static analysis is valuable, but we live in a dynamic world. The various types of time series attempt to analyze changes that take place over a period of time. The most frequent movements that are measured are known as (a) secular trends, (b) cyclical fluctuations, and (c) seasonal variations.

(a) SECULAR TRENDS. Over a long period of time a dominant characteristic of the United States has been growth. The population has increased, industries have grown, production has moved ahead, transportation facilities have been enlarged. Although the growth of population has been an important factor, it is not entirely responsible for other increases. This type of long-term movement is known as a *secular trend*. As this country or others become more mature, there is a tendency for the rate of growth to decrease, and it may be that a downward curve will eventually result.

In general, the secular trend in the United States has meant that business could expand in almost any direction. More people with more money means demands for food, housing, clothing, amusements, and other necessities, conveniences, and luxuries. To apply this logic to a particular industry, however, may prove to be a serious error. In the early days of the twentieth century there was a considerable expansion of the traction lines connecting various cities. With the advent of the large passenger bus and the automobile, the traction lines lost so much business, despite an increased population, that many were forced out of business.

(b) CYCLICAL FLUCTUATIONS. Although the secular trend in this country has been upward over many decades, there have been years of prosperity and years of depression. Ups and downs in the economy as a whole that tend to recur with some measure of regularity and that extend over a period of years rather than months are called *cyclical fluctuations*. A complete sequence from a stable economy to an expanding one followed by a period of contraction and then back to the starting point of stability is called a *business cycle*. A business cycle has a definite pattern of movement from one stage to another, but the duration and extent of any part of the complete cycle is unpredictable. The average duration of a business cycle in the past has been approximately seven years, but individual cycles have varied so extensively that this norm has little value.

Cyclical fluctuations have been accepted by economists as a natural result of our free-enterprise system. It is hoped that the severity of a downward swing, such as occurred in 1933, can be modified by government action on public works programs, subsidies, social security payments, and unemployment insurance payments. Only time will tell whether our economy can be kept at a point of equilibrium or whether the upward and downward swings of the past will continue. At the moment it appears that various controls have been successful only to the extent of smoothing the peaks and valleys of cyclical fluctuations.

(c) SEASONAL VARIATIONS. Many businesses are subject to regular month-by-month changes during the calendar year. Department stores have an increase in trade before Easter and Christmas. Travel agencies are patronized heavily during the summer months and have a smaller boom in the mid-winter season. Such changes are known as *seasonal variations*.

Weather and holidays are reasons for many seasonal variations, but they are not the only factors responsible for month-by-month changes. If a manufacturer of automobiles brings out a new model each year, he can determine his own seasonal variation because of the large number of people who want to own the most up-to-date product and who place orders as soon as the new car is on display.

■ Probability

Underlying the various methods of statistically measuring and analyzing business data is the theory of probability. *Probability* is the likelihood that a particular form of an event will occur. It may be thought of as a scale of values ranging from one to zero. Thus, the probability of obtaining a head or a tail with a toss of a coin is one; the event is certain to happen. The probability of obtaining a head when a coin is tossed is one half.

The following table shows the probability of obtaining different numbers of heads when six coins are tossed simultaneously, which allows for 64 different combinations when each coin is considered separately.

NUMBER OF HEADS	NUMBER OF COMBINATIONS PRODUCING THE COUNT OF HEADS	PROBABILITY
0	1	1/64
1	6	6/64
2	15	15/64
3	20	20/64
4	15	15/64
5	6	6/64
6	1	1/64
	64	64/64

Examining the table, it can be seen there is only one combination which will be all tails; there are 20 combinations in which 3 heads can appear, but there are only 6 chances out of 64 that 5 heads will appear. The chances that 1 or 2 heads will turn up is 21 out of 64.

A further examination of the frequency distribution shows that it is symmetrical. It also possesses *central tendency*, that is, there are more frequencies in the center of the distribution.

The theory of probability provides a framework by which a statistician can judge the range of accuracy of sampling, correlation, and other statistical techniques. It is the foundation of industrial quality control methods, of much market research, of various applications of game theory, and of PERT. It is the theory that changes the field of statistics from one of mere quantitative description into the basic method of making decisions in the face of uncertainty.

■ Presentation of Statistical Material

In order to present statistical material in a manner that will be useful for purposes of analysis, two devices are commonly used. These are summary tables and graphic presentations. A statement that production in 1968 reached 10,000 tons, which was an increase of 25 percent over the 1967 output of 8,000 tons, might well be expressed in this narrative form. If the number of yearly production figures were increased, however, a summary table or graph would be more effective.

1 / Summary tables. A considerable amount of statistical material can be presented in a table (see page 533). Years, geographical areas, types of products, income groups, and nationalities may be the basis of the comparisons.

Gross National Product in Current Dollars, 1950 to 1965
(In Billions of Dollars)

ITEM	1950	1955	1960	1965
Personal Consumption Expenditures	191.0	254.4	325.2	428.7
Gross Private Domestic Investment	54.1	67.4	74.8	105.7
Net Exports of Goods and Services	1.8	2.0	4.1	7.1
Government Purchases of Goods and Services	37.9	74.2	99.6	134.8
Gross National Product	284.8	398.0	503.8	676.3

Source: Department of Commerce, Office of Business Economics.

2 / Graphic presentations. The pictorial presentation of statistical data has the great advantage of interest to the reader by presenting a visual analysis of the facts. Several forms are used.

One of the most common graphic statistical presentations is the *line* or *curve chart,* which uses a line or curve to indicate changes or a trend over a period of time. Two or more lines may be used in the same chart to indicate changes in related items.

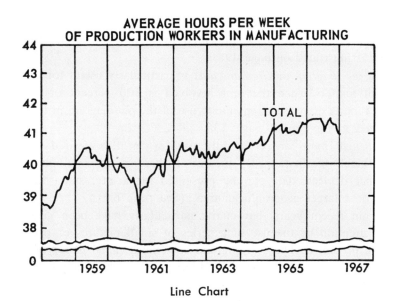

Line Chart

Another common form of graphic presentation is the *bar chart,* which is used for the comparison of figures. The bars in the chart may be horizontal or vertical.

Who owns corporate stock

By income		By occupation *
Less than $5,000	12.5%	34.6% Managers
5,000 – 9,999	14.0	18.8 Professionals
10,000 – 14,999	11.4	4.0 Clerical
15,000 – 24,999	14.1	6.4 Sales
25,000 – 49,999	15.9	3.2 Farmers
50,000 – 99,999	12.7	6.5 Other employees (Including armed forces)
100,000 – 149,999	4.7	18.2 Retired
150,000 – 199,999	3.2	8.3 Others not employed (Including widows and minors)
200,000 and over	11.4	

Data: Wharton School of Finance and Commerce; B. W.   * adjusted to eliminate "not known" category

Horizontal Bar Chart

When the item represented by a bar includes two or more parts, each part of the bar can be indicated by a different color, shading, or design, as illustrated on page 49.

The *pie diagram* or *circular chart* is particularly useful for explaining financial matters when the unit involved is 100 percent or $1. Many annual reports of corporations make use of the pie diagram in the manner illustrated at the top of page 535.

Statistical maps are commonly used when it is desired to present geographical information. By means of shading, coloring, pins, circles, and other devices, data can be presented for a city, state, the United States, or a larger geographical area. (See page 640.)

Within recent years, bar charts particularly have been given added reader attention by the use of a series of small pictures or drawings of the data presented. These graphs are sometimes called *pictographs*. They are effective for comparisons of subject matter, which can be presented by a self-explanatory drawing.

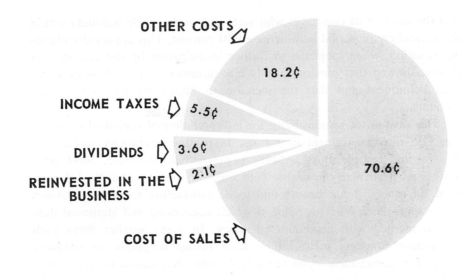

Corn Products Company

Distribution of Sales Dollar

■ Interpretation of Business Statistics

The final stage in the role that statistics may play in aiding management to make decisions and to control operations is that of interpretation. At this point two questions need to be resolved—"What conclusions can properly be drawn from the data?" and "Who should be responsible for this interpretation?"

As to the first question, considerable judgment needs to be used. In this country we have a great faith in figures, which, in most cases, is probably justified. If a controller reports to the board of directors of a corporation that its profits last year were $2.18 a share, this statistic is accepted as a fact. Caution, however, should be used in relying on statistical measurements to influence decisions, particularly those affecting the future operations of a firm. Despite the best of intentions, several types of errors can creep into a computation. Arithmetic errors are likely to occur, particularly when the quantity of data to be processed is extensive. In surveys, the sample selected may not be representative of the whole. If a computer is used, the programmed instructions may be faulty.

Even more inexcusable is a situation where the statistician is prejudiced in his views and uses only such information as supports his preconceived ideas, or where he manipulates accurate figures in such a manner as to arrive at a faulty conclusion. For example, it was reported to executives that the number of customers who were not paying their accounts within the normal credit period had increased 50 percent. This apparently alarming situation, when subjected to further investigation by the executive in charge, showed that previously only ten customers out of thousands had been delinquent and that the increase to fifteen involved only small accounts.

The location of responsibility for interpretation of statistical measurements to top management or for use in routine operations varies with the size and complexity of a firm's organizational structure. Most large businesses, particularly insurance companies, maintain a statistical department. In others, it has been found to be satisfactory to center activities in the controller's office, a point at which accounting and statistical data can be merged with maximum efficiency. In many smaller firms each department conducts such studies as it deems necessary or produces figures for management upon request. A somewhat common variation of these possibilities is found in companies that maintain a market research department but rely on the controller or other individuals for compiling statistics involving finance and production. As management tends more and more to make decisions backed by adequate evidence, the tendency is to create statistical departments or to designate a statistical officer for the company.

PROFESSIONAL ASSOCIATION IN STATISTICS

One of the oldest professional associations in the United States, the American Statistical Association was founded in 1839. At the present time it has over 8,000 members organized into 41 chapters. In addition to the quarterly *Journal of the American Statistical Association,* the *American Statistician* is published five times yearly, and *Technometrics,* which is cosponsored with the American Society for Quality Control, is published quarterly. A national convention is held each year. Full-time students may join the Association at a special rate of $6 a year.

BUSINESS TERMS

(a) business statistics (520)
(b) sampling (521), universe (521), random sampling (521), controlled sampling (521)
(c) primary data (522), secondary data (522)
(d) averages (525), array (525), frequency distribution (525)
(e) mode (526), median (526), arithmetic average or mean (526)
(f) index number (527), relatives (528), weighted index number (528)
(g) correlation (529), simple correlation (530), multiple correlation (530)

(h) secular trend (530), cyclical fluctuations (531), business cycle (531), seasonal variations (531)
(i) probability (531), central tendency (532)
(j) line or curve chart (533), bar chart (534), pie diagram or circular chart (534)
(k) statistical map (534), pictograph (534)

QUESTIONS FOR DISCUSSION AND ANALYSIS

1. It is probably a fair statement to say that accountants are more important to a firm than statisticians. How can this situation be reconciled with the broader scope of business statistics compared to accounting?
2. Do you believe that individuals who complete questionnaires give honest answers to all of the questions asked? Why?
3. What technique would be most satisfactory to sample student opinion on some campus question?
4. How do you account for the fact that the federal government is the most valuable source of secondary data for business use?
5. Can you give some examples in addition to those mentioned in the text where different meanings are attached to the term "average"?
6. The Dow-Jones Industrial Stock Average was described in Chapter 20. Is this average an index number? Discuss.
7. Can you give some examples other than those mentioned in the text of two sets of variables that might have a high degree of correlation?
8. Do you believe that the concept of a business cycle is now outmoded?
9. Accounting presentations consist largely of what might be termed summary tables. Why does statistics make more extensive use of other forms of presentation?
10. Do you believe that most people are inclined to accept facts and figures that they hear and see as accurate and true? Discuss.

PROBLEMS AND SHORT CASES

1. The following grades were received on a final examination taken by students in a section of an introduction to business course: 84, 72, 68, 90, 32, 72, 63, 81, 60, 17, 72, 98, 70, 55, 77, 96, 72, 45, 70, 61, 48, 75, 89, 21, 71, 92, 66, 72, 58, 84, and 69.

   (a) Compute the median, mode, and mean of these final grades.
   (b) The instructor, in posting these grades, wishes to indicate the class average. Which one of the three computations do you think is preferable for this series? State reasons for your choice.

2. The following tabulation shows the distribution of the income received in a fiscal year by the North American Metal Products Co. Compute the percentage of each classification to the total, and construct a chart to present this information in graphic form.

ITEM	AMOUNT
Material and supplies	$2,080,000
Wages and salaries	3,200,000
Expenses	1,040,000
Taxes	880,000
Dividends	480,000
Retained income	320,000
Total income	$8,000,000

3. The management of a corporation that produces and distributes a popular soft drink has been approached by a can manufacturer with the suggestion that the corporation shift from glass bottles to cans as containers for its product. It is claimed that such a change would be well received by the public since cans eliminate the bottle return problem and are more easily stored in the home.

The corporation, while recognizing the merit of cans, wonders whether the public would be willing to accept a change from the traditional bottles. A shift in the type of container would involve a sizable expenditure for new equipment, and many other problems would be involved. Faced with this dilemma, the management turned to its statistical department to seek an answer. It voted to add $50,000 to the budget of this department and requested that a report be submitted within six months.

The Director of the Statistical Department has hired you as a consultant. What is your advice as to the procedures he should follow to obtain consumer reaction to soft drinks available in cans rather than bottles? The only limitation on the alternate methods is the $50,000 allotted for this study.

SUGGESTED READINGS

Bryant, E. C. *Statistical Analysis,* Second Edition. New York: McGraw-Hill Book Company, 1965.

Leabo, D. A., and C. F. Smith. *Basic Statistics for Business and Economics,* Revised Edition. Homewood, Illinois: Richard D. Irwin, Inc., 1964.

Neter, J., and M. Wasserman. *Fundamental Statistics for Business and Economics,* Third Edition. Boston: Allyn and Bacon, Inc., 1966.

Richmond, J. B. *Statistical Analysis,* Second Edition. New York: The Ronald Press Company, 1964.

Stockton, J. R. *Introduction to Business and Economic Statistics,* Third Edition. Cincinnati: South-Western Publishing Company, 1966.

Wessel, R. H., E. R. Willett, and A. J. Simone. *Statistics as Applied to Economics and Business,* Revised Edition. New York: Holt, Rinehart and Winston, Inc., 1965.

Magazines: *Journal of the American Statistical Association, Review of Economics and Statistics.*

Chapter 25

DATA PROCESSING

Many people within a business organization rely on facts for performing their functions. They need facts in order to answer questions or to make reports to others inside or outside of the company. They must rely on, and consequently should have a vital interest in, the company's *data processing system,* which is an organized method of gathering, storing, and processing data.

■ Nature of Data Processing

Six basic operations may be performed in processing data: classifying, sorting, calculating, summarizing, recording, and reporting. All data processing, whether done manually, mechanically, or electronically, is an application of one or more of these operations. If both mechanical and electronic equipment are employed, the term *automated data processing* (*ADP*) is applicable; if all processing is done electronically, the term *electronic data processing* (*EDP*) is more descriptive.

Data are the "raw" facts that must be converted into information. There are many classes of data, but the common ones used in business are those which identify individuals, locations, objects, quantities, and monetary values. The word "data" might be defined as all the facts that have been gathered, and the term "information" may then denote the particular facts management wants to know. *Information* is the result of data processing and may be made available to company personnel as operating documents, reports, and analyses of problems. The procedure used to convert data into information is *data processing.* The goal of an efficient system of data processing is to produce the maximum amount of useful information for people within an organization in minimum time at reasonable cost.

■ History and Importance of Data Processing

Man's first data processing tools were simple—his fingers, pebbles, notched sticks, and knotted ropes. A primitive nomad could classify his wealth into cattle, sheep, and chickens. By using different colored cords for each class of livestock and by tying knots in the cords, he could count and record the number of animals he owned.

The evolution of these simple counting and recording devices into high-speed electronic data processing systems took several thousand years. During this time many inventions helped to pave the way to the present level of development; notable among these were the following:

The abacus	1860—Babbage's differential analyzer
1642—Pascal's calculator	1889—Hollerith's punched card equipment

The first truly electronic computer was made at the University of Pennsylvania in 1946; it was called ENIAC (Electronic Numerical Integrator and Calculator) and was conceived to produce mathematical tables required for the accurate firing of projectiles.

Within the last twenty years the growth of computer utilization has been phenomenal. In 1966, more than 25,000 computers were in use by industry, government, educational institutions, and service organizations. It has been estimated that in 1970 the number of computers used in all applications will be nearly 60,000 and the sales volume of computers and computer services will exceed $5 billion.

Without the computer, the problem of organizing data to uncover facts was dependent on the time and personnel available. For example, in a single sale on account of one hammer, a saw, and an assortment of nails in a large multiproduct hardware store, about all that could be done was to record the transaction as a sale and to see that the customer was charged properly for the merchandise. To secure additional information about this sale, such as the type of hammer purchased to determine which hammers were selling the fastest, the salesman to whom credit for the sale should be given, and the determination quantitatively as to when hammers needed to be reordered based on a perpetual inventory, required additional time, more clerks, and more detailed records.

With the computer, once the system is established, the basic transaction of recording the sale can be made on a punched card. Additional information can be punched into the card letting the machine do the storing, reorganizing, sorting, and collecting the various other bits of information that are needed.

■ Types of Computers

There are two general classes of computers, analog and digital. There are also hybrid computers that combine the features of both.

An *analog computer* carries out its calculations by making measurements. It deals with continuous quantities; it translates such physical conditions as temperature, pressure, angular position, or voltage into related mechanical or electrical quantities.

The operating principle of an analog computer may be compared to the operating principle of an ordinary weather thermometer. As the weather becomes cooler or warmer, the mercury in the glass tube rises or falls. The graduated marks on the tube permit the interpretation of the climatic changes. The expansion and contraction of the mercury has a relationship to the conditions of the weather. The thermometer provides a continuous measurement that is analogous to the climatic temperature. Other examples of devices that make analogous measurements include the slide rule and automobile speedometer.

Commonly, analog computers are used in industry to make scientific computations, to solve equations, and to control manufacturing processes. An analog computer is used by the National Aeronautics and Space Administration to measure the speed, direction, and trajectory of manned space vehicles. In 1966, a firm in Princeton, New Jersey, designed and marketed a desk-top analog computer to assist investors in making decisions to buy, hold, or sell stocks.

Digital computers deal solely with numbers. Whereas analog computers measure physical relationships, digital computers count numbers. A digital computer differs from the ordinary rotary calculator in four ways:

1. It is faster; it can perform arithmetic operations according to directions at speeds measured in billionths of a second.
2. It has the capability to make logical decisions, such as comparing one number with another and determining which is larger.
3. It has the capacity to store data and have them available for almost instantaneous recall.
4. It can follow a set of written instructions.

The remainder of this chapter will be devoted to digital computers because they are the type most commonly used in business.

■ Binary Code

Digital computers process data fundamentally by a system of counting, a form of arithmetic that is different from the decimal number system used in everyday calculations. In the decimal system ten numbers are used, zero through nine; and if a digit is moved one space to the left and a zero is placed after it, the resulting number is ten times the original number.

The arithmetic of computers is based on the binary code. The *binary code* is a system of arithmetic based on two digits, zero and one. A digit, either the zero or the one, in the binary code, is called a *bit,* which is a contraction of "binary digit." If a binary digit is moved one space to the left and a zero is placed after it, the resulting number is two times the original number.

In the binary code, the value of 1 depends on the position of the 1 in a binary number, reading from right to left. A digit doubles its value each time it moves one place farther to the left. For example, 0001 means 1; 0010 means 2; 0100 means 4; 1000 means 8, as shown in the following illustration.

Binary Number Positions

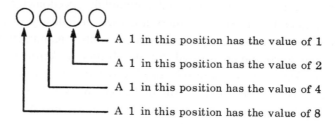

A 1 in this position has the value of 1

A 1 in this position has the value of 2

A 1 in this position has the value of 4

A 1 in this position has the value of 8

Binary Number Position Value

	8	4	2	1	
To write 3	0	0	1	1	The value of 1 in the 1 position, plus the value of 1 in the $\frac{2}{3}$ position equals
To write 5	0	1	0	1	The value of 1 in the 1 position, plus the value of 1 in the $\frac{4}{5}$ position equals
To write 9	1	0	0	1	The value of 1 in the 1 position, plus the value of 1 in the $\frac{8}{9}$ position equals

The following table compares decimal numbers with binary numbers.

Decimal	0	1	2	3	4	5	6	7	8	9
Binary	0	1	10	11	100	101	110	111	1000	1001

Using six binary digit positions, a code may be developed, a portion of which is illustrated on page 543.

DECIMAL NUMBER, LETTER, OR SYMBOL	BINARY CODE
1	000001
5	000101
9	001001
A	010001
B	010010
E	010101
I	011001
+	110000
$	111011
%	111100

Letters of the alphabet are indicated by a 1 appearing in the fifth or sixth positions. Symbols are indicated by a 1 appearing in the fifth and sixth positions.

In a computer only four digits (right to left) are used for the expression of numbers (0-9). Each digit in a decimal number is expressed by four binary digits. For example:

	(hundreds)	(tens)	(units)
142 equals	0001	0100	0010

	(thousands)	(hundreds)	(tens)	(units)
4,283 equals	0100	0010	1000	0011

The binary code may seem awkward in comparison to the decimal system, but it fits the computer ideally. Each electronic circuit inside a computer can exist in only two possible states—the current is on or the current is off. Symbolically, the zero can indicate one state (off) and the 1 can indicate the other (on).

The binary code, thus, is the language into which data are translated. This language is then converted within the computer into electrical impulses.

■ Components of a Computer

Basically a computer consists of the following five component sections or units.

1. Input
2. Memory
3. Arithmetic
4. Control
5. Output

A schematic diagram of these five basic component units of a computer is shown at the top of the following page.

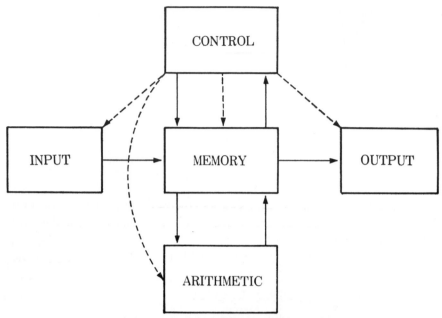

Schematic Diagram of Basic Digital Computer Components
Solid lines indicate information flow; dashed lines indicate control.

1 / Input unit. The purpose of the *input unit* is to permit the computer operator to "communicate" with the computer. It carries out its function by translating codes from the external form in which the data are represented, such as holes in a punched card, to the internal form in which data are stored in the memory unit. The data thus translated and stored may be numbers used in calculations, instructions that tell the computer what to do, or numbers or letters to be used as names and addresses.

Input consists of data to be processed and the instructions required to process the data. The input unit of a computer involves devices that "read in" data and instructions from various media. The *input media* may be punched cards, punched paper tape, magnetic tape, magnetic disks or drums, optical characters, magnetic ink characters, or a console typewriter. Various types of input media are illustrated on the opposite page.

2 / The memory or storage unit. The *memory or storage unit* is the distinguishing component of a computer. It is the center of operations. All data being processed by the computer pass through the memory unit. By means of this unit immense quantities of data are immediately available to the commands of the computer. The memory holds the input data, the intermediate results of calculations, the final results to be "read out," and the program of instructions telling the computer what to do.

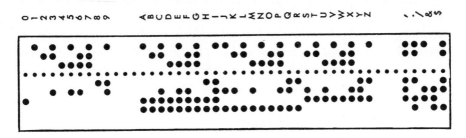

Magnetic tape is tape upon which data are recorded by the presence and absence of magnetized areas arranged according to code. Actual tape is one-half inch wide.

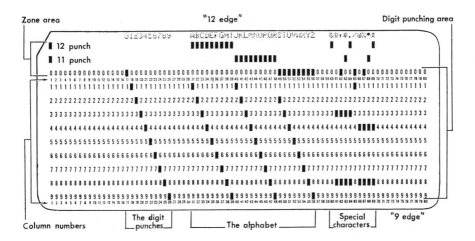

Punched paper tape is a special tape upon which data may be stored in the form of punched holes. Holes are located in columns across the width of the tape. Each column usually contain 5 to 8 positions, which are known as channels.

A *punched card* is made of heavy, stiff paper of constant size and shape. Data are stored in the form of punched holes arranged in 80 vertical columns. All holes in a single column are sensed simultaneously when a card is read by automated equipment. In each column there are 12 punching positions; (0-9) are identified as numeric punches and 11 and 12 are identified as zone punches.

Input Media Containing Data

Several types of memory devices are used in computers, but *magnetic cores* are used in most of the high-speed computers. Magnetic cores are made of special magnetic material shaped into circles or "doughnuts" the size of pinheads. Each core can be magnetized at any time in one of two directions. One direction stands for the binary 0, and the other direction for a binary 1. Thousands of these cores are strung on criss-crossed wires, arranged like the strings of a tennis racket, inside a square frame. The frames are stacked one on top of another to make a basic memory unit. A large-scale computer may have as many as eighteen basic units, each with more than 150,000 cores.

The stacking arrangement places the cores in columns. Each of the columns is assigned an *address,* which is a specific location within the memory unit. Each column of cores can store either one fact or one instruction expressed in binary code. The stored data can be instantly "read out" from any address and used in working a problem. If desired, data can be erased from any address and be replaced with a new fact or instruction.

There are other types of memory devices, such as disks, drums, and magnetic tapes, but in each case the computer performs the same basic operation. It converts data according to instructions into a series of magnetic charges and stores these charges.

The *capacity* of a memory device is measured in words. A *word,* which is a technical term, is defined as a group of binary digits that is treated as a unit and is stored in one location. A *location* is a unit-storage position in the main internal storage where one computer word may be stored or retrieved. Large-scale computers have memories with capacities of 32,768 words or more.

3 / **Arithmetic unit.** The *arithmetic unit* of a computer performs the operations of addition, subtraction, multiplication, and division, as well as comparison operations.

4 / **Control unit.** The *control unit* has the function of interpreting the program or instructions stored in the memory. It directs the various processing operations, issues proper commands to computer circuits to execute instructions, and checks to see that the instructions are properly carried out.

Register is a term commonly used in discussing the arithmetic and control units. A register is a device for temporarily storing a unit of data, a word, while or until it is used for arithmetical, logical, or transferral operations.

5 / Output unit. The *output unit* has the function of "reading out" or translating into convenient form the results of processing or the contents of the memory. The *output* is the end product of the computer. The output media used to "read out" may be punched cards, magnetic or paper tapes, or printed pages. Printed pages are the most important medium for obtaining information from a computer if the output is going to be used solely by human beings. High-speed printers are capable of printing 1,200 lines a minute. Some of the types of information that can be produced by a printer are accounts, journals, financial statements, bills and invoices, and checks.

In some kinds of research, it is desirable to have the results of computer processing graphically presented in the form of curves. In this case, the output can be flashed on a cathode ray tube (CRT) similar to a TV screen. If future reference to the graphic output will be made, its pattern on the cathode ray tube may be photographed.

■ Hardware

Each of the five components of a computer—input, arithmetic, control, memory, and output—may be an individual piece of physical equipment. One or more of the components may be located a few feet or many miles away from the central processing unit. The term *hardware* describes the central processing unit and its peripheral equipment. The *central processing unit* contains the circuits that control and perform the execution of instructions. *Peripheral equipment* is the collective term for input and output units, supplementary storage (memory) units, and printers that are linked to the main computer. For example, the General Electric Compatibles/400 system consists of seven pieces of hardware: the GE/415 computer, console, card reader, card punch, high-speed printer, magnetic tape units, and disk storage units. The last five of these are classified as peripheral equipment.

It is convenient to speak of the developments in computer hardware in terms of three generations, beginning in 1955, 1960, and 1965. These are not precise time demarcations, but they are useful in placing the developments in perspective. In the first generation of computers, the circuitry was based on vacuum tubes, such as were used in radio sets. The speed of operations was in the neighborhood of 500 additions a minute. By 1960, the vacuum tubes were replaced by transistors and speed had increased sevenfold. In the current generation of computers, the circuits are based on silicon chips much smaller than the eraser of a pencil and speed has reached the level of 20,000 additions a minute.

Other recent improvements in computer hardware have been the development of larger memories; optical scanning devices, which can read printed matter or handwritten material and convert it into data for the computer; data transmission equipment, which links distant computers over standard communications facilities; and information retrieval instruments, which automatically store and recall filed data.

▓ Software

One of the most significant aspects of a computer system is its program. A *program,* or *software,* may be defined as a series of operating instructions to be performed in processing the data supplied to the computer, the results of which will give the required answer. The actual writing of a program is done by a person called a *programmer.* A program is prepared by listing in complete detail the logical steps which the computer must take in order to obtain the desired results. There are four basic considerations in the preparation of a program: (1) definition of the problem to be solved; (2) outlining each logical step required to reach the solution; (3) writing the program in machine or symbolic language; and (4) translation of the program into machine language, if the program were written in symbolic language.

Each computer is wired to respond to basic combinations of characters or words. A *machine language* is a collection of words which a particular computer "understands." There is an IBM 1620 machine language, an IBM 1401 machine language, and so on. For example, in IBM 1620 language, the word, 21 02005 11509, would be understood by the computer to add (the symbol 21 means add) the number stored at location 11509 to the number stored at location 02005, and to store the resulting sum in location 02005. This instruction, 21 02005 11509, would be keypunched on a card, and the card would be "read" by the input device. Then the computer would carry out the operation.

Symbolic languages enable the programmer to write instructions in English and algebraic symbols, rather than in machine language. Two of the most popular of the symbolic languages are COBOL and FORTRAN. *COBOL* is the abbreviation for Common Business Oriented Language, and *FORTRAN* is the contraction of Formula Translation.

In the foregoing example, using the IBM 1620 machine language, the number 21 was the symbol for "add." In FORTRAN a plus sign would be used, and in COBOL the word "ADD" would be used. The computer would translate these symbols into the correct binary code instructions. The computer can automatically do this translation because a special program, known as an assembler, has been written. Assemblers convert symbolic programs into fundamental machine language, the binary code. Once the symbolic program has been converted into binary code, it can move as electronic impulses into the computer's memory unit.

To write programs in machine language, the programmer must keep track of what is contained in the various memory addresses and does not have the benefit of many shorthand statements that are available in symbolic languages. In FORTRAN, the programmer is relieved of the task of keeping track of storage locations. Using FORTRAN, the programmer could give the computer the same instruction as that given above in the IBM 1620 machine language by writing: $A = A + B$.

■ Flow Charts

The importance of outlining the logical steps required to arrive at the solution of a problem has been mentioned. One way to do this outlining is by means of flow charts. Not only in computer programming, but also in general logical thinking, flow charts are most useful.

A *flow chart* is a graphic representation of the logical steps to be used in solving a problem. It helps the programmer to do the following: (1) to break down a problem into workable segments; (2) to ensure that each step is accomplished in correct sequence; (3) to bring to light areas of the problem that need further clarification; (4) to prevent or to detect errors in a proposed solution; (5) to discover laborsaving and timesaving shortcuts to the solution.

Basically, a flow chart is a drawing of boxes, lines, arrows, and comments, which indicate what is to be done. A well-designed flow chart will reveal all of the specific steps that are necessary for a completely logical solution to a problem.

For example, there may be as many as eleven distinct steps in solving the problem of crossing an intersection where there is a traffic light but no oncoming automobile traffic. The problem may be stated, how does one go from corner A to corner B without diagonal crossing? The diagram of the problem and its flow chart are presented at the top of the following page.

■ The Systems Concept

As the flow chart and its related program are developed for each data processing operation, computer specialists seek ways of combining, expanding, and coordinating them into larger units of operation. The systemization of data processing operations for the purpose of eliminating

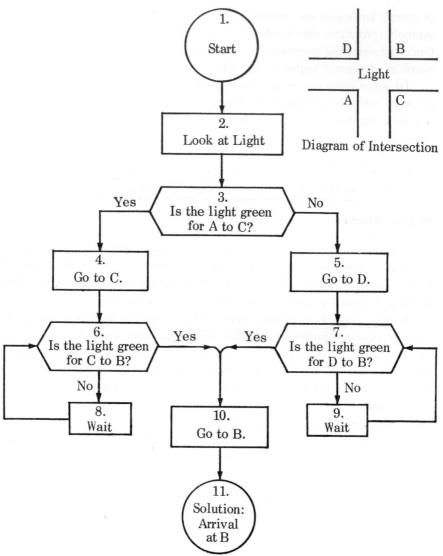

Flow Chart for Crossing Intersection from A to B with No Automobile Traffic

retranscriptions of data and of limiting the rehandling and resorting of data from one stage to the next is termed *integrated data processing* (*IDP*). The term is broadly used and may be applied to a particular group of operations of a company or to its entire operations. When the integrated data processing system is very comprehensive, it is called a *master systems plan* or *total systems concept*.

How subsystems may be coordinated into larger integrated data processing plans may be seen in the following illustrative steps.

1 / Sales subsystem. When a sales order is received from a customer, all pertinent information—name, address, items ordered, quantity of each, and delivery instructions—become input data and are recorded on magnetic tape. If the stock on hand is sufficient to fill the order, the output unit, acting upon instructions stored in the memory unit, will print the customer's name and address on the invoice, together with a description of the items, their quantities, sales prices, and total amount of the sale. Simultaneously a shipping order is prepared.

2 / Credit control subsystem. The current accounts receivable balance and credit limit for the customer, which are stored in the memory unit, are then automatically transmitted to the computer. The total of the sales invoice is added to the customer's previous account balance, and the new balance is compared with the credit limit. If the comparison indicates adequate credit, the invoice and shipping order are released. The calculation and comparisons are made during the time the output unit is printing the invoice and shipping order. If the customer's credit limitation has been reached, the sales invoice goes to the credit department for approval. If the credit department approves the sale, the invoice and shipping order are released. If the credit extension is not approved, sales cancellation data are entered into the system to cancel the data recorded for the order.

3 / Inventory subsystem. When the merchandise and quantity data from the sales order enter the system, comparisons are made with the perpetual inventory record contained in the memory unit. If the stock on hand is adequate to fill the order, the inventory balance, after providing for the order, is compared to the reorder quantity. If a reorder is indicated, a purchase order is printed. If the stock of the commodity is insufficient to fill the order, a lesser quantity and its sales price are recorded on the invoice and a "back order" is printed for the remaining quantity. Later, when the back-ordered goods are available, a sales invoice and shipping order for the quantity required to complete the original order are automatically prepared.

4 / Other subsystems. Details of cash receipts, purchases, and cash disbursements may be processed in a similar manner. Payrolls are also handled in a like fashion with the output media being payroll checks. At the end of a day, week, or month, totals of the various accounts may be printed and financial statements prepared.

Commonly the installation of electronic data processing equipment has been the piecemeal application to routine subsystems. These subsystems are those which are best understood by the firm's employees. They are usually characterized by a high volume of transactions and a large amount of routine processing (sorting, calculating, etc.) that must be performed with each transaction. The potential cost savings from the application of electronic data processing is high. For these reasons, it is typical to include billing accounts receivable, inventory control, the payroll, and similar subsystems in developing programs for a computer as first steps toward integrated data processing.

A growing number of companies are developing and experimenting with plans for a total systems concept. These comprehensive plans would give unity and coherence to the financial, production, marketing, and personnel functions of an enterprise. The total systems concept can properly subordinate departmental goals to the overall objectives of the company and give top management a broad, critical perspective of all the operations of the company.

■ Real-Time Systems

One term frequently occurring in discussions of the total systems concept is real time. *Real time* is a type of data processing that is performed concurrently with a physical process or business transaction. The purpose of this type of information for management is to produce results that are immediately useful in the control of the physical process or business transaction that is transpiring. A real-time computer system has three major characteristics. First, data are maintained *on-line*; that is, all data and instructions to be used in the processing are directly available to the computer by either being stored in the memory of the computer or capable of being read in as required. Second, data are updated as events occur. Third, the computer can be "questioned" from remote terminals; that is, information stored in the computer can be obtained on request from a number of locations at a distance from the computer.

1 / **SABRE.** One of the first commercial applications of real-time data processing is SABRE, a system built by IBM for American Airlines. This information system receives data pertaining to airplane passenger reservations from the company's agents throughout the country. It can immediately process the information and send a virtually instantaneous output message to the agent. SABRE is designed to handle tens of thousands of telephone inquiries every day together with requests for prices, passenger reservations, inquiries regarding seat availability to and from other airlines, and sales of tickets. On certain days, American

Airlines has nearly 600,000 passenger records in its electronic files. The processing of a reservation through SABRE takes approximately three seconds.

2 / Westinghouse Tele-Computer System. An example of real-time data processing within the total systems concept is the Tele-Computer System of Westinghouse Electric Corporation. The company installed its first computer in 1956, established a headquarters Business Systems Department in 1959, and built its Tele-Computer Center on the outskirts of Pittsburgh in 1962. The center of the system is a Univac 490 computer supplemented with 71 other computers placed in other localities. Among the numerous functions this system performs are the following:

a. Ninety percent of the industrial orders have their shipping instructions transmitted to the warehouse nearest to the customer in three seconds.
b. Orders for nonstock items are immediately sent to the proper manufacturing plants.
c. Inventory is maintained on a real-time basis, giving almost instantaneous answers to questions concerning stock levels.
d. A running cash balance on each of the corporation's 230 bank accounts is maintained.
e. Every sale is immediately recorded at the sales offices, transferred to regional sales headquarters and thence to the central sales office in Pittsburgh on a daily basis.
f. Checks are regularly prepared for 20,000 employees, 15,000 pensioners, and 200,000 stockholders for wages, pensions, and dividends.
g. Daily income statements and balance sheets are prepared for use by top management.

Top management of this corporation points out that the system is a management tool which processes information but that it does not make decisions. The system demands that a manager think about how he does things rather than just do them, and about how his actions mesh with those of other managers.

■ The Future

Several trends sketch in broad outline the future role of computers in business. Computers are becoming increasingly faster, smaller, and less expensive. Within the last ten years, electronic data processing equipment has become approximately 100 times faster, 10 times smaller in size, and 1,000 times less expensive in handling a unit of information. Increasing simplification of programming has accompanied the improvement in hardware. Within the next few years, new symbolic languages will be developed, each more closely geared to ordinary English and algebra. Moreover, computer services will become increasingly available in much the same way as electricity and telephone services have become widely available. These trends will change the concept of a computer from that of a lightning-fast electronic calculator to that of an information processing device which will handle data in any form—numbers, words, sounds, pictures, or symbols. The computer will provide new types of data that will give powerful new decision-making tools for management. New mathematical techniques are developing that will enable management to simulate through the use of the computer the operations of a company under varying conditions, and from the results of these simulations management will be able to make more timely and more accurate decisions concerning the future of the company. All of these trends indicate that the total impact of computers on the economy will be greater productivity from the resources of capital and labor.

BUSINESS TERMS

(a) data processing system (539), automated data processing (ADP) (539), electronic data processing (EDP) (539), data (539), information (539), data processing (539)

(b) analog computer (541), digital computer (541)

(c) binary code (542), bit (542)

(d) input unit (544), input (544), input media (544)

(e) magnetic tape (545), punched paper tape (545), punched card (545)

(f) memory or storage unit (544), magnetic cores (546), address (546), capacity (546), word (546), location (546)

(g) arithmetic unit (546)

(h) control unit (546), register (546)

(i) output unit (547), output (547)

(j) hardware (547), central processing unit (547), peripheral equipment (547)

√(k) program (548), software (548), programmer (548), machine language (548), symbolic language (548), COBOL (548), FORTRAN (548)

(1) flow chart (549)

(m) integrated data processing (IDP) (550), master systems plan (550), total systems concept (550)

(n) real time (552), on-line (552)

QUESTIONS FOR DISCUSSION AND ANALYSIS

1. If the decimal numbers 1, 2, 4, and 8 are represented in the binary code by 0001, 0010, 0100, and 1000 respectively, what are the binary code numbers for 13 and 65?

2. Explain how a six-space binary code may be used to denote decimal numbers, letters, and symbols.
3. What parts of the diagram on page 544 would represent the central processing unit, and what parts would represent peripheral equipment?
4. Explain the nature and the function of a program for a computer system.
5. Is the equals sign in the FORTRAN expression, A=A+B, used in its usual way or does it mean something different? Explain.
6. In most card games, the cards are shuffled to place them in random order before dealing. Explain how a skillful card player uses the basic operations of data processing after receiving the cards from the dealer.
7. Explain how the basic operations of data processing are used in preparing an income statement.
8. When we speak of the "solar system" and a "business procedures system," are we using the word "system" in the same sense? Explain.
9. Under a pen-and-ink data processing system, sales slips for charge-account customers are placed in batches and posted to the customer accounts once a week. Is this a real-time system? Explain.
10. What might cause inadequate or inaccurate information to be produced by a data processing system?

PROBLEMS AND SHORT CASES

1. In the discussion of flow charts, the problem of crossing an intersection of two streets was outlined. The problem assumed that there was no automobile traffic. Redo the problem assuming that there is automobile traffic and present a neatly organized flow chart.
2. You have six electric lamps arranged in a row, left to right. Each has a separate switch so that each lamp may be individually turned on or off. Starting at the right-hand side of the row, you designate the first four lamps with the numbers 1, 2, 4, and 8 respectively. When the last two lamps are off, the lights of the first four are used to signal numbers from zero to nine. When either of the last two lamps is on, the lamps will signal a letter.

   Thus, if all the lamps are off, the signal is that of zero; if the first lamp on the right is on, the signal is for one; if the fourth and the first lights are on, the signal is for nine (8+1); if the first and fifth lights are on, the signal is for the letter *A*.

   Write out a code for the numbers zero to nine inclusive and for all the letters of the alphabet. In writing out your code, use a zero to indicate that the light is off and a one to indicate that it is on.
3. The Polar Parts Company employs 1,500 people and has annual sales of approximately $40 million a year. It manufactures 150 different products that are sold throughout the world. It has been using a manual accounting system supplemented by the services of an electronic data processing center. The center prepares the weekly payroll and maintains inventory records. These services are purchased on an annual contract basis from the independent center.

Two years ago, under the stimulus of the controller of the company, Polar Parts began to study the feasibility of installing a company-operated computer system. The task force that has been carrying out the study has gathered evidence that the company should gradually progress, after the computer is installed, toward a total systems concept. The controller believes that the task force's recommendation is "too far-reaching." The total system concept, he contends, is "day-dreaming," and that it calls for more hardware and software than the company presently needs. He favors the quick installation of a simple computer system for handling accounts receivable, accounts payable, payroll, and inventory. He believes that the computer is primarily a device to perform bookkeeping operations efficiently.

In recent discussions, questions have arisen concerning who should head the new computer department. The controller favors a man from his own staff, who is presently chairman of the task force. He says that the head of the data processing department should report directly to the general accountant, who is a subordinate of the controller. The chief engineer is opposed to this view. He believes that this arrangement will provide little or no time to use the computer for engineering studies; moreover, he is afraid that the task force chairman is not sufficiently acquainted with the engineering uses of a computer. The vice-president in charge of sales is concerned that he and his staff will not receive detailed sales analysis reports promptly or effectively presented. The chairman of the task force is privately recommending that the head of the proposed data processing system should be independent of all functional area executives and should be a vice-president in charge of systems and procedures and report directly to the president.

You have been appointed chairman of a subcommittee of the task force to resolve this conflict. What factors would you consider in arriving at a recommendation?

SUGGESTED READINGS

Awad, E. M. *Business Data Processing.* Englewood Cliffs, New Jersey: Prentice-Hall, Inc., 1965.

Arnold, R. R., H. C. Hill, and A. V. Nichols. *Introduction to Data Processing.* New York: John Wiley & Sons, Inc., 1966.

Gregory, R. H., and R. L. Van Horn. *Automatic Data Processing Systems,* Second Edition. Belmont, California: Wadsworth Publishing Company, Inc., 1963.

Laurie, E. J. *Computers and Computer Language,* Second Edition. Cincinnati: South-Western Publishing Company, 1966.

Martin, E. W., Jr. *Electronic Data Processing: An Introduction.* Homewood, Illinois: Richard D. Irwin, Inc., 1965.

Wheeler, G. J., and D. F. Jones. *Business Data Processing.* Reading, Massachusetts: Addison-Wesley Publishing Company, 1966.

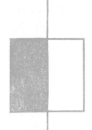

Chapter 26

BUDGETING AND FORECASTING

Whenever the functions of management are discussed, two terms—planning and control—are invariably mentioned. The first of these, planning, involves looking ahead, sometimes for only a few weeks or months and, at other times, for several years. Regardless of the length of time, predicting the future is hazardous but is a risk that cannot be avoided. Executives must make decisions today that only time will determine to have been good or bad for their firms.

The inherent uncertainty of the future makes it imperative that management use every scrap of information and every technique that can be of assistance in making decisions affecting future operations. Accumulated accounting and statistical data will usually prove helpful even though most of this information has the handicap of being historical. To help fill an apparent void, the techniques of budgeting and forecasting have been developed. Their use can result in decisions being made on the basis of scientific estimates of what is likely to happen in the future rather than on the hunches or whims of executives.

Budgeting and forecasting have a common ground in that both involve predictions. Although forecasting does not involve a budget, a budget can be termed a forecast. Despite this seeming confusion, the commonly accepted meaning of the two terms is quite distinct. *Budgeting* is the estimating by a firm of its anticipated incomes and expenditures over a definite future period, most frequently a year, and the use of this information not only for planning but also for purposes of control. The budget often appears as a projected income statement, and its construction is based very largely on past experience as measured by internal data. *Forecasting,* on the other hand, usually involves a longer period of time, frequently several years, is based almost entirely on external data, and arrives at conclusions regarding the economy as a whole or some major segment of it. This knowledge is then analyzed in light of its probable effect on the individual firm.

Relying on these definitions, which admittedly are somewhat arbitrary, this chapter will first discuss the budgeting process and its uses, following which some principles and practices of business forecasting will be described. These explanations will emphasize that budgeting is short-term planning for a firm whereas forecasting is a tool used by executives to help in arriving at long-range decisions.

BUDGETING

Budgets were first adopted in this country by governmental units, and today their use by states, counties, townships, cities and villages, school districts, the federal government, and other political subdivisions is universal. Income, usually from taxes, can be predicted quite accurately; and expenditures, unless borrowing is authorized, must be kept within the bounds of the anticipated receipts. Personal budgets are also widely used by individuals and families who realize that their expenditures must be kept in line with their known incomes. In addition to these better known uses of budgets, all large companies and many smaller progressive concerns also use this tool as an aid in management planning and control.

When a business undertakes the preparation and use of a budget, three major steps are involved. First of all, it is necessary to establish a budget organization and to reach agreement on some basic policies. After this has been accomplished, it is then possible to proceed with the preparation of a budget. This task should be completed prior to the first day of the budget period. Finally, as operations move into the budgeted period, controls must be established so that corrective measures or revisions can be made promptly. Each of these steps will be explained in some detail with particular emphasis on the actual preparation of budget figures.

■ Organization and Policies

Assuming that a business has not previously used budgets, a number of preparatory steps must be taken in order to make certain that maximum managerial results will accrue. Some of the problems that need to be resolved are:

1. Budget organization
2. Extent of budget adaptation
3. Length of budget period
4. Control procedures

1 / Budget organization. At the very outset, someone should be named as the budget officer. Frequently he is the controller because of

his contact and familiarity with the accounting system, although sometimes the president or general manager assumes this position. The direction
of budgetary procedure is a task for top management; and, while the
budget officer may function as a clearinghouse for the assembly of estimates and the transmission of performance data to and from the operating
departments, the policy decisions that are required from time to time
must emanate from the top. To carry out these policies and provide
supervision at the operating level, a common practice is the appointment
of an individual in each department to handle any budget matters that
require attention during the budget period.

Many companies set up a budget committee, consisting of the president and the heads of the major departments, whose job is that of
reviewing the figures that are collected and of counseling with the budget
officer and the president as the program proceeds. This group may
possess authority to pass on policy matters that arise, but in any case
its decisions are subject to the approval of the president.

2 / Extent of budget adaptation. Before installing a budget, management must determine the extent of its coverage. In most businesses it is
possible and desirable to include every phase of its operations. Occasionally, because of innate irregularities such as might be found in a research
department, a few activities may not lend themselves to the limitations
imposed by budgeting. Since a hoped-for goal of a budget is a projected
income statement, it is more satisfactory if budgeting is adopted on a
company-wide basis.

3 / Length of budget period. It is inherent in a budget that it cover
a specific period of time. The customary coverage for an operating budget
is a year, which is then broken down into quarters or months. This subdivision is particularly important for firms that have seasonal variations
although the major purpose is to make it possible to check the budget
against actual operations at frequent intervals. A few budgets, such as
one covering repair and replacement of machinery, may be for longer
than a year although an annual breakdown would provide necessary information for an estimated income statement.

4 / Control procedures. A budget will not work unless it is carefully
coordinated with the accounting procedures used by a firm. In addition
to performing its usual functions, the accounting department must keep
its accounts in such a manner that comparisons with the budget can
be made quickly and easily. The installation of a budget may require

revamping accounting procedures that were formerly considered satisfactory. Control procedures must also be established that will assure management that when any operating result is out of line with the budget estimate, this variance will be promptly called to the attention of the proper company official.

Preparation of a Budget

The actual preparation of a budget should begin several weeks or even months before the beginning of the budget period. A typical procedure would involve the following steps:

1. Sales budget
2. Sales expense and advertising budgets
3. Production budget
4. Other departmental expense budgets
5. Cash budget
6. Estimated statements

1 / **Sales budget.** In view of the fact that all of the activities of a business depend primarily on the volume of sales, the first step in the preparation of a company budget is customarily to establish the sales budget. This involves the submission of the estimated sales volume by the sales manager, revision of this estimate by the budget committee in light of information furnished by the firm's statisticians, and the establishment of the revised figures as the goal for the sales budget. All of the other departmental budgets are then set up on the basis of their relation to the sales budget and involve only the single step of compiling and submitting the figures.

The most common method used by the sales manager to compile his estimate of total sales is to require each salesman to submit a detailed estimate of the sales, by items, that he believes he can make in his territory during the coming budget period. For example, salesmen of food lines, such as frozen fruits and vegetables, know how many grocery stores and supermarkets are in their territories, what new ones are to be opened, and what old ones may be closed. They also know conditions of employment and industrial activity that will affect the purchase of their products by consumers. Accordingly, they are in an excellent position to submit intelligent estimates of the sales of frozen foods in their areas. These estimates are then accumulated for each of the territories and finally for the company as a whole.

At the same time, the statisticians in the home office compute a tentative overall sales total, based on a consideration of past sales and a knowledge of general economic trends. The estimate submitted by the sales force is then compared with that developed by the head office, and any differences are composed by the budget committee unless they have been reconciled by the top sales executives. This final figure becomes the basis for determining the sales expense and advertising budgets that will be necessary to attain the agreed-upon sales goal and, as mentioned above, is the determining factor for all other budgets as well.

2 / **Sales expense and advertising budgets.** Two budgets are closely allied to the sales budget. These are the sales expense budget and the advertising budget. The *sales expense budget* consists of an estimate regarding the anticipated cost of securing the sales volume that is projected for the coming budgetary period. It includes sales office expense, traveling expense, salesmen's salaries or commissions, and sales supervision expense. It may also include storage costs for finished goods.

As a corollary of the sales expense budget, the *advertising budget* sets forth the expected cost of advertising the product as a means of helping to secure the planned sales. It is made out in great detail and usually embraces all advertisements and the dates of their scheduled appearances. Unusual advertising plans with a complete explanation of the reasons for them and the sales results that are expected because of the extraordinary expenditure are presented. For example, one company planned to spend $100,000 on a campaign to introduce its products on the West Coast. In making up his advertising budget, the advertising manager of the firm placed this item together with the required explanation in a section of his budget estimate separate from that in which his regular advertising expenditures were listed. Thus the budget committee was able to note quickly the increased advertising that was planned and to discern the reasons for it.

3 / **Production budget.** The drawing up of the *production budget* consists of determining the amounts of all products that will be made during the coming period and setting up the production schedules so that these goals can be attained. In most companies the production budget is dependent upon the development of the sales budget. In some firms the manufacturing division decides what and how much is to be made, and the sales budget is based on this estimate. This practice, however, is becoming less frequent.

Occasionally the manufacturing division takes issue with the sales department's budget figures, with the result that changes are made in the latter estimate. This situation may arise due to the production department's feeling that the sales department is asking it to do the impossible in agreeing to manufacture goods in the quantities asked. Perhaps a major alteration in the plant that will take a sizable part of the productive facilities out of action for a time is scheduled for the coming period. Or possibly a planned addition to the factory is behind schedule because of material or machine shortages. These or any number of other causes may force a revision of the sales budget to bring it in line with the productive capacity of the manufacturing division.

(a) MATERIALS BUDGET. After the production budget has been established, it is necessary to plan for the materials that are required to make up the finished products. This involves the planning of purchases so that the needed materials will always be available to the production department on schedule. The *materials budget* thus serves as a guide to the activities of the purchasing department.

(b) LABOR BUDGET. The personnel department is charged with the task of providing the workers needed to make the planned volume of production. It sets up its plans to procure and have on hand the number and types of laborers that will be required for the job.

(c) MANUFACTURING EXPENSE BUDGET. The *manufacturing expense budget* consists of an estimate of the expenses that will be incurred by the manufacturing division in producing the quantity and types of goods called for by the production budget. It is broken down into account classifications similar to those shown on page 509 under the heading of Factory overhead. Although the total of this as well as other expense classifications is of more interest to top management, within the department the details are necessary in order to pinpoint items that may become responsible for budget variations, such as Heat, light, and power or Factory supplies expense.

4 / Other departmental expense budgets. In addition to the sales expense, advertising expense, and manufacturing expense budgets, it is a common practice to budget the expenses of operating the other major departments of a business. The department heads submit their estimates to the budget committee that approves or amends them.

5 / Cash budget. When a firm sets up a budget to control its selling and manufacturing operations, a cash budget should be established also. The purpose of the *cash budget* is to make certain that the company has sufficient cash on hand to meet its current needs as they arise. Bills of all kinds must be paid when due, and money must be available to meet the payrolls as they occur.

In order to accomplish this objective, estimates of all cash receipts and disbursements must be drawn up for each month (or even on a weekly basis) in the budget period and examined carefully to determine whether the amount that will be on hand from time to time will be adequate. If, at any time during the period under scrutiny, the supply of cash will not take care of the needs for it, it may be necessary for the company to negotiate a bank loan or to sell short-term notes. This condition frequently exists in those industries that have year-round production schedules but seasonal sales periods. The toy industry is an excellent example. Toy manufacturers produce throughout the year, but most of their orders, which constitute the source of their cash receipts, are secured during the late spring and summer months. Many firms in this business, therefore, must negotiate bank loans to carry them through the months when sales are not being made.

THE EDWARDS CORPORATION

Cash Budget

	JANUARY	FEBRUARY	DECEMBER
Cash on hand— beginning of month	40,173.00	85,038.40	24,535.86
Receipts:			
Cash sales	39,285.00	14,250.00	40,500.00
Collections	57,280.00	50,220.00	52,200.00
Total receipts	96,565.00	64,470.00	92,700.00
Total cash available	136,738.00	149,508.40	117,235.86
Disbursements:			
Purchases	33,460.00	48,052.00	20,500.00
Selling expenses	9,586.00	9,824.00	22,660.00
Administrative expenses	8,653.60	7,185.40	7,743.60
Other expenses	....	....	5,200.94
Total disbursements	51,699.60	65,061.40	56,104.54
Estimated cash at end of month.	85,038.40	84,447.00	61,131.32

Cash Budget

Related to the cash budget, but frequently prepared separately, are budgets that cover major repairs, replacements, and additions to plant and equipment. Although these budgets are likely to cover a period of time such as five or ten years, the applicable portion of the expenditures for any one year must be included in the cash budget for that year. Also, routine disbursements, such as paying interest on bonds outstanding or dividends on stock, plus nonroutine expenditures, such as retiring all or a portion of a long-term debt, must also be incorporated in the cash budget.

6 / Estimated statements. If all departments of a business are budgeted, it is possible to construct an estimated income statement that will show the anticipated income and expenses as well as net income for the budget period. It is also possible to construct a balance sheet that reflects these operating results, although this statement is less commonly prepared.

The 1967 income statement and the 1968 budget shown on page 565 for Loomis Rugs, Inc., indicate that this retail firm expects to increase its sales 20 percent in the budgeted year. The increased volume of purchases necessary to support the higher sales is expected to result in lower prices paid to manufacturers and to yield a higher gross margin of profit. Selling expenses are expected to rise proportionally to the increase in sales, but it is not anticipated that the increased volume will materially affect general expenses. Assuming the attainment of budgeted goals, Loomis Rugs, Inc., can anticipate a net income of $25,000 in 1968 as opposed to the low and unsatisfactory return of only $7,840 in 1967.

■ Budgetary Control

The third and last step in installing and using budgeting as a management tool is that of control. When the budget committee has coordinated and reviewed the estimates received from divisions and departments, its final figures, assuming the approval of the firm's president or executive committee, become the goal toward which all activities are directed. The sales department subdivides its total into quotas for districts and individual salesmen, the production department sets up manufacturing schedules, and similar procedures are followed by other operating units. By the time all this has taken place, the chances are excellent that the beginning of the budgeted period is only a matter of days away.

Control is achieved by the use of forms that show the budget figures for a period of time, such as a month, with a space for inserting actual performance reports as soon as they are compiled. A comparison between the planned and actual results indicates how well each department is doing in measuring up to its budgeted figures. These performance reports

LOOMIS RUGS, INC.

Income Statement for 1967 and Budget for 1968

	ACTUAL 1967		BUDGET 1968	
Sales		$220,000		$264,000
Cost of merchandise sold:				
Merchandise inventory,				
Jan. 1	$ 70,000		$ 66,700	
Purchases	159,250		190,000	
Merchandise available for				
sale	$229,250		$256,700	
Merchandise inventory,				
Dec. 31	66,700		75,000	
Cost of merchandise sold ..		162,550		181,700
Gross profit on sales		$ 57,450		$ 82,300
Operating expenses:				
Selling expenses:				
Sales salaries	$ 22,725		$ 26,000	
Advertising	6,250		9,000	
Delivery expense	2,790		3,200	
Misc. selling expenses ..	1,805		2,000	
Total selling expenses ..	$ 33,570		$ 40,200	
General expenses:				
Office salaries	$ 8,400		$ 9,000	
Rent	3,600		3,600	
Taxes	1,865		2,000	
Insurance	1,225		1,300	
Misc. general expenses ..	870		900	
Total general expenses ..	$ 15,960		$ 16,800	
Total operating expenses ..		49,530		57,000
Net income from operations .		$ 7,920		$ 25,300
Other expense:				
Interest expense		80		300
Net income		$ 7,840		$ 25,000

Estimated Income Statement

are available to the budget committee and the chief executive officer of the company who may review them with the department managers concerned. Any variations will be noted and remedial steps, if required, can be instituted. For example, if sales in a certain territory are running below the budget, the sales manager can get in touch with the salesmen in that area to discover where the trouble lies.

The important point in this procedure is that the deviation from the budget is brought quickly to the attention of the responsible executive, who is enabled thereby to investigate the matter and do something about it while there is time for remedial action. This practice, which is also used for many other situations, is known as *management by exception*. It is a valuable means of conserving managerial energy, through the planning of a firm's records, so that only the exceptions to the company's plans are brought to the attention of the executives. As long as things are progressing according to plan, no special need exists for the management to exert other than the customary supervision over operations. It is when something that upsets these plans occurs, an exception to the plans, that management should be immediately notified. Intelligent administration calls for records that will provide this kind of information.

There is another facet to budgetary control and this occurs when evidence accumulates that the estimated figures are out of line with actual performance. The variance can be either over or under although plans are more likely to be optimistic than pessimistic. Assuming that five months of a budgeted year have gone by and sales are consistently running 10 percent below estimates, a revision of the budget for the remaining seven months may be in order. This will have far-reaching effects on almost every department and division of the firm, but there is no point in adhering slavishly to goals that seemingly cannot be attained.

Actually, many firms prepare flexible budgets before the start of the budget period based on different sales estimates. In any event, the budget should be closely geared to actual conditions as they develop and necessary adjustments should be a part of the control process. A requirement of this element of control is that the accounting department be able to release operating figures promptly, a task that has been speeded up in recent years through the use of electronic data processing equipment. With both flexibility and prompt access to operating data, a budget becomes a managerial tool of great value.

FORECASTING

As has been emphasized in this chapter, businessmen find that looking into the future is a necessity despite its uncertainties. In preparing a budget, such figures as sales, labor costs, and expenses are actually forecasts; but these are dollar value estimates for a relatively short period of time, such as a year, that immediately follows a like time span for which operating facts are available. It is frequently important to gain some idea of what general business conditions will be in a number of months or years ahead. Forecasting attempts to make such estimates and, in so doing, places major reliance on external data.

Forecasting can be, and frequently is, a complicated process. Even though the intricacies of some calculations are beyond the grasp of the average business executive, he should have a basic understanding of the mechanics involved. Without such knowledge he cannot appreciate the strengths and the weaknesses of the predictions. In the remainder of this chapter some explanations will be offered of who prepares forecasts, how they do it, and the reliability and uses that can be made of the conclusions reached.

■ Who Prepares Forecasts?

There are three major groups who prepare and issue forecasts of the types that are of interest to business. Various agencies of the federal government play an important role in forecasting; there are several well-known private agencies, usually of the nonprofit variety, active in the field; and most large companies maintain their own staffs of economists. All three groups make use of any and all figures released by each other, and they also draw on other sources of information.

1 / **Agencies of the federal government.** In 1946 Congress passed the so-called Full Employment Act. Among other provisions it created a Council of Economic Advisers who were instructed to report to the President of the United States. This Council makes reports that are published every six months and, on the basis of its work, the President issues an Economic Report each January. The basic idea of the Act was to provide jobs for everyone by maintaining a healthy economy with the government providing employment on public works when necessary. Forecasts, obviously, become an important part of the duties of the Council. Some of these are made for the Council, at its request, by other federal agencies. Notable among these is the monthly *Business Cycle Developments* of the Bureau of the Census, which is available for business use.

The Federal Reserve Board is another governmental agency that releases a vast amount of statistical data including the Industrial Production Index published each month. In the forecasting area, its annual survey of the anticipated spending and saving habits of consumers provides information about this important but difficult-to-measure segment of future economic activity. Using a sampling technique, composite data are compiled on what people think their financial habits will be in the future.

Many other departments and divisions of the federal government are deserving of mention. As described on page 528, the Bureau of Labor Statistics publishes the Consumer Price Index. In connection with the budget the Treasury Department must make forecasts of general business conditions. The Department of Agriculture forecasts the crop situation as part of its concern with price supports. The Department of Commerce publishes some predictions in its monthly publication *Survey of Current Business.*

2 / Private agencies. One group of private agencies that frequently make forecasts includes the trade associations. The American Iron & Steel Institute indicates the expected rate of steel production in the months ahead, and the National Association of Purchasing Agents publishes figures in its weekly bulletin on the anticipated rate of placing orders.

Another group of private concerns includes such organizations as the National Bureau of Economic Research, the National Planning Association, the Chamber of Commerce of the United States, and the National Industrial Conference Board. In specific areas, the F. W. Dodge Corporation's figures on construction and the forecast of security prices by the Standard and Poor's Corporation are well known. Several universities also maintain research bureaus interested, in part, in forecasting; and some business magazines publish articles on anticipated future developments.

3 / Corporation economists. One of the functions of a staff of economists on the payroll of a corporation is to make forecasts and to relate these to the company. For example, a manufacturer who is a heavy user of basic raw materials, such as coal, rubber, and copper, can either buy on a hand-to-mouth basis or practice forward buying. An accurate prediction of future price trends could easily produce savings amounting to hundreds of thousands of dollars.

■ **How Are Forecasts Made?**

Although there are almost as many systems and devices for making forecasts as there are forecasters, an explanation of a few will serve our purposes. Three will be mentioned here—projections, leads and lags, and gross national product.

1 / Projections. *Projections* as applied to business forecasting are the extensions of known trends of the past into the future. This is done by plotting data for past years on a chart and extending a line from the latest date that follows the pattern of prior years. This extension of a trend line is known as *extrapolation.* For example, the Troy Manufacturing Company, which was organized in 1923, was interested in the average hourly rate of pay that might prevail in its factory for the next fifteen years. Payroll records revealed that rates paid at five-year intervals between 1923 and 1968 were as follows:

YEAR	HOURLY RATE	YEAR	HOURLY RATE
1923	$.40	1948	$1.00
1928	.50	1953	1.40
1933	.35	1958	1.80
1938	.45	1963	2.15
1943	.70	1968	2.25

These rates were plotted as shown in the chart on page 570, and a line was drawn that reflected, as nearly as possible, the trend over the past 45 years. By extending this line to 1983, the company determined that its hourly rate of pay would probably be approximately $2.50 in 1973, $2.75 in 1978, and $3.00 in 1983. Although the trend line shown is a straight line, as is the extrapolation, a curved line is more accurate in some instances.

This oversimplified illustration of a projection was based on internal data. A more meaningful estimate could be made by reference to the monthly reports on the labor force issued by the Bureau of Labor Statistics and relating its statistics to the firm. Hourly rates of pay are influenced by national, regional, and local levels in comparable industries. It is possible that the Troy Manufacturing Co. has recently been unionized, and this status could invalidate an extrapolation based on its own historical rates of pay.

Despite the possibility that other factors may enter the picture and invalidate an extrapolation, projections are a very useful forecasting device. The influences that acted in the past to establish a specific trend can be assumed, with some degree of assurance, to continue to affect the future. So many indexes are available covering so many different economic indicators that projections of one or more of these may well provide a firm with a sound basis on which to base a business decision.

2 / Leads and lags. Past figures are available on literally hundreds of different types of economic data. Quarterly reports can be obtained on

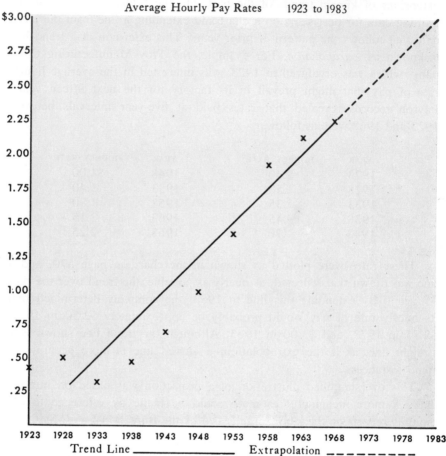

Troy Manufacturing Company
Average Hourly Pay Rates   1923 to 1983

1923 1928 1933 1938 1943 1948 1953 1958 1963 1968 1973 1978 1983

Trend Line _____   Extrapolation _ _ _ _ _ _ _ _ _

such items as barrels of oil refined, business failures, government spending, man-hours worked, and many other series of data covering every conceivable type of economic activity. The *Survey of Current Business* and related publications of the Department of Commerce contain data on approximately 2,600 different series, which provide some idea of the vast extent of statistical data available. It has been the aim of forecasters to locate among the various series available some that have led the rest of the economy either into an upturn or a downturn, and others that lag behind general economic conditions. On the lead side, forecasters have favored common stock prices, machine tool orders, housing starts, business failures, hours worked per week, and approximately 25 other series. On the lag side a common indicator used is consumer debt.

It might appear that by combining several lead indicators and averaging the number of months by which they led an upturn in general business activity a foolproof forecast could be made. Actually, forecasters using this composite method have not been much more successful than others who have relied on a single series. It seems to be impossible to predict the future, but this statement does not mean that leads and lags do not constitute a valuable forecasting tool. The past has demonstrated enough consistency to warrant making an estimate of the future by this device that has a reasonable chance of being proved accurate.

3 / Gross national product. A concept that has come into much favor with economists since World War II is that of *gross national product,* or GNP as it is commonly called. It is the nation's output of goods and services expressed as so many dollars per year or quarter. It may be defined as the total market value of all final goods and services produced during a stated period. There are four major components of the gross national product: (a) personal consumption expenditures, (b) gross private domestic investment, (c) government purchases of goods and services, and (d) net foreign investment.

Personal consumption expenditures include the amounts consumers spend for durable and nondurable goods and services. Gross private domestic investment represents expenditures for capital goods, chiefly by business concerns. The expenditures of local political subdivisions, the states, and the federal government are totaled to arrive at the item of government purchases of goods and services. In the case of foreign investment only the net difference between goods and services exported and imported is used in this calculation.

Current GNP figures show the level of total business activity at that date. A forecaster can project each of the components to whatever period of time he wishes to measure and arrive at an estimate of the dollar value of the gross national product at that date. Since many decisions affecting the future of a firm are closely related to overall business conditions that will prevail in the years ahead, a projected GNP total may provide the best basis for judgment. In other cases one segment, such as personal consumption expenditures, can be more helpful than the overall figures.

■ Reliability and Uses of Forecasts

No one has yet found a satisfactory way to look into the future, and this statement applies to forecasting. So far no method attempted seems to work consistently, but there is no doubt that predictions made on the basis of the techniques here described and many others are reasonably accurate in a majority of instances. Reliance placed on forecasts made by trained personnel is certainly to be preferred over any other known method of predicting the future.

The uses of forecasts are many and varied. Some of the more obvious managerial decisions based on the business outlook include plant expansion and location, inventory stock-piling, the sale of stocks or bonds, and the introduction of new products.

■ Operations Research

One of the latest developments in the area of managerial decision making is *operations research* or *OR* as it is popularly called. OR is characterized by the application of quantitative techniques to a wide variety of management problems, frequently by a team consisting of accountants, engineers, statisticians, economists, scientists, and mathematicians. The use of high-speed computers is almost a necessity; in fact, the ability to apply complicated mathematical formulas to business problems is interwoven with the programming of a computer to handle the data.

Some of the techniques used in operations research, such as linear programming, are used to solve production problems. Other techniques are primarily useful in forecasting what may happen if one or another course of action is followed. These include such OR devices as game theory and simulation among several of the analytical tools available to management.

1 / **Game theory.** The purpose of *game theory* is to decide the strategy that is most likely to achieve maximum profits in a competitive situation. The businessman does not know what his competitors may do, but he must plan his moves to offset those of one or more of his opponents. For example, if his goal is to increase sales, he may be able to do so by lowering prices, by launching an advertising campaign, or by employing more salesmen. He does not know what his competitors will do to offset any one or a combination of his moves, but he can make any number of assumptions and by mathematical computations arrive at a plan that indicates maximum profit potential.

2 / **Simulation.** *Simulation* provides a technique for observing the interaction of a number of important elements in a business problem by using various mixes in an attempt to see what will happen if some elements remain constant and others change. A business seeking more profits may wonder whether increased production would reduce manufacturing costs

so that lower prices could be offered that would result in the needed additional sales. The extent of the cost saving per unit as well as the size of the reduction in sales price would be important as would labor costs, advertising expenses, general economic conditions, and the competitive situation. By trying numerous combinations, which a computer can process rapidly, management may determine that one course of action seems to offer more promise than other alternatives.

These oversimplified illustrations of operations research as applied to forecasting indicate the gigantic strides made since World War II in applying quantitative analysis to the solution of business problems. The electronic computer has made it possible to process masses of data in ways and at a speed previously beyond man and machine capabilities. Staunch advocates of OR see it as a technique that can produce definitive answers for management; others believe it no more than a useful tool, particularly when applied to budgeting and forecasting.

PROFESSIONAL ASSOCIATION IN BUDGETING

The Budget Executive Institute, founded in 1951 as the National Society for Business Budgeting, now has over 2,500 members who are organized into 52 chapters located in cities in the United States and Canada. A publication *Budgeting* is published bimonthly and is available to students at a special rate of $3 a year. Regional conferences as well as a national convention are held each year. Chapters cooperate with colleges and universities by furnishing speakers on budgeting.

BUSINESS TERMS

(a) budgeting (557), forecasting (557)
(b) sales expense budget (561), advertising budget (561)
(c) production budget (561), materials budget (562), manufacturing expense budget (562)
(d) cash budget (562)
(e) management by exception (566)
(f) projection (569), extrapolation (569)
(g) gross national product (571)
(h) operations research or OR (572), game theory (572), simulation (572)

QUESTIONS FOR DISCUSSION AND ANALYSIS

1. Budgeting is usually considered more accurate than forecasting. Is this solely because budgeting is normally for a shorter period of time than forecasting?
2. Why cannot budgets be established and operated at a middle management level?

3. In compiling a budget, does not a request for estimates from divisions and departments tend to result in each submitting inflated figures for expense items? Explain.
4. Can you name any divisions of a business other than research to which it might be difficult to apply budget limitations?
5. Why is the customary operating budget compiled for one year? Would it not be satisfactory to budget for two, three, or five years?
6. Why should sales potential rather than production facilities, labor supply, or financial resources be the first step in the preparation of a budget?
7. To what areas other than budgeting is management by exception applicable? Give a specific example.
8. Why is the federal government so heavily involved in forecasting? Is its motive selfish or to be of assistance to business? Explain.
9. Of the three methods of forecasting described in this chapter, which one do you believe to be more reliable? Why?
10. Staunch advocates of operations research believe that game theory and simulation can provide solutions to certain types of problems far superior to those rendered on the judgment of executives. Do you agree? Why?

PROBLEMS AND SHORT CASES

1. Below is an income statement for the Paxton Manufacturing Company for 1968. The management is disturbed at the small net income on a million dollars in sales and has asked the sales force whether volume might be increased in 1969 with the hope that added profits would result from increased sales. The consensus of the salesmen is that a 50 percent gain in units sold could be attained provided the price of each unit was reduced 10 percent.

Prepare an estimate of income, expense, and net income for 1969, taking into account the information given and also the following:

(a) Cost of each unit will decrease 12 percent with increased volume of production.

(b) Selling expenses will increase 25 percent due to need for an advertising campaign and increased sales commissions.

PAXTON MANUFACTURING COMPANY
Income Statement
For the Year Ended December 31, 1968

Sales (50,000 units)		$1,000,000
Cost of merchandise sold		600,000
Gross profit		$ 400,000
Selling expenses	$200,000	
General expenses	180,000	380,000
Net income		$ 20,000

On the basis of your budget, do you think that the management should reduce prices and expand production or that it should look elsewhere for a solution to the problem of low net income?

2. The population of the United States including Alaska and Hawaii but excluding citizens living abroad was as follows for the ten-year periods of the twentieth century:

	POPULATION (Thousands)
1900	76,212
1910	92,228
1920	106,022
1930	123,202
1940	132,165
1950	151,326
1960	179,323

Plot the above statistics on graph paper allowing room for expansion to 250,000 thousands of people and for the years 1970, 1980, 1990, and 2000. Plot the known population figures and draw a trend line to the year 1960 that is the best possible fit to the data plotted. Then, starting with the year 1960, continue this line to 2000 in a manner similar to the chart on page 570.

On the basis of this extrapolation, what estimates could have been made after 1960 of the population in 1970, 1980, 1990, and 2000? Do you believe this projection is a satisfactory method of estimating the population of the United States?

3. The Budget Committee of the Madison-Jones Corporation, a steel fabricating concern, consists of the following corporate officers: President, Executive Vice-President, Vice-President—Sales, Vice-President—Manufacturing, Vice-President—Finance, Vice-President—Personnel, and a Budget Director. The President serves as chairman of the group, which has final authority for determining the budget for the following year.

Preliminary budget figures were assembled several weeks ago, and the Budget Committee has held three meetings. On the basis of these discussions the Budget Director has now presented a tentative budget that, in condensed form, appears as follows:

	CURRENT YEAR	BUDGET
Sales	$3,600,000	$4,200,000
Cost of merchandise sold	2,340,000	2,800,000
Gross profit on sales	1,260,000	1,400,000
Selling expenses	540,000	558,000
General expenses	375,000	395,000
Total operating expenses	915,000	953,000
Net income from operations	$ 345,000	$ 447,000

The Vice-President—Sales has agreed that the budgeted increase in sales is a realistic figure and one that is attainable but only if he is given a substantial increase in the amount allocated to advertising. During the current year selling expenses included $135,000 for advertising, and the budget prepared by the Budget Director shows an allocation of $140,000 for this item. The Vice-President—Sales is adamant in insisting that he must have an increase of $85,000 over the $5,000 added by the Budget Director.

When it was pointed out to the Vice-President—Sales that an added expense of $85,000 would reduce profits to a level only slightly better than the current year, he insisted that the increased number of units to be manufactured would provide savings in the cost of goods sold that could easily offset the increased advertising cost and not affect the budgeted net income from operations. The Vice-President—Manufacturing took an opposite viewpoint and argued that any economies accruing from a more efficient use of plant facilities would be offset by higher costs of raw materials and of labor.

The matter finally came to a vote when it became apparent that both vice-presidents were firm in their convictions. The Executive Vice-President, a former sales manager, and the Vice-President—Personnel supported the Vice-President—Sales, and the Vice-President—Finance and the Budget Director voted with the Vice-President—Manufacturing. This left the decision up to the President, who announced that he wanted a day or two to make some investigations on his own before rendering his decision. He immediately turned to a statistician in the market research department and requested projections of the wholesale price index and of wage rates. Both showed that an increase of 3 percent could be anticipated in the coming year, and the President determined that these items accounted for approximately one half of the cost of goods sold.

If you were the President of the Madison-Jones Corporation, how would you decide this issue? Support your conclusion by reference to the data available and make any assumptions you believe necessary consistent with the figures and facts supplied.

SUGGESTED READINGS

Dauten, C. A. *Business Cycles and Forecasting,* Second Edition. Cincinnati: South-Western Publishing Company, 1961.

Knight, W. D., and E. H. Weinwurm. *Managerial Budgeting.* New York: The Macmillan Company, 1964.

McKinley, D. H., M. G. Lee, and H. Duffy. *Forecasting Business Conditions.* New York: The American Bankers Association, 1965.

Silk, L. S. *Forecasting Business Trends.* New York: McGraw-Hill Book Company, 1965.

Wolfe, H. D. *Business Forecasting Methods.* New York: Holt, Rinehart, and Winston, Inc., 1966.

Magazines: *Business Budgeting, Federal Reserve Bulletin, Operations Research.*

Part VIII

LEGAL AND REGULATORY ENVIRONMENT OF BUSINESS

CHAPTER

27 Business Ethics and Law

28 Regulation of Competitive Business

29 Regulated Industries

30 Taxation and Business

LEGAL AND REGULATORY ENVIRONMENT OF BUSINESS

Many laws and regulations are to the advantage of the businessman in the orderly conduct of his affairs, while others have a restraining influence. Although several laws and governmental agencies have been discussed in previous chapters, notably in the areas of marketing, labor, and finance, this part provides a comprehensive survey of the extensive relationships between government and business.

In order for business to function smoothly, it must rely on good faith as well as legal safeguards. Chapter 27 discusses the importance of ethics in the business world as well as the basic laws that are applicable to business transactions.

Chapters 28 and 29 are concerned with the regulation of business by government, which seems to be expanding year by year. The first of these two chapters examines the impact of government on competitive enterprises and the consequent abridgment of the freedoms associated with capitalism. The second chapter discusses the extent and methods used by government for the regulation of public utilities, railroads, and other noncompetitive industries. These chapters provide a contrast between laws passed to promote competition and those designed to regulate prices and services.

Without much question the most important influence government has on business centers on taxes. Chapter 30 describes the taxing systems used by local, state, and the federal governments. Because the impact of these levies on a business is so extensive, emphasis is placed on the tax consequences that frequently affect decisions reached by management.

Chapter 27

BUSINESS ETHICS AND LAW

The millions of transactions that take place every working day in this country rely, to a great extent, on a mutual trust between the parties involved. For example, a customer chooses a model of a television set in a department store, charges it to his account, and later an unopened carton is delivered to his home from the store's warehouse. The customer expects the carton to contain a set in perfect working order identical to the one he selected in the store, and the store expects him to pay what he owes when his account is due. This trust, that is so necessary for the operation of our economic system, is based in part on business ethics and in part on business law.

Business ethics consists of the principles and practices that are concerned with morals and good conduct as related to business situations. It has to do with what is right or wrong, good or bad, desirable or undesirable, as judged by the public rather than the individual firm. *Business law,* on the other hand, is concerned with constitutions, statutes, court decisions, rules, and regulations administered by judges, administrators, and numerous other law-enforcement officials. It guarantees an orderly conduct of business affairs and the settlement of disputes that may arise in connection with business transactions. To the extent that it enforces fair business practices, it legalizes good business ethics.

This chapter will first discuss business ethics and the role it plays in modern-day business. Then, after an explanation of our legal system and the way it operates, the types of law that affect business transactions will be examined. Every person engaged in business, even though he is honest and trustworthy, needs to know some law and, at the same time, should understand the limitations of his knowledge. All business transactions have some legal overtones; and even though a businessman acts in what he believes to be an ethical manner, he may discover that he did not fulfill the necessary legal requirements.

BUSINESS ETHICS

Throughout recorded history the concept of business ethics has meant different standards of conduct to different people at different times. As an example, the ownership and use of slaves was rarely considered a moral issue in this country until a few years before the Civil War. Even today there is no common denominator that applies to businessmen throughout the world. In this country we have a heritage from the religious traditions of Western Europe, based on the Bible. The Ten Commandments and the Golden Rule established standards of conduct for business as well as personal behavior.

Prior to the onset of the Industrial Revolution, business had been largely dominated for several centuries by rulers of kingdoms, city states, and countries. Business ethics was largely subordinated to the needs and decrees of kings who ruled by so-called divine right. Piracy on the high seas, slave trading, and oppression of colonies were commonplace. *Mercantilism,* an economic system consisting of government domination of business to the end that the wealth of the country would be increased, held full sway. The ethical ingredient of personal choice was largely missing.

There was much dissatisfaction with mercantilism, particularly in England in the eighteenth century, and a growing support for what was called natural law. This concept, which held that man had certain rights that could not be invalidated by laws, was written into the Constitution of the United States. The economic doctrines stemming from this concept were first expounded by Adam Smith when, in 1776, his famous book *The Wealth of Nations* was published. This work had a profound influence in England and, somewhat later, in the United States.

◼ Ethics in the Nineteenth Century

The latter part of the eighteenth century, when Adam Smith's treatise was gaining favor, saw the advent of the factory system, the invention of machinery, the application of mechanical power in industry, and, in brief, the beginnings of the Industrial Revolution. By the early 1800's it also brought forth a capitalistic economic system of the laissez-faire type. The new theory was that business and economic progress would be advanced more rapidly and effectively if each individual was free to pursue his profit-making activities without governmental restraint. What was good for the individual would, in the long run, prove to be best for the nation.

The acceptance of this doctrine, which placed responsibility for business decisions on individuals, might have produced business ethics on a high plane. Actually, in the United States, particularly after the Civil War, the inherited concept of a golden rule in business transactions was eagerly replaced by a belief that any action a businessman could take to increase his profits was moral because it would prove to be good for the public and for the country. The doctrine of caveat emptor held full sway and individuals who reaped huge profits, regardless of the methods used, were held in high esteem. The so-called "robber barons" were deeply religious on Sunday but during the week were ruthless competitors.

Toward the close of the nineteenth century a wave of public indignation against unethical practices in business gave rise to legislation that gradually had an effect on the whole moral tone of business. One of the offenders had been the railroads whose rate structure had harmed farmers and given favored business units exorbitant profits. In 1887 Congress passed the Interstate Commerce Commission Act to bring the railroads under government control. Another direction taken by business had been the creation of monopolies in certain areas of business. The Sherman Antitrust Act, passed in 1890, made combinations and conspiracies in restraint of trade illegal. These laws will be discussed in later chapters, but at this point it will suffice to note that laissez faire, with its resulting lack of acceptable business ethics, had not worked to the benefit of the public.

■ Modern Trends in Business Ethics

It is probably fair to say that most businessmen today recognize that the maintenance of high ethical standards in their dealings with each other is also good for their firms. Considerable evidence supports the contention that "honesty is the best policy," which is, perhaps, another way of saying that good ethics makes for good business. A firm with a reputation for using questionable practices in its dealings is likely to find itself without customers and, in some instances, on the receiving end of a legal action.

Both industries and individual companies have taken positive steps to indicate their belief in and support of ethical practices. Many trade associations have adopted a Code of Ethics that is expected to serve as a guide to their members. These codes are printed, and framed copies are frequently found hanging in the offices of the individuals or firms who comprise the association. A large number of business firms have drawn up codes that are binding on their employees. Some of these are stated in general terms, but others deal with specific problems, such as accepting bribes or expensive gifts and conniving with competitors.

The importance of business ethics received national recognition in 1961 when the Department of Commerce of the federal government organized a Business Ethics Advisory Council consisting of a group of outstanding American businessmen, educators, clergymen, and journalists. This Council made its first report in 1962 in a publication titled *A Statement on Business Ethics and a Call for Action*. Following is an excerpt from this pamphlet:

> Business enterprises, large and small, have relationships in many directions—with stockholders and other owners, employees, customers, suppliers, government, and the public in general. The traditional emphasis on freedom, competition, and progress in our economic system often brings the varying interests of these groups into conflict, so that many difficult and complex ethical problems can arise in any enterprise. While all relationships of an enterprise to these groups are regulated in some degree by law, compliance with law can only provide a minimum standard of conduct. Beyond legal obligations, the policies and actions of businessmen must be based upon a regard for the proper claims of all affected groups.

■ Application of Ethics to Business Decisions

A basic concept in a capitalistic economic system is that the major function of the management of business units is to maximize profits for the benefit of the owners. As long as actions are legal and not immoral, any decision that might enhance the return on the investment would appear to be a proper course of action. At this point, however, a question can be raised that has ethical overtones. Is a business run for the benefit of its owners or should it be operated as well for the benefit of its employees, its customers, its suppliers, the government, and the public in general?

As an example, in recent years some firms have closed down inefficient plants and moved to new locations. This is legal and certainly not immoral. But what about the effect on the employees who live in the community and on the community itself? In some instances, ethical rather than profit motives have resulted in a decision to modernize the old plant rather than to move. Or, what should management do with an old and valued employee who has lost his executive ability but who still lacks a year of reaching retirement age? The profit motive would certainly dictate that he be fired.

The efforts to create a favorable corporate image, while they may eventually prove valuable to a business, involve decisions based on what is right and good rather than the most profitable. Corporate giving to universities and colleges, community chests, and support to civic undertakings is considered the right thing to do although it is doubtful if such acts make even an indirect contribution to profits. Producing goods for the government, particularly in time of war, is frequently less profitable than using the same facilities for consumer goods.

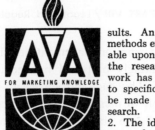

FOR MARKETING KNOWLEDGE

The American Marketing Association, in furtherance of its central objective of the advancement of science in marketing and in recognition of its obligation to the public, has established these principles of ethical practice of marketing research for the guidance of its members. In an increasingly complex society, marketing management is more and more dependent upon marketing information intelligently and systematically obtained. The consumer is the source of much of this information. Seeking the cooperation of the consumer in the development of information, marketing management must acknowledge its obligation to protect the public from misrepresentation and exploitation under the guise of research.

Similarly the research practitioner has an obligation to the discipline he practices and to those who provide support for his practice—an obligation to adhere to basic and commonly accepted standards of scientific investigation as they apply to the domain of marketing research.

It is the intent of this code to define ethical standards required of marketing research in satisfying these obligations.

Adherence to this code will assure the users of marketing research that the research was done in accordance with acceptable ethical practices. Those engaged in research will find in this code an affirmation of sound and honest basic principles which have developed over the years as the profession has grown. The field interviewers who are the point of contact between the profession and the consumer will also find guidance in fulfilling their vitally important role.

For Research Users, Practitioners and Interviewers

1. No individual or organization will undertake any activity which is directly or indirectly represented to be marketing research, but which has as its real purpose the attempted sale of merchandise or services to some or all of the respondents interviewed in the course of the research.

2. If a respondent has been led to believe, directly or indirectly, that he is participating in a marketing research survey and that his anonymity will be protected, his name shall not be made known to anyone outside the research organization or research department, or used for other than research purposes.

For Research Practitioners

1. There will be no intentional or deliberate misrepresentation of research methods or results. An adequate description of methods employed will be made available upon request to the sponsor of the research. Evidence that field work has been completed according to specifications will, upon request, be made available to buyers of research.

2. The identity of the survey sponsor and/or the ultimate client for whom a survey is being done will be held in confidence at all times, unless this identity is to be revealed as part of the research design. Research information shall be held in confidence by the research organization or department and not used for personal gain or made available to any outside party unless the client specifically authorizes such release.

3. A research organization shall not undertake marketing studies for competitive clients when such studies would jeopardize the confidential nature of client-agency relationships.

For Users of Marketing Research

1. A user of research shall not knowingly disseminate conclusions from a given research project or service that are inconsistent with or not warranted by the data.

2. To the extent that there is involved in a research project a unique design involving techniques, approaches or concepts not commonly available to research practitioners, the prospective user of research shall not solicit such a design from one practitioner and deliver it to another for execution without the approval of the design originator.

For Field Interviewers

1. Research assignments and materials received, as well as information obtained from respondents, shall be held in confidence by the interviewer and revealed to no one except the research organization conducting the marketing study.

2. No information gained through a marketing research activity shall be used directly or indirectly, for the personal gain or advantage of the interviewer.

3. Interviews shall be conducted in strict accordance with specifications and instructions received.

4. An interviewer shall not carry out two or more interviewing assignments simultaneously unless authorized by all contractors or employers concerned.

Members of the American Marketing Association will be expected to conduct themselves in accordance with the provisions of this Code in all of their marketing research activities.

American Marketing Association

Marketing Research Code of Ethics

The truth is that many management decisions are based on more than the data so painstakingly prepared by accountants, statisticians, budget officers, and others. This fact introduces an element in decision making that is not susceptible of measurement and that cannot be fed into a computer. It raises a question about the validity of the concept of maximizing profits when ethical considerations come into conflict with an otherwise profitable course of action. From the public viewpoint, it is comforting to discover that many business units have a heart as well as a mind and are recognizing their social responsibilities.

BUSINESS LAW

Although it might seem preferable that business ethics rather than business law should be the dominant regulating force in business transactions, this is not the case. For one reason, even if there were an agreement on good business ethics, there is no method by which many of these standards of conduct can be enforced. Another factor is that business procedures are necessary, and these are frequently stated in the law. For example, when a person indorses a check in favor of another party, he is fulfilling a legal requirement that has no ethical ramifications.

In the remainder of this chapter some of the topics comprising the area of business law will be described after a brief look at legal systems, legal procedures, and our system of courts.

■ Legal Systems

There are essentially two legal systems in operation throughout the world, common law and civil law. Common law began in England centuries ago and, considering the relationship of the thirteen colonies with that country, we logically inherited this system when we became an independent nation. The basic premise of *common law* is that each decision rendered by a court becomes a precedent for successive cases of a similar nature, which is known as the *doctrine of stare decisis,* a Latin phrase meaning "to stand by decided matters." These decisions, modified by changing times, regularly find their way into constitutions and statutes drawn up or enacted by the people or their duly elected representatives. Further interpretation then follows, creating more precedents for guidance in subsequent decisions or as a foundation for further legislation.

Civil law is based on codes, which consist of compilations of laws, rules, and regulations. Ancient Roman law was codified. The Code Napoleon of France was another example of a civil law code. In countries using civil law, courts interpret the code. The legal system of many

European countries is based on civil law; and in this country Louisiana, long under the domination of France, still uses some civil law. Common law, based on decisions, is frequently called unwritten law as opposed to the written law of the civil law system. As of today, however, so much common law has been written into laws passed by all levels of government that the differences between the two systems are inconsequential.

■ Legal Procedures

If a businessman believes he has been wronged, either because another party has broken a law or has taken unfair advantage of him, he may initiate legal action. He is called the *plaintiff,* and the other party is known as the *defendant*. The plaintiff's attorney files a complaint with the proper court and a *summons* is issued, which requires the defendant to appear in court to answer the charges.

If the case involves a point of law, it will be tried before a jury unless both parties waive this privilege. Assuming that a jury does hear the facts as presented by witnesses for both parties, it renders a decision in favor of the plaintiff or defendant. If a jury does not hear the case, the decision is rendered by the presiding judge.

■ Courts and Laws

In the United States there are systems of federal courts and of state courts. The lower courts in each case are known as *courts of original jurisdiction*. These are the courts in which the cases referred to above are heard. If the loser believes a principle of law has been violated, he may carry this issue into an *appellate court,* which is a higher court that has been established to hear appeals from the decisions of lower courts. If this court believes the case was improperly tried in the first instance, it may dismiss the decision or refer it to the original court for a retrial. The Supreme Court of the United States is the highest appellate court for matters under federal jurisdiction, and the supreme court of a state is the highest court for disputes having no federal implications.

If a case involves an alleged violation of a federal law or interstate commerce, it will be heard in a federal court. Most legal disputes, however, are of such a nature that they are tried in state courts. One of the resulting problems has been the lack of uniformity among the laws of the 50 states. To improve this situation, a National Conference of Commissioners on Uniform State Laws was formed several years ago with representatives from each state. This Conference promotes uniformity in state laws and over a period of years was successful in securing the passage by many state legislatures of a number of uniform laws including the Uniform Negotiable Instruments Act, the Uniform Sales Act, and the Uniform Conditional Sales Act.

In 1957 the National Conference of Commissioners on Uniform State Laws in conjunction with the American Law Institute drafted a Uniform Commercial Code. One of the stated purposes of this Code was to simplify, clarify, and modernize the law governing commercial transactions. It has now been adopted by most states. In the ensuing discussion, the provisions of this Code, where applicable, have been followed.

■ Scope of Business Law

The major topics that comprise the area of business law are business torts and crimes, contracts, property, agency, negotiable instruments, business organizations, insurance, sales, bailments, and bankruptcy. Some of these have been adequately covered in previous chapters. An examination of the remaining topics will indicate the types of legal information that the average businessman should understand and will illustrate the tremendous value of a system of law to the business community.

■ Business Torts and Crimes

A _tort_ is a private wrong as opposed to a public wrong, which is a _crime_. As applied to business, torts are concerned primarily with moral wrongs that one person may do to cause damage or loss to another. Business crimes include conspiracies and restraints on commerce, such as were declared against public policy in the Sherman Antitrust Act. An act may be both a tort and a crime.

1 / **Business torts.** The day-by-day operations of a business continually present problems that may involve torts. A businessman may not indulge in fraud or deceit, make libelous statements, induce others to break a contract, make threats, try to intimidate those with whom he deals, or, in general, engage in unfair trade practices. For example, a restaurant owner in a small town repeatedly and untruthfully claimed that a rival establishment served horsemeat. It was proved that his intention was to destroy the competitor's business, and he was forced to pay damages.

A particularly vulnerable area for many businesses is the possibility of the infringement of patents, copyrights, and trademarks. If the federal government grants a patent, it gives the holder the exclusive right to its use for 17 years. Copyrights are good for 28 years and may be renewed for a like period. A registered trademark does not have an expiration date. Such well-known names as Kodak, Nabisco, and Frigidaire are the property of the corporations that registered these names, and others may not copy them or use any similar name that might mislead the public. Regardless of whether an infringement is deliberate or unintentional, the holder of a patent, a copyright, or a trademark can sue for damages, as it is the responsibility of each business to be sure that it does not commit torts of this nature.

2 / Business crimes. Business crimes involve breaking laws that have been passed for the public good. In many instances the businessman is aware of his crime when, for example, he forges checks or receipts, operates lotteries, swindles the public, or sells goods on a short weight or measure basis. In other situations a matter of interpretation may be involved, such as the clause "unfair or deceptive acts or practices" as contained in the amended Federal Trade Commission Act. Whether advertising that a particular remedy will positively cure a cold within a week is a crime or merely a harmless exaggeration may be determined by the courts if an FTC cease and desist order is appealed.

■ Contracts

A *contract* is a voluntary agreement between two or more competent persons by which, for a consideration, one party acquires the right to have the other party do or not do some lawful act. In a general sense, the entire field of business law is one of contracts because agreements between parties are essential to practically all business transactions. This subject therefore is not discussed as something apart from other applications of business law but rather as a fundamental background. The following features of contracts will explain the terms used in the above definition as well as discuss other aspects of this important area of business law.

1. Voluntary agreement	4. Lawful acts
2. Competent persons	5. Forms of contracts
3. Consideration	6. Performance, discharge, and remedies

1 / Voluntary agreement. The essence of an agreement is an offer and an acceptance. The offer must be communicated in definite terms and with the intent to create a contract, and the acceptance must be indicated within a reasonable time or before the offer is withdrawn. Any means of communication may be used and, if the mail or telegraph is involved, the contract is in force just as soon as the acceptance is deposited with the post office or telegraph company. A reply that fails to conform to the exact terms of the offer, known as a *counteroffer,* does not constitute an acceptance because there is no mutual agreement or common understanding of the subject matter of the contract.

Contracts must also involve agreements in which both parties act in good faith and of their own free will. The term "voluntary" is used in the sense that there has been no fraud, duress, or undue influence brought to bear on one or the other party. Tricking someone into signing a written contract or threatening a person at the point of a gun to agree to a contract will provide grounds for relief. Even some mutual mistakes, such as agreeing to sell a building that, unknown to either party, burned down the night before will void the contract.

2 / Competent persons. Most people are legally competent to enter into a contract, but some groups, such as insane persons, are without the capacity to make a contract. In most states persons under 21 years of age are classed as *minors* and usually cannot make enforceable contracts. If a dealer sells an automobile on time to a minor who, after making a down payment and one or two installments, wrecks the car, the minor can return the vehicle and demand his money back.

3 / Consideration. *Consideration,* which is something of value received by one party or parted with by the other party, is essential to every contract. If Jones pays Smith $50 for an option to purchase property at a certain price within 30 days, the payment of the $50 is the consideration for this option contract. Smith gives up his right to sell the property for 30 days and Jones parts with $50. Also, any possible gain to one party or loss to another will serve as satisfactory consideration. For example, a wealthy uncle agrees to pay $1,000 to his nephew if he does not smoke until he is 21 years of age. The fact that the young man gives up a legal right provides adequate consideration. An offer to sell merchandise at a stated price, followed by an acceptance, includes adequate consideration.

4 / Lawful acts. The subject matter of a contract must involve lawful acts. A contract made with a person in which a promise is made to burn down a building illegally is not enforceable, nor is one with the intent to restrain trade unduly. Other contracts that are against public policy or that would violate specific laws are not enforceable. For example, most states have laws against gambling and promises to pay gambling debts, whether written or oral, are not enforceable. Likewise, if a lender attempts to collect interest in excess of the legal rate permitted in the state, as a general rule he forfeits the right to collect any interest, although the debt is still owed.

5 / **Forms of contracts.** Most contracts do not need to be written, and oral agreements are fully enforceable although there may be difficulty in proving the facts. Under what is known as the *Statute of Frauds,* certain types of contracts must be in writing, including sales of real estate, of personal property in excess of a certain value (usually $500), and agreements that cannot be performed within one year. The reason for the unusual name for this rule of law dates back to England when persons wishing to prove the validity of an oral contract would induce friends and relatives to give false testimony in court.

6 / **Performance, discharge, and remedies.** Most contracts are discharged by full performance on the part of both parties. Some contracts are not completed, however, and this condition may or may not give rise to a court action. In some instances, the defendant may be excused under the operation of a law, such as bankruptcy; or, if special conditions, such as illness, have arisen in a personal service contract, the courts may excuse performance.

When a contract has been broken, the remedy is to obtain from a court an order that requires the payment of damages or, in a few instances, compliance with the terms of the contract. If damages are in order, the court issues a *judgment* in favor of the plaintiff, which can be executed against the defendant. If necessary, a sheriff will sell enough property of the debtor to satisfy the judgment.

Of interest to many businessmen is the situation in which a person, against whom a judgment has been rendered, has no real or personal property that can be sold to satisfy the claim. If this person is a wage earner, it is possible in most states to force the employer to pay the amount owed by withholding a portion of the wage usually paid to the employee each payday. This is known as *garnishment.* Operators of business establishments not only may find it desirable to garnishee the wages of individuals who owe them money, but also may be served with an order to impose a garnishment on one or more of their own employees.

■ **Property**

Ownership of, or an interest in, anything subject to ownership is known as *property.* A businessman is vitally concerned with the laws on this subject because his daily transactions and the place in which they are carried on directly or indirectly involve rights and interests in property. When he buys merchandise, any subsequent loss that may occur falls on him even though payment has not yet been made for the goods. If he improves a building on which he has a lease, such improvements become the property of the owner when the lease expires.

The term property, when it refers to possessions or things owned, may be given several classifications, but the most important distinction from a business viewpoint is that of real property and personal property. *Real property* normally refers to land and buildings or, in a general way, to things immovable. *Personal property* refers to things owned that are movable. Personal property may be further subdivided into *tangibles* and *intangibles,* the former referring to merchandise in stock, fixtures, machinery and equipment, and the latter to stocks and bonds, notes and checks, bank accounts, and accounts receivable. The businessman is interested in these classifications because, if for no other reason, he may be required to pay taxes at different rates on each grouping.

1 / Ownership. If a person has every possible right that can be attached to ownership, he has absolute ownership. In the case of real property, this common form is known as an *estate in fee simple.* Aside from the various types of restrictions that may be imposed by government, the owner may make such use of his property as he wishes. He can sell it, give it away, leave it to his heirs by drawing up a will to this effect, lease or rent it, or use it as security to borrow money. A customer who owns a fair amount of property usually has a satisfactory credit standing, but the businessman will do well to remember the rights of this individual concerning the property that has been used as a basis for granting credit. If it is given away or used as security for a loan, it is no longer available to satisfy claims of general creditors.

Ownership rights in real property that fall short of the extent of absolute ownership are usually for a fixed period of time. A common example is the relation of landlord to tenant. When a proprietor leases a store building for 10 years, the tenant has a right in the property for that period of time if he pays the stipulated rent. Unless there is a specific agreement to the contrary, he may sublet his lease. Repairs and improvements that he may make will usually revert to the owner at the conclusion of the ten years.

2 / Security for loans. Property is frequently used as security for the extension of credit. If personal property is involved, the customary procedure is to execute an obligation known as a chattel mortgage. As described in Chapter 19, the use of chattel mortgages is an optional way of selling goods on an installment basis. The buyer has title to as well as physical possession of the goods and, if he completes the schedule of payments, the mortgage is canceled. If he fails to make the prescribed payments, the seller can, if necessary, take legal steps to regain possession of the goods. Such an action is known as a suit in *replevin.*

If real property is used as security, the obligation created is a real estate mortgage. This mortgage, as well as a chattel mortgage, should be recorded in a county courthouse. If the loan is not paid in accordance with the terms, the mortgage is usually foreclosed and title is transferred to the creditor. Intangible personal property, such as stocks and bonds, is also used as security for loans, but a mortgage is not necessary because the lender can take physical possession of the securities.

■ Agency

An *agent* is one who is authorized by another person, known as the *principal,* to deal with third persons in behalf of his principal. Many businessmen find it necessary to appoint agents to act for them in either a general or a specific capacity, and it is important that there is a complete understanding of the exact relationship. A *servant*, on the other hand, is an employee who does not have authority to act for his employer in contract situations.

A principal is liable for all acts of his agent within the actual or apparent scope of the authority vested in the agent. For example, the manager of a chain store held a contract that permitted him to operate the store at his discretion but with a limitation that all cash was to be deposited in a specified bank to the credit of the principal. On several occasions he indorsed checks on hand and cashed them at the bank in order to obtain change for the store. The principal did not object. One day the manager indorsed several days' accumulation of checks and disappeared. In this case the bank had the right to assume that the manager was an agent with authority to cash the firm's checks.

Agents are bound to follow instructions, to serve loyally, to render proper accounts, and to use intelligence and due care in the acts that they perform. If they exceed their authority, they may become personally liable to their principals.

■ Negotiable Instruments

A *negotiable instrument* is a form of business paper that can be transferred from one party to another as a substitute for money. Negotiable instruments can be classified as either drafts, which include checks, or promissory notes. In most states the law applicable to negotiable instruments is contained in Article 3 of the Uniform Commercial Code. Under the Code, negotiable instruments are also referred to as *commercial paper*.

The Code provides that an instrument to be negotiable must conform to all of the following requirements: (1) it must be in writing and signed by the maker or drawer; (2) it must contain an unconditional promise or order to pay a sum certain in money; (3) it must be payable on demand, or at a definite future date; (4) it must be payable "to order" or "to bearer"; and (5) where the instrument is addressed to a drawee or payee, he must be named or otherwise indicated with reasonable certainty. Some of the acceptable forms of negotiable instruments, such as checks, promissory notes, drafts, and trade acceptances, have been described in Chapter 19.

A person who receives a negotiable instrument is a *holder in due course* if the instrument is complete and regular on its face, if it is acquired before it is overdue, if it was taken in good faith and for value, and if there was available at the time of negotiation no knowledge of any infirmity in the instrument or defects in the title of the person from whom it was received. For example, when a merchant accepts a check from a student who has received it from his father, the merchant is a holder in due course if the check is presented for payment within a reasonable time. If the check were over thirty days old or bore signs of an erasure, the merchant might not be a holder in due course.

Negotiable instruments, such as notes and time drafts, must be presented for payment at their maturities if the last holder wishes to hold indorsers as well as the maker or drawee. For demand paper, such as checks, unnecessary delay may relieve indorsers from liability. If a negotiable instrument is not paid when presented at the proper time, a *notice of dishonor* should be given to the maker or drawee and to each indorser. This notice can be either written or oral, although the safest procedure is to have a notary public complete a *notice of protest*. This is then mailed or delivered to all parties concerned. In order to avoid the expenses incurred by a formal protest, some businessmen stamp "No Protest" on checks and other negotiable instruments received, which means that they waive a notice of dishonor.

■ Sales

A *sale* is an exchange of goods or property between two parties for money paid immediately or to be paid in the future. It involves a contract, and most of the comments on contracts are applicable to sales. A *bill of sale* is evidence of the transfer of title to personal property that is signed by the seller.

1 / **Who bears the risk of loss?** One of the problems involved in a sale is the answer to the question, "Who bears the risk of loss?" If a customer walks into a store and buys a gallon of vinegar bottled in a glass container, which he drops and breaks on the sidewalk outside the store, who assumes this loss? Title generally passes immediately in a cash transaction, and the purchaser in this illustration must assume the loss. When goods are shipped f.o.b. factory, the risk of loss passes at the time they are delivered to a common carrier. The buyer, however, may specify a *c.i.f.* (cost, insurance, and freight) contract. Under these terms, if the merchandise is lost or destroyed while enroute to the purchaser, he is protected by insurance, the cost of which is added to the purchase price and transportation charges.

Sometimes wholesalers and manufacturers wish to sell their products through dealers whose credit standing is not adequate. In this case, goods can be sent on *consignment,* which means that title remains in the hands of the shipper until such time as they are sold by the retailer. This fact is important to the retailer because he need not insure the goods against loss nor need he pay personal property taxes on such merchandise. For like reasons, the ownership is important to the wholesaler or manufacturer. The consignor has the right to repossess the goods should the retailer become bankrupt while the goods are still in his possession.

2 / **Warranties.** An *express warranty* is a statement on the part of the seller that the goods have certain characteristics, such as quality, which is made to induce the buyer to make the purchase. If an antique dealer states that a chest of drawers is over one hundred years old and if it is subsequently discovered that ten years is a more accurate estimate, the dealer can be sued for damages.

An *implied warranty* covers title and quality. The buyer has a right to assume that he receives a clear title to the goods and that the merchandise agrees with a sample or description and is usable for the purposes for which it was sold. A purchaser of stolen goods must return them to the original owner or pay for them, but he has a right of action against the seller because there was an implied warranty of clear title.

3 / **Conditional sales.** Merchants who sell goods on long-term credit can make a contract under which title does not pass to the buyer until

all of the purchase price is paid. This is known as a *conditional sale* and is used in connection with installment sales of air-conditioning units, television sets, radios, refrigerators, automobiles, furniture, and other durable consumer goods. It permits possession of the goods by the buyer while title remains with the seller. The main purpose from the seller's point of view is to permit the repossession of the goods in case the monthly or weekly payments are not continued as scheduled.

■ Bailments

A *bailment* is a relationship in which one party, known as the *bailor,* leaves property with another, known as the *bailee,* for a certain purpose with the understanding that the goods will be returned to the bailor or delivered to someone else after the purpose is fulfilled. There is no passage of title, which means that a bailment is not a sale. Leaving a watch at a jeweler's for repairs or with a pawnbroker as security for a loan are examples of bailments.

Under common law more than reasonable care was enforced against an innkeeper for loss or injury to the personal property of his guests and to common carriers who transport merchandise. Today, most hotels avoid their liability by notifying guests to deposit valuables in their safes. Railroads and other forms of public transportation must pay for loss or damage to goods in transit unless excused for such reasons as a flood (act of God) or seizure (act of public authority or enemy). Poor packaging or crating or shipping perishable goods in nonrefrigerated cars may also relieve the carrier from responsibility.

■ Bankruptcy

As noted in Chapter 22, an insolvent firm may go into bankruptcy on its own initiative, which is called *voluntary bankruptcy,* or it may be declared a bankrupt by a federal court, which is known as *involuntary bankruptcy.* In either case, the court-appointed referee calls the creditors together and they elect a trustee. As a general rule, the trustee then liquidates the assets and distributes the proceeds.

It would be very rare for the trustee to be able to pay all creditors in full, for a bankrupt owes more than he owns. The courts have established a system of priority of claims that recognizes five classes of *preferred creditors,* as follows:

(1) The actual and necessary costs of preserving the estate subsequent to the filing of the petition.

(2) Wages due to workmen, clerks, traveling or city salesmen, or servants, that have been earned within three months prior to bankruptcy, not to exceed $600 to each claimant.

(3) Reasonable expenses of creditors in opposing an arrangement or a plan for the discharge of a bankrupt.

(4) Taxes due the United States or any state or subdivision.

(5) Debts owed to any person who by law is entitled to priority.

Court costs are included in (1) above as are fees for the referee, trustee, and lawyers. Number (5) most frequently involves the holders of a first mortgage on the bankrupt's property. If this property is sold for more than the mortgage, the preferred creditors will be paid in full. If the property brings less than the amount of the mortgage, the lenders will receive the entire proceeds and join the general creditors for the balances due them.

Assuming that there is money available for distribution after preferred claims are settled, the *general creditors* will receive a percentage of their established claims. A final accounting is then filed with the court, and the debtor is legally discharged from further payments on the amounts owed. Although there are a few liabilities that cannot be cleared in a bankruptcy proceeding, in general the bankrupt can start a new business or take employment with a clean financial slate.

Banks, incorporated cities, insurance companies, railroads, and savings and loan associations may not become bankrupts. Wage earners whose annual income is less than $1,500, nonbusiness corporations, and farmers cannot be forced into bankruptcy. Other persons, partnerships, or corporations can become a bankrupt on either a voluntary or involuntary basis if debts of $1,000 or more are owed.

PROFESSIONAL ASSOCIATION IN BUSINESS LAW

The American Business Law Association was organized in 1924 at which time it was known as the American Association of Instructors of Business Law in Collegiate Schools of Business. In 1954 a number of regional divisions were established, and regular meetings are now held on both a national and regional basis. Its constitution provides for both active and associate memberships. Annual dues are $7, which include a subscription to the *American Business Law Journal*.

BUSINESS TERMS

(a) business ethics (579), business law (579)

(b) mercantilism (580)

(c) common law (584), doctrine of stare decisis (584); civil law (584)

(d) plaintiff (585), defendant (585); summons (585)
(e) courts of original jurisdiction (585), appellate court (585)
✓(f) tort (586), crime (586)
(g) contract (587); counteroffer (588), minor (588), consideration (588)
(h) Statute of Frauds (589), judgment (589), garnishment (589)
(i) property (589); real property (590), personal property (590); tangibles (590), intangibles (590)
(j) estate in fee simple (590)
(k) replevin (591)
(l) agent (591), principal (591); servant (591)
(m) negotiable instrument (591), commercial paper (592)
✓(n) holder in due course (592)
(o) notice of dishonor (592), notice of protest (592)
(p) sale (592), bill of sale (593); consignment (593)
(q) express warranty (593), implied warranty (593)
(r) conditional sale (594)
(s) bailment (594); bailor (594), bailee (594)
(t) voluntary bankruptcy (594), involuntary bankruptcy (594)
(u) preferred creditors (594), general creditors (595)

QUESTIONS FOR DISCUSSION AND ANALYSIS

1. What is your opinion of the ethics of the businessmen with whom you have come into contact? Give some specific examples to bolster your conclusions.
2. Would it be helpful if all good ethical practices were enacted into law? Why?
3. How effective do you believe industry Codes of Ethics are in actual practice? Are codes drawn up by individual firms likely to be more influential on its employees? Why?
4. As long as a proposed action is legal and not immoral, should business decisions stress profit maximization? Explain.
5. Does common law tend to perpetuate decisions that may not recognize social and economic changes? Explain.
6. Why do we have a system of appellate courts? If an individual has had "his day in court," why should he be given the privilege of another day?
7. Does the granting of patents, copyrights, and trademarks tend to give governmental sanction to monopolies completely at odds with extensive legal efforts to enforce competition? Explain.
8. Should the age limit be lowered for the classification of minors who are also, in legal language, frequently termed infants? If you favor lowering the age below 21, what age should it be?
9. Do individuals in this country place considerable emphasis on the ownership of property? Does the same prevail throughout the world?
10. Should an individual be permitted to wipe his financial slate clean by going into voluntary bankruptcy?

PROBLEMS AND SHORT CASES

1. (a) Mr. Green was interested in buying some stock in a local bank and learned that Mrs. Little had inherited 100 shares from her father's estate. He wrote inquiring whether she would be willing to sell and at what price. Mrs. Little replied stating that she preferred to hold her shares but would sell them for $300 each. Mr. Green replied that he thought her price resembled highway robbery but that he accepted her offer and was enclosing his check for $30,000. Mrs. Little was incensed at his remarks and returned his check stating that she would not sell her shares to him at any price. Mr. Green sued for performance of contract. Was there a contract? Why?

(b) Mr. Goodwin drove his delivery truck into a parking lot and turned it over to the attendant. When he returned a few hours later, he paid the fee but when his car was delivered to him he noticed a sizable dent in the hood. Investigation proved that this was caused by a brick that had fallen from the roof of a building adjacent to the parking lot. Mr. Goodwin felt that the operator of the parking lot was responsible for the cost of removing the dent, but the operator insisted that he had not been responsible for the accident and that Mr. Goodwin should present his claim to the owner of the building. Is Mr. Goodwin entitled to reimbursement for the cost of the repair and, if so, who should pay the bill?

2. Mr. Romano invested all the money he had saved plus what he could borrow in a restaurant. After operating the business for five years with a consistent record of annual losses, he found he could not pay his current debts and decided to become a voluntary bankrupt. The trustee elected by the creditors found the following situation according to Mr. Roman's books:

ASSETS		LIABILITIES	
Cash	$ 120	Wages Payable .... $	500
Food and Wine Inventory	8,260	Taxes Payable	1,850
Dining and Kitchen Fixtures	14,900	Accounts Payable	23,500
Land and Building (net)	62,400	Mortgages Payable	80,000
	$85,680		$105,850

The trustee sold the food and wine inventory for $4,100; the fixtures, on which there was a mortgage of $10,000, for $9,500; and the real estate, on which the mortgage amounted to $70,000, for $72,200. The cost of the sales, lawyer's fees, and court costs amounted to $3,750.

Compute the amount available for general creditors. How much did they receive on a cents-on-the-dollar basis?

3. The T. X. Electronics Co. maintains and generously supports a research laboratory. It has in its employ over one hundred scientists, ably assisted by technicians, and the latest types of equipment. Each research worker, when accepting employment, signs an agreement that any discoveries he may make are to be the property of the T. X. Electronics Co. If the invention or process is patentable, the necessary papers are to be filed by company lawyers, and the patent rights are to be assigned to the employer.

Dr. Edmonds, a physicist, was in the employ of the T. X. Electronics Co. and diligently performed all research projects assigned to him. A man of considerable energy, he had equipped, at his own expense, a laboratory in the basement of his home. Working nights and weekends, he pursued an idea that he had held for some time that heat could be directly converted into electricity. Unknown to Dr. Edmonds, a similar project was under study at the research laboratory.

After two years of work, Dr. Edmonds devised a method of converting heat directly into electricity, and he was successful in securing a patent on his device. When this was issued, the T. X. Electronics Co. became aware of the outside activity of Dr. Edmonds and insisted he sign over the patent rights to the firm. Dr. Edmonds refused to do so unless he was paid $50,000.

What is your opinion of the business ethics of Dr. Edmonds? Should the T. X. Electronics Co. discharge Dr. Edmonds and sue him for breach of contract, or should they pay him the $50,000 he demands, which is considered a bargain for his discovery?

SUGGESTED READINGS

Anderson, R. A., and W. A. Kumpf. *Business Law,* Seventh Edition. Cincinnati: South-Western Publishing Company, 1965.

Bartels, R., Editor. *Ethics in Business.* Columbus, Ohio: The Ohio State University, 1963.

Dillavou, E. R., and Others. *Principles of Business Law,* Alternate Seventh Edition. Englewood Cliffs, New Jersey: Prentice-Hall, Inc., 1964.

Howard, L. B. *Business Law: An Introduction.* Woodbury, New York: Barron's Educational Series, Inc., 1965.

Johnston, H. *Business Ethics,* Second Edition. New York: Pitman Publishing Company, 1961.

Lusk, H. F. *Business Law: Principles and Cases,* Uniform Commercial Code Edition. Homewood, Illinois: Richard D. Irwin, Inc., 1966.

Smith, L. Y., and C. G. Roberson. *Business Law,* Second Edition. St. Paul: West Publishing Company, 1966.

Towle, J. W., Editor. *Ethics and Standards in American Business.* Boston: Houghton Mifflin Company, 1964.

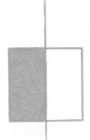

Chapter 28

REGULATION OF COMPETITIVE BUSINESS

The right of government to regulate competitive business stems from constitutions approved by citizens at both the federal and state levels. The Constitution of the United States, which was drafted in 1787, has been amended only twenty-five times in over one and three-quarters centuries. The thirteen states that comprised the United States and adopted the Constitution already had state constitutions, a practice that has been followed by all other states. All of these constitutions provide for a separation of powers into three branches, legislative, administrative, and judicial. This division of authority is of importance to the business world as each branch is frequently involved in the regulation of competitive business.

Historical Background

At the time the thirteen colonies declared their independence from England, they were very jealous of their newly acquired rights and powers as states. Consequently, they granted only limited powers to the federal government. In Article I, Section 8, of the Constitution of the United States, such items as the power to tax, to coin money, to borrow, and to establish the post office, were specifically stated. Of even greater importance to business was the right to regulate commerce among the several states—commonly called the interstate commerce clause—that is the basis for almost all federal regulation of business today.

Of the twenty-five amendments mentioned above, ten were adopted at once; in fact, some of the states ratified the federal constitution only with the understanding that these ten amendments—called the *Bill of Rights*—would be approved. The Bill of Rights, in addition to guaranteeing personal liberties, closed with an amendment stating that all powers not specifically delegated to the federal government were reserved to the states or to the people. It is obvious that the original intent of the framers of the Constitution of the United States was to create a federal government with limited powers as opposed to strong state governments limited only by certain inalienable rights of their citizens.

For approximately one hundred years, as far as the regulation of competitive business was concerned, the separation of powers between the federal government and the states proved satisfactory. Here and there states took over a measure of control of such industries as banks, insurance companies, and railroads; but, for the most part, businessmen were free to pursue their profits unhampered by laws, commissions, bureaus, agencies, and adverse court decisions. It was a century of laissez-faire capitalism that worked because business in the United States was conducted by a large number of relatively small units. In this kind of an economic climate, competition was an effective regulator of the prices business charged for its goods and services.

Forces were at work, however, that started a trend toward governmental regulation of competitive businesses that has continued and, in recent years, accelerated. A fundamental cause was the growing awareness on the part of business units that they could make larger profits if they could eliminate competition. An early example was an agreement on the part of nine firms who owned the grain warehouses in Chicago through which practically all shipments from the west to the east had to pass. The State of Illinois enacted a law regulating the maximum storage charges permitted, which the warehouse owners considered an invasion of their right to set their own fees. In a famous case, *Munn* v. *Illinois,* the Supreme Court of the United States in 1876 upheld the state on the grounds that when private property is used for a purpose in which the public has an interest, the public can control it.

The doctrine enunciated by the Court in the *Munn* case was not extended except in the case of railroads and, at a later date, public utilities. The regulation of these industries will be discussed in Chapter 29. In the meantime, other businesses under a trustee arrangement were taking joint actions for the enhancement of their profits to the detriment of the public. The device used was to have the shareholders of competing firms turn their stock over to trustees who then controlled and operated the several firms in such a manner as to maximize profits and minimize competition. Such organizations became known, quite logically, as *trusts.* Some of the most famous monopolies organized by using the trustee device were the Oil Trust (1879), the Whiskey Trust (1887), the Sugar Trust (1887), and the Tobacco Trust (1890). When state efforts failed to destroy or regulate these trusts, an aroused public sought relief by appealing to the federal government, which resulted in the first of a series of legislative curbs on business, as will be noted below.

Because the laws enacted by the Congress of the United States, the administration of them by federal agencies, and their interpretation by the Supreme Court are so far reaching in their effects on business throughout our nation, this chapter will first discuss the federal regulatory picture as applied to competitive businesses. State and local regulations will then be examined, following which attention will be devoted to some of the problems faced by management in making decisions in a regulated economy.

Federal Laws and Regulations

Reference has already been made to the interstate commerce clause of the Constitution of the United States. The majority of the laws passed by the Congress regulating competitive businesses have asserted that such legislation was necessary to accomplish proper regulation of commerce among the several states. Rulings and orders issued by various federal agencies (administrative law) under the authority of legislation were, and still are, frequently objected to by the business community. As a result, these disputes usually end up in the courts and, in many instances, are finally decided by the Supreme Court of the United States. This body then determines whether the law was constitutional in the first place and, if so decided, whether it was properly applied to the specific problem at hand.

Some of the laws passed by the Congress have been directed to general areas of business, such as labor, finance, and marketing. The constitutionality and impact of many of these laws have been explained in previous chapters. Other laws passed had the objective of promoting competition or of regulating a specific industry. These laws, some of which have been mentioned briefly in previous chapters, will now be examined in some detail.

Federal Laws to Promote Competition

Laws against trusts were the first of a series of acts and amendments passed by the Congress of the United States designed to benefit the public by assuring a healthy competitive business climate. Over the years the emphasis in legislation shifted from monopolies to illegal or unfair trade practices, although even today many businesses find their efforts to merge with competitors or companies in allied lines opposed by the Department of Justice or the Federal Trade Commission. The following laws are the ones most effective today in restraining businesses that would, if unchecked, limit competition or otherwise create unhealthy competitive conditions.

1. Sherman Antitrust Act
2. Clayton Act
3. Federal Trade Commission Act
4. Robinson-Patman Act
5. Wheeler-Lea Act
6. Celler-Kefauver Act

1 / Sherman Antitrust Act. In 1890 the federal government moved against the trusts that had been formed by enacting the Sherman Antitrust Act. The extent of opinion favorable to such a measure can be judged by the fact that this law was passed by both houses of Congress with only one dissenting vote. It provided that "every contract, combination . . . or conspiracy in restraint of trade or commerce among the several states . . . is hereby declared to be illegal," and that "every person who shall monopolize or . . . combine or conspire to monopolize . . . shall be deemed guilty of a misdemeanor." Persons convicted of violating the Act were subject to a fine of $5,000 and/or imprisonment for one year. Triple damages were to be awarded to those injured by the actions of trusts.

The Sherman Act was predicated on the fear, not without foundation in 1890, that large organizations were automatically detrimental to the best interests of the public. Bigness and badness were considered synonyms. The Act gave the Attorney General of the United States the authority to take action against the trusts and, after extensive legal delays, most of them were broken up. The Act was, however, weakened when the federal Supreme Court adopted the *rule of reason.* Under this rule a combination, contract, or conspiracy was judged as to whether or not it constituted an undue or unreasonable restraint on interstate commerce.

Furthermore, as time went on, the fear of large corporations subsided as more than one giant company appeared in several industries. In rubber products, for example, Goodyear, Firestone, Goodrich, and the United States Rubber Company are all large corporations; but several somewhat smaller companies do not hestitate to compete with these giants. The same situation exists in automobiles, steel, chemicals, food retailers, department stores, insurance, banking, and many other industries. Once a business is large enough to gain the advantages of mass production and distribution, it is questionable whether there are any competitive advantages in further growth.

These remarks should not be construed as an indication that the Sherman Act is obsolete. The Department of Justice of the United States institutes several suits each year against a company or a group of companies that seem to have entered into a combination, contract, or conspiracy in restraint of trade. A few years ago the DuPont company was charged with monopolizing the cellophane market, but it won this case as the Supreme Court found that it did not dominate the market for flexible packaging materials.

2 / Clayton Act. By 1914 it was apparent that the legislation of 1890 was not a complete answer to the trust problem. The Clayton Act was the second attempt by Congress to deal with monopolies. The new law, which was more specific than the Sherman Act, recognized that the trust problem was no longer one of size but rather one of business practices.

The Act stated that it was unlawful for persons engaged in interstate commerce to "discriminate in price between different purchasers of commodities . . . where the effect of such discrimination may be substantially to lessen competition or tend to create a monopoly in any line of commerce." Exceptions could be made where such discrimination took into account differences in grade, quality, quantity, or cost, or where such discrimination was made in good faith to meet bona fide competition. The law also prohibited exclusive agreements "for the sale of goods, wares, merchandise, machinery, supplies, or other commodities . . . for use, consumption, or resale within the United States," if the result of such an agreement "may be substantially to lessen competition or tend to create a monopoly in any line of commerce."

Still another restriction on marketing practices was a prohibition against *tying contracts,* under which a buyer was required to take certain undesirable goods in order to secure more desirable merchandise.

The *interlocking directorate,* a situation that exists when the majority of the members of two or more boards of directors are the same individuals, was declared unlawful if the firms are large and in competition with each other. The purchase by one corporation of another corporation's stock, if the effect was substantially to lessen competition or to tend to create a monopoly, was prohibited. Individual officers of a corporation were to be deemed guilty along with the corporation in antitrust suits successfully prosecuted. Labor unions and agricultural organizations were specifically exempted from the provisions of the antitrust laws.

3 / Federal Trade Commission Act. The Federal Trade Commission Act was passed in September, 1914, a month earlier than the Clayton Act. It provided that unfair methods of competition in commerce were illegal. To enforce this law, as well as many of the provisions of the Clayton Act, it also created the Federal Trade Commission. This is a federal agency that consists of five commissioners aided by a large staff of accountants, economists, and lawyers. It investigates alleged unfair methods of competition, issues complaints against offending firms, conducts hearings, and, where necessary, issues cease and desist orders against those found guilty of engaging in forbidden practices.

Over the years the powers of the FTC have been expanded and its current activities include making surveys into various business practices, which sometimes result in "trade practice conferences" designed to secure voluntary agreement among firms in a particular industry as to what constitutes unfair competitive methods. Out of these may come a set of Trade Practice Rules that are mutually agreeable to the Commission and to the members of the trades affected. The mere fact that the FTC is in existence is a deterent to the actions of firms that might be tempted to violate either laws or ethical principles, which is one of the reasons that the Commission is sometimes called "the policeman of the business world."

4 / Robinson-Patman Act. Price discrimination, which was covered in Section 2 of the Clayton Act, was clarified with the passage of the Robinson-Patman Act in 1936. This Act was designed to eliminate the lower prices that had been available to large purchasers, such as the chain grocery stores. Even though price differentials might be justified on the basis of quantity, if the results gave the buyer a monopolistic advantage, they would be illegal. The Act also provided for penalties if larger discounts were given or received, and a seller could be fined if goods were sold at low prices with the intent of eliminating competition or a competitor. Other details of this Act were described in Chapter 9.

5 / Wheeler-Lea Act. The Wheeler-Lea Act was passed by the Congress in 1938 as an amendment of the Federal Trade Commission Act. One of the important features was the change in wording from the original statement that "unfair methods of competition" were illegal to "unfair methods of competition in commerce, and unfair or deceptive acts or practices in commerce are hereby declared unlawful." Formerly, it had been necessary to prove that competitors had been injured by the unfair methods used by the offender. Under this Act any unfair or deceptive act is illegal, which has the effect of protecting the public. For example, if all cigarette companies claimed that it was healthful to smoke, the original Federal Trade Commission Act would not be violated since competition would not be lessened. Under the Wheeler-Lea Act, a claim of this type would be considered an unfair or deceptive act and would be illegal. Other provisions of this Act were discussed in Chapter 10.

6 / Celler-Kefauver Act. Although the Clayton Act stated that it was illegal for a corporation to buy stock in another corporation when the effect was to create a monopoly or to lessen competition, it did not prohibit such acquisitions in different geographical areas or where the companies sold identical goods but in different price ranges. In 1950 the Celler-Kefauver Act was passed as an amendment to the Clayton Act to strengthen the hand of the federal government in bringing action against proposed or completed consolidations. It provided that the use of stock ownership in any line of commerce in any section of the country in such a manner as to lessen competition or tend to create a monopoly was illegal.

▣ Federal Regulation of Specific Functions or Industries

In addition to the regulation of business by laws that attempt to maintain healthy competition, the federal government has passed numerous acts affecting specific business functions or specific industries. The labor and financial legislation described in earlier chapters has an impact on almost all firms, even those not engaged in interstate commerce. Agriculture has been extensively regulated with new farm programs announced practically every year. In one instance, a constitutional amendment instead of a law crippled the liquor industry for fifteen years. During the interval between the ratification of the eighteenth and twenty-first amendments to the Constitution of the United States (1919-1933), the manufacture, sale, importation, or export of intoxicating beverages was illegal.

The following laws that exert some measure of control over one industry or another are of enough public interest to warrant a brief description of how the major provisions of the several acts protect the best interests of consumers.

1. Food, Drug, and Cosmetic Act
2. Labeling acts
3. Quotas and price fixing laws

1 / Food, Drug, and Cosmetic Act. Although the Food and Drug Administration, now a part of the Department of Health, Education, and Welfare, was established in 1906, its authority was increased with the enactment of the Food, Drug, and Cosmetic Act in 1938. Powers of the Administration include insistence on sanitary methods of manufacture, purity of content, and proper labeling. The package must show the accurate weight, ingredients in proportion, and whether coloratives or preservatives have been used. Drugs must be labeled as to use and, if the drug is habit-forming, a statement to this effect must be included.

New drugs cannot be distributed until they have been proved safe to use. Heavy penalties are provided with a limit of a fine of $1,000 and/or imprisonment for one year for a mere infraction of the law, and maximums of $10,000 and imprisonment for three years for deliberate intent to defraud or mislead.

Other legislation has given the Food and Drug Administration the power to control adulteration of insecticides, labeling of caustic poisons for household use, and maintenance of standards for imported tea and silk. Major amendments in 1962 to the 1938 Act gave the Administration authority to make semiannual inspections of factories manufacturing drugs, make checks on the quality of products, and withhold approval of new drugs until it has been demonstrated that these are safe and effective. Also, drugs already on the market can be removed from an approved list.

2 / Labeling acts. In order to protect consumers against unfair or deceptive trade practices as applied to clothing, the Congress has enacted several laws requiring that labels attached to garments must show the types of materials used. The Wool Products Labeling Act of 1939 requires that each product be labeled to show the total fiber weight of the wool; whether it is new, processed, or reused; the percentage of nonwool filling; and the name of the manufacturer. The Fur Products Labeling Act of 1951 requires that the correct name of the animal that produced the fur, as well as manufacturing details, appear on the label of each such item offered for sale. The Textile Fiber Products Identification Act of 1958 requires labels showing the percentage of natural and synthetic fibers used in the manufacture of cloth and other materials.

The above laws are enforced by the Federal Trade Commission. In 1960 Congress passed the Hazardous Substances Labeling Act, and jurisdiction over this law was given to the Food and Drug Administration.

Another labeling act of interest that is concerned with price rather than raw materials is the Automobile Information Disclosure Act of 1958. Under this legislation the manufacturer is required to show the suggested retail price of each new car itemized as to base cost, extras, and transportation. Further efforts by the Congress to protect consumers are evidenced by passing or giving consideration to laws on automobile safety, packaging requirements, and disclosure of lending costs.

3 / Quotas and price-fixing laws. The Secretary of Agriculture of the federal government has been granted authority in certain areas of considerable interest to consumers. Under the Sugar Act of 1948 he is responsible for determining each year the amount of sugar that will be needed in this country, and he then assigns quotas to local producers as well as to foreign countries that sell sugar in the United States. For many years, as authorized by the Packers and Stockyards Act of 1921, he has determined the commission charges allowed for handling shipments of cattle, sheep, and hogs. Under the Agricultural Marketing Agreement Act of 1937, he may designate milk marketing areas and prescribe minimum prices to be paid producers in these areas.

■ Other Types of Federal Regulation

In addition to general and specific laws designed to regulate competitive businesses, the federal government exercises its influence in at least two other areas. One of these is regulation through taxation, which will be discussed in Chapter 30. Another is that of competing with private business through government-owned facilities. For example, the postal service competes with other forms of transporting goods and messages, and its rates have a marked effect on what competitors can charge. The same is true for governmental versus private recreational facilities, shipbuilding and repair, generation of electrical power, sales of merchandise to servicemen and their families, printing and publishing, and many other areas. Since the federal government need not operate these facilities at a profit, it is fortunate for business that its manufacturing and retailing activities are not extensive enough to warrant too much concern on the part of private enterprise.

■ State Laws and Regulations

Cities, villages, townships, counties, parishes, and other governing units within a state are created and exist under the constitution of that state. Consequently, state regulation of business encompasses all legislation passed by the state legislature and any of its political subdivisions that have legislative authority. As long as these laws do not conflict with the state constitution, the federal constitution, federal legislation, or the inalienable rights of its citizens, they are legal and enforceable.

The rights of the citizens of a state are protected in the same manner and to the same extent that they are from the federal government. The Fourteenth Amendment to the Constitution of the United States repeated part of the wording of the Fifth Amendment in stating that "no state may deprive any person of life, liberty, or property without due process of law." The phrase *due process of law* means that proper legal procedures must be taken before any punishment or liability can be enforced. As applied to business it means, for example, that the state cannot arbitrarily take a punitive action against a firm, such as canceling a charter it has granted to a corporation or padlocking a tavern against which no charges have been filed.

On the other hand, under what is known as the *police power,* it is not only the right but also the duty of a state to maintain law and order; to protect the health, the safety, and the morals of its citizens; and to promote the general welfare. This power is not dependent upon state constitutions or enabling legislation although specific laws cover practically all areas of business regulation. For example, many states have established weighing stations on their highways. Trucks moving in both interstate and intrastate commerce must stop and, if they are overloaded, are not permitted to continue their journeys. This is legal under the police power whether the state has or has not enacted a specific law covering this hazard to the safety of the highways.

Considering that there are fifty states and thousands of political subdivisions, it is obvious that the regulation of competitive businesses varies considerably among these governmental units. There are, however, some areas that are quite commonly considered by governing bodies as proper restraints on business activities as follows:

1. Labor legislation
2. Health and sanitation laws
3. Prices
4. Usury laws
5. Zoning ordinances and building codes
6. Licenses

1 / Labor legislation. State laws dealing with labor have long been recognized as a valid field for legislation. At the outset, the chief concern was with necessary minimum standards for working conditions. Most states provide that factory buildings shall be fireproof or have adequate protection against fire hazards to workers. Each employee is entitled to a certain amount of space. Adequate washrooms and other sanitary facilities must be available. Safety devices must be installed where the occupational hazard is excessive; for example, mines must be equipped with ventilating devices, emergency exits, and proper shafts.

Hours of work have been frequently specified for women and children. In some occupations, a woman may not work more than eight hours a day, and she must be given a certain amount of rest time including a lunch hour. Children cannot be employed before a specified hour in the morning or later than a specified hour in the evening. Wage minimums for women and children are also effective in many states.

The Labor-Management Relations Act of 1947 granted permission to the states to pass laws designed to protect the right of workers to continue their employment without having to join a union. Over the past twenty years a number of states enacted so-called right-to-work laws although a few of these were subsequently repealed. The Congress of the United States has been under constant pressure from labor unions to repeal Section 14b of the Taft-Hartley Act, which is the applicable portion of the 1947 law. If and when the Congress takes such an action, state right-to-work laws would be illegal as applied to firms engaged in interstate commerce.

2 / Health and sanitation laws. In addition to the application of health and sanitation rules to factories, laws to protect customers of retail establishments have been passed. For example, a restaurant is usually subject to a periodic inspection and, if certain minimum standards of cleanliness are not maintained, the owner's license to operate can be withdrawn. His employees who handle food may also be subject to annual health examinations.

3 / Prices. The price at which a retailer is permitted to sell a certain product may be affected by state legislation. As described in Chapter 9, fair trade laws and unfair trade laws have been passed by a considerable number of the states.

Sellers of commodities in intrastate commerce are very likely to find that the state has copied many of the federal laws against monopolies, trade practices, and pricing policies. Goods of like grade and quality must be sold at the same price to all purchasers unless the difference can be justified on the grounds of manufacturing, selling, or delivery costs. Any other price practices that might tend to create a monopoly or in any other manner restrain trade would also be illegal.

4 / Usury laws. Laws passed by states stipulating the maximum rates of interest that can be charged on different types of loans are known as *usury laws*. Many people find it necessary to borrow money, and those with little or no credit standing cannot expect lending agencies to compete for their business. If they do locate a source of funds, however, the interest and other charges that the financial institution can charge will be limited by the state usury law. These charges vary with the type of loan and terms of repayment, but a maximum of 3 percent a month is common.

5 / Zoning ordinances and building codes. Most people who build a home do not want their residential area invaded by hot dog stands, pool halls, and other similar types of business enterprises. Laws establishing areas that are available for business sites and others that are restricted to homes are known as *zoning ordinances*. Such laws are passed by village, town, or city councils, and recently townships and counties have established zoning boards to control the use of suburban and rural land areas. Zoning ordinances interfere with the right of a property owner to use his land in any manner that he may desire, but this interference is considered a necessary protection for his neighbors and others who own land in the same geographical area.

Assuming that the requirements of a zoning ordinance have been met, there may still remain the restriction of a building code. *Building codes,* both state and local, are regulations that provide minimum specifications for construction details. For example, a code may provide that only fireproof buildings can be constructed in a certain area, or that electric wires must be laid within a pipe or cable. After work is completed, a building inspector checks it and, if the specifications provided by law have not been followed, necessary corrections must be made.

6 / Licenses. A *license* is a formal document issued by a governmental body to a business or a person authorizing the holder to engage in an activity that would otherwise be illegal. Licenses are issued by states, counties, cities, and towns. Most licenses are on an annual basis, although some are for an event only, such as a circus or carnival permit. Theoretically, licenses are required primarily for regulatory purposes as opposed to the revenue features of most taxes. Practically, licenses may become substantial revenue producers, as shown by the income that states derive from the sale of license plates for automobiles.

Several states list over one hundred different types of businesses that must secure a license. Some of the firms most frequently singled out are restaurants, barbershops, dry cleaning establishments, hotels, ice plants, laundries, motion-picture houses, soda fountains, and dealers in tobacco, fireworks, office machines, and automobiles.

In some areas local licenses are more numerous than state licenses. Pool halls, bowling alleys, and other places of amusement are frequently licensed, and a permit for the use of public sidewalks and streets, such as for farmers' markets or parades, is almost always required. Of special interest to retail merchants are the various types of licenses that may be required of itinerant peddlers.

The use of licenses as regulatory devices plays an important part for businesses that sell liquor, for the professions, and for some types of occupations. Stores that sell liquor in bottles, other than those that may be operated by a state, are required to secure a special license. Also, hotels, inns, taverns, and other places where liquor is sold for consumption on the premises are licensed. By refusing to issue a license or to renew one, the state can control the number and types of outlets. The practice of medicine, law, accounting, dentistry, and other similar professions are usually regulated in that the individual concerned must secure a license from the state before he can offer his services to the public. Brokers, real estate salesmen, barbers, insurance salesmen, and many other workers in occupations not classed as professions must also secure a license from the state. Since most licenses are on an annual basis, the ability of the individuals concerned to continue in business is based on keeping their licenses in force.

■ Decision Making in a Regulated Economy

The managements of business firms of all sizes must be alert to the consequences of taking actions that might prove illegal. Many decisions must be reached in a variety of areas that are affected by regulatory legislation. Fines, damage suits, and even imprisonment await the firm and its management who knowingly or otherwise violate one or more of the laws that have been described in this chapter. Although some offenses, such as failure to secure necessary licenses or violating a building code, are generally clearcut, others are subject to interpretation by the courts. Four areas in which many businesses have found themselves involved in recent years are monopolies, trade associations, prices, and trade practices.

1 / **Monopolies.** Although size is no longer the prime consideration, conspiracies in trade as outlawed by antitrust acts are an ever-present threat to competition. One device used is *collusive bidding* in which supposedly competing firms agree either to submit identical prices or to agree that one of them is to be the low bidder on a contract. In the latter case, geographical areas might be assigned for the exclusive benefit of each firm, resulting in a *territorial pool.* In 1960 a number of manufacturers of heavy electrical goods were found guilty of these practices with resulting fines, prison sentences, and damage suits. Management has found that it must be careful that no official of the firm ever discusses prices or proposed bids with his counterpart in a competing company.

Firms that hold patents have a monopoly grant for 17 years, but during this period they may wish to allow others to use the patent upon payment of a royalty. *Patent licensing,* as it is called, is legal provided the agreement does not restrain trade; but any management engaged in issuing permits to others is treading on dangerous ground. In all cases where patents are involved, it has been held illegal to make use of tying contracts. The Eastman Kodak Company formerly sold colored film at a price that included finishing but, following court action, agreed to sell the film only, thus allowing others to enter the processing field. The International Business Machines Corporation used to lease its patented equipment in the computing field with the understanding that tabulating cards and other supplies would be purchased from the company. This provision was ruled illegal by the Supreme Court as early as 1936.

Interlocking directorates are clearly illegal under the Clayton Act, but a similar situation can exist if the dominant or majority shareholder or shareholders in two competing concerns are in a position to dictate the composition of the boards of directors of two or more companies. The members may be different individuals; but if they are dependent for election to the same individual or individuals and the actions they take are such as to eliminate or reduce competition between the two firms, this *community of interests* may be judged illegal.

2 / Trade associations. Although monopolies and monopolistic practices are illegal, business firms can and do associate with each other for their mutual advantage. Not all joint activities are illegal as, for example, an agreement by a local Retail Merchants Association to close all member stores on Wednesday afternoons during the summer months. The most extensive cooperation among businessmen is attained through organizations known as trade associations. A *trade association* is an organization formed by and composed of firms engaged in a particular industry. Examples include such organizations as the American Iron and Steel Institute, the National Retail Hardware Dealers' Association, the American Bankers Association, and literally hundreds of others.

These trade associations usually maintain a headquarters with a paid staff. Many issue a trade journal, publish trade statistics, devise model accounting systems, conduct educational programs, and help their members with specific problems. An additional function is to conduct lobbying activities in the nation's capitol and with state legislatures. The National Lumbermen's Association, for example, is interested in opposing building codes that might exclude the use of lumber in the construction of commercial and residential properties. As long as the activities of trade associations are devoted to rendering assistance to members and to the trade without conspiring to restrict production or raise prices, their actions are not considered illegal. Unfortunately, in their zeal to help the members make profits, some trade associations have overstepped the legal boundary with the result that its members have been prosecuted.

In addition to the associations that are so prevalent in specific business areas, there are two national organizations that are generally considered to represent business on a broader basis. One of these, the National Association of Manufacturers, represents only firms engaged in manufacturing, but these form a very important segment of our economy. The other is the United States Chamber of Commerce, which is composed of state organizations that, in turn, include the local Chambers of Commerce that flourish in most cities. The Chamber of Commerce publishes a monthly magazine, *The Nation's Business,* and carries on extensive research and lobbying activities.

3 / **Prices.** Decisions made by managements as to prices to be charged for their products are affected by fair trade laws, unfair trade laws, loss leader laws, and antitrust laws. If several competing concerns agree that it would be desirable to raise prices, and if such a price increase does take place, this is called a *gentlemen's agreement,* which would be illegal if the government can prove a conspiracy in restraint of competition.

A somewhat similar situation arises when a company acknowledged as the price leader in a particular industry announces price increases in certain products it manufactures. If all of the competitors quickly make similar increases, this "follow the leader" action might or might not be the result of previous discussions among the executives of the companies involved. In any event it is frequently suspect, and an investigation by the Department of Justice or Federal Trade Commission may well follow such uniform action.

One of the most important decisions a manufacturer must make in the field of prices is whether to market his products under the fair trade laws. If he fails to do so, he may lose all of his independent outlets. If he does establish minimum resale prices on his branded products, this price may be so high that it encourages private brands and he may lose the volume business available from discount houses and other retailers who feature price cuts. There is also the problem of policing price cutters.

4 / **Trade practices.** A decision by management to engage in any number of trade practices designed to give the firm a competitive advantage may be ruled illegal. Many of these involve advertising, such as false endorsements of products or making claims for the efficacy of a remedy that cannot be backed by scientific evidence. Imitating a competitor's trademark, attempting to confuse names, using lotteries as a means of sale, or making false statements about a competitor's product or his methods of manufacture are illegal. Misbranding or failure to provide adequate information under the various labeling acts may result in action against the firm, as would use of false weights and measures.

Most of these illustrations would seem to indicate that illegal trade practices are also dishonest or, at least, unethical. Actually, there are many situations where management is not sure whether the proposed practice is proper or improper. Is it, for example, either dishonest or unethical to use the endorsement of a famous athlete for a breakfast food? Should a retailer of men's clothes, whose name and business for many years has been Ben's Clothing and Tailoring Company, drop the phrase "and Tailoring" when it decides to sell only ready-to-wear suits?

These illustrations point up the difficulty management may have in making decisions in a regulated economy. Other governmental influences are felt in the financial and labor areas, and many business decisions hinge on the tax problems involved. There is no question but that entrepreneurs must operate their businesses with constant regard for the legality of their actions.

BUSINESS TERMS

(a) Bill of Rights (599)
(b) trust (600), rule of reason (602), tying contract (603), interlocking directorate (603)
(c) due process of law (607), police power (608)
(d) usury law (609)
(e) zoning ordinance (609), building code (610)
(f) license (610)
(g) collusive bidding (611), territorial pool (611), patent licensing (611), community of interest (612)
(h) trade association (612)
(i) gentlemen's agreement (613)

QUESTIONS FOR DISCUSSION AND ANALYSIS

1. Is the separation of governmental powers into three branches of help or hindrance to business? Why?
2. Now that there are several large firms in almost all business areas, why would not laissez faire capitalism work today?
3. The organizers of trusts were responsible for the Sherman Act. Would not they have been better off to have allowed some competition in the fields they dominated? Explain.
4. Should the Clayton Act be labeled as an antitrust law or a trade practices act? Discuss.
5. Does the passage of the Celler-Kefauver Act in 1950 seem to indicate a revival in antitrust legislation based on the size of firms? Explain.
6. Why should not other industries, such as packaged foods or fast frozen fruits and vegetables, be subject to as much regulation as the drug business?

7. Do you believe the Automobile Information Disclosure Act has improved trade practices in the sale of new cars? Discuss.
8. Would business be better off if all regulation of it was enforced by the states rather than by the federal government as well? Why?
9. Judging from the types of regulations enforced against business by the states, does it appear that they have acted wisely? Why?
10. Despite general knowledge of federal and state regulations, businessmen not infrequently violate these laws. Why?

PROBLEMS AND SHORT CASES

1. A local personal loan office, which operated in a state with a usury law that specified a maximum rate of 3 percent a month, made a loan to Mr. Galloway on the following terms:

   Size of loan—$3,000
   Length of time—1 year
   Interest at an annual rate of 20 percent deducted in advance
   Monthly payments on loan—$250

   When Mr. Galloway explained this loan to a lawyer friend, he was told that he was being charged an illegal rate of interest. Do you agree? Show calculations on which your answer is based.
2. The Vance Furniture Corporation had been a large manufacturer of furniture for home use for many years. It had been buying its raw lumber from several suppliers, although recently the Holton Lumber Company had enjoyed a substantial percentage of its business. The finished products were marketed through wholesalers, manufacturer's agents, and the Mason-Wardell chain of furniture stores with 210 outlets, mostly in the Midwest. A brand name, Georgian Furniture, had been pushed and was well regarded by consumers.

   The management of the Vance Furniture Corporation had become well acquainted with the officials of both the Holton Lumber Company and the Mason-Wardell chain. On the basis of discussions among each other, it appeared that if the Vance Furniture Corporation bought all of its lumber from the Holton Lumber Company, it would be assured of a steady supply of this raw material that would be adequate for its needs and that the Holton Lumber Company would not need other customers. Likewise, there was evidence that if the Mason-Wardell chain handled only the Georgian brand, it could dispose of the entire output of the Vance Furniture factories.

   A proposal to amalgamate the three companies into a new corporation to be called the Georgian Furniture Company was voted on favorably by the stockholders of each of the three concerns, and plans were progressing to complete the details of the merger. At this point the Attorney General of the United States secured a temporary injunction to stop proceedings and to require that the companies continue operating as independent units.

Prepare a list of arguments that might be used by the attorneys for the proposed new corporation and also by government lawyers. If you were the judge in these proceedings, what ruling would you make and what would be your reasoning to support your decision?

3. The Pot Luck Co. owns and operates a chain of drive-in restaurants in five southern states. All are standardized as to external and internal construction, menus, supplies, nonfood items sold, costumes for waitresses and busboys, etc. The units of the chain are supplied with every possible item needed for their operation from central warehouses.

In order to expand its operations, the Pot Luck Co. decided to license independent owners who would build their own establishments from plans furnished by the company. Each independent owner was required to sign an agreement that he would purchase all items used from the Pot Luck Co. at a schedule of prices stated in the contract. Central warehouses were established as rapidly as enough independent operators were signed up in a new territory.

Harold Thompson, a licensee of the Pot Luck Co., was approached by a local meat packer who quoted prices for comparable products at a saving over the terms of the contract. Thompson notified the Pot Luck Co. that he was transferring his meat purchases elsewhere although he would continue to purchase all other items from it. The Pot Luck Co. notified Thompson that his action was a breach of contract. but Thompson refused to cancel the agreement he had made with his new meat supplier, whereupon the Pot Luck Co. sued Thompson.

A lower court held for Thompson on the ground that the contracts of the Pot Luck Co. were in violation of the Sherman and Clayton Antitrust Acts. The management of the Pot Luck Co. is now considering what action it should take. It can appeal the case and hope for a reversal by a higher court, or it can attempt to change the contractual relationships with its licensees. Its future expansion program is at stake, and the management is faced with a difficult decision. What should it do?

SUGGESTED READINGS

Anderson, R. A. *Government and Business,* Third Edition. Cincinnati: South-Western Publishing Company, 1966.

Dimock, M. W. *Business and Government,* Fourth Edition. New York: Holt, Rinehart and Winston, Inc., 1961.

Isaacs, A., and R. E. Slesinger. *Business, Government and Public Policy.* Princeton, New Jersey: D. Van Nostrand Company, Inc., 1964.

Mund, V. A. *Government and Business,* Fourth Edition. New York: Harper & Row, Publishers, 1965.

Wernette, J. P. *Government and Business.* New York: The Macmillan Company, 1964.

Wilcox, C. *Public Policies Toward Business,* Third Edition. Homewood, Illinois: Richard D. Irwin, Inc., 1966.

Chapter 29

REGULATED INDUSTRIES

The type of capitalistic system operating in the United States today, as has been repeatedly stressed, assumes that competition will automatically provide consumers with the goods and services they want and need at the lowest possible prices. There are, however, some areas of business in which competition is neither desirable nor in the best interest of the public. For example, two competing telephone companies in one city would cause endless confusion and unnecessary expense. But when a monopoly is preferable over competitive units, it seems obvious that a substitute for competition becomes necessary in order to regulate such items as price and service.

This situation has been recognized in this country for many years and, whenever a business is permitted to attain and continue a monopolistic status, it must submit not only to the types of regulation affecting competitive enterprises but also to extensive additional supervision by a governmental body. This added control over its operations extends to rates (prices) and services rendered, and also affects many decisions that would otherwise be the sole prerogative of management. Although privately owned, the concept of maximization of profits for the benefit of shareholders is untenable for a regulated monopoly. Rather, the firm's objectives are to provide maximum service to consumers at the lowest possible prices consistent with providing a fair return to the owners.

PUBLIC UTILITIES

The types of businesses that are currently considered as desirable monopolies, using the term in a broad sense, are classified as public utilities. A *public utility* may be defined as a private industrial concern that is regulated by a federal or a state commission or by a city to at least the extent that the prices it charges for the services it renders are controlled. Under this definition, electric, gas, water, telephone, and telegraph companies qualify as do railroads, street railways and buses, subways, oil and gas pipelines, and air, water, and motor transport companies. Sometimes steam heating, cold storage, irrigation, and sewage disposal companies are also included.

In modern usage, the term "public utility" refers to all of the preceding categories except the railroads and some other forms of transportation, and will be so used in this chapter. Although the problems of both groups are similar, the regulation of public utilities is primarily an intrastate matter, while transportation regulation is more likely to be on an interstate basis. This chapter will first describe the characteristics and the regulation of public utilities, but most of the general principles apply with equal force to all types of approved monopolies. The regulation of the various forms of transportation and communication will then be discussed with emphasis on the predominately interstate nature of these industries.

■ Characteristics of Public Utilities

The major classifications of public-utility companies have certain characteristics that are lacking in other forms of private business. An examination of these differences will explain, in part, why government regulation has replaced competition as the means by which the public secures reasonable prices and satisfactory services.

1. Public necessity
2. Natural monopoly
3. Large investment
4. Special privileges

1 / Public necessity. Most public utilities provide a service to the general public that it could not do without under present-day living conditions. For this reason, millions of individuals are vitally concerned with the problems of services and rates. If a water-softening service company charges high prices and renders poor service, the user can discontinue his contract. He cannot, however, do the same with the water service itself. If he lives in a city, he is dependent upon the water company to furnish a continuous flow of clean water at rates he can afford to pay. This specific example points up the fact that there is no acceptable substitute for many of the services rendered by a public utility, the need for them cannot be postponed, and the consumer has no choice but to pay whatever he is charged.

Because the services rendered by a public utility are necessary, some municipalities have established departments or created governmental corporations to own and operate the water system, street buses, and, less

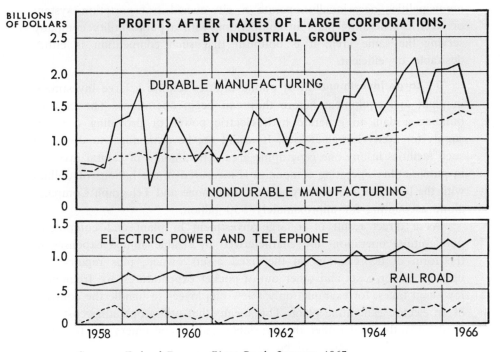

BILLIONS
OF DOLLARS

PROFITS AFTER TAXES OF LARGE CORPORATIONS,
BY INDUSTRIAL GROUPS

DURABLE MANUFACTURING

NONDURABLE MANUFACTURING

ELECTRIC POWER AND TELEPHONE

RAILROAD

1958   1960   1962   1964   1966

Source: *Federal Reserve Chart Book,* January, 1967.

frequently, an electric plant. Despite these encroachments into areas in which private enterprise would be happy to operate, the facts are that public-utility companies, as previously defined, render most of the services that the public needs and demands.

2 / Natural monopoly. A second characteristic of public utilities is that they function in business areas where the existence of competing units would be inefficient and undesirable. It is in the public interest to permit one firm to have all the business of its type available in a given community. As previously mentioned, two competing telephone companies in one city would be completely unsatisfactory. Subscribers to one service could not be connected with individuals who patronized the competing company, and business establishments would have to install at least two telephones in order to be in contact with all potential customers. Furthermore, there would need to be a duplication of poles or underground cables throughout the entire community.

In a similar manner, there is a disadvantage in having two gas companies, two electric light companies, two water companies, or two street railway companies serving the same community. Despite the fact that municipalities occasionally operate a city-owned transportation system or electric generating plant in competition with a public-utility company serving the same area, it is doubtful that such competition is either desirable or efficient.

3 / Large investment. Most public utilities require a large investment in plant and equipment before they can begin operations. The cost of building a dam to generate hydroelectric power or providing a water supply for a city is tremendous. It would not be economical to duplicate such facilities in any one geographic area. The amount of capital invested in public-utility operating companies is measured in the billions of dollars with the total assets of The American Telephone and Telegraph Company alone accounting for approximately $30 billion.

As a direct result of a large investment in plant and equipment, public-utility operations are characterized by sizable annual expenses in the form of depreciation on the fixed assets owned, plus repairs and upkeep. Labor costs and other out-of-pocket expenditures are frequently low, as it takes, for example, only a few employees to handle the controls of an electric generating plant. This means that utility operating costs are predominantly fixed rather than variable and, if consumers are to enjoy low rates, a large volume of business is necessary.

An oversimplified example may clarify this problem. If a water service company has an investment of $10 million in fixed assets on which an average depreciation rate of 3 percent is effective, the cost for this item is $300,000 annually. If the cost can be spread over a 300 million gallon output, one mill per gallon will absorb the depreciation charge. If sales are only 30 million gallons, however, the amount of this item will remain the same, but one cent a gallon will enter into production costs for depreciation.

4 / Special privileges. Another characteristic of many public utilities is the right to secure special privileges from governmental units. These usually take the form of franchises or the right of eminent domain. A *franchise,* which is a privilege conferred by a governmental body, will be granted by the elected officials to a gas company, for example, giving it the exclusive right to lay pipes under the city streets and to serve the community for a specified number of years without any threat of competition. When the franchise expires, negotiations are conducted for its renewal. Frequently, there is no competing company available, and government ownership is the only alternative to a renewal.

The *right of eminent domain* is the power of a government to take private property by the payment of a fair price that, if necessary, will be determined by a court. This privilege may be extended to telephone, telegraph, gas, electric service, and other quasi-public companies. For example, many of the long-distance electric transmission lines run overland on a straight line between two points and make use of private property for the erection of support towers regardless of whether or not such use of the land is agreeable to the owner.

■ Public-Utility Regulatory Agencies

As previously pointed out, part of the burden that a public utility must carry for its special privileges, such as monopoly status and the right of eminent domain, is to be subject to much more extensive regulation than is or can be legally imposed on competitive businesses. Such additional regulation is largely centered on rates and service. The determination and enforcement of what constitutes fair rates and satisfactory service falls under one or more of three levels of government depending on the territory served by the utility.

If the public utility is a street railway or a bus line, a local water or electric company, or any other privately owned organization selling its services exclusively within the confines of a municipality, it will be regulated by the city council or a comparable counterpart. At the time a franchise is granted, regulatory conditions are imposed and, customarily, a committee of the council is charged with the responsibility for overseeing that the rates charged and the services rendered are in accord with the terms of the franchise. Because elected officials are not always competent in the area of public-utility regulation, their efforts to cope with the complexities of this task have not always been satisfactory either to the company or its customers.

More commonly, a utility serves more than one community within a state. In this event, its regulation will fall under the jurisdiction of a state public-utility commission, which is a branch of the state government. Although the utility must still obtain a franchise to operate in each city, this commission can overrule the terms of a franchise if these would obstruct the overall regulation of the utility company. For example, if a city insisted on a very low rate structure before granting a franchise to a natural gas company, it might mean that the company would have to charge high rates in other areas it serves in order to earn a fair profit. Under these conditions, the state commission could overrule the municipality, although it is more likely that it would have entered into the negotiations before the franchise was granted. Although the competence of the commissions varies widely among the fifty states, the appointment of intelligent commissioners, who employ a staff of experts, has frequently resulted in efficient and capable state regulation.

From 1907, when the first state utility commissions were established in New York and Wisconsin, until 1935, when the first of several laws affecting utilities was enacted, the federal government did not regulate public utilities. During this time it became increasingly clear that the interstate operations of some utilities, notably electric and natural gas companies, were so extensive that state commissions could not regulate these companies effectively. The federal government, as will be discussed later, has now established several agencies that either regulate a phase of public-utility company operations or the interstate rates and services of a particular industry. These agencies cooperate with the state commissions whenever a problem is of both an interstate and an intrastate nature and, in general, have filled a previous void in a competent manner.

The actions of regulatory bodies, at all levels, are subject to court actions whenever a ruling is not acceptable either to the public-utility company or to the consumers of the service. So many decisions have been rendered that it seems fair to say that the courts have also played an important part in the regulation of utilities. This role will become apparent in the examination of the techniques of public-utility regulation that follows. Since state commissions play a dominant role in the determination of rates and service, the methods they use will be described in some detail although the basic concepts apply with equal force to all public-utility regulatory agencies.

■ State Regulation of Public-Utility Rates

Of prime importance to the public utility and to its customers are the rates charged for its services. Although many business firms have found that a low profit on a high volume of sales produces maximum profits for the owners, there is a justifiable fear that a monopoly would not follow this price policy. Consequently, all of the states regulate the rates that public utilities may charge for their services.

As a general working principle, commissions have tried to establish rate structures that permit each public-utility company to earn a fair return on a fair value of its property. This principle follows a line of argument adopted by the Supreme Court of the United States in a decision that read, in part, as follows: "A public utility is entitled to such rates as will permit it to earn a return on the value of the property which it employs for the convenience of the public equal to that generally being made at the same time and in the same general part of the country on investments in other business undertakings which are attended by corresponding risks and uncertainties."

1 / **Fair rate of return.** A rate of return that is fair to the utility and to the public is extremely difficult to establish. In most instances the rates allowed have varied from 5 to 8 percent on the fair value of its property, with 6 and 6½ percent favored over the extremes. Of course, once a rate of return is established, there is no guarantee that the return will equal the rate. If operations produce a loss or a very low rate of return, the company can apply for an adjustment in rates. If the commission should refuse to grant such a request, the courts on an appeal would probably decide that the allowed rates were too low. On the other hand, if operations result in a high rate of return, the public will soon bring pressure to bear on the commission to reduce the charges.

It has been charged, and with some truth, that there is no incentive for efficient management of public utilities. If a particular company finds many ways to economize without decreasing the scope of its operations, the result should be a higher profit. As soon as the commission notes the increased earnings, lower rates may be ordered. On the other hand, inefficient operation may produce such a low yield on value that the company feels justified in asking for an increase in rates.

Most state commissions have solved this problem, at least partially, by requiring that uniform accounts be kept and that reports be made at periodic intervals. If one company seems to be spending more for certain items than other similar organizations, the commission can disallow the added expense when it considers rate revisions. Excessive salaries paid to officers and payments made to other companies in the same holding company group are examples of expenses subject to close scrutiny.

2 / **Fair value of property.** Assuming that a fair rate of return has been determined, it must also be decided what is a fair value of the public-utility property that is used and useful for the public good. This involves placing a price tag on every item owned by the company that can reasonably be said to be essential. For example, an electric-service company frequently owns more production facilities than are normally used. Such *stand-by equipment,* as it is called, is available should an unusual peak load be created at any time. Obviously, this equipment is necessary and desirable. On the other hand, if a public utility owns and operates a vacation resort for its employees, a question might be raised as to whether the cost of such facilities was necessary and should be included in the fair value of the utility properties.

Disputes involve not only the items to be valued, but the method of arriving at this value. Two experts, both perfectly sincere, may arrive at fair-value figures that are as far apart as $100 million and $200 million. Usually, the commission is supporting the claim that the lower figure is correct, and the experts representing the company have agreed upon the higher amount.

The reason for wide variations in value is the lack of agreement as to a method that should be used in arriving at true value. The two most widely used measures are (a) cost less depreciation and (b) reproduction cost new, less depreciation. In Ohio, for example, the statutes specify that reproduction cost must be considered, while in other states more emphasis may be placed on historical cost. Courts, including the Supreme Court of the United States, have given sanction to both methods.

(a) COST LESS DEPRECIATION. An examination of the books of a company will disclose the original or *historical costs* of the properties now in use. Assuming that they were properly recorded and that depreciation has been charged on a consistent basis in accord with generally accepted accounting principles, the total of the book values of all assets owned will give the fair value of the utility. In a general way this corresponds to the value of the assets of any private corporation as shown on its published balance sheet.

A variant from historical cost less depreciation is known as *prudent historical cost* less depreciation. At times, a utility in its desire to expand has paid too much for a property, and commissions have raised the question as to whether the public should be forced to pay for the lavish expenditure. For example, an electric-service company bought a local installation because it wished to add this operation to its network of lines. Considerable resistance was encountered in making this purchase, which was finally overcome by an offer of twice what the local plant was really worth. Under the prudent-historical-cost theory, the utility would not be allowed to include more than the fair value of the purchased property.

(b) REPRODUCTION COST NEW, LESS DEPRECIATION. In a period of rising prices the utilities try to bring reproduction costs into the picture. The method used is to value all of the assets now in use at their current purchase prices, and to substitute these values for the actual costs. Depreciation is charged in the same manner as when historical costs are used, except on the higher base. The argument for using reproduction costs is not without some justification. Why should Area *A* enjoy lower rates than Area *B* simply because a utility was organized in *A* at a time when prices were low, and in *B* at a time when prices were high?

Strictly speaking, *reproduction cost new* implies that the assets in use will be valued at current prices. It does not take into consideration the technological improvements that have taken place over the years. One way of bringing current prices into the picture is to compute the cost of a modern plant that would be capable of rendering exactly the same service as do the existing properties. In this case reproduction cost new actually becomes the cost of reproducing the service. This method has much to be said for it and, in these days of miniaturization, it is conceivable that the cost of reproducing the service might be less than historical cost. Actually, any such result is highly unlikely so that either concept of reproduction cost new is likely to show a higher value for a utility than figures based on original cost.

3 / **Rate differentials.** One of the special problems that arise in determining fair rates is that all customers of a particular public utility cannot be charged the same rates. In a given locality, like users of the street railways, water service, electric service, and telephone service do pay the same amount. Rates may vary between two communities located some distance apart, however, even though they are served by the same company. This condition may result from negotiating franchises in different years or under other diverse circumstances. Of even more importance is the difference between rates charged to classes of consumers, such as the homeowner and a manufacturing company. The kilowatt-hour rate charged for electricity in the case of the individual is much higher than that charged to the manufacturer.

There is a sound economic reason for lower rates to large users of gas, water, and electricity. Once the investment in plant and equipment is made, it costs very little to increase the output. The public-utility company is anxious to sell the added volume of business available from large companies. Unless the rate is favorable, a manufacturing company can install its own system, which introduces a competitive situation not usually encountered by utilities. Commissions recognize the general desirability of volume sales and allow rate variations just so long as there is no discrimination among users in the same category. This means that all large users must be given the same schedule of lower rates. The principle of volume sales also explains the lower unit rate applicable to the higher consumption brackets generally available to domestic consumers of electricity.

In general the rates that public utilities have been permitted to charge have resulted in profitable operations for most companies. With the exception of many street railways and interurban lines, which have been faced with competition from buses and privately owned automobiles, the public-utility companies have been moderately prosperous. Over the years they have been able to earn a fair return on a fair value.

■ State Regulation of Public-Utility Services

Several features of the problem of service might not be apparent to a casual observer. The public takes most of these for granted without recognizing that its best interests are being protected by the commission.

1 / Entry into public-utility field. A public-utility company cannot enter the field in any locality without first of all securing permission from the commission. This usually takes the form of a *certificate of convenience and necessity*. If a group of men want to form an electric company to serve a geographic area, they need to secure a certificate from the state regulatory body. If the area includes a municipality, it will also be necessary to secure a franchise from the local authorities.

There are good reasons why it is desirable to control entry into the public-utility field. If a company is serving the territory adequately, a competitor would eliminate the advantages the monopoly formerly possessed. In the long run, the public would suffer from the inefficiencies of competitive rather than single, large-scale operations because, generally, only one company could be expected to attain the size necessary to render good service at the lowest possible cost.

2 / Standards of service. Most public-utility commissions have the right to insist on certain minimum standards of service. A bus route must maintain regular schedules, which means that equipment and drivers must be available to meet published timetables. The heating value of gas furnished to homes must not fall below established minimums. Water must be pure, and the pressure must be maintained in order to ensure protection against fire losses.

Other types of standards are also required. The utility must be safe for the user. For example, buses and street railways must be equipped with proper safety devices. Meters for gas, water, and electricity must be accurate, and the customer can usually secure an inspection by the commission if he is willing to pay a small fee. Complaints must be handled promptly. If a service has been suspended, even for a good reason, it must be restored just as soon as practicable. Many utilities have advertised, with justifiable pride, how rapidly they have repaired the damage caused by hurricanes, floods, ice storms, and other similar disasters; but, for the most part, such action could have been required by a commission.

3 / Service without discrimination. A public-utility company cannot choose its customers or render different classes of service to like users. Every person whose residence is on a street that carries gas, telephone, and electrical connections has a right to demand the use of these services. Furthermore, he is entitled to the same service and rates as exist for other like users of the services. If a utility is granted the exclusive right to serve a certain area, it must do so without discrimination among its customers.

This feature of service is subject to a considerable amount of interpretation by state commissions. If a resident rents a telephone and does not pay his bill, the utility company has the right to remove the instrument and discontinue the service. If a water main has been tapped up to the limit of its capacity to serve the connected outlets, the utility would not be ordered to render a service that would require the installation of a new or duplicating main. In other words, the utility must render equal service within limits of reasonableness.

4 / Extension and abandonment. A public utility usually may not extend, reduce, or abandon the service it renders in any territory without first securing approval from the state commission. In the case of extension, problems similar to those mentioned above in the matter of entry might be created. Some commissions have the right to order an extension of service where such a move would be economically sound and of benefit to the public served. An electric-service company, for example, might be ordered to extend its lines into a rural area if enough customers were available for profitable operation of this addition.

Partial or complete abandonment of service is also restricted by the commission. If a company is losing money, it can, of course, liquidate. If it is losing money on one of its operations or on a particular extension of its service but is earning an overall profit, it may not abandon the losing service without prior commission approval.

■ Federal Regulation of Public Utilities

Although the operations of public utilities are primarily intrastate, electricity and natural gas move in interstate commerce. Furthermore, although the financing and the ownership of public utilities are not related to state boundaries, these items can have a bearing on a fair rate of return. Recognition of the inability of state commissions to cope with these interstate complications became so widespread in the early 1930's that there was a strong demand for remedial action by the federal government. In 1935 the Congress of the United States responded by passing a law that, for the first time, brought interstate activities of public utilities under federal supervision. State regulation, although still dominant, is now supplemented by federal regulation so that both the intrastate and interstate operations of public utilities are supervised.

The chief difficulty encountered by the state commissions in discharging their duties arose in connection with the tremendous increase in public-utility holding companies, which took place in the period from 1920 to 1935. Usually, the holding company was incorporated under the laws of a state in which it conducted no business, and its operating subsidiaries were located in several states. If these were integrated into a single system, many interstate relationships developed. It became exceedingly difficult for the state commissions to control matters that had been removed from their direct jurisdiction.

1 / Public Utility Holding Company Act of 1935. The main purpose of this Act was to eliminate the evils that had grown out of the holding company device as applied to gas and electric public utilities. It required that such companies register with the Securities and Exchange Commission and that this Commission could order the liquidation of such holding companies as were not part of a single integrated public-utility system. One of the tests applied was whether the operating companies were engaged in the same business and were located in one state, or in adjoining states. Another test was whether the holding company was more than two levels higher than the operating companies and, if so, it was to be dissolved. This meant that a holding company could control two or more holding companies that, in turn, owned operating companies, but it could not be owned by another holding company. This provision was commonly called the *death sentence clause* of the Act.

As a means of forcing the holding companies to register, the law provided that unregistered companies were forbidden to use the mails and other instrumentalities of interstate commerce. Registered companies were not allowed to borrow from subsidiaries, to pay excessive dividends, or to make political contributions. Sales, service, and construction contracts between the holding company and the subsidiaries were subject to review by the Commission.

The above features were contained in Title I of the Act. Title II was also extremely important from the standpoint of rate regulation. It gave to the Federal Power Commission the right to regulate interstate electric rates at the wholesale level. This eliminated one of the problems that had vexed the state utility commissions and provided complete control over charges for electric service through the creation of joint boards of federal and state commissions. Title II also gave the Federal Power Commission direction to coordinate and interconnect the transmission lines in the United States, and to control sales and purchases of companies transmitting electricity in interstate commerce.

The Federal Power Commission was not a new government agency. Originally created in 1920 to be composed of members of the President's cabinet, it was reorganized in 1930 with five full-time commissioners. The original purpose had been to license the use of waters for power purposes to private companies, with the proviso that they could be purchased by the federal government. The licenses were to be in the public interest, and about all the Commission had been able to do until 1935 was to require such reports as would demonstrate proper use of the permit and to make studies of the hydroelectric power problem.

2 / Natural Gas Act of 1938. As in the case of electric service, the Natural Gas Act of 1938 gave the Federal Power Commission jurisdiction over the rates charged by companies engaged in the interstate transmission of natural gas. The reason that manufactured gas was not included was that almost all gas so produced is consumed in the city in which it is manufactured or in nearby areas and does not, normally, enter into interstate commerce. This Act added to the jurisdiction of the Federal Power Commission another important interstate public-utility operation.

▤ Regulation by Public Ownership

An activity of the federal government that is regulatory only by indirection is that of outright ownership of electric-power facilities. Within comparatively recent years the federal government has entered the business of generating electricity by constructing dams and hydroelectric plants. The Tennessee Valley Authority, created in 1933, was the first of such projects and has been followed by similar developments in the west, notably at Hoover, Bonneville, and Grand Coulee Dams. The TVA has now expanded its operations to include a generating plant using coal as its source of power and will soon have a nuclear-powered station.

The proponents of public ownership of electrical generating facilities believe that such plants can be used as a "yardstick" to show that privately owned companies charge excessive rates. Actually, the TVA and other public power projects include problems of navigation, flood control, irrigation, and control of soil erosion. The allocation of costs among these objectives has made it impossible to determine accurately the cost of the facilities devoted to producing electricity. Nevertheless, the low rates charged by the TVA have had a far-reaching effect, particularly in convincing privately owned utility companies that electricity has an elastic demand and that increased profits can be earned by selling a higher volume at a lower price.

It is interesting to observe, at this point, that public ownership of manufacturing and distributive enterprises, a characteristic of socialistic and communistic economic systems, is more prevalent in the United States in the electrical-energy field than any other area of business. Furthermore, the Congress in creating the TVA and other similar projects specified that municipalities and nonprofit cooperatives were to be given priority among its customers. Staunch advocates of capitalism view this trend with alarm and as another example of what they call "creeping socialism" in this country.

TRANSPORTATION AND COMMUNICATION

Railroads and other industries engaged in various forms of transportation have much in common with public utilities. These enterprises are a public necessity, have monopoly characteristics, represent large investments of capital, and enjoy special privileges. Consequently, their rates and services are regulated; and all of the principles of a fair return on a fair value, discussed in the preceding pages, are applied to these industries. The main distinction between public utilities and transportation companies is the predominantly interstate character of the latter with the obvious result that federal regulation is more extensive than regulation by states or municipalities. Although the communications industries are not, strictly speaking, a form of transportation, their interstate operations, except for local telephone service, have many elements in common with the transportation industries.

■ Railroad Regulation

As early as 1870 the farmers in the midwestern grain-growing states became so incensed concerning the high rates charged by the railroads that they insisted in their state legislatures that commissions be created to control these monopoly prices. State commissions, however, could regulate only intrastate transportation, and practically all railroads operated in interstate commerce. Since the federal government is the only legislative body authorized to control interstate commerce, pressure was exerted on the Congress to take appropriate action. As a result, the Interstate Commerce Act was passed in 1887. This legislation, designed to regulate the transportation of goods across state lines, represents a milestone in the history of the federal regulation of business.

The 1887 law created the Interstate Commerce Commission and gave it the right to end rate discriminations, stated that rates were to be just and reasonable, and required schedules of rates and fares to be published. It also included a *long-and-short-haul clause,* which made it illegal for a railroad to charge a higher rate for a short haul than for a long haul under substantially similar conditions. Some railroads had been charging a low competitive rate between two points served by another line, but between cities not served by another carrier they charged a high monopoly rate. Although the Commission was not given the necessary authority to enforce the provisions of the 1887 Act and several adverse court decisions further weakened the law, subsequent acts and amendments have corrected these deficiencies.

The early recognition of the public-utility characteristics of the railroads and of the need for extensive regulation of common carriers in interstate commerce has, over the years, resulted in more and more legislation expanding the scope and extent of Commission control. Currently, the Interstate Commerce Commission has extensive jurisdiction over practically all facets of railroad operations. Rates, service, valuation, security issues, consolidations, safety appliances, accounting, and many other phases of this industry are controlled by the seven commissioners, aided by a large staff of experts. Problems involving both intrastate and interstate commerce are handled cooperatively with the state commissions.

A recent concept that seems to be gaining adherents is that railroads are actually in competition with other forms of transportation and with each other to such an extent that all regulation over them should be abandoned. Furthermore, if left to their own devices, they would combine, as they have been doing anyway with slow Commission approval; and there would emerge a handful of strong companies such as dominate the automobile, steel, and numerous other industries. It is too early to predict the ultimate course of events, but in time the most heavily regulated privately owned industry may be returned to the competitive arena.

■ Motor Truck Regulation

Motor trucks engaged in interstate hauling are under the jurisdiction of the Interstate Commerce Commission, although those engaged strictly in intrastate traffic are subject only to regulation by state commissions. All of the states exercise a certain amount of control over trucks using the roads within their boundaries; that is, they regulate the length, width, height, and the gross weight of the vehicle and its contents. Safety regulations, covering the operation of motor vehicles, have been prescribed by the Interstate Commerce Commission, and the states generally follow such regulations.

The regulation of interstate trucks was first recognized as a duty of the federal government with the passage of the Motor Carrier Act of 1935. Previous to this time only state governments had regulated motor carriers, but so many interstate problems had arisen that the addition of some measure of federal control became desirable. Under this Act, the Interstate Commerce Commission assumed power over interstate motor transport carriers very similar to the extensive supervision that existed for railroads. Under provisions of a "grandfather clause" all lines in existence were allowed to continue, but new routes could not be opened until a "certificate of convenience and necessity" was secured. The extent of control varies for common, contract, and private carriers. *Common carriers* operate on regular schedules and offer service to the general public. *Contract carriers* hire their services for special hauls, such as moving household goods. Trucks and buses used by the firm owning them are known as *private carriers*. Common carriers are subject to rate and service regulations. Contract carriers must have permits and minimum rates are prescribed, while private carriers are subject merely to safety regulations.

■ Regulation of Air Transport, Water Transportation, and Pipelines

In addition to interstate traffic by rail and truck, raw materials and other types of merchandise move by air, water, and pipelines. In each of these areas an appropriate agency of the federal government regulates rates, services, and other details in a manner more or less comparable to that described for railroads. In each instance a different regulatory body is involved insofar as the controls are on an interstate level.

Air transport is subject to control by local or municipal, state, and federal agencies. The first two deal with the construction and operation of airports and regulations concerning their use. The federal regulation of air transport under the Civil Aeronautics Act of 1938, the Reorganization Act of 1939, and the Federal Aviation Act of 1958 is vested in two groups, the Civil Aeronautics Board and the Federal Aviation Agency. The Civil Aeronautics Board is empowered to prescribe reasonable rates; to remove discrimination in rates; to fix fair and reasonable rates for air mail; to prescribe routes for the airline companies; and to investigate aircraft accidents and to recommend measures to the Federal Aviation Agency for reducing accidents and preventing their recurrence. The Federal Aviation Agency is concerned with the development and safety of airports and landing fields; with the scrutiny of the methods of operation of air transport companies; and with the issuance and enforcement of safety rules and regulations.

Water transportation between the states was placed under the control of the Interstate Commerce Commission in 1940, although from its beginnings this Commission had the authority to fix rates involving joint water-rail interstate transportation. Regulation of water transportation is similar to that for motor trucks, but several types of contract and common carriers are exempt from supervision over rates. Where rates are controlled, they are usually established at a 10 to 20 percent reduction from the charges allowed the railroads for similar classes of goods.

The interstate shipment of oil by pipelines has been under the jurisdiction of the Interstate Commerce Commission since 1906. As noted earlier, however, when natural gas shipments by pipelines was placed under regulation in 1938, the authority to regulate these common carriers was given to the Federal Power Commission. Actually, most oil pipelines are owned by the companies using them even though they become common carriers on occasion by transporting oil of independents. Gas pipelines are generally owned by companies that buy natural gas at the fields and sell to companies engaged in the business of retailing to consumers. The rates charged for this transportation service are an important element in the cost of natural gas delivered to those who consume it.

■ Regulation of Communications Industries

In the areas of telegraph, interstate telephone, radio, and television, the federal government has seen fit to establish a regulatory agency with varying degrees of authority over companies engaged in these businesses. This is the Federal Communications Commission, which received most of its authority under the Communications Act of 1934.

To all intents and purposes the telegraph business in the United States is a virtual monopoly of the Western Union Telegraph Company, and the long-distance telephone lines division of the American Telephone and Telegraph Company handles practically all interstate telephone calls. The regulation of these companies by the FCC is on the same basis as prescribed for other companies allowed to attain a monopoly status. The same degree of control extends to companies engaged in interstate communication by means of cable or by radio when used for this purpose.

In the fields of commercial television and radio, since stations do not charge the public for their programs, there is no rate regulation. Rather, the Federal Communications Commission has concentrated its attention on allocating television channels and radio frequencies. Each station is licensed for three years, and must follow prescribed rules or endanger its chances of having the permit renewed. One of the problems faced by the Commission was that only twelve channels were available in the VHF (very high frequency) band, which led to station interference in some areas of the country. To solve this problem, seventy new channels were allocated space in the UHF (ultra high frequency) band. In order to make effective use of these new channels, since many TV sets could not receive UHF programs, Congress amended the Federal Communication Act specifying that, after April, 1964, all television sets manufactured had to be able to receive programs broadcast by stations using channels 2 to 83. This requirement is an interesting example of the effect regulation may have on the freedom an industry usually has regarding the products it manufactures.

BUSINESS TERMS

(a) public utility (617)
(b) franchise (620), right of eminent domain (620)
(c) stand-by equipment (623)
(d) historical costs (624), prudent historical cost (624), reproduction cost new (625)
(e) certificate of convenience and necessity (626)
(f) death sentence clause (628)
(g) long-and-short-haul clause (631)
(h) common carrier (632), contract carrier (632), private carrier (632)

QUESTIONS FOR DISCUSSION AND ANALYSIS

1. If it is in the best interests of consumers to have only one telephone company serving a community, why would it not also be preferable to have only one regulated supermarket?
2. A pure monopoly would have no competition. Does this situation exist for any or all public utilities? Discuss.
3. Does not the right of eminent domain violate the property rights of an owner? Is it necessary for government to extend this privilege to public utilities and railroads? Discuss.
4. Would it not be preferable for a state commission to have exclusive control over all public utilities operating intrastate including those whose activities are limited to a single municipality? Discuss.
5. From personal experience, do you believe the concept of a fair return on a fair value has led to inefficient management among public-utility companies? Give specific examples supporting your conclusion.
6. Is prudent historical cost less depreciation a better method of valuing a public utility than reproduction cost new less depreciation? Why?
7. The abandonment of service, particularly of passenger trains on the railroads, has been a hotly contested issue in recent years. Why should

a public utility or railroad not be allowed to discontinue any branch of its operations that loses money?

8. Why is the issue of public ownership of electrical generating facilities not just as prevalent in other public-utility areas such as, for example, natural gas?

9. Would you favor the abandonment of all regulation for railroads? Give reasons for your position on this issue.

10. The United States has five regulatory agencies that have jurisdiction one way or another over public utilities, transportation, and communication. Why would it not be preferable to have but one commission?

PROBLEMS AND SHORT CASES

1. The rates charged to resident consumers by an electric public-utility company are as follows:

First 100 kilowatt hours . . . . 5.0¢ per kilowatt hour
Next 100 kilowatt hours . . . . 4.0¢ per kilowatt hour
Next 900 kilowatt hours . . . . 3.5¢ per kilowatt hour
Additional kilowatt hours . . . . 2.5¢ per kilowatt hour
Minimum monthly rate $2.00

On the basis of the above schedule of charges, compute the amount of the monthly bill if the consumer uses the following number of kilowatt hours: (a) 35, (b) 80, (c) 160, (d) 450, (e) 2,100.

2. Prior to 1968 a locally owned electric public utility was producing its own current at an average cost of 3.4 cents a kilowatt hour based on an output of 1,000,000 kilowatt hours a month. This was being sold at an average price of 4.2 cents a kilowatt hour, and the monthly bill of the average domestic consumer was $14.70.

A public-utility holding company purchased the local company, abandoned the local generating facilities, and connected the city distribution system with long-distance transmission lines owned by another subsidiary. It charged the local company, now owned by the holding company, 2.8¢ per kilowatt hour. However, the local company was also required to use the services of a management concern owned by the holding company at a monthly cost of $15,000 in return for which it received engineering, sales, research, and accounting services.

On the basis of these facts and assuming that the local utility was entitled to the same profit in cents on the sale of each kilowatt hour it formerly earned, which had been determined to be a fair return on a fair value, what was the amount of the average domestic consumer's monthly bill after the purchase? How much of an increase or decrease did this represent? Show calculations.

3. The State Line Electric Co. has filed a rate increase application with the utility commission of a midwestern state. The company has been valued for rate-making purposes at $50,000,000 based on historical

costs, and its earnings for the past three years have averaged $2,500,-000. It is the contention of the company that it should have been allowed to earn at least $4,000,000 a year, and it also disputes the method used for valuing its facilities. It has produced detailed figures to show that its value computed on the basis of reproduction cost new less depreciation is $72,000,000.

An examination of the company's statements shows that it secured 60 percent of its capital by selling bonds that carry an interest rate of 4 percent and that do not mature for 20 years. Another 20 percent was obtained from an issue of 5 percent nonparticipating preferred stock. The company admits that, because it was organized and financed at a most favorable time for selling bonds and preferred stock, the common stockholders have been receiving generous dividends.

Lawyers for the company appearing before the commission state that the decision of the United States Supreme Court, quoted on page 622, is not being followed. They contend that, because of the optional use of gas and of industry-owned generating plants, the State Line Electric Co. is in competition for large portions of its business and that its risks and uncertainties are comparable to those of manufacturing plants located in the area. They have submitted evidence showing that these businesses have been earning, on the average, 9.6 percent on their total assets.

If you were a member of the commission involved, how would you form your opinion on this request for a rate increase? How would you vote?

SUGGESTED READINGS

Anderson, R. A. *Government and Business,* Third Edition. Cincinnati: South-Western Publishing Company, 1966. Part III.

Garfield, P. J., and W. F. Lovejoy. *Public Utility Economics.* Englewood Cliffs, New Jersey: Prentice-Hall, Inc., 1964.

Isaacs, A., and R. E. Slesinger. *Business, Government and Public Policy.* Princeton, New Jersey: D. Van Nostrand Company, Inc., 1964. Chapters 17 and 18.

Locklin, D. P. *Economics of Transportation,* Sixth Edition. Homewood, Illinois: Richard D. Irwin, Inc., 1966.

Mund, V. A. *Government and Business,* Fourth Edition. New York: Harper & Row, Publishers, 1965. Chapter 23.

Redford, E. S. *American Government and the Economy.* New York: The MacMillan Company, 1965.

Wilcox, C. *Public Policies Toward Business,* Third Edition. Homewood, Illinois: Richard D. Irwin, Inc., 1965. Part III.

Chapter 30

TAXATION AND BUSINESS

The trend in this country is for governmental units, at all levels, to spend more and more. Expenditures for national defense, space exploration, and welfare programs plus a growing public demand for services such as better roads, schools, and recreational facilities, to name a few, all contribute to higher governmental spending. The funds necessary to finance these activities must either be borrowed or secured from taxes. Although both sources are used at all levels of government, taxation accounts for a very high percentage of the total money involved. The overall burden of taxes is a heavy one and, although every person is a taxpayer either directly or indirectly, businesses carry at least their fair share of the total load.

Because taxes play such an important role in the efforts of businessmen to earn what they term "net profit after taxes," they constitute the most important relationship between business and government. It is probably safe to say that the tax effect of a contemplated course of action enters into more business decisions than any other single factor. For example, such routine matters as trading in old equipment or writing off bad debts have tax overtones as well as such major decisions as locating a new plant or choosing between issuing bonds or stock when funds are needed for expansion purposes.

This chapter, after a brief statement of some principles of taxation, will examine the taxes levied by the states and the federal government. Although in some instances the specific taxing authority involved will be named, the word "state" will be used to encompass all forms of nonfederal political units including counties, townships, cities, villages, and school districts, as well as the state proper. After the various types of taxes have been explained, some of the effects these levies have on business decisions will be discussed.

■ Principles of Taxation

The problem of enacting a suitable program of taxation for any governmental unit is most difficult. The total revenue secured should be adequate to meet necessary current expenditures. The burden should be distributed on an equitable basis. The tax law must be reasonably simple and the funds easy to collect. In some instances it may be desirable to use the tax as a means of regulation as well as revenue.

If a tax rate remains constant regardless of the size of the tax base, it is called a *proportional tax*. In a particular locality, for example, the same tax rate on the appraised value of real estate is used regardless of the amount of property owned by one person. Many fiscal experts believe that taxes should be based on the ability to pay, which calls for a system of *progressive taxation*. Income taxes are usually designed so that higher rates apply to the upper brackets of income. Likewise, inheritance and estate tax rates are higher for large estates or bequests. The opposite of a progressive tax is a *regressive tax*. Rates of regressive taxes become lower as the tax base increases in size. The cost of securing a corporation charter, when based on the number of shares authorized, involves lower rates on the shares in excess of a stated minimum.

From the businessman's point of view, the impact and incidence of taxes are important. *Impact* refers to the person who is liable for the tax and who keeps the necessary records and mails out a check in payment of the amount due. In many instances it is possible, through a process known as shifting, to pass the tax on to others, usually the final consumer. The place at which the ultimate burden falls is known as the *incidence* of the tax. A gasoline tax may be paid by the man who owns the service station but, if he is able to add this tax to the purchase price paid by the customer, he is merely serving as a collection agency for a governmental unit. If the tax cannot be shifted, the businessman must absorb the amount. If the incidence can be made to fall elsewhere, the tax, aside from the burden of record keeping, does not affect his operations except to the extent that his prices are necessarily higher.

■ Types of State Taxes

The following partial list of the taxes that are most frequently levied by the several states and their various political units will indicate the nature and extent of this relationship between business and government. Some of these are duplicated by the federal government while others are not. Although there have been some efforts to allocate different types of taxes to the various taxing units, the need for revenue is so great that a good source, such as income, is used by cities, states, and the federal government.

1. Sales taxes
2. Income taxes
3. Property taxes
4. Payroll taxes
5. Corporation taxes

6. Special business taxes
7. Inheritance and estate taxes
8. Severance taxes
9. Assessments

1 / Sales taxes. A tax on the sale of commodities or services or both, levied on consumers, is a *sales tax*. It provides the largest single source of revenue for government at the state level, and several cities and counties also make use of this source of income. Some states levy a general sales tax that applies to all, or nearly all, retail sales. A selective sales tax on such items as gasoline, cigarettes, and liquor, is found in all states.

(a) GENERAL SALES TAXES. Forty-two states and the District of Columbia have enacted some form of a general sales tax. Rates vary between 2 and 5 percent of retail prices with 3 percent used by over half of the states. City and county sales taxes vary between 1 and 3 percent. Some states allow certain exemptions, such as food purchases not consumed on the premises or sales under a minimum amount. To supplement the general sales tax, states have enacted a *use tax,* which is a sales tax on goods entering the state from another state. Out-of-state firms that are licensed to do business in a state must collect the use tax on sales to consumers even though such transactions are interstate in character.

(b) SELECTIVE SALES TAXES. The taxation of gasoline sold for consumption on the public highways is the most widely used selective sales tax as all states and the District of Columbia secure revenue from this source. Rates vary from a low of 5 cents per gallon to a high of 8 cents with more than one half of all states using a 7-cent levy. Substantial revenues are derived from this tax and, in general, these funds are used for building and improving highways, roads, and streets. Payments are made to the state, but a common practice is to return a proportion of the amount collected to the county, township, city, or village on the basis of the collections originating in the various political subdivisions.

The gasoline tax is a good example of assessing the cost of a government activity against those who use the facilities provided at government expense. From this viewpoint, it is unfortunate that some state legislatures have increased this tax burden in order to divert a portion of the funds collected to other uses such as unemployment relief or aid to schools.

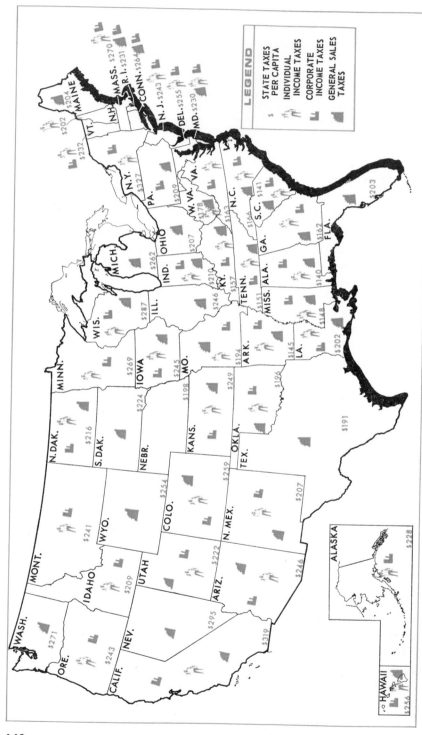

Other common examples of selective sales taxes are those on alcoholic beverages and cigarettes. All states levy a tax on alcoholic beverages and in some, where the liquor business is a state monopoly, as it is in sixteen states, profits from the operation of retail stores provide additional income. All of the states except North Carolina tax cigarettes with rates ranging from 2 cents to 11 cents per package.

(c) CITY AND COUNTY SALES TAXES. In nine states either cities or counties, or both, have also turned to a general sales tax as a means of raising additional revenue. In all cases rates are 1 or 2 percent of the value of goods sold at retail, with the exception of New York City where the rate is 3 percent. In a few cities a selective sales tax is effective on such items as gasoline, cigarettes, gas and electric bills, and beverages.

2 / Income taxes. Thirty-six states have enacted a personal income tax, and thirty-seven states tax the incomes of corporations. In several of these states income taxes are the major source of revenue although twenty-four of these states also levy sales taxes. An *income tax* is one that is levied against wages, salaries, commissions, dividends, interest, rents, and other similar sources of income to individuals and against net profits of corporations. Most states allow certain deductions and exemptions from gross income, such as $600 for each member of a family, following which rates are graduated upwards with a range of from 1 to 12 percent. For example, a person with a taxable income of $50,000 might live in a state that taxes the first $2,000 at 1 percent, the next $2,000 at 2 percent, and so on until the maximum rate applies.

In the case of corporations, the tax rate is most commonly a flat percent of all net income, such as 5 percent, although some states apply graduated rates. Foreign corporations are taxed in the same manner as domestic corporations to the extent that the income of the foreign corporation can be allocated to activities conducted within the state levying the tax.

Within recent years several cities, hard pressed for funds with which to meet rising costs of government, have also enacted income tax laws. Rates are usually 1 percent on payrolls and profits of resident individuals and firms; nonresident individuals and firms pay the same rate on wages or incomes attributable to employment or sales within the corporate limits. One of the justifications for a city income tax is that persons who use the numerous facilities provided by these municipalities are required to share in the necessary costs even though they may live in the country or in suburban areas not annexed to the city.

3 / Property taxes. *Property taxes* are levied against the value of real estate, tangible personal property, and intangibles owned by the taxpayer. Counties, cities, villages, and school districts rely on real estate taxes as their major source of revenue, and some state governments secure income from this source. Local assessors value the land and buildings, and a rate is applied against this appraised value. A rate is determined each year for all political subdivisions. The total rate might be computed at $32.48 on each $1,000 of assessed valuation. This would mean that a factory building and land valued at $500,000 for tax purposes would have an annual real estate tax of $16,240.

From a business viewpoint, a tax on tangible personal property usually includes the value of machinery, stocks of raw materials, goods in process, finished merchandise, and office, store, and factory equipment. Some localities assess the values of these tangibles in the same manner as real estate, and the same rates apply. In other taxing districts cost minus depreciation is used as a basis for valuation, and special rates that have no relationship to real estate tax rates apply against the value of tangible personal property.

An intangible personal property tax is the weakest form of the general property tax in that it is easy to conceal assets of this type. Intangibles subject to taxation include stocks, bonds, mortgages, and notes. Some states have laws that apply special rates to such values; others include intangibles in the total value of all property owned.

4 / Payroll taxes. Two types of payroll taxes may be paid by employers into the state treasury. The federal Social Security Act of 1935 provided for a nationwide plan of *unemployment insurance,* which is a program designed to pay weekly benefits to workers who are laid off and are unable to find suitable employment. The employer of four or more persons (except for exempt employment) pays a payroll tax of 3.1 percent on the first $3,000 of wages and salaries paid to employees. An amount equal to a .4 percent payroll tax goes to the federal government to cover supervisory costs. The remaining 2.7 percent is paid into the state treasury. States use such receipts to finance unemployment insurance payments to workers. In general, an employee who finds himself out of work and who is unable to locate another job can draw unemployment benefits for a stipulated number of weeks. The size of the payment and the length of time such benefits will continue vary among the several states.

Another payroll tax for *workmen's compensation,* which is a form of accident insurance for employees who are injured on the job, is compulsory in most states. Although some states permit employers to purchase a policy from a private insurance company, several states operate the fund from which such benefits are paid. The cost is assessed against the employer as a percent of his payroll, with rates that vary according to the hazard of the industry. A contractor who builds bridges and skyscrapers pays a higher rate than does a retail merchant. The subject of workmen's compensation insurance was discussed in greater detail on page 463.

5 / Corporation taxes. Various types of taxes are levied on domestic and foreign corporations as a prerequisite to organizing and conducting a business in the state under this form of business ownership. At the time a corporation secures a charter from a state, it is charged an organization tax, termed an *incorporation fee,* as was explained in Chapter 5. An *entrance tax* is similar except that it refers to a foreign corporation that wishes to conduct business in states other than the one from which it received its charter. Incorporation fees are usually based on the amount of stock authorized, and some states assess their entrance taxes on the same base. More commonly, entrance taxes are a fixed amount such as, for example, $100.

In addition to incorporation fees and entrance taxes, states levy an annual tax on both domestic and foreign corporations. The amount of the tax for domestic corporations is normally based on the amount of stock either outstanding or authorized. For foreign corporations the base may be the amount of stock owned by residents of the state, the value of the assets located within the state, or a flat fee. The annual fee levied on domestic corporations is known as a *franchise tax,* whereas for foreign corporations the term *privilege tax* is commonly used.

6 / Special business taxes. Many of the states have enacted *special business taxes* that are levied against the incomes of businesses in selected industries. The most common ones chosen for these special taxes are insurance companies, railroads, public utilities, and banks. Less frequently, taxes in this classification are levied against railroad terminals, express companies, mining companies, lumber producers, and grain elevators.

The customary method of taxing insurance companies is to levy a gross premium assessment of 2 percent. All premiums collected within the state are subject to this rate regardless of whether the company is organized under the laws of the state or of another state, although some laws favor domestic corporations. Before a company can sell policies within the state, it must be licensed and agree to pay the tax applicable. Sometimes the amount is payable to the county, village, or city, although most states provide for central collection.

Banks, both state and federal, in addition to paying taxes on all property owned, are frequently taxed on the basis of total deposits on hand at a specific date. This type of tax may also apply to other financial institutions, such as savings and loan associations.

Railroads, whether interstate or intrastate, are frequently taxed on the regular real estate basis. This means that the value of the property in each state must be determined, which is a difficult problem. In order to lessen these complications, some states tax the railroads on the basis of the gross earnings. Even this method is cumbersome, because it becomes necessary to apportion the earnings among the several states in which the railroad may operate.

Public utilities are usually taxed on the basis of gross earnings. Many utilities confine their operations within the borders of a particular state, which eliminates the interstate problems faced in the taxation of most railroads. For those that cross state lines, the problems of allocation are involved. The taxes are determined on the basis of volume of business in the state or by calculating the pro rata share of assets owned in the state.

Another type of a special business tax is based on the occupation in which the business is engaged rather than on its income. These taxes are more prevalent in the southern states and are usually restricted to such industries as the manufacture and wholesale distribution of malted drinks, bottling companies, and the manufacture and wholesale distribution of tobacco products. Chain-store taxes, when based on the number of stores in the chain, are also an example of a special business tax based on occupation.

7 / Inheritance and estate taxes. Both estate and inheritance taxes are levies against the wealth passed on to heirs by a deceased person. They are frequently called *death duties*. The difference between the two is that *estate taxes* are assessed against the entire net value of the holdings formerly belonging to the deceased, while *inheritance taxes* are based upon the separate bequests made to individual heirs. Inheritance tax rates usually vary depending upon the directness of descent; for example, widows and children pay a lower rate than do nephews and grandchildren.

All states except one levy inheritance and/or estate taxes. Because the rates vary in the several states, businessmen have sometimes found it advantageous to transfer their holdings and legal residences to a more favorable state prior to the time at which they expect to die.

8 / Severance taxes. A *severance tax* is a fee levied upon the owner of timberland or mineral deposits whenever the timber is cut or the minerals are removed from the ground. It is the fairest way of taxing these items. If a real estate tax is assessed against timberlands on which trees are being allowed to mature, a pressure is brought on the owner to conduct logging operations in order to raise enough money to pay the taxes. This is contrary to rules of conservation. If a severance tax is imposed, the owner can pay the state a fair amount in the years in which profits would be available.

9 / **Assessments.** Although assessments are purely a local problem and should not be classed as a tax, the general effect is the same as a tax. An *assessment* is for government services presumed to be of direct benefit to the property owner involved. Ordinary real estate taxes usually support the fire department, police, schools, parks, and other municipal functions, whereas a special assessment is made for building a sidewalk, highway, or sewer system available to a particular property owner. This type of improvement is supposed to add to the value of the property, which is the justification for taxing, or more properly, assessing those who benefit from the improvement. A $1,000 unimproved lot might easily be worth $2,000 after the street on which it faces is paved, sidewalks are laid, and a sewer connection is available.

■ **Types of Federal Taxes**

The federal government in recent years has been spending more than $100 billion annually. Practically all of the funds necessary to support these high levels of expenditures have come from tax receipts. An examination of the types of taxes levied by the federal government will indicate the sources from which billions of dollars are collected each year as well as the relative importance of the various bases used. In order to aid in an understanding of these taxes, specific rates will be used; but it should be kept in mind that these rates are subject to change at each legislative session of the Congress as are, for that matter, the sources from which tax revenues are obtained.

1. Income taxes
2. Excise taxes
3. Employment taxes
4. Estate and gift taxes
5. Communications and transportation taxes
6. Miscellaneous taxes
7. Customs duties

1 / **Income taxes.** Income taxes are levied on the gross receipts of individuals not engaged in business as sole proprietors or partners, and on the net profits of all businesses including proprietorships, partnerships,

and corporations. They comprise the largest single source of revenue for the federal government. In recent years income taxes have produced receipts in excess of $78 billion annually, which is more than two thirds of federal income from all tax sources. Of this huge sum, individuals pay approximately two thirds and corporations the remaining one third. The rates and methods of computation vary considerably between individuals and corporations and will be discussed separately.

(a) PERSONAL INCOME TAX. Every citizen or resident of the United States, whether an adult or minor, who has an annual income in excess of a prescribed amount (in 1966 it was $600 for a person under 65 and $1,200 for an individual 65 or over) must file a tax return and may be liable for taxes on his income. This income includes money received from such sources as wages, dividends, interest, sale of property, and the net profit from a business or profession. Sole proprietorships and partnerships that are engaged in any form of business have their net income taxed on the basis of such profits forming all or a part of the income of the individuals concerned. Also, the owners of close corporations having ten or fewer stockholders may elect to be taxed in the same manner as if the firm were organized as a partnership.

All individuals are entitled to a personal exemption and are also allowed to deduct certain nonbusiness expenses such as interest paid, charitable contributions, most state and local taxes, and medical expenses when these exceed certain stated amounts. A taxpayer is also allowed an exemption for his wife if a joint return is filed and for each child who had less than $600 gross income or was under 19 years of age or was a student. Exemptions may also be claimed for relatives and for persons living in the taxpayer's home if more than one half of their support was furnished by said taxpayer. In 1966 the allowance for each exemption claimed was $600, which would have entitled a married taxpayer with three young children to $3,000 in exemptions.

One of the merits of the personal income tax is the application of the principle of "ability to pay." This is accomplished by levying progressively higher rates on each unit, known as a *tax bracket,* of taxable income. The first four tax brackets for married taxpayers filing joint returns are $1,000 each, the next ten brackets are $4,000 each, and higher brackets include larger amounts. Rates in 1966 for these taxpayers started at 14 percent for the first $1,000 of taxable income, increased 1 percent for each of the next three brackets, and continued upward at an accelerated rate until the maximum rate of 70 percent on incomes in excess of $200,000 was reached. Rates for single taxpayers, married persons filing separate returns, and taxpayers unmarried who qualify as the head of a household are somewhat different from those applying to married taxpayers filing joint returns although tax brackets are used for all classifications.

Individuals who are married are permitted to allocate one half of the taxable income to the wife and one half to the husband regardless of which one produced the revenue. Since the rates increase with each tax bracket, the tax liability is usually less for married couples who have over $500 in taxable income if the so-called "split-income" feature is used, which is reflected in the rates given above. The reason for this is that each is allowed up to $500 in the first bracket, which means that the second bracket of 15 percent does not apply until income is in excess of $1,000. Single taxpayers pay 14 percent on the first $500 of taxable income and 15 percent on the second $500. Separate returns for married persons are permissible, however, and in a few instances will provide a lower total tax.

An illustration of the actual tax calculation of a businessman and his wife will show the application of 1966 rates on 1965 income. Mr. Albert Dunham operates a hardware store and also owns a one-third interest in a garage that was purchased by a partnership. The income statement for the store showed a net income of $31,840 and the partnership return allocated $9,375 to Mr. Dunham as his share of the profits earned by the garage. In addition, Mrs. Dunham received interest income from accounts in savings banks and savings and loan associations and from investments in United States bonds totaling, in all, $7,335. These items constituted their entire income. Mr. and Mrs. Dunham have one son enrolled in college and a daughter attending high school. The calculation of their income, exemptions and deductions, and tax is as follows:

Income from hardware store		$31,840.00
Share of profits from partnership		9,375.00
Interest income		7,335.00
Total income		$48,550.00
Exemptions, 4 at $600 each	$2,400.00	
Deductions for contributions, etc.	1,000.00	
Total exemptions and deductions		3,400.00
Taxable income		$45,150.00
Computation of tax: (Married Taxpayer's Table)		
Tax on $44,000.00		$14,060.00
Excess over $44,000.00 ($1,150.00 at 50%)		575.00
Total tax on $45,150.00		$15,635.00

Personal income taxes were placed on a pay-as-you-go plan as early as 1943. Employers are required to withhold a portion of each salary or wage payment and, if the employee has no other source of income, these deductions approximate his total annual tax liability. Persons, such as Mr. and Mrs. Dunham who receive taxable income from sources other than salaries and wages are required to estimate their total tax a year in advance and make quarterly payments thereon. These payments are due on April 15, June 15, September 15, and January 15 of the following year. If profit or income prospects change during the year, an amended declaration can be made.

The individual income tax is far more involved than this discussion might indicate. The computation of net profits from businesses, the taxation of capital gains and losses, a tax credit against dividends received, and allowable deductions for persons not using the standard deduction are just a few of the complications that face many taxpayers. Penalties for failure to report the correct amount of income and to pay the tax thereon may result in severe monetary penalties as well as the possibility of a prison sentence.

(b) CORPORATION INCOME TAXES. Corporations engaged in industry or trade are subject to two rates known as normal taxes and surtaxes. These rates on profits earned in 1966 were 22 percent and 26 percent, respectively. The 26 percent surtax rate did not apply to the first $25,000 of taxable net income, which supplied some relief for the small corporation. Larger corporations do not benefit to any great extent from the lower normal tax as, for example, the tax on $1,000,000 of net income amounts to $473,500.

Beginning with income earned in 1955, corporations were required to make a prepayment of one half of their tax liability in excess of $100,000, which was a start toward placing corporations on a pay-as-you-go basis. As amended in 1964, this provision of the law provided for gradual increases each year until by 1970 one fourth of the estimated tax in excess of $100,000 will be payable on the 15th of April, June, September, and December. Payment of the first $100,000 of income taxes continues to be payable in two installments on March 15 and June 15 following the taxable year.

Some types of corporations do not pay a tax and others, such as life insurance companies and savings and loan associations, pay on a different schedule of rates. Examples of corporations that are exempt from the federal income tax are labor organizations; fraternal societies; religious, charitable, scientific, literary, or educational corporations; and other corporations that are operated on a nonprofit basis. If profits are earned, these may not be distributed to individual shareholders or to members in

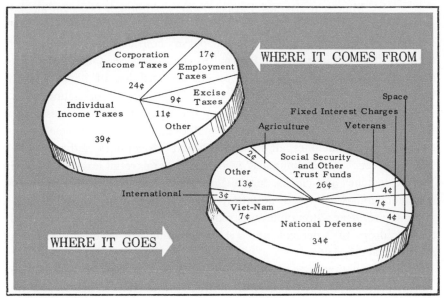

Source: *Statistical Abstract of the United States*, 1966.

Federal Budget Dollar

the case of nonstock corporations. Most tax exempt corporations are required to file an information return, which is examined to make sure that they are entitled to their favored status.

2 / Excise taxes. An *excise tax* is a duty levied on the manufacture, sale, or consumption of goods within the country. Such taxes are similar to selective sales taxes as only certain products are subject to the tax; but they differ from sales taxes in that the impact of the tax, under the current tax law, is on the manufacturer. Excise taxes constitute an important source of federal revenue with annual collections exceeding $12 billion. The levies on alcohol, tobacco, gasoline, and automobiles produce the major portion of this revenue. The different types of excise taxes that are levied by the federal government can be classified as alcohol and tobacco taxes and manufacturers' excise taxes, although this division into two categories is somewhat arbitrary.

(a) ALCOHOL AND TOBACCO TAXES. Taxes on the production of alcoholic beverages total over $3½ billion each year, and the taxation of tobacco products yields more than $2 billion annually. Rates are high in relation to selling prices, e.g., the federal tax on a package of cigarettes is 8 cents. The taxes on alcoholic beverages include all forms of distilled spirits, wines, and beer. Tobacco products taxed are cigarettes and cigars.

(b) MANUFACTURERS' EXCISE TAXES. Although taxes on alcohol and tobacco qualify as manufacturers' excise taxes, their importance as a source of federal revenue warrants separate consideration, which is in accord with the practice of the Internal Revenue Service. Other such taxes are collected from manufacturers on an assorted list of items, usually based on their selling prices or at so much per gallon or pound.

In 1965 the Congress repealed a long list of manufacturers' excise taxes that had been levied on such items as phonograph records, musical instruments, business machines, air conditioners and refrigerators, and radios and television sets. Also eliminated were the federal retail excise taxes on jewelry, watches and clocks, furs, luggage, and cosmetics. On other items rate reductions were voted, i.e., the 10 percent levy on the manufacturer's price of passenger automobiles was reduced to 7 percent; on April 1, 1968, the rate drops to 2 percent; and a 1 percent rate will be effective on and after January 1, 1969.

An examination of the following schedule of rates in effect in 1967 will indicate the types of manufactured articles that the Congress did not remove from the list of articles subject to an excise tax as well as the tax burden borne by these goods.

> Items taxed at 10 percent of the manufacturer's sales price are tractors for highway use with trailer or semitrailer, a bus or truck chassis or body, truck and bus type trailer and semitrailer chassis or body, pistols, revolvers, and fishing equipment. An 11 percent rate applies to other firearms as well as shells and cartridges, an 8 percent rate to truck parts and accessories, and 7 percent on passenger car chassis or body. Rates levied on weight or quantity are 4 cents a gallon on gasoline and other fuels, 6 cents per gallon on lubricating oil, 10 cents per pound on inner tubes and highway type tires, and 5 cents per pound on other types of tires and tread rubber.

3 / Employment taxes. Each employer and each employee affected by the Federal Insurance Contributions Act must pay a tax on wages paid or received in order to provide for old-age, survivor's, and disability insurance benefits and for medicare. Rates effective for 1967 and 1968 are 4.4 percent on both employer and employee on wages paid or received up to a maximum of $6,600. These contributions will increase to 4.9 percent for the years 1969-1972. Self-employed persons are subject to special rates amounting to 6.4 percent and 7.1 percent for the years indicated above. In addition, as mentioned earlier, .4 percent on the first $3,000 paid to covered employees for unemployment insurance goes to the federal government. Employment taxes provided over $17 billion in receipts for the federal government in 1965 and will rise sharply beginning in 1967.

4 / Estate and gift taxes. The federal government did not enter the field of estate taxation until 1926, and the first gift tax law was enacted in 1934. These laws complement each other in that it is no longer possible to avoid estate taxes by gifts made prior to death. Despite the fact that there is an exemption of $30,000 for gift tax purposes, plus $3,000 each year to any number of donees, and an exemption of $60,000 for estates, these two taxes produce a sizable amount of revenue each year.

Gift tax rates start at 2¼ percent and increase, by brackets, to a high of 57¾ percent on taxable amounts in excess of $10 million. The estate tax rate is 3 percent for the first bracket and reaches a high of 77 percent at the $10 million level. The effect of these taxes is to make it almost impossible for large concentrations of wealth to remain in one family for many generations. This leveling factor provides a contrast between the distribution of wealth in the United States and many South American and European countries. In these lands it has long been the right of the eldest son, under the doctrine of primogeniture, to inherit the whole of his father's estate without regard for the fact that there may be a number of younger children in the family.

5 / Communications and transportation taxes. Local and toll telephone service and teletypewriter service are taxed at 10 percent, but this rate is scheduled to be reduced to 1 percent after March 31, 1968, and will expire on January 1, 1969. The transportation of persons by air is subject to a 5 percent tax on the cost of the ticket purchased.

6 / Miscellaneous taxes. In searching for suitable sources of revenue, the federal government has singled out a number of miscellaneous sources on which taxes are levied. Motor vehicles are charged $3 for each 1,000 pounds of weight in excess of 26,000 pounds. Wagers placed with book-makers and lottery operators are subject to a 10 percent tax, and persons accepting wagers must pay a fee of $50 each year. Occupational taxes are assessed against brewers and rectifiers of distilled spirits, retail and wholesale dealers in liquor and beer, and fairs, outings, etc., selling beer or wine must pay a fee of $2.20 a month.

In some instances a tax seems to have been levied primarily for purposes of regulation rather than income, in which case it is known as a *regulatory tax*. An example of such a tax is an annual tax of $250 for all slot machines. If states and the federal government did not derive such substantial amounts of revenue from liquor and tobacco taxes, these levies would also provide examples of regulatory taxes. Although in our affluent society the regulatory features of high taxes on liquor and tobacco products seem ineffective, it is probable that retail prices that are approximately double what they would otherwise be do have an effect on the consumption of these items.

7 / Customs duties. *Customs duties,* commonly called tariffs, are taxes levied on the importation of foreign goods. Unlike all of the federal taxes described above, they do not constitute a part of the internal revenue system of the United States and are not supervised by the Internal Revenue Service. Congress enacts separate legislation on customs duties, and the collection of these taxes is under the jurisdiction of the Bureau of Customs of the Treasury Department.

All importations of merchandise from sources outside the United States are either on the free list or subject to duties. Goods of the types that are not grown, mined, or made in this country are frequently permitted to enter the country tax free. Coffee is a good example of a commodity on the free list. Other goods that compete with goods produced in this country are charged a tax, which discourages imports or at least affords protection to local producers against lower prices for the foreign goods. The import rate of 7 cents a pound on butter is obviously protective in nature. Foreign insurance policies as well as deeds conveying property (until January 1, 1968) are taxed by requiring that documentary stamps be attached to the contracts.

During the early history of the United States, the receipts from customs duties were considered a major source of income to the federal government. More recently, newer forms of tax legislation have overshadowed the receipts from this source, even though the amount collected has grown in total. At present the receipts from customs duties approximate one and one-half billion dollars annually. The subject of tariffs, including levies for protection and for revenue, was discussed in Chapter 11.

■ Taxation and Business Decisions

Taxation plays an important part in numerous business decisions to say nothing of the record-keeping expense involved. Although only a few of the many areas will be covered, the following illustrations and problems may serve to point up the complexities of the tax problem. Because of their outstanding importance in business decision making, the discussion of tax problems will be centered about federal income taxes and state taxes.

1 / Federal income taxes and business decisions. When new capital is to be raised, every corporation must consider the desirability of selling bonds instead of stock. Interest on bonds is a legitimate business expense, whereas dividends on stock are considered a distribution of profits after taxes. If the corporation is in the 48 percent bracket, which is the tax rate on taxable incomes over $25,000, the advantage of securing this interest deduction is obvious.

Small corporations that cannot qualify to be taxed as a partnership might well consider the tax-saving advantage of changing to this form of ownership.

Most businesses have some flexibility in allocating income to one year or another. Depreciation charges, the write-off of worthless accounts, selling machinery or investments, and even sales can be routed to the year that seems better taxwise. Contributions to charitable and educational organizations, bonuses to employees, and payments to pension plans are policies that must be examined in light of their reduced cost when taxes are considered.

In recent years many corporations have given key employees stock options in order to induce them to remain with the company. If members of top management are receiving a salary that places them in the high brackets of the income tax on individuals, further increases are of little value since most of the added salary will be taxed away. When stock options are granted and the price of the shares goes up, the employee has either built up an estate or he can sell the stock and pay the 25 percent capital-gains rate.

2 / State taxes and business decisions. One of the obvious local tax problems is that of plant location. Other factors in location are also important, but the tax rates in a state may well determine the final decision. Corporations are interested in states that do not have an income tax and in a county or township where property taxes are relatively low. If a retail product is involved and the proposed location is near a state line, the tax structure of the adjacent state is important. Only a few miles may separate two towns but, if the gasoline tax is 5 cents a gallon in one state and 8 cents a gallon in the other, it might not be wise to open a filling station in the high tax state.

In recent years states have enacted use taxes to supplement their sales taxes. If a business has an outlet and is licensed to do business in these states, it must collect the use tax on shipments even though these are in interstate commerce. Firms that are not registered with the state generally do not pay use taxes, and states cannot bar shipments that cross state lines. A business may well find it costly to open sales or branch offices in states that enforce their use taxes.

PROFESSIONAL ASSOCIATION IN TAXATION

The National Tax Association, which was organized in 1907, is a nonprofit organization devoted to promoting the scientific study of taxation and public finance. It welcomes individual as well as corporate members. Publications include the quarterly *National Tax Journal* as well as the *Proceedings* of an annual conference. Annual dues for students in recognized institutions of higher learning, which entitle the member to all publications, are $12.50 a year.

BUSINESS TERMS

(a) proportional tax (638), progressive taxation (638), regressive tax (638)
(b) impact, (638), incidence (638)
(c) sales tax (639), use tax (639), income tax (641), property tax (642)
(d) unemployment insurance (642), workmen's compensation (642)
(e) incorporation fee (643), entrance tax (643), franchise tax (643), privilege tax (643)
(f) special business taxes (643)
(g) death duties (644), estate taxes (644), inheritance taxes (644)
(h) severance tax (644)
(i) assessment (645)
(j) tax bracket (646)
(k) excise tax (649)
(l) regulatory tax (651)
(m) customs duties (652)

QUESTIONS FOR DISCUSSION AND ANALYSIS

1. Do businesses carry more than their fair share of the total tax burden, both state and federal? Give reasons for your opinion on this controversial issue.
2. Is a progressive tax more equitable than a proportional tax? Should those who have more be required to pay more? Why?
3. Theoretically, income taxes cannot be shifted. Is this true or do businesses, particularly corporations, charge higher prices in order to earn a satisfactory "net profit after taxes"? Give reasons for your answer.
4. Although sales taxes are levied on a proportional basis, they are considered to constitute a greater burden to low-income families than to high income families. Why is this so? Explain?
5. Why do most counties, townships, cities, villages, and school districts rely so extensively on property taxes as their major source of income? If this type of tax is satisfactory to these political subdivisions, why is not this base used by all states and the federal government?
6. Income taxes provide an illustration of a source of tax revenue used by cities, counties, states, and the federal government. Would it not

be preferable to restrict each taxing authority to separate and distinct bases on which to levy taxes? Give reasons for your answer.

7. In the United States most taxpayers seem willing to pay their taxes even though, as is particularly true for the federal income tax, the amount involved is frequently substantial. What reasons can be given for this compliance, which is reputed to be in contrast with the attitude prevailing in many other countries?

8. Why does the federal government collect manufacturers' excise taxes on some items and not on others, i.e., fishing equipment and firearms but not other sporting goods? Do you see any logic in the items selected for this type of taxation?

9. Why should customs duties not carry a larger share of the total federal tax burden? Would you advocate higher tariffs?

10. Would our private enterprise system function better if so many business decisions were not influenced by tax considerations? Give reasons for your answer.

PROBLEMS AND SHORT CASES

1. The Keltner Arms Company manufactures a line of shotguns, revolvers, pistols, and ammunition. The finished products are produced in factories located in the United States, but some raw materials and parts arc imported. The company employs 6,200 workmen. Sales are made throughout the world by company salesmen and company representatives, branch offices are located in all states, and retail stores are operated in a few large cities.

   Itemize the different types of state and federal taxes this firm would be likely to incur.

2. During the last calendar year Mr. Roscoe Gilcrist earned a net profit of $16,400 from his business as a manufacturer's agent. In addition he received $1,200 for his services as a member of the City Council, $600 for serving on the board of directors of a local bank, and $780 in interest on money deposited in a savings and loan association.

   Mr. Gilcrist is married and has five young children. Allowing a $600 exemption for each person in the family and $1,000 for charitable contributions, personal taxes, and other deductions, how much income tax will Mr. Gilcrist owe the federal government at the time of filing his return? He has already paid $2,500 on a pay-as-you-go basis.

   Use the appropriate rate from the ones listed below and follow the form on page 647.

MARRIED TAXPAYER'S TABLE

Taxable Income	Amount of Tax
Over $ 8,000 but not over $12,000	$1,380 plus 22% of excess over $ 8,000
Over $12,000 but not over $16,000	$2,260 plus 25% of excess over $12,000
Over $16,000 but not over $20,000	$3,260 plus 28% of excess over $16,000

3. At a session that lasted most of one night, the legislature of a state, in a rebellious mood against the governor, took action to repeal all taxes that produced revenue for the state. The next day responsible legislators realized that this situation was intolerable, but they also recognized an opportunity to enact a tax law that would be an improvement over the former patchwork series of laws. It was decided by leaders of the legislature that, while adequate income for the state was a necessity, the new law should take into account the federal tax system and also the taxes currently levied by local governmental units to support their functions.

You are called in as a tax consultant to a legislative committee appointed for the purpose of recommending a new law to the state legislature. What would be your recommendations, and what reasons would you advance for each type of tax selected?

SUGGESTED READINGS

Due, J. F. *Government Finance: An Economic Analysis,* Third Edition. Homewood, Illinois: Richard D. Irwin, Inc., 1963.

Goode, R. *The Individual Income Tax.* Washington, D. C.: Brookings Institution, 1964.

Groves, H. M. *Financing Government,* Sixth Edition. New York: Holt, Rinehart and Winston, Inc., 1964.

Maxwell, J. A. *Financing State and Local Governments.* Washington, D. C.: The Brookings Institution, 1965.

Netzer, D. *Economics of the Property Tax.* Washington, D. C.: Brookings Institution, 1965.

Niswonger, C. R., and P. E. Fess. *Accounting Principles,* Ninth Edition. Cincinnati: South-Western Publishing Company, 1965. Chapter 24.

Pechman, J. A. *Federal Tax Policy.* Washington, D. C.: The Brookings Institution, 1966.

Schultz, W. J., and C. L. Harriss. *American Public Finance,* Eighth Edition. Englewood Cliffs, New Jersey: Prentice-Hall, Inc., 1965. Part III.

Sharp, A. M., and B. F. Sliger. *Public Finance.* Homewood, Illinois: The Dorsey Press, 1964.

Comprehensive Cases

CASE 1—BOZART METAL COMPANY

On May 8, 1967, at a rather informal meeting of the board of directors, John Petersen had been appointed President of the Bozart Metal Company. Two weeks earlier, his father-in-law, Albert Zarzar, who had served as President since 1945, had died while on a sales trip.

John Petersen had worked for Bozart Metal for ten years. He joined the company in 1957, three years after he was graduated from college during which time he had been employed by a firm of certified public accountants. A major consideration in his taking the position of Assistant Controller at that time had been the fact that James Boscam, Controller-Treasurer, was 64 years of age. In 1960 he married Joan Zarzar, Albert Zarzar's only daughter. A year later, James Boscam retired and John Petersen was elected Vice-President for Finance.

The Bozart Metal Company had been founded in Fort Wayne, Indiana, as a partnership for the cutting, bending, and plating of steel tubing. It operated as a job shop for furniture and toy manufacturers. The original capital investment was $21,000 divided equally among James Boscam, Albert Zarzar, and Paul Thomas.

In 1945 Albert Zarzar obtained two major sales contracts. The first was from the Southern Furniture Company for production of chrome-plated chair frames and dinette table legs. The second was from the Chicago Restaurant Supply Corporation for barstool parts. The partnership was converted to a corporation. Three thousand shares of $10 par value common stock were issued. The original shareholders were:

James Boscam	700 shares	Roger Johnson	400 shares
Albert Zarzar	700 shares	Pietro Cellini	300 shares
Paul Thomas	700 shares	Josiah Collins	100 shares
		Lila Baker	100 shares

Roger Johnson was President of the Southern Furniture Company; Pietro Cellini was President of the Chicago Restaurant Supply Company; and Josiah Collins and Lila Baker were long-time employees, having joined the company shortly after it was founded. These individuals were permitted to purchase their shares at $25 each ($10 of this amount was credit to the capital stock account and $15 to paid-in surplus). The

657

partners accepted 700 shares each, reflecting their original investments, even though their partnership accounts had grown to $37,000 each.

In 1954 the company agreed to buy back the stock of Paul Thomas at book value. In return for the stock, the company agreed to give Thomas half of the value of the stock in cash and the balance in a 10-year note bearing 8 percent annual interest. In 1964 the last installment on the note was paid. The treasury stock is shown on the balance sheet as a subtraction from the value of the original 3,000 shares issued.

The first board of directors consisted of the original shareholders. When Pietro Cellini died in 1952 and when Paul Thomas sold his stock to the corporation, no one was elected to replace these men on the board. Under the terms of his will, the shares purchased by Pietro Cellini were transferred on the books of the company to his widow, who is still living.

At the board meeting that appointed John Petersen as President, the following were present: James Boscam, who had flown in from Arizona for the meeting; Mrs. Albert Zarzar, the former president's widow; and Lila Baker, who had always performed the secretarial duties at the annual meetings. Mr. Zarzar's will, which had been read but not probated, provided that 100 of his shares were to be distributed to his widow and 200 shares each to his daughter Joan, his son-in-law John Petersen, and his son George.

Marketing

The Bozart Metal Company had enjoyed steadily increasing sales since 1945. In the next 20 years, sales had grown from $701,000 to $1,930,000 in 1965. Sales for 1966 were $2,001,000 and the expected sales for 1967 were $2,100,000.

For the past three years the distribution of sales, by customer, had been approximately as follows:

Southern Furniture Company	45%
Chicago Restaurant Supply Corp.	8%
Toy manufacturers	20%
Kitchen appliances distributors	12%
Hospital supply houses	5%
Job shop orders and subcontracts to defense companies	10%

Typically, sales to the Southern Furniture Company constituted 43 to 48 percent of sales. Sales to the Chicago Restaurant Supply Corporation were almost constant in amount each year, averaging $165,000 for five years. Other categories of sales were subject to large annual variations.

One of Albert Zarzar's skills was his ability to find new customers to counter-balance declines in orders from other customers. For example, the trip during which Mr. Zarzar had died was for the purpose of exploring a new market in the event the Cellini estate decided to liquidate the Chicago Restaurant Supply Corporation.

While Mr. Zarzar was the chief salesman for the company, he was assisted by three manufacturer's representatives; by his only son George; and by William Collins, the son of Josiah Collins. George Zarzar is 32 years of age and holds the position of Purchasing Agent for the company; he, however, spends a portion of his time in making sales contacts. William Collins works in the factory under his father. He is 26 years of age and is a sports car enthusiast. As a result of his hobby, he has regularly brought to the company job shop orders for the chrome-plating of automotive parts.

Production

The production process of the company is simple: (1) raw strip steel is processed into tubes; (2) the tubes are buffed to remove welded spots; (3) the buffed tube is cut to desired lengths; (4) the cut tube is bent into the desired shape; (5) the bent tube is pierced at specified locations; (6) surface irregularities are removed; (7) the pieces are then nickel- or chrome-plated; and (8) the pieces are wrapped and shipped.

The equipment of the company varies from the most modern to that which is 20 or more years old. A substantial amount of new machinery was purchased six years ago to handle the need for more production. The cost of this equipment was financed by signing a mortgage note that was repaid in 1966. Four full-time skilled repairmen maintain and rebuild the equipment.

The company employs 103 workers, most of whom are unskilled or semiskilled. Twenty-two of the factory employees are women, engaged chiefly in wrapping and packaging operations. Eighty-two employees have been with the company for more than five years.

There is no formal program of inspection or quality control. Each foreman is responsible for the quality of output of his department.

Personnel Policies

The factory employees are not unionized. Albert Zarzar believed there was no need for a union in any company that provided continuous employment at the going community wage rate supplemented by a profit-sharing plan.

When the company was started in 1940, Albert Zarzar told the employees: "We are all in this together. If we make a go of this company, no one should be out of work. Unless you're a drunkard or a thief, you've got a job for life." Since no one was laid off during the first five years of operations, he later told the employees at a dinner celebrating the formation of the corporation: "We've all had our probation. Our new employees will do the same. During the first five years they will be on probation. When times get rough, they'll be laid off. But you, who have passed the probation, and the others that follow, after their probation, will not be laid off."

Every year in March, James Boscam used to make a survey of wage rates in Fort Wayne and then posted it on the bulletin board. The posted rates became the rates for the jobs in the company for the next year. When John Petersen succeeded Mr. Boscam, he continued this practice.

Each year in January the company posted its financial statements on the bulletin board. Mr. Zarzar attached to it his letter explaining that 15 percent of net operating income would be divided among the employees in proportion to their annual earnings. The profit share for each employee was then computed and a check for the proper amount mailed to his home, together with an explanatory letter.

Organization

The company had never prepared an organization chart. Albert Zarzar and James Boscam had both agreed that it seemed unnecessary. A chart would "freeze" people to jobs and duties. The need for a growing, competitive firm was flexibility. "A man should pitch in and do anything he can. Teamwork, not a fixed job, is the key to flexibility."

The Board of Directors

Albert Zarzar had been quite blunt about the role of the board of directors. After Paul Thomas had been bought out, he stated: "Boscam and I are the major shareholders and, inasmuch as we operate the company, the board can be nothing but a rubber stamp."

John Petersen knew he could not operate in the manner of Albert Zarzar with respect to the board. It was his opinion that any board of directors should be an active one. Moreover, unless the board fully understood the plans and operations of the business, there would be pressure for dividend payments. The company had not declared a dividend since 1960, primarily because it seemed necessary to conserve cash. Prior to 1960, a regular rate of $3 a share per annum had been maintained.

Finance

The books and other financial records of the company are, in Mr. Petersen's view, in excellent order. The last certified financial statements are shown below:

Balance Sheets
Bozart Metal Company
December 31, 1965, and December 31, 1966

ASSETS	1965	1966
Current Assets		
Cash	$ 66,000	$ 32,000
Accounts Receivable (net)	152,000	135,000
Inventories	292,000	333,000
Prepaid Expenses	9,000	9,900
Total Current Assets	$ 519,000	$ 509,900
Plant Assets		
Machinery and Equipment (net)	$ 527,000	$ 531,000
Building (net)	136,000	129,400
Land	8,400	8,400
Total Plant Assets	$ 671,400	$ 668,800
TOTAL ASSETS	$1,190,400	$1,178,700
LIABILITIES		
Current Liabilities		
Notes Payable	$ 108,000	$ 38,000
Accounts Payable	120,000	132,000
Total Current Liabilities	$ 228,000	$ 170,000
Long-Term Liabilities		
Mortgage Payable	$ 130,000	$........
TOTAL LIABILITIES	$ 358,000	$ 170,000
CAPITAL		
Capital Stock—3,000 Shares Issued	$ 30,000	$ 30,000
Less: Treasury Stock	7,000	7,000
Issued and Outstanding	$ 23,000	$ 23,000
Paid-in Surplus	73,500	73,500
Retained Earnings	735,900	912,200
TOTAL CAPITAL	$ 832,400	$1,008,700
TOTAL LIABILITIES AND CAPITAL ..	$1,190,400	$1,178,700

Income Statements

Bozart Metal Company

For Years Ended December 31, 1965, and December 31, 1966

	1965	1966
Sales (net)	$1,930,000	$2,001,000
Cost of Goods Manufactured and Sold	1,448,000	1,498,000
Gross Profit on Sales	$ 482,000	$ 503,000
Operating Expenses	96,000	119,000
Net Income from Operations	$ 386,000	$ 384,000
Profit Sharing	57,900	57,600
Net Income Before Income Tax	$ 328,100	$ 326,400
Federal Tax on Income	151,000	150,100
Net Income After Income Tax	$ 177,100	$ 176,300

On the basis of the foregoing information and any reasonable assumptions consistent with the known facts, what problems are facing John Petersen and what should he do about them? Your solution to this case should provide answers to the following questions as well as any others that may seem relevant.

1. What should Petersen do about the board of directors? Should he take steps to be elected rather than appointed as president? Considering the fact that there are only eight shareholders, is the corporation the best form of ownership for this business?

2. Is an organization structure needed? If so, what type should be recommended? Construct a chart to show a specific proposal that might be adopted.

3. Should new sales policies be adopted? If so, how should they be carried out?

4. Should new products be developed? What particular new product lines should be investigated?

5. Should the company modify the current personnel policies?

6. What are the financial strengths and weaknesses of the company? How can the weaknesses be overcome? Considering the fact that half of the shareholders are not on the company payroll, should dividend payments be resumed?

CASE 2—FARR SOAP COMPANY

In 1930 a chemist, Dr. G. W. Farr, who had been employed for the past five years by a manufacturing firm in St. Louis, Missouri, became acquainted with Dr. R. S. Endicott, a local surgeon. Dr. Endicott complained that he was dissatisfied with the antiseptic soaps available for hospital use, and asked Dr. Farr why a more satisfactory product could not be compounded. The problem intrigued Dr. Farr and, after two years of experimentation in a laboratory he had equipped at his own expense in the basement of his home, he developed a liquid soap that proved to have unusual germicidal properties.

Dr. Endicott was pleased with the product and not only induced his hospital to order a supply but also praised the soap to colleagues in other hospitals in St. Louis and elsewhere. Dr. Farr, confronted with unexpected orders, resigned his position, hired an assistant, and set up a shop in a building originally used for the storage of machinery on a farm property that he had recently purchased. Dr. Farr, when hired by the St. Louis firm, had not been required to sign an agreement stipulating that any discoveries he might make would belong to his employer. Consequently, no conflict of interest was involved, and his resignation was accepted with regret and best wishes for success in his new venture.

At the outset Dr. Farr and his assistant mixed, bottled, labeled, and shipped the orders received. Gradually, more and more employees were added until by 1941 the staff had grown to twelve men and women, and the business had outgrown its quarters even though a sizable addition had been made to the original building. The advent of World War II brought an added demand for the product, and Dr. Farr decided to take such steps as were necessary to expand his operations.

Although the business had been profitable from the beginning, Dr. Farr had not been able to accumulate enough wealth to finance the proposed expansion from his own resources so he decided to form a corporation to be known as the Farr Soap Company. Instead of using the services of an investment banking company, Dr. Farr personally undertook the sale of 50,000 shares of no-par common stock at $10 a share. Of the $500,000 involved, he issued $200,000 to himself for the business assets including his formula. Ten employees subscribed to $100,000, and twenty of his doctor friends purchased the remaining 20,000 shares.

With over $300,000 cash in hand, Dr. Farr leased a factory building, purchased modern machinery for all of the operations, and doubled his labor force. The board of directors, which he had handpicked from employees and doctors who had purchased shares, elected him President and General Manager of the company. In this capacity he continued to handle most of the management functions except those delegated to four long-standing employees who were in charge of production, bottling, shipping, and the office. Reliance for sales continued to be placed on repeat orders, plus sales resulting from an occasional advertisement in a hospital supply magazine and on orders from the military services.

By 1955 sales volume had grown to $12 million a year, the factory had been purchased and enlarged, and the work force had expanded to 120 employees. Shipments to all parts of the country and overseas were made from St. Louis as surgeons who had used the product during the war years took up civilian practices in cities and areas not formerly in the Farr Soap Company sales territory. Profits had been excellent, and through the use of retained earnings the corporation had grown to become a $10 million concern.

The original stock had been split on two occasions, the first a five-to-one split in 1950 and the second a two-to-one split in 1960. There were now 500,000 shares outstanding. Dividends had been paid every year since the corporation had been formed until the board of directors passed the dividend in 1968. Between 1960, the date of the last stock split, and 1968, the rate had been $1 a share although earnings in 1966 barely exceeded $500,000 and in 1967 were less than the dividend payout.

Between 1955 and 1968 sales had shown a modest increase, but profits failed to keep pace due to increased costs of labor and materials without a corresponding increase in selling prices. Other suppliers had improved their competitive products and had promoted them through advertising and the employment of a sales force who made regular calls on hospital administrators. In the face of such competition, the Farr Soap Company had been able to retain most of its customers, partially because it had not raised prices. With a product that was certainly as good as, if indeed not superior to, others on the market, satisfied users were willing to reorder at the old price despite the pressures exerted by salesmen representing competing firms.

One of the reasons for the continued success of the Farr Soap Company had been Dr. Farr's insistence, almost from the beginning of his firm, that it was necessary to maintain and support a research laboratory. In earlier years he had been able to spend some time in it; but, as he turned more of his attention to the problems of running the business, he employed a chemist and then another until by 1969 there were five full-time employees in the laboratory. Although considerable time was spent in routinely checking the quality of raw materials purchased and of the finished product, the laboratory had been able to develop several significant improvements in the liquid soap. It had also recently devised a method of producing and wrapping a bar soap so that the germicidal qualities of the liquid soap could be substantially retained in this new form. Since the production of a bar soap would require entirely new types of machinery, production processes, etc., no steps had been taken in the direction of producing this product. Over the years, however, Dr. Farr had received numerous inquiries about the availability of his liquid soap in a bar form and was aware that such a product might well have a very substantial sales potential.

At the annual stockholders meeting held in March of 1969, to the complete surprise of Dr. Farr, his candidates for the board of directors came within a few votes of being replaced, which would have resulted in Dr. Farr losing his position as President and General Manager. One of the surgeons to whom he had sold stock in 1941 had managed to assemble a number of proxies and, had it not been for supporting votes from some of the shares originally sold to employees, Dr. Farr would have lost control of his firm. Although only one of the ten employees who had purchased stock in 1941 was still on the payroll, most of the others, or their widows, were still living. The cause of the uprising, as was brought out when the surgeon nominated a rival slate of candidates for the board of directors, was the fact that dividends were suspended in 1968 and that Dr. Farr, who was now 70, did not seem disposed to relinquish the management or to take steps to restore the firm's former profitability.

After the meeting had adjourned, one of Dr. Farr's former employees, who had voted for him, explained that he and most of the other retired employees, or their widows, had come to depend on the dividends received to supplement their other sources of retirement income, which consisted, for the most part, of monthly payments under social security. He believed that continued support for Dr. Farr would not be forthcoming unless dividends were resumed. He also expressed concern about the drop in value of his shares, which had fallen from $30 a share to $12 a share in the over-the-counter market.

Greatly disturbed by the turn of events, Dr. Farr realized that some action was required. At the next monthly meeting of the board of directors, he surprised the members by requesting permission to employ a firm of management consultants to make a thorough analysis of the Farr Soap Company. He reported that he had investigated costs and the reputation of several organizations and wished to recommend the selection of E. P. Cutler Associates, a nationally known firm that maintained a branch office in St. Louis. This recommendation received the unanimous approval of the board members and Dr. Farr was commended not only for seeking the advice of his board but also for his willingness to bring in management consultants.

Following this action, Dr. Farr invited Mr. William Sherlock, the partner in charge of the St. Louis office of E. P. Cutler Associates, to visit the plant and adjacent offices of the Farr Soap Company. Mr. Sherlock spent a day with Dr. Farr and, on the basis of this preliminary investigation, decided to send four technically qualified men to the company. The individual specialties of these experts were marketing, production, personnel, and finance and accounting. Each spent several days at the plant and in the office examining procedures, interviewing workers, analyzing data, and observing every detail that might be pertinent to their investigations.

After completing the field work, each specialist wrote a long, well-documented report. These were submitted to Mr. Sherlock who subsequently discussed them with the individuals separately and also in a group. It was his responsibility to submit a final report to Dr. Farr that would include the recommendations his firm wished to make. Following is a brief digest of the reports made to Mr. Sherlock by each of his four staff members.

Digest of Report on Marketing

The marketing organization of the Farr Soap Company is practically nonexistent. No salesmen have ever been employed. A small advertisement has been regularly inserted in *Hospital Supply,* a monthly trade magazine read by hospital administrators, but reliance for sales is still placed on repeat orders and the recommendations of surgeons who make contacts with new hospitals.

If a decision is reached to produce a bar germicidal soap, several problems would need to be settled. The soap could be sold to hospitals only, but it would probably be necessary to employ some salesmen in order to obtain the minimum sales volume necessary for efficient operation of a production line. It is also highly probable that the purchase of a bar soap by hospitals would, in a significant number of cases, decrease the demand for liquid soap. On the other hand, the market for such a soap might well extend into the offices of doctors and dentists and even into the home. If it is decided to expand the market for a bar soap beyond hospital use, an entirely new system of distribution would seem necessary.

Digest of Report on Production

The production methods of the Farr Soap Company, although not antiquated, leave much to be desired. Approximately half of the machinery in use is modern and efficient but the remainder should be replaced. In addition, several operations now performed by hand should be automated, for standard equipment is available that can take over these tasks. It is estimated that the cost of trading in the somewhat obsolete equipment and purchasing new machines would total $1 million. Floor space in the building is more than adequate, and almost half of the area could be made available for other uses by a more efficient arrangement of the machines in use plus the elimination of some work space now devoted to hand operations.

An investigation of the costs involved in producing a bar soap indicated that the cost of machinery necessary to produce this product efficiently would amount to $1,750,000. Operating 40 hours a week the capacity of this production line would be 2 million bars of soap a month of a size that would sell for 10 cents each, f.o.b. factory.

Digest of Report on Personnel

Although personnel policies have never been formalized, employee-employer relationships have been satisfactory in that all of the workers are known by Dr. Farr and he has taken a personal interest in their problems. He has always paid hourly wages slightly higher than those that prevailed in the St. Louis area, and the *esprit de corps* of the employees is excellent. One effort was made in 1956 to organize the workers, but interest was so lacking that even an alternate proposal for a plant employee representative plan was defeated.

As to organization, it is obvious that Dr. Farr is the only "boss" in the company. He spoke of the four employees who were "in charge" of production, bottling, shipping, and the office, but admitted that he was consulted on all but routine decisions. In his daily tours about the plant he feels free to make any corrections and changes he believes desirable without reference to the individuals in charge. Much of his office time is taken up with correspondence and telephone calls having to do with sales, an area in which he has no assistance other than adequate clerical help.

Despite his age, Dr. Farr is an intelligent, energetic, and dedicated President and General Manager of the Farr Soap Company. He is on the job every day and seems proud of his record of rarely missing a day's work either for reasons of illness or to take a vacation. He admitted that he should have been giving some thought to delegating duties and responsibilities and to a successor. His excuse was that he was too busy, that his four managers did "run their own show" most of the time, and that as far as sales were concerned he was the only person known by name and reputation to his customers.

The only child of Dr. and Mrs. Farr, a daughter, has been married for some time to a successful lawyer. Although the son-in-law has given free legal advice when requested, he is not interested in associating himself with the Farr Soap Company in a managerial capacity.

Digest of Report on Finance and Accounting

The books and other financial records of the Farr Soap Company were found to be in excellent order. From these, the following comparative balance sheets and income statements were prepared and verified:

Balance Sheets

Farr Soap Company

December 31, 1967, and December 31, 1968

ASSETS	1967	1968
Current Assets		
Cash	$ 1,250,000	$ 950,000
Accounts Receivable (net)	540,000	720,000
Inventories	3,200,000	3,300,000
Prepaid Expenses	215,000	240,000
Total Current Assets	$ 5,205,000	$ 5,210,000
Plant Assets		
Machinery and Equipment (net)	$ 3,460,000	$ 3,525,000
Building (net)	1,800,000	1,590,000
Land	225,000	225,000
Total Plant Assets	$ 5,485,000	$ 5,340,000
TOTAL ASSETS	$10,690,000	$10,550,000
LIABILITIES		
Current Liabilities		
Notes Payable	800,000	600,000
Accounts Payable	$ 1,690,000	$ 1,548,000
Total Current Liabilities	$ 2,490,000	$ 2,148,000
Long-Term Liabilities		
Mortgage Payable	$ 900,000	$ 850,000
TOTAL LIABILITIES	$ 3,390,000	$ 2,998,000
CAPITAL		
Capital Stock, 500,000 shares	$ 500,000	$ 500,000
Retained Earnings	6,800,000	7,052,000
TOTAL CAPITAL	$ 7,300,000	$ 7,552,000
TOTAL LIABILITIES AND CAPITAL .	$10,690,000	$10,550,000

Income Statements

Farr Soap Company

For Years Ended December 31, 1967, and December 31, 1968

	1967	1968
Sales (net)	$13,086,000	$13,475,000
Cost of Goods Manufactured and Sold ..	12,234,000	12,809,400
Gross Profit on Sales	852,000	665,600
Operating Expenses	178,000	183,000
Net Income from Operations	674,000	482,600
Other Expenses	9,800	10,400
Net Income Before Income Tax	664,200	472,200
Federal Tax on Income	312,000	220,200
Net Income After Income Tax	$ 352,200	$ 252,000
Dividends Paid	$ 500,000	......

In addition to these reports, Mr. Sherlock had available information on other clients of his firm. One of these companies, although considerably larger than the Farr Soap Company, obtained most of its revenues from sales of miscellaneous supplies to hospitals. Since the two firms were similar, at least to the extent that they served a common customer, Mr. Sherlock made a percentage analysis of the Income Statement of the larger firm that, in brief, showed the following:

	Percent
Sales	100.0
Cost of Goods Manufactured and Sold	71.7
Gross Profit on Sales	28.3
Operating Expenses	15.0
Net Income from Operations	13.3
Other Expenses	.6
Net Income Before Income Tax	12.7
Federal Income Tax	6.1
Net Income After Income Tax	6.6

On the basis of the facts, opinions, and information provided, plus any reasonable assumptions consistent with known data, what recommendations should the firm of E. P. Cutler Associates make to the Farr Soap Company? Your solution to this case should provide answers to the questions listed on the following page and also to other problems you believe are pertinent.

1. Is an organizational structure needed? If so, what type should be recommended? Construct a chart to show your specific proposal.

2. Is it desirable to create a marketing organization? If so, what type? Should new sales policies be adopted?

3. If a bar soap is to be manufactured, to whom should this new product be sold?

4. Should the new equipment for manufacturing the liquid soap be purchased?

5. Should the machinery be purchased to produce the bar soap?

6. What changes, if any, should be made in the area of personnel relations?

7. If any or all of the new equipment purchases are recommended, how should the necessary funds be raised?

8. What type of a dividend policy should be adopted? Would this satisfy the needs of the retired employees? Is this group entitled to special consideration?

9. Are there any steps that Dr. Farr can take to prevent a possible loss of his position as President and General Manager?

10. What are the strengths and weaknesses of the Farr Soap Company as revealed by an analysis of its financial statements?

11. What seem to be the most promising moves the company can make in an attempt to restore its former profitability?

12. Should the Farr Soap Company be advised to seek out a larger company, such as the client of the E. P. Cutler Associates, that might be willing to buy it for stock or cash?

Appendix

OPPORTUNITIES IN BUSINESS

Selected References by Textbook Parts

PART II / OWNERSHIP, MANAGEMENT, AND ORGANIZATION

A Business of Your Own? Washington, D. C.: Changing Times, 1960.

Business Proprietor, Retail. Moravia, New York: Chronicle Guidance Publications, 1963.

Career as an Administrative Executive in Business and Industry. Chicago: Institute for Research, 1964.

Career Opportunities for Women in Business. King, Alice G. New York: E. P. Dutton & Son, 1963.

Careers in Business Management. Mann, R. New York: Henry Z. Walck, Inc., 1963.

Gift and Art Shop Operation as a Career. Chicago: Institute for Research, 1964.

The Hardware Business. Indianapolis, Indiana: National Retail Hardware Association, 1962.

Should You Go into Business for Yourself? Southeimer, Morton. New York: New York Life Insurance Company, 1960.

Small Business Owners. Chicago: Science Research Associates, 1966.

PART III / MARKETING

Marketing as a Career—A Bibliography. Chicago: American Marketing Association, 1964.

Marketing Research Workers. Chicago: Science Research Associates, 1961.

Career Opportunities in Wholesaling. Washington: National Association of Wholesalers, 1963.

Manufacturer's Representative. Largo, Florida: Careers, 1961.

Career Opportunities in National General Merchandise Chains. Chicago: Institute for Research, 1963.

Careers as a Retail Merchandise Buyer. Chicago: Institute for Research, 1962.

Comparison Shopper. Moravia, New York: Chronicle Guidance Publications, 1963.

Careers for Women in Retailing. Washington, D. C.: Women's Bureau, U. S. Department of Labor, 1963.

Department Store Occupations. Detroit, Michigan: Michigan Employment Security Commission, 1963.

Men's Clothing Store Operation as a Career. Chicago: Institute for Research, 1961.

Retailing as a Career. Boston: Boston University, 1962.

Your Future in Retailing. Scott, George. New York: Richards Rosen Press, 1961.

Supermarket Manager. Largo, Florida: Careers, 1963.

Supermarket Occupations. Detroit, Michigan: Michigan Employment Security Commission, 1962.

Advertising Manager—Store. Largo, Florida: Careers, 1963.

Advertising as a Career. Chicago: Institute for Research, 1963.

Career Opportunities in Advertising. New York: The American Association of Advertising Agencies, 1965.

Careers and Opportunities in Advertising. Boland, Charles M. New York: E. P. Dutton & Co., Inc., 1964.

Employment Outlook for Advertising, Market Research, and Public Relations Workers. Washington, D. C.: Bureau of Labor Statistics, U. S. Department of Labor.

Careers in the Export, Import, and Foreign Operation Field. Angel, Juvenal L. New York: World Trade Academy Press, 1961.

PART IV / OPERATIONAL FACTORS

Employment Outlook for Purchasing Agents and Industrial Traffic Managers. Washington, D. C.: Bureau of Labor Statistics, U. S. Department of Labor.

Purchasing Agent. Moravia, New York: Chronicle Guidance Publications, 1963.

Career as a Production Manager in Manufacturing. Chicago: Institute for Research, 1960.

Employment Outlook for Industrial Designers. Washington, D. C.: Bureau of Labor Statistics, U. S. Department of Labor, 1964.

Industrial Designer. Moravia, New York: Chronicle Guidance Publications, 1961.

Time-and-Motion Study Man. Largo, Florida: Careers, 1962.

PART V / PERSONNEL

Employment Outlook for Personnel Workers. Washington, D. C.: Bureau of Labor Statistics, U. S. Department of Labor.

Employment Manager. Moravia, New York: Chronicle Guidance Publications, 1963.

Job Analyst. Moravia, New York: Chronicle Guidance Publications, 1964.

Personnel Administration. Boston: Simmons College, 1963.

Personnel Specialist. Moravia, New York: Chronicle Guidance Publications, 1963.

Your Future in Personnel Work. Pond, John. New York: Richards Rosen Press, 1962.

PART VI / FINANCE

Banking: A Career for Today and Tomorrow. New York: The American Bankers Association, 1963.

Bank Officers. Chicago: Science Research Associates, 1965.

A Career for Women in Banking. New York: National Association of Bank Women, Inc.

Careers in Banking. Chicago: Institute for Research, 1964.

Careers in the Trust Departments of Banks and Trust Companies. Chicago: Institute for Research, 1962.

Employment Outlook in Banking. Washington, D. C.: U. S. Department of Labor, 1966.

Your Future: Careers in Consumer Finance. Washington, D. C.: National Consumer Finance Association, 1963.

Careers in the Securities Business. Chicago: Institute for Research, 1964.

Employment Outlook for Securities Salesmen. Washington, D. C.: U. S. Department of Labor, 1966.

Opportunities in the Securities Business. Shulsky, S. New York: Vocational Guidance Manuals, 1963.

Securities Salesmen. Chicago: Science Research Associates, 1966.

Careers in Insurance. New York: Insurance Information Institute, 1964.

Careers in Property and Casualty Insurance. Chicago: Institute for Research, 1966.

Employment Outlook in Insurance Occupations. Washington, D. C.: U. S. Department of Labor, 1966.

Insurance Agents. Chicago: Science Research Associates, 1966.

Life Insurance as a Career. Chicago: Institute for Research, 1965.

Employment Outlook for Real Estate Agents and Brokers. Washington, D. C.: U. S. Department of Labor, 1966.

Real Estate and Insurance Business as a Career. Chicago: Institute for Research, 1960.

Employment Opportunities for College Graduates for the Position of Financial Analyst. Washington, D. C.: Securities and Exchange Commission, 1962.

PART VII / QUANTITATIVE CONTROLS FOR DECISION MAKING

Accountancy as a Career. Chicago: Institute for Research, 1964.

Accountants. Chicago: Science Research Associates, 1964.

A Career as a Certified Public Accountant. New York: American Institute of Certified Public Accountants, Inc., 1964.

Career as a Certified Public Accountant (CPA). Chicago: Institute for Research, 1966.

Careers and Opportunities in Accounting. Cashin, J. A. New York: E. P. Dutton & Company, Inc., 1965.

Careers in Accounting. Ashworth, J. New York: Henry Z. Walck, Inc., 1963.

Certified Public Accountants. Chicago: Science Research Associates, 1966.

Employment Outlook for Accountants. Washington, D. C.: U. S. Department of Labor, 1966.

The Field of Management Accounting. New York: National Association of Accountants.

Mapping Your Future. Chicago: American Women's Society of Certified Public Accountants and American Society of Women Accountants, 1964.

Opportunities for Accountants in the Federal Government. Washington, D. C.: Federal Government Accountants Association.

Young Eyes on Accounting. Evanston, Illinois: American Accounting Association.

Your Future in Accounting. Locklear, E., Jr. New York: Richards Rosen Press, 1963.

The Field of Internal Auditing. New York: Institute of Internal Auditors, 1965.

Statistical Workers. Chicago: Science Research Associates, 1963.

Employment Outlook for Computer Operating Personnel, Programmers. Washington, D. C.: U. S. Department of Labor, 1966.

Occupations in Electronic Computing Systems. Washington, D. C.: U. S. Department of Labor, 1965.

Programmers. Chicago: Science Research Associates, 1964.

PART VIII / LEGAL AND REGULATORY ENVIRONMENT OF BUSINESS

Careers in Government. Sullivan, M. B. New York: Henry Z. Walck, Inc., 1964.

Careers in the Treasury Department of the United States Government. Chicago: Institute for Research, 1961.

Federal Career Directory. U. S. Government Printing Office, 1966.

Federal Careers for Women. Washington, D. C.: U. S. Civil Service Commission, 1964.

Federal Civil Service Workers. Chicago: Science Research Associates, 1966.

Futures in the Federal Government. Washington, D. C.: U. S. Civil Service Commission, 1965.

Government Work as a Career. Chicago: Institute for Research, 1962.

Internal Revenue Service. Washington, D. C.: U. S. Treasury Department, 1966.

Treasury Enforcement Agent. Washington, D. C.: U. S. Treasury Department, 1965.

Public Utility Workers. Chicago: Science Research Associates, 1961.

Index

A

Absentee management, 113
Absolute advantage, theory of, 228
Acceptances, bank, 418
Accident insurance, 462
Accommodation indorser, 419
Accountants, certified public, 498; governmental, 498; public, 498; types of, 498
Accounting, 498; careers in, 58; organization chart for, department, 498; professional associations in, 514
Accounting procedures, 498
Accounts, charge, 413; checking, 424; open-book, 413
Accounts receivable, 420
Accumulation bonds, 393
Acid-test ratio, 511
Actuary, 466
Address, 546
Administered prices, 182
Administrative law, 32
Administrative management, 110
Advantage, theory of absolute, 228; theory of comparative, 229
Advertisements, are, false or misleading, 221
Advertising, 139, 203; business papers, 212; catalogs, 212; chain store, 174; class, 204; commodity, 204; criticisms of, 219; direct mail, 210; does, make goods cost more?, 220; effectiveness of, 213; ensuring truth in, 221; industry self-regulation of, 222; in small business, 218; institutional, 205; magazines, 207; mass, 204; merchandise sampling, 212; name, 205; newspaper, 206; outdoor, 210; point-of-purchase, 212; poor taste in, 220; primary, 204; radio, 208; regulation of, by action of media, 222; relationship of, to selling, 203; selective, 204; television, 209; testing radio and television, 215; transportation, 211; types of, 204; volume of, 213
Advertising agency, 139, 215; organization chart of a typical, 216
Advertising budget, 561
Advertising Council, 224
Advertising manager, 218
Advertising media, 205; flexibility of, 206; geographic selectivity, 205; identity of the audience, 206; interest selectivity, 205
Advertising specialists, 212
After-acquired clause, 395
Agency, 591; advertising, 215

Agency shop, 370
Agent, 591; manufacturers', 157; merchandise, 157; purchasing, 279; selling, 158
Agreement, voluntary, 587
Agricultural Marketing Agreement Act, 607
Airplanes, 258
Air transport, regulation of, 632
Alcohol taxes, 649
Alien corporation, 102
Alliance for Progress, 242
Amalgamation, 488
American Accounting Association, 514
American Business Law Association, 595
American Federation of Labor, 375
American Federation of Labor—Congress of Industrial Organizations (AFL-CIO), 375; structure of, 375
American Finance Association, 408
American Institute of Certified Public Accountants, 515
American Management Association, 128
American Marketing Association, 152
American Personnel and Guidance Association, Inc. (APGA), 340
American Risk and Insurance Association, 472
American Society for Personnel Administration (ASPA), 340
American Statistical Association, 536
Analog computer, 541
Analytic process, 298
Antichain laws, 176
Antiloss-leader laws, 190
Appellate court, 585
Apprenticeship system, 334
Aptitudes, 50
Arbitration, 378; compulsory, 378; voluntary, 378
Arithmetic average, 526
Arithmetic unit, 546
Array, 525
Articles of association, 84
Articles of partnership, 75; illustration of a, 77-78
Asked price, 404
Assembly process, 298
Assessments, 645
Assets, 389, 499; current, 389, 500; fixed, 389, 422, 502; intangible, 502; plant, 502; rate of net income on, 514
Associations, accounting, 514; budgeting, 573; business law, 595; finance, 408; financial management, 492; insurance, 472; management, 128; marketing, 152; personnel, 340; statistics, 536; taxation, 654; trade, 612; unincorporated, 85

Atomic Energy Commission, 258
Auction companies, 158
Audimeter, 215
Authority, delegation of, 117; subdivisions of supervisory, 117
Automated data processing (ADP), 539
Automation, 16, 39, 302
Automobile insurance, 460; bodily injury liability, 461; collision or upset, 461; comprehensive coverage, 461; medical payments endorsement, 461; property damage liability, 461
Averages, 524; arithmetic, 526; comparison of, 527
Avocations, 51

B

Baby bonds, 392
Bailee, 594
Bailments, 594
Bailor, 594
Balance of trade, favorable, 234; unfavorable, 234
Balance sheet, 499
Balance sheet equation, 500
Bank acceptances, 418
Bank discount, 416
Bank draft, 425
Bankruptcy, 491, 594; involuntary, 594; voluntary, 594
Banks, commercial, 424; correspondent, 425; savings, 407
Bar chart, 534
Bargaining, collective, 376; collective versus individual, 376
Bargaining theory of wages, 347
Bargaining unit, 370
Barter, 181
Bears, 437
Behavioral sciences, 40
Beneficiaries, 468
Better Business Bureaus, 223
Bid price, 404
Bill of Material, 310
Bill of sale, 593; conditional, 422
Bills of exchange, 238; use of, 238
Binary code, 541, 542
Binary digit, 542
Binary number, 542; decimal numbers compared with, 542
Bit, 542
Blacklist, 373
Blue-collar workers, 366
Blue-sky laws, 440
Board of directors, 90, 92
Bodily injury liability insurance, 461
Bond averages, 448
Bond discount, 397
Bonded public warehouse, 421
Bond premium, 397
Bond quotation, 447
Bonds, 392, 447; accumulation, 393; as security, 395; baby, 392; callable, 396; chattel mortgage, 395; collateral trust, 395; convertible, 397; coupon, 393; debenture, 395; denomination of, 392;

fidelity, 465; for bonds, 481; fully registered, 393; general features of, 392; maturity dates of, 393; method of repayment, 395; provision for trustee, 392; real estate mortgage, 395; redeemable, 396; refunding of, 396; registered versus coupon, 393; security for, 394; serial, 396; sinking-fund, 396; special features of, 394; stocks for, 481; surety, 465
Bonus payments, 355
Boycott, 373; primary, 373; secondary, 373
Broadsides, 218
Brokerage, false, 192
Brokerage firms, 404
Brokers, 157; merchandise, 158; odd-lot, 435
Budget, advertising, 561; cash, 562; departmental expense, 562; labor, 562; manufacturing expense, 562; materials, 562; preparation of a, 560; production, 561; sales, 560; sales expense, 561
Budget adaptation, extent of, 559
Budgetary control, 564
Budget control procedures, 559
Budget Executive Institute, 573
Budgeting, 557, 558; professional association in, 573
Budget organization, 558
Budget period, length of, 559
Building and loan associations, 407
Building codes, state, 609
Bulls, 437
Bureau of Deceptive Practices, 223
Business, 3; and government, 31; and society, 29; big and little, 34; characteristics of present-day, 19; classification of, 23; commercial, 23; competitive, federal laws and regulations of, 601; competitive, historical background of, 599; competitive, regulation of, 599; historical setting of, 27; industrial, 23; international, 243; international aspects of, 227; large-scale, 21; opportunities in, 47; multinational, 245; social responsibilities of, 44; taxation and, 637
Business combinations, 486; horizontal, 486; vertical, 486
Business crimes, 587
Business cycle, 33, 531
Business decisions, federal income taxes and, 652; state taxes and, 653; taxation and, 652
Business ethics, 579, 580; modern trends in, 581
Business Ethics Advisory Council, 582
Business firms, size of, 22
Business games, 41
Business law, 579, 584; professional association in, 595; scope of, 586
Business ownership, other incorporated forms of, 103
Business papers, advertising media, 212
Business profit, 16
Business risks, types of, 454
Business specialization, 48
Business statistics, 520; interpretation of, 535

Business taxes, special, 643
Business torts, 586
Buying, 137, 277; versus manufacturing, 284
Buying committee, 292
Buying cooperatives, 104
Buying ethics, 286
Buying personnel, retailers', 290
Buying plans, 293
Buying procedure, initiating the, 282; retailers', 293; wholesalers', 290
Bylaws, 92
Byrnes Antistrikebreaker Act, 383

C

Callable bonds, 396
Callable preferred stocks, 400
Call price, 396
Capacity, 546
Capital, 10, 389; circulating, 389; debt, 390, 477; equity, 390, 477; fixed, 389; types of, 389; working, 411, 508, 512
Capital funds, 10
Capital goods, 10
Capitalism, 3; basic freedoms of, 4; classical theory of, 17; economist's concept of, 17; modified, 4; other aspects of, 10; paradox of, 151; role of individuals in, 6
Capitalists, 10
Capital structure, 475
Car cards, 211
Carriers, 632
Cash budget, 562
Cash discount, 193
Cash dividends, 484
Cash flow, 509
Cashier's check, 425
Cash surrender value, 468
Casual sale, 182
Casualty, 460
Casualty insurance, 458, 460
Cathode ray tube (CRT), 547
Caveat emptor, 439
Celler-Kefauver Act, 605
Central American Common Market, 242
Centralization, of purchasing function, 280
Centralized management, 113
Central processing unit, 547
Central tendency, 532
Certificate of convenience and necessity, 626
Certified check, 424
Certified public accountants, 498
Chain stores, 173; advertising by, 174; buying by, 173; merchandise specials of, 174; merchandising policies of, 174; operational policies of, 175; policies, 173; warehousing by, 174
Chains, corporate, 173; voluntary, 175
Chance, a factor in plant location, 260
Change, as an environmental ingredient, 38
Character loan, 419
Charge accounts, 413
Charts, bar, 534; circular, 534; curve, 533; flow, 549; line, 533

Chattel mortgage, 422; as security, 395
Chattel mortgage bonds, 395
Check, 424; cashier's, 425; certified, 424; clearing a, 427; stop payment on a, 424; traveler's, 425
Checking accounts, 424
Checkoff, 370
Choice, freedom of, 5
Circular chart, 534
Circular combination, 487
Circulating capital, 389
Civil Aeronautics Act of 1938, 632
Civil Aeronautics Board, 632
Civil law, 584
Civil Rights Act of 1964, 6, 328
Class advertising, 204
Classical theory of capitalism, 17
Clayton Act, 603
Clearing a check, 427
Climate, a factor in plant location, 258
Close corporation, 102
Closed-door discount houses, 169
Closed-end issue mortgage bonds, 395
Closed-loop control, 302
Closed shop, 369
Code, binary, 541, 542
Code, Uniform Commercial, 586
Code of Ethics, 581
Coinsurance clause, 459
Collateral trust bonds, 395
Collective bargaining, 376; versus individual bargaining, 376
Collision insurance, 461
Collusive bidding, 611
Comaker, 419
Combination, circular, 487; complementary, 486
Commercial banks, 424; functions of, 426; regulation of, 426
Commercial business, 23
Commercial consumer, 149
Commercial draft, 417; drawer of, 417
Commercial finance company, 427
Commercial goods, 136; channels of distribution for, 146
Commercial layout, 273, 419
Commercial paper, 592
Commercial paper houses, 429
Committee for Industrial Organization, 375
Committee organization, 125
CSO 1958 Mortality Table, 466
Commission merchant, 158
Commission payment, 356
Commodity advertising, 204
Commodity exchange, 456
Commodity prices, 449
Common Business Oriented Language (COBOL), 548
Common carriers, 632
Common law, 584
Common stocks, 401
Common trust fund, 405
Communication, 118, 630; importance of, 322
Communications Act of 1934, 633
Communications industries, regulation of, 633

Communications mix, 148
Communications Satellite Corporation, 101
Communications taxes, 651
Communism, 24
Community of interests, 612
Company schools, 334
Comparative advantage, theory of, 229
Compensation, employee, 343; workmen's, 642
Competent persons, 588
Competition, 13; among laborers, 344; federal laws to promote, 601; foreign, 35; handicap, 13; innovistic, 14; monopolistic, 13, 187; nonprice, 199; other concepts of, 13; pure, 13; seller's attitude toward, 198
Competitive business, federal laws and regulations of, 601; historical background of, 599; regulation of, 599
Complementary combination, 486
Composition agreement, 490
Comprehensive coverage, 461
Computer, analog, 541; arithmetic unit, 546; components of, 543; control unit, 546; digital, 541; input unit, 544; marketing and the, 148; memory or storage unit, 544; output unit, 547; types of, 541
Compulsory arbitration, 378
Compulsory investigation and delay, 378
Conciliation, 377
Conditional bill of sale, 422
Conditional sale, 593
Conglomerate mergers, 487
Consideration, 588
Consignment, 593
Consumer, 8, 149; as final arbiter, 30; commercial, 149; industrial, 149; ultimate, 149
Consumer buying, aids to, 150
Consumer co-ops, 104
Consumer demand, 8
Consumer finances, 423
Consumer finance companies, 429
Consumer goods, 136; channels of distribution for, 145
Consumer-oriented management concept, 134
Consumer pretest, 214
Consumer Price Index, 527, 568
Continuous process, 267, 299
Contract, 587; discharge of, 589; forms of, 589; freedom of, 6; futures, 456; partnership, 75; performance of, 589; remedies of, 589; tying, 603
Contract carriers, 632
Contract purchasing, 285
Control, budgetary, 564; inventory, in wholesaling and retailing, 293; materials, 287; numerical, 302; of materials, 287; of merchandise, 289; span of executive, 118
Controlled sampling, 521
Controlled shopping centers, 265
Control unit, 546
Convenience goods, 136
Convertible bonds, 397
Convertible preferred stock, 401

Cooperative associations, producer, 104
Cooperatives, 104; buying, 104
Co-ops, 104; consumer, 104
Copartners, 81
Corporate chain, 173
Corporate image concept, 31
Corporate news items, 448
Corporate ownership, disadvantages of, 97
Corporate structure, 90; chart of, 91
Corporation economists, 568
Corporations, 89; advantages of a, 94; alien, 102; board of directors of a, 90, 92; bylaws of a, 92; charter restrictions, 99; classification of, 101; close, 102; definition of a, 90; domestic, 102; ease of expansion of, 96; efficiency of management of a, 96; foreign, 102; governmental, 101; government restrictions and reports, 98; income taxes, 648; industrial classifications of, 102; lack of personal interest in, 99; lack of secrecy in, 99; larger size of, 95; legal entity of, 96; length of life of a, 95; nature of the, 89; nonprofit, 101; nonstock, 101; officers of a, 90, 93; open, 102; organization expenses of a, 97; organizing a, 100; private, 101; profit, 101; relative lack of credit of, 99; shareholders of a, 90, 91; stock, 101; taxation of a, 97; transfer of ownership in a, 95
Corporation taxes, 643
Correlation, 529; multiple, 530; simple, 530
Correspondent bank, 425
Cosigner, 419
Cost, direct, 220; historical, 624; indirect, 220; joint, 182; prudent historical, 624
Cost, insurance, freight (c.i.f.), 593
Cost less depreciation, 624
Cost-of-capital concept, 479
Cost of goods, 197
Cost of goods manufactured, schedule of, 508
Cost of merchandise sold, 505
Cost-price relationship, 197
Council of Economic Advisers, 34, 567
Counseling service, employee, 337
Counteroffer, 588
Coupon bond, 393; partial registration of, 393
Courts, and laws, 585; appellate, 585
Courts of original jurisdiction, 585
Craft unions, 375
Credit, intermediate, 390; letters of, 418; line of, 425; money and, 449
Credit control subsystem, 551
Credit information, 414
Credit insurance, 470
Credit life insurance, 470
Creditor agreements, 489; composition, 490; extension, 490
Creditors, general, 595; preferred, 594
Credit rating, as security, 395
Credit terms, length of, 414
Credit unions, 105
Crimes, business, 587
Critical path method (CPM), 314

Cross elasticity of demand, 186
Cumulative preferred stock, 398
Cumulative voting, 91
Current assets, 389, 500
Current liabilities, 411, 502
Current ratio, 511
Curve chart, 533
Custom manufacture, 300
Customs duties, 652
Cutting a melon, 484
Cycle, business, 33
Cyclical fluctuations, 530

D

Data, 539; analysis of, 523; collection of, 520; measurement of, 523; primary, 522; secondary, 522; sources of, for business, 522; summarization of, 523
Data processing, 539; automated, 539; electronic, 16, 40, 539; history and importance of, 540; integrated, 549; nature of, 539
Death duties, 644
Death sentence clause, 628
Debenture bonds, 395
Debt, ratio of ownership to, 513
Debt capital, 390, 477
Decentralization, of purchasing function, 280
Decentralized management, 113
Decimal numbers, compared with binary, 542
Decision making, 110; in a regulated economy, 611
Defendant, 585
Defense contracts, and space technology, 41
Demand, cross elasticity of, 186; for labor, 344; inelasticity of, 186; supply and, concepts of, 196
Demand deposits, 427
Demand elasticity, 186
Departmental expense budgets, 562
Departmentalization, 116
Department stores, 166; branch, 166
Deposits, demand, 427
Descriptive labeling, 141
Dictionary of Occupational Titles, 52
Differential Aptitude Tests of the Psychological Corporation, 51
Digit, 541; binary, 542
Digital computer, 541
Direct costs, 220
Direct mail advertising, 210
Directorate, interlocking, 603
Discount, 192; bank, 416; bond, 397; cash, 193; chain of, 192; quantity, 193; trade, 192
Discount houses, 169; closed-door, 169
Discount policy, 192
Discount supermarkets, 170
Dishonor, notice of, 592
Dispatching, 311
Distribution, channels of, 145; channels of, for consumer goods, 145; channels of, for industrial and commercial goods,
146; of goods, 11; shift in emphasis from production to, 41
Distribution mix, 148
Distributors, industrial, 156; wagon, truck, 157
Dividend policy, conservative, 485; regular, 484; variable, 485
Dividends, cash, 484; pass the, 398; scrip, 485; patronage, 104; securities, 485; stock, 485
Divisionalization, 113, 114
Doctrine of stare decisis, 584
Dodgers, 218
Domestic corporation, 102
Domestic system, 29
Dormant partner, 82
Double-name paper, 416
Dow-Jones Averages, 445
Draft, bank, 425; commercial, 417; sight, 417; time, 417
Drawee, of commercial draft, 417
Drawer, of commercial draft, 417
Drawing account, guaranteed, 356
Due process of law, 607

E

Earnings, distribution of, policies, 483; rate of, a security selection factor, 478; stability of, a security selection factor, 478
Economic goods, basic types of, 135
Economic systems, 24
Economist, concept of capitalism of the, 17; corporation, 568; role of, 36
Economy, industrial, shift from an, to a service economy, 43
Effective rate of interest, 423
Elastic demand, 186
Electronic data processing (EDP), 16, 40, 539
Electronic Numerical Integrator and Calculator (ENIAC), 540
Eligible paper, 427
Eminent domain, right of, 620
Employee, discharge of, 332; health, 338; layoff of, 332; promotion, 331; retraining of, 335; safety, 338; transfer, 331
Employee compensation, 343
Employee counseling service, 337
Employee selection, nature and background of the problem of, 322
Employment Act of 1946, 34
Employment opportunities, areas of, 54
Employment procedures, 327
Employment taxes, 650
Endorsement, fire insurance policy, 460
Endowment life insurance, 469
Enterprise, private, 5
Entrance tax, 643
Entrepreneur, 6
Equal Employment Opportunity Committee (EEOC), 329
Equal Pay Act, 345
Equilibrium theory, assumptions in the, 195; factors not included in the, 196; of prices, 194

Equipment, expenditures for, 11; install-
ment purchases of, 417; stand-by, 623
Equipment trust certificates, 395
Equity, trading on the, 478
Equity capital, 390, 477
Equity receivership, 490
Escape clause, 240
Esprit de corps, 115
Estate in fee simple, 590
Estate taxes, 644, 651
Estimated statements, 564
Ethics, application of, to business decisions,
582; business, 579; buying, 286; in the
nineteenth century, 580
European Common Market, 36, 241
European Economic Community (EEC),
241
European Free Trade Association (EFTA),
242
European Recovery Plan, 242
Exchange, bills of, 238; commodity, 456;
foreign, 237, 426; rates of, 238
Exchange restrictions, 239
Excise tax, 649; manufacturer's, 650
Executive control, span of, 118
Executive training, 335
Expenditures, by business for new plant
and equipment, 11
Expense, operating, 507; other, 507; sell-
ing, 507
Export control, 239
Exporters, 157
Export-Import Bank, 240
Exports, dollar volume of, 231; merchan-
dise, 230
Export sales, piggyback, 245
Express warranty, 593
Extension agreement, 490
Extractive process, 298
Extrapolation, 569

F

Fabricating process, 298
Factoring company, 428
Factors, 428
Factory buildings, flat-roof type, 270;
multistory type of, 270; types of, 270
Factory system, 28
Fair Employment Practices Codes, 329
Fair Labor Standards Act, 345, 348
Fair rate of return, 623
Fair trade laws, 188
Fair value of property, 623
False brokerage, 192
Favorable balance of trade, 234
Featherbedding, 371
Federal Aviation Act of 1958, 632
Federal Aviation Agency, 632
Federal Communications Commission, 633
Federal Deposit Insurance Corporation,
407
Federal Deposit Savings and Loan Asso-
ciation, 407
Federal Food, Drug, and Cosmetic Act of
1938, 223

Federal government, agencies of, who pre-
pare forecasts, 567
Federal Home Loan Bank System, 407
Federal income taxes, business decisions
and, 652
Federal Insurance Contribution Act, 650
Federal laws, and regulations of competi-
tive business, 601; to promote competi-
tion, 601
Federal Mediation and Conciliation Ser-
vice, 377
Federal Power Commission, 628
Federal regulation, of public utilities, 627;
of specific industries, 605
Federal Reserve Board, 426, 443, 567
Federal Reserve System, 426, 427
Federal Securities Act of 1933, 440
Federal Securities Exchange Act of 1934,
441
Federal taxes, types of, 645
Federal Trade Commission, 31, 223, 603
Federal Trade Commission Act, 31, 603
Fee, incorporation, 100, 643
Feedback, 119, 302
Fidelity bonds, 465
Field warehousing, 140
Finance, careers in, 57; consumer, 423;
market, 142; professional association in,
408
Finance company, commercial, 427; con-
sumer, 429; personal, 429; sales, 428
Financial Executives Institute, 492
Financial institutions, for long-term capital,
402; for short-term capital, 423
Financial management, organization for,
430; professional association in, 492
Financial news, 443
Financial news items, 448; corporate, 448;
government, 449; international, 450
Financing, long-term, 389, 390; long-term
corporate, 391; long-term noncorporate,
390; short-term, 411
Financing statement, 418
Finished goods, 289
Fire insurance, 458; allied coverages, 460;
coinsurance clause, 459
Fishyback freight, 257
Fixed assets, 389, 422, 502
Fixed capital, 389
Fixed liabilities, 503
Flat-roof type of building, 270
Flow charts, 549
Flow control, 309
Food and Drug Administration, 223, 605
Food, Drug, and Cosmetic Act, 223, 605
Forecasting, 557, 566
Forecasts, how made, 568; private agen-
cies that make, 568; reliability of, 571;
uses of, 571; who prepares, 567
Foreign competition, 35
Foreign corporation, 102
Foreign exchange, 237, 426
Foreign trade zones, 241
Foreign Trade Zones Act, 241
Foremanship training, 334
Formula Translation (FORTRAN), 548

Forward buying, hand-to-mouth buying versus, 284
Forward stock, 294
Franchise, 620
Franchise tax, 100, 643
Franchising, 35
Freedom, of choice, 5; of contract, 6
F.o.b. destination, 191
F.o.b. shipping point, 191
Freight, fishyback, 257; piggyback, 257
Frequency distribution, 525
Fringe benefits, 359, 371
Fuel, a factor in plant location, 255
Full employment act, 34
Fully registered bond, 393
Functionalization, 114
Functional middleman, 157
Functional organization, 114; Taylor's, 122
Funds, capital, 10
Fur Products Labeling Act, 223, 606
Futures contract, 456

G

Game theory, 572
Garnishment, 589
General Agreement on Tariff and Trades (GATT), 241
General Aptitude Test Battery of the United States Employment Service, 51
General creditors, 595
General expenses, 507
General partners, 82
General partnership, 81
General sales taxes, 639
General stores, 165
Gentlemen's agreement, 613
Geographic selectivity, 205
Geographic wage rate differentials, 254
Gift taxes, 651
Goods, capital, 10; commercial, 136; cost of, 197; consumer, 136; convenience, 136; distribution of, 11; establishing specifications for, 281; finished, 289; industrial, 135; receiving the, 283; semi-finished, 289; shopping, 136; specialty, 137; steps in ordering and receiving, 281; types of, 278
Goodwill, 502
Government, business and, 31; labor and, 33
Governmental accountants, 498
Governmental corporation, 101
Government publications, 522
Government service, careers in, 60
Grade labeling, 141
Green River Ordinance, 171
Gross margin, 507
Gross national product (GNP), 571
Gross profit on sales, 505
Group incentive plans, 354
Group life insurance, 470
Guaranteed annual wage, 357
Guaranteed drawing account, 356
Guideposts, wage and price, 187

H

Handicap competition, 13

Hand-to-mouth buying, versus forward buying, 284
Hardware, 547
Hazardous Substances Labeling Act, 606
Health, employee, 338
Health and sanitation laws, state, 609
Health insurance, 462
Hedging, 456
Hiring policies, legal restrictions on, 328
Historical costs, 624
Holder in due course, 592
Holding companies, 488
Horizontal combination, 486
Hours, fewer, higher wages, 352
House-to-house selling, 171
Huckster, 171
Human relations, industrial, 321

I

Impact of tax, 638
Implied warranty, 593
Importers, 157; dollar volume of, 232; merchandise, 230
Impulse merchandise, 136
Incentive plans, group, 354
Incentive wages, 353
Incidence of tax, 638
Income, net, 508; net, from operations, 507; other, 507; rate of net, on assets, 514; rate of net, on proprietorship, 513; rate of net, on sales, 513
Income-expenditure analysis, 19
Income statement, 504; estimated, 564
Income taxes, 641; corporation, 648; federal, 645; personal, 646
Incorporation fee, 100, 643
Indenture, 392
Independent retailers, 172
Independent unions, 376
Index number, 527; weighted, 528
Indirect costs, 220
Indorsement, 416
Indorser, accommodation, 419
Industrial businesses, 23
Industrial consumer, 149
Industrial distributors, 156
Industrial economy, shift from an, to a service economy, 43
Industrial fatigue, 338
Industrial goods, 135; channels of distribution for, 146
Industrial human relations, 321
Industrial revolution, 28
Industrial strife, 371
Industrial unions, 375
Industries, regulated, 617; service, 43
Industry contacts, 53
Inelasticity of demand, 186
In escrow, 405
Information, 539
Informative labeling, 141
Inheritance taxes, 644
Injunction, 373
Inland marine insurance, 464
Innovation, 40; experimental, 178
Innovistic competition, 14

Input, 268, 544
Input media, 544
Input unit, 544
Inquiry test, 214
Insolvency, 489
Inspection, 314; devices, 315; place of, 315; quality control and, 314; quantity, 316; time of, 314
Installment purchases, of equipment, 417
Institutional advertising, 205
Insurable risks, characteristics of, 456
Insurance, accident and health, 462; automobile, 460; bodily injury liability, 461; casualty, 458, 460; collision or upset, 461; credit, 470; credit life, 470; endowment life, 469; fire, 458; group life, 470; inland marine, 464; life, 465; limited payment life, 469; marine, 464; miscellaneous casualty coverages, 464; ocean marine, 464; on owners or executives, 471; product liability, 463; professional association in, 472; property, 458; property damage liability, 461; public, 463; straight life, 468; term life, 466; theft, 462; unemployment, 642; workmen's compensation, 463
Insurance companies, 406, 453
Insurance coverages, types of, 458
Insurance policy, 453
Insurance underwriters, 457
Intangible assets, 502
Intangibles, 590
Integrated data processing (IDP), 550
Intelligence tests, 50
Inter-American Development Bank, 242
Interest, 50; effective rate of, 423; nominal rate of, 423
Interest selectivity, 205
Interest tests, 51
Interlocking directorate, 603
Intermediate credit, 390
Intermittent process, 267, 300
International Bank for Reconstruction and Development, 240
International business, 243; factors in the growth of, 244; future of, 245; major aspects of, 244
International financial news, 450
International Franchise Association, 35
International marketing, 242
International marketing manager, 243
International Monetary Fund, 240
International trade, 227; business reasons for, 228; characteristics of, 232; economic reasons for, 228; extent of our, 230; historical role of our government in, 234; political reasons for, 229; recent developments in, 239
Interstate Commerce Act, 630
Interstate Commerce Commission, 31, 631
Inventories, as security for a loan, 420
Inventory control, 277; importance of purchasing and, 277; in wholesaling and retailing, 293
Inventory subsystem, 551
Inventory turnover, 512
Investment Advisers Act, 406

Investment banking companies, 402
Investment companies, 406
Investment Company Act, 406
Investments, 502
Investment trusts, 406
Investor, 437
Involuntary bankruptcy, 594

J

Job, introduction to the, 329
Job analysis, 325
Jobber, 157
Job cycles, 308
Job description, 325; illustration of, 326
Job evaluation, 360
Job shop, 300
Job specification, 325
Joint cost, 182
Joint-stock companies, 84
Joint venture, 83
Journal, 499
Judgment, 589
Judgment pricing, 182
Junior partner, 82
Jurisdictional strike, 372

K

Keynes, John Maynard, 36
Kuder Preference Record, 51

L

Labeling, descriptive, 141; grade, 141; informative, 141
Labeling acts, 606
Labor, a factor in plant location, 253; and government, 33; incomprehensibility to, of many common business methods, 365; management's concept of, as a cost of production, 364; reaction of, to management, 365; sources of annoyance to, 364
Labor budget, 562
Labor disputes, methods of settling, 377
Laborers, competition among, 344
Labor leaders, belligerence of, 367
Labor legislation, 379; state, 384, 608
Labor Management Relations Act, 381
Labor-Management Reporting and Disclosure Act of 1959, 383
Labor organizations, emergence of unions as preferred, 367; reasons for growth of, 367
Labor peace, prospects for, 378
Labor practices, unfair, 382
Labor problems, 363
Labor turnover, 324
Lags, leads and, 569
Laissez faire, 4
Land and building costs, a factor in plant location, 261
Land and the people, 27
Language differences, 232
Large-scale business, 21
Law, administrative, 32; business, 579, 584; civil, 584; common, 584; courts and, 585

Lawful acts, 588
Layoff, 332
Layout, 266; amount of labor required, a factor in plant, 268; characteristics of customer traffic, a factor in retail-store, 272; commercial, 273; customer parking, a factor in retail-store, 273; internal transportation, a factor in plant, 268; lighting, a factor in retail-store, 272; manufacturing policy, a factor in plant, 267; method of moving customers, a factor in retail-store, 272; need for flexibility, a factor in plant, 268; office, 273; plant, 267; retail-store, 270; store service requirements, a factor in retail-store, 272; type of manufacturing process, a factor in plant, 267; type of merchandise, a factor in retail-store, 271; type of product, a factor in, 268; type of service, a factor in retail-store, 271; ventilation and heating, a factor in retail-store, 272; volume of work, a factor in plant, 268; wholesale, 270
Layout procedures, 274
Lea Act, 383
Leads and lags, 569
Ledger, 499
Legal entity, 90; of a corporation, 96
Legal procedures, 585
Legal restrictions, on hiring policies, 328
Legal systems, 584
Legislation, price, 188
Letters of credit, 418
Letters of inquiry, 282
Leverage factor, 479
Liabilities, 500; current, 411, 502; fixed, 503; long-term, 503
Liability, limited, of shareholders, 95; unlimited, of sole proprietorship, 72; of partnerships, 80
Licenses, 610
Life insurance, 465; business uses of, 470; cash surrender value of, 468; credit, 470; endowment, 469; group, 470; limited payment, 469; straight, 468; term, 466
Life insurance policies, types of, 466
Lighting, a factor in retail-store layout, 272
Limited liability of shareholders, 92
Limited partners, 82
Limited partnership associations, 83
Limited partnerships, 81
Limited payment life insurance, 469
Limited-price variety stores, 170
Line-and-staff organization, 123; line departments, 124; staff departments, 125
Line chart, 533
Line departments, 124
Line of credit, 425
Line organization, 121
Listed securities, 434
Load ahead schedules, 311
Loans, business, from the bank, 416; character, 419; security for, 590; short-term, 425
Location, 251, 546; climate, a factor in plant, 258; fuel, a factor in plant, 255;

importance of proper, 251; of offices, 266; of other types of business, 261; of retailers, 262; of service establishments, 266; of wholesalers, 262; plant, labor a factor in, 253; plant, power a factor in, 254; plant, production factors involved in, 252; transportation, a factor in plant, 256; water, a factor in plant, 255
Location of competitors, a factor in plant location, 259
Location of retailers, availability of adequate parking space, a factor in, 263; character of neighborhood, a factor in, 263; customer traffic, nature of, a factor in, 263; downtown vs. suburbs, 265; nearness to a trading center, a factor in, 263; nearness to competitors, a factor in, 265; parking space, availability of adequate, a factor in, 263; rental or sale price, a factor in, 265
Lockout, 373
Logistics mix, 148
Long-and-short-haul clause, 631
Long-term capital financial institutions, 402
Long-term financing, 389, 390; corporate, 391; for short-term, 482; noncorporate, 390
Long-term liabilities, 503
Loss, net, 508; net, from operations, 507
Loss leaders, 174
Loyalty, loss of workers', 366

                              M

Machine language, 548
Macroeconomics, 17
Magazines, 207
Magnetic cores, 546
Magnetic tape, 545
Mail-order house, 171
Maintenance-of-membership, 370
Maker, of note, 415
Management, 7, 109; absentee, 113; administrative, 110; centralized, 113; concept of labor as a cost of production, 364; control by, 113; decentralized, 113; development of scientific, 304; efficiency of, of a corporation, 96; functions of, 112; ignoring of workers' goals, 365; impersonality and arbitrariness, 365; levels of, 110; materials, 287; middle, 110; operating, 110; organization and operation by, 112; organization for financial, 438; planning and policy making by, 112; preoccupation with profits, 364; production, 303; professional associations in, 128; scientific, 305; separation of ownership and, 93; sources of annoyance to, 366; Taylor's philosophy of, 304; top, 110; weakening of, authority, 366
Management by exception, 566
Management-organization theory, 126; historical background, 126
Manager, advertising, 218; international marketing, 243; marketing, 144; merchandise, 291; product, 144; sales, 143

Manpower Development and Training Act (MDTA), 336
Manufacturers' agents, 157
Manufacturer's excise taxes, 650
Manufacturers' sales organization, 143
Manufacturing, buying versus, 284; careers in, 57
Manufacturing expense budget, 562
Margin, selling stock on, 438
Margin requirements, 443
Marginal productivity, 346; theory of wages, 346
Marginal revenue, 346
Marine insurance, 464; inland, 464; ocean, 464
Markdowns, 193
Market, a factor in plant location, 258; investigating the supply, 282; over-the-counter, 404; spot, 449
Market conditions, a security solution factor, 478
Market finance, 142
Market information, 142
Marketing, 133; and computers, 148; approaches to the study of, 135; as a career, 56; changed emphasis in, 133; international, 242; professional association in, 152; scope and cost of, 134
Marketing concept, total, 134
Marketing functions, 137
Marketing institutions, 135
Marketing manager, 144
Marketing mix, 148
Marketing research, 147
Marketing Research Code of Ethics, 152
Marketing risk, 142
Marketing strategy, 147
Markup, formulas for, calculations, 184
Markup percentage, 183
Markup table, retail price, 183
Marshall Plan, 36, 242
Massachusetts trust, 84
Mass advertising, 204
Mass picketing, 372
Mass production, 20
Master schedule, 310
Master systems plan, 550
Materials, 277; control, 287; handling and control, 287; methods of handling, 288; new, 301; purchase of, 278; raw, 289; raw, factor in plant location, 253; storage of, 289; types of, stored, 289; worked, 289
Materials budget, 562
Materials management, 287
Maximization of profit, 346
McCarran Act, 407
McGuire Act, 176, 189
Mean, 526
Median, 526
Mediation, 377
Medical payments endorsement, 461
Memory unit, 544
Mental ability, 50
Mercantilism, 580
Merchandise, 277; cost of, sold, 505; impulse, 136; purchase and control of, 289

Merchandise agents, 157
Merchandise brokers, 158
Merchandise inventory, turnover of, 512
Merchandise manager, 291
Merchandise sampling, 212
Merchandise specials, by chain stores, 174
Merchandising policies, of chain stores, 174
Merchant, commission, 158; wholesale, 156
Merchant wholesalers, 156
Mergers, 487; conglomerate, 487
Microeconomics, 17
Micromotion study, 309
Middle management, 110
Middlemen, 135; functional, 157
Miniaturization, 302
Minimum wage legislation, 348
Mining partnership, 83
Minors, 588
Mode, 526
Models, 41
Monetary standards, different, 233
Money and credit, 449
Money wages, 350; versus real wages, 350
Monopolies, 611
Monopolistic competition, 13, 187
Monopoly, natural, 619
Monopoly price, 186
Mortgage, chattel, 422
Motion and time study, 306; to aid in planning production, 306; to control operating costs, 306; to determine the best methods of performing each task, 306
Motion study, 308
Motor Carrier Act, 632
Motor truck regulation, 631
Motor trucks, 257
Movable property, 421
Multinational business, 245
Multiple correlation, 530
Multistory type of factory building, 270
Multiunit organization, 173
Mutual companies, 105
Mutual funds, 406

N

Name advertising, 205
National Association of Insurance Commissioners, 466
National Bankruptcy Act, 489
National Conference of Commissioners on Uniform State Laws, 585
National income theory, 19
Nationalism, 233
National Labor Relations Act of 1935, 33, 380
National Labor Relations Board, 254, 380, 381
National product, gross, 571
National stock exchanges, 441
National Tax Association, 654
Natural Gas Act of 1938, 629
Natural monopoly, 619
Negotiable instruments, 416, 591
Neo-Keynesian theory, 19
Nepotism, 327, 332

Net income, 508; from operations, 507; rate of, on assets, 514; rate of, on sales, 513; rate of, on proprietorship, 513
Net loss, 508; from operations, 507
Net sales, 505
Newspapers, 206
Nominal partner, 82
Nominal rate of interest, 423
Noncumulative preferred stock, 398
Nonmanufacturing enterprises, purchasing in, 289
Nonnotification plan, 420
Nonparticipating preferred stock, 399
Nonprice competition, 199
Nonprofit corporation, 101
Nonsigner clause, 189
Nonstock corporation, 101
Nonvoting preferred stock, 399
No-par preferred stock, 400
Notes, discounting customers', 416; promissory, 415
Notice of dishonor, 592
Notice of protest, 592
Notification plan, 420
Numerical control (N/C), 302

O

Occupational selection factors, 50
Ocean marine insurance, 464
Odd-lot broker, 435
Office layout, 273
Office management, careers in, 59
Officers, location of, 266; of a corporation, 90, 93
Oligopoly, 13
One-price system, 196
Open-book accounts, 413
Open corporation, 102
Open-end issue mortgage bonds, 395
Open-loop control, 302
Open shop, 370
Operating expenses, 507
Operating management, 110
Operations research (OR), 21, 572
Option, stock, 480
Order, placing and following up the, 283
Order bill of lading, 418
Order control, 309
Organization, 109, 115; and policies, 558; budget, 558; committee, 125; for financial management, 430; functional, 114; line, 121; line-and-staff, 123; manufacturers' sales, 143; of production, 306; of purchasing department, 279; theories of, 127
Organizational picketing, 383
Organizational structure, 115; importance of, 115; types of, 119
Organization chart, 119; of a personnel department, 324; of a production department, 307; of a purchasing department, 279; of a typical advertising agency, 216
Organization expenses, of a corporation, 97
Organization planning, classification of business activities, 116; clearly defined

duties, 118; communication, 118; delegation of authority, 117; departmentalization, 116; factors in, 116; flexibility, 118
Other expense, 507
Other income, 507
Outdoor advertising, 210
Outer Seven, 242
Outlaw strike, 372
Output, 268, 547; restriction of, and job retention, 370
Output unit, 547
Over-the-counter market, 404, 445
Ownership, 590; public, regulation by, 629; ratio of, to debt, 513; separation of, and management, 93

P

Packers and Stockyards Act, 607
Partial registration, of coupon bond, 393
Participating preferred stock, 399
Partner, dormant, 82; general, 82; junior, 82; kinds of, 81; limited, 82; nominal, 82; number of, in partnerships, 75; secret, 82; senior, 82; silent, 82; sleeping, 82; special, 82; unlimited liability of, 80
Partnership, 73; advantages of the, 76; articles of, 75; characteristics of, 74; combined judgment and managerial skills, 79; credit standing of, 79; definite legal status of, 79; definition of a, 73; disadvantages of the, 80; frozen investment in, 81; general, 81; lack of continuity of, 80; larger amount of capital in, 76; limitation on size of, 81; limited, 81; managerial difficulties of, 80; mining, 83; number of partners in, 75; personal interest in business, 79; retention of valuable employees by, 79; special types of, 82
Partnership contract, 75
Par-value preferred stock, 400
Patent licensing, 611
Patronage dividends, 104
Payee, of note, 415
Payroll taxes, 642
Pension plans, 471
Pensions, 358; portable, 359
Performance follow-up and control, 311
Peripheral equipment, 547
Personal evaluation, 50, 330
Personal finance companies, 429
Personality tests, 51
Personal property, 590
Personal property floater, 464
Personal selling, 138
Personnel, careers in, 57; professional association in, 340; retailers buying, 290
Personnel audit, 330
Personnel department, 323; employment division of, 324; organization chart of a, 324; personnel research division of, 339; personnel services division of, 336; safety and health division, 338; training division of, 333
Personnel services, 336; types of, 336

Picketing, 372; mass, 372; organizational, 382

Pictographs, 534

Piece-rate wage payment, 355

Pie diagram, 534

Piggyback export sales, 245

Piggyback freight, 257

Pipelines, 257; regulation of, 632

Placement bureaus, 54

Place utility, 139

Plaintiff, 585

Plant, expenditures for new, 11

Plant assets, 502

Plant location, a threefold problem, 252; chance, a factor in, 260; climate, a factor in, 258; fuel, a factor in, 255; human factors in, 261; labor, a factor in, 253; land and building costs, a factor in, 261; local inducements, a factor in, 260; markets, a factor in, 258; of competitors, a factor in, 259; other factors involved, 258; power, a factor in, 254; production factors involved in, 252; room for expansion, a factor in, 260; site selection procedures, 261; special characteristics of business, a factor in, 259; transportation, a factor in, 256; water, a factor in, 255

Plant layout, 267; amount of labor required, a factor in, 268; internal transportation, a factor in, 268; manufacturing policy, a factor in, 267; need for flexibility, a factor in, 268; type of manufacturing process, a factor in, 267; type of product, a factor in, 268; volume of work, a factor in, 268

Point-of-purchase advertising, 212

Police power, 608

Population growth, and suburbanization, 42

Portable pensions, 359

Portfolio, 406

Postemployment procedures, 329; follow-ups, 330; introduction to the job, 329

Power, a factor in plant location, 254

Preferential shop, 370

Preferred creditors, 594

Preferred stocks, 397; callable, 400; convertible, 401; cumulative, 398; general features of, 398; noncumulative, 398; nonparticipating, 399; nonvoting, 399; no-par, 400; par value, 400; participating, 399; preference as to assets, 401; preference as to dividends, 398; redeemable, 400; series issues, 401; special features of, 400; voting, 399

Premium, 453; bond, 397

Price, 12, 181, 613; administered, 182; asked, 404; bid, 404; call, 396; commodity, 449; delivered, 191; elements affecting, sought by sellers, 197; elements involved in the, buyers are willing to pay, 198; equilibrium theory of, 194; factors in determining, 183; high, 190; importance of, 14; in relation to supply and demand, 194; low, 190; monopoly, 186; odd, 191; one, versus varying price, 191; stable,

191; state regulation of, 609; suggested, 185; wages and, 351

Price determination, approaches to, 181

Price developments, 200

Price-fixing laws, 606

Price guideposts, 187, 350

Price leadership, 185

Price legislation, 188; state, 188

Price lines, 185

Price markup table, retail, 183

Price policies, 190

Pricing, judgment, 182

Primary advertising, 204

Primary boycott, 373

Primary data, 522

Principal, 591

Printers' Ink statutes, 224

Private carriers, 632

Private corporation, 101

Private enterprise, 5

Private property, 4

Privileged subscription right, 480

Privilege tax, 643

Probability, 531

Producer cooperative associations, 104

Product differentiation, 13

Production, 11; for stock, 267; mass, 20; organization of, 306; recent developments in, 301; research and, 303; shift from emphasis from, to distribution, 41; speculative, 138; to order, 267; wages as a cost of, 351

Production budget, 561

Production control, 309; flow, 309; order, 309; performance follow-up, 311; planning, 310; routing, 310; scheduling, 310; steps in, 310; types of, 309

Production control procedure, flow of paperwork in a, 312

Production department, organization chart of a, 307

Production factors, involved in plant location, 252

Production management, 303

Production processes, 297; analytic, 298; continuous, 267, 299; extractive, 298; fabricating, 298; intermittent, 267, 300; new, 301; synthetic, 298; types of, 298

Product liability insurance, 463

Product manager, 144

Product mix, 148

Professional associations, accounting, 514; budgeting, 573; business law, 595; finance, 408; financial management, 492; insurance, 472; management, 128; marketing, 152; personnel, 340; statistics, 536; taxation, 654

Profit, 16; management's preoccupation with, 364; maximization of, 346

Profit corporation, 101

Profit in sales, gross, 505

Profit philosophy, 198

Profit sharing, 356

Program, 548

Program evaluation and review technique (PERT), 313

Progressive taxation, 638
Projections, 569
Promissory note, 415
Property, 589; fair value of, 623; movable, 421; personal, 590; private, 4; real, 590
Property damage liability insurance, 461
Property insurance, 458
Property taxes, 642
Proportional tax, 638
Proprietorship, 500, 503; rate of net income on, 513
Prospectus, 440
Protective tariff, 235; favorable-balance-of-trade-agreement, 237; home-industry argument for, 236; infant-industry argument, 236; military argument for, 235; wages argument for, 236
Protest, notice of, 592
Proxy, 91
Prudent historical cost, 624
Prudent-man rule, 405
Psychodrama, 335
Public accountants, 498
Publicity, 204
Public liability insurance, 463
Public necessity, 618
Public opinion, 29
Public ownership, regulation by, 629
Public utilities, 617; careers in, 60; characteristics of, 618; federal regulation of, 627; large investment of, 620; natural monopoly, 619; regulatory agencies, 621; special privileges of, 620
Public-utility field, entry into, 626
Public Utility Holding Company Act of 1935, 628; death sentence clause of the, 628
Public-utility rates, fair rate of return, 623; fair value of property, 623; state regulation of, 622
Public-utility services, extension and abandonment of, 627; standards of, 626; state regulation of, 626; without discrimination, 627
Punched card, 545
Punched paper tape, 545
Purchase order, 283
Purchase requisition, 282
Purchasing, 277; importance of, and inventory control, 277; in nonmanufacturing enterprises, 289; prime objectives of, 281; value analysis and, 286
Purchasing agent, 279
Purchasing department, 279; extent of authority of, 280; organization and status of, 279; organization chart of a, 279
Purchasing function, centralization versus decentralization of, 280
Purchasing negotiations, starting, 282
Purchasing policies, 283; buying ethics, 286; buying versus manufacturing, 284; contract, 285; hand-to-mouth buying versus forward buying, 284; reciprocal buying, 285; speculative, 285; use of sealed bids, 286
Pure competition, 13

Q

Quality control, 314; and inspection, 314; statistical, 316
Quantity discount, 193
Quick ratio, 511
Quotas, 606

R

Radio, spot, 208
Radio advertising, 208; coincidental method of testing, 215; testing, 215
Radio commercial, 209
Railroad regulation, 630
Railroads, 256
Random sampling, 521
Rate differentials, 625
Rates of exchange, 238
Ratio, acid-test, 511; current, 511; of ownership to debt, 513
Raw materials, 289; factor in plant location, 253
Readership reports, 214
Real estate mortgage bonds, 395; after-acquired clause, 395; closed-end issue of, 395; open-end issue of, 395
Real property, 590
Real-time systems, 552; SABRE, 552; Westinghouse Tele-Computer System, 553
Real wages, 350; money wage versus, 350
Receipt, warehouse, 421
Receiver, 490
Receivership, equity, 490
Recession, 33
Reciprocal buying, 285
Reciprocal Trade Agreements Acts, 239
Redeemable bonds, 396
Redeemable preferred stocks, 400
Rediscount rate, 427
Referee in bankruptcy, 491
Refinancing programs, 480
Refunding, 396
Register, 546
Registrar for stock issues, 405
Regressive tax, 638
Regulated industries, 617
Regulation, by public ownership, 629; motor truck, 631; of air transport, 632; of communications industries, 633; of pipelines, 632; of water transportation, 632; railroad, 630
Regulatory tax, 651
Registration statement, 440
Relatives, 528
Reorganization, 489
Reorganization Act of 1939, 632
Reorganization plans, 491
Replevin, 591
Reproduction cost new, 624; less depreciation, 624
Requisition, purchase, 282
Research, and development, 21; and production, 303; growing importance of, 21; in retailing, 178; in wholesaling, 163; marketing, 147; personnel, 339

Resident buying offices, 291
Retailers, buying personnel, 290; buying procedures, 293; chain stores, 173; classified by types of operation, 165; classified on the basis of ownership, 172; independents, 172; location of, 262; service, 171
Retailing, 163; inventory control in, 293; research in, 178; scrambled, 164
Retailing revolution, 176, 177
Retail price markup table, 183
Retail-store layout, 270; characteristics of customer traffic, a factor in, 272; customer parking, a factor in, 273; lighting, a factor in, 272; method of moving customers, a factor in, 272; store service requirements, a factor in, 272; type of merchandise, a factor in, 270, 271; type of service, a factor in, 271; ventilation and heating, a factor in, 272
Retained earnings statement, 504
Retirement plans, 471; early, 359
Retraining of employee, 335
Revenue, marginal, 346
Rider, 460
Right, 480
Right of eminent domain, 620
Right-to-work laws, 384, 609
Risk, 15, 453; insurable, characteristics of, 456; market, 142; protection against, 455
Robinson-Patman Act, 176, 604
Role, 127
Round-lots of stock, 435
Routing, 310
Rule of reason, 602
Rural Electrification Administration, 105

S

Sabotage, 373
SABRE, 552
Safety, employee, 338
Salary, straight, 354
Sales, 505, 592; bill of, 593; casual, 182; conditional, 593; gross profit on, 505; net, 505; piggyback export, 245; rate of net income on, 513; revenue from, 505
Sales budget, 560
Sales expense budget, 561
Sales finance companies, 428
Sales manager, 143
Sales organization, manufacturers', 143
Sales promotion, 139
Sales subsystem, 551
Sales taxes, 639; city, 641; county, 641; general, 639; selective, 639
Sales test, 214
Sampling, 521; controlled, 521; random, 521; techniques, 521
Savings and loan associations, 106, 407
Savings banks, 407
Schedule, load ahead, 311; master, 310; weekly departmental, 310
Schedule of cost of goods manufactured, 508
Schedule performance reports, 311
Scheduling, 310
Schools, company, 334; vestibule, 334

Science, 39; behavioral, 40
Scientific management, 305; development of, 304
Scrambled retailing, 164
Scrap reports, 311
Scrip dividends, 485
Sealed bids, 286
Seals of approval, 151
Sears' stores, 167
Seasonal variations, 531
Seat on stock exchange, 434
Secondary boycott, 373
Secondary data, 522
Secret partner, 82
Secular trends, 530
Securities, listed, 434; methods of selling, 479; regulation of sales of, 439; state regulation of the sale of, 440; unlisted, 404
Securities and Exchange Commission, 440, 628
Securities dividends, 485
Security, chattel mortgages as, 395; excellent credit rating as, 395; for loans, 590; of bonds, 394; real estate mortgages as, 395; stocks and bonds as, 395
Security exchanges, 434; operation of, 434; seat on, 434; trading procedures, 435; value of, 439
Select-a-Market, 207
Selective advertising, 204
Selective sales taxes, 639
Self-insurance, 455
Selling, 138; advertising, 139; does direct, lower costs, 161; personal, 138; sales promotion, 139; specification, 150
Selling agents, 158
Selling expenses, 507
Selling short, 437
Semifinished goods, 289
Seniority, 332
Senior partner, 82
Serial bonds, 396
Series issues of preferred stock, 401
Servant, 591
Service economy, shift from an industrial to a, 43
Service establishments, location of, 266
Service industries, 43
Service mix, 148
Service retailer, 171
Services, rendered by wholesalers to manufacturers, 159; rendered by wholesalers to retailers, 159; wholesale, 158
Servo-mechanisms, 303
Set-up time, 311
Severance pay, 359
Severance taxes, 644
Shareholders, 90, 91; limited liability of, 95
Sherman Antitrust Act, 602
Shift premium plan of wage payment, 355
Shop, agency, 370; closed, 369; open, 370; preferential, 370; union, 369
Shopping centers, controlled, 265
Shopping goods, 136
Shop stewards, 353

Short-term capital, financial institutions for, 423
Short-term financing, 411; advantages of, 412; cost of, 422; for growth requirements, 412; long-term for, 482; for seasonal needs, 412
Short-term loans, 425; security for, 419
Short-term obligations, 413; types of, 413
Sight drafts, 417
Silent partner, 82
Simple correlation, 530
Simulation, 41, 572
Single-line stores, 167
Sinking-fund bonds, 396
Sitdown strike, 372
Site saturation, 260
Site selection procedures, 261
Size of business firms, 22
Sleeping partner, 82
Slowdown strike, 372
Small Business Administration, 35
Small loan companies, 429
Socialism, 24
Social Security Act of 1935, 642
Society, business and, 29
Society for the Advancement of Management, 128
Software, 548
Soldiering on the job, 372
Sole proprietorship, 68; advantages of the, 69; characteristics of a, 68; disadvantages of the, 72; difficulties of management of, 73; ease and low cost of organization of, 70; ease of dissolution of, 72; freedom and promptness of action in, 70; high credit standing of, 71; lack of continuity of, 73; lack of opportunity for employees of, 73; limitation on size of, 72; ownership of all profits, 69; personal incentive and satisfaction in, 71; secrecy of, 71; tax savings in, 71; unlimited liability of, 72
Source and application of funds, statement of, 508
Space technology, defense contracts and, 41
Span of executive control, 118
Specialist, broker, 435
Specialization, 20; business, 48
Special partner, 82
Specialty goods, 137
Specialty shops, 168
Specialty stores, 167
Specialty wholesalers, 156
Specifications, 281
Specification selling, 150
Spectaculars, 211
Speculative production, 138
Speculative purchasing, 285
Speculator, 437
Spin-offs, 483
Sponsor system, 333
Spot announcement, 209
Spot market, 449
Spot radio, 208
Spread, 403
Staff departments, 125
Standard and Poor's Index, 443

Standardization, 141
Standard manufacture, 300
Standard-of-living theory of wages, 348
Stand-by equipment, 623
State building codes, 609
State health and sanitation laws, 609
State labor legislation, 384, 608
State laws and regulations, 607
Statement of source and application of funds, 508
Statements, estimated, 564; interpretation of, 510
State regulation, of prices, 609; of public-utility rates, 622; of public-utility services, 626
State taxes, business decisions and, 653; types of, 638
State usury laws, 609
State zoning ordinances, 609
Station breaks, 209
Statism, 37, 38
Statistical maps, 534
Statistical material, graphic presentations of, 533; presentation of, 532; summary tables of, 532
Statistical measurement, types of, 524
Statistical quality control, 316
Statistics, business, 520; careers in, 58; professional association in, 536
Status, 127
Statute of Frauds, 589
Stewards, union or shop, 353
Stock, 444; as security, 395; common, 401; company registration of, 441; cost of trading, 437; for bonds, 481; for stock, 482; forward, 294; preferred, see Preferred stocks
Stock averages, 445
Stock certificates, 101
Stock control, 277
Stock corporation, 101
Stock dividends, 485
Stock exchanges, national, 441
Stockholders, 90; see Shareholders
Stock option, 480
Stock quotations, 436, 444
Stock split-up, 485
Stop order, 440
Storage, 140; of materials, 289
Storage unit, 544
Store-door delivery, 139
Straight life insurance, 468
Straight salary, 354
Strike, 372; jurisdictional, 372; outlaw, 372; sitdown, 372; slowdown, 372; sympathy, 372; wildcat, 372
Strike insurance funds, 373
Strong Vocational Interest Blank, 51
Structural unemployment, 34
Style life inventory management (SLIM), 294
Subjective value, consumer's, 199
Subscription right, privileged, 480
Subscription warrant, 480
Subsidiaries, 488
Suburbanization, population growth and, 42

Suggestion box, 322
Summons, 585
Supermarkets, 168; discount, 170
Supervisory authority, subdivisions of, 117
Supplementary unemployment benefits, 358
Supply, and demand, concepts of, 196; of labor, 344
Supply market, investigating the, 282
Surety bonds, 465
Symbolic language, 548
Sympathy strike, 372
Syndicates, 83; underwriting, 83
Synthetic process, 298
Systems analysis, 127
Systems concept, 549; credit control subsystem, 551; inventory subsystem, 551; other subsystems, 551; sales subsystem, 551

T

Taft-Hartley Act, 381
Tangibles, 590
Tariff duties, ad valorem, 237; compound, 237; specific, 145
Tariffs, for revenue only, 235; protective, 235; types of, 235
Tariff system, flexible, 237
Taxation, and business, 637; and business decisions, 652; of a corporation, 97; principles of, 638; professional association in, 654
Tax bracket, 646
Taxes, alcohol, 649; a security selection factor, 477; communications, 651; corporation, 643; employment, 650; entrance, 643; estate, 644, 651; excise, 649; franchise, 100, 643; gift, 651; impact of, 638; incidence of, 638; income, 641; income, federal, 645; inheritance, 644; manufacturer's excise, 650; miscellaneous, 651; payroll, 642; privilege, 643; progressive, 638; property, 642; proportional, 638; regressive, 638; regulatory, 651; sales, 639; severance, 644; special business, 643; tobacco, 649; transportation, 651; types of federal, 645; types of state, 638
Taylor, Frederick W., 122, 304
Taylor's functional organization, 122
Technology, space, defense contracts and, 41
Television advertising, 209; coincidental method of testing, 215; testing, 215
Telstar, 35
Templates, 274
Tender, 489
Tennessee Valley Authority (TVA), 255
Term life insurance, 466; level-term contract, 468
Territorial pool, 611
Tests, aptitude, 50; intelligence, 50; interest, 51; personality, 51
Textile Fiber Products Identification Act, 223, 606
Theft insurance, 462
Throw-aways, 218
Ticker tape, 437

Time drafts, 417
Time series, 530
Time study, 306, 308
Time utility, 139
Time wages, 354
Tobacco taxes, 649
Tolerance, 315
Top management, 110
Torts, business, 586
Total systems concept, 550
Trade, favorable balance of, 234; international, 227; unfavorable balance of, 234
Trade acceptance, 417
Trade activities in Europe and Latin America, 241
Trade associations, 612
Trade barriers, 233
Trade discount, 192
Trade Expansion Act, 239
Trade Practice Rules, 222
Trade practices, 613
Trade puffery, 221
Trading centers, 263
Trading on the equity, 478
Trading posts, 435
Trading stamps, 176
Training, executive, 335; foremanship, 334; for the job, 334; on the job, 333
Training programs, 62
Transfer agent for stock issues, 405
Transportation, 139, 630; a factor in plant location, 256; airplanes, 258; careers in, 60; internal, a factor in plant layout, 268; motor trucks, 257; pipelines, 257; railroads, 256; taxes, 651; waterways, 257
Transportation advertising, 211
Transportation costs, in international trade, 233
Traveler's checks, 425
Treaty of Rome, 241
Trust, Massachusetts, 84
Trust companies, 404
Trustee, 392; in bankruptcy, 491
Trust Indenture Act, 405
Trusts, 600; investment, 406
Trust shares, 84
Turnover of merchandise inventory, 512
Tying contracts, 603

U

Ultimate consumer, 149
Underwriters, insurance, 457
Underwriting, 453
Underwriting syndicate, 83
Unemployment, structural, 34
Unemployment benefits, supplementary, 358
Unemployment insurance, 642
Unfair labor practices, 382
Unfair trade laws, 188, 189
Unfavorable balance of trade, 234
Uniform Commercial Code, 586
Uniform Partnership Act, 73
Unincorporated association, 85

Union groups, 375
Union hiring halls, 369
Union objectives, 368; effects of, 371;
    higher wages and shorter hours, 369;
    security, 369; seniority provisions, 369
Unions, craft, 375; credit, 105; emergence
    of, as preferred labor organizations, 367;
    independent, 376; industrial, 375; types
    of, 375
Union security, 369
Union shop, 369
Union stewards, 353
Unit of supervision, 118
Universe, 521
Unlimited liability, sole proprietorship, 72;
    partnership, 80
Unlisted securities, 404
Upset insurance, 461
Usury laws, state, 609
Utility, place, 139; public, 617; time, 139

V

Value analysis, and purchasing, 286
Vending machines, 172
Vertical combination, 486
Vestibule school, 334
Vocation, 47
Vocational-aim values, 62
Vocational literature, 52, 671
Voluntary agreement, 587
Voluntary arbitration, 378
Voluntary bankruptcy, 594
Voluntary chains, 175
Voting, cumulative, 91
Voting control, a security selection factor,
    477
Voting preferred stock, 399

W

Wage, guaranteed annual, 357
Wage and Hour Act of 1938, 348
Wage and price guideposts, 187
Wage and salary administration, 360
Wage guideposts, 350
Wage incentives, 353
Wage legislation, minimum, 348
Wage payment, bonus, 355; commission,
    356; methods of, 354; piece-rate, 355;
    shift premium plan, 355; straight salary,
    354; time wages, 354
Wage rate differentials, geographic, 254
Wages, and price, 351; as a cost of pro-
    duction, 351; bargaining theory of, 347;
    economic theories of, 346; factors ac-
    tually determining, 349; higher, fewer
    hours, 352; marginal productivity theory
    of, 346; money, 350; money vs. real,
    350; real, 350; standard-of-living theory
    of, 348; time, 354; variation of, among
    individuals, 344; variations of, between
    industries, 345
Wagner Act, 380
Wagner-Lea Act, 406
Wagon, truck distributors, 157
Walkout, 372
Walsh-Healey Act, 383
Wards' stores, 167
Warehouse, bonded public, 421
Warehouse receipt, 421
Warehousing, by chain stores, 174; field,
    140
Warrant, subscription, 480
Warranty, express, 593; implied, 593
Water, a factor in plant location, 255
Water transportation, regulation of, 632
Waterways, 257
Weekly departmental schedule, 310
Weighted index number, 528
Welfare state, 37, 38
Westinghouse Tele-Computer System, 553
What the traffic will bear, 185
Wheeler-Lea Act, 223, 604
White-collar workers, 366
Wholesale layout, 270
Wholesale merchants, 156
Wholesalers, buying personnel, 290; buying
    procedures, 290; bypassing, 160; devel-
    opment of private brands by, 162; for-
    mation of voluntary chains by, 163; in-
    creased efficiency of, 162; location of,
    262; merchant, 156; reaction of, 162;
    specialty, 156; why manufacturers by-
    pass, 161; why retailers bypass, 161
Wholesale services, 158
Wholesaling, 155; inventory control in,
    293; research in, 163
Wildcat strike, 372
Wool Products Labeling Act, 606
Word, 546
Worked materials, 289
Workers, 8; blue-collar, 366; sources of,
    325; Taylor's attitude toward the, 304;
    white-collar, 366
Work experience, 52
Working capital, 411, 508, 512
Workmen's compensation, 463, 642

Y

Yellow-dog contract, 373

Z

Zoning ordinances, state, 609